FDR
The New York Years
1928-1933

❧ FDR ❧
The New York Years
1928-1933

Kenneth S. Davis

Random House   New York

This work was originally published in hardcover by Random House, Inc., in 1985.

Portions of the Prologue and Epilogue were included in "FDR as a Biographer's
Problem," *American Scholar,* Winter 1983/84. That part of Chapter 4 that tells of
Eleanor Roosevelt's trip to Europe in the summer of 1929 first appeared in
somewhat different form as "Symbolic Journey," *Antioch Review,* Summer 1979.
The portion of Chapter 13 telling of the attempt to assassinate the President-elect
appeared, with additional material, as "Incident in Miami," *American Heritage,*
December 1980. Most of Chapter 24 and a small portion of Chapter 27 first
appeared as "The Birth of Social Security," *American Heritage,* April/May 1979.

Grateful acknowledgment is made to Warner Bros. Music for permission to
reprint lyrics from "Brother, Can You Spare a Dime?" by E. Y. Harburg and Jay
Gorney. Copyright 1932 (Renewed) Warner Bros. Inc. All Rights Reserved. Used
by permission.

Library of Congress Cataloging in Publication Data

Davis, Kenneth Sydney
F.D.R., the New York years, 1928–1933.
Bibliography: p.
Includes index.
1. Roosevelt, Franklin D. (Franklin Delano), 1882–1945.
2. Presidents—United States—Biography. 3. New York
(State)—Governors—Biography. 4. United States—Politics
and government—1933–1945. 5. New York (State)—Politics
and government—1865–1950. I. Title. II. Title: FDR,
the New York years, 1928–1933.
E807.D35 1985   973.917′0924   84-42529
ISBN 0-679-75301-X

Manufactured in the United States of America
24689753
First Paperback Edition

Yet again
to Flo
with all my love

A history . . . is worthless except as a documented way of talking about the future.
—Kenneth Burke, *Attitudes Toward History*

Modern politics is, at bottom, a struggle not of men but of forces. The men become every year more and more creatures of force, massed about central power-houses.
—Henry Adams, *The Education of Henry Adams*

In a thousand ways the art of politics is directly affected by moral considerations. Nevertheless, politics cannot properly be regarded as a branch of virtuous conduct; for though the two things are often intertwined, each has its own separate root and stem. The prime motive of the politician is not to do good to humanity or even to his own country, but simply to gain power for himself. Yet he will inevitably fail if he refuses homage to the moral standards of his particular age. And moreover—though this is a different matter—the great majority of politicians are to some extent restrained and impelled by their own consciences. In taking stock of a politician, however, the first question is not whether he was a good man who used righteous means, but whether he was successful in gaining power, in keeping it, and in governing . . . [for] these are the special business of a politician, just as it is a working bee's business to make honeycomb and honey. But we are entitled to ask—how did he gain power? how did he keep it? and what did he do with it when he had it? And the answers to these questions are always mixed up with morals. . . . Morals indeed are waiting for us on the very threshold of our inquiry; for it is not merely the business, but the *duty,* of a politician to govern. The first need of human society is to be governed.
—F. S. Oliver, *The Endless Adventure; Personalities and Practical Politics in Eighteenth-Century England*

Either/Or is the key to heaven; both/and is the road to hell.
—Sören Kierkegaard, *Either/Or*

Contents

PROLOGUE

—»»X««—

Midstream:
October Ferry to
Hoboken

MIDDLENESS there was—a middleness of Time, a middleness of Place, even a middleness of Mind, of Spirit—as at midmorning of a day in the middle of the week and month (it was Wednesday, October 17, 1928) the ferry that crossed from Manhattan to Hoboken plowed its way through gray-blue waters, under an autumnal sky of purest deepest blue, into the Hudson River's midstream, bearing as its most distinguished passenger a man of middle age whose fame, though national, was yet of a middling quality.

Franklin Delano Roosevelt, forty-six years old, sat in an open car beside the ferryboat's railing.[1] He was casually if not carelessly dressed. His shirt's soft collar, in a year when starched collars remained the rule for dressed-up men, loosely clasped his thick strong neck; the unbuttoned coat of his coarse tweed suit hung loosely down from his broad, heavily muscled shoulders; and across his high forehead slanted the brim of an ancient, battered, imperfectly cleaned felt hat. He was smoking. Between his strong but uneven teeth, tilted upward at a jaunty angle by the outward thrust of his heavy jaw, was a long ivory cigarette holder from which the burning cigarette itself protruded. The smoke of it was whipped by the wind from his finely modeled lips and nostrils.

For the moment he was relatively alone. For the moment, and such moments became more and more rare, no wanting, asserting, importuning face leaned over him, demanding responsive smiles and words. He was free to let his blue-eyed gaze wander interestedly or absently over the busy scene, to think his own thoughts within a narrow private cone of silence, and to feel in full surging force the approach of the far shore, with all that awaited him there. He anticipated this shore with an eagerness qualified by apprehension. He knew opportunities for glory grew atop and beyond the distant Palisades. They flamed with color. But he also knew that dangers were there, too, darkly lurking.

It was upon the river, however, that his present vision was focused—a watery expanse that was actually more tidal sea than flowing stream and, to all appearances, wholly in man's dominion, having been ruthlessly wrested away from nature. Along its flanks were tied great sleek ocean liners. Over its body rode at that moment, at almost any moment of day or night, two or three rusty freighters, long strings of barges, an oil tanker or two, various smaller craft. And everywhere the mingled landscape and seascape were shaped and colored by gigantic forces of which economic man was instigator and agent, of which humane man was increasingly the victim. The river was so overwhelmed by these that only its largest outline remained approximately as it had been when Henry Hudson first looked upon it, and even this relatively unal-

tered portion, traced by tall granite cliffs on either shore, was blurred in the
sight of a midstream passenger by smoke from 10,000 chimneys, by the exhaust
fumes from many million iron pipes. As for the mingled waters themselves,
fresh with salt, they were so churned, stained, polluted by the engines of man's
commerce and the refuse of his industry that they had taken on here and there,
in streaks and patches, a metallic sheen.

How different the river here, its mouth opening to the ocean beside the
multitowered world city, from the river ninety miles northward, gently drifting
past the hill-mounted country house where Roosevelt had been born and
raised!

Here, though the same in name, the river bore no resemblance whatever to
the slender youthful stream of sparkling water from which, high in the Adirondack wilderness, it was descended. It bore little resemblance to "itself" in
midcareer. In these upper (earlier) stages of its being (becoming), the river
remained much the same as it had been a half century before. The Hudson as
it bent around Crum Elbow just below the village of Hyde Park—the Hudson
across which Franklin Roosevelt had looked every day as a boy at home, and
continued to look every day he was truly home; for the house of his birth,
where his mother yet lived, remained the one true homeplace for him—this
Hudson might flow somewhat less sweetly, cleanly than it had in the year of
his birth. It carried a lighter traffic of polluting steamboats now than then, but
it was now more harshly used as dump and sewer by upstream towns and cities,
whose populations had grown. In appearance, however, it remained unchanged and so, for the most part, did the landscape of which it was the central
theme—a pastoral and agricultural landscape that reached in long rolling
curves of fertile land, dotted with woods and farmsteads and small villages,
under smokeless skies, to the blue-misty Catskills, which formed the western
horizon.

His abnormally fond mother fondly recalled that he had been an unusually
"good" baby and little boy—sweet-tempered, kind, sensitive, eager to please,
hence tractable, anxious to do the "right thing," naturally courteous and
thoughtful of others. When on his good behavior, and he was generally well
behaved, he was a perfect little gentleman.

But his mother also recalled that he evinced at an early age an instinct for
power, a habit of command, when dealing with his contemporaries. Playing
with other children, *he* gave the orders; the others obeyed him with, it seemed
to his mother, a surprising alacrity and lack of rancor on most occasions.[2] It
was as if he were born knowing he was meant for posts of leadership, was
meant to be a center of activity, and so felt actually *obliged* to exercise authority over his associates in problem or decision-making situations.

Thus there strongly operated in him two natural tendencies, or attractions
—one toward power, the other toward conformity—that easily might have
contradicted each other in ways destructive of spiritual integrity, or else fused
with each other in ways perversely sadomasochistic. In the event they did

neither. They became healthfully complementary, mutually reinforcing.

And for this his parents were in large part responsible.

By both of them, if chiefly by his prideful mother, he was trained to ancestral pride and encouraged in his innate conservatism, his natural love for tradition and for collecting things—stamps, bird skins, books, prints, historical memorabilia of all kinds; this is to say that his power drive was curbed and molded by a deferential sense of the past (the past was beyond his control or any change) and a concomitant commitment to time-tested values and institutions. By both parents equally he was encouraged in his love for outdoor country living, and from each was fed into his bloodstream, as he might believe, the veritable passion he had for the sea, for blue-water sailing and all things naval.* And this, too, served as a curb upon a prideful lust for power: in the solitude of open country, upon the ocean under wide and empty skies, or alone within the green-arched cathedral of a forest, one comes face to face with the infinite, the eternal, and learns humility. Both parents taught him that privilege breeds responsibility, that one's duty to society is proportionate to the height of one's position in society—a teaching that happily linked together the instinct for power and the instinct for conformity in an ideal of service. Wrote Franklin Roosevelt at Harvard: " . . . [the Roosevelts] have never felt that because they were born in a good position they could put their hands in their pockets and succeed. They have felt, rather, that being born in a good position there was no excuse for them if they did not do their duty by the community."[3]

But though both parents impressed this moral teaching upon him, it was more his father than his mother who did so. James Roosevelt was fifty-four years old when Franklin was born, the only child of his second marriage.† During Franklin's childhood, he was a vigorous, active outdoorsman, an English-type country squire. Along with an acute sense of community responsibility joined to an equally acute sense of being born "in a good position" (not a few of James Roosevelt's Hyde Park neighbors thought him a snob, though even those who resented him respected him), he instilled in his son the manly virtues. He was an enthusiastic horseman; he actively supervised the farming of his acres, the management of his woods and herds of fine dairy cows; he loved iceboating, hiking, tennis, sailing on the Hudson—loved even more sailing in the Bay of Fundy off the island of Campobello, where he established

---

*His paternal grandmother was born Mary Rebecca Aspinwall of the wealthy sea-trading Aspinwalls. Her mother was a Howland, and in the 1850s the New York firm of Aspinwall & Howland owned the largest fleet of clipper ships in the world. His maternal grandfather, Warren Delano II, was of a family whose every male generation had gone to sea since the 1660s, prospering hugely as whaling captains and in the China trade.

†An instance of the interconnectedness, a manifestation of the exclusiveness, of New York's aristocracy was the fact that James Roosevelt's first wife, Rebecca Howland, was the daughter of his mother's first cousin. By her he had a son, James Roosevelt ("Rosy") Roosevelt who, old enough to be Franklin's father (Rosy was only six years younger than Franklin's mother), was like an uncle to the boy. He lived next door to Springwood, Franklin's boyhood home at Hyde Park, with his second wife (his first, who died, was a daughter of *the* Mrs. Astor who ruled New York Society in the 1890s). He died there in 1927 at the age of seventy-three.

his summer vacation home when Franklin was in the second year of life. He involved his son in all these activities. But all through Franklin's adolescence he was slowly fading out of life, becoming increasingly dim, increasingly an invalid (he died, aged seventy-two, during Franklin's freshman year at Harvard). And in a very real sense the role of father in the boy's life during this period was assumed by the headmaster of Groton School, Endicott Peabody, whose lessons for living were essentially an extension and intensification of those already impressed upon the boy.

Because his doting mother could not bear to part with her darling son, Franklin did not enter Groton at age twelve, as he was supposed to do, but at age fourteen. This meant that he found himself initially an outsider. Others in his form, the III Form,* had already established circles of friendship, from which he was excluded. They had already established themselves individually in recognized positions in the community; he had no defined status whatever. And he lacked the outstanding abilities as athlete or scholar that might have enabled him to shape for himself, quickly, easily, a position of prestige. He suffered from homesickness two years after his form mates had got over theirs —achingly lonely hours during which he doubted his own adequacy—and was in general more nakedly, vulnerably exposed than most Grotonians to the force of the headmaster's character and personality. This was a powerful force. Endicott Peabody, then in his prime, was a man of commanding physical presence: big, strong, handsome, virile, a natural athlete. He was also a man of immense conviction and iron-hard integrity, sure of himself, certain of the correctness of his opinions, as few men are, and his temperament was unabashedly authoritarian. Not a few sensitive boys of as yet unformed character, lacking an inner strength of resistance, were overwhelmed by him, with unhappy effects upon their future character and conduct.

Upon Franklin Roosevelt, however, his effect was, on the evidence, altogether wholesome, a fact bespeaking the boy's likeness to the teacher (who was also like the boy's mother) in several respects, though in other important respects he was very different. The authority Peabody exerted was, in his own deep belief, imposed from on high. He was an ordained minister of the Protestant Episcopal Church; Groton School and the village were an Episcopalian parish, of which he was rector. Authority and responsibility, the right to command and the obligation to serve, were therefore joined in his Christian teaching of boys who came exclusively, like those of the great English public schools, from the elite and seemed destined by their class position to rule in the America of the future. By Peabody's powerful influence the boy Franklin was confirmed in the religious faith already instilled in him by his parents and by the services of St. James Church in Hyde Park and St. Anne's on Campobello. He was encouraged in the belief, evinced even before he entered Groton, in a universal drama authored and directed by God wherein his own

---

*Peabody's school was modeled on Thomas Arnold's Rugby: British "form" was substituted for American "class."

life, being an assigned "part" and an immensely important one in the total scheme, had its own specific plot or pattern.[4]

What caused him to believe that *his* role was so important?

He was the adored only child of a highly privileged couple, to the manner and the manor born, and the family name he bore had become, by the time he left Groton, one of the most famous in America. From his father's lips he as a small child had heard about the immigration to New Amsterdam from Holland of Claes Martenszen Van Rosenvelt in the 1640s and about Claes's namesake son, who, after New Amsterdam became New York, anglicized his name to the simpler Nicholas Roosevelt. This first Nicholas Roosevelt, he knew, was a common ancestor, the last common ancestor, of Franklin and the man who became the great hero of Franklin's boyhood—a great hero to all the nation, as a matter of fact, after San Juan Hill—namely, Theodore Roosevelt, whose niece, Eleanor, became Franklin's wife shortly after TR became President of the United States and whose career had been the model for Franklin's own. From his mother's lips he as a small child heard about Philippe de la Noye, who landed in Plymouth in 1621, reputedly the first Huguenot to set foot in Massachusetts; who married Hester Dewsbury some thirteen years later; and who fathered many children on his farm near Duxbury.[5]

It was from the seventh son, Jonathan, that Franklin's maternal line was descended. Having served with much valor in King Philip's War, Jonathan was rewarded with a land grant of 800 acres near New Bedford. And from New Bedford, destined to become the most famous of all whaling ports, Jonathan's son Ephraim sailed in the 1660s as the first of the seafaring Delanos (so the family name was by that time, or soon thereafter, spelled). The Delano family seat was established at Fairhaven, across the narrow harbor from New Bedford. There, in 1809, was born Franklin's beloved maternal grandfather, Warren Delano II, who became in his young manhood a senior partner in the great Boston shipping firm of Russell, Sturgis and Company (later Russell and Company) and chief of his firm's China, largely tea-exporting, enterprise, with headquarters on Macao, across the harbor from Hong Kong. Warren Delano II was thirty-three years old—a mature, self-assured, wealthy gentleman with charming manners and a considerable sophistication, though rigidly conservative in his economic, political, religious, and moral views—when, during a return visit to his homeland, he met and married eighteen-year-old Catherine Robbins Lyman of Northampton, Massachusetts.

She, too, explained Franklin's mother, was of distinguished New England lineage on both her mother's and father's sides, numbering among her ancestors heroic Indian fighters, soldiers of the Revolution, a speaker of the Massachusetts House, a lieutenant governor of the commonwealth, several prominent clergymen (the paternal grandmother of Harriet Beecher Stowe was a Lyman), and the founders of Hartford, Connecticut.[6] For three years after her wedding she lived with her husband in his magnificent house on Macao. Then he retired from the China trade, a wealthy man, and returned to America. In 1851 he bought sixty acres of orchard and woodland and lawn, with a substantial farmhouse on a hill commanding splendid views in all directions, on the west bank of the Hudson a couple of miles or so north of Newburgh and only a few miles south and across the river from James Roosevelt's place, called Springwood, at Hyde Park. The property was developed at an expense many times greater than the original purchase price into a multigabled and many-towered mansion of forty rooms, with wide verandas opening upon a beautifully landscaped private park. It was named Algonac. Franklin was brought there for a visit only a week or so after he was christened Franklin Delano Roosevelt (he was named after his mother's uncle Franklin Delano), which was seven weeks after his birth, on January 30, 1882. He was a frequent visitor at Algonac, often for days at a time, all through his boyhood. He knew well the large and airy second-floor bedroom, its windows looking far out across the river, where his mother was born in 1854 as the seventh child of her parents. (She was christened Sarah after a spinster aunt who lived in Algonac, but her name was soon spelled "Sara," and she was nicknamed Sallie, to avoid a confusion of names in the household.) At Algonac Franklin heard many an exciting tale of Delano seafaring days and celebrated many a joyous Christmas and Thanksgiving among a crowd of jolly, active, vital aunts, uncles, and cousins—until Grandmother and Grandfather Delano died within two years of each other while he was a student at Groton.

All this nourished a family pride that could not but nourish, in turn, his sense of his own importance.

And by the time he had graduated from college, married his distant cousin Eleanor, fathered two children, and become a lowly clerk, though with an assured lucrative future, in a rich and prestigious New York City corporate law firm, he felt that he knew quite precisely the objective nature of his importance—knew, in other words, what the plot or pattern of his life must be.

In broad outline it followed closely the career of his wife's uncle the ex-President of the United States, with the important difference that TR was a Republican, whereas Franklin, like his father, was a Democrat. (But was TR really a Republican? Franklin didn't think so in later years. TR was a Progressive and, as such, would have been happier in Democratic ranks after 1912 than he ever was in Republican ranks.) He, Franklin, would go into politics, win election to the New York State legislature, be appointed Assistant Secretary of the Navy, become governor of New York, and then move from the Executive Mansion in Albany to the White House in Washington. He spoke of this in a rare burst of candor to his fellow law clerks one day in 1908, and with such calm conviction that *they* were more than halfway convinced.[7] The conviction was strengthened in the years immediately following. For in 1910 the young Democratic Roosevelt did go into politics, won election to the State Senate by a substantial majority in the overwhelmingly Republican Twenty-sixth Senatorial District (Putnam, Dutchess, and Columbia counties), promptly gained by bold stratagem a more than statewide reputation as Progressive reformer, and then won reelection in 1912.

The 1912 triumph, crucial to Roosevelt's career, was largely due to the man who in that year became his most trusted intimate adviser and closest working associate and whose friendship strengthened his belief in the greatness of his future. This man was Louis McHenry Howe.

In 1912 Howe was a newspaperman of uncertain employment, meager income, and wretched health—he suffered from chronic asthma and a heart condition. Forty-one years of age, but appearing older, he stood barely five feet tall, weighed less than one hundred pounds, and presented to the world a sour and wizened countenance from which a cigarette perpetually protruded (he smoked three or more packs of Sweet Caporals a day) and which appeared perpetually dirty because of a childhood bicycle accident, in which fine gravel had been ground into the skin. He had a shrewd, well-informed political intelligence and a brusque irritable manner, in part determined by his bad health and in part a protective coating for his sensitive inner self. Beneath this coating, looking out through fine brown eyes, was a rare sweetness (bittersweetness) of personality, revealed only in flashes and then, generally, only to the very few whom he loved. At once cynical and idealistic, tough and tender, iconoclastic and hero-worshipful (Carlyle was his favorite author), he hated sham and was harshly contemptuous of all posing, yet shared with Franklin Roosevelt, to whom he was initially drawn in part for this very reason, a strong histrionic bent. Like Roosevelt he delighted in playacting and had a flair for the theatrical, along with a sense of all the world as theater. Like Roosevelt, too, he was encouraged by his boyhood religious training toward a belief that the world as theater was cosmically authored, that it was therefore purposeful beyond human understanding, that consequently the individual lives within it were predestined, preordained. The Howe family's Presbyterian Calvinism differed greatly in mood from the Roosevelt family's Episcopalianism. Also, Howe himself differed from Roosevelt in that he professed no strong Christian faith but inclined instead, as a disciple of Carlyle, toward a heroic destiny-concept, a strictly attitudinal inclination in his case, since he never consciously thought much about it. But the similarities between the two men were great, and almost from the moment he first saw the tall, young, handsome, vibrant Roosevelt in action upon the Senate floor in Albany, early in 1911, Louis Howe saw him as future President. He saluted him as "Beloved and Revered Future President" in a letter written the day after the Democratic National Convention at which Woodrow Wilson was nominated.[8] He longed to join forces with Roosevelt in pursuit, or realization, of this supreme object.

Hence the eager excitement with which he responded in September 1912 to a summons from Roosevelt, who lay seriously ill with typhoid fever in his New York City home on East Sixty-fifth Street. Wholly incapable of the vigorous campaign that, in view of his district's traditional Republicanism, appeared necessary for his reelection to the state Senate, Roosevelt faced in that dark hour the extinction of the political career he had barely but promisingly begun. TR had launched his Bull Moose campaign, virtually assuring Wilson's election to the Presidency and assuring victories also to the New York Democracy in state office campaigns. How could a Democratic Roosevelt hope for future political preferment if, in the prevailing favorable circumstances, he went down to defeat? Louis Howe saved him. The little man took over the Roosevelt campaign and ran it brilliantly, innovatively, virtually on his own. And on Election Day Roosevelt's triumph was by a considerably larger majority than he had had in 1910. A few months later, in further fulfillment of the prediction he had made to his fellow law clerks five years before, Roosevelt was appointed Assistant Secretary of the Navy by President Wilson. He took Louis Howe with him to Washington as his top assistant.

Ever since, Howe had been at his side, helping him to avoid career mistakes, to make the most of career opportunities, and serving as his alter ego in many an important transaction. Howe lived through Roosevelt; he had virtually no life apart from Roosevelt, though he was married and had two children. He was therefore, for Roosevelt, an extra energy, an extra brain, an objectification and consequent reinforcement of the Roosevelt will. And in the last capacity, he was of decisive importance to Roosevelt's career on two other crucial occasions.

The first of these was during the closing years of the World War, when Roosevelt made an astonishing, almost incredible departure from his long-term purpose and design: he fell in love with his wife's social secretary, Lucy Mercer. He seriously considered divorcing Eleanor so that he might marry Lucy. This would have meant the end of his political career, as Eleanor, wounded almost to death, pointed out to him in offering him his freedom. It would also have meant the loss to him of the family fortune, or the bulk of it, for Sara Delano Roosevelt had absolute legal control of this and she, morally outraged (there were now five children, *her* grandchildren), said flatly she would cut off her son without a cent if he went through with the divorce. Lucy herself was opposed to divorce on religious grounds: she was a Roman Catholic, and her marriage to a divorced man could have received Church sanction only through a special dispensation from Rome. Nevertheless, the decision finally arrived at, in family conclave, was a close one. FDR and Lucy agreed to part (two years later she married the wealthy socialite Winthrop Rutherfurd, a widower old enough to be her father). The Roosevelt marriage, at least as regards public appearances, was preserved, and the scandalous gossip that had begun to be whispered quickly died away. But the opposite of this could easily have happened if Louis Howe had not thrown upon narrowly balanced scales the full weight of his commitment to FDR's future greatness, organically joined to his conviction that what FDR seemed about to do was in every respect—religious, moral, practical—a grievous wrong.[9]

The second crucial occasion was in the summer of 1921, when FDR, after running as the Democratic candidate for Vice-President in 1920 and subsequently launching what he intended to be a lucrative interim career as a Wall Street lawyer and business executive, was struck down by polio while vacationing on Campobello. Louis Howe was there. With Eleanor, he nursed the desperately sick man through the nearly fatal initial phase of the attack. He skillfully, unscrupulously managed the news of the attack in such a way as to prevent the abrupt termination of FDR's career as a public man. (He virtually *was* FDR, in career matters, during the months of his friend's total incapacitation, enlisting Eleanor's aid in a campaign to restore FDR's morale and provide him with opportunities for a return to active politics.) And without Howe's iron determination that FDR would continue along the road to the White House, crippled or not, FDR might well have given up and retired to Hyde Park, an invalid country squire, as his imperious mother wished and tried to persuade him to do. Instead, the stricken man began and continued without letup an essentially grim but outwardly gay struggle to regain the use of paralyzed legs while entering more and more into public life. He engaged in exercises strenuous and painful beyond most men's bearing. He swam in the thermal spring waters of Warm Springs, Georgia, where in 1926 he bought a rundown resort and began its transformation into a treatment center for infantile paralysis victims. By 1928 he had strengthened himself sufficiently to permit his standing on steel-braced legs and even "walking" on them with the aid of a cane and somebody else's brawny arm. Simultaneously, he had developed, from the waist up, a magnificent physique—an iron-muscled torso, an enormous chest, the thick neck of a wrestler—and was in better general health than he had been before his illness. He had also returned prominently to political life with his rousing "Happy Warrior" speech nominating Al Smith for President in the ill-fated Democratic National Convention of 1924.

And by this long ordeal he was strengthened in his conviction that his life was being lived within a framework of higher purpose, that he was a "chosen one" of the Almighty.

In the darkest hours he had ever known, when he lay near death on Campobello following his polio attack, he had despaired utterly. He believed God had "abandoned" him, as he later confessed to a friend. And one may suspect, though he certainly never confessed it to anyone, that what he then suffered seemed to him a retribution, divinely imposed, for his transgression, his willful departure from God's design, in the affair of Lucy Mercer. But when his "punishment" proved less than capital and he had stubbornly fought his way back to health and career prosperity, he *knew* absolutely that what had happened to him and through him, including his waywardness, even, was integral to God's design. His had been, as Eleanor called it, a "trial by fire."[10] He was being tested and purified for the great historic tasks he must ultimately undertake.

Gulls wheeled above him, hoarsely crying. Boat engines throbbed beneath his feet. A passing freighter's whistle deeply roared. And if these sounds broke through the cone of private silence that encased him, the middle-aged man beside the ferry's railing might feel again, through memory, the sea's various moods as he had experienced them in boyhood and youth—how the sea had ebbed and flowed in huge violent tides around Campobello, how it far more gently, meagerly flooded and shrank away from the sloping sands of Buzzards

Bay—and he might be particularly reminded of a harbor scene very different in appearance from the one before his eyes but very like it in certain ways of meaning. . . .

At Fairhaven, Massachusetts, on Buzzards Bay, stood The Homestead, the large house built in the Federal style in the early nineteenth century by the original Warren Delano, Franklin's great-grandfather, a whaling captain. In the library of that house were bound volumes of illustrated magazines of the 1850s, with woodcuts and steel engravings of the American whaling fleet at home and at sea, over which the boy Franklin pored for hours. On one wall of the library hung "a lithograph of the Stone Fleet—mile after mile of vessels headed South to be sunk at the mouth of a Confederate harbor." It was a picture made richly meaningful to him by the tales told him at Fairhaven by his grandparents and other Delano relatives about Confederate fighting ships viciously attacking Yankee whaling vessels, including Delano ships, during the Civil War. Again and again he listened to "stories of how the *Florida,* the *Shenandoah,* the *Sumter* and the *Alabama* drove the whaleships off the seas —or burned them."

And even more fascinating than the magazines, the pictures, the family stories, was an old trunk he found, or was directed to, in The Homestead's fourth-floor attic. The trunk was filled with packets of time-faded letters and canvas logbooks, wherein the boy read with avid interest, especially as he grew older, laconic dated reports of ships spoken, of whales sighted and chased and killed, of shipboard injuries and deaths, of mountainous seas during storms that blew sometimes for days on end with near-fatal violence in far northern and southern latitudes, of remote ports ("Fayal, . . . the Falklands, . . . Unalaska") visited during voyages lasting two years and more—bare-bones accounts fleshed out by the boy's imagination into wondrous tales of adventure in the farthest, loneliest quarters of the globe.

All of which rendered more poignant, sharpened with a sense of loss, the boy's musings as he sat solitary upon the stringpiece of his great-grandfather's stone wharf at Fairhaven, looking out across the harbor. He saw battered old whaleships anchored in the stream, saw "a dozen tall spars" aspiring above granite warehouses "near the old winding stone bridge" on the New Bedford shore. Even as a seven-year-old in 1889, or so the middle-aged Roosevelt would say in print a few months hence,[11] he realized that those spars had been "superseded" by the "tall stacks" of New Bedford's cotton mills as "the focal point of the busy community," that the ships were but "survivors" of "a mightier age" now lost to roaring monsters of iron and steam. 'Twas a pity, he felt. The tall-masted vessels, so beautifully designed for the clean, noiseless, nondestructive use of an unprocessed environmental energy, were a lovely sight. The clanking smoking factories, on the other hand, were ugly and often as offensive to the nostril as they were to the eye and ear.

The whole of this boyhood scene was colored, therefore, in Roosevelt's memory of it, by a quality of sadness, a nostalgic yearning toward the simpler, more natural world of his ancestors. High indeed was the price that must be paid in vital coin, paid out in terms of an impoverishment, as he felt, of individual living experience, for a progress that was inevitable. He could not but regret it.[12] His regret, however, was untinged by resentment and unaccompanied by hostility toward its object. It never occurred to him as a boy, and he would not permit himself as a man, to place quotation marks around "inevitable" and "progress" in a bitterly negative commentary upon the latter. Essentially he accepted and even affirmed that which he regretted. And this was highly significant of his temperament, his mind, his basic pieties; it bespoke a self-conception and world view that, because they were to become of determining historical importance upon that shore of Time he now approached, would be subjected by future historians to a far more critical and searching examination than he himself ever made.

One such historian would find it useful to compare Roosevelt's sense of reality, and of his place in the world, with central conceptions of a massive philosophy of history that in 1928 was making a great stir in intellectual circles. The first volume of the American edition of Oswald Spengler's *The Decline of the West* had been published to great fanfare in the spring of 1926; the second was to be published only three months after Roosevelt's mid-October ferry crossing (publication day was November 9, 1928). And though it is unlikely that Roosevelt himself ever read a word of this gloomily prophetic, often insightful, and always perversely romantic work, a significant portion of what he essentially was can be defined in terms of it.

Basic to Spengler's philosophy was a distinction between two kinds of time. One is actual living time, time as we experience it, a continuous vital flux (duration) whose hallmark is direction and irreversibility. The other is recorded clock time, which is not really temporal at all but spatial. It is time that has been intellectualized, mathematicized, eternalized, and thus killed in the sense that duration and irreversible direction, which are of its very essence in our living experience, have been removed from it. Its dead body, so to speak, is stretched out in space, in an eternal *now*, where it is measured and numbered as a reversible succession of moments, each of precisely the same length or width as the others. Associated with actual living time are what Spengler calls the "Destiny idea" and the "world-as-history." Associated with time as a fourth dimension of space are the "Causality Principle" and the "world-as-nature." He writes: " . . . there is, besides a necessity of cause and effect—which I may call the *logic of space*—another necessity, an organic necessity of life, that of Destiny—the *logic of time.*" From this it follows that there are "born destiny-men and causality-men" with "a whole world" separating the two. The causality-man is an "intellectual, . . . subtle and fact-shy," who *thinks* about living, mostly in the past or future, instead of actively presently living, whereas the destiny-man, the man of action, "lives in the *actual* world, the world of political, military, and economic decisions, in which concepts and systems do not figure or count." The causality-man is a partial man. In him "a single organ [the intellect] can operate without (and even against) the body." From him "we get all those ethico-politico-social reform-projects which demonstrate, unanswerably, how things ought to be and how to set about making them so—theories that . . . have not in one single instance affected the slightest alteration in life."[13] The destiny-man, on the other hand, is a "whole man" who, "active, and contemptuous of thought," has always a "belief in his star . . . which is something wholly different from belief in the correctness of a standpoint" and has "voices of the blood that speak in moments of decision, and the immovably quiet conviction that justifies any aim and any means," all of which "are denied the critical, meditative man." What the destiny-man knows instinctively, intuitively, without having to earn his knowledge by any arduous process of study or thought, is of the substance and rhythm of History, to which his heartbeat is attuned. He, in the Lawrencian-Hitlerian phrase, "thinks with his blood."

Now, Roosevelt, if one accepts and limits himself to Spengler's flat distinctions, must be classified as a destiny-man. Certainly he was not a causality-man. He had always been possessed and driven by an immense and restless physical energy. Writing to a friend in 1922 apropos of his friend's literary endeavors, he had said, " . . . I can't help feeling that you are built a bit like me—that you need something physically more active [than writing], with constant contact with all sorts of people in many kinds of places."[14] During his years of formal schooling he had evinced no interest whatever in the abstract, the purely speculative; he had shied away from courses in mathematics or philosophy and from whatever seemed to him "merely" theoretical, rather than realistically, objectively descriptive, in such courses as economics, government, and political science. Nor had he ever evinced any faith in the efficacy of abstract ideas or of generalized thinking in that world of practical affairs by which he was almost totally engaged. Quite the contrary. If never openly contemptuous of pure thought—certainly he was never assertively so —he had nothing to do with it, personally. It was irrelevant to his vital concerns. It could even be hazardous to these—it might prevent his making the right career decision at a crucial moment—by distracting his attention from small but important signs or cues presented him by and through his immediate environmental situation. For, to repeat, at the root and core of his conception of self and world was the inward certainty that he was a "chosen one" of the Almighty, his career a role assigned him by the Author of the universe, and that the "part" he must "act" or "play" to the best of his ability, feeling himself into it, even identifying with it, up to a point, was of major historical importance.

But if Roosevelt thus manifested in action the "belief in his star" that characterizes the Spenglerian Man of Destiny, there was a profoundly significant difference between his and Spengler's conceptions of the nature of this guiding star. For Spengler, of course, the star was Destiny itself, while for Roosevelt, it was God, and between the pagan Spengler's assertion of Destiny and the Christian Roosevelt's belief in God the difference was actually an opposition. The assertion was complicated, egotistic, dark with doom; the faith was simple, humble, bright with hope.

Destiny, in Spengler's conception, was the vital force, the living Time or Direction of a Culture—and every Culture (Classical, Egyptian, Chinese, Western, *et al.*) was a distinctly individual organism with its own unique life-style and life cycle, or History.[15] It was mortal. Having been born, and having gone through a childhood and youth, a middle and old age—or a Spring, a Summer, an Autumn, a Winter, to employ another Spenglerian metaphor—it must surely die, even as you and I. The West, upon which Spengler naturally concentrated, since he was himself a Western man, though transcendent, had now entered the autumnal or declining years of its life. Nearly all of its genuinely creative possibilities had been realized. Which is to say that its Destiny was less and less a life force and more and more a process of dying—a malevolent force, therefore, for those who stubbornly persisted in their preference of life over death, freedom over bondage—and the Man of Destiny in the West was more and more the agent, the administrator, of death. Indeed, he was more even than this, since in Spengler the destiny-man actually ultimately fused or identified with Destiny. He was or became "himself a Destiny (like Napoleon)" between whom "as a fact" of his own perception and the "other facts" he perceived around him there was "a harmony of metaphysical rhythm [*sic*] which gives his decisions their dreamlike certainty."[16]

No such fusion or identification with the moving force of History was implicit or even possible in Roosevelt's plain, simple, matter-of-fact Christianity. Believing absolutely in God the Father and Jesus Christ as the Son of God; believing that God, caring for each individual human being, was infinitely kind and good as well as all-wise and all-powerful; believing or *feeling* that History was a working out of Divine Purpose, that every truly fundamental historical force was a manifestation of Divine Will—believing all this, he must and did believe that History, though it had at any given extended period of time a tidal ebb and flow, had in the long run a surging flow in one direction. It was away from polar Evil and toward polar Good. This was the essential Progress, from worse to better, a process flowing out of gloomy mountains of barbarism through sunlit uplands of increasingly civilized order toward an ultimate shining sea of goodness, happiness, tranquillity (if he had no love of the world city as it now stood at the river's mouth, neither did he doubt that the city, too, was an element or stage of Progress), and it was inevitable because it was God's will. As a "chosen one," he himself was the instrument of Progress, a special agent on Earth of Divine Beneficence. But *only* an instrument. *Only* an agent. The notion of attempting a mystical union with God, becoming one with Him, had it ever occurred to him, would have been rejected as an absurd, outrageous presumption. And similarly with regard to efforts to understand God in any deep metaphysical sense. What his heart accepted should not be questioned or even examined by his mind. "I really never thought about it," he said to his wife when she pressed him, too hard, to say whether or not he was really convinced, intellectually convinced, that Christian doctrine was true. "I think it is just as well not to think about things like that too much."[17]

Thus, Roosevelt's attitude toward power, his attraction by it, and his exercise of it were characterized by a humility, a selflessness, wholly foreign to the Spenglerian Man of Destiny. By his religious faith and his self-conception in terms of it (his sense of his role in History) he was required actively to seek great power. The greatest earthly power. But he never did so with the feeling that he himself would *become* the power he exercised, or even that it would become his personal property, to be used in service of his purely personal will. It was assigned, imposed, from on high. It remained God's. And the ultimate responsibility for his use of it was therefore also God's. This conviction would enable him to act, often, as if he were indeed possessed of a "dreamlike certainty" of decision. On that shore of Time he now approached, he would often move swiftly, boldly, with a seemingly fully informed decisiveness, as if he knew exactly what he was doing and what the results would be, when others in posts of decision—more cerebral than he, more weighed down by a sense of personal responsibility for large-scale consequences—were paralyzed by doubt and fear. His inward experience of such moments, however, was very different from a Napoleon's, or a Nietzschean Superman's, in that his act was not at all the exercise of an iron and conquering will. It was almost the opposite of this. Role and game playing fused: his experience became that of a pious gambler whose risk taking, teleologically motivated, is a form of prayer and an act of faith.

It may be compared, in essence, to that of a man pursued by enemies through a moonless night to the edge of an abyss. Pitch-black darkness fills the void, its depth unknown. To skirt it is impossible; to remain where one is means certain capture; to leap is to risk fatal injury, though there is the alternative possibility of safe landing on safe ground, beyond further pursuit. Roosevelt, brought to such a pass, did not hesitate for long. Quickly he made the leap, the blind existential leap, in his belief (his act a test of his faith) that this was God's intention. Otherwise, would he, a "chosen one," find himself in so precarious a situation? And was not the end of his leap bound, therefore, to be a happy landing?

He was, in fact, making such a leap—the most important, insofar as his career was concerned, that he had ever made—as he crossed the river on this mid-October day.

In late June the Democratic National Committee had assembled in steaming hot Houston, Texas, and had nominated for President, on the first ballot, Governor Alfred E. Smith of New York. Franklin D. Roosevelt had been a key figure in these proceedings. He had been Smith's floor manager; he had made the speech placing Smith in nomination, an eloquent speech that, broadcast over a national radio network, had brought him great and glowingly favorable national publicity. Ever since, he had been harried and pursued by Democratic politicians who wanted him to run to succeed Smith as governor of New York. He was by far the strongest available Democratic gubernatorial candidate. He could, by his victory, assure Al Smith of New York's electoral vote. And Smith had to have these votes if he was to defeat his Republican opponent, Coolidge's Secretary of Commerce, Herbert C. Hoover. So the argument had run.

But it had come hard against Roosevelt's counterargument. Or plea.

Roosevelt was making definite and obvious progress toward walking again. Four years before, when he appeared before the Democratic Convention to make his "Happy Warrior" nominating speech, he had appeared on crutches. He had had to prop himself most carefully against the lectern, his iron-braced legs spread far apart and his strong hands gripping the lectern's sides, as he made his address. This year he had walked, on his still iron-braced legs, at least he had *seemed* to be actually walking, across the convention hall platform, leaning upon a cane clasped in his right hand while with his left he clasped his son Elliott's right arm, and he stood at seeming ease before the lectern, waving gaily to the cheering multitude. The demonstration of his physical recovery had been dramatic. But he still had some way to go. Give him another year, or two; let him continue his swimming and other exercises at Warm Springs; and *then* he would return, with a vengeance, to the political wars as a candidate for elective office, if his party wished it. For by then, he confidently predicted, he would be able to throw away the hated leg braces. He would walk unaided.

Nor was this the whole of his counterargument, or plea. He had used his own capital to buy the Warm Springs resort. He had organized in early 1927 the Georgia Warm Springs Foundation, Inc., a nonprofit corporation that was developing the place into a first-class hydrotherapeutic facility. He had committed to this enterprise the bulk of his personal fortune and had assumed a moral responsibility for its success; he simply could not afford to give less than major attention to it until it was solidly established as a going concern, and that could not be for another two or three years. As for the necessity of his running in order to ensure Smith's carrying the state, Roosevelt refused to concede it. Smith's great record as a four-term governor was "so clear to the voters" that he was bound to carry the state "regardless of who is nominated" to succeed him. So said Roosevelt to the Smith camp.[18]

All this had been given added point, as argument and plea, by Roosevelt's departure from Hyde Park on September 17, his arrival at Warm Springs a day or so later. He would stay there, he announced, for several weeks. At Warm Springs he was ostentatiously out of touch with developments in New York, as final preparations were made for the Democratic State Convention. Pressures upon him to become a candidate were weakened by the fact that they could no longer be exerted directly, face to face, but must be transmitted across a thousand miles through letters, telegrams, long-distance phone calls, which might or might not be answered. And as pressures were thus softened, his resistant will was hardened—and hardened, in part, *because* of his physical remoteness from the places where state party decisions were being made.

For as he exercised in the warm mineral waters of the spring-fed pool and relaxed in the hot Georgia September sun, his mind was released to run freely over his present circumstance and all that had brought him to it. He could trace his resolve, over and over again, back and down to its deepest root, testing it there, confirming it. He and Louis Howe were privately convinced that 1928 was likely to prove a very bad year for Democrats almost everywhere. Even in the solid South. Even in New York. Despite his outwardly confident assertions to the contrary, Roosevelt was far from certain that Smith would carry his home state "regardless," and he considered it distinctly possible, even likely, that he himself would be defeated if he permitted himself to be inveigled into the gubernatorial race. The event could severely harm his political career and might be fatal to it. Far better, therefore, that he wait until 1932—Howe's target year—to run for governor, diligently using the interim to better his physical condition and increase his political following. His victory then, followed by reelection two years later, would make him a front-runner for the Democratic presidential nomination in 1936. And by 1936 the tide of "Republican Prosperity," on which Hoover would probably now ride into the White House, would almost certainly have receded, given the normal ebb and flow of events, providing solid ground on which a Democrat such as he could run to victory.

His conviction was nourished by his strong disapproval of the kind of campaign Al Smith was waging. For campaign manager and chairman of the Democratic National Committee Smith had chosen a fellow Roman Catholic, John J. Raskob, who was a key executive of General Motors (the national campaign headquarters were in the General Motors Building in New York City), a vice-president of E. I. Du Pont de Nemours, and a director of some of the nation's largest banks. The Smith-Raskob campaign, financed in large part by contributions from big-business men, was on fundamental issues virtually indistinguishable from the Hoover-Republican one. Neither candidate recognized, or admitted, that there were large bodies of workers and farmers who did not share to any fairly proportionate degree in the generally prevailing, widely ballyhooed prosperity. Not only did the two candidates agree that this prosperity was real and enduring, they also argued that it was due to the genius of businessmen whose operations had been unhampered, had indeed been encouraged, by the governmental policies of the last eight years. Smith had even abandoned his party's traditional opposition to high tariff walls and appeared as fervently committed to a big-business rule of America, under the guise of *laissez-faire*, as Hoover and the Republicans were. This meant that the electorate, presented with no truly alternative choices on what seemed to Roosevelt essential matters, focused on the nonessential—upon the "phony" issues of religion and Prohibition—and on these Smith's position was less popular than Hoover's.

With Roosevelt at Warm Springs, of course, for she accompanied him everywhere, was his personal secretary, Marguerite LeHand, whom everyone called Missy. During the 1920 vice-presidential campaign, she, then twenty-two years old, had been secretary to Roosevelt's campaign manager, Charles McCarthy. At the Democratic National Headquarters she met and became a friend of Eleanor Roosevelt. And it was at Eleanor's request that she had come to Hyde Park for several weeks following Election Day to help Roosevelt handle the correspondence and other paperwork that had piled up to an intimidating height while he campaigned. She was tall, slender, and graceful of figure, rather too long of face and strong of jaw to be conventionally beautiful but with large, lovely blue eyes and a ready and radiant smile. Quickly proving herself to be a remarkably capable stenographic secretary, she was able to impose efficient order swiftly upon an initially unmanageable chaos. Though far from robust physically, having suffered permanent heart damage from rheumatic fever while a child, she was a tremendous worker. She and FDR got on famously from the first day of their work together. She had an unusually sweet and even temper, and no egotistic assertiveness at all. Her manner was open, simple, unassuming, and unfailingly cheerful, obscuring from many (her value to her employer was enhanced by this disarming concealment) a steely strength of character and a hard-headed realistic intelligence that made her a generally sound judge of character, quick and accurate in her appraisal of motives and shrewd in her assessment of relative factors in a situation. Entering Roosevelt's permanent employ in early 1921, Missy had become indispensable to him following his polio attack, as indispensable as Louis Howe. She was now a member of the Roosevelt household, like Louis Howe. She was totally devoted to FDR, hence an extra energy and mobile extension of his mind and will, like Louis Howe. On occasion she was almost as important to his career decision-making as Louis Howe.

And like Louis Howe she was adamantly opposed to FDR's running for governor that year. Her reason for such opposition, or the distribution of emphasis among the several reasons, differed somewhat from Howe's. Her whole concern was FDR's personal welfare; purely political considerations weighed with her only to the extent that politics might add to, or subtract from, his good health and happiness. Though she must admit that the rate of improvement in his legs had greatly slowed since the fall of 1925, she believed he would continue improving and might actually walk again, as he insisted he would, if only he were permitted to continue his present strength-building regimen for another few years. She knew, moreover, that his life in general was happier now than it had been in any other years since she first met him, that his multitudinous interests were harmonized, balanced against one another, as never before in her experience of him. The proposal that he risk all this in the service of Al Smith's ambition, and perhaps destroy in the process his chance for future preferment, was utterly outrageous, in her view, especially since Smith's ambition was so unlikely to be achieved, no matter what was done for it, Smith's handicaps being what they were. If a sacrificial "goat" was needed, why not Bob Wagner?* So said a nearly frantic Howe in a telegram to Warm Springs in late September.[19] Missy thoroughly agreed.

---

*Robert F. Wagner had won election to the U.S. Senate in 1926, in a campaign greatly aided by Eleanor Roosevelt's work on his behalf. He wanted to stay in the Senate; he dreaded the possibility that he would be forced by the Smith organization to accept the gubernatorial nomination.

She therefore happily dispatched to Al Smith the long telegram FDR dictated to her on the last day of September, reiterating his "compelling" health reason "not to accept the nomination," and she happily joined in an all-day picnic on Dowdell's Knob, some miles from the cottage, a picnic designed to frustrate any attempt to communicate with her employer by telephone or telegraph on October 1, when the New York State Democratic Convention met in Rochester to decide the slate of party candidates. By the same token she was dismayed when Al Smith in Rochester managed to overcome the obstacles to communication, reaching Roosevelt by long-distance telephone on the night of October 1.

Missy may also have been puzzled by the part played in this transaction by her employer's wife. Certainly future historians would be. For though Eleanor Roosevelt was fully aware of the reasons why her husband did not wish to run, and had excellent reasons of her own for not wanting him to, it was she who in Rochester facilitated the decisive contact. Moreover, her facilitation was indispensable to the contact's being made. She knew, as every leading Democrat in the state convention knew, that FDR would accept a Rochester call from no one but her when, at Smith's earnest behest, she placed a person-to-person call to Warm Springs and then, when she had her husband on the line, handed the phone to Smith at her side. . . .

How came she to do this thing? *Why?*

In that year, Anna Eleanor Roosevelt (so she had been christened) was yet in the midst of a long struggle to free herself from an anguished, stultifying past and to define herself as a strong, effective, independent person. Hers had been a remarkably somber childhood. Awkward, owlishly solemn, buck-toothed, and plain-featured, she as a very little girl had been called Granny and labeled "queer," a psychologically devastating operation, by her mother, who, born Anna Hall, was famous in high society for her graceful beauty. The little girl, who was a very sensitive little girl, could not but sense that she was a sad disappointment to her mother, whose own celebrated charm thus became an emphatic commentary upon her daughter's lack of it. The little girl had adored and been adored by her father, Elliott Roosevelt, younger brother of Theodore, Jr. But he, alas, had become a hopeless alcoholic by the time she was five or six and lived apart from his family, visiting them only occasionally. He had been wholly incompetent to assume parental duties when his wife, Eleanor's mother, her resistance no doubt weakened by the sorrows he had brought upon her, died of diphtheria when Eleanor was eight. He himself died two years later, a death whose traumatic effect upon his daughter's psyche was permanent, if of changing quality. Eleanor and her brother Hall, six years her junior, were then being raised by their widowed grandmother, Grandmother Hall, and they continued to be raised by her, very strictly, with little apparent affection, mostly in a gloomy mansion called Oak Terrace at Tivoli on the Hudson's east bank, some fifteen miles north of Hyde Park. One of the grandmother's sons, Eleanor's uncle Vallie, remained in the household as a generally depressing and sometimes actively terrifying presence, for he was as hopeless an alcoholic and as dangerously violent when deep in his cups as Eleanor's father had been. One of her daughters, Eleanor's very pretty aunt Pussie, also remained in the household, her presence almost as disturbing and depressing as Vallie's, for she was possessed of a neurotic self-indulging "artistic" temperament, whose emotions were always extreme: she plunged from heights of elation into depths of despair, where, typically at the end of her numerous love affairs, she threatened suicide. From all this gloom and doom Eleanor had escaped, or had been partially freed, when she was fifteen. She was then sent across the Atlantic to a finishing school in England called Allenswood, just outside London, where she was wholesomely subjected through three school years to the influence of a most remarkable teacher and personality, Mlle. Marie Souvestre, the headmistress. She gained much in physical as well as mental poise, in actual as well as potential spiritual growth. She was liberated from some of the worst emotional and intellectual confinements imposed by her grandmother's stern religiosity. She was strengthened in her idealism, her determination to be and do good in the world, and inspired by Mlle. Souvestre's personal example to a passionate commitment to liberal political causes. Always a great reader, she developed standards and guiding patterns for future reading that would stretch her mind and pour into it insightful wisdom, along with factual knowledge. She returned to America a tall, slender, willowy girl whose large and wonderfully expressive eyes, silky long brown hair, and freshly glowing complexion offset considerably the ugliness of protruding teeth and who, particularly to the more intelligent among those who met her, was more interesting in general than she herself realized.

She was a far from "finished" person, however, and none could have found her actually beautiful. Many found her excessively tense and earnest when, aged eighteen, she was forced by her mother's family to "come out" into New York society, which she hated. She remained basically insecure, docile, uncritically trustful of and dependent upon those she loved (her need to love and be loved was overwhelming), and astonishingly unworldly in most respects (in others she was only too full of the knowledge of evil), when she met in society her distant cousin Franklin. She had known him only distantly before her debut, but soon became an increasingly intimate friend of his, and then, a year later, despite the veiled but stubborn efforts of Sara Roosevelt to force a postponement of the event, became his bride. Two letters to her prospective mother-in-law, one from her, the other from Franklin, written immediately after she and Franklin had revealed their intention to marry, defined the role she thought she wished to play. " . . . I do so want you to learn to love me a little," she wrote. "You must know that I will always try to do what you wish." And he wrote: " . . . dear Mummy, you know that nothing can ever change what we have always been and will always be to each other—only now you have two children to love & love you—and Eleanor as you know will always be a daughter to you in every way."[20] Her role, then, was to be that of a submissive and obedient daughter who was also a dutiful wife and mother, and this is the role she actually did play for a dozen years after her wedding.

During these years, she bore six children, one of whom died in infancy. At Hyde Park and in New York City she lived in houses legally owned by her mother-in-law; on Campobello she lived in a house that was a gift from her mother-in-law; she and Franklin were dependent upon her mother-in-law's largess to maintain them in their accustomed style of living. Every major decision of her life was made for her by her husband and mother-in-law, who even chose the governesses for Eleanor's children, until, in 1917 and 1918, there came down upon her the rending, crushing misery of the affair of Lucy Mercer —the ultimate betrayal, the final disillusionment—whereby she was presented with the ultimate choice, the final flat alternatives.

To be, or not to be, that was her question.

There opened then between her and her husband a gap that could never be closed. Indeed, it might easily have widened within a few years into a total separation, for they did wholly cease to have sexual relations, had not his polio affliction made demands upon her sympathies, her need to be of use, which she, being the kind of person she was, simply could not refuse. The tables were turned, for a time: his need for her was greater than hers for him. *He* became the dependent one. And, paradoxically, it was in the process of supplying *his* need, at Louis Howe's urgent promptings, that she began in the spring of 1922 the conscious struggle to supply her own. Silently, but with iron determination, she declared war upon all that had theretofore stifled her, belittled her, prevented her from becoming the person she longed to be, a war she had waged unremittingly ever since.

And by 1928 she had won many victories.

Out of a number of close working associations in various civic and political organizations with women who were making their own independent ways in the world had grown a number of warm personal friendships—with Rose Schneiderman and Maude Schwartz of the Women's Trade Union League, with Esther Lape and the lawyer Elizabeth Read of the League of Women Voters, with the wealthy pacifistic Caroline O'Day in the Women's Division of the New York Democratic State Committee, and, most important of all, with the executive secretary of the Women's Division, Nancy Cook, and Nancy's close friend and lifelong companion, the educator Marion Dickerman, who was joining the staff of the exclusive Todhunter School for girls in New York City when Eleanor first met her in 1922. Nancy, Marion, and Eleanor had in fact been inseparable for the last half-dozen years. They joined together as active substitutes for the crippled FDR on long camping trips with the two youngest Roosevelt sons, Franklin, Jr., and John, and in the summer island life of Campobello. (FDR had not returned to the island since his removal from it, in agony, following his polio attack.) At Louis Howe's suggestion, and with his initial help, they published and edited a printed monthly, *Democratic Women's News,* for the Women's Division. At FDR's suggestion and with his active supervisory help, on Hyde Park land owned by him to which he gave the three a lifetime lease, they built Val Kill Cottage, using fieldstone and lumber from his land. This became Nancy and Marion's home. Eleanor herself lived there as much of the time as she could, and FDR came often for recreation in the swimming pool and picnic area that were developed on the cottage grounds. The three women jointly purchased the Todhunter School for girls, of which Marion became principal, and Eleanor associate principal, and where Eleanor taught literature, history, and public affairs for two and a half days a week during the school term. They made political organizing tours together through upstate New York, forming local units of the Women's Division; they thus helped to reduce the traditionally overwhelming Republican majority upstate and, consequently, the dependence of the state Democracy upon New York City machines for election triumphs. Together, too, the three women women started Val-Kill Industries in a shop built at Eleanor's expense beside the cottage and actively managed by Nancy, who was a phenomenally skilled handcraftsman—an enterprise through which furniture of Early American design, pewter objects, and textiles were produced, with local labor under Nancy's supervision, for sale by mail order and in New York City department stores. The very closeness of this threefold friendship might have militated against the growth of a unique independent selfhood, especially in Eleanor, who was initially the least clearly and strongly defined of the three, had it not been a *working* relationship as well as a personal, emotional one. Concerned with getting things done in the great world, it was thus saved from a self-devouring, self-depleting subjectivism and had the contrary effect of encouraging an expanding individuality. "Miss Cook and Miss Dickerman and I had become friends . . . through the work which we were doing together," wrote Eleanor years later. "This is, I think, one of the most satisfactory ways of making and keeping friends."[21] Talents that had lain dormant were stimulated into active use. On her own, with coaching and editorial help from Louis Howe, Eleanor became sufficiently effective as a public speaker to command respectable lecture fees, and a writer whose articles appeared in high-paying mass-circulation magazines. Admittedly, her speeches and writings were originally bought in part because she was Mrs. Franklin D. Roosevelt, the wife of a "name"; but they were definitely, exclusively her own productions and had their own listener or reader appeal.

With each of her victories, as the very essence of each, had come a growth of mind, character, personality. It was only incidentally as FDR's wife and primarily because of her demonstrated abilities as a leader and organizer, her sound judgment, and her enormous capacity for hard work that she had become one of the key women on Al Smith's presidential campaign staff, performing important tasks in the party's national headquarters in New York City, while her husband retired to Hyde Park and then fled to Warm Springs in the summer and autumn of 1928. She was now recognized by her personal acquaintances as a woman of force; she was respected and admired by a widening general public. And she knew that this was so.

But she also knew, only too well, that the public life she had made for herself had derived its first impetus and a good deal of its first substance from her husband's career; that its encouragement by her husband and Howe, without which it could not have prospered, was motivated by their desire and need for help in keeping FDR's political career alive during the years of his private struggle against his crippling affliction; that it must come to an end, insofar as it was an independent process, whenever FDR's interests demanded this; and that the demand would be made whenever her husband won election to high office. From that time forth she must, as a public person, function wholly in her husband's shadow, her every published word, her every act and gesture, conditioned by his official need and will. She dreaded the prospect; she frankly admitted as much to her closest friends. And her dread was accompanied by a rebellious resentment that strained at the leash of her self-control. Considering what had been done to her and what she herself had done for others, what justice could she see, justice as fairness, in this enforced shrinkage of her life, this requirement that she eliminate from it active interests that had latterly made it increasingly rich in meaning and happiness?[22]

Nevertheless, on the night of October 1, 1928, from a room on the fifth floor of Rochester's Hotel Seneca, with all eyes of the half-dozen people in the room, including Nancy Cook, focused upon her and all ears attuned to her voice, she put through the crucial call to her husband, knowing well that, given the circumstances, the mere fact of her doing so must mean that she stood on Smith's side of the argument between the two. Franklin must further infer that she stood there because she felt morally *obliged* to do so, felt that not only his practical career interests but also his own moral obligations to the party and the general good required his acceptance of the gubernatorial nomination. Hers, then, was the voice of duty, not of mere expediency—and the voice of duty was the voice of God.

There can be no doubt that this was a voice FDR listened to with an inner ear as, outwardly, he listened through the receiver to Smith's loud rasp, then Raskob's soft speaking, then Herbert H. Lehman's more forceful speech. Raskob promised to underwrite FDR's financial commitment to Warm Springs. Lehman, slated to run for lieutenant governor, offered to serve as acting governor for months at a time, leaving FDR free to continue his health-building regimen at Warm Springs—and Lehman, a leading New York City investment banker with experience as a labor negotiator, was certainly capable of handling the job. But the offer was insulting to Roosevelt in its implication that he was but a piece of lightweight window dressing, to be manipulated in another's interest, and his secret resentment of it added emphasis to his rejection of it when Smith came back on the line. Smith, however, was now actually pleading, in tacit admission of what FDR himself now believed to be true, namely, that Smith, who might not carry New York in any case, would certainly not do so unless FDR entered the gubernatorial race. " . . . I told you I wasn't going to put this on a personal basis," said Smith, "but I've got to." Yet all of this Roosevelt might have resisted, with Missy at his side whispering fiercely, "Don't you dare!" whenever he gave signs of weakening. What he could *not* resist, in the end, was the force brought to bear upon him by Eleanor's part in this affair; he must regard her doing what she had done as a fateful cue, requiring him to respond according to the overall plot or pattern of his life, though he could and did limit his response to the barest minimum of immediate commitment. In reply to a final question from Smith, he indicated—tentatively, reluctantly—that he might not refuse the nomination if, on the morrow, it were tendered to him by a Rochester convention fully cognizant of his private wish and will.[23]

The effect was the same (he knew it would be the same) as if he had shouted from the housetops that he wanted to be drafted. . . .

And so it was that he had come to this present time and place, this midmorning of a mid-October day in a middle year of his life, with the Hudson a flowing extension of his Rubicon and his inward experience that of a man in midleap across the stream. He was falling now through an air of suspense toward a dangerous shore: the ferry's speed seemed to increase as it drew nearer Hoboken, where, within the hour, he would board an Erie Railroad train for Binghamton; that night he would make the first speech of his upstate campaign for governor of New York. Naturally he was apprehensive. But the hazards of the shore just ahead measured small in his eyes against the opportunities for glory that loomed upon the horizon, and in his most immediate anticipations there was far more eagerness than anxiety. There was no actual fear at all.

For the event was in the hands of God, the loving Father of us all.

God's will be done!

BOOK ONE

The Test of Albany

I

-»>X<<-

From Warm Springs to Albany

"MESS is no name for it," read a telegram dispatched to Warm Springs by Louis Howe on October 2, 1928, within an hour after the Rochester convention had nominated Roosevelt for governor by acclamation. The little man was furious at what he deemed Roosevelt's spineless betrayal of their mutual interests, if not of a sacred trust. "For once I have no advice to give," he said. "By way of congratulations dig up the telegram I sent you when you ran in senatorial primaries."[1] *

Eleanor wired from New York City, to which she had returned from Rochester to meet her morning classes in the Todhunter School: "Regret that you had to accept but know that you felt it obligatory." Later, interviewed by reporters in the Democratic National Headquarters, she said, or was quoted as saying, that she was "very happy and very proud" though she "did not want him to do it." He felt that he had had to, she said. "In the end you have to do what your friends want you to do. There comes to every man, if he is wanted, the feeling that there is almost an obligation to return the confidence shown him."[2]

His mother wrote her sentiments in a letter that day: "Eleanor telephoned me before I got my papers that you have to 'run' for the governorship. Well, I am sorry if you do not feel you can do it without too much self-sacrifice, and yet if you run I do not want you to be defeated! . . . However, all will be well whatever happens." She labeled *"really private"* two of her sentences: "In case of your election, I know your salary is smaller than the one you get now. I am prepared to make the difference up to you."[3]

In Warm Springs, Missy LeHand told her employer with considerable feeling that she hoped he would lose the election, a hope that Roosevelt himself may have shared at that moment. He may even have told Missy "just between ourselves" that he did so. Almost certainly he indicated as much to Louis Howe over the telephone, for Howe, when he wrote on the following day to his wife, Grace, said flatly, "We are much upset and are praying that we get licked." Howe's initial campaign advice to Roosevelt the candidate was that he limit his speeches "to the four big cities with a radio hookup and generally make your campaign on a never mind me, vote for Al basis that will have the advantage of avoiding the necessity of debating on state issues with practically no preparation." The rest of the campaign could be left to Lehman. "He wants

---

*In the summer of 1914, at a time when Louis Howe was away from him, on vacation, FDR had impulsively announced his candidacy for the U.S. Senate from New York and had gone down to a humiliating defeat in the Democratic primary.

to relieve you of all routine work as Governor, and it is a grand time to start now."[4]

But if this is how Roosevelt and Howe felt in the immediate aftermath of the nomination, it was, even then, with a crucial reservation: the defeat must be of a special quality. Roosevelt must emerge from the campaign more heroic than before, his heroism actually enhanced, as in his 1924 preconvention campaign for Smith, by his failure to achieve the immediate ostensible objective, so that his defeat would have the seeds of future triumph embedded in it, seeds that could be nourished toward the flowering originally projected by the two of them for 1932, then 1934, then 1936, the culmination.

And Roosevelt, who was in any case temperamentally unsuited to the kind of passivity Howe recommended, was soon driven to conclude that his long-term purposes could be served, in the present circumstances, only by a strenuous, hard-fought campaign.

For within a few hours after his nomination, New York Republicans were exploiting to the full his well-publicized health reasons for not wanting to run, using these not only as an argument against his election but also, and even more so, as a whip with which to castigate Al Smith. "There is something both pathetic and pitiless in the 'drafting' of Franklin D. Roosevelt by Alfred E. Smith," said a New York *Evening Post* editorial. "Stung by the Presidential bee . . . the Governor made this most loyal of friends agree to serve his ambition at a price that is beyond all reason." The *Post* averred that Roosevelt's "own friends, out of love for him, will hesitate to vote for him now." The *Herald Tribune* said, "The nomination is unfair to Mr. Roosevelt. It is equally unfair to the people of the state, who, under other conditions, would welcome Mr. Roosevelt's candidacy for any office." Al Smith struck back. In a press conference on his train, leaving Rochester on October 3, the Democratic presidential nominee said, "Frank Roosevelt today is mentally as good as he ever was in his life. Physically he is as good as he ever was in his life. His whole trouble is his lack of muscular control of his lower limbs. But the answer to that is that a Governor does not have to be an acrobat. . . . The work of the Governorship is brainwork. Ninety-five percent of it is accomplished sitting at a desk." With this sentiment, the *World*, a normally Democratic organ, thoroughly agreed, though in a way that but slightly mitigated the force of the attack on Smith's "ruthlessness." Said the *World*: "Mr. Roosevelt is not risking his life or his general health; he is risking retardation in the recovery of the use of his legs. If he is elected . . . the Governor of New York will be physically as well qualified for his duties as any war veteran who has lost an arm or leg in battle."[5]

It was in the light of this controversy that Roosevelt, about to depart for Cleveland to deliver a long-scheduled Smith campaign speech there, issued on October 5 a press statement denying that he had been "dragooned into running by the Governor. On the contrary," he went on, "he [Smith] fully appreciated the reasons for my reluctance and was willing to give up such advantage as he felt my candidacy might bring him in deference to my wishes." The draft had been accomplished because party leaders were convinced "that the whole splendid structure of State Government built up by Governor Smith and ... the high ideals of service to the people" that Smith stood for were in grave peril; Roosevelt's nomination and election were "the best assurance" that what Smith had accomplished "would be continued." This meant that Roosevelt was "in this fight, not to win personal honor, but for the carrying forward of the policies of Governor Smith." He did not believe that "appeals to personal friendship should form any part of a plea to the electorate," he said. "But if I did, my appeal would be: 'Not only do I want my friends to vote for me, but if they are my real friends I ask them to get as many other people to vote for me as possible.' "[6]

When he returned to New York City on October 8, he made to assembled reporters a joking reference to his all-too-obvious physical disability. The Republican *Herald Tribune* reported next morning that he entered the hotel room where the press conference was held "supporting himself on the left side with a crutch and on the right side with a cane, and leaning forward on these supports so that he could draw his feet after him in a sliding gait." He was quoted as saying "that most people who are nominated for the Governorship have to run, but obviously I am not in condition to run, and therefore I am counting on my friends all over the state to make it possible for me to walk in."[7]

At that time, the odds quoted by professional gamblers against Roosevelt's winning the race were two to one. His Republican opponent appeared formidable in himself, and general circumstances seemed to favor him. Albert Ottinger, who had been elected attorney general of the state in 1924 and reelected two years later, was a Jew, the first of his religion ever to win a major party nomination for governor, and this should give him strong voter appeal to the large Jewish population in New York City, enabling him to reduce the city's normally huge Democratic majority. Moreover, Ottinger as attorney general had gained much favorable publicity for himself by warring effectively against loan sharks, adulterated-food dealers, dealers in phony stocks, and petty grafters of all kinds. This enabled him to campaign as a champion of "little people" against those who would defraud them; it lent weight to his promise of stern action against graft and crime once he was in the governor's chair. Even by Republican standards he was an extreme conservative: he favored high tariffs and the abolition of the personal income tax; he opposed every public measure that might hamper in the slightest the pursuit of private profit by businessmen. But in the prevailing climate of opinion, in that year of "Republican Prosperity" and liberal disarray, such conservatism seemed to constitute no serious political liability. His stand regarding the then hotly debated Prohibition question was an obvious straddle, which might equally alienate fervent wets and fervent drys; but then Roosevelt's own public position on this question was also a straddle, and his tactic would be to ignore it, for the most part, claiming that it was a problem for the federal government, not the state. On one clear issue between himself and Roosevelt, the Republican candidate appeared at a vote-getting disadvantage: Ottinger stood four-square for the private owner-ship and development of water-power resources, Roosevelt for public owner-ship of these, and Al Smith had gained much popular support for public ownership in his battles against giant utility interests in the past.

Roosevelt intended to exploit to the fullest possible extent the water-power issue. He also planned to strike out against the scurrilousness, the anti-Catholic bigotry, of the campaign against Al Smith. He would do so out of profound personal conviction. He was outraged and incensed by the vicious propaganda being disseminated by the Anti-Saloon League, the Ku Klux Klan, fanatically racist Fundamentalist sects all over the country, and Bishop James Cannon, Jr., of the Methodist Episcopal Church, South—a propaganda whose spread was covertly encouraged if not actually facilitated by the national Republican campaign organization while Herbert Hoover, no doubt sincerely, publicly deplored it. Roosevelt was inclined to react more strenuously against all this, in published statements, than seemed wise to the two intimate advisers upon whom Al Smith most heavily relied, namely, Judge Joseph M. Proskauer and Belle (Mrs. Henry) Moskowitz.

II

AMONG the first with whom Roosevelt held a campaign-planning conference after his return from Warm Springs was Edward J. Flynn, the Bronx Demo-cratic boss, who, with Al Smith's blessing, had detached himself from the presidential campaign in order to devote himself wholly to the gubernatorial race. Flynn, the son of a prosperous Irish family, was a graduate of Fordham's Law School. Urbane, suave, astute, knowledgeable not only about immediate electioneering but also about general trends, he was almost as reticent, almost as addicted to behind-the-scenes manipulation, as the late Tammany boss, Charles Murphy, whose protégé he had been. He was, for a politician, remark-ably aloof, solitary by personal taste. He actively disliked the indiscriminate back-slapping cordiality of lodge and fraternity and service club; he insisted upon a total separation of his home from his political life. Yet he was perfectly at ease and conversationally adroit in social situations involving intellectually sophisticated people and, when not in one of the moods of black depression that now and then overwhelmed him, was pleasant, stimulating company. These qualities had already recommended him to Roosevelt, who was destined to have with him, from this point on, a confidential relationship more deci-sively important to his political career, perhaps, than was his relationship with any other one man save Howe. The latter was at Roosevelt's side that day, and it was agreed between Flynn and the candidate "that Howe should have active charge of the campaign."[8]

But in point of fact Howe had already taken charge. Having ceased crying over spilt milk, he had made the best of a bad bargain, as he had done in analogous circumstances in the summer of 1914. He was setting up and staffing a campaign headquarters at the Biltmore and establishing an Independent

Committee for Roosevelt and Lehman. Flynn, at the very first meeting with him, was favorably impressed, a fact in evidence of Flynn's shrewdness as a judge of men. " . . . I began to get an insight into his fine political judgment," Flynn would remember nearly two decades later. Soon thereafter he became, and he would remain, one of the few among Roosevelt's working associates who actually personally liked the sour-visaged, bittersweet little man. "His loyalty to Roosevelt was a beautiful thing. . . . Yet this devotion never turned him into a rubber stamp for his chief. No one could be more alert in watching Roosevelt's rather volatile temperament for dangerous signs of bad judgment, and no one could be more outspoken and critical of his beloved 'Franklin.' "[9] Thus spoke Flynn of Howe, who liked and trusted Flynn in return. As for Howe's campaign management that year, it made much use of techniques he had employed on Roosevelt's behalf in 1912, 1914, and 1920. He concentrated upon the issuance of publicity, the gathering of campaign-relevant information, and the engineering of a vast letter-writing factory, with people specifically trained to forge the candidate's "personal" signature to form letters issued by the hundreds.

He recruited or helped, with Flynn, to recruit several people who, drawn thus into Roosevelt's orbit, were destined for future fame because of it.

One of these was Raymond A. Moley, summoned from his teaching post at Columbia University to play a part-time and peripheral role as speech draftsman and developer of issue ideas, especially with regard to crime prevention and criminal justice. He was forty-one years old. A native of Ohio, he had been much influenced in his youth by Cleveland's great reform mayor Tom Johnson, whose example had stimulated him to read Henry George's *Progress and Poverty* when in his teens, and by Newton D. Baker, who followed Johnson as mayor. He called himself a Progressive Democrat. But like not a few who had joined in the Progressive movement, he was at heart profoundly, invincibly conservative. He admitted it, even boasted of it when dealing with social idealists, saying he felt "no call to remedy evils" and "not the slightest urge to be a reformer"; he fancied himself a practical man, a realist who viewed the world and men without "sentimental" illusions.[10] Deficient in the emotions of generosity, he was almost as worshipful of big-business men and contemptuous of "woolly-minded theorists" (he so classified virtually all leftists) as Calvin Coolidge. His special academic field was political science: he had taught political science at Western Reserve before coming, in 1923, to Columbia. His professional interest in the problems of crime and criminal justice had brought him into working contact with Howe on the National Crime Commission.* His appearance seemed expressive of his instinctive nature. An inveterate pipe smoker, he was tight-lipped and small-mouthed, his eyes preternaturally pierc-

---

*The National Crime Commission was a private organization established to study and recommend solutions to the country's increasingly serious crime problem. Roosevelt had associated himself with it in 1925 and had secured Howe's appointment as assistant to the commission chairman— a part-time job paying between $300 and $400 a month, relieving FDR of some of the financial burden of providing for Howe's livelihood during these interim years.

ing, his face ill-suited to smiles of much breadth or warmth. Since few men were more self-assured or convinced of the correctness of their opinions, relatively few among his acquaintances found him particularly attractive as a personality. There were few whom he particularly cared to attract. None who knew him well had any doubt about his ability, however. His wide-ranging well-informed mind had great toughness and practical efficiency; he had unusual self-control and self-discipline though he was also a man of fiery, impatient temper; his integrity and personal honesty were absolute; and he was a rarely gifted writer and editor.

Another recruit was William H. Woodin, who became one of the gubernatorial campaign's two principal fund raisers, the other being Raskob's very rich Republican friend, Arthur C. James. Woodin was a shy-mannered little man whose appearance was invariably described as "elfin." He had a passionate creative interest in music, and some of his compositions had achieved publication. His dominant personal characteristics seemed incongruous with his being one of the nation's leading bankers—he had been a director of the New York Federal Reserve Bank—and a top officer of the American Car and Foundry Company.

James A. Farley of Rockland County, elected secretary of the Democratic State Committee in August 1928, was assigned, or perhaps assigned himself, the crucially important task of reviving on Roosevelt's behalf the theretofore moribund upstate Democratic organizations, working closely on this project with Howe, his efforts aided by those already made by Eleanor and her friends in the Women's Division of the state Democracy. Farley, whom absolutely everyone called Jim, was a big, bald-headed, immensely likable, insatiably gregarious Irishman, who would become professionally Irish, signing all his innumerable letters and notes in green ink. He was known among the Elks all across the country as one of the most fervent of Lodge members and had made a name for himself statewide as the New York State athletic commissioner. His warmly humane personality and impressive physical presence could effectively implement, as Howe's meager equipment along these line could never implement, a tactical political shrewdness that was, or soon became, the equal of Howe's or Flynn's and was even less complicated than theirs by a concern for issues.

Personally recruited by Roosevelt was Henry Morgenthau, Jr., a move encouraged by Eleanor. Since 1920 Morgenthau and his wife, Elinor (née Fatman), had been among the closest of the Roosevelt's social friends, the Morgenthau country home being at Hopewell Junction, only ten miles southeast of Hyde Park. It was natural for him to be called upon to work on the agricultural side of the campaign. He was well equipped for such an assignment. His appearance was as little like the typical farmer's as any man's could be. He, too, was tight of lip, generally unsmiling, tense-looking, with vertical frown lines drawn in his forehead above pince-nez spectacles, his bearing stiffly upright. It was hard to imagine him milking a cow or husking corn or pitching hay—and of course he did not do these things save in fun. He was very far from being a dirt farmer. But he *had* made money from the operation of his large Dutchess County acreage, even during recent farm depression years, had made a success, too, of the weekly *American Agriculturist,* of which he was publisher. He was as honorable a man, concerned to do good in the world, as he was able an administrator. He was no more interested in general ideas than Franklin Roosevelt. He shared with Roosevelt a deep abiding love of trees and fields and country life, a profound commitment to natural-resource conservation; he also shared a basic conservatism, and was thoroughly orthodox in his economic views.

But the recruit who was of the greatest immediate personal service to the candidate was one whom neither Roosevelt nor Howe had specifically chosen and toward whom Howe soon developed a lasting antipathy. Roosevelt, acutely aware that he "was not adequately familiar with the details of the recent legislative history of both parties in New York State"[11] and lacked both the time and means with which to prepare himself for a well-informed discussion of state issues, had asked Maurice Bloch, leader of the Democratic minority in the New York Assembly, to pick out a man who could supply his deficiencies while traveling with him during the campaign. Bloch chose Samuel I. Rosenman.

Rosenman was a native of San Antonio who had become a New Yorker when young. A lawyer of recognized ability, he was only thirty-two years old in 1928. He seemed older than that to most of those who knew him in Albany, where he had been an elected member of the Assembly for five years and a member of the Bill Drafting Commission for three. Stocky of body and broad of face, serious of mind and stolid of mien, kind, gentle, soft-spoken, unassertive in social intercourse, remarkably methodical in all things, a swift facile writer capable of prolonged bouts of concentrated labor, he was the kind of man who seems ageless, neither youthful when young nor elderly when old.

III

BY his own account, Rosenman had "had no experience at all with the preparation of speeches" when Bloch asked him to take on the assignment.[12] He had contributed speech material to Al Smith on numerous occasions. But Smith had an aversion to speaking from a prepared script, feeling that it interfered with his audience rapport and with his effective presentation of facts that, neatly stacked in his remarkable memory, were always at the fingertips of his agile mind. He spoke from notes, sometimes very sketchy notes. And Rosenman's own speeches as candidate and legislator on the Assembly floor had been of the same extemporaneous nature. Nor did he "expect actually to write any speeches"[13] for Roosevelt when he first met the candidate on the ferryboat crossing from Manhattan to Hoboken on October 17. He expected to function through the weeks immediately ahead as a kind of living mobile reference library, supplying information to the candidate and checking the candidate's speeches for errors of fact and interpretation. He had prepared himself for this task in a characteristically methodical way, gathering great masses of material on housing, labor, old-age pensions, education, water-power development, etc., which he then separated into appropriately labeled red manila envelopes. He had with him several large suitcases stuffed full of these envelopes when he boarded the ferry.

It was Maurice Bloch who introduced young Rosenman to the candidate, an introduction Rosenman had anticipated with no great eagerness ("I was going along just to do a chore") and with only the mildest curiosity. He "knew Roosevelt's family and cultural background"—so highly privileged, so different from his own—and felt it probable that the candidate "was going to be a letdown for me and for all Smith liberals." Moreover, he "had heard stories" of Roosevelt's "being something of a playboy and idler, and of his weakness and ineffectiveness." But this description, given him by Belle Moskowitz, Robert Moses, and others of Smith's inner circle, emphatically did not fit the man he now met. Roosevelt was certainly very different from Al Smith. Friendly, even cordial in his acknowledgment of introduction, he had "an unspoken dignity which held off any undue familiarity," and his great personal charm, of which Rosenman had been told and which exerted itself at the instant of handshaking, was accompanied by a personal force for which Rosenman was wholly unprepared. Rosenman would never forget the vivid initial impression made upon him by "the broad jaw and upthrust chin, the piercing, flashing eyes, the firm hands" of Franklin Roosevelt.[14]

And this impression was reinforced during the next three days, days in which Rosenman's initially slightly patronizing attitude toward the man he was to serve gave way to a respect for him that had in it an element of anxiety. He developed a concern for Roosevelt's good opinion coupled with a dismaying belief that he was failing to obtain it, for during these days, he and his stuffed suitcases were ignored.

In Binghamton on October 17, Roosevelt spoke in support of the national Democratic ticket, mentioning state matters only in the most general terms and only to glorify Smith's handling of them. Boldly, in tacit recognition of the fact that the Ku Klux Klan had been and remained stronger in the Binghamton area than anywhere else in New York, he excoriated "the religious bigotry of this campaign," equating it with lack of education (it "is more glaring in the out-of-the-way farms and hills and valleys and small towns, where there is no contact with the outside world") and saying that "we have never had a governor . . . who has done more for the cause of education than Alfred E. Smith." He believed, he said, "that the day will come . . . when education in our own State and in every other State, in the cities and the hamlets and the farms, in the back alleys and up on the mountains, will be so widespread, so clean, so American, that this vile thing that is hanging over our heads in this Presidential election will not be able to survive."[15] He spoke extemporaneously in somewhat the same vein, though with a less explicit equating of ignorance with farms and small towns and a greater stress on the problems of farm relief and rural taxation, at Oswego and Elmira on the following day and at Corning, Hornell, Wellsville, Olean, Salamanca, and Jamestown on the day after that.

The Jamestown speech was particularly impressive of Sam Rosenman. Though its main thrust was in support of the Democratic presidential nominee, it laid heavy stress on two planks of the state Democratic platform relating to agriculture, one of them pledging the establishment of "a commission of experts to study the problems of [agricultural commodity] distribution and . . . make definite constructive recommendations," the other pledging a "scientific study and investigation" of the "whole farm assessment and tax situation." Roosevelt proposed to go farther than this: as governor he would broaden these "scientific" studies "to cover . . . other factors so that we may have . . . recommendations covering the entire economic farm situation." He stated in "plain language" the goal of his farm policy. "I want to see the farmer and his family receive at the end of each year as much for their labor as if they had been working not on a farm, but as skilled workers under the best conditions in one of our great industries," he said. "I want our agricultural population . . . to be put on the same level of earning capacity as their fellow Americans who live in cities." His closing words were devoted wholly to the national campaign and, delivered in "cultured accent and inflection" (Rosenman's description) with perfect timing, were highly effective with his immediate audience. "It is just possible," he said, "that after the war in 1920 it may have been in some respects a good thing for the United States to have a period of—what shall we call it, politely?—beauty sleep under President Harding and President Coolidge. It may have been a good thing for us to quiet our nerves after the struggle of the Great War. Some of the farmers of this country do not think that that beauty sleep did them much good, and some of us are beginning to realize that we have fallen pretty far behind during that beauty sleep. But be that as it may, the time has come for us to wake up; and I believe that it is better for us when we wake up, instead of stretching and yawning comfortably and putting our head back to doze upon the Hoover pillow, that it is better for us to get up and take a cold Al Smith shower and feel fit for another four years."[16]

That evening, Roosevelt and Rosenman arrived in Buffalo. By then, the strong words spoken in Binghamton had provoked strong reactions, and a wire from Louis Howe had informed Roosevelt of them. The Binghamton speech as reported in the *Times,* said Howe, was "being twisted by Republicans as meaning that those who do not vote for Smith because of religious scruples should be deported." Headquarters had received "several violent comebacks on this," one of them from a Democratic Congressman of Jewish faith who was running for reelection. "Belle [Moskowitz] suggests that religion now be dropped from campaign and that you take up one weak point at a time."[17] At Buffalo, Rosenman was handed a wire from Bloch: "Tell the candidate that he is not running for President but for Governor . . . and . . . to stick to State issues." But by then Rosenman had far too great a personal respect for the candidate and far too little assurance of his own status to do ("probably at that time I would not have dared") what Bloch requested. Instead he was about to ask to be relieved of an obviously useless assignment ("I and my suitcases of red envelopes were excess baggage") when, a short time later, in the Buffalo hotel where they were staying, he was for the first time consulted by the candidate in a way that made him begin "to feel of some use."[18]

Roosevelt said he planned to discuss labor in his Buffalo speech on the following night, October 20. Did Rosenman have material on this? Rosenman did, of course, several fat envelopes of it, in fact. "That's one subject on which you can lambaste the Republican leaders all night," he said. He took the envelopes from a suitcase and handed them to Roosevelt, who was obviously immediately impressed by this display of order and efficiency. Roosevelt skimmed through a number of documents with astonishing speed, asked a few questions whose pertinence seemed to indicate he had read with understanding, then, with a casualness that left his young assistant breathless, asked Rosenman to "knock out a draft of what you think I ought to say" and "let me have it in the morning." He himself then departed for an evening of personal politicking "with the local political brethren," saying airily as he was wheeled from the room: "Don't stay up all night."[19]

But Rosenman did stay up, of course, well into the early hours of the following day, working furiously, tirelessly, having been given no leads or guidelines by the man who was to speak his words. By breakfast time his completed manuscript was in Roosevelt's hand. The two men went over it after breakfast. A stenographer was called in. Roosevelt dictated various revisions and insertions, made others in pencil on the script, his swift labors transforming what had been a "pretty good" speech "but a little on the dull side," as Roosevelt had described it, into a speech that had verve and sparkle, expressive of the speaker's personality, while retaining the solid, accurate information Rosenman had culled from his files. Listening to it that night, and to the audience's response to it, Rosenman lost whatever last lingering doubts he may have had about Roosevelt's general abilities.

The two most memorable passages of the speech were wholly the candidate's own, dictated by him during the morning draft session. One was obviously suggested by Rosenman's manner of filing campaign information. "Somewhere in a pigeonhole in a desk of the Republican leaders in New York State is a large envelope, soiled, worn, bearing a date that goes back twenty-five or thirty years," said Roosevelt. "Printed in large letters on this old envelope are the words, 'Promises to labor.' Inside the envelope are a series of sheets dated two years apart and representing the best thought of the best minds of the Republican leaders over a succession of years. Each sheet of promises is practically the duplicate of every other sheet in the envelope. But nowhere in that envelope is a single page bearing the title 'Promises kept.' " He pledged himself, in the words of the Democratic platform, "to complete Governor Smith's labor and welfare program, including an eight-hour day and forty-eight hour week for women and children in industry."

The other passage was "one more crack at religious bigotry," as Roosevelt had said to Rosenman, adding that he knew some people in his own campaign headquarters "won't like it" but that he was more concerned to elect Al Smith President than to be himself elected governor. Its tone, its rhythms, were reminiscent of Woodrow Wilson's last address, the one delivered at Pueblo, Colorado, in late September 1919, a few hours before Wilson's collapse. "I go back in my memory ten years ago—ten years ago this autumn," Roosevelt said. "I go back to the days when I saw Chateau Thierry; . . . I go back to a day in particular when several miles behind the actual line of contact between the two armies I passed through wheat fields, wheat fields with ripened grain uncut; wheat fields in which there were patches, little patches of color . . . and some of these patches were a dark uniform and others of those patches were an olive drab uniform. And as we went through those fields there were American boys carrying stretchers, and on these stretchers were German boys and Austrian boys and American boys being carried to the rear, and somehow in these days people were not asking to what church these German boys or these American boys belonged. Somehow we got into our heads over there and we got into our heads back here that never again would there be any question of a man's religion in the United States of America. And I want to say to you very simply, very solemnly, that if there is any man or woman whose mind can go back ten years; if there is any man or woman who has seen the sights that I have seen, who knows what this country went through; any man or woman who knows what Germany, Poland, France, Austria, England went through—even more than we did—in those years; if any man or woman, after thinking of that, can bear in his heart any motive in this year which will lead him to cast his ballot in the interest of intolerance and of violation of the spirit of the Constitution of the United States, then I say solemnly to that man or woman, 'May God have mercy on your miserable soul.' "[20]

Thereafter Rosenman had no doubt that he was useful, even indispensable, to a candidate whose stamina, courage, and unfailing good humor aroused in him a steadily increasing admiration. He was also more impressed by Roosevelt's intellectual capacity than many others were, remembering in a later year that he "had never seen anybody who could grasp the facts of a complicated problem as quickly and thoroughly as he."[21]

And in that later year he would remember the closing three weeks of the campaign as a blur of activity, a quick succession of vivid moments looming through a thickening haze of weariness: solitary speech drafting in a hotel room through most of each night; an early breakfast with Roosevelt the next morning, during which Roosevelt dictated inserts, revisions, and instructions for preparation of a final draft; travel by automobile to the scene of the next night's address, with Roosevelt giving extemporaneous talks in one town or village after another, standing up on his braced legs in the back of his touring car, while Rosenman worked in a bus fitted out with typewriters and stenographers, mimeograph machines and their operators; then the consummation of the preceding twenty-four hours of speech preparation, Roosevelt's major address of the day, followed by another night of writing in preparation for the major address of the next day. Never had the countryside, flaming with autumn colors, been more beautiful. The air of October was like chilled wine on the palate. All the sights and sounds and smells of October were there to feed a thin sweet nostalgia, a pleasant melancholy of spirit. And Roosevelt might enjoy these things in brief snatches as he rode in his car, looking up now and then from the inevitable manuscript in his lap. But there were no such restful intervals for his hard-driven assistant. For Rosenman, all of space and time was shrunk to the dimensions of a sheet of paper, the blank page that he and he alone must fill with words.

IV

AT Rochester the words focused on "the human functions of our State Government," the candidate copiously praising Smith's record of welfare legislation and administration and proposing to build upon it. Roosevelt called for an "immediate study" leading toward passage of "a proper and adequate old-age pension law" that would enable the "repeal . . . forever and ever" of the state's sadly outmoded Poor Law. In the meantime, that Poor Law must be drastically revised in the name of common humanity. " . . . it just tears my heart to see these old men and women in the County Poorhouse," Roosevelt said. He followed Smith in the assertion that the care of "crippled children, and indeed of cripples of any kind," was a proper and necessary function of state government, and as he made this assertion he felt compelled to recognize, although he disliked doing so thus publicly, that he himself, in his audience's view, might be peculiarly suited by personal experience to discuss the problem of cripples, that he himself might be taken as "a perfectly good example of what can be done by the right kind of care" of a person struck down by infantile paralysis. His had been "a perfectly normal attack," he said, deprecatingly, yet he had been, "for the moment, out of any useful activities." It had been his "personal good fortune . . . to get the best kind of care, and the result . . . is that today I am on my feet"; but the great majority of New Yorkers who became incapacitated as he had been "are unable to afford the cost and time necessary for rehabilitation. It seems to me," he went on, "that it is the clear duty of the State and local governments to make up what is needed to bring about the splendid definite results that medical science can now provide."[22]

At Syracuse the speech focused on the state's water-power resources and their development, a subject that had engaged his interest since his early years in politics, one about which he was well informed and had strong feelings. These determined the tone of an address whose substantive opening was: "This is a history and a sermon . . . , and I preach from the Old Testament. The text is 'Thou shalt not steal.' " He spoke of the subterfuge, the design for thievery, implicit in the passage by a Republican legislature and the prompt signing by Republican Governor Nathan Miller of the Water Power Commission Law in 1921. The commission thereby created wore the guise of an agency to defend the public interest in the water-power resources that the state clearly owned; actually it was wholly subservient to the big private utilities, which were determined to steal these resources form the people. Witness its composition. On it were "the Speaker of the Assembly, the Majority Leader of the Senate, the Conservative Commissioner, the State Engineer, and the Attorney General"—all of them Republican that year and one of them, Assembly Speaker Machold, "the open and avowed champion" of the utilities. To this commission the Republican legislature gave "the broadest sort of power to grant licenses to private persons or corporations authorizing the diversion and use for power or other purposes of the water resources of the State." Roosevelt made no mention of the Frontier Corporation's attempt to grab, through stealthy commission action, several of the state's best power sites in late November 1922, a move frustrated by Governor-elect Smith,* but he told in some detail how Smith as governor was in turn frustrated by the Republican legislature when he attempted to obtain repeal of the Water Power Commission Law; how the power interests, led in the legislature by Speaker Machold, then attempted to circumvent the governor's veto power by proposing an amendment to the state constitution (this would go "straight to the voters" for action, without crossing the governor's desk) "allowing the use of the waters of the [state] forest preserves"; how they carefully "camouflaged that amendment" in their propaganda "to make the voters think that it would allow the use of these waters up in the Adirondacks only for municipal canal or stream-flow purposes" when in point of fact "it contained a little joker . . . allowing the development of power by lessees under leases not to exceed fifty years," which of course "would have enabled the construction of water-power plants throughout the Adirondack Park"; and how Governor Smith promptly recognized this "little joker" and, dubbing the amendment "the Adirondack raid," campaigned personally against it so effectively that it was defeated by the voters "965,000 to 470,000, a little over two to one."

But this was by no means the end of the story.

Smith, insisting that "the people of the State are opposed to the principle of leasing the power sites which they own," since "leases for long-term periods, such as fifty years, are in effect perpetual grants," proposed legislation creating a state water-power authority "on a principle similar to that of the highly successful Port of New York Authority." He was, of course, blocked in this by "the Republican Senate and Assembly" but managed to push through a state government reorganization, a consolidation of agencies, which, when it went into effect in January 1927, would do away with the Water Power Commission, transferring its powers to the office of the conservation commissioner, who was appointed by the governor. Moreover, in his campaign for reelection in 1926, while his opponent harped on a trumped-up New York City "milk scandal," Smith stressed his water-power policy as the

*See pages 719–720 of *FDR: The Beckoning of Destiny, 1882–1928* (New York: Putnam, 1971, 1972), predecessor of the present volume.

major issue, so that, when he won a decisive triumph at the polls, "it seemed clear that the people of the State had set the seal of their approval upon his policy." The power interests grew desperate. They must consummate their steal while the old Water Power Commission, with its Republican majority, still operated, and they quickly moved to do so after 1926's Election Day. "They induced . . . the Commission to consent to grant them a lease on the St. Lawrence River"—the same lease, permitting the development of Niagara Falls power, that they had tried for in the aftermath of the 1922 election. That lease was about to be signed by the four Republican commissioners, one of whom was Roosevelt's present opponent, Attorney General Ottinger, when the private power interests themselves, quailing and flinching under the glare of hostile public opinion that Governor Smith focused upon them and faced with an investigation of the legality of the proposed leases to be conducted by the formidable Samuel Untermeyer as special governor's counsel, "lost their nerve." Suddenly, "in the nick of time," they withdrew their application. " . . . they decided that rather than arouse public opinion any further, they would wait until they could control . . . not only the Attorney General, but the Governor of the State. They were waiting until the election year 1928. Yes, . . . Attorney General Ottinger and his colleagues had lost their nerve. It was a drama that had a happy ending in the first act; the curtain is about to ring up on the second act."[23]

This was the most effective single speech of Roosevelt's campaign. Ottinger was provoked into bitter reply. Reminding his opponent of another biblical text, namely, "Thou shalt not bear false witness against thy neighbor," he "explained" his and the commission's action in terms designed to show his profound devotion to the public interest. But there was no letup in Roosevelt's furious electioneering. During the ten days following his Syracuse address on October 23 he gave a half-dozen major addresses and approximately a dozen minor ones in as many different places, speeches that continued to aim less directly at gubernatorial votes for himself than they did at presidential votes for Smith, their general theme being the conflict of Smith's constructiveness vs. Republican obstructionism in New York, Smith's commitment to the general welfare vs. Republican commitment to special interests, Smith's warm humanity vs. Hoover's cold engineering efficiency.

In Yonkers he spoke of an article just published in "a leading magazine" under the title "Is Hoover Human?" in which the author "labored heavily . . . to prove that the Republican candidate has the human qualities which the title of his article puts in question" Roosevelt asked his listeners if they had ever, "in their wildest moments, put the question 'Is Al Smith Human?' " He went on to quote Hoover's *American Individualism* in evidence of the Republican candidate's antidemocratic attitudes, his contempt for common people. Hoover had written: "Acts and deeds leading to progress are born of the individual mind, not out of the mind of the crowd. The crowd only feels, it has no mind of its own with which to plan. The crowd is credulous, it destroys, it hates and it dreams, but it never builds. It is one of the most profound of exact psychological truths that man in the mass does not think, but only feels." Roosevelt chose to interpret this as meaning "that there exists at the top of our social system . . . a very limited group of highly able, highly educated people, through whom all progress in this land must originate. . . . It seems to me," he continued, "that the whole life of the man whom we still refer to as 'Our Al Smith' is a refutation of this innate theory of his opponent." The Hoover "attitude" of elitism was inimical to Smith's "great humanitarian achievements and accomplishments in this State," the "magnificent park-development program," for instance, and to Smith's water-power policy. " . . . taking that same Hoover theory of the crowd, and of the little tin gods on wheels up at the top who have got some kind of heavenly right to rule, it is quite safe to say that if that Hoover type of mind had been given full authority over this nation during the past generation, not a single lake or river or stream or waterfall capable of developing electric energy would remain in the possession of the people of the United States, or of any individual State. There is such a thing as too much engineering."[24]

He seemed to thrive on incessant controversy, incessant hectic activity. He claimed he actually gained physical strength as the strenuous days added up to two weeks, then three, and others of his entourage grew irritable and even, in some cases, were rendered fumblingly ineffective by strain and fatigue. Rosenman marveled more and more at his courage and stamina, noting that merely to stand up and sit down in the back of a car several times a day was, for Roosevelt, "almost as much exercise as the ordinary man takes during an entire day." Getting in and out of auditoriums was a "harrowing ordeal," with the candidate often being carried up flights of stairs, though never in the sight of the crowd. Yet "he never got ruffled" and appeared always before his audiences smilingly at ease. In Troy on October 26 he himself spoke to a laughing, cheering audience of the stamina he was displaying—also of the crowds he was attracting. He reminded his listeners with gay boastfulness of the "sob stuff" that "Republican editorial writers" had published about his physical condition when he was first "drafted." He told of covering nearly 200 miles by automobile and making seven speeches in seven different towns in a single day, of having traveled almost that far and made five speeches that very day. " . . . and now here we are in Troy. Too bad about that unfortunate sick man, isn't it?"[25]

By that time, the excitement generated by his whirlwind campaign and the admiration he personally aroused with his exhibition of courage, physical vigor, forthright exposition of issues, and loyalty to his friend Al Smith had been joined by serious disaffections in Republican ranks (the Republican candidate for attorney general was a personal enemy of Ottinger's) to produce a dramatic shift in betting odds on the election. The gamblers who had been betting two to one on Ottinger's victory in early October were betting two to one in Roosevelt's favor as October drew to a close. It was generally conceded that he ran considerably ahead of Smith in his native state.

V

ROOSEVELT ended his campaign on November 5 in Poughkeepsie, where some 20,000 people paraded down Main Street in his honor. That evening he stood upon the porch of the Hyde Park house and acknowledged the greetings and good wishes of 200 or so of his fellow townsmen, gathered in the yard before him.

A little later he sat before the fire in the fireplace of the library of his mother's house and spoke in the presence of reporters about "that old hat of mine," whose disreputable appearance throughout a campaign that had covered 1,300 miles and involved more than four dozen speaking appearances had aroused comment and curiosity. "I have a peculiar superstition about hats," dating back, he said, to 1910, when he engaged in his first political campaign. One day he ran to catch a moving Lexington Avenue streetcar in New York City, missed his grip as he tried to swing aboard, and fell backward. His head "hit the pavement," but the old brown felt hat he was wearing "saved me from serious injury." Since then "I have had a feeling that old brown felt hats bring me good luck."[26]

The next morning, the first Tuesday in November, he voted at the Town Hall in Hyde Park, then went down to New York City, where that night, in his Biltmore Hotel headquarters, he and Eleanor hosted a buffet supper for friends and associates in the campaign. Afterward, they retired to a private room of the suite and there—sitting with a small group that included at various times Rosenman, Farley, Flynn, Howe, Frances Perkins of Smith's Industrial Commission, and the candidate's mother, son James, and daughter, Anna— received by phone and radio reports of the election returns.

From the very first these spelled defeat for the national Democracy. By the time Al Smith dropped by, shortly after ten o'clock, having been with fellow members of the Tammany Society in the Sixty-ninth Regiment Armory earlier in the evening, it was evident that he had lost by a wide margin. The margin grew wider still as the evening wore on. When Emily Smith Warner, Al's daughter, phoned Herbert Bayard Swope of the New York *World* to check on a report that even the solid South was melting, she was told in terms of violent disgust that the reports were true. Virginia, North Carolina, Florida, were all giving their electoral votes to a Republican presidential candidate for the first time in history. Worse, in Swope's view, was the fact that Smith was losing New York, possibly by as many as 100,000 votes. "Well," Smith reportedly said to his intimates grimly, "the time just hasn't come when a man can say his beads in the White House."[27] At midnight he sent a telegram of concession and congratulations to Herbert Hoover, donned his overcoat and the brown derby he had made famous, and left the hotel.

At that time it seemed to Roosevelt that he, too, was going down to defeat under the Hoover landslide. At midnight, Ottinger's upstate lead remained great enough to more than offset Roosevelt's lead in New York City. When the first editions of November 7's morning papers announced, during the midnight hour, that Ottinger had been elected, Roosevelt accepted the verdict "with his usual good nature, . . . philosophically," as Flynn later recalled ("Louis Howe was brokenhearted"), and left the Biltmore to go to his East Sixty-fifth Street home for much-needed sleep.[28]

But he did not accept this negative verdict unequivocally. The race remained too close to permit any thought on his part of immediately conceding defeat. His wary rapprochement with Tammany had evidently increased his strength in New York City, where he ran only slightly behind Smith (ultimately only 30,000 votes behind). Moreover, it seemed not to have injured him upstate, where he had worked carefully to retain and enhance his reputation as an antiboss, rurally oriented Progressive. All through the campaign he had stressed, as he had said at Jamestown, that his "fight" was "not with the Republican rank and file" but with a Republican leadership unrepresentative of that rank and file, being "barren of imagination, . . . stupid."[29] And obviously he was taking many thousands of normally Republican votes away from Ottinger. Not as many as he believed he should be taking, however.

Before leaving his headquarters he took note of the slowness of the returns from certain upstate counties and the surprisingly small vote for him in districts where he knew he had strong support. It looked as though the Republican officials entrenched in those districts were "up to their old tricks of delaying the vote and stealing as many of them as they can from us," he said to Rosenman. So he put through phone calls to the several county sheriffs, voiced his suspicions, told them he counted on them to ensure honest ballot-counting and to call him personally at the Biltmore "if you need assistance" so that he could "ask Governor Smith to authorize the state troopers to assist you."

And Ed Flynn went still further along the same lines after Roosevelt had gone to bed. At two o'clock in the morning, the Bronx boss issued a statement to the press saying that "the extreme delay with which approximately 1,000 districts upstate are sending in election returns" had convinced the Democratic State Committee of "fraud . . . being committed" and that key figures of the committee "with a staff of 100 lawyers" would leave New York City "on the Empire State Express Wednesday morning for upstate cities . . . to uncover such frauds as have been committed and to prevent any further frauds."[30]

The bluff, for that is what it was, apparently worked. Within minutes, teletypers were clicking out this "news" in upstate newspaper offices, whence the word sped to polling places. Within an hour, upstate returns came in more rapidly, and Roosevelt's portion of them was significantly enlarged. Frances Perkins, who remained at headquarters, took note of this, and took heart. . . .

She had known Roosevelt for nearly twenty years, ever since he was a young lawyer in New York City and she, a recent graduate of Mount Holyoke and impassioned convert of the social justice movement, was working toward a master's degree at Columbia. She hadn't liked him much in those days, nor had she been much impressed by his performance as state senator in the immediately following years, a performance she had closely watched as a lobbyist for the National Consumers' League. He had seemed to her just another "correct" and "respectable" young man who had "gone to Harvard." He was, she thought, rather cold and supercilious, a son of privilege who thought himself a superior human being simply *because* he was privileged and who had no real sympathy for the common folk. She had been disgusted by his failure to act as she thought a self-proclaimed progressive reformer was morally obliged to act on legislative proposals for the alleviation of obviously evil factory working conditions, proposals unpopular with his farm constituency. But his long polio agony had "transformed" him, in her eyes. After Governor Smith appointed her to the three-member Industrial Commission of the state, a post in which she became the governor's chief labor adviser, she was brought into frequent contact with Eleanor Roosevelt. Through Eleanor she was brought again into personal contact with FDR. And she was now wholly committed to him as man and politician, being convinced of his broad and deep concern for human rights and betterment and of his seriousness as a political liberal. None other longed more fervently than she, that election night, for a Roosevelt victory.

"I made up my mind to sit out the night on the ridiculous theory that if I didn't give up somehow the result would be changed," she later remembered. "Only one other person seemed to have that idea—Sara Delano Roosevelt. Almost everyone else went home. . . . About two o'clock in the morning surprising returns began to come in. Forty votes here, one hundred votes there, and seventy-five votes somewhere else. They mounted up." Shortly before dawn of November 7, Flynn and other experienced tally analysts were convinced that Roosevelt had won after all! "Mrs. Sara Roosevelt and I had a private if exhausted jubilation and I saw her home as dawn was breaking," Frances Perkins would remember. And Flynn, too, before going to his own home for his first sleep in thirty-six hours, called at the Sixty-fifth Street house. Roosevelt, in bed, received him and "the good news with undisguised astonishment."[31]

The victory margin was about as thin as it could be. Farley dared not go to bed for three days for fear something might happen while he slept to reverse the verdict. Ottinger stubbornly refused to concede as Roosevelt prepared to depart for Warm Springs, and did depart on November 9, and thereafter happily engaged in recreational and therapeutic activities in his beloved pool while dealing simultaneously with his political concerns. On November 17, Roosevelt wrote the governor of Louisiana—a flamboyant personality of Populist stripe named Huey P. Long, whose pudgy face and figure had become nationally familiar through news photographs during the preceding four years —declining with regret Long's invitation to attend the upcoming Governors' Conference in New Orleans. His reasons were two: "First, . . . I am taking daily treatments here for the next three weeks and cannot possibly leave. The other [reason] is that . . . my opponent in the recent campaign has not conceded my election." Ottinger finally did so two days later. He sent a wire to Roosevelt saying that "the final count of the official canvas" would "undoubtedly . . . declare" Roosevelt the governor-elect and offering the traditional "heartiest good wishes for a successful administration." ("I have just heard from my *late* opponent," chuckled Roosevelt in a letter to Archie Roosevelt that day. " . . . he is going to permit me to go to Albany."[32])

The official count showed Roosevelt the victor by a mere 25,564 votes out of a total of 4,234,822—a plurality of 0.6 percent—while Smith ran 103,481 behind Hoover in the state. Ottinger had run 88,715 behind Hoover, due in no small part to undercutting by Hamilton Ward, the Republican candidate for attorney general. Ward, in his home area of Buffalo, encouraged a swap of Republican votes to Roosevelt for Democratic votes for himself and managed to squeak through to victory over his Democratic opponent, Albert Conway. "I do wish that we could find enough votes to elect Albert Conway," wrote Roosevelt to Maurice Bloch on November 16. "It is going to be difficult to have a Republican Attorney General."[33] Lehman won election as lieutenant governor by a somewhat wider margin than Roosevelt's, though trailing Smith and Roosevelt upstate, and so did William Randolph Hearst's protégé, Dr. Royal S. Copeland, to a second term in the U.S. Senate.

VI

BUT, as Roosevelt and Howe at once recognized, the total overall vote, nationally and statewide, had far less significance for Roosevelt's future than did its pattern of distribution among city and town and village, between areas highly industrialized and those predominantly agricultural. A comparison of this pattern with those of the canvasses of 1920 and 1924 indicated a trend that, from Roosevelt's point of view, was hopeful, being confirmative of the validity of the coalition strategy he had pursued, with an increasingly precise awareness, ever since his return to active politics in 1924.

Even the total vote, taken by itself, proved upon contextual analysis to be less disastrous for the national Democracy than it seemed at first glance. In the electoral college, Smith's vote was the lowest that any second-running party candidate had received since 1868. He won only 87 electoral votes,* compared with Hoover's 444. But his popular vote of 15,016,433, compared with Hoover's 21,392,190, amounted to 40.8 percent of the total, and this was a marked improvement over the Cox-Roosevelt showing (34.1 percent) in 1920 and an even greater improvement over the Davis-Bryan showing (28.8 percent) in 1924. He had gained 6,630,847 more votes than Davis won four years before —had in fact come within less than a half percentage point of equaling Coolidge's 1924 total. Moreover, his loss of eight traditionally Democratic Southern and border states (Texas joined Florida, North Carolina, and Virginia in going to a Republican presidential candidate for the first time ever) was clearly

---

*In 1912, when the decisive contest was between Wilson and TR, Taft, the Republican candidate, received only 8 electoral votes. TR received 88.

due to strategical campaign errors deplored by Roosevelt at the time they were made, coupled with personal political liabilities (Smith's Romanism, Smith's East Side accent, Smith's Tammany connection, Smith's intellectual and cultural parochialism) that would not attach to such a candidate as Franklin Roosevelt.

The most important facts in terms of trend, however, became evident in a study of the vote in Northern big cities, in the industrialized Northeast, and in the states of Pennsylvania, Illinois, and Wisconsin. The facts thus descried were three: (1) the Democrats in a national election, for the first time since the Civil War, had carried Massachusetts and Rhode Island; (2) though Smith had failed to carry Pennsylvania, Illinois, and Wisconsin, he came closer to doing so than had Davis or Cox; (3) the national Democracy had won a net plurality in the nation's twelve largest cities, namely, New York, Chicago, Philadelphia, Pittsburgh, Detroit, Cleveland, Baltimore, St. Louis, Boston, Milwaukee, San Francisco, and Los Angeles. The plurality was tiny in figure—only 38,000, a fraction of 1 percent—but big with meaning for the coming years to one who knew that the voting balance of those dozen cities had never tipped toward the Democracy before, that it favored the Republicans with a net plurality of 1,683,000 in 1920 and 1,252,000 in 1924.[34]

Obviously, the continuing shift of population away from farms and small towns into increasingly larger cities, which Roosevelt as Jeffersonian deplored, was creating an urban electorate to whom Al Smith had a special appeal, and obviously the event pointed toward future Democratic victories, provided it was accurately assessed by the party leadership and responded to with creative flexibility, as Roosevelt was prepared and preparing to do. Embedded in this growing urbanization was a process of change wherein the voting strength of the old "pure" American stock, which had derived its traditions and essential politics from seventeenth- and eighteenth-century England, declined relative to that of the children and grandchildren of immigrants from geographic areas and cultural backgrounds far distant from the Anglo-Saxon—Russian Jews, olive-complexioned southern Europeans, Slavs from central and eastern Europe, joined with Negroes, who, as they moved into Northern cities, increasingly exercised the franchise that had been forcibly denied them in their native South. The shift of majority party allegiance in Massachusetts and Rhode Island, for instance, was unquestionably due in part to the influx of French Canadian industrial workers and to the Irish immigration of earlier decades. This also Roosevelt might deplore or at least regret, in a carefully politic secrecy. He was himself an "Old American." But it encouraged him to believe that the strong stand he had taken against religious and racial bigotry since 1924, though with no specific mention of the Negro, was not only good morals but also good politics for him personally, provided he simultaneously maintained and further exploited, as he intended to do, his vital connection with Georgia and his status as a Southerner by adoption.

In general, the 1928 experience further encouraged Roosevelt's long-held belief that America, over the long run, like the rest of the civilized world, "was trending to the left," as Ed Flynn put it. ("This . . . world-wide trend [was one] that few people saw as early as he did," Flynn would remember.) Hence the political position Roosevelt had defined for himself "a little left of center"; it was a recognition in strategic terms of basic realities. But he was not purely opportunistic in this. Out of his conservationist's conservatism, out of his moderate's abhorrence of extremes, out of his gradualist's instinctive avoidance of sharp deep breaks or fundamental discontinuities, came his intention to make of his necessary yielding to historic force a process analogous to a scientific technologist's dealings with natural force. That is, he would yield in *purposeful* ways—ways designed to give him a measure of directional control over that to which he perforce yielded—and the predominant purpose of the control he sought would be to place "reasonable" limits upon the leftward drive. He wanted, as Flynn put it, "to preserve the capitalist system," which he, like Flynn, identified with "freedom," with "democracy."[35] He strove to prevent the effective rise of American Communism or of any other movement toward totalitarian change.

Within a few weeks he would receive from a fellow Hudson River aristocrat, Herbert Claiborne Pell of Hopewell Junction, a neighbor of Henry Morgenthau, Jr., a letter expressing angry disgust with the election's outcome nationally and with the present state of the Union. Pell had in general the hereditary landed aristocrat's disdain for the bourgeoisie, with its "trader morality," and he felt more than justified in this by the current policies and practices of the business community. "The destinies of the world were handed them on a plate in 1920," he would say a few years later. "Their piglike rush for immediate profits knocked the whole feast over in nine years. These are the people, who with an ignorance equaled only by their impudence, set themselves up as the proper leaders of the country." Much the same harsh tone characterized his letter to Roosevelt. He was inclined to despair of the future ("Of course," he said, "I am more of a radical than you"), being convinced that American big business "would stop at nothing to keep in office the Administration that let off Sinclair and Doheny."* To this Roosevelt made soft reply, significant alike of his personal moderation and of his carefully calculated design upon the immediate future. "You are right that the business community is not much interested in good government and it wants the present Republican control to continue just so long as the stock market soars and the new combinations of capital are left undisturbed," wrote Roosevelt. "The trouble before Republican leaders is that prevailing conditions are bound to come to an end some time. When that time comes, I want to see the Democratic party sanely radical enough to have most of the disgruntled ones turn to it to put us in power again."[36] Otherwise, he clearly implied, these "disgruntled ones" might em-

---

*Harry F. Sinclair and Edward L. Doheny were lying, thieving, corrupting heads of giant oil corporations who became central figures of the Teapot Dome oil scandal of the Harding administration.

brace a radicalism so "insane" as to alter fundamentally the structure of American society.

There was a similar "toning down" of a form letter Louis Howe prepared for Roosevelt's signature to be sent, as in the aftermath of 1924, to a selected mailing list of some 2,000 Democrats. Its purpose was to promote a national Democratic organization that would bring victory to the Democracy in 1932. As telegraphed to Roosevelt at Warm Springs on November 12, the Howe letter pooh-poohed the notion that the Democratic Party, because of Al Smith's decisive defeat, was "in any danger of extinction. On the contrary," Howe had written, "the fact that an organization largely composed of inexperienced people hastily thrown together two weeks after the nomination was able in six weeks to convince so many millions of people that Governor Smith was the proper man to be selected for our next President shows that the Democratic Party and the Democratic principles are very much alive in this country. When you consider that this was done against a powerful organization which had been working for four years to perfect its machinery of reaching the public and that the machinery was unscrupulously but effectively used to arouse bigotry and passion by the dissemination of unspeakable slander, I feel certain that had we kept our national organization going in between elections we certainly would have won. I think the time has come to immediately start work in between elections."[37] Howe had gone on to say that no thought should now be given to "who should be the candidate or what should be the issues four years from now" but that every effort should be bent toward the development of local, state, and national Democratic organizations, financed initially by "modest" contributions from each of the letter's recipients. This original version of the letter totaled some 400 words. Roosevelt cut it down to 158 words, eliminating all harshness and including a sentence of his own composition: "Of the additional votes cast in the election the Democratic nominee apparently received many more than half, and the casting of fifteen million votes for our ticket shows that our party has gained tremendous strength since 1920 and 1924." He was sure, he continued, "that had we kept our national organization going between elections we should have done better and I hope that steps will be taken to have this carried out during the next three years. This is no time to discuss candidates but it is time for putting into effect a permanent working organization. I hope you will write me your views."[38]

He moved to stimulate Democratic organization in upstate New York. "Dear Jim," he wrote Farley on December 1. " . . . When the final figures [for the New York election] are prepared in the Secretary of State's office, will you make a definite comparison of the vote for Governor, going back every two years to 1918. This should be complete down to the election districts. I want it only for up-State—New York City can be left out. It is my thought that the leaders in every County should have a copy sent them for their County and it will serve as an excellent talking point when you and Bill Bray [William Bray of Utica was chairman of the Democratic State Committee] and I meet them from time to time. . . . I . . . don't have to tell you how very grateful I am for all the splendid work you did during the campaign. We have a splendid opportunity to go forward and consolidate our gains."[39]

But of course he meant to "go forward" on a national front, not merely statewide, though he continued to be careful not to say so out loud.

Louis Howe, in the opening sentence of his November 12 telegram to Warm Springs, reported receipt in New York City of "six hundred letters" to Roosevelt that very morning "of which four hundred [were] out-of-state . . . [and referred] to national matters." When the replies to Roosevelt's form letters came in, Howe, with Roosevelt's blessing, would hire a young Kentucky newspaperwoman named Lela Stiles to prepare detailed analyses of them, state by state, providing, as Howe had done with the replies to the form letter of 1924, an invaluable overview of the national political scene. Bound into a volume entitled *National Political Digest,* these analyses, and the letters themselves, read by Roosevelt with close attention, greatly aided his continuing Whitmanesque effort to "hear America singing" toward the next presidential election year.*

VII

ELEANOR, who had taken almost no part in her husband's campaign, who had continued all through October and the first days of November to work intensely hard for Al Smith, received the first news of her husband's election with mixed feelings, of which, it would seem, joy was not one. Nor even pleasure. A reporter for the New York *Post* asked her how she felt about it. Her reply, as printed on November 8, read strangely to many. "If the rest of the ticket didn't get in, what does it matter?" she reportedly said, as if she felt that the sole justification for her husband's running had been the assurance of Smith's victory, as if all her own emotional investment had been in Smith's lost campaign. "No, I am not excited by my husband's election," she went on. "I don't care. What difference can it make to me?"[40] Which seems to mean that she *did* care intensely in that hour of letdown following prolonged tension, but bitterly; she cared because her husband's election *would* make a difference in her life, a profound and, as she believed, unhappy difference.

But this recurrence of her "Griselda mood," as she herself called it, with its core of resentful martyrdom, was of brief duration. She soon decided that, governor's wife or no, first lady of the state or no, she would continue her active association with the Val-Kill factory and the Todhunter School. ("I teach because I love it," she told a New York *Times* reporter on the day following her husband's departure for Warm Springs. "I cannot give it up.") And though she necessarily resigned from the Democratic State Committee and refused to speak in public "on any subject bordering on politics," she continued to be active in political matters—intensely though covertly so. The women with whom she had worked in various women's organizations counted upon her to

*See pages 783–785 of *FDR: The Beckoning of Destiny.*

transform the role of First Lady from a passive "society" one into an active one on their behalf, on behalf of women's concerns and rights in general. She herself was eager to do this. Soon she was urging her husband by letter to "consider making Frances Perkins Labor Commissioner," replacing Dr. James A. Hamilton, whose handling of the Labor Department had come under sharp criticism, with whom Smith himself was dissatisfied, and whom Roosevelt subsequently described as a "complete stuffed shirt."[41] She suggested that the post of chairman of the Industrial Board, which Frances Perkins had filled, be now filled by "one of the men" already on the board and that *his* place be filled by the appointment of Nell Schwartz, currently with the Bureau of Women in Industry. Thus there would continue to be a woman member of the Industrial Commission. Eleanor also engineered an invitation from her husband to Mary W. (Molly) Dewson to come to Warm Springs, to present to the governor-elect in persuasive terms the legislative program of the New York Consumers' League, which Molly headed.

At the same time, Eleanor was much involved with family and household matters. She was required to journey to Groton, where all three of her sons enrolled in the school were ailing at the same time. Franklin, Jr., was in the infirmary with "a belly-ache in his right side"; young John was on crutches, having badly bruised a knee accidentally (his knee would be operated upon successfully in February 1929); and Elliott, who had not told school authorities about the rupture he had suffered as a child for fear they would then deny him permission to play football, was being painfully threatened by a recurrence of his old trouble. Having dealt with the problems these ailments imposed, she went from Groton to Cambridge, where her son James casually informed her that he was engaged to be married, though he was not yet twenty-one (he would not be until December 23 of that year), was only a junior at Harvard, and had no definite career yet in mind. His fiancée was a slender lovely blonde named Betsey Cushing, daughter of the world-famous Boston brain surgeon Dr. Harvey Cushing, and James took his mother to meet his fiancée's parents that very day. "She [Betsey, whose name Eleanor misspelled, leaving out the 'e'] is a nice child, family excellent, nothing to be said against it," wrote the disturbed mother to her husband, "but I regret that he wished to tie himself down so young, however perhaps it will be a good influence & in any case we can do nothing about it. He tells me they expect to be married 2 years from now."[42] A little over a week later, accepting an invitation from Mrs. Smith, Eleanor went over with great care the huge Victorian pile that was the Executive Mansion in Albany and decided upon the specific uses of key rooms— where Roosevelt should have his study, which room should be Missy's, etc. —and upon the changes that should be made in the Mansion's interior and grounds in preparation for the Roosevelts' moving in. An elevator and ramps must be installed for the new governor's wheelchair use.

Amid all this she kept her eyes and ears open to hazards for her husband's governorship that were developing during the interregnum.

On the day after the election, Smith made a brief appearance at his campaign headquarters in the General Motors Building in New York City, where, doffing his brown derby and removing from between his tobacco-stained teeth a well-chewed cigar, he said to reporters, "I certainly do not expect ever to run for public office again. I have had all I can stand of it. . . . I will never lose my interest in public affairs, that's a sure thing; but as far as running for public office is concerned—that's finished."[43]

Eleanor was willing to believe, as others did, that Smith meant exactly what he said that day. He was deeply hurt and thoroughly confused by the outcome of a campaign that, at the very last, he seems to have expected to win, his hope having fed on the fact that his crowds had been much larger and more enthusiastic than Herbert Hoover's. But Eleanor also believed that she "understood Governor Smith better than Franklin did" (her commitment to Smith's presidential candidacy had involved no equivalent commitment to Smith personally), and her knowledge of the man and of those most closely associated with him as governor inclined her toward concern over the form that his continued "interest in public affairs" was likely to take. Smith was not the kind of man who yields easily to another reins of power that have been firmly grasped in his own hands, and Eleanor sensed that his willingness to do so in the present instance would be reduced by the belief, it might even be a secret wish, that her all-too-charming husband would prove too weak and frivolous a character to succeed on his own as the Empire State's chief executive. Joined to this would be Smith's natural anxiety over the fate of state programs and institutions established under his regime and over the outcome of battles (for hydroelectric-power-site control, for an executive budget, etc.) that he had initiated but that were not yet won. The net result might well be a Smith "regency." Roosevelt would reign as titular governor while Smith ruled through his close political friends and agents— through Belle Moskowitz, who would be retained as principal speech writer and strategist in the governor's office; through Belle's protégé Herbert Lehman, who, in Roosevelt's absence from the state, was supposed to operate for months at a time as acting governor; and through hard-driving, immensely egotistical, immensely capable Robert Moses, who would be retained as secretary of state while performing functions and exercising powers far outside those specifically assigned that office.

Beware of "B.M." and "R.M.," Eleanor warned her husband in a letter written four days after his departure for Warm Springs. They "mean to cling to you" and would certainly do so "unless you take a firm stand," she said. In a letter dated November 19 she repeated her warning in terms indicative of her awareness of rivalry, as yet unacknowledged but potentially explosive, between Smith and her husband. "Don't let Mrs. M. get draped around you for she means to be," wrote Eleanor. "It will always be one for you and two for Al." And Frances Perkins, who was drawn into very close communication at this time with Smith, Belle, Eleanor, and, subsequently, Roosevelt, became convinced, and remained so to the end of her life, that Roosevelt, had it not been for Eleanor, "might well have drifted into acceptance of Mrs. Moskowitz," as Frank Freidel, to whom Madame Perkins confided this view in a personal interview, has recorded.[44]

Perhaps he would have.

But the conclusion is rendered dubious by the available evidence, including evidence supplied by Frances Perkins herself. On the evidence, Roosevelt's appetite for power was at least as great as Smith's. His instinct for locating, acquiring, then retaining it amid changing circumstances was more acute, more profound than Smith's. His empathic awareness of other people, his consequent sensitivity to subtle psychological pressures, were far greater than Smith's. Roosevelt had a superb actor's ability to play many different roles, impressing upon others intended images of himself. The very impression Smith now had of him as a man of the second rank, possessed of an excessive eagerness to please, a need for someone of superior strength upon whom he might lean, hence easy to manipulate, had been in part deliberately imposed by Roosevelt, or at least calculatedly risked by him, in order to prevent Smith's viewing him, dangerously, as a possibly serious future competitor for the highest office and power. Moreover, he had long been perfectly aware of Belle Moskowitz's total commitment to Al Smith and had no reason for liking her personally. She had scarcely bothered to conceal her contempt for him as a "lightweight" in the recent past. She had often treated him cavalierly.

At Warm Springs, Roosevelt plunged literally as well as figuratively into recreative and therapeutic activities, giving no evidence of fatigue from the campaign just ended and every evidence of serene confidence in his ability to handle the immediate future. He received daily treatment from the physiotherapist Helena T. Mahoney. He swam and loafed and played for hours at a time, as if he had not a care in the world. On many a late afternoon there was a cocktail hour, necessarily severely restricted as to guests and highly secret because of Prohibition, with Roosevelt mixing the drinks. There were picnics at Dowdell's Knob. On Thanksgiving Day there was the celebration that had already become a Warm Springs tradition, with Roosevelt presiding over the feast and displaying his remarkable skill with carving knife upon a huge turkey, slicing thick, medium, or thin, even paper-thin, dark meat or white, according to the expressed wishes of guests. And this year there was also, that day, the dedication of a glass-enclosed pool made possible by Edsel Ford's contribution, followed by "water football" and a "crab race" in the new pool, games in which Roosevelt enthusiastically participated. A few days later, there was a barbecue in Roosevelt's honor at a nearby town, where a local speaker referred to Roosevelt's Warm Springs cottage as "the Summer White House after 1932," though, according to a close Roosevelt political associate who was present, "no one . . . took it seriously; it was merely some oratory in behalf of a favorite son—an adopted one." Yet the New York *Times* made this quoted "oratory" part of the lead of a story filed from Warm Springs that day and, a little later, editorialized that Roosevelt "by a most extraordinary combination of qualities, political fortunes and diversified associations . . . , is within reach of the elements of [national] party leadership."[45]

But there was also, despite the appearance and reality of careless pleasure, much hard work. Every afternoon, seated in a wicker chair before a card table beside the fireplace in his cottage, where a wood fire was often lit in the late afternoons to take off the chill, he worked effectively to reduce the mountainous pile of personal and political correspondence that had accumulated over the weeks and on memoranda and notes for his inaugural address and his initial message to the legislature.

Missy LeHand, always physically delicate, had fallen ill shortly after her boss's nomination and had consequently remained in Georgia while he went north to campaign. Some of her duties had devolved upon a pretty, vivacious Irish Catholic girl named Grace Tully, who had been secretary to Cardinal Hayes for several years, had been released by him to work in the Smith presidential campaign, and had been assigned as stenographer to Eleanor Roosevelt in the Democratic National Headquarters. She had come to FDR, upon Eleanor's high recommendation, when FDR began his gubernatorial campaign, and he had at once developed with her a warmly paternal as well as efficient working relationship. "Child," he said to her during a session of dictation at the Biltmore shortly before Election Day, "win or lose, I am planning to go to Warm Springs immediately after election and stay there until the middle of December. . . . Would you like to come down with us?" She accepted "with alacrity" and so became one of a party that included Roosevelt's law partner Basil O'Connor, several New York newspapermen, including James M. Kieran of the New York *Times,* and a male stenographer, V. Warwick Halsey, who, with her, "made up the staff" during the journey down. She had been warned that, coming in as "second girl" to the now almost fully recovered Missy, she might find herself in a difficult position. Missy might resent her. But the careful tact, the deference, she had come prepared to exercise proved unnecessary. "From the moment we met, Missy and I liked each other tremendously and our relationship . . . was like that of two sisters who never quarreled." The working relationship soon developed in such a way that Missy took relatively little dictation. Instead, guided sometimes by penciled notations ("Missy to ack" or "Missy tell him sorry") or by more detailed instructions from the boss, but often guided only by her own judgment, she herself dictated many of the letters that the governor-elect signed. It was Grace Tully who took most of Roosevelt's dictation. She found working for him less of a strain than working for Eleanor, though the work load he handled with her was as heavy as Eleanor's. "He dictated more slowly. . . . There was less of the hurried atmosphere in his manner." He thoroughly enjoyed "doing his mail" and made it pleasantly exciting to his secretaries by his running side commentary upon the personalities, the masked motives, the problems involved in his correspondence.[46]

At the end of November, Sam Rosenman was one of "a gay group" that came down from New York for planning conferences with Roosevelt—a group

including Maurice Bloch; Bernard Downing, Democratic minority leader of
the New York Senate; Herbert Lehman, and William Bray, chairman of the
Democratic State Committee. On the long train ride down they speculated
about the kind of governor this new man would make, following the brilliant
Smith regime. They wondered if, or in some cases expressed the belief that,
Al Smith would continue to "run the show" and raised and failed to suppress,
despite Rosenman's assertion to the contrary, doubts about his physical ability
to stay on the job at Albany through the long periods of labor and strain
required to deal effectively, as top executive, with a recalcitrant legislature
dominated by the opposition party. They found a man whose buoyant general
good health was so obvious that his withered legs were soon almost forgotten.
The sight of them shocked those who saw him for the first time in a swimsuit
at poolside, but when he plunged in and engaged, splashing and laughing, in
the strenuous water games he loved to devise, it became evident that he
possessed more physical vitality than most men his age. He gave his visitors
the impression of living easily with his disability, of not being embarrassed by
it, as if it were a minor annoyance, like the astigmatism requiring him to wear
glasses; if his general physical health was excellent, his psychological or
spiritual health was magnificent. He appeared absolutely secure within himself, fearful of nothing; his zestfulness was seemingly inexhaustible.

By the end of their first day at the resort, his visitors were disabused of "any
thought . . . that Smith was going to run things," to quote Rosenman.[47] Nor
had Rosenman by then any doubt of Roosevelt's capacity for command. It was
a capacity all the more impressive, to one who studied power, for operating
in winning rather than coercive ways. Clearly, overwhelmingly, he was the
dominant figure of this Warm Springs world he had largely made, as much so
as Endicott Peabody ever was of the Groton world. But had his visitors known
Peabody at Groton they would have noticed a great difference between the
schoolmaster's kind of dominance and Franklin Roosevelt's. Roosevelt, whose
manner was wholly disarming rather than intimidating, was no God the
Father. Rather, he was a brilliant star, the radiant magnetic center of a solar
system. He compelled by attraction; he ruled through appeals to inward tendencies to respond on the part of those drawn into his orbit. Always he was
at his best at Warm Springs, most true to his highest self; always he brought
out the best in others. He radiated charm, fun, eagerness, vitalizing energy.
Those around him shone in reflection of these qualities and, if normally deficient in them compared with Roosevelt, as almost everyone was, came unwontedly alive. The "Spirit of Warm Springs" that quickly infected his visitors, and
obviously largely emanated from him, dissolved formalities that tend to render
human relations less than human. It made possible vital communications
between living individuals, in place of prescribed signals along lines drawn
between integers on some abstract organization chart. It thereby engendered
something rare at any time and place but especially so, perhaps, in the America
of the New Economic Era, namely, a truly human community in the direction
of which humane values were given the highest priority.

Yet none of the party regulars who conferred with the governor-elect at Warm Springs during this interregnum—men like Bloch and Bray—could fault him for a; lack of practical realism as he approached his gubernatorial problems. In his planning conferences with his visitors from New York he gave as much weight to the maintenance of a strong Democratic Party organization in New York City and to the creation of one upstate as he did to the development of his legislative program. The two matters, he would later stress in conversations with Rosenman, were not really separate, independent of each other; they were interactive elements of the same political process. The "first thing" a political executive had to do "in order to put through good legislation," he would say to Rosenman, was "to get elected," and to get elected he must have not only a personal and programmatic appeal to the majority but also a party organized "to get out the vote" on Election Day.[48]

His legislative program, as his campaign had promised, would be a continuation of Smith's, aiming to complete Smith's announced agenda. But his priorities would differ from Smith's, and there would be innovations designed to woo rural New York away from its traditional Republicanism. Already he had conferred about agricultural policy with Henry Morgenthau, Jr., whom he had invited down to Warm Springs for this purpose. An unofficial agricultural advisory committee was to be set up, with Morgenthau as chairman and with a membership of unpaid "experts," nearly all of them Republicans, representative of all agricultural interests: individual farmers, farm organization officials, representatives of farm-related economic enterprises, agricultural journalists, conservationists, and professors from the agricultural college of Cornell University, a land-grant institution. This group, as Morgenthau later told the press, "would make a study of the whole tax situation as it affects . . . highways . . . the rural school situation, rural health, and the whole problem of making homelife on the farm more satisfying."[49] Holding its meetings in the offices of Morgenthau's *American Agriculturist,* the committee would ultimately make a series of specific legislative proposals to the governor.

Already, too, Roosevelt had moved toward the implementation of the water-power policy he had espoused during the campaign—or toward a clarification of it, for it had been vague on every point save that of a retained public ownership of the power sites still held by the state, notably those of the St. Lawrence, Niagara, and upper Hudson rivers. " . . . I followed the platform declaration which was in favor of State owned [power] sites," he wrote to his favorite uncle, Frederic A. Delano, on November 28, responding to a letter from Delano advising him to make no definite commitments on power policy until he had studied material gathered in a U.S. Chamber of Commerce study in which Delano had been involved. "This does not, of course, include [State ownership of the] distribution of power." He was particularly in need of "data on the capitalization of existing Water Power companies," he said. "It seems to me that the fundamental difficulties with the existing rates . . . is [sic] that these rates are based on a capitalization far greater than the actual investment." The rates were in fact being set to produce a return of around 8 percent, *not* of what the utility company facilities had actually cost but of what it would cost to replace them at the current, much higher prices. He mentioned as a "political difficulty" the fact that the chairman of the Republican State Committee was "Mr. Machold, President of the North Utilities Company." He went on, "Do send me the data as soon as you can do so because I have more opportunity here to study it than I shall have later."[50]

As regards personnel appointments, he was more than willing to follow political recommendations for posts of minor importance, so long as the people recommended where honest and capable, for he wanted to strengthen the party organization. He planned to retain most of Smith's top bureaucratic appointees and would, in the event, keep sixteen of the eighteen department heads that his predecessor had appointed, including Colonel Frederick Stuart Greene, state superintendent of public works, who was a Republican. But he made it clear that his closest advisers would be people whose primary personal loyalty was to him, not to Al Smith. A few days after Rosenman arrived at Warm Springs, Roosevelt asked him to become counsel to the governor. "We'll have a fine, stimulating time together," Roosevelt said. Rosenman hesitated, and explained why. The post of counsel under Smith had been "not much more than a political sinecure," since Smith's "kitchen cabinet" of intimate advisers had performed the functions normally assigned a counsel. Roosevelt shook his head over this. "I do not expect to continue to call on these people whom Al has been using," he said. "I shall expect the Counsel to do much of the work they have been doing." A little later, while Rosenman was still carefully considering the governor-elect's offer, he read in an afternoon paper that his appointment as counsel had been announced by Roosevelt. "I made up your mind for you," said Roosevelt with a laugh when Rosenman phoned him to find out if the newspaper report were true.[51]

Thus, on the evidence, there was little if any danger at any time that "R.M." or "B.M." would be permitted to "cling" to the new governor as, in Eleanor's words, "they mean to." Even before he left New York for Warm Springs, Roosevelt had moved to replace Moses as secretary of state. He had offered the post to Ed Flynn. Flynn had refused it for personal reasons that seemed to him conclusive.* He had then sailed with his wife for Europe, intending to stay abroad "for at least six months" and, upon his return, retire altogether from politics, devoting himself to his lucrative law practice. But Roosevelt persisted. From Warm Springs he sent Flynn several cables, begging him to reconsider. He talked to Flynn by transatlantic telephone, saying he was under increasing pressure to reappoint Moses. Finally he sent a cable whose language convinced Flynn that an open break between Smith and Roosevelt might occur —a break that could not but be harmful to the general welfare of the state and

*"We had lost our first child at birth. This was a tragic blow . . . to Mrs. Flynn and me. Since my political duties had taken me away from home so consistently over the years, I now felt an obligation to my wife to eliminate needless intrusions into our private lives." Edward J. Flynn, *You're the Boss* (New York, 1949), p. 73.

disastrous for the Democracy—unless he, Flynn, a friend of both Smith and Roosevelt, returned to New York at once "to talk over the entire situation," as the governor-elect asked him, pleadingly, to do.

VIII

ROOSEVELT arrived back in New York on December 11. Three days later, he and Smith conferred for four hours in Roosevelt's home on East Sixty-fifth Street.

It was, for both men, a difficult interview. Smith still felt bitterly his loss of his native state in the national election, a humiliation whose sting was increased by Roosevelt's victory. He was oppressed by and rebellious against a sense of having come to the end of his career. He felt also that Roosevelt, whom Bob Moses had so often described as "not very bright," owed his present position largely to him. Had not Smith persuaded him to run? Had he not run on Smith's gubernatorial record? Was not his present national political standing due in considerable part to the fact that he had tied his political fortunes to Smith's in 1922 and that Smith had chosen him to present the "Happy Warrior" speeches of 1924 and 1928? Roosevelt, on the other hand, was very sure he owed Smith absolutely nothing. Whatever benefits he had derived from his relationship with the governor had been offset, or more than offset, by benefits Smith had derived from it, and he knew full well that Smith at no point had been motivated to any great extent by a personal affection for him, or by a generous concern for his personal well-being. Roosevelt might even believe, with at least plausible objective reasons for his belief, that he would have won his election victory by a wider margin and that Smith would have lost the state by a wider margin if less of the gubernatorial campaign had been devoted to the Democratic presidential candidacy and more to Roosevelt's independent self. As for Smith's privately announced intention to remain in Albany for an indefinite period following the inauguration (he had reserved a suite in the DeWitt Clinton Hotel) in order to "help" the untried new governor, Roosevelt did not appreciate it at all. He resented it, as a matter of fact, and feared its consequences.

But the governor-elect was very careful during this interview to disguise his resentment, along with the anxiety he felt over the direction in which his relationship with Smith now pointed. He wanted no quarrel with his predecessor. He must have the support of Smith's hero-worshipers among the city electorate and of Smith's special friends in the state's legislative and executive branches. And to avoid a quarrel he was willing to go to almost any length short of yielding up any part of the governing power that was properly, legally his. He exerted himself to lubricate the transfer of power, to make it as smooth and easy for Smith as possible. He was cordial, notably voluble, high-spirited, and flatteringly deferent. But from Smith's point of view he was strangely reluctant to talk seriously about state business. It was the still-incumbent governor who, with some difficulty, brought the talk around to specific matters for decision. He gave advice about the handling of the new "scientific" executive budget, concerning which there were important unanswered questions having to do with the division of authority between the legislature and the executive. Roosevelt nodded in seeming agreement. Smith spoke in glowing terms of Mrs. Moskowitz, of her brilliant abilities and the invaluable service she had rendered, and he assured "Frank," as if it were a longed-for reassurance, that she was "willing" to continue to serve. What "Frank" should do, said Smith, was assign Mrs. Moskowitz the position of governor's secretary: this would give her an assured, well-defined position "from which to work." Roosevelt again nodded in seeming agreement. Only when Smith proposed the retention of Robert Moses as secretary of state did he encounter a Roosevelt negative. This negative was firm. Roosevelt was willing to retain Moses in posts for which Moses had proved himself exceptionally well qualified—as chairman of the State Council for Parks, for instance, and as president of the Long Island Park Commission, posts Moses now held in addition to the cabinet position —but he wanted him in no post requiring or encouraging close and frequent contact with the governor. "He rubs me the wrong way," said Roosevelt. Smith, by his own account, accepted this without argument (Roosevelt later alleged that "Al was furious" about it); he may even have half expected it, knowing as he did how Moses and Roosevelt had clashed in the past.[52]

The one matter that Roosevelt himself brought up was the possibility—and he seems to have presented it as no more than a possibility—that he might name Frances Perkins to the post of industrial commissioner, replacing "old man" Hamilton. What did Smith think of the idea? Smith thought very poorly of it. He had the highest regard for Frances Perkins, whom, after all, he had appointed to her present position, which had never before been filled by a woman. He liked and admired her personally, and she had abundantly proved her ability as a public servant. But the industrial commissioner, as administrative head of the Department of Labor, had directive control over "all the men who work as factory inspectors and on the compensation boards," and it was Smith's "experience" that men, though willing to accept advice from a woman, provided it was sound, of course, were *not* willing to take orders from one.[53]

Yet again Roosevelt nodded, as if in agreement.

And so the interview ended on a high note of mutual personal good feeling.

But if Roosevelt thus succeeded in soothing Smith's sensibilities, he did so at some cost: there was encouraged a continued view of him as an essentially frivolous character, admirably fitted to serve as a façade but too deficient in willpower and serious purpose actually to govern a great state. A week later, according to Roosevelt's own testimony, "Al came to see me and told me that Mrs. Moskowitz was preparing my Inaugural Address and Message to the Legislature." Roosevelt, recalling the episode long afterward, was willing to concede that Smith "probably did this in complete good faith, wanting to help"; but of course such "help" would never have been offered if Smith had not had "the rather definite thought that he would continue to run the Governorship. His first bad shock came," Roosevelt continued, "when I told him that I had already prepared my Inaugural Address and that my Message to the Legislature was nearly finished."[54]

Even this rebuff, however, was evidently thickly coated by a charming deference and display of naïveté. Roosevelt told Smith he would of course submit both draft speeches to Mrs. Moskowitz for her review before he went to Albany on January 1 (" . . . my recollection is that I did not find the opportunity to do so," he later said, "though I really meant to at the time"),[55] as if he, surprised by the proffered help, had proceeded in the way he had only because he had not known that such help, which he would have welcomed, was available to him. Smith, now puzzled and uneasy, still did not realize that his effort to have Belle Moskowitz established as secretary to the new governor had failed and that further effort along that line would be worse than futile. He couldn't believe it! Surely Roosevelt must realize that Belle's continued active service would virtually assure him of a successful administration, enabling him to advance the programs for which he had campaigned! So Smith continued to press for this appointment. He employed an intermediary. He asked Frances Perkins to talk to Roosevelt about it, and she, with some misgivings, agreed to do so.

Meanwhile, Ed Flynn had returned to New York City. Basil O'Connor met him at the boat when it docked on Christmas Eve and took him at once to the Sixty-fifth Street house, pleading with him all the way to reconsider his refusal of the post Roosevelt had offered him. "When I arrived at Roosevelt's home all the great charm and persuasiveness of that remarkable man were turned on," Flynn recalled decades later. Flynn, Roosevelt made clear, was the one man whose appointment as secretary of state in place of Moses would be accepted by Al Smith without rancor, and it was of the utmost importance, as Flynn well knew, to prevent any rift with Al that might widen into a party split. Moreover, Flynn was the only man who could function for Roosevelt as Robert Moses had for Smith, as a general adviser on matters of state concern, and the new governor was badly in need of the political knowledge and judgment and skill that Flynn was uniquely equipped to supply him. "Finally he [Roosevelt] said to me, 'Eddie, when you were insisting that I run for Governor, you said that I owed a duty to the party to accept. I am now saying to you that you owe a similar duty to the party to accept this office.' " When the request was "put . . . on that basis, I could not refuse."[56]

Frances Perkins would always remember in vivid detail the interview with Roosevelt during which, as promised, she again raised the question of Belle Moskowitz. He listened to her reiteration of Smith's argument. He agreed that Mrs. Moskowitz was certainly "very, very able," that she had done "a great deal for Al," as she would "for any man who is Governor." But, he went on, she was a very masterful person who had become "accustomed to running and planning everything." If appointed the governor's secretary, "she would inevitably plan and develop the work of the Governor" as if she, not he, were the executive. It just wouldn't do. " . . . I've *got* to be Governor of the State of New York and I've got to be it MYSELF." If he weren't, "something would be wrong in here," he said, tapping his chest. He was "awfully sorry if it hurts anybody, particularly Al."

His expressed concern for Al's feelings did not, however, prevent his telling reporters four days before the inauguration that he had had no conferences, not a single one, with Mrs. Moskowitz, and on the very eve of inauguration day he told Smith that he had decided to appoint Guernsey Cross as secretary to the governor, largely because Cross was a "great, big, strong man" upon whom he could "lean . . . physically." Small wonder that, as Madame Perkins recorded nearly two decades later, a "self-conscious tension" developed between Smith and Roosevelt.[57]

2

-»>X«-

The New Governor: Is He Tough Enough?

I

BUT there was no outward sign of inner tension when, in the afternoon of December 31, 1928, Al Smith, who had celebrated his fifty-fifth birthday only the day before, welcomed Franklin Roosevelt to the Executive Mansion in Albany. Nearly a thousand people were gathered along the Mansion's front drive when the Roosevelt motorcade, preceded by a motorcycle escort, arrived from Hyde Park at around three-thirty. Among them were sharp-eyed reporters who had published rumors and surmises of possible friction between the incoming and outgoing regimes and were on the lookout for the slightest indication of it in the behavior of the principals of this transaction in power. They saw none. They saw instead a display of warm personal affection.

Before the Roosevelt automobile was completely stopped under the ornate portico, Mr. and Mrs. Smith came down the front steps, Al with his hand outstretched, a wide smile on his face. "God bless and keep you, Frank," he said. "A thousand welcomes. We've got the home fires burning and you'll find this a fine place to live." Mrs. Smith, a plump and pleasant lady, kissed the governor-elect before the applauding multitude. Smith embraced Eleanor. And Roosevelt, turning to those around him, said wistfully, "I only wish Al were going to be here for the next two years. We certainly will miss him." He continued wistful, or seemed so to at least one reporter, when, standing inside the Mansion a few minutes later, he watched through a window the Smiths' departure. The crowd, which obviously had gathered more to say goodbye to Smith than to greet Smith's successor, sang "Auld Lang Syne" as the great governor and his lady seated themselves in the limousine; scores of voices, some of them tearful, cried out, "Goodbye, Al," as the car moved down the drive, and Al, on the verge of tears himself, lifted and waved his brown derby.[1] The Smiths were driven to the DeWitt Clinton. They would sleep in the hotel that night.

They were back in the Mansion within two or three hours, however, and as master and mistress of the house. Smith's legal term as governor did not expire until midnight. He was therefore the host at a dinner in the Mansion whose guests were the governor-elect, Roosevelt, and the lieutenant governor-elect, Lehman, with their wives and several members of the Smith, Roosevelt, and Lehman families, including Roosevelt's mother and son James, all of them, Roosevelt and Eleanor especially, exerting themselves to make the occasion as warm and smooth as possible, a soothing salve upon whatever sore spirits might be at that table.

After dinner they all went into the drawing room, or parlor. This was the room in which Theodore Roosevelt had been sworn in as governor three decades before. And there Franklin Delano Roosevelt, his face solemn, almost stern, took the oath of office as governor of the state of New York. The oath was administered by Judge Irving Lehman of the Court of Appeals, who immediately thereafter administered it to his brother, the new lieutenant governor. As Roosevelt took the oath he rested his left hand upon a Bible brought up from Hyde Park for this purpose, an ancient Dutch Bible that may have come to New Amsterdam in the 1640s with Claes Martenszen Van Rosenvelt and certainly had been a treasured possession of the first Jacobus (James) Roosevelt, father of Isaac the Patriot. Thus Roosevelt went to bed late that night as chief executive of the Empire State, armed with full authority to deal with any state emergency that might arise before he was formally inaugurated the next day.

No emergency arose.

Nor did the new governor himself, until rather late in the morning of Tuesday, January 1, 1929. He awoke no doubt in happy anticipation of the most important ceremonial day of his public life thus far and may well have displayed rather more than his usual good cheer as his valet helped him into the formal morning attire proper to his public appearance. He could feel that the script assigned him from on high was still being "religiously" followed: he stood at age forty-seven where TR had stood at age forty, and there opened up before him vastly enlarged opportunities to express that instinct for power, to exercise that faculty of command, that his mother had noted in him as a child. He, who in his boyhood had habitually given orders to his playmates because "if I didn't . . . nothing would happen," was now in a place where he could make things happen on a, for him, unprecedentedly large scale. More fully than ever before he was in his element. He entered eagerly upon a job he knew he was born to do.

But there was no diminution of his resolve to defer, in outward show, to the sensibilities of the man whose place he took. The weather, he at once noted through his bedroom window, was more in keeping with Al Smith's probable mood than with his own. It was gloomy. A leaden sky wept a thin chill rain upon snow that had accumulated overnight, washing that snow into gray slush upon the streets, into black mud in the Mansion's winter-killed gardens. The whole of the day's atmosphere was suited to melancholy farewells, not joyous welcomes, and it increased Roosevelt's sensitivity to what Al must be suffering. "No man ever willingly gives up public life—no man who has ever tasted it," Roosevelt would say to the journalist Ernest K. Lindley, self-revealingly, a few months hence. And poor Al on this dreary morning must contemplate the bleak fact that for the first time in a quarter century save for the two years 1921–1923, recognized at that time as a mere interval, he held no public office, nor had any prospect of one. Roosevelt was glad that the ceremonial arrangements he had approved if not in part suggested were rather more in Smith's honor than his own. He wanted Al to have the best possible send-off, while at the same time making it clear to Al that it *was* a send-off, a fond but very firm farewell.

The ceremony began at noon. Because of the weather, it was held in the Assembly Chamber of the Capitol. A remarkably large crowd of loyal Democrats was present, thanks to invitations Roosevelt had sent to virtually every important party figure in America (most had of necessity declined, but not a few came from neighboring states) and thanks also to his scheduling of conferences with state and county party officers later that day and on the morrow. There was a departure from the usual procedure: the outgoing governor was called upon to present a farewell address. And never had Smith been in better speaking form, never had he had a more sympathetically responsive audience, than on this occasion. He spoke extemporaneously, as he almost always did, reviewing with pardonable pride the great achievements of his four terms, and as he drew toward a close, he turned to his successor. "Frank, I congratulate you," he said. He spoke so warmly, so earnestly, that few took note of the far from flattering implications of his following words: "I hope you will be able to devote that intelligent mind of yours to the problems of this state."

He referred, emotionally, to the presence of Sara Delano Roosevelt upon the platform, bringing tears to that lady's eyes and to the eyes of his own wife. "My mother [she had died only a few weeks before the 1924 convention] was on the platform with me for two inaugurations," he remembered. "I know how she enjoyed it and how she felt about it."[2]

Then it was Roosevelt's turn.

The crowd was impressed by the difference between Al Smith's presentation and that of this new man—by the contrast between Al's gruffness, Al's total lack of literary style, and the musical tones, the cultured accent, the occasional eloquence, of Roosevelt's voice and words. After a graceful tribute to his predecessor, in which he said the day was notable more as a farewell to a great governor than as the inauguration of a new one, he effected a smooth transition to a discussion of that conception of state government, of its necessary role amid "the interdependence on each other" created by "modern civilization," that Smith had triumphantly implemented and to which Roosevelt himself subscribed. He appealed to the legislature for a burial of the enmities that had in former years arisen "between the Legislative and Executive branches." Pointing out that "on many of the great State questions . . . the platform and public pledges of both parties are substantially agreed," he called for a new Era of Good Feeling. He pledged that he would not permit "the business of the State . . . to become involved in partisan politics" and would "not attempt to claim unfair advantage for my party or for myself, for the accomplishing of those things on which we are all agreed."[3]

There followed the inaugural parade. The weather continued miserable, the thin rain of the early morning having turned back into snow that fell in soft wet flakes upon the ex-governor and the new governor as they stood side by side on the flag-bedecked reviewing stand. The parade was followed by a huge reception at the Mansion, hosted by the new governor. The Smiths attended it only briefly. Having already checked out of the DeWitt Clinton, they went directly from the Mansion to the railroad station, where, as thousands shouted

goodbyes to them, they boarded a train for New York City. It was evident that
Al, to Franklin Roosevelt's relief, had given up his plan to remain in Albany.

The next day, in his annual message to the legislature, the new governor
sounded again the note of conciliation as he outlined his legislative program,
inherited for the most part from his predecessor. "He best serves his party,"
said Roosevelt, "who best serves his State. . . . I urge you all, individually, to
come to me with problems, with suggestions, with honest differences of opinion
as often and as freely as I hope you will let me come to you. The verdict on
our relations that I most desire is that I have at least been fair and reasonable
and friendly."[4]

II

IN the audience were some who interpreted Roosevelt's sweet reasonableness,
his appeal to "the better angels of our nature," in much the same way as
Southern hotheads and Northern Abolitionists interpreted, in 1861, the closing
words of Lincoln's first inaugural address. They deemed the words an expression of personal weakness, a cowardly fear of combat. And they were encouraged in this view by Roosevelt's persistence in pacifist attitudes and in efforts
at conciliation during the weeks that followed, despite increasingly bold provocations by Republican legislators.

Only once during these weeks did he publicly slip from his lofty perch above
party politics.

It had been decided that Louis Howe would not accompany his chief to
Albany, where he was suited to no available post, but would remain in New
York City, where his principal concern would be the undercover promotion
of Roosevelt's presidential ambitions. (This decision was painful to Howe: he
feared his place as Roosevelt's most intimate adviser might be usurped by Sam
Rosenman, and he hated Rosenman to the extent of this fear.) And it was in
pursuance of his national concern that he prepared for Roosevelt's release to
the press on Sunday afternoon, January 13, a lengthy statement based on the
"three thousand" epistolary responses allegedly made to Roosevelt's postelec-
tion letters to leading Democrats all over the nation. The statement was strong
and bitter. "Bigotry, ignorance of democratic principles, the spread by unspeakable and un-American methods of the most atrocious falsehoods, unfair
and improper pressures brought to bear upon workers in specially favored
Republican industries, false claims for prosperity of the country and kindred
propaganda cheated, my correspondents feel, our party out of the Presidency."
So said Roosevelt in print under big headlines in Monday morning's newspapers. There had been, he implied, a "theft of the Presidency" as palpable as
"in the case of Mr. Tilden" in 1876. Equally strong and bitter were the reactions
this provoked, and not only from Republican politicians and newspapers but
also from newspapers normally Democratic and voters who, casting their
ballots for Hoover and Roosevelt the preceding fall, deemed themselves intelli-

gently "independent." Even the Democratic national chairman, John J. Ras-kob, himself the target of much campaign abuse, let it be publicly known that he thought Roosevelt's statement unwise.[5]

The new governor, badly stung, defended himself forcefully in private talk and correspondence. His distant cousin Nicholas Roosevelt, who had voted for him the previous fall while also voting for Hoover, angrily protested in a private letter against his statement—and Nicholas' position as editorial writer on the New York *Times* made him worth answering at length. Roosevelt replied that his statement had been a summary of what the "thousands" of letters had said, not an expression of his personal views; he was personally convinced, however, that what the letters had said was true. There certainly *had* been a carefully organized, hugely expensive campaign of viciously lying propaganda directed against Smith. " . . . the mere printing and postage bill of the Fellowship Forum* alone must have run up into a figure between two and five million dollars. Add to this the other similar papers, . . . the handbills and finally the undoubted fact that many poverty-stricken Protestant ministers —mostly Methodist or Baptist, received some form of emolument or pay, and it is very certain that the funds to put forth this propaganda did not come just from the Anti-Saloon League and similar sources but must have been raised or guaranteed by outside organizations. . . . I am personally convinced that large sums were handed over by people pretty high up in Republican Organiza-tion Headquarters for the purpose of paying for and accelerating this propa-ganda." He was very sure that "Dear Nick" would "sympathize with my thought that if a very un-American, a very disgraceful and a very vile cam-paign has been proven, the answer is not just to pull a veil over it with the hope that it will not happen again. I am red-blooded enough to believe that it sometimes pays better for the country to talk things out."[6]

But he made no further public pronouncements along this line.

The image he projected of himself more strongly now than ever before, and upon a larger and more swiftly enlarging public than ever before, continued to be an accurate if partial reflection in the public mind of what he really inwardly was: warm, kind, zestful, joyous, incredibly even-tempered under stress, eager for new experience, interested in everything—a man who, liking everybody, wanted everybody to like him and was exceptionally well equipped to ensure their doing so. The huge red-brick Executive Mansion, a cluttered Victorian pile of cupolas and bay windows and towers square and rounded, a porch on every story of each tower, became under the Roosevelts a less formal and exclusive place, a more public and "democratic" one, than it had been under the popular and democratic Smiths, and life within it was more abundantly characterized by fun and laughter. The nine guest rooms were continually occupied, and there were additional guests at virtually every lunch-eon, at the substantial tea Eleanor presided over every afternoon when she was home, at every dinner, even at Sunday suppers, and at the motion-picture show

---

*One of the most vicious and widely circulated of the propaganda publications.

presented at least once a week in the "theater" that was set up in a third-floor hallway, for few Americans were more addicted to "the movies" than Franklin Roosevelt. The incessantly vigorously active Roosevelt boys romped through the place during school holidays and vacations, engaging with their friends in a bewildering variety of pursuits. There were fairly frequent public receptions only slightly less crowded than the inaugural day festivities. "The people of New York have always liked their governors to entertain a good deal, and when invited to . . . the Executive Mansion, they came in droves," Frances Perkins would remember. Roosevelt "seemed to enjoy these large evenings" and managed to impart to them "an atmosphere of pleasure."[7] Every guest, warmed by the cordial hospitality of the governor and first lady, was made to feel perfectly at home. Many were stimulated into an unwontedly wide range of simultaneous awarenesses by a Roosevelt "proclivity" of which Ernest Lindley took note. "Roosevelt gives the impression that he is not fully occupied unless he is doing two or three things at once," wrote Lindley.* " . . . he will grant a newspaper interview while swimming in his pool [he had a heated pool installed in what had formerly been the Mansion's greenhouse], carry on a discussion while correcting a speech or while arranging his stamps."[8] (Roosevelt allotted at least a few minutes to his stamps every day that he was home.)

And Lindley also told of his experience of a typical late-afternoon visit to the Mansion. "You arrive . . . at five-thirty. An impressive delegation is just coming out. You go inside, the tea-table has just been trundled into the study and Mrs. Roosevelt is pouring. The Governor, two unidentified persons who look as though they might be old friends from Hyde Park, a secretary and a stenographer are there. They all get their tea. Sergeant Earl Miller, the handsome state trooper [he was assigned to guard Mrs. Roosevelt on her travels, and he became her fast friend and fervent admirer] and Sergeant Gus Gennerich [he was assigned to guard the Governor, and he, too, became a fast friend of the family's] drift in and get their cups." There was much banter about the troopers' horses, Miller's Ford, and similar inconsequentials, until the "brief interlude" was ended. "One of Roosevelt's secretaries arrives from the Capitol with two brief cases filled with letters dictated earlier in the day. Roosevelt reads and signs the letters, occasionally altering one and putting it aside for retyping. As he does so he answers questions [Lindley's] at length," Mrs. Roosevelt "slips in, hands him a piece of paper with a head pasted on it, and whispers he will have to draw a valentine for Howe [it was Valentine's Day and Howe, spending the night in the Mansion, as he did almost every weekend, was at work in the adjoining dining room with cardboard and scissors and paints, making a centerpiece for the table and individual comic

---

*When a boy, Franklin had often worked on his stamp collection while his mother read aloud to him. One day he seemed so utterly absorbed in what he was doing, so oblivious to what she was reading, that she grew annoyed. "I don't believe you are hearing a word," she protested. He then promptly repeated to her, word for word, the whole of the last paragraph she had read, adding, "I would be ashamed of myself if I couldn't do at least two things at once." (*Gracious Lady: The Life of Sara Delano Roosevelt,* by Rita Kleeman [New York, 1935], page 189.)

valentines for staff members who were to be the dinner guests that night]. He puts aside his correspondence for a second, swiftly draws an absurd picture of a man in a long nightgown, holding a candle, and puts on a nightcap for a finishing touch. He puts some caption beneath it which makes them both burst into laughter. Mrs. Roosevelt exits and he returns to his work." When one of his department heads arrived a few minutes later, unexpectedly it seemed, the governor, his letter signing done, asked him to "come along and talk to me upstairs" while he dressed for dinner. The conversation with the department head, Lindley noted, was "serious."[9]

It was now remarked more widely and frequently than ever before that the former amateur ornithologist of Hyde Park and Campobello could "charm the birds off the trees." But this of itself alone served more to raise than to reduce, in critical minds, questions as to Roosevelt's bravery and strength of character. Such charm, because it can be used so easily as a substitute for hard effort, is often linked to a deficiency of willpower and a failure to develop genuinely productive faculties; those having it run the risk of being spoiled by it, as children of the rich are spoiled by too many unearned possessions and undisciplined pleasures, or a beautiful woman, by attentions showered upon her in tribute to nothing more than her appearance. There were many in Albany who were inclined to believe, in agreement with the covertly expressed opinions of Al Smith and Smith's "kitchen cabinet," that Roosevelt had been thus weakened, thus spoiled. They ignored or discounted, as was easy to do since he himself made light of it, the evidence presented by his long struggle against crippling polio; they stressed instead his evident reluctance to meet opposition head-on or to come to grips with thorny issues. Others, like Rosenman, having initially shared this view, changed their minds. These others agreed that Roosevelt's strength of character was less obvious than his charm, but they had no doubt of its active existence; its precise nature would prove difficult to assess even by those who had had a long experience of him.

From the moment of his first meeting people, Roosevelt habitually called them by their first name and was likely subsequently to speak of them as "dear friends," but it was notable that very few people addressed him by *his* first name. He loved to engage in persiflage, he never "put on airs," he treated his servants as friends, and he thoroughly enjoyed a session of poker in shirt-sleeved informality, all of which became widely known among the people of the state. But that "unspoken dignity" that Rosenman had felt upon the Hoboken ferry was felt equally by others and continued to protect him, as governor, against "undue familiarity." He was never quite "one of the boys," as Al Smith had been. In Albany, as at Hyde Park, where, because it was so near Albany, he was able to spend much time and transact much public business, he remained the country squire, possessed, for all his seeming self-revelations, of impenetrable reserves, which others sensed and which generally imposed a considerable measure of respect for him personally, even upon those who still believed themselves contemptuous of him as a mere charmer.

From his first day in office he operated as though he had been governor for

years, and thanks to his predecessor he was instrumentally equipped truly to
govern; he could administer New York's $300,000,000-a-year business with
efficiency and dispatch. This had been impossible for any governor to do when
Smith first took office in 1919. The state's administrative operation and authority then had been distributed among more than 200 separate boards and
commissions, many of them virtually laws unto themselves and some of them
authorized to enter into large financial contracts with private businesses. The
opportunities for waste and graft and corruption were immense, and those for
honest efficiency correspondingly limited. Smith, relying here especially heavily upon Robert Moses, had changed this. Through a series of bitter battles
with the legislature he had managed to gain such wide popular support for his
reorganization plan, devised by Moses, that it was adopted, eliminating many
of the formerly separate bodies altogether and consolidating the others, or their
functions, into a mere eighteen departments, whose heads reported directly to
him.

Roosevelt, therefore, stepped into a going concern.

And he worked hard at his job. Often his Albany workday began with
breakfast conferences in the Mansion, and always, at breakfast or immediately
thereafter, he swiftly scanned some eight newspapers selected as representative
of various parts of the state. After breakfast he dealt with the mail, mostly
personal, addressed to him at the Mansion, dictating two or three dozen letters
before going to his office in the Capitol, where he dealt with some forty
additional letters. At 11:00 A.M. began his appointments, an uninterrupted
stream of interviews and conferences lasting until 5:30 or 6:00 P.M.; even
during his lunch hour he conferred, for he had lunch brought to his office,
where he ate it at his desk. Nor did his workday end with his return to the
Mansion: always there were guests, generally with official business to transact,
at tea, at dinner, and after dinner, and always there were documents to peruse
and speeches or messages to prepare.

He easily dominated whenever he wished to dominate the meetings over
which he presided. He did so sometimes under very trying circumstances. In
the first weeks of his administration he "established the habit," as Frances
Perkins put it, "of holding conferences or informal hearings on matters not yet
embodied in bills." She never forgot the first of these she attended. It was held
in the Capitol's Executive Chamber, an ornate audience room large enough to
accommodate gatherings of a hundred or more people. Approximately a hundred people were assembled, "including many strangers to the Governor,"
when a small door opened from the executive's adjacent office. Roosevelt
entered. Everyone stood up and remained standing in "natural common courtesy" as the governor, one hand grasping a thick cane, the other the muscular
arm of Guernsey Cross, made his way toward his desk. "It took him a long,
long time," for the desk was far across the room from the door, no one having
thought to move it nearer; and those who watched felt increasing dismay and
anger at an ordeal, a humiliation, needlessly imposed upon so pitiably helpless
a man. But then something humanly magnificent happened. When he was

about halfway to the desk, Roosevelt suddenly "realized the tension of the audience. He began to smile and nod, tossing his head up gaily. He waved the cane, saying cheerfully, 'That's all right. I'll make it.' "[10] His audience, its tensions at once relaxed, smiled back at him and wordlessly cheered on the man who, in self-mastery, had so gracefully eased this awkward situation. Pity was transformed into admiration.

Yet in the minds of several in the room that day, the truly vital questions about him in his present role remained unanswered. Roosevelt's ability to achieve this kind of dominance sufficed for his rule of Warm Springs, where Sam Rosenman had first observed it in its fullest flower. Warm Springs, however, was a world he had largely made, and in his own image. Albany, as the governing center of the Empire State, was a different world, a world he emphatically had *not* made. It had harsh dissonances and conflicts built into its very structure. And to master it, charm, fortitude, perseverance, hard work, and the courtesy of an unusually kind and sensitive man, though helpful, were not enough. He faced a long series of the toughest kind of adversary proceedings in which his opponents would be coldly ambitious men incapable of the finer vibrations, committed wholly to organized selfishness, and ruthlessly determined to knock him down. To deal with them successfully he must himself be tough in combative ways. He must be prepared, instrumentally and psychologically, to exercise a form of power involving no element of willing assent or acquiescence on the part of those subjected to it—a power of coercive force, including threats. Did the new governor realize that this was so? Or did he actually believe, as his inaugural and message seemed to say he believed, that conflict could be avoided and his goals achieved through a mutual agreement on "fundamentals" and a consequent strategy of compromise, conciliation, cooperation?

III

IN point of fact, Roosevelt on the morrow of his election victory was perfectly well aware that he faced "a strenuous two years" during which he could "expect to be the target of practically all of the Republican artillery." The quoted words are from a letter he wrote to the widow of William Jennings Bryan shortly before Christmas of 1928. Nor did he shrink from this aspect of the prospect before him. "I am a little like my dear friend, Mr. Bryan, in liking a good fight,"* he wrote to Mrs. Bryan.[11] His style of fighting differed greatly from Al Smith's, however, not only because his nature was radically different from Smith's but also because his political aims were different. Smith, who lacked any sympathetic understanding of the rural mind and temper, who had

---

*During the Wilson administration, Assistant Secretary of the Navy Roosevelt's contempt for Secretary of State Bryan as man and statesman had been profound. Bryan's pacifism, which led to his resignation from the Cabinet following Wilson's second *Lusitania* note, was deemed weak, cowardly, and sentimental by the young FDR.

long ago written off upstate farmers and villagers as hopelessly lost to Republicanism, never pretended that the essential relationship between a Democratic governor and a Republican legislature could be other than hostile. His habit was to focus upon his enemies the full fire of his wrath, lambasting them with the harshest language of scorn and ridicule whenever, presented with a major welfare or governmental reform proposal, they engaged in blindly partisan obstructionism. (They almost invariably did so; the level of intelligence among New York Republican leaders was not high.) Roosevelt, on the other hand, habitually called himself a farmer and identified himself with the rural interest when he toured the upstate countryside. He had already succeeded in splitting off from the state Republican Party a significant portion of its upstate support, else he could not have won the election, and he intended to split off more. Also, of course, he played his persuasive role very consciously before a national audience. Hence his soft words, his conciliatory gestures, his determination to appear before a normally Republican rank and file as the very personification of good feeling, and his determination to maintain this stance for as long as he could in the face of predictable Republican provocations.

At the same time, he very realistically mobilized his resources for battle, organizing them into instruments of persuasion that, as they worked upon the general public, could become instruments for the coercion of recalcitrant legislators.

It was at his suggestion that a permanent state Democratic Party press bureau ("information service"), with an annual budget of $100,000, was established in Albany by the end of January to send out, primarily to rural editors, *not* party publicity but "straight news" of a kind not theretofore readily available to them—news of such undoubted local interest about specific issues, the local expenditure of state moneys for new or improved facilities, the attendance records of local legislative representatives, how they voted on important bills, and so on, that the most partisan of Republican papers printed it. The immediate impact upon Republican strongholds upstate was so great that the Republicans hurriedly reactivated a state publicity apparatus of their own, originally intended for use only during the campaign.

Similarly with regard to radio. Sooner and more clearly than almost any other major politician, Roosevelt realized the importance of radio, the revolutionary change in communications being wrought by it. "One can only guess at the figure," he told the Tammany Speakers' Bureau on January 17, "but I think it is a conservative estimate to say that whereas five years ago ninety-nine out of one hundred people took their arguments from the editorials and news columns of the daily press, today at least half the voters sitting at their own firesides listen to the actual words of the political leaders on both sides and make their decisions on what they hear rather than what they read."[12] A few days later the Democratic Party arranged by contract for one hour a month of statewide radio network time. Roosevelt would make good use of it. His radio reports to the people, during which he "chatted" with his listeners in tones of frank and friendly intimacy, as if physically present in their homes and addressing himself to them individually, proved tremendously effective from the first and became increasingly so as he further mastered the techniques of radio speech. He learned to slow down his speech rhythms and to employ homely concrete illustrations, drawn from the everyday lives of his listeners, to illumine complexities normally dealt with in abstractions. If his use of radio did not of itself alone overcome the advantage that accrued to the Republicans from their control of virtually all the daily press outside New York City, and of most of the papers in that city, it went far toward doing so.

He continued to pay close attention to the formation of effective Democratic organizations in upstate districts where none had existed in more than name for decades, if ever. Smith had generally brusquely denied requests from rural Democrats for state campaign funds: the requested assignment would be a foolish waste of money, he said. The new governor took a different view. He talked in early January of making a serious effort to win upstate Assembly seats for Democrats in the fall of 1929 (assemblymen were still elected to one-year terms). His talk continued to stimulate upstate workers with its implied promise of funding even after Roosevelt had soft-pedaled it, as he soon did, in the interests of "harmony" with Republican assemblymen who had his legislative program in hand. Stressing far more than Smith had ever done the importance of women in politics, he gave Eleanor, Nancy Cook, Caroline O'Day, and other Democratic women workers advice on ways and means of overcoming a prejudice against Democrats in general, on grounds other than purely political, that was particularly strong among rural women—the tendency to regard Democrats as socially inferior to Republicans, to look down upon them as predominantly of the "wicked city's" immigrant "lower classes," essentially alien to the American way of life. (Of any such general view, the Roosevelts themselves were of course a living contradiction as they pursued their well-publicized lives in the Mansion, at Hyde Park, on East Sixty-fifth Street, in Warm Springs.)

But though he thus stressed upstate organization with an energy unprecedented for a Democratic governor, Roosevelt did not do so at the expense of good working relationships with the New York City machines. He cooperated with these machines, conferring on patronage matters with George Olvany, the Tammany boss; John McCooey, the Brooklyn boss; and of course his secretary of state, Boss Flynn of the Bronx. Moreover, he defended such relationships in correspondence with those who criticized him for having them. When a Western Republican wrote that Roosevelt had "out here . . . the brand of Tammany Hall" and that "the Democratic standard will . . . doubtless go down again in defeat in '32" unless Roosevelt helped "to eliminate the unworthy men in your party," he replied, signing a letter drafted by Howe, in unwontedly strong language: "I suppose it is rather useless for me to attempt to convince you that your ideas of Tammany Hall and its relation to the Democratic National Party are founded on untruth and vicious propaganda. . . . It is very hard for the Democrats, with a press so hopelessly Republican, and in the face of such enormous sums of money spent for the dissemination of the most atrocious libel, to get the truth before the people."[13] Roosevelt strove mightily toward a consummation of his long effort, initiated in the aftermath of his 1920 defeat, to make the New York Democracy a smoothly functioning amalgam of city *and* country and to become himself, in his public image, a symbol of the process and of its end. As he did so, he became considerably more partisan in his political appointments, over the state as a whole, than Smith had been. "When vacancies arose in any of the upstate counties, . . . Roosevelt in practically every instance appointed men and women recommended by the organizations," Ed Flynn would remember. " . . . he eventually made the New York City members of the Port Authority all Democrats, where previously this group had been bipartisan." He even "appointed Democrats to succeed Republicans on the various visiting boards of the state institutions," positions that were "purely honorary" and had always before "been filled without regard to the politics of the appointee." This "break with precedent . . . caused the Republicans some concern," added Flynn in bland understatement.[14]

Roosevelt gave no public sign that he recognized for what they were, at the outset, acts by the Republican legislative majority that were clearly solely designed to gain an "unfair partisan advantage," since they had to do with matters on which the two parties were substantially agreed. Yet he defended himself against these with subtle skill on several occasions.

For instance, five days after the delivery of his conciliatory message he announced the formation of an advisory body on farm relief, which he had proposed in that message. Calling it the Agricultural Advisory Commission, he appointed to it the same twenty-one people who had served upon the agricultural committee that he, as governor-elect, had asked Henry Morgenthau, Jr., to form and chair. Morgenthau was again chairman. Eighteen of the twenty-one, Roosevelt pointed out, "happened" to be Republicans. Nevertheless, the Republican legislature immediately summoned a conference of state agricultural "experts" to meet with legislators on the same day as the Agricultural Advisory Commission was originally scheduled to meet, that is, on the day of the annual meeting of the New York Agricultural Society. Roosevelt's commission was now unnecessary, the Republican leaders announced. The governor ignored this. He indicated to reporters that he and the Republican speaker of the assembly were delighted with each other's proposals, an expression of good feeling that virtually forced the Republicans to invite him to address their agricultural conference, since their failure to do so would be an open admission of their partisan motivations. Roosevelt accepted with pleasure; he moved to make the most of his opportunity.

He encouraged Morgenthau to advance the time of the meeting of the commission so that its report could be issued before the rival conference opened in the Assembly Chamber. Morgenthau barely managed to do so. The commission met in all-day session on January 16, met again on the morning of January 17, which was the day of the legislature's conference, and reported its recommendations only an hour before that conference was called to order.

The recommendations were ones upon which all the major farm organizations of the state had agreed—for farm tax relief, for a gasoline tax of 2½ cents per gallon to pay for road construction and maintenance, for improved rural schools, for studies leading to a more rapid extension of rural electrification, for more agricultural research. Consequently, most of the bills embodying them were virtually certain of passage during the current legislative session. It was a great boon to Roosevelt, therefore, to be able to present himself to the conference as a fellow farmer eager to inform his colleagues of what his commission was proposing for the benefit of them all. He also seized the occasion to recommend, as if it were his own idea, what he knew the Republicans were planning to do, namely, appoint a committee of "experts" to advise the legislature on agricultural matters. "After I go downstairs* to my desk," he closed, "you will find an Executive who wishes to go along with you the whole way."[15] If the applause he then received from the Republican legislators was something less than wholehearted, it was perforce required to appear so.

Thus did he prove his mastery of the art of political jujitsu, and he amplified its effectiveness through his equal or even greater mastery of the art of publicity. He promoted his farm program, stressing the proposed gasoline tax, which Republican legislators were initially inclined to oppose, in an address to a meeting of rural newspaper publishers and editors on February 1; he also talked individually to several dozen of them. On February 16 he delivered a major address on farm relief to approximately 3,000 country people assembled for the annual Farm and Home Week of the Agricultural College at Cornell, achieving a "grand success," as he wrote soon after to his son James.†[16] In early March he talked about his agricultural program over the statewide radio network—talked in studiously nonpartisan terms about the problems facing them all and the progress thus far made toward their solution.

All of this ensured his receiving most of the credit upstate for the farm measures that the legislature finally adopted. He was so credited despite the fact that every agricultural bill he proposed through Democratic legislators was killed by the Republicans so that they might pass a practically identical measure of their own.

Equally skillful though less immediately fruitful was his political handling of a problem of poverty most acute in cities, namely, that of the elderly indigent, stressed by him during the election campaign. "No greater tragedy exists in our civilization than the plight of citizens who find themselves, after a long life of activity and usefulness, unable to maintain themselves decently," he said to the legislature and to the public as he called for the establishment of a commission to study and propose legislation on old-age security. With regard to this, he also demonstrated his mastery of the art of publicity. A bill

---

*The Assembly Chamber was on the third floor, and the governor's office on the second, of the Capitol.
†James was then in Thomasville, Georgia, where he had gone to recuperate from a severe attack of pneumonia suffered soon after the holidays.

to establish the commission having been introduced, he proposed in his budget a sum of $25,000 to fund it. The Republicans wished to smother the proposal to silent death in committee, but Roosevelt on February 27 sent a special message on it to the legislature, stimulated organized support of it by welfare workers, civic groups, and religious bodies, and forced the Republicans to hold a public hearing on March 5. It proved to be a crowded, heated session, rendered particularly newsworthy by the forceful, colorful appearance of Rabbi Stephen S. Wise in favor of the measure.[17] Roosevelt and Wise, who was one of the most famous and influential of the nation's liberal religious leaders, had developed together the main outlines of testimony presented by the rabbi, who was particularly effective in his scathing ridicule of real-estate interests who opposed old-age security because it might ultimately boost property taxes. As a result, even though Roosevelt failed to win from the Republicans the kind of commission he wanted, a commission *was* set up. Sharpened, clarified as an issue in the public mind, old-age security was firmly established on the agenda for future action.

IV

But such displays of tactical skill provided no clear affirmative answer to the question of whether the new governor was brave enough or strong enough really to tame a rebellious special-interest legislature as Al Smith had done time and again, forcing it ultimately to enact major portions of his legislative program. Indeed, a negative answer to this question was indicated by the preponderance of evidence as spring came and the 1929 legislative session drew toward a close.

Consider the fate of the governor's long-awaited and greatly publicized hydroelectric-power proposal. In a special message delivered in person to the legislature on March 12, he referred to "a series of court decisions, especially in the Federal courts" that now enabled utility companies to fix rates to consumers not in terms of a "fair return" on actual cash investment but in terms of what it would cost to replace the facilities. This "made legally possible investment returns as high as fifty percent or even one hundred percent annually on the original investment" and, of course, nullified the "protection . . . for the consumer" that New York's Public Service Commission was intended to provide when it was established, with rate-making authority, a quarter century before. Roosevelt proposed therefore to circumvent the PSC by creating a five-member body "to be known as the Trustees of the Water Power Resources on the St. Lawrence River" and armed with authority "as the duly constituted instrumentality of the State" to finance, build, own, and operate generating facilities on "natural power sites . . . now owned by the people . . . or hereafter to be recovered." The power thus developed was to be "transmitted and distributed, if possible," by private companies, but only at the "lowest rates to consumers compatible with a fair and reasonable return on actual cash investment." He stressed the latter point, accompanying it with a threat. "They [consumers] must not be left for their sole protection to the existing methods of rate making by Public Service Commissions," said he. "Are the business men of this State willing to transmit and distribute this latent water power on a fair return on their investment? If they are satisfied, here is their opportunity. If not, *then the State may have to go into the transmission business itself.*"* He also set a time limit. The trustees were to shape "a definite carefully worked out plan" and on the basis of it negotiate a "specific contract," reporting both "for the approval of the Legislature on January 15, 1930."[18]

The message had national reverberations. It established Roosevelt in the public mind as a champion of public power at a time when the power issue was coming to the forefront of those by which several state election campaigns across the country would be decided in 1930. But it also raised questions among active public-power advocates as to the effective nature of this championship, namely, doubts regarding Roosevelt's grasp of the problem he addressed and of his ability or even willingness to arrive at what seemed to the advocates the only true solution.

Thus, Senator George W. Norris of Nebraska, the great public-interest warrior in this field, praised Roosevelt's message with its appended "suggested act" as a "very brave step in the right direction" while deploring the fact that the governor had confined himself to this single step, with only a "threat" of possible steps to follow it.[19] Why not go all the way right now, since a failure to do so was only too likely to render the one step, however brave, a futile risk? Technologically, the facilities for generating electric power and the facilities for transmitting it were joined in a seamless web; so should be the administrative facilities by which the technology was applied to human purposes. What was obviously needed, said Norris, was public ownership and operation of the entire hydroelectric process, from dynamo to consumption outlet, since the giant private utilities had abundantly demonstrated their contempt for ethical standards, their ability to corrupt and frustrate regulatory agencies, and their greedy hostility to any means by which light and power could be brought to the people, including rural residents now denied it altogether, in the amounts and at the cheap rates clearly indicated by available technology. He pointed to Canada. In Ontario, just across the St. Lawrence River from New York, electricity was delivered at cost from government-owned and government-operated generating plants and power lines and in Ontario electric rates were drastically lower than in New York.

Roosevelt's answer to this, in a face-to-face meeting with the senator, would doubtless have been an appeal to practicality: what he proposed, he would have said, derived from a realistic appraisal of hard facts and stood at the outermost limit of the politically possible. But Norris would have been unpersuaded by this. Surely a bill embodying a truly comprehensive solution to the problem would have had *at least* as good a chance of passage that year, or the next,

*Present author's italics.

as Roosevelt's half measure! It might well have a better chance. For it would have enlisted, as the half measure could never do, the persuasively enthusiastic support of those most knowledgeable in this area, who were also most strongly committed to the public interest.

Seeming partial confirmation of this view was swiftly provided by the action, or inaction, of the 1929 legislature. The governor's proposal got nowhere. In public statements the Republicans dismissed Roosevelt's plan as "nothing new," a mere warming over of Al Smith's rejected proposal of a Power Authority. They carefully refrained from comment upon the governor's new departure, his insistence upon a drastic change in rate-making machinery and policy. They then killed the measure and others stemming from it by straight party votes in committee, without holding public hearings, thereby preventing floor discussion. Their only response to increasingly widespread and bitter criticism of prevailing electric-power practices was their reluctant permission to have a nine-member committee investigate the Public Service Commission, which, under the chairmanship of Republican William A. Prendergast, almost invariably decided rate cases as the utility companies wished them decided. Even this became a meaningless gesture insofar as the Republicans could make it so, for they permitted the governor to appoint only three of the nine committeemen. They themselves appointed the other six, and the three Republican senators and three Republican assemblymen whom they named were "not merely conservative but definitely reactionary," as Roosevelt complained disgustedly in a private letter.[20] Thus was made certain a majority report strongly approving of the special-interest favoritism habitually practiced by the PSC under Chairman Prendergast.

A similar fate befell every other new departure proposed by the new governor. All were contemptuously rejected by the Republicans, who by late March had long since abandoned any pretense of that good feeling Roosevelt had called for and continued to maintain, in ostentatious forbearance, wherever and whenever he could. The 1929 session was "ending in a burst of profane glory against practically every one of my recommendations," wrote Roosevelt to George Foster Peabody* on March 27.[21] Hundreds of bills, including important measures that had strong backing from civic and welfare organizations, were being killed in committee, without hearings or debate. All of Roosevelt's proposed social and labor legislation was slaughtered save that establishing an old-age study commission, but on Republican terms, not his, as regards composition. His recommendation of a $50,000,000 bond issue for the construction of state hospitals and other buildings was ignored, as was his recommendation of a constitutional amendment to create a four-year gubernatorial term. He had recommended a commission to study and propose revisions of civil and criminal judicial administration, and the legislature had passed a bill establish-

---

*Peabody, a native of Georgia who had become a New York City banker and then established for himself a reputation for philanthropy that some knowledgeable observers thought questionable, was the man from whom FDR had bought the Warm Springs resort.

ing one but allowing him to appoint only a minority of the commissioners and requiring that all his appointees be lawyers. Such a commission would be "interested only in strictly legal and technical phases of judicial administration rather than broad general questions of policy and fundamentals," and its establishment "would be a wanton waste of sixty thousand dollars of public moneys," the governor would say in his veto of this measure. He had also recommended the establishment of a Saratoga Springs Commission, to study and plan for the development of the Saratoga Springs state park and spa into a modern resort on European models, a proposal in which Louis Howe, who had grown up in Saratoga Springs, took a special interest, as did Bernard Baruch, the wealthy stock-market speculator who had headed the War Industries Board during the Great War and whom Roosevelt wished to appoint as the commission's chairman. The legislature found it politic, for it pleased certain vested interests, to establish the commission, but it did so again on lines inimical to stated purposes. "Instead of a real commission of experts, they have two Assemblymen, two Senators, and three to be appointed by me," complained Roosevelt in his letter to Peabody. "I doubt if Mr. Baruch will take an appointment under these circumstances." Simultaneously with this massacre and mutilation of the governor's proposals came the passage of hundreds of bills, nearly a thousand of them altogether, dumped abruptly onto the governor's desk for his signature or veto within thirty days. Many of them were routine and most of them were trivial in nature, but among them were scores of petty "pork barrel bills of all varieties," to quote Ernest Lindley, along with numerous "bills empowering local authorities to authorize bond issues without local referenda."[22]

Then the legislature adjourned. The Republicans left Albany, wickedly happy in the belief, fulsomely proclaimed by the Republican press, that the session had been a "howling success" for them and a "complete 'flop' " for the Democrats[23] and that they had wholly emasculated a governor whose fighting manhood, had been slight to begin with, unlike his predecessor's. The New York *Herald Tribune* believed, or editorially said it believed, that Roosevelt in the closing weeks of the session had attempted to emulate Al Smith's tactics but, lacking Smith's political acumen and skill, had failed abysmally.

V

AND, indeed, on one crucial issue—the issue shrewdly chosen by the Republicans as their main *casus belli* when they declared open war upon him—Roosevelt faced bitter alternatives. It was an issue too technical, too complicated to lend itself to the tactic he intended to employ with regard to other items of his legislative "defeat," namely, a persuasive appeal over the heads of the legislators to the general public for understanding and support. Yet if he lost upon this issue, his personal prestige and official authority would be much reduced; conceivably, his very capacity to govern might be destroyed.

The federal Budget and Accounting Act, for which Roosevelt had agitated as a general proposition when Assistant Secretary of the Navy and candidate for Vice-President of the United States, was passed by Congress in 1921. It enabled a Republican President, in the year that followed, to establish the Bureau of the Budget as a major administrative arm of the federal executive, this in order to reduce logrolling and pork-barreling—evils that were inevitably rampant in budgets originated by the legislative branch—and to strengthen the President's control over executive departments. Its example had stimulated Smith's effort to do much the same thing by constitutional amendment in New York while at the same time undermining the New York Republicans' opposition to his doing it, the result being the adoption of the needed amendment by the people in the fall of 1927. During Smith's last year as governor, the office of director of the budget for the State of New York was established, empowered to review the operations of the various departments in order to determine whether their appropriations were being efficiently spent and to make judgments as to the accuracy of estimates of needed funding for the fiscal year ahead. Each department was required to submit an itemized budget request by October 15. These estimates were then revised by the executive, through consultation with representatives of the department and of the Senate and Assembly finance committees, and an overall budget was developed by the governor. He was required by the state constitution to present it in a message to the legislature on or before February 1. Until he did so, no appropriations bill could be passed. After he did so, the legislature could eliminate or revise up or down any budget item, could add new items, which were to be explicitly separate from the governor's proposals, and could revise or reject any or all of the executive's revenue-raising proposals, though it could do this only by substituting tax proposals of its own to raise the appropriated moneys.

Special difficulties, aside from the novelty of the enterprise, attended the development of the first executive budget in New York history (it had necessarily been substantially prepared under the Smith administration), which was submitted by Roosevelt to the legislature on January 28, 1929. The governmental reorganization voted for so reluctantly by the legislature was not yet completed. In several departments major structural and procedural changes were still under way, and this made it impossible to itemize every specific appropriation. Accordingly, the budget submitted by Roosevelt on January 28 for the fiscal year beginning July 1, 1929, contained several lump-sum appropriations. They totaled about $25,000,000 out of an overall budget of more than $260,000,000, and to them was attached the provision that the governor, and the governor alone, would segregate, that is, itemize, them if and after the money was voted.

After some hesitation, the Republicans protested heatedly against the latter provision, even though they knew they ran political risks in thus shattering unilaterally the façade of Good Feeling. They dubbed it executive tyranny and charged that the governor employed the lump-sum device to obscure his use of tax moneys for increased Democratic patronage and special favors. They slashed nearly $3,500,000 of the proposed lump sums out of the budget and then, in contradiction of their own initial protest against the procedure, pulled many previously segregated items into lump sums of their own, so that the aggregate size of these was more than doubled. The lump sums now totaled $54,000,000. And to this "perfected budget," as they called it, was attached a provision denying the governor authority to segregate lump sums by himself; he must call in the chairmen of the fiscal committees, Republicans, of course, and make all segregations jointly with them.

From the governor's point of view, this last was intolerable. He said so, mildly but firmly, in a message to the legislature on February 27, the very day on which the Republican-revised budget was reported out of committee. Hurling no charges of selfish partisanship, he spoke in the tones of a schoolmaster correcting the errors of pupils. He questioned the "constitutionality of requiring the approval of two members of the legislature before appropriations made in the spring by the legislature can be spent during the following fiscal year." Such requirement blurred the distinction between the legislative and executive branches; it assigned "executive functions" to members of the legislature. He also condemned the proposal as administratively unsound. He pointed out that there was a period each year, the interval between the final adjournment of one legislature and the organization of another, when there *were* no legally existent fiscal chairmen. During this interval, if the proposal became law, the governor would not be able legally to spend any money at all that had been appropriated in lump sums.[24]

The mildness of the governor's language, however, failed to prevent a great show of outrage and wrath by his opponents. On the contrary, by encouraging the lingering suspicion that he was too "nice" or afraid to fight, it probably increased the angry force of their response to his message, a response so disproportionate to its presumed incitement that it seemed ludicrous to reasonable and informed onlookers. "The very foundation of the State is in danger from this message of avarice, usurpation and presumption," proclaimed one Republican assemblyman, who referred to Roosevelt as "that man downstairs." There were Republican charges of "arrogance and presumption" on the part of an "over-zealous executive," of "sinister" ulterior motives, of "audacity and insult" to the legislators and people of the state.[25] Roosevelt refused to reply in kind. He made no overt response at all until March 13, when, with a boldness that surprised, he sent the appropriations bill back to the legislature with every one of the lump-sum items vetoed.

"I am forced to take such drastic action because the future of the Executive Budget is at stake," he said in his veto message. "Either the State must carry out the principles of the Executive Budget, which embody fifteen years of effort to place the affairs of the State on a modern efficient business basis, or we shall drift into a hopeless situation of divided responsibility for administration of executive functions. It is wholly contrary to the whole plan of the American form of representative constitutional government to give two-thirds of a purely executive duty to the legislative branch of the government. . . . I will not assent to a precedent depriving the present Governor and future Governors of a large part of the constitutional duties which are inherent in the office of the Chief Executive."[26]

To newspaper reporters he remarked in tones of weary disgust that, while the executive had been modernized by Al Smith's long and valiant struggle toward that goal, "upstairs in Albany conditions have not changed; it is the same old crowd of Senators and Assemblymen that used to be there back in the years when I was a member of the Legislature."[27]

But even at this juncture Roosevelt remained conciliatory. He was dissuaded from his initial plan to test the constitutionality of the Republican proposals in the courts by Smith, Moses, and others whom he consulted, and perhaps also by the opinion of the attorney general, the Republican Hamilton Ward, who was sure the legislature had *not* exceeded its authority. For one thing, Roosevelt couldn't do so, or he didn't see how he could, unless the legislature agreed to the test, and he was virtually certain that if he asked for such agreement, it would be refused him by the Republican majority. It would be refused simply *because* he asked it, blind obstructionism being the Republican rule of life. Hence he told reporters who interviewed him concerning his veto message that the "court case is out the window." Instead, he offered to eliminate the lump-sum appropriations altogether, difficult and inefficient though such a procedure would be in the circumstances, substituting for them bills in which expenditures were itemized in detail. He seemed at first to have persuaded the Republicans to accept this compromise arrangement. They soon reverted to form, however. In late March they killed every one of the item-bills he had submitted, restored the budget as a whole to precisely the form in which he had vetoed parts of it, then passed it on straight party vote. "We restored the lump sum for the Departments of Labor and Law, because the department heads want to be free to reorganize their departments," said Senator Knight virtuously, in partial explanation. "The Governor's segregation for these departments was hasty and unscientific."[28]

Hence the bitter alternatives.

Since there apparently could be no appeal to the courts and since no appeal to public opinion in so complicated a business seemed likely to be effective, Roosevelt was reduced to a flat either/or choice that would probably prove to be no real choice at all. His signing of the Republican budget bill, thereby yielding a portion of the executive's power to the legislature and permanently impairing the state's constitutional government, would be an immediate open admission of his impotence in dealings with men whom Smith had generally managed to master. On the other had, his vetoing of the budget, then calling the legislature back into special session, would merely delay such forced admission and ensure its greater personal humiliation of him. The Republicans would simply repeat their regular-session performance; there seemed nothing the governor could do to prevent it.

3

→>>X<<←

The Answer: A Highly Qualified "Yes"

I

YET if Roosevelt sighed as he gazed upon the towering stacks of bills he was supposed to examine and decide upon judiciously during April, and there was a sighing note in his personal letters at this time, it was a sigh of disgust and natural aversion to needlessly heavy labor, not a sigh of despair. He had not expected to have his way without war, as we have seen. Indeed, as his quoted letter to Mrs. Bryan indicates, he may well have *preferred* war, assuming he won a fighting victory, to a peaceful cooperative enterprise, devoid of color and drama, for whose outcome he personally could claim little exclusive credit. And he knew that in the war so obviously forced upon him he had gained certain strategic advantages in the very process of suffering his seemingly grave tactical reverses. In considerable part, from his point of view, his seeming reverses added up to an enemy's blindly aggressive momentum into the grip of one whose skill in jujitsu could be employed on a grand scale quite as effectively as it was in minor skirmishes when the need arose. "They [the Republican legislators] have come out in the open and shown their hand," he had said to the banker Peabody as the session ended, "which makes the record very clear and will give a splendid opportunity for carrying matters straight to the people."[1]

He promptly seized the opportunity.

On April 3, over the statewide network, he made the first of what were to become annual radio reports to the people of New York on the doings of their legislature. " . . . I feel I have a distinct duty to keep the people of the State informed . . . as to what goes on in State Government," he began, "and I am very mindful of the fact that I am Governor not just of Democrats, but of Republicans and all other citizens of the State. That is why this talk . . . will be, just as much as I can make . . . [it], non-partisan in character. I want merely to state facts and leave the people of the State to draw their own conclusions." He then proceeded to define the conclusions they should draw. He did so by comparing 1928 Republican platform pledges with 1929 Republican legislative performances, easily showing that the latter were flatly contradictory of the former on one important matter after another. He suggested the reason for this. Republican legislators, in order to be elected, had to pretend that they would represent the people of their districts; actually they were the hired representatives, in many cases, of narrow special interests. "For all practical purposes this year's Legislature consisted of the chairmen of a few committees who in most cases have themselves been acting on orders from others, and the majority of the members of the majority party have been merely rubber stamps to register other august wills. I hope the people of this State will realize how completely undeliberative this Legislature has been and that they will insist next year that their representatives sent to Albany, whether they be Democrats or Republicans, will really represent their districts, have minds of their own, and insist on free discussion of important questions and their right to vote as their conscience and their judgment lead them to believe is desired by those who have elected them to the Legislature."[2]

In the following days and weeks he proceeded to drive this lesson home and to give a public impression of remarkable executive energy and attention to administrative detail, through his well-publicized handling of the bills that had been so hugely piled upon his desk. With a flourish he signed the agricultural bills. Under protest against the prescribed composition of the commissions they established, he signed the old-age study bill and the Public Service Commission investigation bill. His vetoes were more numerous than Al Smith's had been, and his veto messages at least as strongly worded. He made headlines with his angrily disgusted veto of the bill to set up a commission for the study and revision of judicial procedures. He vetoed scores of petty pork-barrel bills, every bill that would authorize a local bond issue without a local referendum, and every bill providing compensation to individuals when compensation, if just, could be provided for by existing general legislation. In the third week of April he disposed of seventy-nine bills of this nature in one sweep, under a single brief, bluntly worded message.

But the most crucial by far of the decisions facing him in early April was, of course, that of the budget. It was soon eased for him by two things. One was an opinion given in conversation to Basil O'Connor, and in a letter to Roosevelt, by the famous Republican lawyer of New York George W. Wickersham, a former Attorney General of the United States, whose appointment to head a federal commission to investigate and recommend action upon the related problems of Prohibition and crime was soon to be announced, with great fanfare, by President Hoover. Wickersham had been among the sponsors of the constitutional amendment establishing New York's executive budget. He was inclined to believe that the amendment permitted such action as the legislature had taken. But he admitted to doubts about it, adding that in his view "the question of the budget legislation might well be submitted to judicial determination."[3] The second easing factor was perhaps causally related to the first, since Wickersham's judgment further encouraged the belief among Republican leaders that they could win their case in court. At any rate, to Roosevelt's great relief, these Republican leaders announced in the second week of April that, should the governor again veto the lump-sum appropriation items, they themselves would appeal to the courts. Roosevelt at once accepted the challenge. On April 12 he vetoed for the second time all the lump-sum items save those for the departments of Labor and Law.

"The Legislature deliberately violated the spirit and letter of the Constitution," he declared. "They cut out whole sections of the Executive Budget without indicating by brackets or in any other way what had been deleted. They then added new items here and there throughout the budget, not in a distinct and separate place [as specifically required by the constitution], and this was done in such a way that no one who did not compare hundreds of pages of each bill could figure out what had been done. They not only cut out and reduced items in this way, but they then restored the same items with different phraseology and conditions so as to produce in effect a totally different result. If this practice is followed to its logical conclusion, all that any subsequent Legislature need do is to cut out all the Governor's budget the minute it reaches them and start an entirely new one of their own, or by altering the controlling language change completely the intent and purpose of every item of the Governor's budget, and set up control of every administrative agency by a committee controlled by two of their members as officers. What is the good of amending the Constitution . . . if the very first Legislature can nullify the reform adopted . . .?"[4]

In late April, when Roosevelt left Albany for a month in Warm Springs, half circles of darkness were under his eyes. Always darkness gathered there when he grew tired, and he admitted that the unwontedly long hours of concentrated mental effort required for his disposal of the thirty-day bills had been wearing, more so than all the first three months of his governorship. But such effort would have worn out any man, he insisted to reporters whose newspapers had printed politically inspired rumors of a nervous collapse; his general health remained excellent. And he did bounce quickly back on a full tide of zestful energy, all darkness erased, as he swam in the Warm Springs pool and sunbathed at its edge. His personal prestige, however, was largely restored with the general public by April's end, if in fact it was not greater than before. Republicans who had taken such joy in his seeming discomfiture were themselves on the defensive, in their public relations, and quite gloomily so. In mid-April, John Knight, the Senate majority leader, and Joseph A. McGinnies, the Assembly speaker, issued a joint statement angrily protesting the "ridiculous and groundless charges" that Roosevelt was hurling at the legislature "through the press and over the air." On April 27, three days after the governor's arrival in Georgia, newspapers quoted Knight as saying that it was the governor, not the legislature, who had fomented strife over the budget issue. The governor, said Knight, had "openly agreed upon the procedure relating to the budget" and then "suddenly and without warning . . . reversed his attitude and charged, in substance, that the Legislature was trying to force secret . . . consideration of budget bills."[5]

II

THUS began the process by which, as the months passed, as an old year died and a new began, Roosevelt managed to convert his seeming defeat into a semblance of victory in the hydroelectric-power fight and into a considerable measure of actual mastery of the legislature in general. As regards the latter, at least, he greatly reduced the capacity of the Republicans to frustrate and humiliate him publicly, and for this happy development the outcome of his court battle over the executive budget was greatly responsible.

To argue the budget case Roosevelt retained an elderly former president of the New York Bar Association, William D. Guthrie. To assist Guthrie, who needed help badly—the old gentleman, who had "good" days and "bad," was overly inclined toward highly technical legalistic arguments—he assigned a comparatively youthful and vigorous counsel to the governor named Edward G. Griffin, held over from the Smith regime chiefly to deal with the budget problem. Meanwhile, the legislature chose as its legal representative ex-Governor Nathan L. Miller, assisted by the Republican state attorney general, Hamilton Ward. It was then quickly agreed that both sides would concur in a statement of fact as to what had happened and what was at issue, so that the argument could be made wholly on legal and constitutional questions, whereupon the case was entered upon the docket of the Appellate Division of the State Supreme Court.

The case was heard by a full bench of the Appellate Division in late May. To Griffin's and Roosevelt's dismay, Guthrie's argument was as technically legalistic as it could possibly be, turning upon points of law so subtle and obscure that no layman and few lawyers could grasp them. It failed to address forcefully the central question of whether legislators could constitutionally assume administrative functions; it also failed to convince the judicial majority. In a split decision handed down on June 21, the court ruled for the legislature and against the governor.

Roosevelt was badly jolted, though he gave no outward sign of it; at this point he was glad the case was too complicated for popular understanding and received, amid smiling summer relaxations, little popular attention. He promptly called for a review of the decision by the Court of Appeals, which agreed to hear the case in mid-October. In the interim, following Griffin's advice, he tactfully but forcefully urged upon Guthrie the importance of changing the nature and style of his argument so that the major emphasis was placed on the separation-of-powers question and that this question was made understandable to laymen. Upon the eve of the oral-argument presentation, Roosevelt bolstered Guthrie's wavering self-confidence with a personal letter full of the warmest praise of Guthrie's handling of the case and expressing absolute assurance that victory would crown his efforts. " . . . I know that you are going to make a ten-strike," he wrote. " . . . you will win the case and cannot fail."[6] Guthrie did do well then—much better than he had in May.

A month later, the Court of Appeals unanimously reversed the lower court's decision and upheld the governor's contention that the participation of the legislature's finance chairmen in the segregation of lump-sum budget items was a violation of the state constitution.

Roosevelt was justifiably jubilant, though he was careful to make no public claim of *personal* victory: it was constitutional democracy that had triumphed, good government that had been served, he said. "From now on I trust that instead of constant bickering . . . we shall have better cooperation and a clearer understanding of the governmental powers in Albany."[7] The Republicans were proportionately depressed, though they of course professed relief that a "vexed point" had been finally settled. The net effect was a palpable and permanent shift of power and prestige away from the Republican legislature toward the Democratic governor. He had dared a head-on collision with his enemies, and it was he, not they, who remained standing on the disputed ground. They had been knocked down. Henceforth he must be regarded with respect, openly if reluctantly shown, by men who had formerly paraded their contempt for him while concealing their suspicion that they just *might* be mistaken about his vacillating "weakness," his "fear" of combat.

It was a respect that had been growing in any case all through the summer and autumn, as he continued to press and maneuver for adoption of his power program against the opposition of private utility corporations and of their henchmen in the legislature and on the Public Service Commission.

He had, of course, numerous other concerns and engaged in many other activities. In June 1929 he received a series of honorary doctorates—from Hobart, Dartmouth, Fordham, and, most gratifyingly, Harvard, where he was also that year's Phi Beta Kappa orator and received an honorary Phi Beta Kappa key. "I have never had such a surprise in my life as when I had a letter from President Lowell [of Harvard] in regard to the degree," he wrote Langdon P. Marvin, a former law partner, on April 11. "I always had it in the back of my head that if I got one at all it would be after I had attained the age of seventy."[8] And his degree was not his chief triumph during his alma mater's commencement festivities. Greater was the honor of serving as grand marshal, in accordance with a Harvard tradition requiring that this supreme functionary of alumni activities be a member of the twenty-fifth reunion class. When told of his appointment by James Jackson, a classmate of his at Groton, president of the Harvard class of 1904, and now a Boston banker active in Massachusetts Republican politics, Roosevelt replied with total sincerity, "I am quite overcome. . . . I had literally no idea even of the possibility of it, and realize to the full the very great honor that has been given to me by the class and the university." He bubbled over in a letter to his longtime friend Livingston Davis: "It certainly is grand to be Chief Marshal. I assure you being Governor is nothing in comparison."[9]

In July he was much concerned with an acute and rapidly growing shortage of state hospital beds—nearly 11,000 more were needed for proper patient care. So concerned was he that he seriously considered calling the legislature into special session to pass enabling legislation for a $50,000,000 bond issue. He abandoned this in the face of adamant Republican opposition, after a meeting with Republican leaders, but only when they pledged their support of an increase of hospital facilities to at least 5,000 beds and agreed to provide the necessary funding. He was also much concerned with problems of crime and prison reform that summer. There was a bloody, destructive riot in the penitentiary at Dannemora in the second week of July, during which three convicts were killed and twenty wounded. Buildings were burned. In the following week a riot in the Auburn prison caused damage estimated at $250,000. Roosevelt promptly ordered the state commissioner of corrections, R. F. C. Kieb, to conduct an investigation into the riots' causes, and on the basis of the investigative report, he moved toward a broad "expert" inquiry into the parole system, the notorious Baumes Law,* and especially state prison conditions, which were horrible after long years of neglect: there was abominable food, intolerable congestion, and a breakdown of discipline that enabled the most vicious of the inmates to prey brutally upon the others. He talked about crime and law enforcement in mid-July at the Governors' Conference in New London, Connecticut, and made national headlines when he appended to his prepared address, drafted largely by Louis Howe, almost the whole of a long letter written him by George W. Wickersham.

Wickersham, upon his appointment on May 28, 1929, as head of the President's commision on crime and Prohibition, the Wickersham Commission, as it was promptly dubbed, had become a highly newsworthy figure. For obvious reasons he had steadfastly refused to answer reporters' questions as to his personal views on the problems his commission would study. He had no notion that he was writing for publication when, on a two-week vacation, with no stenographer available to him, he replied in longhand to Roosevelt's request for ideas to be used in the New London address—and Roosevelt had not bothered subsequently to ask permission to quote him directly. One can imagine his unhappiness when he read front-page news stories under big headlines directly quoting his suggestion "that the Governors' Conference . . . consider approaching the Federal Government on some feasible proposal to share" the burden of enforcing Prohibition, a burden that "thus far the Federal Government alone has borne."

The letter having been read, Roosevelt dramatically proposed that the governors go into executive session to discuss, in the absence of reporters, Wickersham's suggestion and those he himself had made in his address. His proposal was not accepted. Instead, the governors embarked upon a heated debate of the Prohibition issue, wet vs. dry, which became the principal news of the entire conference and from which Roosevelt, having sparked it and gained much personal publicity by doing so, stood prudently aside.

But the hydroelectric-power struggle was his overriding public concern during that summer and fall. Its urgent importance was emphasized in mid-June by the announcement of a pending merger, under Morgan auspices, of New York's three greatest electric-power systems into a single giant ($500,-000,000) combine. A leading organizer of the merger was the state Republican Party chairman, H. Edmund Machold, who would become a principal executive officer of the Niagara-Hudson Corporation thus formed†—and Niagara-

---

*Named after state Senator Caleb H. Baumes, a typically obtuse "law-and-order" zealot, this law forced the imposition of life sentences upon all fourth offenders against the criminal code. The predictable result had been that third offenders who continued in crime did so with increased ferocity and desperation, knowing that their punishment would be no greater for a major than for a minor crime.

†Machold, a former Assembly speaker (see pages 41 and 58) would resign his party chairmanship when he assumed the corporation post, but this would mean no reduction, and possibly even an increase, of his effective control of Republican policy with regard to utilities.

Hudson would have a virtual monopoly of the transmission and final distribution of electricity in the state. This would, on the face of it, render totally ineffective Roosevelt's plan to assure fair electricity rates to consumers through sale "on a contract basis" of state-generated power along the St. Lawrence River, for it would destroy the possibility of competitive bidding for such a contract. Roosevelt at once asked the state attorney general for an opinion on the legality of the merger. Ward, a Republican, after some delay and considerable gubernatorial prodding, naturally gave it as his view that there were no state laws under which the merger could be ruled illegal.

On July 4, 1929, as he had last done on July 4, 1917, Roosevelt addressed the great Independence Day assemblage of Tammany Hall, an occasion especially newsworthy in 1929 because it was the formal dedication of Tammany's newly built brick clubhouse on Union Square. He capitalized on the popular fears that the pending power merger had caused and that he shared. He spoke extemporaneously, and no stenographer recorded his words, or so at least he claimed (he seems to have become somewhat alarmed by his own temerity) when later asked for manuscript copies of what he had said. But he was reported at length in the New York *Times*, summaries of his remarks were printed across the country, and the speech was praised by Will Rogers, the Cowboy Humorist, then at the height of his fame, who asserted in his syndicated column that Roosevelt's words "just about" assured him of becoming "the next Democratic candidate" for President.[10]

The burden of the speech, as reported in the *Times*, was that the "vast economic changes through which the country was passing," particularly the "creation" of a "highly centralized industrial control" in private hands, made it necessary "to reconsider the whole problem of liberty." The "independence" of small business was now "a thing of the past." "Can a man today run a drug store, a cigar store, a grocery store as an independent business?" he asked rhetorically. He admitted the possibility that "the question presented by the ever-growing aggregations of capital . . . may find a natural solution,"* but they could do so only "if government and business are kept separate." They now most emphatically were *not* being kept separate. On the contrary, they were linked in closer and closer partnership. As an example of this he cited the "new tariff bill," the measure that would become the Hawley-Smoot Act, which was then under congressional debate. Consequently, there was rising and casting a dark shadow over the land "a new kind of economic feudalism," which would "have to be combatted just as was the power of the old barons and the earlier kings." The citizens of the United States might have "to don

---

*The use of "natural" in this context betrayed his continuing economic orthodoxy, while his use of the tentative "may" indicated the unwelcome intrusion of certain doubts concerning it. He retained an eighteenth-century conception of "natural law" and "natural rights" operating in a "free market" (the only "natural" market) to determine gross "natural" patterns of social and economic behavior, but he had an increasingly uneasy realization that this conception might prove, upon close examination, to have fundamental flaws. One sees here echoes of an address Roosevelt made as state senator in Troy, New York, in 1912, and it is historically and biographically instructive to compare the two. See pages 266–267 of *FDR: The Beckoning of Destiny.*

again the liberty caps of their Revolutionary forefathers and fight anew for independence." To the wise doctrine of total separation of church and state, therefore, he would add and "preach a new doctrine: A complete separation of business and government."*

It was promptly noted in the press, by critics of both left and right, that Roosevelt had said nothing specific about how the separation of business and government was to be achieved or how the swift recurrence of giant mergers was to be prevented if those now in existence, or in the process of coming into existence, were actually dissolved. The governor engaged in an "intellectual sham battle," according to the conservative New York *Evening Post*; the "dangers to our democracy" against which he inveighed "seem to have singularly little substance in the life of the nation today." Roosevelt, concluded the *Post,* was sadly muddle-headed: " . . . clearer phrases would have come from a mind that was more clear on the question at issue."[11]

The *New Leader,* a Socialist Party organ, thoroughly agreed with this conclusion. Its commentary on Roosevelt's speech was written by Norman Thomas, the Socialist candidate for President in 1928 and currently a candidate for mayor of New York City. Acidly remarking that the separation of business from government was "a funny thing to talk about before Tammany Hall," Thomas wanted to know how a reversion to the "trust-busting" of TR's rhetoric in 1904, which Roosevelt *seemed* to favor, could be of any permanent effect unless severe limits were placed upon the growth of "legitimate" (that is, "small") businesses, restrictions that would be tantamount to a repudiation of capitalism in favor of some kind of planned society. The governor's evident wish to apply nineteenth-century "solutions" to twentieth-century problems was "sentimental." One could understand the governor's dismay in the face of the announced private power merger, since it of course rendered futile the proposed use of contract sales of public power as a device for consumer protection and state regulation. But that had been a perfectly predictable response to the proposal before he made it. The real answer to the problem, the only true answer, was that of Ontario, Canada, namely, the complete socialization of the power industry.[12]

But was Roosevelt concerned with a "real" answer to his or any other problem, save insofar as it might serve his political ambition? Thomas doubted it, having been given what seemed to him good and sufficient reason to doubt it that summer and fall as he conducted his mayoralty campaign against Tammany graft and corruption. Roosevelt, thought Thomas, was primarily concerned with appearances and their manipulation for his advantage. He was involved in image making. And it must be admitted, with a reluctant admiration on Thomas' part, that the Independence Day speech, judged by the end it seemed designed to serve, was notably successful. It further established Roosevelt nationally as a progressive in the general tradition of TR, Gifford

---

*The "partnership" of business and government was obviously, in his view, an "unnatural" phenomenon.

Pinchot, George Norris, even, to a degree, the elder Robert Marion La Follette
—his attack on big business pleased farmers and small-business men everywhere, while his championship of the principle, at least, of public power had
strong appeal throughout the power-starved West and Midwest—and it cost
him nothing statewide. Indeed, it gained more than it lost of voter support for
him in Republican strongholds upstate.

And as he moved to consolidate his political gains on this issue through the
ensuing weeks—as he furthered his education concerning it and sought ways
and means of countering the private utilities' strategic reactions against his
stated purpose—he moved ever closer, publicly, to the policy position advocated by Norris and Thomas.

He had been permitted to appoint only three of the nine members of the
Public Service Investigations Committee; all that they could do, he wrote in
a private letter, was "make the scope of the investigation as broad and as
fundamental as possible and see to it that the progressive side of the case
obtains adequate publicity."[13] Consequently, he sought to appoint men who,
wholly free of interested commitment, were recognized as outstanding authorities in this field and whose conclusions were therefore bound to be widely
persuasive. He had turned for advice to several students of the utilities problem, including the Harvard Law School professor Felix Frankfurter. Frankfurter, a quick-moving, bright-eyed little man whose students almost wor-
shiped him, had served as counsel in the War Department when Roosevelt was
Assistant Secretary of the Navy, had worked with Roosevelt on various matters at that time, and had been striving since the day of Roosevelt's entrance
into the gubernatorial race to make himself Roosevelt's chief personal unofficial consultant.* He would succeed in this. He possessed and fully exercised
in his dealings with FDR the unctuous arts of a courtier, who laid on flattery
with a trowel, but he also possessed and exercised a shrewd and remarkably
well-informed intelligence, along with sound judgment, as Roosevelt increasingly realized. Thus, when he strongly recommended for the committee Professor James C. Bonbright of Columbia University ("I don't know anybody
. . . who has a more penetrating understanding of the fundamental problems
relating to utilities and utilities regulation, nor one who could bring a more
disinterested expert attitude to bear on these problems"),[14] Roosevelt promptly
made the appointment. He also appointed Frank P. Walsh, a longtime close
associate of George Norris', and David C. Adie of the Buffalo Council of Social
Agencies. Adie was no utilities expert, but from Bonbright and Walsh, the
governor learned much about utilities financing and the crying public need for

---

*A few years before, Frankfurter had been among the leaders of bitter protest against the judicial
murder of Sacco and Vanzetti by the Commonwealth of Massachusetts, a matter of international
concern on which FDR made no recorded comment, public or private. This had given Frankfurter
a justified reputation for courageous commitment to legal justice (Harvard's President Lowell,
asked to review the Sacco-Vanzetti case by the governor of Massachusetts, had upheld the death
sentence imposed by the courts); but it had also given him a wholly *un*justified reputation for
"radicalism." He was a Brandeisian liberal.

a substitution of prudent-investment criteria for those of current replacement cost in the setting of electricity rates. He learned much, too, from the Syracuse University professor William E. Mosher, not only through talk and correspondence with him but also from a report of a study committee Mosher had headed at Syracuse; published as the book *The Electric Utilities: A Crisis in Public Control,* the report was read by Roosevelt with unwonted care. He had Louis Howe gather data on widely varying electricity rates within the state and on the difference between these and the rates in Ontario. Howe found that the rate for 250 kilowatt-hours, the estimated monthly use of an average family, varied from $19.50 in Albany (it was just $9.30 in Schenectady, fifteen miles away) to a low of $5.53 on the American side of Niagara Falls, whereas the rate in Ontario was a mere $2.79.[15] During extended inspection tours of the state that summer, Roosevelt made a point of discussing electricity at every stop and asking for local information and opinion about it.

There could be no doubt in his mind by summer's end that his was the popular side of the power controversy and that it provided him with a political issue on which he and his party could abundantly capitalize in the 1930 election. This was as true in rural areas, normally Republican, as it was in urban areas, generally Democratic. The private power companies had long refused to make the slightest serious effort to supply electricity to farms. They claimed that doing so was uneconomic for them: farmers could not pay rates high enough to make country transmission lines profitable. Hence farmers were bound to find highly attractive Roosevelt's proposal, as yet tentative and unpublished, for a Rural Power Authority—an agency that would become part of an overall New York Power Authority if one were ultimately established, as Roosevelt now believed it should be. In connection with the development of this proposal was a study of rural electricity rates being made by George F. Warren, a Cornell professor of farm management, at the request of Agricultural Commissioner Henry Morgenthau, Jr.

All this encouraged him, as autumn came, to implement the threat he had made in his special message to the legislature on March 12, namely, that New York State would "go into the transmission business itself" if businessmen refused to transmit and distribute power from state-owned plants at reasonable rates. Such rates should provide no more than a "fair" return—8 percent—on "prudent" investment in the necessary facilities.

He authorized Professor Mosher to make a study of how and in what amounts electricity would be used in both city and country under a state-owned statewide system of transmission lines. To Bonbright, in response to a query as to whether the PSC investigation should explore the issue of public vs. private ownership and operation of power development and distribution, Roosevelt indicated that, while the committee should "primarily examine" the question of regulating "existing private utilities," he could not completely rule out examination of the issue Bonbright raised, for "there is always the possibility in the future of public competition with private utilities, at least as a 'yardstick.'" As he said this, he was preparing an article that was to be published in the December 1929 issue of *Forum* magazine. In this article he spoke of the establishment of federal and state authorities to develop the water power of the St. Lawrence River, of Muscle Shoals on the Tennessee River, of Boulder Dam on the Colorado River, and cited as a "most important argument" the fact that such authorities "will remain forever as a yardstick with which to measure the cost of producing and transmitting electricity."[16]

III

BUT, of course, his political opponents could also read the signs of the times. Some of them did so as accurately as he. And the difference between those who did and those who did not became sharp enough that fall to cut through the normally monolithic Republican Party hierarchy, splitting it into factions.

One faction was headed by the young and fiery W. Kingsland Macy of Suffolk County; possessed of an astute intelligence rare indeed among New York Republican politicians, he was convinced that his party had no chance to defeat Roosevelt's bid for reelection if water power remained a central issue. True, only 60,000 more New Yorkers voted Democratic in 1929 than in 1927, the last off-year election. True, the bulk of this shift had been in New York City and was obviously due to the successful mayoralty campaign waged by the incumbent mayor, Jimmy Walker. Upstate, the Democrats had gained a mere 3,000 votes, despite a vastly improved upstate Democratic organization, and only three seats overall in the Assembly, which remained firmly in Republican control. But it was the Republicans who *should* have gained that year, given the circumstances, in the opinion of young Macy, who continued to regard Roosevelt as personally weak and ineffective, compared with Al Smith. They *would* have if the power issue had not been hung as an albatross around their collective neck, and if that albatross remained in that position, the Democratic victory in 1930 would be overwhelming. "It's the issues the . . . party is licked on," said Macy at a party council on legislative policy held early in January. He then boldly called for the resignation of William J. Maier as state Republican chairman because Maier, in the popular view, was "on the wrong side of the water power question."[17] Maier had been Machold's personal choice for this post when Machold resigned it, and Macy had aspired to it.

Macy failed to force Maier's resignation. He did help force a shift in his party's operative policy, however, since his appraisal of the political prospect was the same as that made by Niagara-Hudson's professional lobbyists. And so a delegation representative of the Republican–Niagara-Hudson homogeny called at the Executive Mansion in Albany a few days before Christmas of 1929 for a private talk with the governor. The visitors included Floyd L. Carlisle, chairman of the board of Niagara-Hudson; Machold; and Majority Leader Knight of the state Senate. Roosevelt received them cordially. He ordered refreshments served. He listened with close attention as they spoke of their wish to end the quarrel between public- and private-power advocates, which had for so long prevented urgently needed hydroelectric developments. It was a wish he fervently shared. Some kind of compromise must be devised that would enable all hands to get on with the job. He thoroughly agreed. They therefore proposed a compromise arrangement, to wit, the appointment of a five-member commission that would study *all* power plans for the St. Lawrence and prepare, for presentation to the 1931 legislature, a report-recommendation of the plan New York should follow. It would be a plan inclusive of proposals for the rigid regulation of the financing, rates, and management and operation of the corporation (Niagara-Hudson) to which state-developed power would be sold for transmission and distribution. They further proposed that the commissioners, all five of them, be appointed by the governor, without the necessity for Senate confirmation! This was their great concession; the governor would be wholly free to appoint men whose basic view of the power question coincided with his own and whose final report, therefore, would be substantially *his*! His visitors eyed him narrowly as he digested this. They were at once relieved. He gave every sign of immense pleasure. He thanked them so warmly that they left the Mansion convinced he had accepted their offer and would act upon it promptly when the 1930 legislative session opened in January.

What followed was a masterpiece of Rooseveltian political jujitsu.

Beneath his outward show of eager gratitude, the governor was perfectly aware from the outset that his pre-Christmas visitors came to him as Greeks bearing gifts. He was properly wary. He at once recognized the great "compromise" for what it basically was—a stratagem for removing from the 1930 election campaign an issue by which his opponents were gravely disadvantaged, while offering him in return little or nothing of a truly substantive nature.

Under consideration for many years had been the development jointly by the United States and Canada of a St. Lawrence shipway, a wholly feasible engineering project, already blueprinted, whereby the St. Lawrence barge canal would be deepened by dredging and by dam construction to permit oceangoing vessels to reach the Great Lakes. Buffalo, Cleveland, Detroit, Chicago, and Duluth would thereby become ocean ports, and the sad effects of railroad rate schedules that discriminated against the Midwest, and supposedly had much to do with the loss of foreign markets for Midwestern farm products, would be overcome. Power development of the river would be incidental to this navigation development: according to the plan, some 5,000,000 electrical horsepower would be produced by the required dams. (An American St. Lawrence Commission, of which Secretary of Commerce Hoover was chairman, had reported favorably on this proposal in 1924, estimating its cost, "after [NB] disposal of the electrical power, as $148,000,000.")[18] And, of course, the power development of the St. Lawrence by New York State must be an integral part of the overall navigation and power development. Equally of course, the project as a whole required treaty arrangements between the United States and Canada.

What this meant in terms of New York political strategy was that the House of Morgan and Niagara-Hudson had two lines of defense against any public-power proposal Roosevelt might make—the first of them formidable, the second seemingly impregnable—and were thereby virtually assured of the last word on the matter. Any such proposal must first run the gauntlet of a Republican majority in the New York legislature, whose leadership remained practically identical with the management of Niagara-Hudson. If it survived this ordeal, it must, in a doubtless weakened condition, come up against a wall of opposition raised in Washington, D.C. International treaty making was the exclusive prerogative of the federal executive, with the advice and consent of a U.S. Senate currently dominated by Republicans, and Herbert Hoover, the Republican President of the United States, with his strong bias in favor of big business,* was certain to listen with a far more sympathetic ear to the Morgan spokesman Carlisle than to anything that might advance the political fortunes of a Franklin Roosevelt, who already, by the end of 1929, was being touted as a likely opponent of Hoover in the 1932 presidential contest.

All this Roosevelt clearly recognized.

So in his annual message to the legislature on January 1, 1930, the governor gave no indication that he had ever heard of the "compromise" proposal he had seemed so grateful to receive barely a week before. He caught his power opponents off guard. He surprised and infuriated them by not only reiterating his commitment to state-owned and -operated generating facilities but also stating for the first time as an official pronouncement his "belief" that any "State agency [that developed and operated the generators] should at least provide the financing of, and retain the fee to, any system of statewide transmission of electricity made necessary by the new power development." The interest on state bonds to finance transmission facilities would be markedly less than the interest private utilities must pay on borrowed money, he pointed out, and "this would reduce the cost of electricity many millions of dollars each year, for the consumer of course pays the interest and dividend charges on the project."

The message provoked violent floor attacks upon Roosevelt by Republicans in both the Assembly and the Senate. They were more vituperative than any Al Smith had ever had to face, in the opinion of at least one veteran Albany reporter;[19] but then Smith, while fighting for state-owned power sites, backed away from the idea of state-owned transmission facilities. Roosevelt was charged with responsibility for the prison riots the previous summer, for corruption in the banking department, for a breakdown in morale and effi-

---

*In August 1929 President Hoover had proposed that all public lands not specifically reserved be transferred from federal to state control and that reclamation projects of the future also be handled by the states. He of course justified this proposal as a "decentralization" from which individuals would have an increase of freedom, but what it actually meant was a shift of power from government to private business. Nationally, even internationally, organized corporations could manipulate state legislatures far more easily than they could the Congress of the United States, and state officials were proportionately less able to withstand big-business pressures than were federal officials.

ciency in the department of public works. He was *not* strongly attacked on the power issue, indeed it went almost unmentioned, since this was the issue that his opponents very much wanted to remove from the 1930 campaign and that he, as they now realized, had no intention of giving up as a political asset in return for an essentially meaningless "compromise."

In the days immediately following there was some rather desperate casting about by Niagara-Hudson politicians.

In an open letter to the governor nine days after the annual message, Carlisle called for a "non-political" meeting of interested parties to discuss the power question, to be held, he suggested, in the Executive Chamber adjacent to the Governor's Capitol office. Roosevelt did not reply for several days, then blandly said in a public statement that the Executive Chamber was far too small to accommodate such a meeting: the Capitol park, then covered with snow and swept by icy winds, was hardly large enough to contain all who would wish to attend. Meanwhile, W. Kingsland Macy had been urging upon his fellow Republicans the strategic advantage of publicly dumping "the water-power problem right in Roosevelt's lap," saying to the governor that it was now *his* problem alone: " 'Go ahead and solve it.' "[20] And on the very day of Roosevelt's reply to Carlisle's open letter, January 13, 1930, the Republican leadership acted in accordance with Macy's advice: Republican Warren K. Thayer of the Senate and Republican John M. Hackett of the Assembly introduced in the legislature a bill that rendered public the proposal that had been privately made by Carlisle and his cohorts in their pre-Christmas visit to the Executive Mansion. There was an added proviso that the governor's five-member commission, for which $200,000 would be appropriated, must investigate the governor's own power plan before inquiring into any other; this proviso was designed to emphasize the disinterestedness, the generous concern for the public's welfare, with which the Republicans sought to answer the power question.

That night Republican leaders went to bed happy in the belief that they had put the governor "on the spot." He would try to squirm his way out of it— he had already found this proposal unacceptable when privately made, and going public with it did not change its essential nature—and as he did so he would become vulnerable to precisely those charges of hypocrisy, insincerity, irresponsibility, that he, or his supporters, were constantly hurling against utility politicians. The tables were turned, the balance shifted. He would stand condemned by public opinion of "playing politics" with the power issue, which would thereby be abruptly transformed from an asset into a liability for a governor seeking reelection. Thus the rosy prospect for Republican–Niagara-Hudson politicos, whose dreams, as they slept into the morning of January 14, may have been warmed and colored by it.

They awoke to a cold gray dawn.

Roosevelt, having obtained a copy of the Thayer-Hackett bill before he left his Capitol office on the night of January 13, sat up until after midnight in his Mansion study reviewing it in careful detail with Sam Rosenman. His reaction to it was reminiscent of the tactic he had employed to transform personal humiliation into personal glory in the affair of "Blue-eyed" Billy Sheehan, in 1911, during his first term as state senator.* To the utter astonishment and quick discomfiture of his Republican foes, at his midmorning news conference on January 14, he announced to reporters his joyous acceptance of this measure he had been expected to shy away from. He did more: he held it aloft as a great triumph for him personally as well as for the general public. "This is one of the happiest days of my life," he declared, "and one of the most important for the people of the State of New York." To Al Smith, vacationing in Coral Gables, Florida, went a telegram: " . . . the Republican legislative leaders have introduced and come out in favor of an electric bill which seems to accept the great basic principle for which you and I have fought so long. There is no doubt it is a great victory."[21]

And his glowing interpretation of the event was generally accepted at face value even by critical minds well informed on the hydroelectric-power struggle. "Happy Congratulations on your great victory," wired back Al Smith. Walter Lippmann, who was very far from being a wholehearted admirer of the governor and who increasingly revealed that fact in his New York *World* editorials, being particularly distressed by the governor's refusal to intervene in the current New York City "mess," was enthusiastic about this "complete triumph." He said so in a personal communication to Roosevelt. From Felix Frankfurter came a letter to "Dear Frank" saying, "All too often public men compromise essentials on a vital issue, accept stone for bread, and then comfort themselves with the metaphor that half a loaf is better than none. By holding out on your water power policy for New York, you have vindicated courage in government. . . . Your achievement means, I believe, everything for the future of water power policy of the whole country."[22]

Certainly his "achievement" was an authentic triumph in public relations and, as such, meant a good deal for his immediate political future. The Republicans could not persuasively claim credit for what he so persuasively described as their "capitulation," and instead of being removed from the 1930 campaign, the power issue remained central to it and, now more than ever, in such form that only the governor could make political capital of it.

IV

ALL the same, the utilities interests had no reason for profound dismay. The Socialist Norman Thomas pointed this out as he struck the one major discordant note amid the sweet harmonies of praise then singing into Roosevelt's ears.

Of *course* the utilities were willing to have the state build dams and plants from which power flowed into their privately owned lines and stations, said Thomas again in public speech. It was from the transmission and distribution

*See pages 246–257 in *FDR: The Beckoning of Destiny*.

of electricity that the big money was now being made. And it would continue so—the water in utilities stock would remain as potent a generator of profits as ever the waters of the St. Lawrence could be of electricity—for as long as the utilities could charge consumer rates based on 8 percent of hugely inflated capital values. Who or what was to keep them from doing so? The state's regulatory agencies? The PSC had been emasculated by court rulings, as Roosevelt himself stressed, and was in any case made up of men highly vulnerable to the covert pressures of threat and bribe continually exerted by the corporations that were presumably being regulated. The contract-sale device? How had this been rendered more effective by the governor's great "victory"? *Vis-à-vis* the private monopoly of transmission facilities, the state's bargaining position remained essentially the same as before, which is to say it remained too weak to force any real reduction in rates or any significant increase in the availability of electricity to those now deprived of it. Virtually nothing, then, had been changed—nothing of real importance. The power interests had lost at most a skirmish on a far frontier of their empire, and the net effect of this would actually be a gain for them if popular attention was diverted from the fact that the empire itself remained yet intact. The diversion could stunt the growth of a public opinion that might otherwise force government toward the one and only true public-interest solution of the problem.

This solution, reiterated Thomas, in agreement with George Norris, was the *complete* socialization of electricity, its transmission as well as its manufacture. Such socialization, for anyone really committed to personal liberty and democratic government, was a clear and necessary implication of the technology involved and of the demonstrated mentality and ethical standards of big-business men. Here was a physical energy upon which the economic life of the whole community was every year more dependent. Its technological development and distribution required increasingly centralized controls over increasingly unified, geographically far-flung networks. This meant in the prevailing circumstances that every year the welfare of the community as a whole was more completely at the mercy of a handful, an ever-smaller handful, of men who had arrived at their decisive posts through processes of self-aggrandizement and ruthless greed and who now made their decisions, ultimately, in terms of their own private profit, not in terms of the general good. Of course, these men insisted in their self-serving propaganda that the two sets of terms were consistent with each other, that no contradiction was indicated by the current labeling of the utilities as both "public" *and* "private," but this was patently untrue. The contradiction was there, and it was glaring. Balefully glaring. It grew ever more dangerous to the functioning of a free society. And so it simply must be removed. The utilities must become wholly and exclusively public property; they must be managed by professional public servants whose decisions were made within a policy framework initially and ultimately determined by the people's elected representatives. And the time for a definite and irreversible move in this direction was right now, else the chance to move at all might be lost.

Most politicians in Roosevelt's position would have ignored Thomas' strictures, though Thomas was at that time an increasingly influential spokesman for the Socialist cause. Instead, the governor took careful account of them, a fact significant alike of his political astuteness and of the political position he had chosen to occupy "a little left of center." He addressed a private letter to Thomas, prudently labeled "entirely confidential and not for publication," in which he expressed surprise at the criticism. "I was under the impression that . . . you . . . were largely in agreement with me as to the need for a better regulation of our public utilities and of the securing of cheaper electrical rates."[23] He asked for a fuller explanation of Thomas' views than had been printed in the *New Leader.*

Thomas issued a prompt reply. He said in effect that while he of course agreed as to the need for cheaper rates and increased availability, he had no faith whatever in the regulatory device as a means to these ends. Nor had he much more faith in "regulation" joined to "yardstick" competition with giant combines that had proved themselves to be inherently corrupt and corrupting of democratic processes. In any case, why settle for so complicated and dangerous a half measure? The full measure was simpler, easier. What the governor ought to do is move definitely toward public acquisition of the entire power system at the earliest possible date; his minimum first step should be to specify the location and extent of the transmission lines he proposed immediately to build and to also specify the rating priority he intended to give to municipally owned distribution systems when state-generated and -transmitted electricity was delivered to users.

In the months and years that followed, the view that Thomas took of this matter at the opening of 1930 might well have come to seem to the governor a prophetic vision. Certainly, the general course of events that Thomas would have predicted, from his assessment of existing realities, was the course they actually followed in 1930, 1931, and 1932.

The governor won every obvious tactical victory in his continuing war with the power magnates during those years.

In February 1930 Roosevelt forced the resignation of Prendergast, the Public Service Commission chairman, by skillfully mobilizing public opinion against him and in favor of his own contention that the commission was intended to be an active policing agency, that is, a defender of the public against the utilities, rather than a passive quasi-judicial body, that is, a mediator of disputes between the utilities and the consuming public. In March he appointed as Prendergast's successor Milo R. Maltbie, long famous as an enemy of corporate gouging. Also in March he signed into law the Thayer Water Power Bill, enabling him to appoint his five-man St. Lawrence Power Development Commission. In May, when the New York Telephone Company attempted to boost rates by adding some $133,000,000 to its phony capital evaluation, Maltbie earned the plaudits of the governor and public by forcing a sharp *reduction* of rates. In January 1931 the St. Lawrence Commission issued a majority report of the kind Roosevelt had wanted: a New York Power Authority should be established to develop hydroelectric power on state-owned sites; this power would be sold to the Niagara-Hudson combine* only if Niagara-Hudson agreed to deliver it to consumers at actual, not falsely inflated, cost plus a reasonable profit, not exceeding 8 percent; if Niagara-Hudson refused to do this, the Power Authority would build its own transmission lines. In early April 1931 Roosevelt forced the legislature to give him the kind of Power Authority he wanted. He accomplished this by covertly organizing a huge "spontaneous" popular protest against an attempted emasculation of the Power Authority bill—letters, telegrams, phone calls, poured in by the hundreds upon Republican legislative leaders—and by announcing a radio speech in which he would "lay the facts before the people." In May 1931 he named an outstanding board of trustees to run it: Frank P. Walsh, chairman; Professor Bonbright; Fred J. Freestone; Delos M. Cosgrove; and, upon the advice of Pennsylvania Governor Gifford Pinchot, who won his office on the power issue in 1930, Morris L. Cooke of Philadelphia, a management engineer and power expert destined to play an important role in Roosevelt's future programs in this field. The economist Leland Olds was named the Power Authority's executive secretary. And in June 1931 the Power Authority began to seek from the federal government official recognition of New York's active interest, which should mean an active role, in the negotiations with Canada for a St. Lawrence development treaty.

But at this point it began to become clear that Roosevelt's tactical victories, however gratifying in themselves and useful to his political ambition, added up to no triumph of grand strategy in his war with utility interests. Quite the contrary.

For at this point his power program came hard against the Morgan–Niagara-Hudson combine's second line of defense. The Hoover administration refused to give the State of New York any such part in the treaty negotiations as the Mackenzie King government of Canada gave the Province of Ontario —refused, in fact, to give the Power Authority any part at all in these proceedings. The Authority could negotiate only with the U.S. State Department, and in these negotiations, very reluctantly entered upon and then deceitfully conducted by Washington, a dispute arose as to the portion of the St. Lawrence developmental cost to be borne by New York, with Washington setting a figure far too high for the state to meet. By the summer of 1932 it seemed highly probable to Chairman Walsh and perfectly obvious to Roosevelt that President Hoover deliberately delayed the conclusion of the Canadian treaty, while giving the public the impression that negotiations proceeded smoothly on this matter between Washington and Albany, in order to remove the power issue from that year's presidential campaign. Roosevelt reacted. On July 9, 1932, he dispatched a lengthy telegram to the White House in which he stressed the importance of a prompt "initiation of this vast project—one which means

---

*If the corporation was not specifically named, it was clearly exclusively indicated; with its private transmission monopoly, it was the only possible buyer.

. . . cheap electricity from the State-owned and controlled resource, to be developed for the primary interest of homes, farms and industries." He concluded, "I hold myself subject to your call and am ready to go to Washington on forty-eight hours notice at your convenience." Hoover replied next day "that negotiations between the United States and the Dominion of Canada are making progress and that it will not be necessary to interrupt your cruise [Roosevelt had embarked on a one-week cruise aboard a forty-foot yawl along the New England coast] by a visit to Washington."[24]

When Roosevelt's gubernatorial term expired, no start had been made on the development of the St. Lawrence's power resources. No reduction commensurate with increases in technological efficiency had been made in the rates charged small consumers. Most important, big business remained in firm control of the final decision-making process, or of a major portion of it, in a field where problems of environmental pollution, energy shortage, and governmental corruption grew. These problems, which had already more than sprouted by the end of the 1920s, would come into full flower in the 1960s and 1970s.

V

BUT let us return to the summer, autumn, and winter of 1930—the seasons when Franklin Roosevelt had his first contacts with Norman Thomas.

At that time, a rather curious psychological relationship was initiated between the two. Seemingly tenuous in the extreme, it was actually of considerable mental substance. It possessed also a considerable historical interest. The two never became personally intimate. They rarely corresponded with each other; they even more rarely met face to face. But each was, on the evidence, always acutely aware of the other's presence on the national scene and more than normally sensitive to the other's judgments of him—each was *bothered* by the other, each making the other uncomfortably conscious of the more dubious elements of his own thought and action patterns—and their dealings with each other were always about historically important matters. Virtually their every exchange of letters, certainly their every personal meeting, became a historically significant encounter. There is enough on the record, therefore, to enable one to look at Roosevelt every now and then, from the mid-1920s to the end of his life, through the sharply measuring eyes of Norman Thomas, and this is very useful to a historian who seeks to define and assess Roosevelt as a historical figure. It helps one to place himself at points of decision in Roosevelt's public life and to view from these vantage points not only the path he chose to follow but also various paths he might have followed, and did not, through the crisis landscape of our time. It thus helps one to trace what happened in history *because* Roosevelt was as he was, distinguishing this from what would probably have happened in any case and also from what might have happened had he been different.

There were few similarities between these men in mind, character, background. Thomas was born in 1884 in a small Ohio town and raised there as the eldest of six children of a typically impecunious Presbyterian minister.* He had begun his own career as a Presbyterian minister after graduating *magna cum laude* from Princeton (a wealthy uncle's largess had enabled him to go there) and taking a degree at Union Theological Seminary. Two of his teachers at Union were Harry Emerson Fosdick and Henry Sloane Coffin, great exponents of the social gospel. His first parish was in the fetid slum of East Harlem, where he "came to the conclusion that it was extraordinarily difficult under the existing economic structure for many men and women of any class to carry out the ethics of Jesus."[25] His first major public activity was as a Christian pacifist passionately opposed to American involvement in the World War, and it was his disgust with the churches' support of the war in the name of Jesus ("the Pacifist of Nazareth") that finally alienated him from the ministry and led him ultimately to reject the Christian theology, though retaining in full force the Christian ethic. He had joined the Socialist Party in 1918. By 1929, having run brilliant educational campaigns as a Socialist candidate for governor of New York in 1924, for mayor of New York in 1925, and for President of the United States in 1928, he had made his party and its cause not merely respectable but actually prestigious among middle-class intellectuals as it had never been before, not even under the great and saintly Eugene Debs, though Thomas' effectiveness as a labor leader and organizer was considerably less than Debs's. Thomas was an adamant foe of every form of human exploitation and an impassioned champion of civil rights and liberties. He was physically impressive. His capacity for moral outrage was immense; so was his ability to communicate it. He was an obviously authentic intellectual, firmly grounded in history and ethical philosophy, and a prolific writer of articles and books. He was utterly fearless. He had become as eloquent and persuasive a public speaker as there was in America.

He had paid increasingly close attention to Roosevelt's developing political career since the 1924 Democratic convention. By the summer of 1929 it seemed clear to him that, of all the potential Democratic candidates for President, Roosevelt was the most likely to win nomination and election. The prospect failed to please him. It pleased him less and less as that year's heated campaign for mayor of New York, in which he was again the Socialist candidate, mounted toward its autumn climax. Few men had a greater detailed knowledge than he of the graft and corruption rampant in city government under the administration of Tammanyite Mayor James J. Walker. He could name names, cite dates, specify crimes, and vividly describe their meaning in terms of ghastly human suffering. He was proportionately outraged, his denunciation of Roosevelt's July 4 speech to the Tammany braves was given special pungency, by what he perceived as the governor's refusal to use his power of office

*When he was twelve, Thomas became a delivery boy for the Marion *Star*, the local daily published and edited by Warren Gamaliel Harding, the future President of the United States.

to help remove these evils. He was actually infuriated by the governor's pretense, and Thomas had no doubt it *was* pretense, that he lacked this power legally, lacked also the definite information needed before such power, even had he possessed it, could be exercised. Certainly such information was not hard to come by for one in Roosevelt's position; indeed, it must require some effort to avoid, a calculated inattention at least.

And in point of fact, Roosevelt *had* been given ample warning that grave troubles impended for the city. As long ago as the spring of 1927 he had heard, via Louis Howe and Ed Flynn, that "wine, women and song" were playing "the very devil with Jimmy Walker."[26] The "song" part of this seemed particularly appropriate to anyone who knew that Walker had actually begun his career as a Tin Pan Alley songwriter;* he still retained the flashy manners and sharp style of dress, the wise-cracking insouciance, the brittle "sophistication" of Broadway show biz. The "devil" had not yet harmed his public image when, on October 2, 1928, with glowing words of praise, he presented Roosevelt's name to the Rochester convention. But a month later, a notorious big-time gambler and industrial and labor racketeer named Arnold Rothstein was shot (he died on the morning of Election Day). Numerous municipal officials, including high police officers, were known to have had dealings with him, and the obvious reluctance of law-enforcement officers to solve the case had sparked a smoldering fire of criticism that grew more widespread with every passing week. Increasingly vehement and persuasive were charges of wholesale corruption of the city's judicial system, this as one element of a total breakdown of law enforcement in widening areas of the working alliance between city government and organized crime. Hurled by taxpayers' associations, civic welfare organizations, leading churchmen, and others prominent in city life, these charges were joined by a growing criticism of the natty little mayor's playboy antics, chronic tardiness, and equally chronic absenteeism. (He was dubbed the *late* Mayor Walker because he could never get anywhere on time; he took seven vacations totaling 147 days during his first two years in office.) He was a married man, a Roman Catholic who had married within the Church in 1912. He had taken a most solemn oath, administered by Judge Robert F. Wagner on January 1, 1926, to uphold the laws of the state and nation. Yet on almost any night he could be seen in one or another of the speakeasies he favored in the company of a beauteous musical comedy star named Betty Compton.†

This last seemed particularly reprehensible to Al Smith, who, for all his

---

*In the early 1900s, when he was a chum and protégé of the songwriter Paul Dresser (Dresser, the composer of "On the Banks of the Wabash" and "My Gal Sal," was an older brother of Theodore Dreiser), Walker had written the lyrics of such hits as "Kiss all the Girls for Me," "There's Music in the Rustle of a Skirt," and, most successfully, "Will You Love Me in December as You Do in May?"

†Walker married Betty Compton in April 1933, a month after his first wife, at his urgent request and presumably with a handsome cash settlement, had divorced him. His second marriage ended in divorce eight years later.

liking of a convivial glass in hand, was exceedingly straitlaced in matters affecting home and family.

In March, as Roosevelt had heard, Smith bluntly asked the mayor, who owed Smith much politically, *not* to run for reelection. "If you do you'll be defeated, and hurt the party," Smith reportedly said. Walker was sure he knew better. His personal popularity with the electorate remained immense. He was not personally identified with any of the alleged crimes attributed to his administration, nor was he likely to be during the months ahead. Indeed, the public mind during these months might well doubt that the allegations themselves were actually true, since the progressive Governor Roosevelt would almost certainly refuse to take any stand concerning them.

Moreover, Al Smith, though still a sachem, had lost most of his once-great influence in Tammany Hall. At nearly the time, perhaps on the very day, of the reported Smith-Walker conversation, Judge George W. Olvany, who had become Boss Murphy's successor as Tammany chieftan but had proved too weak of mind and will to handle the job, was deposed and replaced by City Commissioner John F. Curry. The event measured the sharp decline of Smith's local authority: Curry, a thoroughly corrupt machine politician whom Walker personally favored for grand sachem, was emphatically not a Smith man. And this was but the latest in a series of instances since the Happy Warrior's presidential defeat in which men committed to him were replaced in posts of importance by men not friendly to him.

Jimmy Walker therefore need feel no external compulsion to accede to Smith's request, which he furiously resented. Smith's "real reason" for making it was not his concern for party welfare, asserted Walker; it was "because I have a girl,"[27] and this was none of Smith's business. The mayor then, at the earliest opportune moment, announced for reelection.

His Republican opponent was the liberal insurgent Congressman Fiorello H. La Guardia, whom Roosevelt had first met in Washington or New York during the World War days and with whom he had held a memorable conversation in August 1918 in Turin, Italy, where La Guardia had been stationed as a captain (he later became a major) in the U.S. Army Air Corps. He was a pugnacious, volatile, tireless, brilliant though erratic product of Manhattan's melting pot (his father was Italian, and his mother, Jewish). Squat of figure, broadly expansive of countenance, he possessed a rare gift for comedy, which he used to leaven his intensely serious purpose. He had absolute integrity, along with a genius for making headlines; he was personally a formidable candidate. But in this year of 1929 he was fatally encumbered, as Thomas pointed out again and again. Running as a Republican, La Guardia could "only be elected with the support of the working Republican leaders"—men who were on the average "worse than Tammany leaders on the principle that a jackal is worse than a lion"[28]—which meant that his attacks upon the iniquities of the Walker regime must be considerably less detailed, less specific, than those Thomas could and did make. Also, since he and Thomas competed for the same constituency, virtually every vote that Thomas gained over the meager Socialist vote of 1925 was a vote lost to La Guardia.

There were some 136,000 of these last on Election Day.* Thomas, who had obtained fewer than 39,000 votes in 1925, had nearly 175,000 in 1929. The size of his vote, joined to the fact that the bulk of it came from middle-class areas, was the most surprising and potentially significant result of the election, as was soon recognized by Roosevelt, Howe, and Flynn. But despite the headline exposures of a corrupt regime, the dapper Jimmy Walker won reelection by an overwhelming majority, running nearly a half-million votes ahead of La Guardia. It was a victory margin that would have been considerably reduced had Roosevelt so much as indicated a concern over the corruption charges; it could have been wiped out altogether had the governor proclaimed a serious concern. But it was *also* a victory margin largely responsible, though the governor received the credit, for the slight gain in Assembly seats and total vote scored that year by the state Democracy, as has been said.

This indicated to Norman Thomas as clearly as to anyone else what a "practical" politician in the governor's position would do on this matter in the future. Such a politician would avoid a sharp clean break with Tammany: he needed Tammany votes to get legislation through in Albany and needed a good legislative record, plus Tammany delegate support in the Democratic convention, to win the presidential nomination. But he would also avoid any close overt ties with a Tiger that seemed bound and determined to revert to the crudely predatory habits of the jungle it had made of city politics in the years of Tweed and Croker. His strategy would be a carefully calculated mixture of aloofness and cooperation, and in the shaping and implementing of it the governor would be greatly helped by his secretary of state, the suave, astute Ed Flynn. Flynn had no use whatever for John Curry personally. He was actively hostile to policies Curry openly avowed, to practices Curry covertly engaged in himself and condoned on the part of others. Immediately upon Curry's elevation, as Flynn later said, a "great coolness developed between Tammany Hall and the Bronx organization."[29]

Norman Thomas understood all this as he understood the general necessity for compromise in politics, for choosing the lesser evil, for even accepting sometimes the worst momentarily in order to gain the best, possibly, at a future date. Moreover, when harshly condemnatory judgments were precipitated from Thomas' mind by his critical observations of Roosevelt in action, there almost always remained suspended in that mind a scattered dust of doubt, a nagging suspicion that he, doubting Thomas, might indeed have a less acute and accurate sense of realities than the man he condemned. Did he, Norman Thomas, *truly* judge the limits of the possible? Did he draw accurately the line between compromise that is morally justified and compromise that is tan-

---

*One reason for this was the unprecedentedly full coverage given by the New York *Times* to Thomas' campaign, with other papers following suit. This stemmed from a casual meeting between Thomas and Adolph S. Ochs, the *Times* publisher, in which the former convinced the latter that coverage of the Socialist's speeches up till then had been inadequate and distorted. Ochs, favorably impressed by Thomas, ordered reporters to pay more attention to him. They gladly did.

tamount to complicity in evil? Might not Roosevelt somehow know better than
he what could and should be done in terms of the long run, having perhaps
consulted an inner oracle of instinct and intuition whose counsels were denied
other men?

All the same, in the present instance Thomas was morally outraged.

His awarenesses of the evils that darkly flourished behind the smiling,
brittle-bright Walker façade were vivid and definite. There were rat- and
roach-infested tenements, filthy firetraps whose landlords escaped code-viola-
tion penalties by regularly paying off city inspectors. There were honest hard-
working men condemned with their families to a life of impoverishment and
terror because they had fallen into the clutches of loan sharks who used
strong-arm hoodlums as collectors and corrupt magistrates as allies. There
were small shopkeepers similarly condemned by their forced payments of
"protection" to mobsters who had bought and paid for key city officials. There
were slum-bred girls forced into prostitution and now enslaved by vicious
pimps, who, in cahoots with vice-squad police, brutally maltreated them.
There were perfectly respectable women, some of them housewives and moth-
ers, who were arrested by members of the vice squad on trumped-up charges
of prostitution and then presented with the brutal choice between paying off
their tormentors or risking court action that would ruin their reputations even
if it did not result, as it almost certainly would, in jail or a heavy fine or both.
There were brave men and women workers who were maimed, even killed,
because they dared protest control of their unions by racketeers having close
ties with Tammany, such as Arnold Rothstein. There were a myriad such
iniquities; they added up to monstrous wickedness.

No decent man who could strike a blow against that wickedness, certainly
none who presented himself to the electorate as a "liberal" and "progressive,"
would hesitate to do so for any reason of personal political advantage.

VI

IN general, Thomas' criticism of Roosevelt as mind and politician was one that
idealists in philosophy traditionally level against pragmatism and pragmatists,
namely, that Roosevelt failed to make essential, internal connections between
one item of information and another, one conception and another. Perhaps he
lacked the mental ability to do this, but if he did possess it, he saw no need
to exercise it, since, being predominantly a man of action, he had less faith in
such inward effort as a guide to outer action than he had in the signs and
portents presented him through his senses. He collected facts, including other
people's expressed ideas, as he did stamps and naval prints. He was content
to pile them up, inert, their relations to one another remaining altogether
external, in capacious compartments of memory, where they were readily
available for reference and whence they could be withdrawn for instrumental
use whenever circumstances (cues) suggested (commanded) that he do so. He
failed, in other words, to transform his collection of facts into an organized,

self-consistent body of knowledge informed by carefully considered principles of his own.

Thomas must have taken note of this failure in Roosevelt's speeches—and not only in those dealing with electric power.

For instance, in his inaugural address, the new governor had stressed the "interdependence on each other" that had been created by "modern civilization," asserting as a "literal" truth "that the 'self-supporting' man or woman has become as extinct as the man of the stone age," and in his commencement address at Hobart he had said that, with each passing day, "a hundred small storekeepers go out of business or are absorbed by the new business device known as the chain store." This meant "that a hundred independent owners of their own businesses either transfer to some other business or become employees of a great impersonal machine," he continued. "We see the same trend in every form of manufacture, in transportation, in public utilities, in banking." There was a similar trend in government—a draining away of governing power from several states, an increasing concentration of it in Washington. He deplored this. It endangered individual liberty. But he made in his speech no clear causal connection between the two trends, economic and political, that he described. The fault politically, he indicated, was a default: power went to Washington because it was rejected at home; state and local governments refused to give it proper employment on its native grounds. There was a demand for "a department of education" in Washington whenever a state failed "to provide adequate educational facilities for its boys and girls," he said. There was a demand for "a department of health" in Washington whenever a state failed "to keep abreast with modern [public health] provisions." And if a state failed "adequately to regulate its public service corporations, the easiest course . . . [was] to ask the Interstate Commerce Commission or the Federal Trade Commission to take jurisdiction."[30]

He had returned to this theme of states' rights, local control, and local responsibility, and of the deplorable trend toward a centralization of governing power in Washington, when he talked about crime and law enforcement at the Governors' Conference in mid-July. Many would later deem it a strange theme for him to pursue. Some surmised that he did so simply because he happened to be governor at the time, was speaking to fellow governors, and had a natural egoistic concern for the power and prestige of the gubernatorial office. In any case, he notably failed in this address as in his Hobart one to trace connections between the trend he inveighed against and its underlying technological, economic causes. "No constitutional sovereign right vested in the forty-eight States . . . has been more zealously defended or clearly established than the right of each State to control the police powers and the administration of justice within its borders," he began. " . . . But there is a tendency, and to my mind a dangerous tendency, on the part of our national Government, to encroach, on one excuse or another, more and more upon State supremacy. The elastic theory of interstate commerce, for instance, has been stretched almost to the breaking point to cover certain regulatory powers desired by

Washington." He conceded, à la his Hobart address, that Washington's lust for power was not the sole reason for this; in many cases there "has been . . . a failure of the States, themselves, . . . to pass legislation necessary to meet certain conditions." And what had happened in other fields was now threatened in the field of law enforcement and criminal justice. "If we wish to retain our control over the criminal laws and police powers we must accept responsibility for their enforcement; we must clean out the antiquated machinery of justice; we must meet new kinds of crime with new kinds of laws [this was his only indication of his awareness of the impact of technological change]; and we must do this, not in this State or that State, but in every State." Otherwise "we shall find the heavy hand of Washington laid upon us by Federal legislation." He made no mention of the automobile, the telephone, the radio, the speedboat, and the airplane as means of a criminal organization and activity having no regard for state boundaries, and on a scale so huge as to overwhelm the law-enforcement facilities of local governments. He did stress, however, the need for more scientific crime detection and the greatest possible uniformity among the states, not only in the collection of accurate crime statistics but also "in our crime legislation and our criminal codes." (Every state should have its own crime commission to work in cooperation with the National Crime Commission "of whose executive committee I happen to be a member."[31]*

By January 1930, Norman Thomas was inclined to believe that American Socialism might have more reason to fear this man as President than any other who could possibly win the White House in the next election. Roosevelt seemed to Thomas to be the kind of politician who dissipates developing forces of change in the very process of seeming boldly to apply them. As governor he was demonstrating a genius—an evil genius in Thomas' opinion—for harnessing to his ambition and then involving in halfway, hence ultimately ineffective, measures, political energies that would otherwise flow leftward toward a truly effective concentration, an actually powerful focus, upon fundamental social and economic transformations. He had the potential, therefore, of performing in twentieth-century America much the same historic function as Bismarck had performed in nineteenth-century Germany, despite, if not in part because of, his great differences from the Iron Chancellor in personal character and political technique.[32]

---

*Some three months before Roosevelt made this speech, the president of the Chicago Crime Commission was one of "a committee of prominent Chicago citizens" who called upon President Hoover at the White House "to reveal" to him "the situation" in their city. "They gave chapter and verse for their statement that Chicago was in the hands of the gangsters, that the police and magistrates were completely under their control, that the governor of the state was futile, that the federal government was the only force by which the city's ability to govern itself could be restored," writes Hoover in the first volume of his *Memoirs* (pages 276–277). The President "at once" ordered federal law-enforcement agencies, though "limited" in their "authority to violations of the income-tax and Prohibition laws," to concentrate attention upon the notorious Chicago gangster Al Capone. Two years later, Capone was convicted of income-tax evasion and sentenced to eleven years in the federal penitentiary. "It is ironic," comments Hoover, "that a man guilty of inciting hundreds of murders, in some of which he took a personal hand, had to be punished merely for failure to pay taxes on the money he made by murder."

And Thomas' sense of this danger to his own cause was sharpened and, as 1930 wore on, became increasingly invested with bitter irony. There was then underway a historical development of the most profound significance, long anticipated by Thomas and his party, from which American Socialism expected immense political gains. With each passing week it became more apparent that the "system" against which Socialists had always inveighed was collapsing. With each passing week opportunities for translating Socialist theory into practice seemed to multiply and shine more brilliantly amid dark and spreading ruin. How ghastly it would be, from Thomas' point of view, if these opportunities were now snatched away and lost by an essentially unprincipled opportunist!

4

The Last Summer of the Golden Glow

I

" 'TIS distance lends enchantment to the view," sang the poet Thomas Campbell, who also averred, in another poem, that "coming events cast their shadows before." The latter statement was, in the late 1920s, inescapably and indelibly impressed upon the public mind by ubiquitous Lucky Strike cigarette advertisements in which Americans fearing obesity were urged to "Reach for a Lucky Instead of a Sweet."[1] Both statements remain applicable to the American summer of 1929 as remembered in later years by those who lived through it. Temporal distance operated in this case, however, chiefly to change the quality of the "enchantment," not its quantity, and to define "shadows" generally unperceived at the time. At the time, the closeup view was pleasing enough to many if not most Americans, to nearly all, indeed, who actively shared, or believed they did, in the prevailing Prosperity; and every perceived "coming event" of major import, far from casting a shadow across the smiling scene, shed a more brilliant light upon it.

Neither war nor serious rumor of war disturbed the Western world.

It is true that Benito Mussolini, the jut-jawed burning-eyed latter-day Roman caesar, engaged in bellicose posturings that summer as he looked down from high balconies upon vast throngs gathered in piazzas below. He praised war as the great uplifter and purifier of the human spirit. But he had been doing this for years, and it was generally agreed among Americans that his posturing was just that and nothing more, a gaudy piece of theater as meretricious as Italian opera, designed exclusively for Italian audiences. Americans could forgive it, even be grateful for it, knowing that Mussolini, in part by means of such theatricality, had brought Fascist order out of Communist-breeding chaos in his native land, imposed work and discipline upon his notoriously wayward and indolent fellow countrymen, and made the trains run on time. Of course, his overt theatricality was reportedly joined to covert brutality. It was alleged that his political opponents were savagely beaten in Fascist jails and forced to drink massive, sometimes fatal, doses of castor oil. But these opponents were Reds, after all, weren't they? A Great Man is by definition one who operates beyond the Good and Evil of ordinary men, is he not? And Benito Mussolini was indubitably a Great Man. Britain's Winston Churchill said so. Thomas W. Lamont of the Morgan bank and Otto Kahn of Kuhn, Loeb said so. The actor-humorist Will Rogers said so. Great industrialists and newspaper publishers on both sides of the Atlantic said so. Famous diplomats said so, one of whom, as a matter of fact, the Honorable Richard Washburn Child, former U.S. ambassador to Italy, had asserted in a widely read essay, published only a few months before, that "the Duce is now the greatest figure of this sphere and time." Like Theodore Roosevelt, he was "boyish and likable" and "gives the impression of an energy which cannot be bottled, which bubbles up and over like an eternally effervescent, irrepressible fluid." With this energy and a genius for "super-statesmanship" he had "built a state upon a new concept of a state" and changed "not only . . . the lives of human beings but . . . their minds, their hearts, their spirits." "Time has shown that he is both wise and humane," said Richard Washburn Child.[2] Obviously no such superman could seriously contemplate involving his people in the catastrophic folly of modern war.

It was also true that there was much angry bickering that summer among delegates from Germany, France, Britain, Belgium, and Italy over terms of the Young Plan, a revision of the Dawes Plan for German war reparations payments that Owen D. Young of General Electric had drafted. Especially vigorous and bitter were protests entered by the German Reichsbank president, Dr. Hjalmar Horace Greeley Schacht,* against some of the proposals. But all obvious signs were that the German economy was still booming; the new payment schedule called for smaller annual installments on the debt than the Germans had actually been meeting; and the proposed establishment of a Bank for International Payments in Basel made excellent practical sense, as Dr. Schacht was among the first to admit. Hence there was little doubt in early summer that the Young Plan would ultimately be adopted as, according to economists and diplomats, a final satisfactory answer to a most vexatious problem. In late summer this happened: the Germans accepted the Young Plan, whereupon the French and Belgians agreed to withdraw their occupation troops from the Rhineland, where they had been since 1923, thereby greatly relaxing Continental international tensions.

By then, President Hoover had proclaimed formally in effect the U.S. signature of the Kellogg-Briand Pact, whereby sixty-two nations renounced war "as an instrument of national policy in their relations with one another." The politically sophisticated might agree with Virginia's crusty Senator Carter Glass that the much-ballyhooed pact was not "worth a postage stamp in bringing about peace," a view Franklin Roosevelt emphatically agreed with, but Glass himself had voted for ratification on the ground that "it would be psychologically bad to defeat it," and it certainly encouraged the general public's belief that war, having been thus "outlawed," was now unlikely in the extreme.[3] Further encouragement of such belief came from preparations being made that summer for another naval disarmament conference involving Britain, Japan, and the United States, to be held in London early the next year.

As for the economic outlook, it was of a dazzling brightness in the eyes of most Americans having savings to invest. A boundless optimism pervaded the business community, along with a boundless self-esteem on the part of individual big-business men. *They* had created this nearly perfect mechanism for the ever-increasing production and consumption of goods. They pridefully said as

*Schacht had lived in Brooklyn as a boy, and it was there that he acquired his middle names.

much in public speech and print, and some of them even essayed to explain, how the mechanism worked and why it would keep on working, better and better, if only businessmen were permitted to run it without hindrance from "radicals" and "academic theorists." For instance, the banker Paul M. Mazur of Lehman Brothers had published in the spring of 1928 the book *American Prosperity: Its Causes and Consequences,* in which he spoke of the ever-lower unit costs resulting from assembly-line Taylorized mass production and glowingly described how the consumer market for this mass production was steadily increased by planned obsolescence (style changes), massive and unremitting advertising, and the wonderful device of the installment plan. "Today American prosperity exists through intensive selling," he concluded. "Let him who would destroy that foundation consider the cost of such an act of Samson upon the basic pillars of the temple of American business. Only he who wishes to destroy this temple for the sake of some principle antagonistic to it can logically persist in his attack upon present-day distribution." But Mazur had no real fear that the "temple" would fall or, to shift metaphors as swiftly as he, be emasculated. "There is every probability of a continued virility in the strength of American business," said he. " . . . There is nothing which indicates any change in the importance of American industrial life, and it will continue to write the most significant pages of American history."[4] Most others who had practical influence upon Americans with surplus income to invest agreed wholeheartedly with Mazur. Thus, in late May, the federal government had issued an economic survey, called the Hoover Survey because it was initiated in 1921 under Secretary of Commerce Herbert Hoover, of which "the keynote, ringingly struck, was that there is no limit to the capacity of the U.S. consumer to consume," *Time* magazine reported. There was, according to the survey, said *Time,* "a non-vicious circle in which the manufacturer constantly produced more merchandise, the consumer constantly consumed more merchandise, and out of the horn of plenty came gifts for all."[5]

This optimism was measured by the New York Stock Exchange. There, on almost every trading day, almost every stock issue moved upward on a trading volume of 3,000,000 to 5,000,000 shares. (In 1919 a series of 1,500,000 share days had caused the Federal Reserve Board to worry about overspeculation.) It is true that, as regards the stock market, warning signals and warning voices had been raised; these, recorded in the cold print of history, would seem in retrospect to have constituted a sufficiency of "shadows" cast by "coming events." In early February 1929, for instance, the Federal Reserve Board had pointed with alarm at the unprecedented volume of brokers' loans,* saying that $5,669,000,000 of these loans outstanding was much too much. *Dangerously* too much. (Such loans had seemed disturbingly large in December 1927, when they totaled $3,500,000,000.) The Federal Reserve Board had then moved to deny its rediscount facilities to member banks who borrowed "for the purpose of making . . . or . . . maintaining speculative loans."[6] The

---

*Loans made by brokers to customers, enabling the latter to buy stocks on margin.

immediate effect had been a sharp break in the "Hoover bull market" that had begun on Election Day, 1928, as an acceleration of the Great Bull Market under way since early March of that year—a break followed by much pulling and hauling, while the market floundered in uncertainty, sometimes sharply up, sometimes sharply down, between those who sought to slow the boom and those who sought to speed it. In late March, though the banks had withdrawn a mere $25,000,000 from an inflated market, the interest rate on call money had shot up spectacularly. The rate was 9 percent at the close of the trading day of March 25. It was 12 percent at the opening on March 26 and quickly rose to 15 percent, then to 17 percent, finally to a dizzying 20 percent, while a wave of selling inundated the market, forcing prices steeply downward on an unprecedented volume of 8,246,740 shares. For the moment it appeared that the financial conservatives of the Federal Reserve Board had succeeded in their efforts to reduce the speculative fever, that they might in fact have been *too* successful, committing the crime of what in later, less happy, seasons would be called overkill. A financial panic seemed to impend. But measures to counteract the Federal Reserve were promptly taken by one of the leading managers of the private money market, Charles E. Mitchell, president of the National City Bank in New York City. He announced that his bank—it was certainly *his* in that he dictated bank policy and used bank money almost as his own —would lend $20,000,000 on call at rates substantially lower than the stultifying prevailing one: Mitchell proposed to lend $5,000,000 at 15 percent, another $5,000,000 at 16, and so on to a top of 20. Other bankers followed suit. What the bankers did in this case, however—the call money rate went down to a fluctuating figure between 6 and 15 percent—was less important than what the managers of giant industrial corporations did. These corporations had coffers swollen with undistributed profits; their managers began to feed these into the market through direct loans to brokers, thus bypassing the flimsy barriers put up by the Federal Reserve and greatly augmenting their corporate incomes.

By mid-May, when the market clearly showed it was on the verge of another big advance, informed people like the chairman of International Acceptance, Paul M. Warburg, who had been a member of the Federal Reserve Board from 1914 to 1918, were saying flatly that the Federal Reserve now had no control whatever over the money market. Warburg deplored this. Others did not. Among the most important of those who did not was the president of the New York Stock Exchange, Edward H. H. Simmons, who expressed in public speech and a pamphlet his grateful pleasure in the fact that brokers need no longer depend upon banks for the nourishment of their margin accounts, that practically all of the recent increase in money going into brokers' loans had come from "private corporations" independent of Federal Reserve controls. Capitalists recognized that call money was "the safest form of investment known in this country," said Simmons, and their increased making of such investment was a great boon to the general economy. For if "the enormous masses of capital today invested in stock market loans" had gone instead into "commercial business," he said, the resultant "huge rise in commodity prices, inflation of inventories, and an artificial business boom" would inevitably have led to "a colossal smash."[7] The stock market, in other words, according to the Stock Exchange president, was a kind of safety valve, through which excess steam was harmlessly expended and without which there would be a catastrophic explosion. He was obviously right in one respect: there was an enormous amount of unemployed steam in the economy. Pouring into the "safety valve" as spring gave way to summer and summer wore on, this "steam" (brokers' loans climbed above $6,000,000,000) forced the market up again, and up, and up, far into the bright blue sky, of which considerable pieces were also traded. Those few who warned of a coming fatal fall, as did the financial forecaster Roger Babson, were increasingly dismissed with ridicule, when listened to at all, by the financial world's presumed masters.

Unnoticed by the New Era spokesmen, or noticed only to be contemptuously denied, was the fact that unemployed steam in the economy meant unemployed workers and that the number of the latter increased simultaneously if not proportionately with the volume of the former. No one could know for sure, at that time, *what* the proportions were. Indicative of the scale of values, the order of priorities, whereby governmental policies were determined during the years of the Republican Prosperity was the total lack of reliable national employment figures. The Coolidge administration could supply precise statistical data on factory production, railroad traffic, bank loans, and "the status of our wheat, prune, cherry, and apricot crops," also "on the cold storage holdings of cheese and pickled pork," complained Senator Robert Wagner in his maiden speech (March 5, 1928) on the U.S. Senate floor, but "when I made inquiry of the Department of Labor as to how many people were unemployed, I was told that they did not know." He introduced a resolution calling upon Coolidge's secretary of labor, James J. Davis, to report on the extent of unemployment and upon the methods by which this was measured, a resolution promptly adopted. But the resultant report was, as expected, highly unsatisfactory. It came to the Senate in two parts: a statistical study by the commissioner of labor statistics, Ethelbert Stewart, and a cover letter by Davis himself, the latter a purported summary of the former. "Commissioner Stewart finds that the actual number now out of work is 1,874,050," asserted Davis, whereupon the Senate Republicans lambasted Democratic "alarmists" who sought to undermine confidence in the prevailing Prosperity and its source, the wondrous free-enterprise system. Actually, as was soon demonstrated by Wagner and others who carefully studied Stewart's report (the dearth of solid data required of Stewart an extreme complexity of mathematical assumptions and projections), unemployment was then at least 4,000,000. Some placed it as high as 8,000,000. And this at the very height of the Golden Glow![8] So conclusive was this estimate that administration supporters fell silent upon the subject, which, in their view, was irrelevant to the proper concerns of a legislative body. " . . . remedies for unemployment cannot be supplied by law," said Utah's Republican Senator Reed Smoot.[9]

Everybody, it seemed, was following the market through press and radio every day if not actually "playing" it through a local broker's office (such offices had sprung up even in small towns all across the land). The once-esoteric language of the financial world had become common parlance.

Thus, when released to the press on a dull day in late June, the spoofing postscript that the governor of New York had appended to a letter mailed to his agricultural commissioner from Warm Springs a month before was immediately understood by millions who read it. Roosevelt and his friend and neighbor Henry Morgenthau, Jr., were playfully cooperating in a squash-growing enterprise on their respective Dutchess County farms, the squash market being, said Morgenthau, a profitable one. And Roosevelt's letter to "Dear Henry" told of instructions given Moses Smith, Roosevelt's farmer, "to get four or five acres ready for the squash seed" at the Hyde Park farm. He signed himself, "Yours for Squashco," no doubt in emulation of Camco, a speculation in which he and Morgenthau were also joined and would soon fervently wish they were not.* This suggested his postscript. "Please write me any further directions as to how the common stock should be planted," he said, "whether it should be watered, whether the distribution should be wide or closely harrowed, whether it carries any bonus (besides bugs), other stock in the same rows, etc. I am writing Moses Smith to visit your Squashco vaults at Fishkill Farms Security Company to inspect the Squashco safe deposit cellar accommodations."[10]

It was in its August issue of this enchanted summer that the *Ladies' Home Journal* published the most widely quoted (by historians) of all the articles it published during the 1920s. "Everybody Ought to Be Rich" was its appealing title. Its author was John J. Raskob. "If a man saves fifteen dollars a week [this was about half the average weekly paycheck for workers that year] and invests it in good common stocks, and allows the dividends and rights to accumulate, at the end of twenty years he will have at least eighty thousand dollars and an income from investments of around four hundred dollars a month," wrote Raskob. "He will be rich. And because income can do that I am firm in my belief that anyone not only can be rich but ought to be rich."[11]

II

WHEN Franklin Roosevelt read Raskob's article in late July, and one can be certain he did read it, since Raskob's views were an important factor in his political calculations that year, he was embarked on what he had laughingly described a few months before as an upcoming "voyage" through upstate New York.

It was in late March that he had written to his old Navy friend Captain Edward J. McCauley, Jr., his chief of staff during his 1918 trip to war-torn Europe and commander of the presidential flagship *George Washington* on which he and Eleanor, with Woodrow Wilson, had returned from France in

---

*See *FDR: The Beckoning of Destiny,* pp. 706–708.

1919. In his letter to "Dear Eddie," he wrote: "This summer I am going on a cruise which makes me laugh whenever I compare it with the old Navy days. I am taking command of the good ship INSPECTOR [literally named—it was the state's inland waterway inspection craft], which has a glass roof, and with the whole family I am navigating the barge canal from Albany to Buffalo, thence to Lake Ontario and the St. Lawrence River and back through the Hudson to the Champlain Canal. It will certainly be a rough and exciting voyage."[12]

He made no mention to McCauley of other travel plans then in the making, which, in the event, were integrated to a degree with the waterway "voyage."

Roosevelt wanted his two youngest sons, Franklin, Jr., and John, to have that summer the educational and recreational experience of a properly conducted European tour. Franklin, Jr., or Brother, as he was called, would be fifteen years old in mid-August, and John was thirteen. Roosevelt was particularly anxious to have them see battlefields he himself had toured in France in 1918, so that they would have some vivid sense of what the World War had meant as a human experience. He longed to take the boys himself, but this was manifestly impossible. So in March he suggested, he in fact urged, that Eleanor do so—and encountered on her part a considerable reluctance.

It will be recalled that on the morrow of Election Day she had bitterly resented the threatened blotting out of her independent career and self by the demands of her husband's high office and yet higher ambitions, but that almost at once she had asserted herself against this threat. She had done so success-fully, had indeed been helped to do so by her husband, who, due in good part to the sympathetic understanding Louis Howe had always had of Eleanor, knew how she felt, greatly respected her abilities and integrity, and realized that these could become valuable political assets for him. She had perforce resigned from the Democratic State Committee, from the boards of such lobbying organizations as the Women's Trade Union League, and from the editorship of the *Women's Democratic News.* But she continued her connection with the Todhunter School and Val-Kill Industries, she continued to spend several days and nights each month in the beloved Val Kill Cottage, she continued to be active behind the scenes in organizations from which she had nominally resigned (she remained in effect top editor of the *News*), and she continued to make speeches and write articles of a "nonpolitical" nature. Each weekend she worked out, with Missy, with her social secretary, and with the Executive Mansion's butler and housekeeper, the schedule for her official "hostessing" during the week to come. On occasion, Missy had to substitute for her at formal luncheons, teas, and dinners. Generally Eleanor managed to allocate her time and distribute her official obligations in such a way as to permit her to preside beside her husband where and when she was supposed to. During the school term, if at all possible, formal entertainments and func-tions were not scheduled for Mondays or Tuesdays or for the morning and noon of Wednesdays; during the school term she took a Pullman down from Albany to New York City each Sunday night to meet her Todhunter classes on Monday morning and thereafter perform her duties as teacher and associate principal, working with the principal, Marion Dickerman, until Wednesday noon. She then took a train back to Albany, arriving at the Executive Mansion in time to receive callers during her official "at home" from 4:30 to 6:00 P.M.

By March she was again attending purely political meetings, her husband having rescinded his order against her doing so provided she made no political speeches that could be reported in the press. (He valued her private reports to him of what transpired at such meetings.) By then, too, she had earned wide recognition as the most remarkable first lady the State of New York had ever had—one who employed her social prestige, along with her ready access to the governor's eye and ear and decision-making judgment, to further particular causes and, in general, the cause of women's rights and an expanded role for women in public affairs. She thus used her husband as a means toward her ends.

She did so, however, in perfect awareness that he simultaneously used her as a means toward his own ends. In this respect the relationship between them became symbiotic in somewhat the same way as the political relationship between Al Smith and Roosevelt had been from 1922 until the autumn of 1928. It was a relationship made possible by the fact that the two sets of ends, hers and his, were sufficiently consistent with each other to make for a general harmony. Yet they were very far from being identical, even in the long run. They were sometimes actually contradictory in the short run. And in the latter case, *his* were invariably the ends that were served, and not always advertently, by Eleanor. To the end of her life there remained, deep in her, a residue of resentment over this, a resentment of the profound contempt for her as a human being that seemed to her implicit in it. (A summary statement she wrote after his death says, bleakly, "I was one of those who served his purposes."[13]) Indeed, in her published autobiographical works and published letters, there are subtle hints of a suspicion that it was more his recognition of her potential usefulness to his ambition than his love for her as a woman that had prompted his initial courtship of her, his proposal of marriage, he having shrewdly assessed the advantages he would gain careerwise from having as wife the niece of a namesake President of the United States. It was a suspicion that could not but have been fed by the kind of filial relationship he had maintained with his mother after the marriage and by his refusal ever to define clearly, much less make a definite choice between, the loyalties he owed his wife and those he owed his mother.* Certainly, by the summer of 1929, Eleanor realized that she increasingly served her husband as a kind of lightning rod reaching up into a turbulent atmosphere shot through with the frictional electricity of liberal vs. conservative, or as a launcher of trial balloons into winds of uncertain direction which, strongly blowing, might quickly veer from right to left or *vice versa*, with unhappy consequences for a politician who was neither braced against them nor prepared to sail with them. She realized that

*See pages 203–204 of *FDR: The Beckoning of Destiny.*

she could be used in this way because there was never any doubt about where she herself stood on issues: her liberal stance was as unwavering as it was greatly publicized. She further realized that this helped him not only to attract the liberal vote but also to hold it when he, on a specific issue, found it expedient to be noncommittal or even to embrace the conservative position. In the latter case, if fervent partisans of the right came raging into his office over something she had said or done, he could simply spread his hands, shrug his shoulders, and say with a rueful smile that his "missus" was a woman of powerful conviction—she had a mind of her own, a will of her own—and though he did not always agree with her, neither could he deny her the right to her opinions and their free expression.

In sum, by means of rigid scheduling, through the exercise of an almost superhuman self-discipline and energy and capacity for a swift shifting of concentrated attention from one object to another, Eleanor had managed to weave the various strands of her interest and activity into a living tapestry that had extraordinary strength and resiliency, since the strands were mutually reinforcing, and that was vividly colored with excitements. At the vital center of this tapestry's design were the personal friendships she had formed during the years since her "declaration of independence" or "coming out" in the aftermath of the Lucy Mercer affair and of the horrible first nine months of her husband's polio. Nancy Cook and Marion Dickerman remained the most intimate of these, as Val Kill Cottage remained the closest to a true home that Eleanor had ever known.[14] But there also remained the lawyer Elizabeth Read, who handled some of Eleanor's personal legal affairs, including her income-tax returns; Esther Lape, Elizabeth's companion in a Greenwich Village apartment, with whom Eleanor continued to be active in League of Women Voters affairs and in efforts toward U.S. participation in the League of Nations; Mary W. (Molly) Dewson of the Women's Civic Club (she lived across the hall from the Greenwich Village apartment that was Marion and Nancy's city home), whom Eleanor had recruited for important work in Al Smith's campaign and who would be involved importantly in every national Democratic campaign thereafter; Molly Goodwin, an attractive and athletic young Englishwoman who had charge of physical education at Todhunter and became so constant a visitor at Val Kill that a room over the garage of the Industries shop was permanently assigned to her; Elinor Morgenthau (Mrs. Henry Morgenthau, Jr.), Eleanor's closest social friend among the families along the Hudson River, as well as an active partner in Democratic politics, though Eleanor was also on warm, friendly terms with Margaret Norrie (Mrs. Gordon Norrie) of Staatsburg, the next town north of Hyde Park; Rose Schneiderman, the fiery labor leader whose impassioned speech in the aftermath of the ghastly Triangle fire of 1911 had helped initiate the factory reform movement in New York; Maude Schwartz, also of the Women's Trade Union League; Agnes Leach (Mrs. Henry Goddard Leach), state chairman of the League of Women Voters; and Caroline O'Day. Especially Caroline O'Day, an absolute pacifist, an uncompromising liberal, who greatly influenced Eleanor's outlook and attitudes and was destined to play a small but significant role in Roosevelt's political future.[15] For the last half-dozen years Caroline had been associate chairman of the Democratic State Committee, *ex officio* head of the party's Women's Division, of which Nancy Cook was executive secretary. She had been one of the founders of the *Women's Democratic News* and took over as editor in chief when Eleanor was forced to resign this post. She had been one of the incorporators of Val-Kill Industries and remained an honorary officer of it.

Thus it was of friendships with women, ardent feminists all, who were themselves unattached to men, having never married or having been separated from their husbands by death or choice, that the vital core of personal relationships was made, around which Eleanor wove her living defense against husband and mother-in-law. There was a single exception at the outset. Louis Howe was very much at the center of things for Eleanor. He was dearly loved by her and absolutely trusted by *both* her and her husband. He was equally trusted and hardly less loved by Marion, Nancy, and others of the most intimate inner circle who came to know him well. This loving trust was a kind of cement that held the vital core together, a kind of bridge for communication across the abyss of alienation between husband and wife. It had in these respects a considerable historical importance.

But to this single exception another was being added in the spring and summer of 1929, a far more emphatically masculine element at the center of Eleanor's life than Louis Howe had ever been.

In 1924 a certain Corporal Earl R. Miller of the New York State Police had become the governor's personal bodyguard, the assignment being made by Major John W. Warner, the state police superintendent who in 1926, with his marriage to Emily Smith, had become the governor's son-in-law. Al Smith became very fond of Miller. When the Roosevelts moved into the Executive Mansion, the post of governor's bodyguard went to a husky New York City policeman named Augustus (Gus) Gennerich, a native of Worcester, Massachusetts. Gennerich had earned many citations for bravery. As a rookie cop he had rescued people from a burning tenement at great risk to his own life; as a motorcycle patrolman he had single-handedly engaged gangsters in gun battle, capturing several of them. And though he was a "rough diamond if ever there was one," as Marion Dickerman remarked,[16] he was essentially kind and gentle and soon won his way into the affections of all the immediate Roosevelt entourage, and especially of Roosevelt himself. But though Corporal Miller was thus removed from his post at the governor's side, he continued on the Mansion's police detail: the police superintendent assigned him to guard the governor's lady.

It was not an assignment that, when first announced, provoked expressions of envy among Miller's fellow troopers in the state police barracks. Instead, they commiserated with him. Miller had little formal schooling and few intellectual interests, but he was more sensitive and intelligent than most of his barracks colleagues, who deemed him especially sensitive and susceptible to feminine beauty. He was a most masculine man. Possessed of a magnificent physique and the swift, precise reflexes of a natural athlete, he had fully developed these during a life that had contained far more of the rough than the smooth. He had been orphaned at the age of twelve and lovelessly raised thereafter. He had served a hitch in the Navy and had subsequently been a circus acrobat, a champion amateur welterweight boxer, and a teacher of judo and boxing in the State Police School. He had also become a superb, enthusiastic horseman who won prizes with his displays of horsemanship at fairs. He had been unhappily married and rancorously divorced while earning, or at least acquiring, a considerable reputation among his colleagues for sexual prowess. Handsome of face as well as body, he was reputed to attract women as strongly as he was attracted toward them, and by repute he was indeed very strongly attracted toward them—provided the women were pretty. Eleanor Roosevelt emphatically was not. As a matter of fact, she was just about the least attractive woman in every way that a man could find in a long day's journey, according to Miller's barracks companions.

But Miller did not find her so. Within a few days after his new assignment began he became utterly devoted to her and angrily defended her against denigrating remarks. She was, he insisted, the greatest and kindest lady he had ever known. She was fun to be with. He was delighted to pay her gallant attentions of a kind (deferent to her, protective of her) that few men, and certainly not her husband or sons, had paid her in many years. She reciprocated by encouraging him to tell her about himself, his past rough life, and to bring to her his personal troubles, of which he had in that year a good many, having been deeply hurt by his marriage and divorce. She gave him advice and sympathy, even tangible assistance on occasion. Soon the two had formed a fast and lifelong friendship of a kind difficult to classify, mingling as it did elements of filial and maternal devotion with a masculine romantic gallantry and some measure at least of its feminine counterpart. Young Miller dined at the Roosevelt table while others of the police detail ate in the kitchen; he was present at every tea over which Eleanor presided and at many or most of the dinners, being introduced to her guests not as "Corporal" but as "Mr." Miller; he accompanied her, often as her sole companion, on the auto trips across the state required by her interweaving activities. He became in all respects one of the Roosevelt inner circle at Val Kill Cottage; in the Big House at Hyde Park, where Sara Delano Roosevelt covertly but definitely resented his presence as an equal at her table; and in the house on Sixty-fifth Street, as well as in the Mansion.[17] Some of this inner circle began to wonder if Eleanor was not "using" Earl or her special relationship with him, perhaps inadvertently, to offset her husband's "use" of Missy's constant companionship, though those who thus wondered also remarked that if Eleanor hoped to provoke from her husband any overt sign of jealousy, or even the mildest concern, she was sadly disappointed. The governor simply accepted the handsome state trooper as one of the intimate family; he did so blandly, cheerfully, indifferently. It was, for instance, at Roosevelt's behest that Miller accompanied Eleanor on long auto trips; she was averse to using the chauffeured official limousine for her travels and Roosevelt was averse to her driving her car alone for great distances, since she had had several minor driving accidents in the past. Miller discounted these last in his talks with her; she was, he insisted, a very good driver really, whose accidents had been of a kind that might happen to anyone. He encouraged her to take up horseback riding again and acquired for her a mare, Dot, whose disposition and gaits were exactly suited to Eleanor's temperament and riding skill. (He also encouraged Roosevelt to try riding again, but this was a failed experiment because Roosevelt's withered legs could not clasp a horse's flanks with sufficient strength.) Joseph P. Lash tells how Miller helped her face newsmen's cameras with a relaxed smile instead of the almost frowning tension that had so often characterized her pictures in the past.[18] (She had dreaded being photographed because she looked "so awful" in the papers.) In general and in sum, Earl Miller encouraged Eleanor's further growth in courage, independence, and self-confidence.

Certainly her friendship with Earl Miller greatly increased her personal happiness. She derived from his companionship an unfailing pleasure.[19] And this friendship was yet in the blooming stage—a new and exciting strand at the heart of her living tapestry's design—when her husband proposed that she take their two youngest sons abroad.

She knew that she could not refuse to do what her husband was so obviously intent upon her doing in this case; for years he had talked of taking the boys himself as soon as they were old enough, by which time he would have regained the use of his legs. Nevertheless, she pointed to certain difficulties. She expressed concern over her ability to exercise adequate control over two unusually rambunctious teenage boys, incessantly active and inclined toward frequent violent quarrels. She worried, too, about the cost of the trip. All four of her sons had incurred sizable medical bills during the preceding months— James with serious digestive troubles,* John with his aforementioned knee operation, Elliott with his aforementioned rupture, Brother with a broken nose —and her husband's income was now much less than it had been the year before. (The governor's annual salary was $10,000; Roosevelt had received $25,000 as vice-president of one of the nation's largest surety bonding firms.) He would not have been able to meet these bills, and Howe's salary plus James's allowance, if the imperious Sara had not come to her son's rescue with a generous gift check. The family finances continued strained.

But the major source of her reluctance to go, expressed more frankly to Marion and Nancy than to her husband, was the pleasure she took in the life she was now making for herself in New York. She hated to be cut off from

---

*James was and is convinced that his lifelong chronic stomach ailment was caused by a sadistic governess he, Anna, and Elliott had been forced to endure as children—an evidently psychotic Englishwoman whom Sara had selected and against whose "strictness" Eleanor, in those years of her profound psychological dependence and insecurity, had lacked the courage to protest. Angered by James, this woman had forced him to eat spoonful by spoonful a whole pot of "hot" mustard, whereupon he had become violently ill. See pages 205–206 of *FDR: The Beckoning of Destiny.*

this life for so many weeks! She would, she was afraid, miss so much!

Then, as May gave way to June, an idea was born that considerably reduced this reluctance, replacing it with pleasurable anticipation. In past summers, Eleanor, Nancy, and Marion had taken John and Brother by auto from Hyde Park to Campobello, camping out on the way across upper New York, Vermont, New Hampshire, and Maine. The first such trip had been made in August 1923 in the seven-passenger Buick touring car that the Roosevelts had then owned. Every seat had been filled; seven-year-old George Draper, the son of Roosevelt's polio doctor in New York City, was along, as was Henry Roosevelt, the son of Eleanor's younger brother, Hall. It had been a wholly memorable and generally enjoyable experience. Since then the three women and two boys had become experienced campers, wise in the selection of camp sites, resourceful in such matters as tent pitching, fire building, bed making, and outdoor cooking. (Nearly all the cooking was done by Nancy, however; she was as expert in food preparation as she was in woodworking, photography, pewter manufacture, gardening, and virtually any manual task to which she applied herself.) Why not put these skills to use during the European trip? Why not take across the sea the two cars that the three women owned (Nancy and Marion had a Buick roadster that year, while Eleanor had a Chevrolet touring car) and the necessary paraphernalia for a camping tour of England and the Continent? The questions were no sooner asked than they were enthusiastically answered by the three women and two boys: there was no reason why not, and they would do it! Nor did Roosevelt raise any objections. " . . . he thought we were perfectly capable," says Marion Dickerman.

But Sara Delano Roosevelt did raise objections—and most emphatically at a Sunday evening dinner in her Hyde Park home in late June.

She sat that evening, as she always did, at the head of the table, with her son the governor at its foot and with Eleanor, Nancy, Marion, Brother, John, and Elliott ranged along its sides. When the subject of the imminent European camping trip came up, she registered her strong disapproval of the whole idea. She doubted that the three women were competent to operate "as chauffeurs" in countries where the rules of the road differed markedly from those of the United States. But even if they were, "the Governor's wife and sons should not visit Europe in such an informal manner." The proposal was unseemly: it betrayed a distressing want of taste and dignity. Her judgment, incisively pronounced in her most regal manner, was of course an insulting commentary upon Eleanor's, and Nancy's and Marion's, judgment. Eleanor had heard it before, however—when the idea of the camping trip was first broached in Sara's presence—and had been unmoved by it. No doubt she would have remained unmoved this time if Brother had not chosen precisely the wrong moment to "venture a wisecrack." He cheerfully opined that his mother probably *would* "land us in the first ditch" and went on to refer to an occasion some years before when she had driven into one of the two stone gateposts at the entrance to the drive into the Big House. Too late he sensed danger. The silence that followed his words was electric, and into that supercharged atmosphere his attempt at retrieval (" . . . but I'm sure we'll be all right") limped helplessly.

Eleanor, who had been sure Brother stood especially firmly on her side in this controversy, felt utterly betrayed. If she looked toward her husband, hoping he would come to her aid, her hope was small: he never did come to her aid in such situations as this. He sat now at the table's foot, silent, seemingly unperturbed, as if unaware that anything was the matter.

She stood up abruptly. She spoke to her mother-in-law.

"Very well," she said, her voice quavering into a high key, "I will see that your grandsons travel in the way in which you think they should be accustomed."

And left the room.

Brother, ordered by his father to go to his mother and bring her back, found her weeping helplessly on the screened porch. With profuse apologies and much abject pleading he did manage to persuade her to return to the table. But she flatly refused, then or later, to return to the camping trip idea, thus greatly distressing her two sons and causing some dismay on the part of Nancy and Marion.[20]

It was a little over a week later that the *Inspector* set out on her "voyage," and if this was neither "rough" nor "exciting," it was by no means devoid of interest, color, activity.

For Eleanor, Brother, and John the "voyage" was to be the initial portion of, and continuous with, their voyage to Europe. While Nancy and Marion drove their Buick in leisurely stages from Val Kill Cottage to Montreal (Eleanor's Chevrolet remained in the garage at Hyde Park), the *Inspector* would journey there in even more leisurely fashion via barge canal and lake and river, arriving sometime during the day on July 26 for what would be publicized as a "good will" visit by the governor of New York and was of course deemed by the public, as it was intended to be, part of the governor's campaign for St. Lawrence hydroelectric-power development. On the evening of that day Roosevelt would give his wife and two sons, and his wife's two closest friends, a bon voyage dinner in the rooftop restaurant of the Mount Royal Hotel, and at midnight the three women and two boys would sail for England aboard the *Regina*, with the Buick in its hold.

All this happened as scheduled.

There were always a good many people aboard the *Inspector*. In addition to the governor's immediate family, including Elliott and, part of the time, Sara Roosevelt, there were Gus Gennerich, Earl Miller, sometimes the governor's Albany secretary, Guernsey Cross, sometimes his New York City one, Louis Howe, sometimes Sam Rosenman. At each of the frequent moorings, beside a sleepy market village or along the waterfront street of a bustling industrial town, a party of local civic leaders, politicians, and selected, often self-selected, plain citizens called upon the governor for give-and-take discussions of their various concerns. At each stop the governor's limousine awaited his use, driven by his longtime personal chauffeur, Montford (Monty) Snyder of Rhinebeck. In it he went to numerous public meetings, where he made impromptu speeches stressing, almost always, agricultural and hydroelectric problems. In it he also went on inspection tours of insane asylums, schools for the deaf, hospitals for crippled children, and other state institutions. Actually it was Eleanor who made the indoor inspections of these facilities. "Walking was so difficult for him [Roosevelt] that he could not go inside an institution and get a real idea of how it was being run from the point of view of overcrowding, staff, food and medical care," she later explained. "I was asked to take over this part of the inspection, and at first my reports were highly unsatisfactory to him."[21] But as a result of his careful coaching and that of Earl Miller, who was knowledgeable about the guile and wiles of officials having something to hide, she soon became, in this as in other matters, a wonderfully efficient extension of her husband's sight, hearing, and judgment.

III

IF there was no lack of personal contacts and personal activity for Roosevelt during this boat tour and the two others he made that summer, tours lasting many weeks, there were yet hours of relative solitude when he sat in silence, unspoken to, in a wicker armchair on the *Inspector*'s glass-roofed decks— hours when his peace and quiet were not disturbed but instead rendered all the more soothing and even, now and then, nap-inducing by the constant low hum and gentle throb of the boat's engine. Especially was this so during his return from the bon voyage at Montreal.

Time slowed almost to a stop. He could drink serenity through his sky-blue eyes until his soul was saturated with it, and he could feel himself really a part of all he saw of the physical state he governed, becoming himself an element of that which he glided through effortlessly at a pace not much faster than that of a fast-walking man, his level gaze not much higher than the fertile topsoil of the richly cropped valleys he looked across toward green pastured or wooded hills. He was vividly in touch: "I would rather see [the natural beauties of the state] . . . while being seated . . . on the deck of a boat going along at a speed of six or seven miles an hour than I would from the most luxurious automobile ever made travelling along at forty or fifty miles an hour," he later said in public speech.[22] The weather, for the most part, was beautiful. Occasionally, the whole of a day was shadowed: curtains of rain rustled and rattled upon the glass roof, and when he looked out from the deck, he found himself confined in a narrow room by dissolving walls of mist. But for the most part the days were bright and wide open, and across them lay no perceived shadows of coming events that were black enough or dank enough to encourage any mushroom growth of anxieties.

There were, however, a few shadows dark enough to give rise to certain tensions in Roosevelt's anticipatory mind. One of them, cast by Jimmy Walker and Tammany Hall, has already been defined. Another was cast by that prophet of wealth for Everyman whose optimism irradiated the current issue of *Ladies' Home Journal.*

John J. Raskob, the continuing chairman of the Democratic National Committee, had done that spring what Roosevelt had long insisted should be done, namely, put the committee on a continuously active basis. A permanent headquarters had been established, financed in large part by personal loans from Raskob to the party, amounting to some $370,000 between 1929 and 1931. A longtime newspaper reporter named Charles Michelson was appointed as its publicity director.[23] A man not unlike Louis Howe in experience, ability, and temperament, Michelson began his career as a Hearst reporter on the West Coast, an employment not encouraging of idealism or ethical sensitivity. He had shifted to Hearst's archrival in New York City, Joseph Pulitzer, becoming in 1917 the chief of the Washington bureau of Pulitzer's *World.* He was cynically romantic or romantically cynical, like Howe, though in him the proportion of cynicism relative to romanticism was considerably higher than in Howe. His quick wit inclined toward acidity, like Howe's, and he had a sense of public opportunities as sharp and dramatic as Howe's. And it is these qualities that were destined to make him, in his new post, a legendary figure in political journalism. This could be foreseen by such people as Howe. It added to the wariness with which Roosevelt viewed the selection of Michelson's immediate superior, the executive director of the new headquarters. The director, Raskob's personal choice, was Jouett Shouse of Kansas City, Kansas. Though Shouse, a wealthy businessman and "fancy dresser" addicted to spats and walking sticks, hence invariably described as "dapper," had great energy and a considerable talent for organization and political manipulation, he shared Raskob's wholehearted devotion to a business-governed America and must therefore be expected to damn as "dangerously radical" proposals emanating from that political position "a little left of center" that Roosevelt had made his own. Of course, Roosevelt had given not the slightest hint of any feeling but enthusiasm when he commented to others on Shouse's appointment. Even in his communications with Howe, from Warm Springs in May, he had said nothing of the doubts they secretly shared over the turn of events. Instead, he spoke of the party advantages to be gained from an energetically active executive director. "Shouse," he said to Howe firmly, "will make an excellent man in Washington."[24] And to "Dear Jouett" he had written, on May 6, 1929, in praise of "a generous and unselfish act" on Shouse's part, adding, "If there is any chance of you making a trip South before June 1st, it would be delightful if you could run down here to Warm Springs. . . . In any event I want to see you as soon as I go North."[25] For he was acutely aware that Shouse would have to be subtly handled if the persistently active headquarters for which Roosevelt had pleaded were not to become a force inimical to Roosevelt's own interests.

Interrelated to a degree with the shadow of coming event that was cast by Raskob were yet others, cast, initially, by New York City's banking troubles.

These came to involve Lieutenant Governor Herbert Lehman and Robert Moses.

When Roosevelt was inaugurated governor, the state superintendent of banks was a Smith appointee, Frank H. Warder, whose term was to expire on July 1 next. But Roosevelt had been barely a month in office when one Francesco M. Ferrari, organizer and president of a private New York City bank called the City Trust Company, died unexpectedly following an appendectomy. City Trust was a bank for "little people," the bulk of them of Italian immigrant extraction, and they were justifiably angry, outraged, and terrified when, eleven days after Ferrari's death, his bank, essentially a one-man concern in which their lifetime savings were deposited, was closed by the bank superintendent. At once there were ugly rumors, increasingly widespread, of criminal misuse of depositors' money by Ferrari, aided and abetted by Warder's deliberate, highly selective neglect of official duty. And when Warder suddenly resigned his post in late April and applied for a passport, having quietly laid plans for a European trip for himself and his family, the rumors became banner-headed news stories. Fortunately, Warder's successor, Joseph A. Broderick, had already been appointed by the governor and confirmed by the state Senate, and was able promptly to take over the vacated office. Roosevelt had by then departed for Warm Springs. In his absence, Lehman, the acting governor, moved swiftly and effectively to protect the administration and the public. Having satisfied himself through immediate inquiries that Warder had been at the very least utterly incompetent and, in all probability, was thoroughly corrupt as well, he immediately appointed a special commissioner armed under the Moreland Act* with full authority and sufficient funds to conduct a thorough investigation of the banking department's operations in the City Trust case. The man he appointed, without prior consultation with Roosevelt by telephone or telegraph, was one whom Roosevelt would *never* have chosen for such an assignment. This man was Robert Moses.

"In the first place, I knew you felt he [Moses] was courageous and of great ability," explained Lehman to Roosevelt, somewhat defensively, in a letter dated April 30; "in the second place, I was convinced that he would work well with the Superintendent of Banks [Broderick] and help in all the steps leading to the reorganization of that department; and, finally, I felt that he would be less likely to disrupt things than would a brand new man. I am sure you will agree with this judgment on my part."[26]

One doubts he was actually so sure of this: he certainly knew of Smith's efforts to have Moses continued as secretary of state and of Roosevelt's flat refusal to do so on grounds of personal antipathy. More probable, more firm, was Lehman's assurance that Roosevelt would (could) express no displeasure

*The Moreland Act was passed by the New York legislature in 1907. It resulted from Charles Evans Hughes's victorious gubernatorial campaign of 1906, waged in the aftermath of, and with reformist energies generated by, Hughes's exposure of criminal practices by the managers of giant New York insurance firms.

over the decision. And evidently Roosevelt did not, though he certainly sniffed danger on this wind of news from the north—a suspicion that Lehman as acting governor just *might* prove more committed to the Smith camp than to Franklin Roosevelt's if faced with an equal choice between the two. The odor of danger, if still too faint to be acknowledged, was rendered more pungent when, at this time, Lehman was invited by Raskob to participate in a national conference on party finances. Was Lehman being groomed by the Smith-Raskob forces as a potential rival of Roosevelt's? The chronically suspicious Howe was at once inclined to think so, though he was also inclined to believe, and said in a letter to his chief after talking to Lehman, that the acting governor had no notion and no intention of being so used.[27] Suspicion allayed, however, was not suspicion destroyed: Lehman would have to be carefully watched and possibly as subtly handled, with extreme covert care, as Jouett Shouse. As for the all-too-brilliant and ambitious Moses, he must of course be prevented from capitalizing on this new opportunity in any way that could seriously endanger Roosevelt's own ambition.

Hence Roosevelt had not been pleased by the amount and kind of publicity given the Moreland commissioner's report and Robert Moses personally when the report was officially presented to the governor on July 9. Nor was he truly pleased by the report itself, despite, or, rather, *because* of, the fact that Moses succinctly summarized an investigation of remarkable thoroughness, derived from it incontrovertible conclusions of guilt and innocence, and based upon it recommendations for sweeping changes in the banking laws, along with a drastic overhaul of the state banking department, which were as logically convincing as they were bold and incisive. Clearly, on the evidence, said Moses, the collapse of City Trust was due to Ferrari's "dishonest management," of which Moses gave details. Warder was a "faithless public official" who, in return for "gifts and gratuities including money and securities," had "deliberately prevented exposure" of Ferrari's criminal operations.* And the whole affair, coming hard on the heels of the Clarke Bros. failure,† pointed unmistakably to the need for drastic revisions of existing banking law. At present, only 10 percent of the private banks were supervised, though the public had been led to believe that all of them were—and certainly all of them should be, rigorously. Under existing law, a distinction was made—in effect, by the bankers themselves!—between thrift and savings accounts, the former being unrestricted as to how they might be invested whereas the latter were regulated, if inadequately. Certainly, savings and thrift accounts in banks other

---

*Warder was eventually tried and convicted of accepting a $10,000 bribe from Ferrari. He was sentenced to a five- to ten-year term in the penitentiary.

†Clarke Bros., a private bank, failed in April 1929 because the bank's managers had used depositors' money for their own speculations and had been caught when the stock market broke badly in late March. Six weeks later, having made full disclosure of their wrongdoing and having promised to liquidate their private holdings to pay off depositors, who eventually received a few cents of every dollar deposited, all four of the bank's top managers received prison sentences, one of them suspended.

than savings banks should be subjected to the same laws that governed investments by savings banks. There should be strict regulation of the issuance of securities "whether they be those of a bank or a utility company." There should be a law prohibiting top officials in the banking department from "holding, owning or speculating" in securities they were supposed to supervise. Moses also strongly recommended that no new private banks be permitted to open, there being "no good reason for them," and that existing private banks "be given a period of two years in which to convert into state or national banks." He singled out for special condemnation the current banking practice of creating affiliates, financed with depositors' money, through which bank officials speculated for their personal profit. The state-chartered, hence deceivingly named, Bank of United States in New York City, which had nearly a half-million depositors of generally modest means, was one of the worst offenders in this as in other respects, said he.[28]

Walter Lippmann editorialized that the Moses Report was the best of its kind he had ever read. Franklin Roosevelt made no public comment on it at all: he referred it without recommendation to the legislature's Joint Committee on Banking and Investment Trusts. Subsequently, he appointed a special Commission on Revision of the Banking Law, to which, in a sharply pointed snub, he did *not* name Robert Moses. Among those he did name was, incredibly, a director and vice-president of the Bank of United States, Henry Pollock by name!

Obviously Roosevelt would not have acted so had he, looking out from placid waters across the smiling summer landscape of 1929, recognized as imminent a most important "coming event," which he had long vaguely anticipated, some of whose causes he had long vaguely perceived and among whose expected consequences was national triumph for the Democratic Party.

One foreshadowing of it may have lain more darkly, more heavily across his mind as his upstate travels continued into August than it had before these travels began: his many conversations with farm folk at stops along the way brought him into vivid contact with the human effects of the worsening farm depression. He had often expressed his belief that a healthy national economy absolutely required a prosperous agriculture, that the inability of farm families to consume their fair share of the total industrial output placed dangerously severe limits upon the growth of the industrial market and could mean a disastrous contraction of it if foreign buying slowed. He was therefore well prepared to recognize current farm troubles as portents of greater trouble to come. He was even better prepared for an immediate sympathetic understanding of these troubles, in human terms, by his own living experience as country gentleman—his love for fields, meadows, woods, clear-flowing streams like Val Kill, his Jeffersonian inclination to equate health and virtue with country life, sickness and wickedness with great cities. Indeed, aesthetic and moral considerations far outweighed economic ones in determining Roosevelt's concern for agriculture as "a way of life." He in fact regarded the economic as wholly a means toward ends that were aesthetic and moral and that required, in his view, a continuation of the individual family farm as the basic agricultural unit. It was therefore ironical, if also typical, that his specific policy dealings with farm economics should contain implicit contradictions of the ends at which they were aimed.

He took sorrowful note of the fact that acres as fertile as they had been two generations ago, when they had "provided a prosperous livelihood for an intelligent and progressive population," could now provide no adequate livelihood for a significantly smaller number of families despite the development of new and improved crop varieties, the scientific breeding of better dairy and meat animals, the increased per acre yields resulting from the use of fertilizers and crop rotations, and the increased per capita productive capacity of farmers through new farm-machinery applications. He expressed no awareness whatever that farm mechanization was itself a threat, a fatal threat as things were then going, to the family farm he longed to preserve. Instead, he said that there was "necessarily a limit to the continuance of the migration from the country to the city" and that he looked "for a swing of the pendulum in the other direction" because the United States had "perhaps come to the period when industrial expansion will slow up,"[29] a wishful thought that, though it accorded with current theories of a "mature economy," was in his case sustained if not basically determined by his religious sense of history and of his own historic role. But at the same time he proposed "solutions" to the "farm problem" that implied, clearly, that the family farm was rapidly approaching its end as a viable self-determining economic unit. In June President Hoover had signed the Agricultural Marketing Act, under which a Federal Farm Board, chaired by Hoover-appointed Alexander Legge, president of International Harvester, was assigned a revolving fund of $500,000,000 of federal moneys to stabilize the farm market. The Farm Board was to do this through loans to national marketing cooperatives, which, stimulated by the act, were being rapidly organized for all the major staples; such loans would enable them to build storage facilities and keep off the market, until prices went up, products currently in market surplus. The Farm Board was further authorized to engage in direct market operations in support of farm prices, but this was a principle-violating amendment to the original bill that Hoover accepted only because doing so seemed necessary to secure the bill's passage through the Senate (Farm Bloc senators insisted upon it); he hoped and trusted it would be unused. The farm proposals that Roosevelt made were also concerned with techniques for increasing marketing efficiency through cooperative action. For instance, he proposed that farmers organize "vegetable sheds" in extension of the "milk shed" device by which dairy farmers planned their production and, through cooperative marketing, strengthened their bargaining position vis-à-vis city processors and distributors. Unlike the President, however, the governor recognized a need for major structural changes in the agricultural economy as a whole, as well as changes in general taxation policy, in order to maintain or restore what he deemed a "healthy balance" (that is, an equality of emphasis) between agriculture and industry, country and city, in the nation's life. Too much emphasis was now being placed on property taxes, he asserted, and too little on the taxation of corporate profits and the high personal incomes derived from industry. This meant that a disproportionate share of the tax burden was being borne by farmers, along with homeowners of low or moderate income. Specifically for agriculture, he pointed definitely toward a considerable measure of "planned economy" involving, necessarily, the direct use of governmental powers and institutions.

"I have long been interested in the general subject of city and regional planning," he said in an address to some 500 members of the Wyoming County Historical Society at Silver Lake on August 15, 1929. In this most important of his summer tour speeches he went on to predict "a day when, throughout the length and breadth of the United States, zones will be established for the production and consumption of whatever the soil within that zone is best fitted to raise and whatever the demands of consumption require." He deplored the fact that a large proportion of the agricultural land was now being used to produce "the wrong kind of crop"—wrong in terms of an efficient economic adaptation to soil, climate, and consumption pattern. He further deplored the dearth of accurate data on which to base intelligent plans and the dilatory fashion in which the needed data were being gathered, when gathered at all. At the present rate of progress, he said, the national soil survey being conducted by the U.S. Department of Agriculture could not be completed for another thirty years! He therefore proposed that New York "lead the way [toward national zoning] with a great farm survey" of its own, a historic "first" in that never before had a "regional plan . . . been extended to take in a whole State." His Agricultural Advisory Commission, he announced, had planned such a survey. It embraced five projects: (1) the swift completion of the soil survey of the state and the preparation of detailed soil maps; (2) the compilation of all available long-term weather statistics for the state; (3) the classification of all land in the state for agricultural, forest, recreational, or residential purposes; (4) the compilation of detailed information on present land use for comparison with "best use . . . including charts for vegetables, forests, and pastures"; and (5) cost studies for milk production under various existing systems of dairying. Obviously all this could not be done in a single year, but it could and should be started at the next session of the legislature, for its beneficial importance was as great as its cost was small. The estimated annual cost for the first three years was a mere $110,000.[30]

Equally obvious, though left unstated, was the fact that "regional planning" involved to a very considerable degree the substitution of governmental decision-making for "free enterprise" in the one major segment of the overall economy in which economic individualism was still, if ever more feebly, the rule rather than the exception. Drastic shifts in land use, with severe limitations of the production of certain crops, were implied, and these changes could not be effected without the use of the coercive powers of the state. . . .

But again, though his mind thus dwelt upon agricultural ills and their cure, though he evinced an awareness that these ills uncured were weakening the economy as a whole, though he was aware of ominous declines in construction* and in automobile sales during the preceding two years, and though he had long predicted an end "sometime" of the Republican Prosperity, Roosevelt gave no sign of recognition in August 1929 that the "sometime" might be tomorrow, and unprecedentedly catastrophic. He did express that month, as he had before, his negative reaction to the current and increasingly blatant prosperity ballyhoo. Raskob's *Ladies' Home Journal* article evidently stimulated him, in an idle hour aboard the *Inspector,* to make an arithmetical examination of its basic assumption, to wit, that the price of "good common stocks" must inevitably and forever rise at approximately the rate currently recorded on the stock exchange. (How otherwise could anyone have "at least" $80,000 as a result of investing $15 in stocks every week for twenty years—a total investment of $15,600? And how could this $80,000 provide thereafter an income of "around $400 a month" unless it was taken out of the stock market altogether and put into a 6-percent savings account? Current stock earnings were much less than 6 percent.) "Do you still feel as I do that there may be a limit to the increase of security values?" he asked a St. Louis banker friend rhetorically, in a letter dated August 5, wherein he disparaged the judgment of "those business circles which can only see a fifty per cent increase in prosperity and values for every year that goes by between now and the year 2000."[31]

Roosevelt returned to Albany and Hyde Park from the first of his waterway tours in early August. After a few days he embarked upon his second tour, and then, when this second was completed, upon a third. He dealt with various and sundry matters relating to utilities, prisons, hospitals, bank regulation. On August 23 he sent to newspapers in all counties outside the New York City area open letters addressed to local taxpayers listing local tax savings resulting from the farm tax relief legislation that had passed the last session of the legislature. And on virtually every trading day he, with millions of other Americans, read on the front page of whatever daily newspaper came to hand the continuing story of the stock market's soaring higher, higher, with only minor dips in the upward climb—until, on September 3, 1929, it touched its highest point ever in the bright blue sky.

On that Tuesday following the Labor Day holiday weekend, 4,500,000 shares were traded. By that date, stock holdings acquired on March 3, 1928, and held through intervening stock splits and rights issues, with the rights fully exercised, had increased in price from 77 to 181⅞ for American Can, from 54½ to 162 for Anaconda Copper, from 128¾ to 396¼ for General Electric, from 92½ to 505 for RCA, from 145 to 413⅝ for Union Carbide, from 89¾ to 203⅝ for Electric Bond and Share, and from 91⅝ to 313 for Westinghouse. Similar gains had been registered for many other stocks. A securities

---

*Of construction industry troubles Roosevelt was especially aware. For six years, 1922–1928, he had been president of the American Construction Council, the building industry's national trade association. The post was unsalaried and carried no executive authority, but it provided Roosevelt with a liberal education in the evils that sprang from the total lack of intelligent overall planning in this crucially important field. See *FDR: The Beckoning of Destiny,* pages 700–704.

price index using 1926 prices as the equivalent of 100, compiled by the Standard Statistics Company, showed an upward movement of 404 stocks from 183.6 in January 1929 to 253.3 in September of that year.[32] Nor was there any widespread conviction that this height of speculative profit was precarious, hazardous not only for those who rode at its top but for everyone beneath it. The majority opinion among those "experts" who published their opinions was that stock prices could continue to rise, or at least remain on that "permanently high plateau" that Yale's brilliant economist Irving Fisher thought he described and would publicly proclaim, to his subsequent great regret, a few weeks hence.

IV

MEANWHILE, Eleanor Roosevelt with her two closest friends and two youngest sons was making in England and on the Continent a journey that might later be deemed symbolic, for it crossed landscapes whose contours were historical and whose vistas were ordered by symbolic structures of the most profound cultural significance—and this on the very eve of a historical event that would prove as traumatic in its effects upon the lives of great masses of Western men as had been the Great War of 1914–1918, to which it was causally linked. Even at the time there were segments of this journey that were like a pilgrimage to sacred shrines for Eleanor and at least one of her companions. As such, they were rich in felt symbolic meanings.

Yet the trip was not truly happy. For this, Eleanor herself was in good part to blame.

As anticipated by her, she had considerable difficulty in controlling the immense, frequently quarrelsome energies of her teenage sons. No doubt she would have had in any case, but she would have had considerably less, and the trip's cost in money, about which she also worried, would also have been considerably less had she not stubbornly literally adhered to the bitter promise made at her mother-in-law's table during that Sunday evening dinner in late June. In England she rented a Daimler with a chauffeur, to whom the boys took an instant violent dislike. And while her two friends drove ahead or behind in their Buick roadster or took side trips to places that interested them, she herself rode with two fuming boys directly from here to there in the luxury car's back seat, and with the boys always very properly "dressed up." It was the same in Belgium, Germany, France, though the chauffeur hired in Belgium, named Willie, happened to be a man the boys liked. Thus did she punish Franklin, Jr., for the grievous hurt he had inadvertently given her ("Poor Brother paid dearly for his mistake!" Marion Dickerman would remember long afterward), but she also punished the others of her party by depriving them of some of the ease and pleasure that would otherwise have been theirs. Eleanor herself would remember that in "every city where we stayed, we climbed bell towers, and I tried to walk my sons in the evenings" because "I wanted them to be so weary that they would not start roughhousing before they went to bed, since roughhousing usually turned into a battle royal." She "many times . . . wrote to my husband how glad I should be to get home."[33]

Of England they made a cultural tour. It ranged from the prehistoric religious mysteries of Stonehenge's huge monoliths to the medieval Christian mysteries of Salisbury and Winchester cathedrals, from the turbulent poetic passions of the Elizabethans (they visited Hampton Court, Stratford-on-Avon) to the nature-loving serenities, the disciplined passions, of Wordsworth (they spent a day or two in the Lake District), and in modern times, from the contemplative academic life of Oxford dons to the active, nervous, highly pressured life of denizens of the City.

To this last they were introduced by a friend whom Marion Dickerman and Nancy Cook had made during the Great War, when these two had served on the all-women staff of the Endell Street Hospital in London. She was Helena Hirst. Her husband was Francis W. Hirst, editor of the *Economist.*[34] And in the Hirst home the three touring women heard and participated in talk of the vast economic dislocations caused by the war, of the close economic interdependence of the United States and Europe, and of the anxieties therefore aroused in European capitals by the new tariff bill (Hawley-Smoot) then being shaped by the American Congress. Dozens of formal protests against the high rates proposed by the new bill had come to the U.S. State Department from foreign diplomats in recent weeks, each of them stressing the rate schedule's threat to foreign trade—its almost certainly fatal threat to any such expansion of U.S. foreign trade as President Hoover had said he desired. How could Europe possibly pay for American goods if Americans refused to buy in Europe? There was talk, too, in the Hirst home, of the dire effect the American stock-market boom was having upon the German economy. Beginning in 1924, with the adoption of the Dawes Plan for German war reparations payments, a tide of American loans, handled by American bankers as private transactions, had poured into Germany, and continued pouring through 1928. These loans had been the chief means and prop of German economic recovery, enabling Germany to make reparations payments to the Allies, who, in turn, were enabled to make payments on war debt to the United States. But now the lending was being sharply reduced. American call-money rates as high as 15 percent were sucking into Wall Street speculation savings that would otherwise have gone, at lower interest, into German bonds (American loans to Germany had totaled $1 billion for the year 1928; they would total less than one fourth that amount in 1929). Consequently, German business had gone into a dangerous slump. Unemployment had risen sharply, providing an increasing abundance of political ammunition for both the Communists and the Nazis. The bloody riots marking 1929's May Day demonstrations across the length and breadth of Germany had been ominous. Francis Hirst was frankly worried. Though he hoped the new Young Plan would prove as efficacious as the Dawes Plan had been in staving off catastrophe, he was far from convinced that it would be, hence far from sanguine about the long-term survival possibilities of the Weimar Republic.

But when Eleanor and her party drove their two cars from Belgium into the

Rhineland a few days later, they saw no sign of economic distress or political unrest. From the cathedral tower of Cologne they looked down upon a peaceful town of ancient, seemingly eternal prosperity. Peace, prosperity, and a scenic beauty akin to that of the Hudson River Valley, if more spectacular, were everywhere about them as they rode a small steamer, their cars in its hold, up the castle-dotted Rhine from Cologne to Coblenz. And in Coblenz, peace of the kind that passeth understanding on its way into the heart was with them through a night they spent in a particularly beautiful and prosperous hotel on the bank of the great river.

It was a soft warm night, lit by a full moon. Over the river-fronting balcony and through the open windows of the room that Nancy and Marion shared came the sound of music drifting up from barges that sailed slowly down the river, filled with young Germans singing sweet, sadly sentimental German songs. Marion took her mattress out onto the balcony. Soon she was joined there by Brother. The woman and boy, who had long had a special rapport, spent most of the night there, listening to the songs and looking up into a sky that was ink-black, though spangled by stars, and down upon the river and across it to the great fort whose grim lines were softened and silvered by moonlight. They talked in desultory fashion of many things, but most memorably of the human meaning of the war whose battlefields they were soon to tour. It was a meaning sharpened for Marion by the juxtaposition of her present sense experience with her remembrance of bloody horrors she had first witnessed in Endell Street during the spring of 1918, when British casualties poured in from the last great German offensive along the Somme. Most of these young masculine voices now singing into the mild air, said the woman to the boy, would have been shouting harsh martial slogans in march time along the streets of Coblenz a dozen years ago, had they then been the age they now were. They would have become part of the collective voice of the hated bestial Hun. And some of them might have become voices screaming into the stinking air of no-man's-land, screaming in the agony of wounds dealt by American boys who were little older than Brother now was. Perhaps only two or three years older.

For while Brother lay upon the balcony that night, he entered upon the first hours of his fifteenth birthday, August 17, 1929.

In morning light, a few hours later, he and Marion begged his mother to grant him, as a birthday present, permission to change places with Nancy Cook for the drive from Coblenz to Luxembourg—let Nancy ride in the back seat of the chauffeured limousine and let him ride in the Buick roadster, with Marion behind its wheel. Eleanor did not reply at once. There was a long moment's struggle between her generalized compassion and her particularized, harshly punitive will. But at last she relented. Permission was granted.

And neither Brother nor Marion ever forgot their ride together that day in the open car (they took the top down because the day was bright, warm, with hardly a cloud in a lapis lazuli sky). They drove up the narrow winding valley of the Moselle along a road over which German armies had marched toward the invasion of France in 1870 and 1914, over which a hundred armies had marched since the last Roman legion made its last retreat southeastward from the Teutonic fury, but where now there was no sign that war had ever come this way or could ever come. A smiling green-mantled peace crowned with gold sat fat and happy upon a harvest landscape of clover and grain and grape as they passed through farming country similar in some respects to that in which Marion had been born and raised (Chautauqua County, New York), a hilly country of vineyards, of wine making. They talked and laughed together in a joy of release, almost as if they were two children playing hookey from school, during a long afternoon, until, tanned by sun and wind, they came near dusk into the mountains of Luxembourg and to the city of Luxembourg, where at the hotel that evening there was a gay birthday dinner for Brother. Toasts were drunk, not in the pale sweet wine of that country but in the sparkling dry white wine of the country toward which they would head on the morrow.[35]

For the next day they drove their two cars southeastward into France toward Champagne, against whose northern boundary on the Marne the iron-gray German hordes had pushed, bloodily, futilely, in August 1914 and again in June 1918. They stopped at Verdun, having driven across Lorraine, and visited there the great monument inscribed "They Shall Not Pass," as well as the underground concrete quarters in which thousands of men had lived for weeks on end as if entombed alive (Roosevelt had told his sons of the miserable sleepless night he himself had spent there in the summer of 1918) before they were killed or wounded as they manned the trenches above. Eleanor pointed out to her sons how grass, the "forgiveness of nature,"[36] was healing the wounds four years of bloody battle had dealt the landscape now spread so peacefully before their eyes, how it now covered "the ditches . . . dug by soldiers for their protection, and the curious holes made by bursting shells." She pointed out, too, that the old Argonne Forest through which they rode, and through which American National Guard divisions had driven in the fall of 1918 as part of the greatest battle operation Americans had thus far ever engaged in, was now a forest of young trees rising above whitened stumps, and that the streets of ancient towns and villages they passed through on their way from Verdun to Rheims were lined by new buildings. She tried thus to convey to the boys some sense of the ruin, the desolation, that had prevailed here, for as far as the eye could see, barely ten years before. She did not feel she succeeded. But the boys *were* visibly impressed by the vast war cemeteries with their endless rows of white crosses (they visited the grave of Quentin Roosevelt, TR's aviator son, who died when his plane was shot down behind the German lines in 1918) and by the fact, upon which Brother remarked, that there were "only boys our age and old men coming out of the fields" at day's end; " . . . there don't seem to be any men of father's age."[37]

It was during their last days in France, the last of their whole European tour, that the portion of the journey was made that was most rich in felt symbolic meanings for Eleanor and Marion.

Their way from Paris to the sea lay through Chartres. There the practical-minded and managerial Nancy Cook took the two boys to a cattle show while Eleanor and Marion went together to the great cathedral and spent hours walking around it and through it. They were well prepared to see and feel significances. On chill summer nights on Campobello, seated before a flaming fireplace in the Roosevelt cottage after the boys had been sent to bed, Eleanor often read aloud to her two close friends from books that especially interested her. Among these had been *Mont-Saint-Michel and Chartres,* conceived by its author to be a study in thirteenth-century unity, and *The Education of Henry Adams,* conceived by its author to be a study in twentieth-century multiplicity. Hence it was with a vision conditioned by the history-haunted symbolic vision of Henry Adams that Marion and Eleanor, riding their separate cars from Paris southwestward across a somber landscape, first saw the great and lovely mismatched spires of the cathedral rising some 300 feet above the clustered roofs of the town.[38] They may well have been reminded of what Adams had said about the shift of religious emphasis from the masculine to the feminine, from God the Father and Jesus the Son to Mary the Mother of God, during the intensely religious century that intervened between the uplifting of the militant archangel upon his towering sea-washed Norman rock and the aspiration of this Notre Dame of Chartres to an even greater height above a flat dull plain. They may well have been struck by the fact, which might have seemed "relevant" to them, that a great gain in beauty had come from this shift of emphasis—and without loss of strength! " . . . no architecture that ever grew on earth, except the Gothic, gave this effect of flinging passion against the sky," Adams had said of Chartres and of the eighty cathedrals, the five hundred churches of cathedral class, that were built in France during the century after Chartres neared completion, under the protection and for the glory of the Blessed Virgin. Of all these, Chartres remained the most impressive. And now, close up, Eleanor and Marion studied the statuary of the church portals, where no cruelty or pain was figured but only love and compassion: the sculpted life of Christ from Nativity to Ascension made no mention of Jesus' torture-death upon the Cross. They then entered upon the vast vaulted spaces and unearthly beauty of nave and apse. They saw and felt the very light of Heaven slanting down upon them through the incredibly brilliant twelfth-century colored glass of perhaps the most beautiful windows ever made in the world. Here, truly, dwelt the Virgin. Here one sensed the ultimate triumph of the feminine princi-ple, Notre Dame as the vital unifying force of the medieval synthesis that reached its height of perfection in the century opened by Chartres' construc-tion. And when the two women emerged at last from the cathedral door into the town square, where Nancy awaited them with the two boys who had been rendered hot, soiled, quarrelsome, by their hours in the cattle fair, it was as if they stepped from a dream of queen-ruled Heaven into an all-too-worldly world—walked out of the infinite peace and silence of eternity into a noisy, crowded, closed-in bustle of male-dominated time—yet with much of the immense hushed dream still clinging to them.

From Chartres they drove the next day to Mont-Saint-Michel.

A flood tide of evening was pouring onto the Norman beach when they arrived, transforming peninsula into island. A setting sun splashed the color of blood across the western sky and over the shining sea. Against that sky, above that sea, the vast pile of Mont-Saint-Michel rose up in darkening silhouette for those who watched from the mainland shore—a masculine erection surely, upthrust from fortress base through vertical castled walls above the granite cliff, then narrowing, tapering, concentrating, until at its ultimate point, pressing into the heavens, it was as sharp as Michael's wrathful sword. No Virgin here. No dualism of masculine-feminine principle. No hint, even, of Holy Trinity. The whole of the silhouette had a single masculine aspiration: it was instinct with the priest-blessed warrior energies of the Norman duke who sailed for England with his host in 1066 and with those of the Normans who in 1097 were the commanding will and chief martial power of the First Crusade.

But scarcely two hours later the travelers saw all this in a different light.

By then the blood had drained from the heavens into the sea, and was from the surface of the sea itself withdrawn, as the sun sank far below the horizon of the English Channel toward an American dawn. Night had come to Normandy, such a night, mysteriously silver-bright and -shadowed, as Marion and Brother had shared upon the balcony above the Rhine weeks before. The air was mild. A bright moon rode high in the sky. So Marion found a boatman who for a fee rowed them around the island, so that they might see the immense church militant from every side and angle but with all its hard upthrusting lines softened, feminized by the moon's radiance as the lines of the great fort of Coblenz had been. It was as if the Virgin, as a force, was triumphing even here, for Saint Michael seemed to yearn toward her as he looked far out across the "immense tremor of the ocean" from his Mount in Peril of the Sea.[39] Yet the strength of the warrior archangel remained unimpaired! Indeed, the aspiring synthesizing unifying force seemed actually greater in this silver light of the night than it had in the red light of evening.

Two days later the travelers sailed from Cherbourg for home. On September 15 they entered New York harbor.

Young John had developed a severe earache in midpassage. He had suffered greatly, and his mother and her two friends had become almost frantic with worry before, quite abruptly, he recovered. All of them were travel-worn, eager for home. "On landing," Eleanor remembered twenty years later, "I breathed a sigh of relief and made a vow that never again would I take a trip on which I had to be responsible for the young."[40] None of them, therefore, was in a mood of symbolic vision when, from the deck of their ship, the *Belgenland,* they gazed upon the Statue of Liberty and the towers of the world city.

Had they been in the mood, Eleanor and Marion might have remarked, as Adams did in January 1901 and again in November 1904, when he, too, voyaged homeward from Cherbourg[41]—might have remarked how different was this skyline of New York City from the Gothic passion that had been flung a half-thousand times and more against the sky of France in the century between 1170 and 1270. That passion's forms remained fixed against the sky. The New York skyline was, in comparison, like the smoke clouds made by a continuous series of explosions. Its shapes, measured by the rhythms of world history, were almost as ephemeral as smoke, a fluid chaos of physical energies tossed up in mindless random, with barely enough viscosity to exhibit the more obvious properties of a solid through a single given hour. And in September 1929 no more, indeed much less, than in January 1919, when she had sailed for France with her husband beside her and Adams' *Education* in her luggage,* could Eleanor have discerned here a pattern of purpose human or divine. There was no rational design whatever. All was anarchy—an anarchy of stupendous forces gone out of control. All was Change—driving and driven Change—with nothing of the Permanent, no hint anywhere of the Eternal.

True it was that the Woolworth Building yet remained, in 1929 as in 1919, the tallest of all these jumbled upthrustings of "twentieth century multiplicity." But this would not be so a few months hence. Rising on Forty-second Street was the Chrysler Building of sixty-eight stories, whose proposed construction had been pridefully announced by the automobile manufacturer Walter P. Chrysler a year before: its height of 1,045 feet would be 254 feet greater than that of Woolworth's Cathedral of Commerce. And just two weeks before, Pierre S. Du Pont and John J. Raskob had announced their organization of a new corporation to raise an office building of 102 stories at the corner of Thirty-fourth Street and Fifth Avenue, where the old Waldorf-Astoria Hotel had stood for decades. Demolition of the latter structure was to begin shortly. The Empire State Building, as the proposed Raskob–Du Pont structure had been named, would be 1,250 feet high, 200 feet higher than the Chrysler Building!

These height statistics had been interesting to Eleanor, Nancy, and Marion when they read them in the Paris *Herald* after a strenuous day of sightseeing. But considerably more interesting to them was the announcement that the president of Empire State, Inc., was none other than Raskob's great and good friend Alfred E. Smith. This was reassuring news to anyone committed, by choice or necessity, to Franklin Roosevelt's political fortunes. It signified that Al yet remained true to his announced resolve never again to seek elective office, a resolve that, if maintained, would greatly simplify matters for any other Democrat possessed of presidential ambitions.

Eleanor continued dubious of this resolve, however. Some two weeks after the *Belgenland* docked she would read on the front page of the Sunday book section of the New York *Times* a review by Henry F. Pringle of Al Smith's just published autobiography, *Up to Now*. The very title suggested to Pringle, as it did to Eleanor, that Smith, for all his disclaimers, yet remained a hopeful as well as potent national political figure. "It is wholly absurd that a man of

*See pages 549–551 of *FDR: The Beckoning of Destiny.*

his talents, with a following of millions," wrote Pringle, "should now devote his time to so relatively trivial an undertaking as the construction of another skyscraper in New York."[42]

V

ARRIVING at 49 East Sixty-fifth Street on that Sunday, September 15, 1929, Eleanor was at once returned to the world of great affairs she had left so reluctantly two months before. If she immersed herself in that morning's New York *Times*, as it would have been natural for her to do who had been so long remote from the flow of events vitally interesting to her, she read chapters of several continuing news stories that were directly or tangentially relevant to her husband's, and her own, political concerns.

Jouett Shouse, chairman of the Democratic National Committee, had spoken at a luncheon meeting of the Massachusetts Democratic State Committee in Boston the day before. He had denounced President Hoover for maintaining silence while the special session of Congress called for farm relief concocted a tariff bill whose higher rates, the highest ever, chiefly benefited big industry.* The Hawley-Smoot bill, said Shouse, was "a monstrosity that, in many of its provisions, is the most vicious, the most reprehensible, the most unnecessary in our economic history." But before thus voicing in harsh generality the discontents that sparked a Democratic–Progressive Republican coalition's battle against the bill in Congress (though the "working man may worry because his shoes cost a dollar or two more, truffles for his *pâté de foie gras* are on the free list," Democratic Congressman McClintic of Oklahoma had remarked acidly two weeks before[43]), Shouse paid glowing tribute to Al Smith, whose tariff views, insofar as the ex-governor's parochialism permitted him to have them, were approximately those of the big industrialist Raskob.† It appeared from the *Times* account that Shouse had joined to this praise of Smith an assertion "that political activity should be continuous and not confined to the few months preceding a campaign," a linkage that may well have induced thoughtfulness on Roosevelt's part. And Eleanor's.

In Washington, D.C., a three-man subcommittee of the Senate Naval Affairs Committee, comprising Republican Senator Samuel M. Shortridge of Califor-

---

*Seldom had a Congress proved more frankly eager to do the bidding of big-business special interests. Republican Senator Hiram Bingham of Connecticut had actually placed on the Senate payroll as a tariff "expert" a high-tariff lobbyist for the Connecticut Manufacturers Association! Bingham then assailed in "discourteous language" on the Senate floor the lobby committee that exposed and criticized this cozy arrangement. He went a bit too far, even in that climactic summer of the New Economic Era. Subsequently, by a vote of 54 to 22, with the Republican old guard voting a solid "nay," the Senate adopted a resolution offered by Senator George Norris in which the Connecticut senator was "condemned" for "action . . . contrary to good morals and senatorial ethics."

†Raskob subsequently joined the chorus of those who begged Hoover to veto the Hawley-Smoot bill, but his reason for doing so was more politically partisan than it was a conviction of the iniquity of high protectionism.

nia, Republican Senator Henry Allen of Kansas, and Democratic Senator
Robinson of Arkansas, was about to open public hearings on sensational
charges made by one William B. Shearer, a self-proclaimed naval expert and
big navy lobbyist. Shearer was suing three U.S. shipbuilding companies for
$250,000 he claimed they owed him, by prior agreement, for his successful
effort to frustrate the purposes of the three-power Geneva Naval Limitation
Conference of 1927. One of the three companies was Bethlehem Shipbuilding,
a subsidiary of Bethlehem Steel, and Senator Shortridge had announced the
day before that Charles M. Schwab, head of Bethlehem Steel, was among the
several big-business executives being called for early testimony. Had Shearer
been called? a reporter wanted to know. No, he had not been, Senator Shortridge replied. Would he be? No doubt, the Senator said. But later on. This
strange reversal of logical procedure, whereby the defense against grave
charges was to be spread upon the record before the charges themselves were
made, had obviously aroused the suspicions of the *Times* reporter. *Why,* he
had asked, were the business executives being called first? Because that was
the way the senators had decided to do it, the senator replied. "Our purpose,"
he said, as if this "purpose" had been questioned, "is to get at the truth." And
eventually much of the unsavory truth *would* be "got at," despite the reluctance of the three conservative senators to press lines of inquiry embarrassing
to the big-business men brought before them. Sworn testimony would show
that Shearer had indeed been hired as a lobbyist and propagandist by ship-
builders and other interests who stood to profit from large naval appropriations and high merchant marine subsidies; that his efforts to prevent naval
reduction at the Geneva conference had been effective; that his efforts to shape
and secure enactment of the Jones-White Merchant Marine Bill a year later
had been equally effective; that his work had been aided by highly confidential
contacts with Navy Department officials; that William Randolph Hearst had
hired him as "patriotic" propagandist at $2,000 a month; that his propaganda
had included vicious personal attacks upon the patriotism of peace and disarmament advocates; and that he had contributed draft speeches and propaganda articles to the Republican National Committee during the 1928 campaign. The point of the Shearer story was sharpened for such minds as Eleanor
Roosevelt's, on this September 15, by an adjacent front-page report that
France, Italy, and Japan were busy establishing their negotiating positions on
naval armaments, now that the United States and Britain had announced they
were "prepared to enter an international conference on naval limitation and
reduction," to open in London a few months hence. Japan, it was said, would
ask for a 10-10-7 ratio (7 for Japan) on cruisers and smaller craft, this conference being called to place restrictions on these as the Washington Conference
had placed them on battleships in 1922.
    Eleanor might also see or feel connections between the Shearer story and
one that had come out of Geneva the day before. There the League of Nations
Assembly, "unanimously and without discussion," had adopted "the protocol
containing the Root formula for satisfying U.S. Senate reservations" regarding

the World Court, thus opening the way for U.S. adherence to the Court. This was gratifying to one who remained fervently committed to U.S. participation in the League and its subsidiary organizations. Of greater, more immediate, concern to her, however, was the report from Washington of a statement issued by Senator Thomas J. Walsh of Montana. Walsh termed "ominous" the recent purchase by the Morgan interests of the Frontier Corporation in New York. It placed in jeopardy the entire St. Lawrence seaway and water-power development project, he said. And Eleanor, when she arrived at the East Sixty-fifth Street house, found her husband preoccupied with a public statement of his own on this same matter, one that would be reported in next morning's *Times* under a two-column headline on the top right-hand side of the front page:

ROOSEVELT DECLARES DEAL
BY MORGAN FORCES STATE
TO ACT TO DEVELOP POWER

5

The Coming on of the Great Depression

I

IT is unlikely that either Eleanor or the governor paid any special attention on that Sunday or Monday to stock-market news, but they may have noted in the financial section, on September 15, a headline, MANY STOCKS BELOW HIGH POINT OF YEAR, under which it was reported that heavy liquidation had obviously been "going on recently" with declines "here and there ranging from 20 to 70 points." (There had, in fact, been a sharp market break on September 5, just two days after the all-time high, whereupon Roger Babson had renewed his prediction of a general collapse "sooner or later" that would drive stocks down 60 to 80 points. But a considerable measure of recovery had immediately followed, encouraging those who wished to believe that the Great Bull Market would soon be again surging onward, upward. It had happened before.)

Roosevelt went to Warm Springs a day or so later, accompanied by Eleanor. After a few days she left him there and returned to New York City to help Marion Dickerman prepare for the opening of the fall school term at Todhunter on October 1. Roosevelt remained in Warm Springs until mid-October with Missy and his beloved "gang" of fellow polio victims—sunbathing, picknicking, engaging in therapeutic exercises, swimming in the thermal pool. He was not wholly out of the news. On October 2 he told reporters he had no intention of replying to repeated demands by Republicans and political independents, such as La Guardia and Norman Thomas, that he initiate an investigation into the murder of Arnold Rothstein. Not while he was in Georgia. He was on vacation, he said. He even made oblique reference to his special health reasons for needing rest and relaxation. A week later, however, he addressed a luncheon meeting of the Macon (Georgia) Rotary Club. In his speech, which was nationally reported, he urged government aid for "1,500,000 defective children in the United States who could be directed to public usefulness" with proper care; the cost, he said, would be $900,000,000 a year. And two days after that he was in Atlanta, where, as the national press reported, he was hailed as the "next President of the United States" and enthusiastically cheered at his every appearance. One appearance was at the Southeastern Fair, where he gave a short talk to a crowd of thousands, many of them children; another was at Grant Field, where he watched North Carolina defeat Georgia Tech 18 to 7 in a football game. In Albany, on that same day, Eleanor issued to the press a statement pledging her aid in the raising of $250,000 for "aged, needy teachers."[1]

Meanwhile, the stock market was again making spectacular front-page news, though emphatically not of a kind pleasing to investors.

On Tuesday, September 24, after stumbling uncertainly over a series of small humps and depressions for nearly three weeks, the market suffered another bad fall—and this with 963 issues, a record number, being traded. The volume was not exceptionally large. It totaled 4,408,900 shares. But more than 1,500,000 of these were traded in the final frantic hour, when the decline was precipitous, an ominous sign.* There was recovery the next day, however. Prices were rising at the session's end, and they continued to rise the following day. After that they resumed the stumbling course they had followed lately, until Thursday, October 3, which saw a repetition of the market experience of September 24, save that this time the fall was farther. Declines of 5 to 10 points were commonplace; declines of 20 to 25 were numerous; and again, on a total volume of 4,747,330 shares, most of the loss came in a final frantic hour during which 1,500,000 shares were traded. Leading stocks fell another 3 to 5 points the next day. There was recovery during the short session on Saturday, October 5, and on high volume, too, but most of the buying appeared to be by investment trusts and financial institutions of various kinds whose managers were said to feel that a continuance of the recent stock declines could have a deleterious effect upon the general business of the country. (This alleged view of the money managers contradicted, of course, their often expressed view that the stock market merely reflected the general state of the economy, upon which it had no determining influence; it contradicted with equal flatness the view, soon to be vastly publicized, that the stock market had no real relationship whatever to the general economy, reflective or otherwise.) For a week and a half thereafter stock prices remained reasonably steady, though on a volume small enough to indicate a continuing uncertainty in that portion of the public that had been bidding up stocks for a year and a half.

On October 16, there was another sharp decline; it was on this day that Irving Fisher, speaking to the Purchasing Agents Association, made his remark about stock prices having reached "what looks like a permanently high plateau." This was followed, after a couple of days of only partial recovery, by what in many respects was the worst break yet. Nearly 3,500,000 shares were traded on Saturday morning, October 19, the second largest volume for a Saturday session in Exchange history, and losses of 5 to 20 points were registered all across the board. On Monday, October 21, stocks slumped again, with losses of 2 to 10 points for those issues normally most active, on a volume of 6,091,870. The *Times* reported "scenes of wild confusion" and unanswered margin calls by thousands of small traders.

On Tuesday there was a sharp gain in the early hours due, it was reported, to "organized support" by banks and to a reassuring statement by Charles E. Mitchell. Mitchell had been on a brief European trip. In England, embarking for his homeward voyage on October 15, he told reporters that while "in some

---

*The break naturally elicited, in automatic response, a flood of optimistic statements by the presumed masters of finance. One hugely publicized speculator, Arthur W. Cutten of Chicago, long a leader of the bulls, sensationalized his continued bullishness on September 29 by proclaiming that even $12 billion in brokers' loans would not be too high. Within a few weeks, Cutten would lose a reported $40,000,000 in the market.

cases speculation has gone too far in the United States," a six-week shakedown in prices had put "the markets generally . . . in a healthy condition." He was more determinedly optimistic when he landed in New York on October 22. The stock price decline had now "gone too far," he declared to reporters assembled at the dock, and the public was paying far too much attention to the amount of brokers' loans. "I know of nothing fundamentally wrong with the stock market or with the underlying business and credit structure." Irving Fisher spoke with similar optimism that same day; the recent market declines had been merely a healthy "shaking out of the lunatic fringe," said he. However, the lift thus given trading spirits, if a market factor at all, failed to last out the trading day: stocks were dipping downward again when the closing bell sounded, and though the market opened in seeming strength the next morning, it soon demonstrated its actual weakness. In the last hour of trading came unprecedented catastrophe. In just sixty terrifying minutes, from two to three o'clock, some 2,600,000 shares of a 6,374,960-share day were traded (the ticker lagged an hour and three quarters behind the trading), with prices plunging downward for a paper loss of $4 billion.

On Thursday, October 24, 1929, the market had barely opened when it was overwhelmed by a flood tide of selling orders from all over the country, many if not most of them forced by unanswered calls for more margin. Selling sparked more selling in chain reaction as buyers bid belatedly, reluctantly, or, on a few issues, not at all. Within an hour the ticker lagged far behind trading more frantic even than that of the last hour of the day before, with prices often falling 2 to 5 points *between sales!* Nothing like it had ever happened before. Every wall and channel devised for orderly market procedure was swept away, and hysterical terror, breeding pandemonium on the Exchange floor, sped thence with the speed of light to every brokerage office in the land. Darkest chaos reigned over what would become known in Stock Exchange history as Black Thursday.

But the blackness did not long outlast the morning hours for those who yet remained in active voluntary trade. At approximately 12:05 P.M. the excited crowd gathered in the street outside the Exchange saw Charles E. Mitchell enter the offices of J. P. Morgan and Company at 23 Wall Street, quickly followed by Albert H. Wiggin, chairman of the board of the Chase National Bank, and William Potter, president of Guaranty Trust. Seward Prosser, chairman of Bankers Trust, was already inside the building; George F. Baker, Jr., chairman of First National, was consulted by phone. Word of this assemblage passed at once to the Exchange floor, where it became as a spreading beam of light into turbulent darkness, a soothing hand laid upon violent breasts. Order was restored. Soon a brisk rally was under way, encouraged by the calm confidence exuded by Morgan partner Thomas W. Lamont when he talked to reporters immediately after the brief meeting had ended (there had been "a little distress selling" on the Exchange, said Lamont) and encouraged still more by the belief that the great bankers met to pool their enormous resources in support of the market. The belief proved justified. At 1:30, Richard

Whitney, the Exchange vice-president and Morgan floor trader—a somewhat stout figure who, however, carried his weight gracefully; a man of arrogant aristocratic pride—strode through the floor crowd to the Steel post (No. 2), where he ostentatiously bid 205 for 10,000 shares of U.S. Steel.[2] His was the last quoted price; current bids were several points less. He then moved to other posts to make with similar ostentation more than fifteen other bids of the same nature. Their size indicated that he was an agent for a pool of unprecedented size. Stock prices began to rise almost as sharply as they had fallen during the morning hours, until, despite renewed heavy selling pressure during the last half hour, the market closed with most stock leaders down only 10 points or so on a record volume of 12,894,650 shares (Steel actually closed higher), a loss far smaller than had been suffered the day before. The day was nonetheless tragic for thousands upon thousands across the land, who, affluent or at least comfortably well off at dawn, were sold out and ruined by noon. The afternoon rally was no tonic for these children of woe; it was gall and wormwood.

The next day, Friday, October 25, the press carried Lamont's encouraging announcement that the bankers' consortium had indeed been formed "to furnish a cushion against the recurrence of any such condition as Thursday." This clearly meant that the consortium's powerfully implemented defensive strategy remained in full force. Also on that day the mightiest in the land sang in chorus a prayerful incantation addressed not to Heaven but to Fundament. Charles E. Mitchell said that "fundamentals remain unimpaired." Charles M. Schwab said that the steel industry was in a "fundamentally sound condition." Walter C. Teagle of Standard Oil of New Jersey said there had been "no fundamental change in the petroleum industry." Samuel Vauclain of the Baldwin Locomotive Works said that "fundamentals are sound." And Herbert Hoover, President of the United States, said that the "fundamental business of the country—that is, the production and distribution of goods and services —is on a sound and prosperous basis."[3] (Franklin Roosevelt spoke before a church organization in Poughkeepsie within a few hours after the President's statement was released. "It is not good to go too far on the theory of getting something for nothing," he said. "Much of the activity of the stock market is legitimate and proper, but in some cases improper schemes and questionable methods have been used in stock promotion, and many investors have lost sight of the real purpose of the Exchange." However, he went on to say, business morality was improving.[4])

Thus sustained and encouraged from above, though not by any push from below, as would soon come clear, the stock market held steady through a day and a half of orderly trading on a volume somewhat greater than the recent average. Many stocks advanced. Never had the prestige of the great bankers and their big-business colleagues been higher with the public in general than it was at high noon of Saturday, October 26, 1929, when the closing bell sounded on the Exchange. They to whom miraculous powers had long been ascribed by the New Era faithful were, it appeared, performing another miracle: the Big Six were Saviors of the Market, Richard Whitney the Hero of the Hour.

That, however, was the ultimate peak of such prestige. From it the fall was swift and fatal.

For over the weekend the seemingly miraculous powers of the great bankers evaporated in feverish air as sell orders piled up to unprecedented heights in brokers' offices. On Monday, October 28, occurred what the New York *Times* described as a "nationwide stampede to unload." Yet Richard Whitney made no appearance on the Exchange floor; there was no sign anywhere of organized market support. When the closing bell rang, with 9,912,800 shares having been traded, the day's overall decline was greater than that of the preceding week. An hour and a half later, the Big Six again assembled in the Morgan bank, joined by Owen D. Young and by the president of Equitable Trust, C. A. Austin. This time the conference did not end in a few minutes. It lasted for two long hours. And when it was over, Lamont handed to reporters a press release that made no mention of any "cushion" against further market declines. He now said that the consortium's purpose had never been to maintain any particular price level or to protect anyone's profit but only to maintain an orderly market; presumably this "orderliness" would "stabilize prices" at *some* level or other. He further said that the situation "retained hopeful features." What these were he did not say.

Immediately there were ugly rumors, spread with lightning speed far and wide, that the Big Six, far from being Saviors of the Market, had been operating only to save themselves—had moved to support prices just long enough to enable them quietly to unload their own holdings without serious loss, or even at a profit—and were now abandoning to a tragic fate the men who had been so foolish as to buy from them, these along with the myriads of other poor suckers. Sell orders piled up overnight higher than they had over the preceding weekend. The way was prepared for Tuesday, October 29, 1929.

And this Black Tuesday, darker by far than Black Thursday—indeed, the most ghastly day ever suffered on the Exchange—was recognized even at the time by scores of thousands of dazed, bewildered people as a historic ending, a breakpoint in history as in their own lives. Within thirty minutes after the opening bell, some 3,000,000 shares had been dumped on the market in huge blocks—5,000, 20,000, even 40,000—and though the volume per minute shrank thereafter, it remained greater than on any day before. Recorded prices plummeted as never before, even on ticker tape that lagged behind the trading as never before. Again there was a noon meeting of the Big Six in the Morgan bank, but no encouraging word came from it. Rumor had it that the consortium was selling, not buying, and when Richard Whitney, "hat tilted on his head at a jaunty angle, sauntered nonchalantly across the floor half an hour before closing time," he bid for no stocks.[5] At the closing bell a brief rally had cut losses on leading issues,* but these losses remained huge and on an unprecedented volume (16,410,030), which would not be equaled for another

---

*It is highly unlikely that Whitney's ostentatious floor appearance had anything to do with this; most experts ascribed it to bargain hunting on the part of those who still had money, and the will, to gamble.

thirty-nine years. The general average loss amounted to almost 25 points, the Dow-Jones industrials were down 48 points, the New York *Times* fifty-stock average was down 43 points, and paper losses for that single day amounted to considerably more than the total national debt, several times the total amount of money in circulation throughout the United States at any time during the preceding year. Nor was there now any real hope for the morrow on the part of the general investing public. The Big Six met again at the Morgan bank that evening, but when this last meeting broke up and Lamont again faced the press, his chief concern was obviously to protect the bankers' reputations against damaging rumor. Reiterating that "the group" had never proposed the maintenance of any particular price level, he flatly denied that "the group" had been "a seller of stocks." He also said that "the group has continued and will continue in a cooperative way to support the market," but these words had, in the circumstances, a hollow ring.

On that same evening, the governor of New York was guest of honor at a Democratic banquet in Springfield, Massachusetts. While the banquet was under way, "local humorists" at one of the tables concocted a one-line telegram: "Will they blame the stock market on the Democrats?" They signed it "Al Smith" and had it delivered to the master of ceremonies, who, in all good faith, read it to the banqueters. There was laughter and applause, and none laughed more heartily than Franklin D. Roosevelt. Al Smith was less amused; the next day he publicly denied having sent the telegram, prompting a newspaper investigation, which uncovered the hoax.[6]

The New York State government, it might be added, profited from the Exchange debacle, collecting some $350,000 in transfer taxes on the transactions of October 29, and the New York governor, it *would* be pointedly added (by Herbert Hoover, for one), had considerably more regulatory power over the New York Stock Exchange than he ever chose to exercise.[7]

II

So came to an end the Jazz Age,* the Roaring Twenties, the Republican Prosperity, the New Economic Era. Recognition of the depth and magnitude of the change did not come, of course, immediately after Black Thursday or Black Tuesday. The truth of Hegel's dictum that the effect of an event is the *cause* of that event's causality, since no event can be cause without effect, is continually impressed upon the mind of a philosophical historian, and it was not until the bitter grinding downward spiral of economic activity, affecting every phase and aspect of human life, had gone on for a year or more that the causal significance of the stock price collapse of 1929 was universally recognized as the triggering, the incitement of the Great Depression.

---

*The Jazz Age "leaped to a spectacular death in October, 1929," wrote the man who gave that age its name, F. Scott Fitzgerald, in "Echoes of the Jazz Age," *Scribner's* magazine, November 1931.

But if the dimensions of the change were not and could not be grasped immediately after the Crash, there was immediate realization by the public at large that a great change had occurred in both the national life and the personal lives of those directly involved with the Exchange—a change in mood, attitudes, patterns of belief, standards of value—and that this change was not only a permanent break with the immediate past but also a continuing, developing process. As Fitzgerald wrote, the "utter confidence that was the essential prop" of the boom years had been dealt "an enormous jolt."[8] But had this confidence been truly "utter," after all? Certainly it had been asserted and assertive in the highest key, but was not that very assertiveness a sign, a shouting down, of secret persistent doubt? Many now realized, who had not before, that even at Prosperity's height they had not believed in its perma- nence, had instead been haunted by an unadmitted sense that it rested upon a foundation of sand, the flowing hour-glass sand of "borrowed time."* The fact was indicated by their use of the word "boom" to describe what had been going on in the America of Calvin Coolidge and the Great Engineer. For in that era of widespread belief in "business cycles" that governed economic activity but were themselves no more controllable by man's will and intelli- gence than wind or tide, it was commonly deemed axiomatic that every "boom" must be followed by a precisely proportionate "bust," as per Newton's third law of motion. Black Thursday and Black Tuesday promptly initiated, therefore, a general feeling that the whole "flimsy structure," as Fitzgerald called it, might soon come tumbling down.[9] And this perceived shadow of a coming event, this sense of impending and developing doom for Coolidge's Business Civilization and Hoover's American System, grew wider, deeper, darker as the last two months of 1929 wore away and a new year came on.

Yet it was not for all Americans a shadow of black despair. There were some who found it a grateful shade wherein spirits long overheated, blasted and withered by harsh blazing suns of materialism, might rest and be refreshed, renewed. This was so for nearly all who lived the life of the mind and were committed to cultural values. For them the prospect immediately ahead, if obviously characterized by risk and danger, was far richer in hopeful promise than any they had viewed these last ten years.

Ever since the Civil War a gulf of alienation had yawned between the intellectual, particularly the literary, community and the business community of the United States. Witness the revulsion against the Gilded Age's mores and ethical standards that underlay so much of Mark Twain's mordant humor. Witness the self-imposed exile to Europe of Henry James. Witness the retreat of Henry Adams from public action into private self-conscious ironies (con- voluted, involuted) and Herman Melville's long, long dying, by deliberate choice, into silence and obscurity. This gulf had become wider still, and deeper, in the aftermath of Wilsonian idealism's ignoble death at Versailles and the taking over of America by big business. A principal dynamic of the remarkably

---

*Said Fitzgerald in the aforementioned article: "It was borrowed time anyhow."

intense intellectual ferment in America all through the 1920s had been the profound antipathy of American writers, painters, musicians, philosophers, educators, to the American businessman as type—to his manners, his morals, his mentality, his general tastes, his politics. During that decade the great fear of the intellectuals had been not that American capitalism would fail but that it would succeed, that in fact it *was* succeeding, and hugely, on its own terms. In the intellectuals' view, these terms were wholly pernicious. They ensured a society in which what rose to the top was not the cream but the scum of humanity, a society that richly rewarded selfishness, callousness, thievery, and deceit while imposing harsh competitive penalties upon generosity, sensitivity, honesty, and strict truthfulness, a society in which human decency and liberty seemed likely to be soon smothered to death as the scum solidified in a crust of fused business and government so hard, so thick that no heavenly air could penetrate it. But now such fear was relieved. " . . . a darkness seemed to descend," wrote Fitzgerald's close friend Edmund Wilson. "Yet, to the writers and artists of my generation who had grown up in the Big Business era and had always resented its barbarism, its crowding out of everything they cared about, these years [the ones that would follow the crash] were not depressing but stimulating. One couldn't help being exhilarated at the sudden collapse of that stupid gigantic fraud. It gave us a new sense of freedom."[10]

Stock prices continued to decline steadily after October 29 until, at the market's lowest point for the year, in mid-November, some $30 billion to $40 billion had been lopped off listed security values at their highest point of two months before.[11] By then, every index of economic activity pointed definitely downward—freight-car loadings, inventory size, commodity prices, industrial production figures, employment figures (though these were very inadequately reported), bank suspensions, that is, all the indicators of that "fundamental business of America" so prayerfully cited in the October incantations of the New Era prophets. Nor was Herbert Hoover slow to respond to these ominous tidings; he grasped their significance more quickly and fully than did most others in his administration or in the business community. When he asked for advice from the Secretary of the Treasury he had inherited from the Harding-Coolidge administrations,* he received pure *laissez-faire* doctrine. "Liquidate labor, liquidate stocks, liquidate the farmers, liquidate real estate," said Andrew Mellon—in short, let the "business cycle" run its course with no governmental interference of any kind, as in the post–Civil War depression of the early 1870s.[12] (Mellon had personal youthful memories of the 1870s.) Instead, Hoover promptly took action that must be judged extreme if measured against

---

*The immense prestige that this Treasury Secretary ("the greatest . . . since Alexander Hamilton") had gained from the business community he acted for made it politically inexpedient for Hoover to dispense with his services, as Hoover would not have been loathe to do, in the spring of 1929. Rumors that Mellon might soon be leaving the Cabinet were cited as one cause of the jittery stock market of September 1929, prompting a White House announcement on October 7 that Mellon would stay on until 1933. Businessmen were reported "relieved" by this news.

established precedents for the conduct of his office and against his own economic pieties. On November 18 he ordered Secretary of Commerce Robert P.
Lamont to set up an organization of "experienced men to assure as much
public and private construction work as possible." On November 19 he held
a conference with railroad presidents and extracted from them a pledge to
"continue and even expand their construction and maintenance programs over
the next year." He elicited a similar pledge from "public utility leaders" a few
days later. On November 21 he held a morning conference with leading manufacturers and financiers and an afternoon conference with labor leaders. He
impressed upon those assembled his view of the seriousness of the situation and
obtained pledges that prevailing wage and employment levels would be maintained, that new wage demands and strikes would be avoided. According to
his *Memoirs,* Hoover spoke at the morning meeting of a "crisis," a "depression" that "must last some time," and of "two or three millions unemployed
by the sudden suspension of many activities," but no hint of this was permitted
to appear in the press. All published statements issuing from the meetings were
of an anxiety-soothing, "confidence"-breeding nature. The next day he met
with leaders of the construction industry, obtaining their promise to maintain
current wage and hour standards. On November 23 he sent telegrams to all
the governors and mayors of large cities asking them to expand public-works
expenditures to the utmost. He also moved to expedite the expenditure of some
$420,000,000 that had been appropriated for federal public works. Further
meetings with larger groups of labor and business representatives were held in
December.[13]

Thus did Herbert Hoover depart from the prevailing conservative view that
government had no responsibility for the economic welfare of the citizenry,
that its sole legitimate function as regards business was the assurance of a
"favorable environment," including subsidies of various kinds, for private
enterprise, with only such regulation of competition as was required to keep
it "free" and "fair." This view was wrong for twentieth-century America, said
the President in action, and this departure from orthodoxy was disturbing to
many of the big-business men who were the Great Engineer's strongest supporters.[14]

Meanwhile, appeals to the Fundament continued as fervent and numerous
as before from those whose word on business matters had long been deemed
the word of higher law. Within a week after Black Tuesday the Secretary of
Commerce had announced, "There are present today none of the underlying
factors which have been associated with or have preceded the declines of
business in the past." Simultaneously, Henry Ford had announced that "things
are better today than they were yesterday," and John D. Rockefeller had
announced that, for some days past, he and his sons had been buying "good
common stocks." On December 10, Charles M. Schwab said flatly, "Never
before has American business been as firmly entrenched for prosperity as it is
today." John E. Edgarton, president of the National Association of Manufacturers, looking forward into 1930, could "observe little on the horizon to give

us undue or great concern." He was less optimistic than Secretary Mellon (the great "leave it alone liquidationist," as Hoover dubbed him), who could "see nothing . . . in the present situation that is either menacing or warrants pessimism" and who was unqualifiedly confident "that during the coming year the country will make steady progress." According to Willis H. Booth, president of the Merchants' Association of New York, there was "no fundamental reason why business should not find itself again on the upgrade in 1930." More cautious in his optimism, yet determinedly optimistic, was the President of the United States: a White House press release reported the President's view "that business could look forward to the coming year with greater assurance."[15]

These incantations were not without effect, joined as they were to efforts by business and labor leaders to live up to the pledges they had made to the White House—joined also to further governmental action in aid of the economy. In early 1930 the Federal Farm Board, unable to halt farm price declines, acted with some vigor to at least slow them, through loans and direct open-market purchases of wheat and cotton—the latter an action very reluctantly acquiesced in by the President. A cut in federal corporate and individual income taxes was made for the stated purpose of increasing purchasing power and stimulating capital investment, an action of the kind recommended by the British economist John Maynard Keynes but amounting to little more than a token gesture in the United States of 1930: thanks to Coolidge-Mellon policies, taxes were exceedingly low to begin with. In Congress bills to increase public-works expenditures were introduced and the Hawley-Smoot Tariff bill was reintroduced (the 1929 special session had adjourned without action upon it) to legislators obviously disposed to adopt them come spring.

But if all this was not without effect, the major effect, it would seem, was a stock-market rally, which, beginning in January 1930, became for three months a plausible if uneasy imitation of the Great Bull Market of 1928–1929. There was a resurgence of legal thievery and blatant lying on the part of pool operators and securities promoters; new holding companies and mergers and investment trusts were formed to issue new stocks for sale to that portion of the gullible public that still had savings to "invest"; and the prices of many stocks rose as steeply, though not as high, on volumes as great as during the preceding summer. There was, alas, no comparable upturn in those "fundamentals" that stock prices were supposed to reflect or discount. Quite the contrary. The New York *Times*'s "Weekly Index of Business Activity," which measured not fluctuating prices but the actual physical volume of car loadings and basic industrial output, had begun to decline in the last week of June 1929; and it continued to do so fairly steadily through the early months of 1930. The reason for this was hinted at by government spokesmen at the time. In early November 1929 Secretary of Commerce Lamont had predicted that the only effect of what he called "recent fluctuations" in the stock market would be "to curtail the buying power, especially of luxuries, of those who suffered losses in the market crash." The general public would be unaffected. This view was echoed by President Hoover in his first annual message to Congress on December 3, 1929, but with a significant addition having to do with employment: "The natural consequences [of the crash, which he attributed to 'over-optimism' generated by the 'long upward trend of fundamental progress] have been a reduction in the consumption of luxuries and semi-necessities by those who have met with losses, and a number of persons thrown *temporarily* out of employment."* The simultaneous collapse of farm prices, which had already been at severe depression levels, was merely a "sympathetic" reaction of the "great commodity markets" to "the stock market," said the President.[16] What Lamont and Hoover failed to recognize or chose publicly to ignore was the fact that a disproportionate share of the total national income, thanks in good part to Republican economic policies, had been going to that relatively small segment of the population that consistently made "luxury" and "semi-necessity" purchases. Workers' wages and farmers' income had not come anywhere near matching the increase in per capita production resulting from technological advances: the bulk of the latter had been translated into the profits and salaries of the affluent. Hence, the "reduction of consumption" on the part of the "luxury" and "semi-necessity" buyers meant an immediate significant contraction of the total consumer market. And this was chain-reactive. Domestic servants were laid off, clerks in expensive stores were laid off, employees of luxury manufacturers were laid off, construction workers employed on expensive housing projects were laid off as new construction was abandoned or postponed. The curtailment of purchasing by those laid off implied further layoffs, elsewhere in the economy, with further contraction of purchasing power. Thus did the Depression, triggered by the Crash, feed upon itself and gain steadily in downward momentum, and thus did it spread human misery in ever-wider circles, as it disastrously involved more and more of the national economy. In retrospect it would seem that this doomful trend should at once have been as obvious to the mighty of the land as it was inevitable unless far more direct and drastic governmental action was taken than had yet been publicly proposed by either the administration or the leading Democrats.

Instead of more action, the administration took less. Herbert Hoover, whose inclination was to deem "confidence" a cause rather than an effect of prosperity, took heed of the "uncertainty" bred in big-business leaders by his unprecedented governmental intervention in business affairs in November. The administration, therefore, made no new departures from strict orthodoxy as wintry 1930 advanced hopefully, anxiously, toward springtime. Simultaneously, the administration's published optimism became less restrained, as well as less constrained by a scrupulous regard for truth in its citation of "fundamental" facts. In late January and early February the Secretary of Commerce asserted, on the basis of no given evidence, that production and distribution were now at "normal" levels; the President asserted that the unemployment climb was halted and that employment was on the increase; and the U.S. Employment Service backed up the White House by announcing a few days

*Present author's italics.

later that the nation would "be on a normal employment basis" within the next "sixty or ninety days" as the prevailing trend continued. A month later, on March 7, the President reiterated his assertion that unemployment was going down and concluded, "All the evidences indicate that the worst effects of the crash upon unemployment will have been passed within the next sixty days." Fifty-four days later, on May 1, 1930, he addressed a convention of the U.S. Chamber of Commerce. Speaking for government he said to business, "Our joint undertaking has succeeded to a remarkable degree." He was convinced that "we have now passed the worst and with continued unity of effort we shall rapidly recover."[17]

But events, which all winter long had covertly belied him on the level of Fundament, now bitterly mocked him in the open light of day.

His Chamber of Commerce optimism was headlined in the morning papers of May 2. The afternoon papers of that same day headlined a "wave of liquidation" on the Stock Exchange, with stock prices plunging as they had not done since the preceding November—and this was the end, once and for all, of 1930's Little Bull Market, the last bull market of any kind for years to come. On the following day, May 3, came "another violent break in stocks," whereupon, day after day, week in and week out, every brief mild upturn in stock prices was succeeded by a prolonged severe downturn, so that the overall trend was down, down, down into the slough of despond. It would come to seem that administration "optimism" actually *caused* downturns, for every major expression of it was immediately followed by an especially steep price decline. And not only in stocks. In the summer of 1930 the chairman of the Federal Farm Board, Alexander Legge, announced that his agency's farm price support program had succeeded. There would be "no further decline in commodities," in his view. Whereupon wheat promptly fell to its lowest price of the century, 45 cents a bushel (it was destined to go yet lower).

By that time the administration's credibility with the general public on economic matters had been damaged beyond the possibility of restoration. It had already been severely damaged when Hoover arose to address the Chamber of Commerce.

Bank suspensions, commercial failures, and mortgage foreclosures were then increasing at any alarming rate; a total of 659 banks, with deposits of nearly $250,000,000, had closed their doors in 1929, and 1,352 banks, with deposits of $853,000,000, would do so in 1930. There were lengthening bread-lines and increasingly crowded flophouses in every major city as local relief agencies, assigned the full burden of relief for the unemployed by Hoover's ideological opposition to any direct federal aid to individuals, began to groan and, some of them, to crumple under unwonted strains. Evidences of growing human distress were everywhere in urban centers for those with eyes to see. Heywood Broun, a nationally syndicated liberal columnist, had eyes to see when, on a bitter day in March 1930, the Little Church Around the Corner in midtown Manhattan opened its first soup kitchen since the Panic of 1907. From the church door to the corner of Twenty-ninth Street and Fifth Avenue, and far up Fifth toward the construction site of the Empire State Building, stretched a single file of hungry men. The sight was distasteful to the denizens of perhaps the richest thoroughfare in the world; the hungry were therefore reformed into a triple line jammed into Twenty-ninth, as Broun reported in a pungently phrased column. He also reported that of the 2,000 in that line, 500 had to be turned away when the food gave out.[18]

No mere words, however glowing with "optimism" and august in source, could any longer persuade the distressed themselves that they were not in the condition they were in.

Hence the damage to presidential credibility. Either the administration was woefully ignorant of actual economic conditions or it deliberately lied about them, and it was the latter harsh judgment that came more and more to be accepted by the general public.

III

RIDING to the State Office Building in New York City on the morning of January 21, 1930, Frances Perkins, New York's industrial commissioner, was "horrified" to read on the front page of the New York *Times* the President's announcement that there had been a national gain in employment during the preceding week. The economic situation in general was improving, he indicated. Commissioner Perkins knew this wasn't so. She suspected that the President knew it, too. At least he *should* have known that the U.S. Employment Service, whose information he now used, "had no information-collecting technique" whatever; that its "announced figures . . . reflected only the number of placements or applications they had had in a particular week, comparing these figures with those of the previous week"; and that, as a measure of unemployment, such figures were worse than useless.[19] They were definitely misleading. Yet there could be no doubt that Hoover's statement, weighted with the immense prestige of the presidency, would be widely believed even among the unemployed themselves and their families, for Hoover's personal credibility was then, in January, still high. It would be cruel to impose such false belief on men laid off through no fault of their own, men struggling desperately and vainly for new jobs—to further slash their already bleeding self-respect ("they would feel that there was something wrong with them personally if . . . the employment situation was better the country over"[20]), and add to their misery the bitter reproaches of their wives and children and the contempt of their yet-employed acquaintances. It was wickedly cruel if done deliberately. By the time she reached the State Building, Frances Perkins was, by her own account, fuming with indignation.

She summoned to her office Eugene Patton, the chief statistician of New York's Department of Labor, a nationally recognized expert in his field. With him and his subordinates she spent a long hard day correlating unemployment figures for the state with the recent movement of unemployment indices for other industrial states, the latter information supplied over the phone from

Washington by the U.S. Bureau of Labor Statistics. ("We had confidence in the Bureau. . . . We were fairly sure that these people were making honest, reliable estimates."[21]) From this correlation careful projections were made to cover the country as a whole. The conclusion reached was indeed conclusive, and flatly contradictory of the President's pronouncement. Employment was decreasing, unemployment increasing, throughout the United States; that is, things were getting worse, not better. The next day, Commissioner Perkins called in newspaper reporters and issued a statement saying the President was wrong and giving her reasons for saying so.

The statement made banner-head front-page news from coast to coast. Telegrams and phone calls, some full of praise, others of abuse, began to crowd the commissioner's office, and inevitably much of this reaction was along partisan political lines. It was naturally assumed that the commissioner acted on behalf of her superior, who thereby further impressed himself upon the popular mind as leader of the President's political opposition.

All the same, according to Frances Perkins' own account, it was not until she was told she had a phone call from the executive office in Albany, at midmorning of January 23, that she realized she should have asked the approval of the governor of New York before issuing her challenge to the President of the United States. She feared a well-deserved reprimand as she picked up the phone. Instead, the "cheerful voice" of TR's distant cousin, who had married TR's favorite niece, boomed out TR's favorite phrase, "Bully for you!," and went on to say, "That was a fine statement and I am glad you made it." She was immensely relieved but remained rueful, apologetic. She was sorry she had not checked the statement with him in advance; she should have. "Well, I think it was better you didn't," said he. "If you had asked me, I would probably have told you not to do it, and I think it much more wholesome to have it right out in the open."

Thus Frances Perkins' story.[22]

The manner of her telling it, however, coupled with one's general knowledge of her psychological and political acumen, raises a suspicion of ingeniousness. One suspects she failed to consult her superior in advance not because she "forgot" but for three shrewd reasons. First, she wanted to impress upon him —she wanted *him,* above all others, to realize—the seriousness of a growing unemployment to which he had not yet paid attention; second, she sensed that, if forced to make a choice, he would feel forced to decide against her doing what she wished and felt it right to do; whereas, third, if she went ahead and did it on her own responsibility, and her statement was as convincing as she expected it to be, she would be doing him a service to which he would react, as in fact he did, with gratitude.

Certainly Roosevelt would appear to have been slow to recognize the stock-market crash for what it was—slower than one might have expected him to be, given his long, if vague, anticipation of the event and his expectation of political profit from it. Historians are fond of citing in evidence of this a letter he wrote on December 1, 1929, to Louis Howe, asking Howe to bid at a forthcoming auction in the Anderson Galleries on certain items he wished to add to his collections. "It is just possible that the recent little Flurry down town will make the prices comparatively low," he wrote, as if the Crash were of no great importance.[23] But the validity of such evidence is rendered dubious by Roosevelt's habitual indulgence in hyperbole and its opposite when attempting "humor." More certainly revealing of his sense of realities was his reply to a wire from a newspaper editor, immediately after Black Thursday, asking his view of economic conditions. He joined the incantative chorus, if more tentatively than most who did. He had no detailed information, he wired back, but believed that "fundamental" industrial conditions were "sound."[24] To Hoover's wire of November 23, 1929, begging him, with other governors, to expand programs of state public works, Roosevelt made essentially negative response. He did expect "to recommend to legislature . . . much needed construction work program," he said; but what he referred to was the prison and hospital construction already decided upon. He indicated no intention to call for new public works to mitigate a developing economic crisis, and he went on to say that whatever new building he proposed would be "limited . . . by estimated receipts without increasing taxes."[25]

In Chicago three weeks later he made a rousing Populist-Progressive speech in the tradition of the Midwestern agrarian revolt as echoed by the congressional farm bloc. He inveighed against Hawley-Smoot tariff-making by big business; he spoke of how big-business combinations, mergers, and holding companies had encouraged, through watered-stock promotions, "the recent wild speculation and senseless inflation" of securities prices; he pointed out how business combinations placed agriculture at a disadvantage in the marketplace, since the farmer on the family farm "was and always must be an individual"; and he described as "recent" a "realization" that had at last "brought . . . [the farmer's plight] prominently before the attention of the public," namely, "that if the farmer starves today we will all starve tomorrow."[26] He made no mention of developing depression or unemployment.

Nor did he do so in his annual message to the legislature on January 1, 1930. He did stress in his message the "need of revision" of the "entire Banking Law." "The meshes of our banking laws have been woven so loosely as to permit the escape of those meanest of criminals who squander the funds of hundreds of small depositors in reckless speculation for private gain," he said.[27] But when his special commission for banking law revision, the one to which he had *not* appointed Robert Moses, made its predictably feeble recommendations to him in late January, ignoring every major reform proposal Moses had made, he passed it on to the legislature without criticism or question. Four bills embodying these recommendations, with some others equally mild, were developed by the legislature's Joint Committee on Banking and Investment Trusts and then enacted by the legislature. The governor then signed them with a flourish on April 22, 1930, declaring them to be "some of the most necessary, important and constructive banking legislation proposed in recent years." No act of omission or commission on Roosevelt's part could have more clearly demonstrated the inadequacy of his perceptions of deepening depression. Norman Thomas was disgusted. The joint committee had engaged in tautology, he said publicly: having "almost completely disregarded" the Moses report, it "solemnly concluded that everything would be all right if everybody put his money in a sound bank."[28]

By that time, however, the governor *was* paying close attention to growing unemployment in New York. His doing so was due in good part to Frances Perkins' efforts to educate him on the subject, though one must add that these were efforts he deliberately encouraged. She became more and more impressed by the openness and flexibility of his mind, by his capacity to absorb and retain immense amounts of new information, and by his proceeding always from the particular to the general or from the concrete to the abstract, never the other way around, when dealing with problems. "I learned in that period that Roosevelt could 'get' a problem infinitely better when he had a vicarious experience through a vivid description of a typical case," she later wrote. "Proceeding 'from the book,' no matter how logical, never seemed solid to him."[29] She was impressed even more by his empathic understanding of how people were thinking, feeling—a general understanding that, again, derived from and was composed of vivid particular understandings of individual human beings. Her belief in the warmth, the breadth, the depth, of his human sympathy was strengthened. He truly cared, she believed.

There was a sweater-manufacturing mill in a small town near Hyde Park, locally owned and employing some 150 local people. Formerly it had made sweaters for sale in "quality" stores at the high price of around $10 each. The market for this "luxury" or "semi-necessity" item collapsed with the stock market, and so, in desperation, owner and employees agreed to accept an order for 5,000 sweaters, shoddily made, to be sold at $2 each, though this meant wages of only $5 a week, a stretched-out workweek at that, and not a penny of profit for the employer. Roosevelt visited this mill, talked with employer and employees, and carried away sharp impressions of how the business slump eroded the self-respect as well as the living standards of hardworking men and women. He became intensely interested in what he and Frances Perkins called "stabilization of employment," by which was meant the ironing out of seasonal fluctuations in employment (he had been much concerned with this while president of the American Construction Council) in order to provide a guaranteed annual wage for workers. He talked with Marion Dickerman about the Welch Grape Juice Company in her hometown of Westfield, New York, and learned that Welch had gone far toward solving the seasonal problem by adding grape jelly to grape juice as a company product. He talked several times with a top executive of the Hills Brothers Company, which imported and packed dates, learning that Hills Brothers had achieved considerable employment stabilization by adding shredded coconut and canned figs to its products and by installing a cold storage plant for its dates.[30]

On March 29, 1930, Roosevelt became the first governor in the nation to stress openly and emphatically that unemployment was a major and growing problem. "The situation is serious," he said in a press statement, "and the time has come for us to face this unpleasant fact as dispassionately and constructively as a scientist faces a test tube of deadly germs, intending first to understand the nature, the cause and effect, and finally the method of overcoming and the technique of preventing its ravages."[31] The effect, added to that of Miss Perkins' late January statement, was a definite divorcement of his public enterprise from the President's effort to cure economic sickness by asserting in "confidence"-breeding ways that this sickness was *already* cured, that convalescence was under way.

Roosevelt diagnosed. There was an "accumulation" of unemployment* "due to three contributing factors: (1) seasonal fluctuations . . . ; (2) technological unemployment . . . [which] has been greatly accelerated in recent years . . . and since it indirectly [sic] correlates with cheap mass production we must expect its continuance; (3) the depression due to the business cycle which is an economic phenomenon recurring with some regularity throughout the Nation as well as in this State." He announced the appointment of a Commission on Stabilization of Industry, made up of businessmen and labor representatives, to develop "a long-time program for industrial mobilization and prevention of unemployment." For the immediate future he called upon local officials all over the state to join in gathering accurate local employment figures, organizing communitywide emergency relief, promoting "small-job campaigns," establishing "local free employment clearing houses," and "starting up local public works immediately."[32]

---

*The state Department of Labor index of employment showed a 9-percent drop in New York factory employment since October.

6

⇶✕⇷

Triumphant Balancing Act,
on a Tightrope in a Rising Wind

I

BUT the deteriorating economy, though it obviously generated a political climate more likely to favor Democrats than Republicans, was yet far from becoming itself a major determinative issue between the two political parties as the spring of 1930 advanced toward summer. To prevent its becoming so was, indeed, as great a concern of the conservative (Raskob-Shouse) wing of the Democratic Party in that season as it was of the Republican leadership: both groups sorely feared the issue's policy implications. In March Raskob publicly expressed worry lest his party "engage in attacks on business" when what it *should* do was "everything to take government out of business and relieve trade from unnecessary and unreasonable government restriction." He wanted the Democracy to concentrate its fire upon the Hoover administration's violation of the sacred tenets of *laissez-faire,* its "tendency to centralize greater and greater power in Washington."[1] Nor did Franklin Roosevelt evince publicly, at that time, any disagreement with the latter view, which he himself had in recent months repeatedly expressed. As he prepared that spring for an autumn gubernatorial reelection campaign whose triumphant success would be great enough, he hoped, to establish him as his party's only logical choice for presidential nomination, he initially laid little stress in public speech upon unemployment or the breakdown of relief agencies or any other element of deepening depression. Instead, he focused upon the electric-power issue, which the New York Republican leadership, especially W. Kingsland Macy, had striven so anxiously to remove from the agenda of partisan political debate.

When, for instance, Roosevelt addressed the Jefferson Day dinner of the national Democratic Club at the Hotel Commodore in New York City on April 26, his speech clearly indicated to a New York *Times* reporter his intention next fall to wage "a vigorous campaign on the public utility issue." He inveighed against the threat posed to America's free institutions, such as the St. Lawrence Power Development Commission, by the growing concentration of American economic power in the hands, the ever fewer hands, of giant corporations, such as the Morgan–Niagara-Hudson combine, as he had done in his address to Tammany Hall on July 4, 1929. He said he had been told recently by a prominent New York banker, a Republican, that fifty or sixty corporations, each controlled by two or three or four men, did "about 80 percent of the industrial business of the country," while many hundreds of thousands of businessmen did the remaining 20 percent. Similarly in the financial world: capital was increasingly concentrated through bank mergers.

"If Thomas Jefferson were alive he would be the first to question this concentration of economic power."

And this issue choice was seconded that night, was emphatically affirmed as a concern of national import, in a memorable address by Montana's great fighting liberal Democratic Senator Burton K. Wheeler, the hero, with his Montana colleague Senator Walsh, of the Teapot Dome investigation and the running mate in 1924's presidential election campaign of Wisconsin's Robert M. La Follette on the National Progressive ticket. Wheeler, who followed Roosevelt at the lectern, proclaimed the "overshadowing issue" before the country to be "the control of electric power and public utilities," with a secondary though yet crucial issue being the "special interest" tariff.[2]

But it was not this endorsement of the preceding speaker's views that made Wheeler's speech memorable. It became so, was even rendered historic to a degree, when the senator went on to endorse the speaker himself for the highest office in the land! Said Wheeler to a hushed, attentive audience: "As I look out over the field for a general to lead the people to victory under the banner of a reunited, militant progressive party I cannot but fasten my attention upon your Governor. The West is looking to Roosevelt to lead the fight and with him I feel sure we can win."[3] Roosevelt was not present to hear this. Having been warned by the former ambassador James W. Gerard* of what the senator proposed to do, he made no protest, raised no objection, but he had no wish to remain at the speaker's table while the senator praised him, his facial expressions measurable by a thousand pairs of inquiring eyes, and so he begged to be excused as soon as his own speech was ended. He pleaded weariness, and could do so legitimately, having worked well into the morning hours every night for the last week, signing or vetoing some 750 bills.

This public endorsement from a major national political figure, the first such that Roosevelt's unavowed presidential candidacy had received, provoked prolonged thunderous applause, interspersed with loud cheers, from its immediate audience, and it made headlines in the next morning's newspapers from coast to coast. Predictably, it aroused no joy in the Democratic National Headquarters presided over by Jouett Shouse in Washington. It even raised alarm there, to the extent it was deemed persuasive of the Democratic rank and file. With Raskob, Shouse preferred a safely conservative, business-oriented candidate who would make Prohibition the predominant partisan issue for 1932. He deplored the Roosevelt-Wheeler emphasis upon the "power question." And in doing so he was in perfect accord with the leaders of the opposition party: a spate of editorials promptly appeared in the Republican press denying, with the fervor of a strong covert fear, that electric-power and

*It was Gerard, then U.S. ambassador to Germany, who overwhelmingly, humiliatingly defeated Roosevelt in New York's Democratic primary for U.S. senator in 1914, the only election defeat Roosevelt had ever suffered. Gerard had then himself been defeated by the conservative Republican James Wadsworth in the general election. But by 1930, Gerard had long felt a warm paternal affection for his onetime rival and was prepared not only to contribute generously from his own large fortune to a Roosevelt-for-President campaign but also to solicit substantial contributions from his wealthy friends.

public-utility control was or could possibly become a major national issue.[4]

As for Roosevelt, he refused any public comment whatever upon what Wheeler had said, while at the same time expressing regret, in his private communications, and with a great surge of irritation, that efforts were being made to push him into presidential politics.

Thus, from Warm Springs, where he went in early May for a stay of three weeks, he complained in a "confidential" note to Nicholas Roosevelt that the date 1932 had "become a positive nightmare" to him "and the whole family." He went on to ask, plaintively, "Why can't reporters, editorial writers [Nicholas Roosevelt was pointedly indicated] and the politicians leave a poor devil alone to do the best he can with a very current job? As a matter of fact, I am trying to put even November, 1930, out of my mind until at least September 1." Two days later he addressed to Nancy Cook a letter approving her "tentative plan of work" for what was to become that fall, at his and Louis Howe's order, an unprecedentedly massive and active election campaign by the Women's Division of the New York Democracy, under the leadership of Nancy, Eleanor, Molly Dewson, Caroline O'Day, and Marion Dickerman. "I would only add one thing to it," he continued, "and that is a definite plan to guarantee having Democratic women attend and speak at the meetings of the League of Women Voters and other women's clubs." The "first literature" would be ready by June 17, he thought, when the state committee met, and Nancy should "get a very careful check in every community of those women who will distribute literature."[5]

To Wheeler he communicated nothing at all for five long weeks, during which time the senator's puzzlement over such unnatural silence grew into an anxious fear that he had given personal offense. Not until Roosevelt returned to Albany did he relieve this anxiety in a warmly friendly but noncommittal letter, dated June 3. "I have been meaning to write you for the past month," he then said. " . . . I want to tell you that personally I was made very happy by your reference to me at the Democratic Club dinner, for the very good reason that I have always thought of you as one of the real leaders of progressive thought and action in this country. Therefore to be considered as [a] real progressive by you means something to me. As to 1932, however, I am in a somewhat difficult position, first, of having no personal desire to run for a national office, and, secondly, because I feel that the more I get into the national limelight the more it is going to hurt my present work as Governor of New York."[6]

He was prudent. He was wary.

One could easily anticipate some such judgment as the Chicago *Journal of Commerce,* speaking for and to the Midwest's business community, would in fact pass upon the Wheeler endorsement a year hence, namely that "Senator Wheeler is for the Governor because the Governor is for Socialism,"[7] and he took steps to belie such allegation, or render it highly dubious, *without* reducing the value to him of the stated fact. This meant keeping a safe but open distance between himself and the senator, carefully avoiding identification of himself in any exclusive way with Wheeler's "radicalism," yet at the same time indicating to the senator and the senator's followers a sufficient sympathy with their position to retain their support—all this in tactical implementation of his long-term strategy.

Hence the curious mingling of liberal attitudes, progressive proposals, and conservative economic doctrine in his address to that year's Governors' Conference in Salt Lake City on June 30.

It was a conference whose announced central concern was unemployment, his own specific topic being "Unemployment and Old Age Pension," and this encouraged his coming closer than he had ever come before to a sharp definition of the state of the economy as an issue between the Hoover administration and himself. (He was actually presented to the conference, openly, as a presidential candidate.*) First, Roosevelt excoriated "government officials" for, in effect, lying to the country—they "juggle figures," they "distort facts"—about the extent of unemployment, which, he insisted, was a national problem requiring national solutions. "We can and we must think nationally." He cited in evidence the abrupt descent upon New York City the previous fall of some 40,000 workers laid off by the automobile industry in Detroit. Then, in words that puzzled liberals at the time, he implicitly blamed the economic collapse upon the Republicans' espousal of "a wholly new economic theory that high wages and high pressure selling could guarantee prosperity at all times regardless of supply and demand." ("Unfortunately for some of our Washington friends this new theory that although a man cannot pull himself up by the bootstraps a nation can, came an awful cropper when it bumped squarely into the old law of supply and demand.") His own pious respect for the ancient and immutable law led him to cast some doubt upon Hoover's current efforts to stimulate public-works spending by the states in order to reduce unemployment. Such works must be paid for from state treasuries, he pointed out, and these, if expenditures were large and prolonged, would be overstrained. Whereupon, in a breathtaking shift of stance, and as the only newsworthy part of his speech, Roosevelt became the first governor to propose unemployment insurance and old-age pensions as one way of steadying the economy and alleviating the human distress resulting from market fluctuations.

Social insurance was then no new idea in the world, nor untried in practice. A half century before, Germany's Iron Chancellor, Bismarck, faced with growing worker unrest and a rising Socialist party in an increasingly urbanized, industrialized German empire (then but a few years old), had pushed through the Reichstag laws severely restrictive of civil liberties and harshly punitive of Socialists, had then provided a "necessary" counterbalance of these

*In his welcoming address to the assembled governors, the Republican mayor of Salt Lake City, John F. Bowman, said, in unmistakable reference to Roosevelt: "If a member of the group here should be the Presidential nominee of his party—and I have in mind one who, I think, if elected, would make one of the great Presidents of the United States—he should, as President, have the support of all the people of the United States." "I feel like crawling under the desk," said a smiling Roosevelt when he stood up to speak a few minutes later, having been introduced by Utah's Governor George Dern.[8]

by securing enactment of a health insurance law (1883), accident insurance laws (1884, 1885), and an old-age insurance law (1889), all of them compulsory contributory insurance schemes involving the buildup of reserves to which the government contributed, along with the workers and their employers.* From Germany, compulsory social insurance had spread to Austria (1888), Hungary (1891), Luxembourg (1901), and England, where a comprehensive National Insurance Act, in 1911, added national health insurance and national unemployment insurance to the old-age pensions that had been enacted in 1908. England's initiatives in this area were largely due to a working alliance between Lloyd George and young Winston Churchill, who had become, respectively, Chancellor of the Exchequer and President of the Board of Trade in the Liberal government of Prime Minister Asquith. Young Churchill's motive for this enterprise was similar to Bismarck's insofar as Churchill's major concern was to prevent a social unrest that would weaken England as it faced the challenge of German militarism. But in the United States the social insurance idea, initially promoted by the American Association for Labor Legislation (AALL), founded by university professors of economics and political science in 1906, had run hard and, for the most part, futilely against a wall of Western frontier attitudes, those of Hoover's "rugged individualism,"† which continued to prevail in the middle-class mind and to dominate the business mind for decades after the frontier itself had disappeared. What Roosevelt proposed to his fellow governors, therefore, though long recognized by sophisticated minds as a necessary social implication of an advancing industrialism, was likely to seem a daring innovation to most Americans and a dangerously radical one to all conservatives.

So Roosevelt made his proposal more cautiously, less emphatically, than Frances Perkins had hoped he would. He drastically cut and modified the "three or four pages about unemployment insurance" that she had written for inclusion in his speech, saying merely that "proper study" could, he thought, develop a plan for insurance against unemployment that would not be a "mere dole [as per the then much-maligned British system] or handout from State or local governmental agencies but would be placed on a self-supporting basis through contributions from public treasuries, employers and the workers themselves." He advocated application of the same "sound" insurance principles to the alleviation of "old-age want," which increased as business and industry tended to employ younger people. Frances Perkins, listening to his address, which was broadcast over a national radio hookup, was initially

---

*Bismarck's idea, as he expressed it to England's W. Harbutt Dawson (see Dawson's *Social Insurance in Germany, 1883–1911,* page 11), was "to bribe the working classes, or, if you like, win them over to regard the State as a social institution existing for their sake and interested in their welfare." He succeeded: German workers, in whom revolutionary passions had flamed high from 1848 into the 1870s, were among the most docile in Europe by the 1890s.

†Yet Hoover himself, as Commerce Secretary in 1923, had actually proposed unemployment insurance, imposed through regional associations by federal authority, as one means of squeezing out part-time coal operators and bringing order and stability to bituminous and anthracite fields that were then a bitter battleground between exploited labor and exploitive management.

disappointed. But the favorable reception given his words by the assembled governors and by the national audience soon convinced her he had been exactly "right" in his judgment of the degree of emphasis required to achieve a maximum of persuasiveness. "If he had been more emphatic, there would have been an immediate shying away by all except the already convinced," she later averred.[9]

II

So it was that Roosevelt became established in the public mind, dangerously early, as front-runner for his party's presidential nomination, and this meant, as he knew only too well, that his gubernatorial reelection campaign must be waged and won, for it would be everywhere viewed as part and parcel of his developing campaign for the White House. Few political observers doubted he would win reelection: his personal circumstances and the general political climate overwhelmingly favored such an event. But for that very reason mere reelection would not serve his larger purpose. A narrow New York victory would be none at all in terms of presidential politics, would even be a defeat in those terms, since it would not give him sufficient political strength to overcome the opposition to his nomination, which, he knew, would be strongly if covertly exerted between now and convention time by those who had literally bought control of the national party machinery. He must win his second term by a large majority in a fashion demonstrative of great vote-getting power,

And it seemed highly likely that he would do so when he surveyed his prospects in early July, after his return to Albany from Salt Lake City.

His first-term record, especially as regards hydroelectric power, public utilities, agriculture, and social welfare, was a good one: Roosevelt could run on it strongly, straightforwardly. Moreover, he had achieved his record in a way that pointed up the poverty of constructive ideas and lack of concern for the general welfare in the opposition party, thereby weakening its voter appeal. His record, his highly effective use of radio speech to publicize it, his careful attention to small but vote-influencing detail (he concerned himself with such matters as the ruffed grouse hunting season), and his astute tactical harmonizing of the often essentially discordant interests of major political power blocs had enabled him to strengthen greatly upstate Democratic organization, yet without impairment of the support from city machines that could deliver to him the required urban majorities. He owed here a great deal to the Women's Division as run by Eleanor and her closest friends, with the advice and guidance of Louis Howe.

There were problems, of course.

For one thing, there was the question of Prohibition as an issue: Roosevelt must handle it in such a way as to retain as many dry votes as possible without loss of wet ones. But this was an issue on which his Republican opponent, whomever that might be, had more to lose than he did. Though more and more New Yorkers, Republicans as well as Democrats, were now as convinced as

Roosevelt had long been that the Eighteenth Amendment was a catastrophic error, a majority of those who remained most fervently committed to the Noble Experiment were residents of upstate rural areas who normally voted Republican. The indicated tactic for Roosevelt was a carefully timed but forthright advocacy of repeal, on the grounds that national Prohibition, without furthering temperance but in fact doing the opposite in New York, vastly encouraged racketeering and contempt for law. Such an advocacy, coupled with the argument for local option and local enforcement of strict liquor-control laws, appeared to be the best means toward true temperance (there must of course be no return of the old-time saloon!) and toward the reduction of crime. Meanwhile, the Republican candidate would almost certainly attempt a straddle on Prohibition. Whether personally wet or dry, he would feel forced to do so. And by this he would lose votes upstate, perhaps to a Prohibition Party candidate (organized dry forces threatened to field a ticket), without gaining any in New York City.

Prohibition, then, was an issue-problem easily solved.

Far more difficult and dangerous for Roosevelt—in fact, the only serious threat to the kind of reelection victory he needed—was the problem of Tammany corruption. It would not go away. The "unknown man" who had shot the gambler Arnold Rothstein before many witnesses in New York's Park Central Hotel nearly two years before was still at large and unidentified for the public. The obvious implications of this continued to agitate reformers and urge ambitious politicians toward further exposures of Tammany wickedness. And the dilemma thus presented Roosevelt was sharp-horned indeed. The corruption issue, he could not afford to forget, had been used up to the hilt against Jimmy Walker by the Socialist candidate Thomas and the Republican candidate La Guardia in the mayoralty campaign barely ten months before. La Guardia had made much of the documented fact that Rothstein had "loaned" $19,600 to Magistrate Albert H. Vitale, who was responsible for delivering the Bronx Italian vote to the incumbent mayor; Norman Thomas had made other persuasive charges of payoffs, blackmail, and extortion in the magistrate's courts. Yet Walker's half-million plurality on Election Day had been the largest any candidate for mayor had ever received! Clearly, the Tiger, wounded or no, remained a powerful animal: if Roosevelt provoked it into raging fury against him, his presidential aspirations could be torn to shreds. Even a passive hostility could defeat him: if he won nomination in spite of it, which would be difficult, he could lose the general election through the denial to him of New York's 47 electoral votes, a denial Tammany might effect simply by "sitting on its hands" during the campaign. On the other hand, if he permitted himself to be put in the position of condoning criminality, or seeming to do so, his presidential hopes would also die. Even his gubernatorial reelection, much less by the needed margin, could be endangered.

The situation, as he studied it for cues from on high, bred greater anxiety than he would ever publicly admit, the cues being far less clear and emphatic than he would have liked them to be. But here, again, there appeared to him in early July no reason for pessimism. He saw good reason to believe that his problem would be solved, was in fact being solved, by the tactics of skillful parry and calculated indirection he had thus far employed.

He drew confidence from the Republican failure to capitalize in Albany upon the New York City mess, despite exposures made *since* 1929's election. The Republican legislative leaders had certainly *tried* to capitalize. Perhaps they would have done so had they followed the lead of Suffolk County's W. Kingsland Macy when he introduced a proposal for a statewide legislative investigation of New York's lower courts. (Macy wished to make it statewide because earlier upstate Republican inquiries into, specifically, the iniquities of the New York City machine, by implying a felt moral superiority of rural over urban folk, had been resented by the latter: the upshot had generally been an increase in downstate Democratic majorities.) Such an investigation, vigorously and intelligently pursued, might have made Roosevelt appear as weak a character, as devious and opportunistic and devoid of moral courage, as Macy believed him actually to be, while at the same time elevating greatly Republican Party prestige. But the Macy proposal had been rejected. Instead, acting upon that assumption of the general public's stupidity that so often led it into disastrous error, the Republican leadership had tried to embarrass the governor with a bill conferring upon him the authority and means—thus, tacitly, the obligation—to conduct a full-scale investigation of New York City government. One immediate, predictable effect had been a move by Tammany to protect itself with a show of housecleaning. Vitale was sacrificed. While the investigative bill was yet in committee, the Walker administration itself produced evidence of the magistrate's wrongdoing, namely, that he had received $30,000 from Rothstein. The Bar Association disbarred him, and on March 13, the Appellate Division of the New York Supreme Court removed him from office. By the time the Republicans passed their bill, much ground had been cut from beneath their feet. In any case, their exclusively partisan motives were too transparently clear to make their move effective. Roosevelt lost nothing and probably gained in popular sympathy when, vetoing the message as soon as it reached his desk, he rebuked its proponents for their "obvious lack of good faith." The proposed special grant of power was redundant, he indicated in the veto message, since he already had power to act in response to specific charges, properly filed, and no legislature could confer upon him the right, which would violate the principle of home rule, to investigate any particular city government in the absence of specific formal charges. The case was different with the legislature, he concluded sarcastically. That body had "the right . . . to go wholly outside of specific charges of specific facts about specific individuals and to go on any general fishing expedition it wishes." He challenged it to do so, a challenge that Macy was eager to accept but his fellow Republicans chose to ignore. They then fell silent on the corruption issue, remaining so when the legislative session came to an end in mid-April.[10]

But then, in May, came new disclosures of the inner workings of the Walker administration, and these more damaging than any before. Charles H. Tuttle,

U.S. attorney for the Southern District of New York, who aspired to the Republican nomination for governor, filed charges that the Tammany Brooklyn judge W. Bernard Vause had received $250,000 from United American Lines, a steamship company, for obtaining a pier lease from New York's Sinking Fund Commission, of which Mayor Walker was *ex officio* chairman; that a former veterinarian and fire department official, one William F. "Horse Doctor" Doyle, had made a highly lucrative practice of obtaining for his contractor and landlord clientele, from the Board of Standards and Appeals, variances from the city's strict zoning and building regulations by splitting fees with, among others, the board's chairman, the Tammanyite William F. Walsh; and that the Tammany magistrate George F. Ewald, who had succeeded to Vitale's post, had been associated with the Tammany district leader Martin J. Healy, now the deputy commissioner of plants and structures, in the sale of worthless mining stock. Tuttle obtained some indictments. He presented local district attorneys with exhibits and sworn testimony they could not ignore. The huge publicity given his findings caused renewed demands from civic reform groups, from Tammany's political opposition, and from leading citizens for executive action in Albany. The Tuttle disclosures came very close to providing the specifics Roosevelt had said he had to have before he could act. All that seemed lacking was a formal request for action, and this the Socialists under Norman Thomas tried promptly to supply when they petitioned the governor for a Moreland Act investigation of the Walker regime. Roosevelt as promptly replied that the Moreland Act authorized investigations only of state departments; it did not apply to municipalities. Whereupon the State Republican legislative leaders—Assembly Speaker Joseph A. McGinnies and Senate Majority Leader John Knight—repeated the tactic that had failed during the legislative session, feeling with some justification that it now had better chance of success: they "demanded" (so Roosevelt and the public interpreted their statement) that the governor summon a special session of the legislature to obtain, by legislative enactment, the power to deal with municipalities as the Moreland Act enabled him to deal with state agencies. Roosevelt, who later privately admitted that he "had to do a lot of hard thinking over . . . [the] Knight-McGinnies demand,"[11] then arranged a meeting to be held on July 22 with the two Republican leaders to discuss the matter.

Meanwhile, a now seriously alarmed Tammany took further steps to protect itself, increasing not only the show but also the actual substance of a housecleaning effort. Vause and Walsh were forced to resign their offices. Magistrate Joseph E. Corrigan, a highly respected Democrat, was elevated to the post of chief magistrate by Walker, who as mayor made all magistrate appointments. Corrigan, whom Tammany had not theretofore seen fit to promote, perhaps because he had proved an able, independent, incorruptible officer of the law, promptly initiated what the reporter Ernest Lindley of the *Herald Tribune* called a "wholesale shakeup of the personnel of the magistrates' courts," his first major step being the forced resignation by Ewald of his magistrate's office. A committee to review and recommend revisions of the procedures of the

Board of Standards and Appeals was ordered by the mayor, who also, and most importantly, ordered his commissioner of accounts to inquire into every alleged misconduct of city agencies and departments.[12]

For this flurry of self-reforming activity, especially the belated application of a Tammany broom, albeit a far from clean-sweeping one, to dirt in the Hall, Roosevelt was profoundly grateful. It enabled him to remain still in the same defensive position he had occupied in mid-April, with the home-rule principle his shield, when in mid-July he embarked on the first of that summer's *Inspector* tours. As in 1929, he met with local officials, citizen delegations, and politicians at every stop. He discussed with them such things as unemployment, electric-power prices and availability, Prohibition, and specific matters of local concern. At Seneca Falls on July 20, for instance, he urged the importance of better country roads. In general, he was relieved to find that, though the topic naturally came up in his meetings with politicians, New York City's scandals aroused no great excitement among his rural constituency; there were few expressions of strong personal concern over them.

All the same, the Tammany problem remained urgently with him, and although the position he had taken with respect to it seemed to him tenable, he was considerably less comfortable in it than he had been three months before. He was also less secure in it now than then, since the constitutional ground he stood upon was exceedingly narrow and, being more loose sand than solid rock, was highly erodible in the high wind of controversy that swirled across it—a wind that would almost certainly grow stronger as the Republicans, desperate for a viable issue in the upcoming campaign, seized upon the Albany executive's alleged scared subservience to the Tiger.

Hence Roosevelt's move to widen somewhat his defensive standing ground and to render it a bit more solid while simultaneously reducing, so far as he could, the wind storm across it. On the same day as he made his public speech about rural roads, which was just two days before his scheduled meeting with Knight and McGinnies, he sent them a letter, which he also released to the press. In this letter, which he called a "state paper," he said he had no intention of calling a special session. There was no need for one. Already he possessed all the power that a democratic state executive should have to act against municipal wrongdoing, he reiterated; but "observance of the home rule principle" dictated that such special action be taken only as a last resort, after it had become crystal clear that specific local officials in specific cases were breaking the law and that there was no further recourse through the courts to assure their removal from office. He reminded Knight and McGinnies that the Appellate Division of the New York Supreme Court now had, under recently enacted law, full power to investigate magistrate's courts. Charges against Manhattan magistrates should be submitted to the department of the Appellate Division covering Manhattan and the Bronx. However, this did not mean that he would shirk his own responsibility. "With respect to the specific matters which the New York City Commissioner of Accounts and the local District Attorneys are now investigating," he wrote, "I shall stand ready to send the Attorney-General . . . to the City of New York for an extraordinary term of court with an extraordinary grand jury whenever it becomes apparent that an investigation is not as complete and as searching as it should be." But such action, he indicated, would be the ultimate limit of proper executive action in this matter. " . . . if action by the Attorney-General in these cases becomes . . . of no avail, it then becomes a matter for the Legislature itself to investigate."[13]

The immediate effect was what Roosevelt had hoped it would be. Newspaper editorials, generally approving the governor's letter, impugned the motives of Knight and McGinnies, who at once retreated. At the scheduled meeting, in the small western New York town of Arcade, Knight read to the press a statement denying that he and McGinnies had ever asked for a special session! "Sam Rosenman and I almost fell backwards," wrote Roosevelt in a letter to Lehman.[14] All they had said was that they would raise no objection to the governor's calling of one. Then, again, they lapsed into silence on this subject.

III

ONLY for the time being, however.

Twelve days later, the ambitious and indefatigable Tuttle, being unable to obtain indictments from a federal grand jury because Tammany witnesses took refuge behind the Fifth Amendment,* submitted to the Tammany district attorney for Manhattan, Thomas C. T. Crain,† incontrovertible evidence that Mrs. George Ewald, on the very day of her husband's appointment as magistrate, had personally delivered $10,000 in cash to his former associate in the phony stock sale, the Tammany district leader Martin Healy. The inevitable conclusion that Ewald thus paid for his office ($10,000 was alleged to be the standard price charged by Tammany for a magistrate appointment) was vehemently denied by Mrs. Ewald when questioned, as she at once was, by District Attorney Crain. She "explained" that the $10,000 was an unsecured "loan" for which, alas, the note signed by Healy had been "lost." It had been a transaction of pure friendship: Healy needed the money to finance a new home he was building on Long Island. Mayor Walker backed her up, indicating that Ewald would have been as likely to throw money "down the sewer" as he would have been to give it to anyone on the assumption it would buy an official appointment. Actually, he had appointed Ewald, Walker said, because the Steuben Society and leaders of the German-American community had urged him to do so.[15]

---

*Federal grand juries were not permitted to grant immunity to witnesses in return for self-incriminating testimony, and Tuttle, in view of his later action on immunity, would probably not have asked for such a grant had one been possible.

†Crain, a personal friend of John F. Curry's, and a former magistrate, had been persuaded by Curry to resign from the New York Supreme Court, where as justice he had been highly regarded, in order to run for district attorney in 1929, though Crain was within a year of retirement age. He had won election by a wide margin.

Such testimony was of course unpersuasive of a now at last thoroughly aroused city public, which watched closely Crain's handling of this test case, exploding in a wrath almost as ominous for Roosevelt as it was for Tammany when, on August 15, Crain blandly announced that he had been unable to secure grand jury indictments in either the Ewald-Healy case or any of the others presented by Tuttle. At once Rabbi Stephen S. Wise of the City Affairs Committee dispatched a public letter to the governor charging Crain with laxity and incompetence in his investigation of the magistrate's courts and calling, again, for state executive action in the matter. So did other prominent citizens who were politically independent, along with the independent press. So did the predominantly Republican leaders of the Bar Association. And so, of course, did Republican politicos—not by letter but by public statement.

Clearly, the time had come when Roosevelt could no longer either parry or sidestep without first delivering a thrust of his own, and at this juncture he acted promptly, vigorously, in accordance with his June 20 pledge.

Though Crain, surprised by the vehemence of the public outcry, was already in the process of reopening the Ewald-Healy case, Roosevelt ordered him to send its grand jury record to Albany, where Roosevelt turned it and the case over to the Republican attorney general, Hamilton Ward, for prosecution. Simultaneously, he asked New York Supreme Court Justice Philip J. McCook, also a Republican, to convene on September 15 an extraordinary (so-called blue-ribbon) grand jury to hear and act upon the testimony Ward developed. There were political risks for Roosevelt in this procedure. If smaller than those of *no* executive action, they were still disturbingly large. Ward had proved in the past to be utterly ruthless in pursuit of his political ambition,* and, like Tuttle, he now aspired to Republican nomination for governor. He could be counted upon to make, with no scrupulosity whatever, the most possible out of the opportunity for favorable personal publicity that the governor now presented to him. This was dangerous for the governor: any "general fishing expedition" into Tammany operations whence stemmed sensational charges of general corruption might hurt him badly in an election campaign having corruption as a partisan issue. So limits were placed, by Roosevelt's instructions, upon the scope of Ward's inquiry. Ward was to confine his investigation exclusively to the Ewald matter.

Roosevelt then moved, a few days later, to offset the criticism bound to be made of this limitation of Ward's activity, namely, that he, cravenly deferent to Tammany, blocked the sweeping and probing inquiry obviously needed. He asked the First Department of the Appellate Division of the New York Supreme Court for a full exercise of its newly acquired investigative and removal powers over the magistrate's courts. Further, he suggested, though this was not generally known, Judge Samuel Seabury, for the post of referee, to conduct the inquiry. Formerly of the Court of Appeals, Judge Seabury was an eminent lawyer of lucrative practice who had been the Democratic Party's 1916 nominee

*See page 47.

for governor of New York. Roosevelt's suggestion was accepted at once. Seabury's appointment was announced on August 26 by the presiding justice of the First Department, Edward R. Finch, some hours before Seabury himself, who was on vacation in London, received formal notification of it. None could now plausibly charge that the needed inquiry would not be made, for Seabury was a man of unquestioned and unquestionable integrity, as greatly respected as he was capable, and he had fought many a bloody battle against Tammany in the past. His investigation would certainly be prolonged and exhaustive. But for that very reason its disclosures could have no effect upon the upcoming election. When Seabury, having sailed home on the *Aquitania* (he landed September 5), met with bar leaders and newspapermen in the county courthouse on September 29, he indicated that weeks and maybe months of unpublicized investigation would precede public hearings. "The essential facts can be ascertained only by laborious investigation," he said. "They do not lie patent upon the surface—they must be brought to light."[16]

And initiation of the Seabury Investigation, as the inquiry came to be known through the press, *did* blunt criticism of Roosevelt's dealings with Tammany. Such criticism was by no means eliminated, however: it remained substantial, and it remained sharp. Indeed, well before Seabury had formally begun his work, Roosevelt had reason to wish he had not so precipitously acted in literal fulfillment of his June 20 promise. There had been reasonable alternatives to his arming of Ward and McCook with weapons they could and did promptly use against him on behalf of the Republican Party. He might have "rebuked Crain and ordered him to submit evidence to another grand jury," or he might have "obtained from Ward an agreement to appoint a competent special prosecutor who would have gone about his business without regard to the requirements of the Republican campaign," as the reporter Ernest K. Lindley would observe.[17] In the event, Ward was denied his golden opportunity for self-promoting publicity. Under extreme pressure from Republican colleagues, among others, he was forced to assign the actual investigation to a lawyer familiar with New York City affairs (Ward, it will be remembered, came from Buffalo); he named, as special assistant attorney general, Hiram C. Todd. But from the outset, Todd, a Republican, evinced to the politically sophisticated as great a concern to embarrass the governor and to advance party interests as Ward could have done, this outweighing the concern to serve justice and promote reform. It was a concern, or imbalance of concerns, fully shared by the judge who presided over the blue-ribbon jury's hearings. At the jurors' very first convening, on September 15, Republican Justice McCook suggested in his charge that they might wish to go into "related matters," once they had disposed of Ewald-Healy—might wish, in other words, to request of the governor a widening of the terms of reference under which they operated, thus enabling them to inquire, with state financing of the inquiry, whether or not the alleged $10,000 bribe paid by Healy was but an instance of the system Tammany employed in making judicial appointments.

The suggestion could not have been better timed for persuasive effect upon the jury and public. It followed hard upon the sensational revelation that a colleague of McCook's upon the State Supreme Court bench, Justice Joseph F. Crater, a Tammany Democrat, was now listed on police records as a "missing person"! He had been for a month! On August 6 he had entered a taxicab in front of a West Forty-fifth Street restaurant where he had lunched with two friends, one of whom was a Ziegfield Follies chorus girl. He had waved gaily to these friends as he rode away and then had vanished as if swallowed up by the earth, never to be seen or heard from again.* The disappearance evidently had been prepared by Crater himself: in the days immediately preceding his farewell he had liquidated all his stockholdings, had closed out all his bank accounts, and had otherwise tidied up his affairs, leaving few loose ends dangling. And the suspicions thus aroused in the blue-ribbon jurors' mind, as well as in the popular mind, were heightened when it was pointed out that Crater was a former president of a Tammany club in the Upper West Side district of which Martin Healy was Tammany leader. Had Crater's appointment, then, to the Supreme Court bench, been bought in the same way and through the same man as Ewald's to the magistrate's court had been?† If the answer was yes, then Roosevelt himself was involved, however innocently, since it was *he* who as governor had made the appointment less than nine months before. Moreover, he had made it in accordance with the wishes of John F. Curry and against those of Al Smith. This had raised eyebrows at the time among those who, aware of the power struggle between Curry and Smith, were equipped to measure Crater's merits against those of the man whom Smith had sponsored for the post. Most knowledgeable observers agreed there was no comparison between the two: Smith's candidate, Bernard L. Sheintag,‡ was much the better man, indeed, a man of such quality as was rarely available to gubernatorial choice.

A week of hearings sufficed for the handing down, by the special grand jury, of criminal indictments against Ewald and Healy. It was a week during which most of the testimony the jurors listened to, from witnesses introduced by Todd, had no direct exclusive bearing upon the case at hand but a great deal to do with "related matters." Thus, on September 24, while Republican delegates were gathering in Albany for their party's state convention, the special prosecutor called before the jury John Curry himself, along with some sixteen of his Tammany subordinates, all of them city officeholders (Walker had named no fewer than eighty-five Tammany district leaders to city posts paying, on the average, $7,500 a year). None remained more that a moment upon the witness stand. Todd addressed to each a single question: would he, the witness, sign a waiver of immunity from prosecution for self-incriminating testimony?

*To this day, Crater's fate remains unknown.
†Soon, sworn testimony and documentary evidence presented in grand jury hearings would disclose that Crater had withdrawn $7,000 from his bank account, in cash, within a day or so following his Supreme Court appointment. An additional $15,500 in cash was withdrawn a few days later, making a total cash withdrawal of $22,500, for which no explanation was forthcoming.
‡Roosevelt subsequently appointed Sheintag to fill the vacancy left by Crater's disappearance.

Each replied with a flat no! Whereupon each was contemptuously dismissed by Todd. This made sensational news, provoking new public cries of outrage with its implication of covert criminality among city officeholders in general. And it was quickly followed by the Ewald-Healy indictments, which, being based almost wholly upon evidence that Crain's grand jury found unconvincing, seemed a disparaging commentary upon Crain's competence as prosecutor, if not upon his commitment to truth and justice. Naturally, the jurors then acted as the presiding judge had suggested they should: they dispatched to the governor a formal request for an expansion and extension in time of their state-funded investigation.

It was on the day following Todd's parade of nontalking Tammanyites before the jury and public that the Republicans opened their convention in Albany with a keynote address by the U.S. Secretary of State, Henry L. Stimson. His choice could be justified by the fact that he was a native of New York City and a former (unsuccessful) Republican gubernatorial candidate; its effect was to point up the national significance of the upcoming state campaign and the Hoover administration's anxiety concerning it. Nor did Stimson's words blunt this point: he extolled the administration's record as if this were at issue in New York's election. The convention delegates, however, pointedly declined to follow Hoover's lead regarding Prohibition, the President being in favor of a postponement of a decision on Prohibition until after the Wickersham Commission had made its report and recommendations. By a vote of nearly three to one they adopted a platform plank calling for immediate outright repeal of the Eighteenth Amendment. They did so with the intent to remove Prohibition from the agenda of partisan debate. In early September, Tuttle, already virtually assured of the nomination he sought, had let it be known that he personally favored repeal. Roosevelt had countered immediately with a highly publicized "Dear Bob" letter to U.S. Senator Wagner, who was to keynote the Democratic State Convention, calling for a new national constitutional amendment that, repealing the Eighteenth, would restore "real control over intoxicants to the several States." There could be no doubt that New York would reject state Prohibition in favor of "a reasonable sale of intoxicants through State agencies," wrote Roosevelt, though there must of course be "some definite assurance that by no possibility at any time or in any place shall the old saloon come back."[18] Similar pious pronouncements about the "old saloon" were made by the Republicans now in convention, after they had crushed the drys in their midst. And so the erstwhile troublesome issue, which was especially troublesome to New York Republicans, seemed disposed of. The delegates in Albany could and did turn their attention to "Tammany corruption" and to the Roosevelt administration's alleged craven failure to deal with it, endorsing a platform that stressed this. Then they nominated Charles H. Tuttle for governor and Caleb H. Baumes for lieutenant governor.

Fortunately for the Democrats, Tuttle's skills as a courtroom lawyer proved not to include any great talent for public speaking. His nomination acceptance address, delivered in the convention's closing hour—a speech in which he

declared "the issue" of the campaign to be the question whether or not the state
would have a governor "bigger than Tammany Hall" and challenged Roosevelt to show in action whether he stood "by his own grand jury or by Tammany
Hall"—had no inspirational effect upon his immediate audience.[19] All the
same, the Republicans departed Albany in a glow of enthusiasm and optimism
that would have been utterly impossible a few weeks earlier.

Nor were they alone in their belief that Roosevelt's political future, which
at summer's height had shone in brightest sunlight, was now, in early autumn,
shadowed by clouds of doubt.

A week before the Republican convention, Walter Lippmann, grown increasingly critical of, as he saw it, Roosevelt's artful dodging and lack of
candor concerning the executive's power to act against manifest Walker regime criminality, had editorialized in the New York *World* that Tuttle would
be a good, strong candidate. Lippmann ticked off reasons: Tuttle's record as
U.S. attorney had earned him the respect and gratitude of the people of New
York; an avowed wet, he would appeal to the so-called Al Smith Republicans,
who, out of opposition to their party's stand on Prohibition, had maintained
a Democratic executive in Albany since 1922; and, most important of all,
Tuttle as governor would exercise fully the state's power to break the grip of
corrupt Tammany upon New York City.[20] The New York *Times,* normally
Democratic, opined that the corruption issue brought hope to a Republican
cause that, only a short time before, had been hopeless. Even among Roosevelt's own advisers there was expressed fear, immediately following the adjournment of the Albany convention, that Tammany scandals would reduce
his New York City plurality by more than 100,000 and might narrow his
statewide margin of victory to a mere 50,000.[21]

IV

AND what of Roosevelt himself? How did he think and feel about his circumstances at this point?

If he felt anxiety, and some of his letters show that he did, it was not about
the outcome of the election at hand. Never, in his gloomiest moments, did he
accept as valid the pessimistic estimates of his gloomiest advisers. On the
contrary, he sensed and accurately assessed the hopeful factors in his New
York situation—factors clearly discernible by historical hindsight—and remained serenely confident that the campaign just before him would produce
a victory of satisfactory proportions.

One such factor, which he had by August definitely decided to stress in a
state campaign having national implications, was the collapse of the Republican Prosperity and the current state of the general economy. He was encouraged in this issue-choice, which would probably be even more effective in 1932,
by the obvious intent of the Hoover administration to campaign overtly against
him, an intent manifest in Stimson's appearance before the Republican State
Convention. "Lack of leadership in Washington has brought our country face

to face with serious questions of unemployment and financial depression," Roosevelt would therefore say in his formal nomination acceptance speech, of which the first draft had already been prepared by Rosenman, Howe, and his erstwhile law partner Basil O'Connor, working under his instructions. "Each state must meet this situation as best it can."[22] On this issue his state victory would clearly be a national one, further impressing him upon the popular mind as leader of Hoover's national opposition.

As regards Prohibition, the Republican leadership had made its usual mistake of underestimating the intelligence of the common folk. Having adopted a platform and named a gubernatorial candidate as wet as those of the Democracy would be, thereby eliminating, as they hoped, Prohibition as a campaign issue, the Republicans had nominated dry "Law-and-Order" Baumes to run against wet Lehman, their evident assumption being that this last would mollify upstate drys. The actual effect would be to convince both wets and drys of Republican Party insincerity with respect to this matter, driving fervent drys to vote for a Prohibition Party candidate, or not at all, while at the same time reducing one of the three advantages Lippmann had seen in Tuttle's candidacy, namely, Tuttle's appeal to "Al Smith Republicans." Roosevelt would make this reduction as great as possible: one of his campaign tactics would be to challenge candidate Tuttle to say whether or not he, Tuttle, as governor would sign a new Prohibition-enforcement bill to fill the vacancy left by the repeal of the Mullan-Gage Act in 1922, if such a bill were presented him by the legislature (there was not the slightest chance that one would be).[23]

Essentially similar, and of immensely greater magnitude, was the mistake made by the Republicans, if what they were virtually *forced* to do could be deemed a "mistake," when they chose Tammany corruption as their major or only issue and "Tiger Tamer" Tuttle as their standard-bearer. Far from reducing Roosevelt's New York City plurality, this issue- and candidate-choice would probably increase it.

One had only to look at the situation from the point of view of Boss Curry, Jimmy Walker, and their cohorts to see that this was so. Tammany's leaders resented Roosevelt's launching of the Seabury Investigation, though Walker had of course said publicly that he welcomed it, an investigation whose disclosures months hence could not but injure them. They resented the letter Roosevelt addressed to Mayor Walker on the day after the refusal by Curry and company to sign the waivers of immunity that Todd requested of them—a published letter saying it was "contrary to public policy" for public officials to "plead immunity . . . in regard to official acts" and that Walker should therefore advise all the officeholding district leaders to "return before the special grand jury," "voluntarily" waive immunity, and "freely answer all questions relating to their official acts."[24] These same leaders would certainly resent the strong denunciations of New York City government corruption, especially of Tammany's buying and selling of judicial posts, that Wagner in his keynote address at the Democratic State Convention and Al Smith in his speech nominating Roosevelt would make with Roosevelt's blessing. In addition, they would also resent Roosevelt's insistence that the platform adopted at that convention include a plank calling for legislation whereby every official, by taking oath of office, automatically waived immunity against self-incriminating testimony regarding official acts. They were bound to protest bitterly, if privately, any further steps Roosevelt was bound to take against their exposed malfeasance during the campaign weeks just ahead. Nevertheless, Roosevelt could confidently expect what did in fact happen: when Tammany delegates arrived in Syracuse for the Democratic convention on September 28, seething with anger against the governor because of the "insult" given Curry by the letter just sent to Walker,* they were promptly soothed by Curry himself, who then "exacted from each [of them] a pledge to do his best for the state ticket,"²⁵ this after Tammany's lawyers had seen saving grace in the governor's careful limitation of the required immunity waivers to "*official acts*" only (every questionable act was, of course, "unofficial").²⁶ Indeed, so long as the governor measured his steps short of an all-out full-scale attack upon their power and persons, the besieged Tammanyites must engage in intense, fervid activity on his behalf, "getting out the vote" for him as they had seldom, if ever, done for an earlier gubernatorial candidate. They must do so because of the horrendous alternative to his reelection that was presented them by the Republicans. They knew that Roosevelt, both by personal temperament and by political ambition during the next two years, would be inclined to give large benefits of doubt to the Walker regime and to temper justice with mercy for those criminals of that regime upon whom his office required him to pass judgment. Tuttle as governor, on the other hand, would necessarily continue to act the role of public prosecutor, pursuing Tammany malefactors with tireless ruthless energy and encouraging, to the fullest extent of his power to do so, the merciless punishment of those convicted of crime.

Hence, the Republicans' choice of issue and candidate could be profitable for them at the polls only if it had enormous voter appeal upstate—and Roosevelt was sure it did not. If it gained any votes upstate at all, as a matter of fact, the gain was unlikely to offset the loss the Republicans would take on the Prohibition issue in rural areas. Other observers confirmed Roosevelt's impression that the upstate electorate saw little connection between New York City scandals and their own concerns and, in any case, did not hold him responsible for them. Upstate he yet retained rather more than vestiges of the reputation he had won as a warrior against Tammany bossism in the affair of Blue-eyed Billy two decades before.†

No, to repeat, the anxieties Roosevelt felt with regard to his political circumstances in late September 1930 did not include the fear he would not be reelected by a satisfactorily large majority. They had to do with the limits that might be imposed upon his governing action, once he had won reelection, by

---

*Jimmy Walker, who had nominated Roosevelt for governor at the 1928 convention, would not even attend the 1930 one.
†See *FDR: The Beckoning of Destiny,* pages 246–247.

the *way* in which he won it. They had to do with the effect his handling of the Tammany corruption issue would have upon those whose support he must have nationally to be nominated and elected President in 1932. And they had to do, more vaguely, with the general historical context in which his presidential power must be won, then exercised in terms of the long-term general goal that he, as God's special agent, felt himself assigned to pursue.

"Before our eyes," Norman Thomas had said to his fellow Socialist Party members a few months before, "the Socialist prediction of the breakdown of capitalism is being fulfilled with a rapidity and completeness which not even the most confident Socialist expected to see in 1928." "We call this country a democracy," the novelist Theodore Dreiser had said in the spring of 1930. "It's really an oligarchy. The seat of government is Wall Street, not Washington. . . . For a long time this country has been moving unconsciously toward communism. Whether it will come to that I don't know. But some change must come." In July 1930 Charles H. McCarthy, who had served as one of Roosevelt's two secretaries when Roosevelt was Assistant Secretary of the Navy (the other had been Louis Howe) and had managed the 1920 Vice-Presidential campaign, was appalled by the sight of some 5,000 women lined up to obtain application blanks for an advertised 200 openings as charwomen in government service in Washington. In a letter to Roosevelt dated July 31 he commented ominously upon what he had seen, saying that the way things were going "we are certainly heading for what took place in Russia. . . . We will all have to join the Reds soon and if present conditions and the present attitude of big business men and women in responsible positions continue any man will be justified in doing so." In August 1930 James W. Gerard lent support to the Dreiserian view of American "democracy" by publishing with sensational effect a list he had drawn up of *the* fifty-nine men who ruled America—a list later expanded to sixty-four names. Only one of them held a government post and he, Andrew Mellon, exercised his primary power not as U.S. Treasury Secretary but as the great Pittsburgh banker who controlled the monopolistic Aluminum Company of America. Two on the list, William Green and Matthew Woll, represented organized labor, and their inclusion seemed to most observers incongruous. All the others were big-business men—Rockefeller, Morgan, Lamont, Charles Mitchell, Samuel Insull, John J. Raskob, William Randolph Hearst, and the Du Ponts. They were "themselves . . . too busy to hold political office but they determine who shall hold such offices," and they dictated national policy.[27] Dozens of similarly expressed opinions and statements of alleged fact crowded in upon Roosevelt's mind that summer and autumn. They fed and strengthened the opinion Roosevelt had himself expressed in mid-May in a letter to Democratic Congressman William I. Sirovich of New York City. "There is no question . . . that there will be a gain throughout our country of communistic thought unless we can keep Democracy up to its old ideals and its original purposes," he had written. "I know that you will agree with me in believing that we face in this country not only the danger of communism but the equal danger of the concentration of all power, economic and political, in the hands of what the ancient Greeks would have called an Oligarchy."[28] Clearly, he who was elected President in 1932 might be hard put to save democratic capitalism from the threat of totalitarianism, left or right, and it behooved Roosevelt to keep this in mind as he, campaigning for gubernatorial reelection, defined the deteriorating economy as a political issue between himself and Herbert Hoover.

Sharper, more specific, more immediate, was his anxiety over the effect his handling of Tammany corruption might have upon national public perceptions of him as a presidential candidate, and there is evidence that this anxiety was joined with a troubled conscience. On October 1, Mayor Walker somewhat belatedly complied with what was in effect an order from the governor: he called in the Tammany district leaders whom Todd had sought to question and gave them twenty-four hours in which either to sign immunity waivers or to resign office. On October 2, these leaders went before the special grand jury and offered to sign the *limited* waivers (confined to "official acts") that the governor's careful wording suggested—offers that Todd, with a great show of angry contempt, refused in a way that made Roosevelt seem, on this matter, tricky. Four days later, Roosevelt refused the special grand jury's request for an expansion of its field of inquiry, arguing that such expansion would confuse and conflict with the Seabury Investigation and that, in any case, he lacked constitutional authority as governor to do what the jurors asked. And three days after that, squirming in the harshly critical light now focused upon him by men of good will, he revealed both anxiety and uneasy conscience in a sharply worded letter to the Reverend W. Russell Bowie, rector of Grace Church in New York City, a leader among civic reformers, who was a Harvard classmate and had been a hero-worshiper of his since college days.*

Bowie had written him on October 4, deploring his manifest reluctance to take the bold forthright action against the Walker regime that justice and human decency required. "It is of the judgment of the whole country and of tomorrow rather than today that I am thinking," Bowie had said, as if in echo of Roosevelt's own long-term concern. " . . . the innate idealism of America is hungering for a leader who in some conspicuous crisis such as this will cut through the entanglements of expediency and stand in the open as the unquestioned assailant of corruption in politics no matter where it is found. This great distinction I covet for you. And the time has come when it seems to me that you must either win it or lose it."[29] Stung, Roosevelt replied with unwonted heat, accusing "Dear Russell" of having "fallen for some of the deliberately untruthful and misleading articles and editorials." At once lofty and profound, by his own account, were the motives and reasons for his acting as he had on the "local situation in New York." The issue was "not . . . between Curry and myself" but "between the retention of constitutional government and a break-

---

*Bowie had succeeded Roosevelt as managing editor when Roosevelt became president of the *Crimson* at Harvard and had been Ivy Orator at commencement ceremonies when Roosevelt and he received their A.B. degrees.

ing down of the safeguards of liberty in the same way that they have been broken down in the Italy of Mussolini and in the Russia of Lenin." New York City, as an executive problem, was by no means unique. "During the past two years I have received anonymous letters, rumors and allegations concerning supposedly corrupt acts of public officials in fifty of sixty-two counties." He could act legally, however, only "on definite specifications relating to a definite case," as he had done when he activated a special grand jury in the case of Ewald-Healy. He lacked "the authority of a Czar regardless of law." He must obey the law, and "the law requires specifications, so there you are!" (A cynical Bowie might have seen as vicious indeed the confining circle that Roosevelt claimed he was legally compelled to draw: apparently the executive could not begin an investigation of city corruption until it had substantially in hand the "definite specifications" that the investigation was designed to discover.) He urged Bowie to "[t]hink over, too, this immunity question. Never in Anglo-Saxon civilization have Grand Juries asked people not suspected of crime [*sic*] to waive immunity; . . . the danger to our constitutions and our personal liberties has always become too apparent. With official acts it is, of course, different. In thinking this over, for the love of Mike, remember that I am just as anxious as you are to root out this rottenness, but that on January 1st, 1929, I took a certain oath of office."[30]

V

BY that time, which was the second week of October, the political campaign was beginning to move into high gear, and it proceeded pretty much as Roosevelt had confidently expected it would.

He was now in total command of state party machinery. He had forced the resignation of Utica's William Bray, originally an Al Smith man, from the chairmanship of the Democratic State Committee, despite strong efforts by several upstate county chairmen on Bray's behalf, and without giving Bray the nomination for attorney general that Bray coveted. He had replaced him with Rockland County's James A. Farley, who continued to work well with Howe (Farley worked well with everyone, but Howe's was a special case, an acid test) and who during the last two years had continually demonstrated major talent and tireless energy as a political organizer. Moreover, Roosevelt had done this with such smooth efficiency that neither Bray nor his supporters could publicly display resentment. Farley would later say that "Bray volunteered to step aside in order to defer to the Governor's wishes."[31] Roosevelt had virtually dictated the party platform, with its immunity-waiving plank, another plank pledging establishment of a special commission to study employment stabilization and unemployment insurance, a plank calling for state action toward old-age security against want, and a plank calling for legislation that would apply to lower court judges the prohibition against the simultaneous holding of business corporation offices, which already applied to superior court judges. Indeed, at Syracuse the governor had so obviously and absolutely dominated the state convention, every element and phase of it, that charges of his "subservience" to any politician or political machine lost credence. All knew that key phrases of the tune he called must sound harshly in John Curry's ears, yet Curry had danced to it on the convention floor.

In his informal nomination acceptance speech, delivered to the delegates at the close of the Syracuse convention on September 30, the candidate Roosevelt struck the dominant note of his campaign, indicating the strategy he would pursue in his quest for votes. He poured contempt upon his opponent, whom he never named, for referring "to the 'issue' and not to the 'issues' of the campaign." Evidently "the control of public utilities, the relief of rural taxation, old-age security against want, the solving of the unemployment problem, cheaper electricity for the people by the exercise of their sovereign rights in their own water power, prison reform, labor laws, the building of hospitals, the bettering of local government, the improvement of dirt roads, the reform of the election laws—all these things, . . . for which I have fought for two long years with the unprogressive, short-sighted Republican legislative majority, are no longer matters at issue. I have apparently converted the entire Republican party to my views." And what of "the sole issue" to which his opponent "limits himself"? It was the "most remarkable . . . ever advanced for being elected Governor. When I . . . read this keynote address of my opponent I was puzzled . . . as to whether he was running for Governor . . . or for District Attorney of New York County." But since this was his opponent's "only issue, let me hasten to assure him that this particular Governor will stand, as he has always stood, for the authority, for the enforcement and the integrity of the law with due respect for the fundamental rights of every citizen concerned, irrespective of political faith."[32]

In his formal acceptance speech, on October 3, he chastised the "Republican leadership" for a mindless obstruction of "progressive government," an obstructionism rooted in "personal interests," nourished by "selfish reasons." But he went on to "make it perfectly clear that in my judgment this Republican leadership does not represent the great rank and file of the men and women of this state who call themselves Republicans." He was "confident" that of this rank and file "large numbers" would "recognize this autumn, as they have recognized before, that Government at Albany must be progressive"; they remained "as out of step with the leadership of their own party as they have been in the past." He poked fun at his "distinguished opponent's" attempt, after two days of hesitation, to answer with "no hesitancy," as Tuttle had said, the "simple question . . . whether or not he would sign a State [Prohibition] enforcement act, a question based on the widespread belief that some agreement of this kind was made to secure the support . . . of dry leaders who have fought for this measure for so many years." The answer had been "a long and lawyer-like way of saying 'yes' and at the same time 'no.' " He rebuked a Tuttle statement that he, the governor, "had given the special grand jury a 'wooden hatchet' with which to do its work," saying, "Permit me to inform . . . my distinguished opponent that I did not give the grand jury a hatchet of any kind.

... Their weapons are the scales of justice and the sword of justice, to protect the innocent as well as to punish the guilty." He then announced that for the next two weeks he would be fully occupied with his constitutional duty to prepare the executive budget for 1931 and so could "give little thought to the campaign or to myself as your candidate." His "distinguished opponent" would be active during those two weeks, having "announced that he is going to proceed upstate and, as he was quoted in the press, 'get down among the people.' " Roosevelt was sure "the people will be properly flattered" and hoped that his opponent would "at the same time . . . inform himself [through conversation with 'the people'] of those great matters of State policy about which he has as yet said nothing, those vital questions affecting the welfare and prosperity of all our fellow citizens," which were "the real issues of this campaign."[33]

A few days later, Roosevelt spoke candidly of his campaign strategy to a reporter for the Kansas City (Missouri) *Star,* who interviewed him in his East Sixty-fifth Street home in New York City. "I will give Mr. Tuttle that time [the time required to prepare the budget] in which to tell the people of New York all he knows about Tammany," said the governor, smiling broadly. "I am being liberal I think. Probably he could tell all he knows in two hours. But I give him two weeks. By that time I predict the state will be ready to hear about the real issues of this campaign."[34]

Actually, the people were already hearing "about the real issues" as Roosevelt defined them. Louis Howe had seized upon the then-new technology of the "talking" motion picture. He had used some of the surprisingly ample funds (surprising, that is, for Democrats in a year of financial depression) that were being collected by the Broadway theatrical producer Howard Cullman to produce one of the earliest documentary sound films, *The Roosevelt Record.* * It was booked into some 200 movie theaters across the state; it was also shown via five hired Movietone sound trucks to scores of outdoor assemblages, enabling the sight and sound of Roosevelt in action to reach hundreds of thousands of voters who would never see him in the flesh. Molly Dewson, whom Eleanor Roosevelt and her women friends had put in charge of the Women's Division campaign with the enthusiastic approval of Howe and Farley, had also tapped party funds for innovative enterprise. She had prepared a printed handbill, its text supplied by Rosenman at Roosevelt's order, wherein the cost of operating electric irons, waffle irons, carpet sweepers, and other appliances in New York towns was compared with the much lower cost of operating them in Ontario, Canada. To every Democratic woman whose name appeared in state committee files, a sheaf of these handbills was sent with a cover letter,

*Cullman was then commissioner of the Port of New York and cooperated with Henry W. Morgenthau, Sr., elderly longtime "angel" of the New York Democracy, and with Gerard and Arthur C. James, the railroad magnate (he was on Gerard's list of America's "rulers"), in raising money for Roosevelt's 1930 campaign. The first commercially produced talkie picture, mingling sound with silent film, starred Al Jolson as the Jazz Singer and was released in the fall of 1927; the first all-talking picture, *The Lights of New York,* premiered in July 1928.

individually typed and addressed by three stenographers employed for this labor, instructing the recipient to give a copy of the handbill to every woman she knew who was neither a fervent Republican nor a fervent Democrat and to explain to that woman what the governor had done and proposed to do to lower New York's electricity rates. The tactic was so successful that many women remembered the 1930 New York campaign forever after as the "waffle-iron campaign."[35]

Meanwhile, Tuttle campaigned as his circumstances compelled him to do, and with no more, indeed rather less, vote-getting effectiveness than Roosevelt had expected. This was so despite developments in the area of Tuttle's single issue that were highly embarrassing to Roosevelt.

It now appeared that the governor's refusal of "his own" special grand jury's request for prolonged, widened investigative powers had been a political blunder. The refusal's all too evident purpose, Roosevelt's claims to the contrary notwithstanding, was to end the special jury's operations by cutting off its state funding. This cutoff did occur. But private funds were then at once sought and forthcoming from civic reform groups and from concerned citizens having well-stuffed pocketbooks, so that the jury continued uninterruptedly in active session,* and the highly publicized testimony presented it by Todd's witnesses all through October increased the persuasiveness of Tuttle's charge at his first campaign rally that, since "the Governor needs the support of Tammany Hall in the current campaign and in preparation for 1932," he, the governor, did as little to curb Tammany criminality and as much to shield it from exposure as public opinion would permit. " . . . the State needs a Governor that leads rather than follows public opinion and is bigger than Tammany Hall," Tuttle had gone on to say.[36] A considerable portion of the Todd testimony had to do with the mysteriously vanished Judge Crater. But to this was now added the case of Judge Amadeo A. Bertini, whom Roosevelt had appointed to the Court of General Sessions just three weeks before New York City's 1929 election—an election whose outcome would profit Roosevelt politically to the extent that it reduced the Republican legislative majority. As a lawyer in private practice, Bertini had won little distinction. He had made his money, a sizable amount, as a businessman. He had almost no experience in criminal law. The Bar Association deemed him unfit for the judgeship and said so in public statement. This, however, counted for nothing against the fact that Bertini was a friend of John Curry's. It was at Curry's behest, and to curry favor with Curry, that Roosevelt had named Bertini to fill the vacancy left when General Sessions Judge Francis X. Mancuso, who had been discreditably involved in the collapse of City Trust,† resigned under fire. Bertini, at the time of his interim

---

*Roosevelt spoke of the special jury, thereafter, as "Ward's grand jury."

†Mancuso had served simultaneously as a judge and as chairman of the board of the now scandalously defunct bank, his being one of the cases leading to New York legislation prohibiting sitting judges from holding private corporation offices.

appointment, had just been nominated by Tammany for the elective post—a nomination tantamount to the election he did then win, by a wide margin, in the Walker landslide. It was now charged or broadly hinted by Todd that, simultaneously with his nomination and appointment, Bertini had made a large cash donation ($30,000 was the figure cited) to his Tammany district leader. Subpoenaed before the grand jury, Bertini refused to waive immunity on grounds that the Todd inquiry was being improperly, unfairly conducted, and so was dismissed without being questioned. He then issued a masterfully devised public statement that not only denied the charge against him but put Todd on the defensive, a statement so effective that Todd declined to press the case. Further damage was nevertheless done to Roosevelt's image as progressive reformer in minds already critical of him.

Roosevelt's campaign strategy with regard to these embarrassments was simply to ignore them.

On October 18, before assembled reporters and photographers, he accepted life-insurance policies totaling $560,000 taken out fifteen days earlier, at normal rates, with twenty-two insurance companies. The beneficiary of the policies was the Georgia Warm Springs Foundation, but the likelihood of the foundation's collecting on them at any early date was exceedingly remote, according to the doctor who had conducted the medical examination of him for the companies. The public was informed that the governor was completely recovered from his polio save for his legs, which showed considerable improvement in the thighs. He weighed 182 pounds, normal for a man standing six feet one and a half inches tall;* his blood pressure was somewhat lower than average for men his age (forty-eight); he had a chest expansion of five and a half inches, which was greater than Jack Dempsey's and two inches greater than average; and he possessed, generally speaking, a magnificent physique.[37]

An hour or so later he took this magnificent physique of his aboard a train bound for Binghamton, where that evening he made the first of his formal campaign addresses. In it he gave a general accounting of his "stewardship" of the state citizenry's interests during the last two years and damned the Republican leadership for its lack of ideas, its hostility to every proposal for social welfare and economic justice. "I can say without fear," he declared, "that every constructive measure of importance . . . has been originated by Democratic leadership since 1910." He made no mention of New York City scandals. Nor did he when he spoke in Buffalo two nights later; instead, he spoke there of depression and unemployment, of the Hoover administration's failure to deal with them adequately, and of his own efforts and plans to increase public-works expenditures and institute rural tax relief. He laid heavy stress upon the claims of credit for prevailing prosperity that the Republicans had issued in 1928, extensively quoting the campaign addresses of Herbert

---

*But Roosevelt, as the public was *not* reminded, did not stand normally. He sat. And his withered legs contributed little to his overall weight. From the hips up he was abnormally thick and heavy of body.

Hoover, with bitterly ironic effect. He also quoted a letter just received from President William Green of the American Federation of Labor. "Your leadership as Governor of the State of New York stands out in the most striking way and the work you are able to do must be classified as a most rare accomplishment," Green had written. "You deserve the support of labor, and of all classes of people who seek to perpetuate our free institutions and who are engaged in preserving our principles of free government." At Rochester, on the following night, October 21, Roosevelt spoke of prisons and parole, of improved hospitals, and of his old-age insurance proposal. "I look forward to the time when every young man and young woman entering industrial or agricultural or business activity will begin to insure himself or herself against the privations of old age," he said. "The premiums which that young man or young girl will pay should be supplemented by premiums to be paid by the employers . . . , as well as by the state itself. In that way, when the young man or young girl has grown to old . . . age, he or she will have built up an insurance fund which will maintain them in comfort in their years of reduced activity. . . . They will be receiving not charity, but the natural profits of their years of labor." At Syracuse the next day he devoted the whole of his address to his program for cheap electricity in the home and on the farm, and at Albany on October 24 he addressed himself exclusively to the problem of public-utility regulation.[38]

Not until his last campaign speech, in Carnegie Hall in New York City on the night of November 1, with Curry and other Tammany bigwigs seated on the platform behind him, did candidate Roosevelt mention the corruption issue. He did so then at full length—and with devastating effect upon his opposition.

By that time, Tuttle's campaign was obviously in a bad way, and had been for weeks. Upstate audiences were interested in the topics Roosevelt chose to talk about; they responded enthusiastically to his personality and to what he said. But they were increasingly irritated, even disgusted, by Tuttle's harping upon his single theme, his silence upon matters that to them were of vital concern. "If he's so worried about New York City's corruption he should have stayed down there and done something about it instead of coming up here to tell us about it. It's none of our business, and it was there long before Governor Roosevelt took office. It'll probably still be there after we're dead and gone." This was a typical reaction of northern New Yorkers to a typical Tuttle speech. Moreover, as expected, and even more than expected, the Prohibition issue was hurting Tuttle's candidacy. Fervent drys were infuriated by the Republican leadership's attempt to make the party, in Roosevelt's words, "an *amphibious ichthyosaurus* equally comfortable whether wet or dry, whether in the sea or on the land or up in the air";[39] they were much more angry with Tuttle on this score than with Roosevelt, whose party had never pretended to represent them. So they nominated a Prohibition Party candidate for governor, a Syracuse University professor named Robert Paris Carroll, who in his speeches ignored Roosevelt altogether but said a great deal about the evil forces promoting Tuttle. It was in obvious desperation and with considerable reluctance that

New York Republicans accepted active help from Washington in the campaign's closing days, a help not so much asked for as thrust upon them by an anxious White House. Into the state came Secretary of War Patrick J. Hurley and Under Secretary of the Treasury Ogden L. Mills, primarily to campaign for Republican candidates for Congress (these, too, were in trouble) and to woo disaffected drys back into the ranks of national Republicanism, but also to aid Tuttle and defend the Hoover administration against Roosevelt's strictures upon it. From Washington via beamed radio broadcast came the voice of Secretary of State Stimson, emphatically agreeing with Tuttle that the transcendent issue before the people of New York was Tammany's corruption of the judiciary and Roosevelt's demonstrated "unfitness to deal with the great crisis." (Next morning's newspaper headline, STIMSON CALLS ROOSEVELT UNFIT, angered Roosevelt as did no other single item of the opposition campaign.)

Thus the governor had been presented with an opportunity to impress upon the national mind, as well as New York's, that his victory in the upcoming election should be interpreted as a victory over the Hoover administration, whose hydroelectric-power policy, approach to unemployment, and handling of Prohibition he opposed. He could do this in the process of rebutting both Tuttle's charges and Stimson's. And he had worked hard to take full advantage of the opportunity as he, with his writing team of Rosenman and O'Connor, prepared the speech whose reading copy was on the lectern before him, in Carnegie Hall, that night of November 1.

As usual, his speech delivery was superb.

Why, he began, had the Republican candidates refused to discuss "the many great issues" that he himself had discussed "with truth and frankness" for the last two weeks? Because on every one of them the Republican record, made in the service of narrowly selfish special interests, was dismal. Hence the decision by Republican leaders "to adopt . . . a policy of misrepresenting and distorting a local situation in the City of New York" to the exclusion of all else. But "after continuing this campaign of calumny against the [New York City] judiciary coupled with utter silence on actual state issues for two whole weeks, the Republican leaders began to realize that the people of the city and state were beginning to resent this hypocrisy as an insult to their intelligence." A call went out for help from "the Republican national Administration," which, "suddenly solicitous for our welfare," then "presumed to send into this State campaign officers of the cabinet itself to instruct us how to manage our State affairs." And what were the qualifications for their assignment of these "estimable gentlemen"? One, Patrick Hurley, came from Oklahoma, had never lived in New York, knew nothing whatever of state problems. The other two, Stimson and Mills, were citizens of the state; but both had run for governor in campaigns similar to the one the Republicans now waged, and both had been defeated. Surely the people who had "repudiated them are the best judges of whether or not any man is fit to be Governor." As for himself, he would make "no personal attack on these three gentlemen," nor would he "dispute their personal fitness to hold the great offices they do." He simply said to them, "We shall be grateful if you will return to your posts in Washington, and bend your efforts and spend your time solving the problems which the whole nation is bearing under your Administration. Rest assured that we of the Empire State can and will take care of ourselves and our problems." He passed in review, in the most favorable light, the actions he had taken in response to specific allegations of judiciary corruption, laying heavy stress on the fact that he, "a Democratic Governor on the eve of a campaign for reelection," had "sent into a Democratic county a Republican Attorney General and a Republican judge with an extraordinary grand jury" to deal with charges "that a magistrate of the city of New York had paid a district leader for his appointment." And how had the attorney general responded? By "using his office in every way possible to pervert the function of the grand jury . . . for the political benefit of Republican candidates," who, in cooperation with "a small section of the local press . . . sought . . . to make the people of this city believe: (1) That the greater part of the 220 judges in this city are corrupt; (2) that as a result the judiciary as a whole is no longer worthy of the confidence of the people; and (3) that neither I nor the Democratic Party in city or State will lift a finger to restore confidence in the courts and punish the guilty." His face was set in grim lines. His voice rose on a singing tide of indignation. "I, as a citizen of this State and as Governor, resent this campaign. . . . I, and the members of my Administration, do not yield place to any Republican candidate or editor in abhorrence of a corrupt judiciary. We do not yield place to anyone in indignation against any holder of public office who is recreant to his trust. We do not yield place to anyone in the sincere . . . desire to punish those judges who have or who may prostitute their positions. If there are corrupt judges still sitting in our courts they shall be removed. They shall be removed by constitutional process, not by inquisition; not by trial in the press but by trial as provided by law. If there is corruption in our courts I will use every rightful power of the office of Governor to drive it out, and I will do this regardless of whether or not it affects or may affect any Democratic or Republican organization in any one of the five counties of New York City, or in any one of the fifty-seven other counties in the state.* That is clear. That is unequivocal. That is simple honesty. That is justice. That is American. That is right." Roosevelt visibly relaxed through a long period of loud applause that then ensued, Curry and his men perforce joining in it. He was again smiling, his voice was again warm and friendly, when he spoke his last words, asking at this campaign's end for the support of New York's electorate.

He closed with a statement of literal truth: "Cheerfully and confidently, I abide the result."[40]

For he was now assured that his victory would be larger than he had at the

---

*The veiled threat in this remark was not lost upon the Republican leadership, whose reluctance to promote a statewide investigation of the lower courts had as one root a fear of what it might disclose of corruption on the part of upstate Republican judges.

outset thought it could be. Jim Farley wanted to issue a statement that night for next morning's (Sunday's) newspapers predicting the governor's reelection by a plurality of more than 600,000. Roosevelt dissuaded him: overconfident Democratic workers might relax last-minute efforts on behalf of Democratic candidates for Congress and the state legislature, might work less hard on Election Day to get Democrats into polling booths. Also, if Farley's estimate of victory size proved too great by far, as Roosevelt, for all his optimism, believed it to be, the credibility of Farley's future political prognostications would be reduced. So Farley scaled his prediction down to 350,000, which was 50,000 more than the highest prediction made (by James Kieran of the New York *Times*) in a voting pool formed by twenty newsmen who had been covering the campaign. Roosevelt's own estimate was a plurality of 437,000, but he did not publish it. When he arrived at Hyde Park on Sunday evening for a day of relaxation and recuperation from a "slight cold," he told reporters he thought that Tuttle's plurality upstate might be cut to as little as 100,000 but that most of his advisers believed him too sanguine; they estimated Tuttle's probable plurality outside New York City at about 200,000.[41]

VI

THE event, on Tuesday, November 4, 1930, proved even Farley's expectations to have been too modest.

At one o'clock in the afternoon of that day, Roosevelt and Eleanor, with Missy LeHand and Sergeant Earl Miller, voted in Hyde Park's Town Hall, Roosevelt casting ballot 494 for himself and the straight Democratic ticket. Then he returned by automobile to his New York City home, accompanied by his wife, his mother, and Henry Morgenthau, Jr. In the early evening he went to his campaign headquarters, a large suite in the Biltmore, where, in a room from which all were barred save the Roosevelt family, others of his closest intimates, and a few invited guests, among them Al Smith, he received election returns that were, from the first, astonishing. By nine o'clock he had in hand Tuttle's telegram of concession and congratulations. By ten, when he returned to 49 East Sixty-fifth Street, it was clear that he was carrying New York City by a vote greater, actually 60,000 greater, than Walker had received in his unprecedented landslide victory of the year before. More astonishing still, to the point of incredibility, were the returns from upstate, which he continued to receive via radio and telephone in his home. Tuttle's plurality was not merely reduced upstate, it was wiped out! Roosevelt was carrying precincts and wards and whole districts that had not before voted Democratic in living memory! It appeared he would have a statewide plurality of over 700,000 (actually it was more than 725,000), nearly twice as great as the theretofore largest gubernatorial plurality in New York's history, that of Al Smith (387,-000) in 1922. It appeared that his upstate plurality would be well over 150,000 (actually it was 167,784) and that he would carry three times as many counties there as Tuttle would (actually he carried forty-three compared with Tuttle's fourteen). It was a day of national triumph for the Democracy. Democrats won control of the U.S. House of Representatives for the first time since 1916 and reduced the Republican majority in the U.S. Senate to a single vote, which meant an antiadministration Senate, for such Progressive Republicans as Norris and La Follette voted with Democratic liberals. Democrats had captured state houses all across the land. But no individual personal triumph elsewhere in the nation was anywhere near as great as Franklin D. Roosevelt's in New York.[42]

An analysis of this astounding triumph could not but enhance Roosevelt's confidence in his judgment and skill as political organizer and campaigner. The event fully justified the careful detailed attention he had given to agricultural matters and upstate organization, and it proved that he had accurately weighed the corruption and Prohibition issues against those he deemed substantially important and that he had shaped with regard to them the correct strategy. Obviously Tammany had made the unwontedly arduous efforts on his behalf, or against Tuttle, that he had anticipated, for an amazing 91.1 percent of the registered voters in New York City had gone to the polls. Upstate, only 70.6 percent of the registrants had voted, and of these, a substantial number who would normally have voted the Republican ticket had voted for Roosevelt (he won more votes than there were Democratic registrants in every county outside New York City) or for the Prohibition gubernatorial candidate: Carroll's upstate total was 181,000, or some 13,000 more than Roosevelt's plurality there. Obviously, too, Roosevelt's stress on hydroelectric power and utility regulation as issues had been highly effective in transforming Republican into Democratic votes: the "waffle-iron" campaign had yielded large vote dividends in precinct after precinct across west central and northern New York.

Many, and of national import, were the signs and portents in these election returns. Not all of them were as immediately obvious as those pointing the way to the White House for Roosevelt and the Democracy two years hence.* Some were seen only by minds prepared to see them through a knowledge and philosophy of history, with an accompanying sensitivity to underlying trends.

The Socialist Norman Thomas, for instance, saw in the statistics a mingling of opportunity and threat for his cause, both enormous; he assessed significances with a consequent, commensurate, joy and dread. The New York Socialist Party had made manifest gains at the polls since 1928. Socialist candidates for its state Senate had won 105,600 votes in 1930, compared with 65,700 in 1928, a gain of 60 percent. Socialist candidates for Congress, among them Thomas, running respectably but third in the Sixth District, Brooklyn, had garnered 127,500 votes in 1930, as compared with 66,800 in 1928, a gain of 92 percent. But the Socialist candidate for governor, Louis Waldman, had done less well: he had won 88,000 votes in 1930, as compared with 49,000 in

---

*"The Democrats nominated their President yesterday, Franklin D. Roosevelt," was the actor-humorist Will Rogers' comment in his nationally syndicated column dated November 5, 1930.

1928, a gain of only 50 percent. Why? Obviously because of the Roosevelt landslide.

And there, for Norman Thomas, was the rub!

The increased Socialist vote, though small in number, was large in significance for the future, in Thomas' belief. It reflected the beginnings of a popular awareness that neither major political party addressed itself effectively to the human consequences of economic depression, if indeed that increased vote did not measure the beginnings of an awareness that capitalism itself, fatally flawed, was in a state of collapse. One might reasonably expect that Socialist sentiment would grow in geometric progression during the years just ahead as the downward economic spiral continued and as Thomas and his party intensified their efforts toward political organization and popular education. The prospect of a continued human misery, a mass misery out of which sprang threats of Fascist or Communist dictatorship, was distressing and frightening, of course. But this fearful distress seemed balanced by an opening of the way toward fundamental changes in American society whereby that society, with its vast technological capability, freed itself from a thoroughly discredited private-business control, organized itself rationally and cooperatively upon generous principles, and dedicated itself to the achievement of genuine personal freedom, of truly human community, within a peaceful world order. All that seemed needed for this was a sharpening focus upon, and clarification of, the fundamental issues between right and left. The issues would then be resolved on the side of left democracy, Thomas believed, given the nature of current social pressures and their operations within the American political tradition.

But what if the focus upon issues were not sharpened, nor the issues themselves clarified? What if there were instead a blurring and confusion of issues?

This was the fear accompanying the growing probability that Franklin Roosevelt would become President of the United States in such minds as Norman Thomas'. For though one saw no profound commitment to humane ideals, no great moral courage or strength of character, in Roosevelt's dealings or refusals to deal with the Walker regime's viciousness—though one saw no sign that the governor really understood the current crisis and had clear ideas for dealing with it, as one examined his handling of hydroelectric power, banking chicanery, and unemployment during his first term—one did see large and clear, in every phase of Roosevelt's operation, a genius for image making, a swift shiftiness of footwork, a quick eye for the main chance, and a remarkable ability to persuade the public that trivial patchwork improvisations were actually major solid achievements. With every passing week of the last eight months, Thomas had been further confirmed in a belief that Socialism had more to fear from Roosevelt than from any other man who could possibly win the presidency in 1932.

BOOK TWO

⇥⟩⟨⇤

The Rocky Road
to the White House

➤➤╳◄◄

7

The Governor as Presidential Candidate

I

AT precisely forty-five minutes after noon on November 5, 1930, from a termi-
nal slot in the Grand Central Station basement, a New York Central train, its
every car brightly lit, began a journey northward so smoothly that no passenger on it had a sensation of motion, none knew his journey had begun on
schedule, unless he happened to be gazing out a window. And there was no
reason, no inducement, for an outward look at this outset. There was nothing
to see. From wide bleak basement gloom the train glided into the narrow
gloom of a tunnel, where it remained, rushing through a dank concrete hole
beneath the bustle of the world city, with increasing noise and speed, for many
minutes.

Nor was there much widening and brightening of outlook when the train
emerged from tunnel into open air.

The light of day was dreary, the open air was a cold gray wind, and even
when the train had moved beyond North Tarrytown into the rolling woods and
fields of Westchester, where the mighty river at the left of the tracks widened
out to the dimensions of a large lake, with whitecaps whipped across it by the
wind from this east bank to that Rockland County shore where, at Grassy
Point, Jim Farley had been born and raised—even then the visible landscape
remained a narrow one. For at that point in temporal space, or spatial time,
what had theretofore been a light thin drizzle became all at once a heavy
curtain of rain and mist that dropped down from ever-lowering and ever-
darkening clouds. Visibility was reduced to barely a half mile in any direction.

Yet aboard the governor's special car at the rear of this northward-roaring
train there was nothing of chilly gloom, no damp drizzly November of the soul.
Franklin Roosevelt rode there with intimate associates only—people tied to
him less by career ambition than by strong bonds of personal affection, people
with whom he could and did relax, since they imposed upon him little necessity
to maintain social distance or appearances greatly at odds with his sense of
realities. Short, thin, sharp-faced, sharp-eyed Basil O'Connor was there, his
former law partner, whose practical talents as organizer had done so much to
make Roosevelt's dreams for Warm Springs come true. Stocky, broad-faced,
methodical, industrious Sam Rosenman was there, whose quick sharp intelligence belied the stolidity of his appearance and whose use of that intelligence
continued to make him indispensable to the governor as legal adviser, editor,
and writer. Wizened, ugly, sickly little Louis Howe was there, whose whole
life since 1912 had been so absorbed into Roosevelt's life and career that
historians would be hard put to determine with any precision what his individual contributions had been to the overall Roosevelt enterprise, knowing only

that the contributions were immense, and who now, on this northward journey, kept as wide a distance as possible between himself and Rosenman, as narrow a one as possible between himself and the governor. Roosevelt's old friend Tom Lynch of Poughkeepsie was there, who with John E. Mack had launched Roosevelt on his first election campaign in 1910, had handled finances for the 1920 vice-presidential campaign, had been at the station to greet the stricken Roosevelt when Roosevelt arrived in New York City on a stretcher following his polio attack at Campobello, and who was currently, by gubernatorial appointment, president of the State Tax Commission. Strong-jawed, slightly built, dignified Missy was there, sweet of face and temper, softly brilliant of eye, wholly feminine in her feeling and manner, but the personification, all the same, deep down, of granite-hard New England conscience—a Puritan conscience, one might say, had she not been, in religion, Roman Catholic. Beside her, laughing with her, was pretty, rosy-complexioned, vivacious Grace Tully, an Irish Catholic whose conscience was strong but less stern, more lyrical and self-forgiving than Missy's could ever be. Both women loved Roosevelt personally. Grace Tully loved him as a beloved daughter adores a handsome, brilliant father. Missy loved him with a self-immolating devotion as great as Howe's, though of very different nature. It was a devotion that often caused Eleanor to feel sorry for Missy, since it destroyed Missy's chance for any truly independent life and rendered her peculiarly vulnerable to, defenseless against, deep and possibly fatal hurts; it even aroused in Eleanor, now and again, a species of contempt for the younger woman, for her naïveté, conjoined with a hurt resentment of implicit violations of her own marital "rights" and prerogatives. Yet she loved Missy, deeply, sincerely, as a human being. Indeed, the whole psychic relationship between these two, compounded of endless variations on the themes of love and hate, loyalty and betrayal, envy and compassion, was complicated beyond the understanding of either of the two principals, much less of any historian, though hints of its quality might have been perceived by a shrewd observer, possessed of the factual knowledge we now have, had one been on this car this day. For Eleanor, too, was there. She had left last night's victory celebration at 49 East Sixty-fifth Street earlier than any other intimate, allegedly because she must meet Wednesday morning's Todhunter class alert and prepared, and just before she retired she had hastily scrawled in pencil a note to her husband that historians might find interesting for its, in the circumstances, curiously detached, faintly patronizing tone. "Much love & a world of congratulations," she had written. "It is a triumph in so many ways, dear & so well earned. Bless you & good luck these next two years."[1] This morning she had taught her class, giving her pupils no sign that anything of great importance had occurred for her, and then had rushed to Grand Central just in time to board this train. She was now glowing with a happiness that had less to do with her husband's triumph, our knowledgeable observer might suspect, than with the fact that the handsome virile Earl Miller was beside her, paying her gallant attentions.

Among all these people the prevailing mood was of sunlit happiness, the prevailing sound was of jokes and laughter. And "a lot of the joking," Sam Rosenman would remember, was "about the Presidency."[2]

This last was a new departure.

Everyone in the car had taken for granted for at least the last year that the governor aspired to the White House and had a more than fair chance to achieve it. Little or nothing had been said about it out loud, however, for somewhat the same reason that teammates of a baseball pitcher who is throwing a no-hit game studiedly refrain from mentioning the fact until the last man is out in the ninth. To speak of presidential victory in 1932 until its indispensable prerequisite, a satisfactorily large gubernatorial reelection victory in 1930, was behind them had been felt to be "bad luck," a needless "tempting of fate." But now the taboo was removed! He who had been dubbed a "Half-of-One-percent" governor following his paper-thin 1928 victory was now, it appeared, the greatest vote getter in the nation! Roosevelt himself, riding into the rain-shrouded landscape of his past, glancing now and then through rain-streaked window into streaming mists along the great thematic river of his life, was acutely aware that the river flowed inexorably southward, that the waters of his future flooded down in seemingly irresistible tide toward Washington, while he in his physical body moved northward toward Albany. He was also acutely aware, however, that the symbolic river had a various width, that the historical river it symbolized might be dammed by designing men at its narrowest segment and there diverted from its "natural" channel and that such tides of event as he now contemplated are unpredictably reversible, ebbing and flowing according to unknown laws of history, unknown purposes of God. Hence, though he shared to the full his companions' happiness, laughed at their jokes, and enjoyed their verbal anticipations of his future glory, he did so with certain unspoken reservations. There was, in his joyous mood, an element of tentativeness, of uncertainty and indeterminateness. He remained reticent and noncommittal regarding his own personal designs upon the two years just ahead.

"I do not recall his saying seriously even once that he was interested in 1932," Rosenman would remember, "—or that he was not."[3]

The train paused briefly at Poughkeepsie. Thereafter it roared northward without pause, past Roosevelt's birthplace, the steep wilderness slope of his boyhood going down to the river, the house that was the one real home he had ever known; past Rhinebeck, where, in Vincent Astor's heated pool, he had begun to "swim back to health" after his crippling illness ("Water got me into this fix! Water will get me out again"[4]); then out of Dutchess into Columbia County and past Tivoli, where, at gloomy Oak Terrace, her maternal grandmother's country home, Eleanor had spent much of her miserably unhappy childhood and whence her alcoholic uncle, Vallie (Valentine Hall), raving in his cups, had descended upon the Executive Mansion only a few months past (it had been in mid-July; Earl Miller had had to subdue him by physical force before transporting him back to Tivoli[5]); then finally into Rensselaer County and the city of Rensselaer and across the lordly Hudson on ringing steel into the county and city of Albany.

The sky was at its darkest, the rain at its heaviest, when the train pulled into Albany's railroad station. In such miserable weather, Roosevelt could not have been surprised or disappointed if but meager results had been produced by the efforts of the local Democratic organization to have a large crowd on hand to hail his triumphant return to the state capital. He *was* happily surprised by what he saw through his window as the train ground to a stop. Jammed round the station and as near the tracks as safety permitted, under umbrellas that reminded one correspondent of a great "cluster of mushrooms" opened beneath the deluge, were perhaps a thousand people.[6] They cheered his descent from the train, his progress to a waiting automobile; they hailed him, so newspapers would report, as the "next President." And, incredibly, thousands more lined the streets as he made triumphant progress, accompanied by a brass band, down Albany's Broadway, up State Street, then along Eagle Street to the Executive Mansion, where again a crowd of many hundreds had clustered, awaiting his arrival. He smiled. He waved. From those who cheered and applauded came loud voices crying their expectation that he would win the White House two years hence. He laughed but shook his head as, here and now, he entered the house of the governor.

And there, within minutes of his entrance, he accepted a phone call from Jim Farley in New York City, a call that was probably not unexpected, since what Farley wanted to tell him about was a press statement that Louis Howe had helped to prepare and that would make front-page headlines in every newspaper in the country. The gist of the statement was that Roosevelt was now, willy-nilly, a candidate for President of the United States. "The Democrats of the nation naturally want as their candidate . . . the man who has shown himself capable of carrying the most important state in the country by a record-breaking majority," Farley had said. "I do not see how Mr. Roosevelt can escape becoming the next presidential candidate of his party, even if no one should raise a finger to bring this about." Farley would later claim he was anxious about the response Roosevelt would make to this "linking of his name to the presidency" for, on Farley's part, the first time, and in the absence of any prior consultation with the governor on the matter. He had no need for anxiety. Roosevelt did not even ask to hear the issued statement. "Whatever you said, Jim," he said with a laugh, "is all right with me."[7]

II

THUS, before the last vote of 1930's election had been counted, Roosevelt and associates were "embarked on another campaign . . . , a campaign for the nomination for the presidency," as Rosenman would write, with Roosevelt only too acutely aware "that everything he said or did from that time on would be interpreted in the light of his candidacy and would affect it."[8] Not separate from but essentially identical with his campaign for the presidency in 1932 would be the remainder of his first term as governor of New York and his second term up until November of the presidential election year.

Yet this identity must be publicly denied by him. Indeed, of the two processes that were in essence and covert practice fused, the very existence of one must, he felt, be publicly denied, for by his interpretation of historical tradition in the light of his special circumstances in this autumn of 1930, and also by the sheer joy he derived from "acting" a "part," he was required to disclaim any concern whatever with the presidency as a future possibility for him.

He did so with a perfectly straight face within minutes of his acceptance of Jim Farley's phone call in the Executive Mansion on November 5. "I am giving no consideration or thought or time to anything except the duties of the governorship," he said to assembled newspaper reporters. " . . . and to be clearly understood you can add that this applies to any candidacy, national or otherwise, in 1932."[9]

He maintained this stance in private as well as in public, even on occasions when there appeared no great need to mention the subject.

" . . . quite frankly I mean what I have said," he wrote a month after Election Day to Mrs. Caspar Whitney, a good friend of Eleanor's who was an extremely active member of the League of Women Voters (and one wonders how or if Missy or Grace Tully kept *her* face straight as she took down the words in shorthand), "—that I am not in any sense a candidate for 1932, partly because I have seen so much of the White House ever since 1892, that I have no hankering, secret or otherwise, to be a candidate."[10]

A little more than two weeks *before* this letter was written, Ed Flynn, having been asked to spend the night in the Executive Mansion, had dined with Roosevelt and Louis Howe on a dark November evening. The three men were alone together. They ate, therefore, not in the Mansion's large formal dining room but in the much smaller, cozier breakfast room. Afterward they went into the library, where Roosevelt, turning at once to Flynn, came directly to the point. "Eddie," he said, "my reason for asking you to stay overnight is that I believe I can be nominated for the Presidency in 1932."[11]

But he did *not* believe this would happen "if no one should raise a finger to bring . . . [it] about." Even a forest of fingers, merely lifted, could not prevail against the strong hands bearing potent weapons that were now being raised against his ambition, as he had known they would be.

On the very morrow of Election Day, simultaneously with Roosevelt's triumphant return from Albany, Raskob and Jouett Shouse, in the name of the Democratic National Committee, had addressed to President Hoover an open letter bearing the signatures of three former presidential nominees—Al Smith, John W. Davis, and James M. Cox—and the two Democratic leaders of Congress—the soon-to-be House Speaker, John Nance Garner, and the Senate minority leader, Joseph T. Robinson, both of whom were politically conservative. The letter pledged Democratic cooperation in the new Congress with respect to administration efforts to promote business recovery. It even promised to forgo, in the interests of constructive harmony, efforts to revise downward the Hawley-Smoot tariff rates (Raskob was unremitting in his efforts to commit the Democracy to high protectionism, in defiance of the most hallowed of party traditions), while saying nothing at all about relief for the unemployed, farm relief, public-power development, or labor reform.

Clearly, from the hands that shaped this epistle, Roosevelt could expect nothing but hostile acts, to the limits of covert hostility, as he aimed for the White House. Clearly, if he was to achieve his object, a major organized effort would have to be made according to carefully calculated designs.

Luckily, or, rather, as the fruit of arduous labor steadily pursued for a decade, Roosevelt and Howe had at hand much of the material, much of the human resource, of such organization. In January 1920, when Herbert Hoover was generally assumed to be a Democrat, not having yet announced a party preference, and when his prestige was at its highest because of his vastly publicized administrative services under Wilson during the war,* one of Roosevelt's college friends, the attorney Louis B. Wehle, a nephew of Louis Brandeis, had sought to promote a national Democratic ticket of Hoover for President and Franklin Roosevelt for Vice-President. Wehle's most telling argument, when he called upon Roosevelt to urge the latter's cooperation in this enterprise, was that Roosevelt in his vice-presidential campaign tours "would make a great number of key acquaintances in every state" and could, if he would "methodically build on them," acquire a "personal following in the Democratic Party" that might lead him to the presidency.[13] When Roosevelt did become his party's vice-presidential nominee that year, Wehle's advice, which was in perfect accord with Howe's own predilections, had been followed. By the end of the campaign, Roosevelt and Howe had on file many hundreds of index cards listing the names, addresses, occupations, special interests, and even, when unique or remarkable, the personal characteristics of influential men and women in every state of the Union. With these people and the hundreds more whom Roosevelt had since met, a sufficiently active personal correspondence had been maintained to assure their willingness, even eagerness, to work for Roosevelt's presidential nomination. (Howe in New York City conducted what Flynn called "a veritable letter-writing mill for the governor.")

But how were they to be "gathered together in a working organization"? This, as Flynn would remember, was the "real problem" faced by the three men in the Mansion library that November night. It was a problem whose solution could not be delayed. Time was of the essence. Roosevelt, now so emphatically established as a front-runner in this race and in consequence so obviously targeted by party conservatives as a man to be shot down, could not for a moment forget that (1) these conservatives had their hands on every lever of the national party machinery, (2) a two-thirds vote of the convention

---

*"He is certainly a wonder, and I wish we could make him President," wrote Roosevelt of Hoover to Hoover's friend Hugh Gibson on January 2, 1920. "There could not be a better one."[12]

delegates was required for presidential nomination by the prevailing Democratic rule, which meant that a man could enter the convention with a majority of the delegates initially committed to him yet still fail to get the nomination (Champ Clark had had eleven more than a majority on the tenth ballot in 1912, yet Woodrow Wilson was nominated), and (3) there was little if any chance that this two-thirds rule could be changed in the 1932 convention. The very fact that Roosevelt was a front-runner worked against such change: Northern conservatives of the Raskob-Shouse stripe would be as anxious to retain the rule as the South, whose peculiar regional interests (agrarian, white racist) it was designed to protect. In view of all this it was imperative that Roosevelt prepare *at once* to take full advantage of his head start. He must strive to forge so swiftly and far ahead that potential rivals would be discouraged from active campaigns of their own; he must strive to invest his candidacy with the overwhelming momentum and inevitability of a landslide by the time the first primaries were held. He needed, therefore, and soon, someone who would function as unannounced campaign manager or, to put it more accurately, as unannounced personal agent until the formal announcement of his candidacy was made sometime early in 1932. The agent should be someone who could travel extensively throughout the nation making organizational contacts with Roosevelt's friends, persuading and cajoling local Democratic politicos into the Roosevelt camp, and lining up delegates committed to Roosevelt in the nominating convention.

"Would you do this for me, Eddie?" asked Roosevelt of Flynn.

In a context that included Roosevelt's now considerable personal experience of Flynn, his question must have seemed to Flynn strange, even astonishing. Flynn had had virtually no national political experience and little working contact with other than urban types. He was tagged a machine politician and, as a big city "boss," was automatically suspect among Democrats whom Roosevelt must recruit in the West and South. Incongruous though it seemed, he was an intensely *private* person, whose distaste for easy backslapping familiarities was profound and who, in his own words, "found it quite difficult to move about with facility among strange people." He suffered now and then spells of deep melancholy, during which his tendency was to withdraw completely from human contact. And Flynn fully "realized my own limitations." He thoroughly agreed, and now said, that the governor had a better than good chance to win nomination; he pledged himself to do all in his power to help bring this about. He could work well as an organizer behind the scenes, dispense experienced and informed strategical and tactical advice, and communicate in Roosevelt's interest with other city bosses. He could also operate with a superior effectiveness as a fundraiser, which would be a crucially needed service in the months just ahead, for Howe had in mind an unprecedentedly elaborate, highly expensive publicity and "personal" letter-writing campaign, joined to an unprecedented use of the long-distance phone for personal communications between Roosevelt and literally hundreds of people. And all these things Flynn promised he would do if Roosevelt wished it. But he "preferred to remain in the background. . . . As a 'front man' I was not to be considered."[14]

Roosevelt showed reluctance to accept this answer. Indeed, that night he refused to accept it as final. He said they'd talk about it again. They did so a few days later, just before Roosevelt left for his annual Thanksgiving visit in Warm Springs, where he was to remain into the second week of December. In this second "conversation with the Governor," writes Flynn, "I convinced him of my unavailability."[15]

Actually, one more than suspects Flynn's response was the answer Roosevelt had expected, even designed to hear, and his "reluctance" to accept it was feigned according to the same design. Certainly the question and answer served for him a a highly useful purpose: it not only recruited the astute Flynn into the innermost core of the developing campaign organization, where he would be invaluable; it also led inevitably to Flynn's suggestion, or wholehearted concurrence in Roosevelt's suggestion, that the needed field agent be the man whom Howe had been grooming for the job and who, during the last two years, had demonstrated superb qualifications for it, namely, Jim Farley. The possibility of future jealousies and friction between Flynn and Farley was, by this stratagem, greatly reduced.

As for Farley, he had the makings of one of the great campaign managers of all time, as Roosevelt and Howe clearly saw. Physically impressive, affable, sweet- and even-tempered, the very personification of Irish charm, he was everybody's friend, almost impossible to dislike. He was insatiably gregarious; he had not the slightest resistance to new acquaintance and, in his own phrase, "never forgot a face." His industry was immense. He worked well in harness, he was absolutely loyal and trustworthy and dependable (for one thing, almost unique among Irish Catholic political types, he neither drank nor smoked), and he could be counted upon to confine himself to vote getting as primarily a game of personal politics and organization, for he had little interest in, hence no compulsion to interfere with, the determination of issue-stands. His judgment, generally excellent within the limits of his professional interest, was occasionally flawed by excessive optimism; but this optimism, a great virtue overall, was for the most part easy to discount in specific instances, and in ways that prevented consequent dangerous errors of decision. Farley had never been a member of Tammany or of any other big-city organization and therefore could not be damned as a machine politician, yet he worked well with Tammany, the Bronx Democracy, and other urban political organizations. Moreover, he had a perfect "cover" for unacknowledged national campaign operations, a fact that, if unmentioned this early, was certainly in the back of at least Howe's mind: Farley was an exalted ruler of the Benevolent and Protective Order of the Elks (B.P.O.E) and, as such, was officially obliged to visit Elk lodges throughout the land and attend Elk conventions at every opportunity.

Roosevelt arrived in Warm Springs on November 20. The next day he addressed to "Dear Jim" a letter Farley would treasure in later life as the only formal explicit expression of gratitude for his campaign labors on Roosevelt's behalf that he ever received. Or so he would claim. It was a warm expression.

"You have done a wonderful piece of work," wrote Roosevelt, "and I don't need to tell you how very appreciative and grateful I am. As I went through the State I got expressions everywhere showing that no man since the days of David B. Hill has such hearty backing and enthusiastic co-operation from the organizations as you have. . . . When I think of the difficulties of former State Chairmen with former Governors and vice versa (!), I have an idea that you and I make a combination which has not existed since Cleveland and Lamont —and that is so long ago that neither you nor I know anything about it except from history books."* He invited Farley to come down to Warm Springs and "roll up" his "sleeves" for work in, though this was not explicitly said, the campaign for the 1932 presidential nomination, an invitation accepted by Farley in a letter wherein he promised to "bring with me all the correspondence I have so that I may go over them [sic] with you and clear up a number of matters that require attention." Thus began for Farley a decade during which the whole of his life would be absorbed into national politics. When he came to Warm Springs, he found Flynn there with Flynn's wife, Helen, the two having arrived with Nancy Cook and Eleanor on the night of November 26. The two men enjoyed, as Roosevelt had promised Flynn, "the pool, the golf course and the riding . . . also the opportunity for a real rest," yet found the last somewhat curtailed, as expected, by conferences with Roosevelt on campaign matters.[16]

III

THEY were conferences in which Roosevelt would have been glad to have Louis Howe participate. But Howe was far too busy in New York that autumn to leave the city for any extended period.

Theretofore the untidy, irritable, asthmatic, chain-smoking little man had functioned on Roosevelt's behalf from his office as secretary of the National Crime Commission in the Equitable Building. This was no longer feasible. The publicity, letter-writing, and fund-collecting operation he now launched in the name of "Friends of Roosevelt" required expanded office space, more staff, and a more frank and open, though still wholly unpublicized, assumption by him of his long-played role as Roosevelt's chief of staff. He searched for suitable new quarters, ultimately renting several rooms on the seventh floor of 331 Madison Avenue, at Forty-third Street, directly across from the Biltmore. He had established himself there by mid-January 1931, with an augmented staff, having rehired the more efficient of the girls who had worked with him during the reelection campaign and adding others, at least one of whom was trained

---

*If Howe saw this letter at the time it was mailed, he could not but have been unhappy over the comparison of Farley to Lamont. Dan Lamont had been night editor of the Buffalo *Argus* when Grover Cleveland became mayor of that city and had subsequently become Cleveland's secretary during Cleveland's administrations as governor of New York and President of the United States. He had been, to Cleveland, invaluable and indispensable, as Howe was to Roosevelt. Howe would have regarded Roosevelt's analogy of Farley with Lamont as a threat to his own position.

to forge Roosevelt's signature on the hundreds of "personal" letters that would go out every few days. By then he was making initial arrangements for the preparation, printing, and distribution by the myriad, during the months ahead, of pamphlets that would bear such titles as *Roosevelt and Human Welfare* and *Franklin D. Roosevelt—Who He Is and What He Has Done.* He encouraged Ernest K. Lindley to write, as Lindley wished to do, a biography of Roosevelt, which, though friendly, would be objective and scrupulously accurate, hence far more effective of vote getting than the typical fawning, adulatory "campaign biography." And Lindley began the book early in 1931, receiving as he did so the active cooperation of Howe, Eleanor, and, to a lesser extent, Roosevelt himself, who reviewed the completed manuscript, excising some items. It would be published in the autumn of 1931 under the title *Franklin D. Roosevelt: A Career in Progressive Politics* and remains to this day one of the best books ever written about Roosevelt. Howe was also adding to already lengthy lists of "contacts" to be "worked" at every opportunity the names of those who acknowledged in surprising number the receipt of a pamphlet as dull as its title, *Officers and Members of the Democratic State Committee of the State of New York.* This pamphlet, which was simply a roster of names, with a few routine remarks on organization, had been sent out by Farley, at Howe's suggestion, to "active Democratic workers" throughout the land soon after the election as a campaign "feeler" that would not be recognized as such.[17] The receipt of each acknowledgment was in turn acknowledged by Farley in a friendly letter, which he signed, invariably, in green ink, and in which he invited future correspondence. Howe seized *every* chance to add a new name to the aforementioned file of index cards, and the chances for this now multiplied swiftly.

Simultaneously, he intensified the workings and increased the size of the network of confidential communicants whereby Roosevelt and he had long been kept informed of subtle shifts in popular opinion, of the prevailing dominant concerns of different geographical regions, different occupations, different economic classes and ways of life. It was a network by no means precisely identical with the "contacts" directly cultivated for a future harvest of votes, and Howe and Roosevelt were now at special pains to keep informed of the thoughts and plans of those party leaders whose unstated but overriding aim was to "stop Roosevelt" while, and by, committing the Democracy to conservatism. Jouett Shouse would become convinced of what was almost certainly true, namely, that Roosevelt and Howe had a "spy" in the Washington headquarters of the Democratic National Committee. For it came to seem to Shouse that Roosevelt was always informed of Raskob's plans in advance of their public announcement and was preparing to counter them by the time their announcement was made.

So it appeared with regard to the first major move Raskob made in follow-up of the letter to Hoover pledging Democratic "cooperation" in the administration's efforts to promote business recovery. That letter was not only designed to protect big business against popular wrath by removing the general economic situation from the agenda for partisan debate; it was also designed, by that token, to block Roosevelt's nomination, since Roosevelt increasingly defined depression-fighting policies as issues between Hoover and himself. To such blockage the only alternative would be, if Raskob had his way, the governor's retreat from "radical" ground into "safe" conservative territory, where, in all important matters, he accepted the dictates of big business. And it was in extension of this design that Raskob issued, on February 10, 1931, a call for a special meeting of the Democratic National Committee "to discuss plans and policies to govern our activities during the next fifteen months." The meeting was to be held on, some thought, remarkably short notice, considering its announced purpose: it was to be held March 5, just a little more than three weeks hence, the day after Congress adjourned.

Roosevelt and Howe at once recognized the move as a hostile act, though Roosevelt, for the time being, discreetly refrained from public comment on it. The two men were warned that Raskob planned to propose resolutions whose adoption would commit the Democratic Party to outright Prohibition repeal and to a high protective tariff, in effect writing two crucial planks into the 1932 platform fifteen months before the opening of the national convention, which was *supposed* to have exclusive authority over platform formulation. And within days political reporters were speculating in print that one of Raskob's intentions might be to embarrass Roosevelt. Up until then, the New York governor had managed to appear merely "damp" rather than "wringing wet" in his stand on the liquor question, thus distinguishing himself from Al Smith in a way that made him far more attractive, or far less obnoxious, to drys, especially Southern drys, than Smith was. Raskob seems to have believed that the distinction would be removed if his maneuver succeeded. Roosevelt could hardly oppose the resolution, having himself come out for Prohibition repeal, but by accepting as official party policy the "wringing wet" language that, one assumes, Raskob would employ, he would become tarred by the same wet brush that so blackened Smith in rural Southern eyes. " . . . the Raskob crowd did not care for whom the South voted as long as it was kept out of the Roosevelt column," Charles Michelson would later explain.[18] As for the tariff proposal, its adoption would widen the gap between the party's stated economic views and the "radical" ones expressed by Roosevelt, thereby further reducing his chances for nomination or else encouraging a shift by him toward conservatism.

But the maneuver was of a piece with Raskob's overall political operation in that it was stupidly conceived, clumsily executed, and easily countered (Raskob's record in politics, conjoined with his success in big business, would seem to suggest, as a general proposition, that intelligence is no absolute requirement for the latter). Roosevelt moved swiftly to counter it in ways that greatly advantaged him. He had been a friend and political ally of Tennessee's Cordell Hull ever since the Democratic convention that nominated Wilson in 1912.* Former Congressman Hull was now Senator-elect Hull, and Roosevelt at once let him know what Raskob proposed to do and of his own strong

---

*See *FDR: The Beckoning of Destiny,* page 276.

opposition to it. This stimulated Hull's public denunciation of Raskob's move and his recruitment of senators and representatives who were similarly opposed and could let the national committee members from their states know that they were. In the process of this recruitment, Hull learned and warned Roosevelt that Raskob, attempting to run the party in the same way he had run General Motors, was obtaining proxies from committee members who would be unable to attend the special meeting (there were many such, in distant states). It behooved Roosevelt to obtain proxies of his own, and as many as possible through a revocation of proxies by those who, unaware of what was at stake, had given them to Raskob supporters. Hence his telegram on March 4 to Arizona's national committeewoman, Mrs. John C. Greenway (née Isabella Selmes, a longtime close personal friend of Eleanor's),[19] telling her he was "wholly" opposed to the making of issue-statements by the national committee ("It is contrary their authority and disrupts harmony"), that he had been "informed present holder your proxy will vote against me," and that she could "supersede present proxy by wiring new one, as follows, quote: James A. Farley, Continental Hotel, Washington; I hereby revoke all previous proxies and designate you as my proxy to cast my vote in meeting of Democratic National Committee, Washington, March fifth, in all respects as if I were myself present. This telegram is sent to you from Tucson, end quote, giving date and hour you send it."[20] Mrs. Greenway immediately did as he wished.

But by that time, Roosevelt had the situation so well in hand that Mrs. Greenway's proxy was really not needed.

At his behest, Farley had summoned a special meeting of the Democratic State Committee of New York, held in Albany on March 2. On the morning of that day, in one of the earliest of the Roosevelt "bedroom conferences" that would become famous, Howe, Flynn, and Farley gathered round the governor's bed in the Mansion to draft, for state committee adoption, a resolution whose gist Roosevelt had dictated in a "Dear Al" letter to Smith, with a copy to Shouse, two days before. " . . . it would be very contrary to the established powers and precedents of the National Committee, were they to pass resolutions *of any kind* affecting party policies at this time," Roosevelt had written Smith, after repeated failed attempts to reach him by phone. " . . . Historically, the National Committee has always recognized that in between Conventions, the spokesmen on policy matters are, primarily, the Democratic Members of the Senate and House of Representatives, together with individuals high in the Party Councils, who, however, speak as individuals."[21] When the Democratic State Committee meeting opened in the early afternoon, Flynn introduced the draft resolution, which was adopted at once and wired to New York's national committeeman, Norman Mack of Buffalo, and to others of influence around the country.

Meanwhile, by telephone and telegraph, the hectic business of garnering proxies proceeded apace. By nightfall, Farley had enough of them in hand to defeat Raskob's proposals two or three to one, and he said so to a newspaper reporter, since it had been decided by then that Roosevelt should make a public announcement of his opposition to any statement on Prohibition or on any other issue by the Democratic National Committee. The announcement was countrywide front-page news next morning, March 3. "Roosevelt's friends suspect that Raskob's call [for a Prohibition-repeal statement] is designed to aid Al Smith," said the story in the New York *Times*. Later that same day, Smith told a reporter he saw no objection to the committee's expressing an opinion on any subject—a statement that sharpened, for penetration into the public mind, the significant point that Smith and Roosevelt were emphatically publicly arrayed against each other, for the first time, on an intraparty political question.[22] Was this the beginning of a Smith-Roosevelt feud? asked political reporters. One may be sure that Republican leaders hoped so and wished Raskob every success in his evident effort to split the party on the same issue as had so disastrously divided it in 1928.

Farley was aboard a train bound for Washington when he read Smith's statement, with such emotions as one can imagine—his own first fame had come as a Smith appointee to the New York State Athletic Commission, and he still counted himself one of Smith's friends. In Washington he faced his first test as a Roosevelt national campaign manager, and he passed it with high marks during the next two days. Affable, modest, deliberately inconspicuous, deferent to those more experienced than he, yet firm and shrewd in his tactical counsels, Farley made a highly favorable impression on Hull, Virginia's Governor Harry F. Byrd (the brother of the explorer Admiral Richard E. Byrd, who was a longtime personal friend of Roosevelt's), and other national leaders whom it was highly important that he impress. He expressed perfectly Roosevelt's concern, a predominant one among party leaders, to prevent another intraparty fracas of the kind that had dealt victory in huge portions to the Republicans in the two preceding presidential campaigns. By this concern, floor strategy was dictated.

Yet the meeting itself was not, could not be, free of acrimony.

By the time it opened, Raskob had been made to realize that the assembled opposition to what he had planned to do was overwhelming. He attempted a retreat from his announced position to a compromise one, with conciliatory gestures. His keynote speech was a fog of generalities about "liberty" (defined as the absence of governmental "interference" with the sacred pursuit of private profit), whence emerged no concrete proposal whatever about the tariff, and only a mild suggestion regarding Prohibition, to wit, a "states' rights" resolution in favor of restoring liquor control to the sovereign states. But there were those among his auditors who were in no mood to be conciliated. Such a one was the chronically choleric Senator Joseph T. Robinson of Arkansas. Though every bit as conservative as Raskob—he was a corporation lawyer whose firm profited greatly from his political office, and he championed "white supremacy" as a matter of course—Robinson was a fervent dry and, in any case, disposed to resent what he saw as Raskob's personal arrogance and egotism. He took the floor to make what Farley later described as "a sizzling attack on Raskob in which he accused the chairman of attempting to steamroller the party."[23] Though not a national committee member, Al Smith was then called upon, by unanimous consent, to pour oil on greatly troubled waters in a speech, jocular in tone, denying as "bunk" the charge that Raskob sought to dictate party policy. According to Smith, the chairman merely exercised his right, the right of every leader of the Democracy, to express freely and forcefully his own opinion. Raskob, personally humiliated by the need for such defense, then refrained from putting even his watered-down Prohibition proposal to the test of a vote. He sensed it had no chance of passage. When he adjourned the meeting shortly thereafter, its single formal accomplishment was the adoption, with little debate, of a fairly routine plan for raising money.

Yet the meeting had been important, as was at once and everywhere recognized, having effects precisely opposite those Raskob had intended. Far from weakening Roosevelt's candidacy by embarrassing him in the South, the event strengthened his candidacy by relieving him of a serious embarrassment in that region—his theretofore widely presumed friendship and alliance with Al Smith and, through Smith, with Raskob. Both Smith and Raskob were anathema to most of the Southern electorate. Smith was so as personification—with his wetness, his Roman Catholicism, his rasping Lower East Side accent—of the wicked immigrant-dominated Northern city. Raskob was so as personification of that Northern corporate giantism that "enslaved" and "exploited" the rural agrarian South by means of high tariffs, discriminatory railroad freight rates (which operated, on purpose, against Southern industrialization), currency manipulations, and similar "special privileges" dispensed through the federal government. The fact, therefore, that the meeting's outcome was clearly a victory for Roosevelt over Raskob-Shouse forces with which Al Smith was now openly aligned greatly strengthened Roosevelt's support in Southern states. Cordell Hull would later claim, in his memoirs,[24] that the event was actually decisive of Roosevelt's ultimate nomination, an assertion of at least negative truth in that, had the outcome been different, had the meeting committed the party to Raskob's views, Roosevelt would certainly *not* have been nominated.

And one may be sure that the governor, in Albany, rejoiced. He was careful, however, to give no outward sign of rejoicing.

For the victory that gratified also sprouted dangers to be removed, or avoided, in view of the fact, to be borne constantly in mind, that a two-thirds vote of convention delegates was required for presidential nomination and that beyond nomination lay a battle for election whose success depended upon party unity. Roosevelt moved quickly to heal wounds. "I think on the whole that largely thanks to you and Jim Farley the meeting did no harm," he wrote to Norman Mack on March 9, "—and indeed I am inclined to think that in the long run the result will be beneficial to the party. . . . The thing we must work for now is the avoidance of harsh words and no sulking [by those who had been defeated] in tents." To Georgia's Democratic national committeeman, Major John S. Cohen, editor and publisher of the Atlanta *Journal,* he wrote on that same day: "Now that the smoke has cleared away from the gathering of last week I am on the whole satisfied that not much harm has been done the party. I hope that none of those who were behind the proposal for a formal commitment of the party will sulk in their tents. I know that you will agree with me on this."[25]

IV

IN New York City, Louis Howe cultivated assiduously, with great show of deference and much flattery, a man of the historic past who, though now elderly (seventy-three years of age), still aspired to be a man of the future and who was therefore eager to grasp the opportunity seemingly presented him by a likely next President of the United States. There ensued a delicious comedy that only Roosevelt and Howe were in a position to appreciate, as an arch-manipulator of important people, accustomed to influencing through ingratiation, was himself manipulated through ingratiation.

Colonel Edward Mandell House, whose winter home was an apartment only two blocks from Roosevelt's East Sixty-fifth Street house, was equipped to appreciate at full value the usefulness of Louis Howe and to understand the pangs and joys of Howe's operation behind the scenes of great events. He had had a relationship with Wilson through seven years of the century's second decade similar in some respects to that Howe had with Roosevelt at this opening of the fourth. Like Howe, he took a Carlylean romantic view of history: Great Men made it, which is to say, history's essence is biographical. Observation had convinced him as a young man that, behind the show of popular democracy, public affairs in America, as in other societies, are actually controlled by a mere handful of men, nearly all of them personally acquainted with one another. Like Howe, House was physically frail, having never fully recovered from a near-fatal accident suffered at the age of twelve. Like Howe, he was physically unprepossessing—a small man, wispy-looking when young and now, in old age, shrunken—though none called him ugly, as many called Howe; but in sharp contrast to Howe, he cared about his appearance, dressing neatly and well, and he took care to lubricate his social relationships with impeccable old-fashioned good manners. Like Howe, he had never sought to exercise great power personally, directly, assuming personal responsibility for consequences; he was sensible, as Howe was, of disqualifications—a lack of personal magnetism and the supreme self-confidence required*—for open heroic mass leadership. Yet, again like Howe, his attraction toward power had been immense—had been, in effect, a compulsion to attain it through vital

---

*But is the confidence implicit in the willing exercise of great power over masses of men truly or exclusively *self*-confidence? Do not powerful individuals always regard themselves as agents of a higher power—of the people, or destiny, or historic Process (dialectical materialism), or God the Father? The test of the sanity of the power-wielding individual would seem to lie in an analytical definition, from evidence, of his conception of the *source* of his power, also of the degree and way of his personal identification with it.

influential attachment to an Other who supplied his deficiencies, being equipped, as he himself was not, for public life.

Here, however, the two men's similarities ended. House was much more cerebral than Howe, hence far more concerned with, and clear in his ideas of, the ends or goals that power ought to serve. He was also far more egotistical and vain. A native Texan and the son of a wealthy man, he had been raised in easy circumstances, had lived much in England, and had increased his inherited wealth through successful operations in Texas banking and cotton planting. Between 1892 and 1904 he had employed his wealth and remarkable manipulative talents to promote the political careers, and subsequently greatly influence the policies, of four successive governors of Texas. In 1912, when he was fifty-four, he had published anonymously a futuristic political novel entitled *Philip Dru, Administrator,* a book that had almost no impact upon the general reading public, then or later, but may have had a considerable impact upon historical developments in which Franklin Roosevelt played a leading part.

Consider the novel's story. Philip Dru, a West Point graduate debarred by ill health from an active military career, nevertheless became an effective leader of a successful armed revolt against the managers of giant business combinations, who, behind the walls of governmental "special privilege" erected for them by elected officials whom they bought and paid for, had by 1920 become the real rulers of the American republic. True democracy was the aim of the revolution, but there must be, in House's conception, a period of transition from oligarchy to democracy during which a benevolent dictator ruled America in the interests of the theretofore deprived, exploited populace. Philip Dru became this dictator. Guided by his chief counselor and intimate friend, a shadowy figure named Selwyn, who never permitted himself to be photographed or interviewed in the press, Dru did away with the protective tariff, established a "flexible currency" destructive of the "credit trust," outlawed holding companies, decreed corporate income taxes and drastic regulation of big-business operations, socialized the telephone and telegraph, imposed federal old-age and unemployment insurance, decreed other legislation designed for "full employment," made woman suffrage the law of the land, and reached out toward the establishment of world law and order by making the United States the prime mover and key member of a league of nations founded on Anglo-Saxon solidarity.

Thus the novel as a political tract was in perfect alignment with, though it went much farther than, Theodore Roosevelt's New Nationalism, inscribed on the Progressive Party's banner in the year of the novel's publication. It was substantially flatly opposed to Woodrow Wilson's New Freedom,* inscribed on the Democratic Party's banner in that same year. Hence the irony of the

---

*House portrayed Dru as one who, initially committed to states' rights doctrine, abandoned this as unrealistic in the face of corporate giantism. Selwyn was obviously House's conception of himself and his role.

fact that Colonel House became the intimate friend and confidential adviser not of Theodore Roosevelt but of Woodrow Wilson—"my second personality . . . my independent self," Wilson called him, one whose "thoughts and mine are one"—and that *Philip Dru, Administrator* came to be regarded by some close observers as the model for Wilson's administrations. "Labor is no longer to be classed as an inert commodity to be bought and sold by the law of supply and demand," said Philip Dru in 1912. Said the Clayton Antitrust Act in 1914: " . . . the labor of human beings is not a commodity or article of commerce," meaning that labor unions should be exempt from prosecution as "combinations in restraint of trade." And there were other striking parallels between Dru's administration and Wilson's, enough of them to cause Wilson's Secretary of the Interior, Franklin K. Lane, to assert in 1918: "All that book [*Dru*] has said should be, comes about, if slowly, even woman suffrage. The President comes to Philip Dru in the end."[26]

Certainly the President came to House "in the end," agonizingly, against his moral will, when he abandoned even the pretense of neutrality following the 1916 election and embraced the Allied cause, as House, a fervent Anglophile, had continually if often subtly pressed him to do from the moment the Great War began. And it was Wilson's reluctance to do this and his stubborn inclination to heed the counsels of his pacifist Secretary of the Navy, Josephus Daniels, that had first brought House and Assistant Secretary of the Navy Franklin Roosevelt into friendly relationship, if not covert working alliance, in the early months of 1917.* The two had remained friendly, though far from intimate, ever since.

For instance, the colonel had been one of those high in party councils whom Howe had enlisted, evidently without direct personal contact with him, in Roosevelt's aborted attempt to promote a national Democratic conference in 1925 to heal the wounds of 1924 and unite the party on Progressive principles. "The Party is thinking of you as one of our principal assets," wrote House to Roosevelt at that time. In 1928, when the colonel congratulated Roosevelt on his first gubernatorial nomination, the candidate had replied, "I would rather have your approval than that of almost any other man I know."[27] And Roosevelt made similar flattering reply when the colonel, congratulating him on his 1930 election triumph, predicted his election to the presidency two years hence.

It was then privately decided by Roosevelt and Howe that the colonel should be recruited for active service in Roosevelt's campaign for the nomination and made to feel, though he would never actually become, one of the candidate's two or three closest advisers. He would be a useful vital link between the Roosevelt candidacy and the so-called Old Wilsonians, despite the fact that many of the latter resented House's portrayal of himself, in his published papers, as the real author of Wilson's successes and the mastermind whose counsel, if heeded, would have prevented Wilson's failures. It was possible that he could persuade New England, where he was known to have a considerable

*See *FDR: The Beckoning of Destiny,* pages 446–447.

personal influence with Democratic leaders and where Al Smith had his strongest support.

Howe conferred with House while Roosevelt was in Warm Springs in late 1930, stimulating a letter from House to Roosevelt in which the governor was solemnly urged to strike a "high and progressive note" in his second gubernatorial inaugural address.[28] But the first major recruitment move was made on March 22, 1931. Howe then came to the colonel's apartment bearing letters addressed to Roosevelt from would-be organizers of Roosevelt-for-President clubs from every part of the country, along with a draft formula-letter reply for Roosevelt's signature, which encouraged such organization *without* admitting that the governor was actually a candidate for the presidency: he was totally absorbed, said the letter, in his important duties as chief executive of the Empire State. The colonel wrote the governor the next day, the tone of his letter indicating the tone of Howe's approach to him. "It was pleasant to read the letters . . . which Mr. Howe brought me . . . ," wrote House. "The draft he submitted [Howe had obviously been very submissive] as a suggested reply was admirable but too long. We decided that the enclosed covered the necessary points. . . . Every word was taken from Mr. Howe's draft for I do not believe that it could be bettered. It is a joy to cooperate with him for the reason that he is so able and yet so yielding to suggestions. We never have any arguments and have no difficulty in reaching conclusions satisfactory to us both. I congratulate you upon having such a loyal and efficient lieutenant."[29]

House was among the first of those from whom Flynn and Frank C. Walker, Flynn's chief colleague in this enterprise, elicited sizable campaign contributions in early 1931.* He had fruitful communication with the Old Wilsonians Breckenridge Long and Daniel C. Roper. Long, a Missourian whose maternal ancestors were the politically famous Breckenridges of Kentucky and paternal ancestors the aristocratic Longs of Virginia and who had married the granddaughter of Francis Preston Blair, had been third Assistant Secretary of State under Wilson. Roper was a North Carolina businessman who had actively aided McAdoo's presidential bid in 1924 and who remained a personal friend of McAdoo's. Both were politically influential; both assured House they were for Roosevelt. House publicly announced his own support of Roosevelt in an interview with Ernest K. Lindley, published in the New York *Herald Tribune* on June 4, 1931, stressing as he did so that, from 1916 till now, he had endorsed not a single presidential candidate. Nine days later he hosted a luncheon for Roosevelt at his Beverly Farms, Massachusetts, summer home (actually the House cottage, though in Beverly Town, was closer to Manchester-by-the-Sea than it was to Beverly and was often linked to the latter in the press). A greatly publicized affair, it was attended by, among others, the Massachusetts senators

---

*Flynn in his *You're the Boss,* pages 84–85, lists thirteen people, in addition to himself and Walker, who contributed $2,000 or more apiece "to get our campaign launched." They were James W. Gerard, Guy Helvering, House, Joseph P. Kennedy, Herbert H. Lehman, Eugene Lorton, F. J. Machette, Henry Morgenthau, Sr., Dave Hennen Morris, Mrs. Sara Roosevelt, Laurence A. Steinhardt, Harry M. Warner, and William H. Woodin.

David I. Walsh and Marcus A. Coolidge; Ellery Sedgwick, editor of the *Atlantic Monthly,* a leading intellectual among the Old Wilsonians; Henry Morgenthau, Sr., who had been Wilson's ambassador to Turkey; and James M. Curley, the highly practical politician who was mayor of Boston.

V

BY that time, Roosevelt's design to forge swiftly so far ahead of any and all possible rivals as to make his nomination a foregone conclusion long before he formally announced his candidacy appeared, in the eyes of many politically astute observers, to have come already near the achievement of its purpose. In late March, only a few days after the aforementioned Howe-House conference, Jesse I. Straus, president of the great mercantile establishment of R. H. Macy and Company, had announced the results of a poll he had taken of delegates to the 1928 Democratic National Convention, in which he asked each delegate to list a presidential preference for 1932. No ballots were sent to the New York delegation, to avoid overweighting the results in favor of the two men most prominent among likely Democratic nominees and to avoid encouraging a party split in that state. No replies were received from the delegations of Oregon, Wisconsin, and Wyoming. Of the 942 delegates who replied, 98 declined to state a preference. Of the 844 who did, 478 named Roosevelt, 125 Al Smith, 73 the industrialist Owen D. Young, 39 Maryland's Governor Albert C. Ritchie, 38 Senator Joseph T. Robinson, 35 Newton D. Baker (the Ohioan who had been Wilson's Secretary of War), and 15 Missouri's ex-Senator James M. Reed. The remaining 41 distributed their votes among 13 favorite-son candidates. In mid-April, Straus announced the results of a second poll he had taken, this one of some 1,200 prominent business and professional men in every state save New York. Of such a poll, Owen D. Young should, in the expectations of most, emerge the front-runner. Actually, he ran far behind Roosevelt (Roosevelt received 562 preferential votes, and Young 256) and Al Smith farther still (Smith had 115, or one fifth as many as Roosevelt), followed by Robinson (95), Ritchie (85), and Baker (16). Unpublicized with the poll results was the fact that Straus was one of the "Friends of Roosevelt" who had made, and would continue to make, large personal contributions to the Roosevelt campaign fund.[30]

Two weeks later, an event in Roosevelt's personal life resulted in publicity that confirmed his position as an overwhelmingly probable presidential nominee.

Roosevelt was about to leave New York for his annual Warm Springs vacation, at the end of April, when a cablegram informed him that his mother, who had been traveling in Europe, was ill with pneumonia in Paris. He at once canceled his vacation and the numerous political visits planned for Warm Springs, sailing instead for Europe on the *Aquitania.* He asked Eleanor to go with him. She refused. "I knew it was the best thing for you to do & the sensible thing for me not to," she wrote him after he'd gone, in tacit recognition that his ties to his mother remained of the essence of his selfhood whereas her relationship with her mother-in-law was not a loving one; his presence at his mother's bedside would do more to benefit her if she, Eleanor, were not beside him.[31] So he took Elliott with him as companion. A flock of reporters and photographers attended his departure, and another his arrival in Paris, where he found his mother, whose illness had been less serious than at first believed, well on the way to complete recovery. He praised to reporters the treatment given her in American Hospital. He toured with Elliott the battlefields "where I had followed the fighting in 1918" and found that the "farms which I had seen smashed and splintered around Belleau Wood and Chateau-Thierry had been completely rebuilt." He had talks with high French officials, notably with André Tardieu, then Minister of Agriculture. He sailed from Cherbourg on May 22 aboard the *Bremen*. Among his shipboard companions was the U.S. ambassador to Great Britain, Republican Charles G. Dawes of Dawes Plan fame and Vice-President of the United States from 1925 to 1929, who recorded in his diary entry for May 24 that, accepting an invitation sent him by Roosevelt via Elliott, he had dined with Roosevelt in the latter's stateroom the night before. "I do not know when I have enjoyed an evening more," wrote Dawes, "and we both were surprised, being still fresh and in full height of conversational activity, to find we had consumed 4½ hours when . . . I left his room. . . . Roosevelt is only 49 years of age. After this evening's visit I feel that if he is the next President of the United States, he will serve with honor to his country and credit to himself. He seems to have strength and equipoise, clarity of mind with soundness of judgment, and to steer his course by the compass of common sense." Two days later, Dawes recorded that he had "[d]ined again with Governor Roosevelt at his stateroom" the night before "and we had a session until midnight, and a fine time." The governor's landing in New York on May 27 received considerably greater publicity than did the arrival of Ambassador Dawes, who, returning to Washington for consultations with the State Department and the President, was Hoover's guest in the White House. Reported the New York *Times*: "Viewed as the outstanding probability for the Presidential nomination next year of the Democratic Party, which until recently has stood firmly against protection in any form, the Governor declared [in a shipboard interview upon his arrival] that France's agricultural tariff has been an important factor in maintaining fairly stable economic conditions there when a large share of the rest of the world was suffering from a business depression."[32] This was interpreted as tacit approval by the governor of tariff protection for American agriculture, a shift from the traditional Democratic position toward the continuing Republican position on protectionism.

A little over two weeks later, on June 13, Colonel House hosted his Beverly Farms luncheon in Roosevelt's honor.

Eleanor accompanied her husband to Boston on the afternoon of June 11, checking in with him at the Statler Hotel, where they shared a suite. There, that evening, he conferred for four hours with a man whom House had strongly recommended as a potential manager of Roosevelt forces in New Hampshire, a state whose importance to presidential candidates was vastly disproportionate to its delegate strength because its primary in early March 1932 would be the first state primary to be held, and its outcome therefore deemed a sign and portent. The man was the industrialist Robert Jackson, a Dartmouth alumnus, long a dominant figure in his state's Democracy, whom Assistant Secretary of the Navy Roosevelt had met during the war, when Jackson was a Portsmouth shipbuilder. When Eleanor at last broke up their lively talk, shortly before midnight ("Franklin, you have a hard day tomorrow," she said. "You should get a good night's rest"), Jackson had received solid assurance that Roosevelt was indeed running for the presidency and had virtually pledged himself to take charge, as in the event he did, of Roosevelt's interests in New Hampshire.[33]

The "hard day" Eleanor spoke of had as its main feature Roosevelt's delivery of the commencement address at Groton School, where their sons John and Franklin, Jr., were students. A large commencement crowd, including many note-taking reporters, heard the governor praised by the Reverend Dr. Endicott Peabody, headmaster, as an alumnus of whom Groton was especially proud, and by the Right Reverend William Lawrence, Protestant Episcopal Bishop Emeritus of Massachusetts, as one who had not permitted severe physical handicaps to stand in the way of a career of great public service. One may be sure that an outwardly gratefully smiling Roosevelt flinched inwardly at this calling of attention to his infirmity, for one of his chief worries at that time was a whispering campaign wherein he was portrayed as a man utterly unfit physically to withstand the rigors of the presidency. Roosevelt then spoke extemporaneously. "I could no more deliver a formal address in my old school than I could in my own home," he began, amid much applause, going on to rebuke the "well-educated" who failed to meet their obligations as citizens of a free society because they refused to take an interest in good government.[34]

That evening, he and Eleanor presided over a family dinner. All four of their sons were there: John and Franklin, Jr., who were doing somewhat better at Groton than James had done and far better than Elliott; Elliott, who was soon to marry Betty Donner, of a wealthy Pennsylvania steel family, and who had appeared at Groton unexpectedly, coming in from Chicago (he was now affiliated with a New York City advertising firm); and James, who had married Betsey Cushing in a much-publicized Boston wedding in June 1930 and was now enrolled in Harvard Law School (he was unhappy in law school and was about to leave it in order to enter the insurance business in Boston, where, in good part because of a conversation his father had had on the train the day before this family dinner, he would be "adopted" by the mayor of that city). The evening was typically Rooseveltian, bursting with vitality, fun-filled, loud with talk and laughter—one of those warmly affectionate affairs by which Roosevelt renewed vital connections with his past and from which he drew much of the serenity and self-confidence he needed to withstand the intense, constant pressures of his public life.

House's political luncheon the next day was designed to be, in political effect, of a piece with the governor's surging progress toward nomination. In the Straus poll, Massachusetts had been the only state in which Smith led Roosevelt by a wide margin; it had been one of the few states Smith carried in 1928, and he had run more strongly there than anywhere else. Hence the strategic importance of a vivid public display of Roosevelt's personal popularity among leaders of the Massachusetts Democracy, a display that the luncheon did certainly achieve. It would be especially discouraging "to . . . Smith and his followers," showing them "how hopeless it was to oppose our man," as House explained in a letter to a friend on the day following the luncheon.[35] "Friends of Mr. Roosevelt now believe that the delegation from this state [Massachusetts] . . . will be found in line for the Governor of New York" in the upcoming presidential nomination race, said the New York *Times* political reporter A. A. Warn in a by-lined front-page story of the luncheon. To assembled newsmen, Henry Morgenthau, Sr., spoke of the Roosevelt nomination as a sure thing: "Governor Roosevelt is the choice, first or second, of at least ninety-five percent of the delegates who will sit in next year's Democratic convention." Said Marcus Coolidge, Massachusetts' new Democratic senator: "I think there is little doubt that Governor Roosevelt will be nominated and elected President of the United States. I favor his nomination strongly." His colleague Senator Walsh was less definite but seemed clearly sympathetic to the Roosevelt cause. "I have always been an admirer of what Governor Roosevelt stands for," said Walsh. "I can only repeat what I said some time ago. It is high time we had a Roosevelt in the White House." Mayor Curley spoke to Roosevelt before Movietone newsreel cameras on the cottage's lawn: "Within the next two years we hope you will come to us in an even more exalted capacity. We expect to welcome you as President of the United States." And the newspapers that reported this solid news also reported what was, for Roosevelt, cheering rumor. Massachusetts Governor Joseph B. Ely, a Democrat who had been unable to accept House's invitation to the luncheon because he was speaking that day at Williams College, was said to favor Roosevelt's candidacy, as was Frank J. Donahue, the Massachusetts Democratic state chairman. Most cheering of all was a remark allegedly "dropped" by Jouett Shouse during a recent visit with his father-in-law, A. Lincoln Filene, in Boston, a remark to the effect that Roosevelt was "as near to the nomination as a man could well be" twelve months before the nominating convention.[36] The remark must have been a grudging concession, if not a sigh of despair, and had clearly not been intended for publication.

But if instant flowers, bright with hope, thus sprang up in this new-planted corner of Roosevelt's flourishing campaign garden, they did so in soil where weed seeds, dark with misfortune, had also been sown—and sown, moreover, by Roosevelt's own reckless hand.

The name of James M. Curley had not been on House's original list of those to be invited to the luncheon. Not only did House have at that time an English aristocrat's disdain for the Irishman and his brand of "low politics," he was also aware that Curley publicly only a few weeks past had favored the presidential nomination of Owen D. Young. This somewhat incongruous choice had been tentatively made by Curley as the lesser of two evils. In 1930, in a bitter struggle for control of the state Democratic organization, he had suffered decisive defeat at the hands of Ely and Walsh, both Al Smith supporters. The defeat frustrated his ambition to advance from his present status as city boss to that of national politician, and the advance could now be made only if he hitched his fortunes to a new rising star who, outshining Smith, captured the Democratic nomination in 1932. Obvious by late spring of 1931 was the fact that the rising star was not Young. It was Roosevelt. And when Curley met Roosevelt on the train from New York City to Boston on June 11, he seized the opportunity to ally himself with the governor. Turning on the full force of that Irish charm of which he had rather more than his fair share, he persuaded Roosevelt that an alliance between the two of them would be irresistible in the Bay State. If Ely and Walsh continued to support Smith (as in the event they did, despite Walsh's kind remark following the luncheon and the then-published rumor about Ely's "leaning" toward Roosevelt),* they would simply be overwhelmed in a primary that committed the whole of the Massachusetts delegation to Roosevelt's nomination. And as Massachusetts went, following the expected New Hampshire triumph, so would, in all likelihood, Connecticut and Rhode Island. Roosevelt, therefore, as soon as he arrived in Boston, asked House to add Curley's name to the luncheon invitation list. Subsequently, he was confirmed in his immediate, but at first tentative, decision to challenge Smith in the Massachusetts primary—a decision he would later bitterly regret: its effects, far from assuring him the first-ballot victory that Farley was predicting, greatly strengthened a "Stop Roosevelt" movement that would come within an ace of success.

But this untoward event was wholly unforeseen when Roosevelt returned to Albany glowing with optimism regarding his candidacy.

VI

A few days later, on Sunday, June 21, he lunched with Howe and Farley at Hyde Park, then retired to his small study on the first floor to confer with his two guests for two hours over, in Farley's words, "a Rand-McNally map of the United States, a flock of train schedules, and the latest available list of Democratic National Committee members and state chairmen."[38] For years past, Farley's annual summer vacation had consisted of travel to, and attendance at, the Grand Lodge (national) Convention of the Elks. This year the convention was being held in Seattle in early July and, as Farley would later say, "I had made plans [to go to Seattle] many months in advance . . . , solely

---

*On June 16, three days after the House luncheon, Walsh told a reporter, "If Al Smith desires to have the nomination, then of course Massachusetts will be for him and none can prevent such a development. Next to Smith, of course, I am for Roosevelt."[37]

with the thought of attending the convention and enjoying a bit of scenery en route. But Louie [Howe] had other thoughts. He saw an opportunity to mix a little politics with good comradeship."* The purpose of this Hyde Park session was to plan Farley's itinerary in careful detail (" . . . [it] was decided upon in large measure by the Governor, who had a keen sense of selection in determining what states it was wise to visit and what states it was wise to shun"), and to agree upon the names of people he should talk to and the kinds of approach he should make to them.[39] This done, Howe by telegram, telephone, and airmail letter informed local leaders of Farley's coming and obtained, from Colonel House, for one, names to be added to the list of those whom Farley would see. "Thus," as Frank Freidel writes, "Howe, like a meticulous promotion manager who has been conducting a vigorous direct-mail campaign, sent out his talented traveling salesman . . . to clinch the sales."[40]

Farley began his cross-country tour on Monday, June 29. When he concluded it nineteen days later, travel-weary but jubilant, he had visited and conferred in seventeen states, attending luncheons and dinners and meetings of all kinds. " . . . I shook hands with thousands of men and women," he remembered a half-dozen years later, "and among them were over 1100 individuals who held 'key' positions in the party. . . . I took careful note of each name and address, and later I sent each one of the 1100 a personal letter."[41] The written reports he made to Howe and Roosevelt en route, the press interview he granted upon his return, and the lengthy detailed oral report he presented at Hyde Park two days after his return were enthusiastically optimistic.

Thus, a week after his tour began, he wrote: "Since I left New York I have visited Indiana, Wisconsin, Minnesota, North and South Dakota, Montana, and am now in Seattle. There is apparently an almost unanimous sentiment for you in every one of these states and the organization in every instance is for you wholeheartedly." Only infrequently had he encountered "sentiment for Smith . . . mostly from ardent Catholic admirers and in some instances from strong wet advocates." Baker's name had been mentioned once or twice "but that is all." He had seen signs that the "power group" was hoping "to tie up some votes for Young and Ritchie, to be used later on when they decide what candidate they are going to support to try to keep you from getting the nomination," but he had seen no sign that this tactic was likely to succeed "because the consensus . . . among the leaders is that you are the one man who can win." From Seattle he had toured southward through Oregon into California, where he found Roosevelt "sentiment" considerably less strong than elsewhere. This was largely due to McAdoo, a power in state Democratic

*This was Farley's remembrance in 1938, when his *Behind the Ballots* was published. In his *Jim Farley's Story,* published ten years later, he remembers it differently: the tour idea, he asserts, was actually originally his, though both Howe and Roosevelt claimed credit for it. The revision of memory was doubtless determined by Farley's bitterness toward Roosevelt following the break between the two in 1940.

politics, who nursed secret presidential ambitions of his own. Replying to a written query from Colonel House in January 1931, McAdoo had written: " . . . I can't see Roosevelt or any other New Yorker at the moment."[42] McAdoo's evident wish was for a deadlocked convention like that which had denied the nomination to either him or Smith in 1924, giving it at last to the dark horse John W. Davis. *This* time, if his wish came true, the dark-horse nominee would be William Gibbs McAdoo.

And so, from San Francisco, Farley had written Roosevelt not only of his attempt "to further the desire on your part for an early [state] convention and to instruct for you" but also of his efforts to persuade state leaders that "they must all get away from the 'favorite son' idea, on the theory that it is only used for the purpose of tying up blocks of delegates to be manipulated." His journey homeward took him through Nevada, Utah, Wyoming, Colorado, Nebraska, Kansas, Missouri, and Illinois. In Kansas City he gave remarkable demonstration of his genius for human relations: he managed to curry favor with both sides of a feud between Missouri's favorite son, Jim Reed, and an anti-Reed faction, "as a result" of which "both . . . factions have gotten together for the first time in many years, and both sides are tremendously pleased."

The quoted words are from a letter Howe wrote on August 17, 1931, to Colonel House, who, in a phone conversation while Farley was on tour, pointed out grave "dangers" in the use of the allegedly inexperienced, parochial Farley as Roosevelt's national field representative. The length, the substance, and the tone of Howe's letter are revealing of the way in which Roosevelt-Howe manipulated the would-be kingmaker. "Indeed I am only too pleased to have you call me Louis instead of the formal Mr. Howe," the letter began, "and I am really flattered and feel that you consider me a well established member of your wide circle of acquaintances." The colonel's attempt to replace Farley with a man of his own choosing met, however, with a rebuff, whose firmness must have been felt through the thick cushions of flattery that enwrapped it. Howe left no doubt that in his and [by unmistakable inference] the governor's opinion, Farley had proved in action to be superbly qualified to fulfill his assignment. The Kansas City episode had been "an excellent test of his political ability and personal initiative as it was necessary to leave it to him to work it out the best way he could," wrote Howe. " . . . Also we have so far managed to avoid any bad feeling or local rivalry in any of the states that Farley has visited, and where there have been factional rows, we have received since Farley's visit, long letters of support from the leaders of both factions. I have gone into this somewhat at length because I realize that [so House had said] the ability and character of the man who represents us is of the utmost importance. May I suggest you drop Farley a little note asking him to come over to Manchester and take lunch with you in order that you may size him up for yourself. He has expressed to me a great many times his desire to meet you and talk things over with you. He has also one very great recommendation. He does not attempt to dictate, but follows implicitly any advice or instructions which the Governor gives him, and his loyalty and unselfishness are beyond question."[43]

A single question nagged, not deeply, at Farley's optimism as he boarded in Chicago the train that took him on the last leg of his journey, which was an uninterrupted ride to New York City. This single question concerned Roosevelt's health, his physical strength to bear the burdens of the presidency. Though absurd on the face of it for Farley or anyone else who had seen Roosevelt personally in action, and though it had been well scotched in New York State by the publicity given his life-insurance examination the year before, the threatful question had cropped up again and again during Farley's tour. But this, too, in its bearing upon the presidential candidacy, had been satisfactorily answered by the time Farley arrived in New York. By then he had read an article by the journalist Earle Looker, who called himself a Republican, published in the July 25, 1931, issue of *Liberty* magazine, entitled "Is Franklin D. Roosevelt Physically Fit to Be President?" The article was initiated three months earlier, when Roosevelt, disturbed by the whispering campaign about his health that had intensified with each passing week, accepted Looker's "challenge" (he had connived in its issuance) to submit to an exhaustive physical examination by a committee of physicians eminently qualified to conduct it, the results to be published by Looker, along with the journalist's own evaluation of the governor's physical stamina as observed in Albany. The doctors' conclusion was "that his [Roosevelt's] health and powers of endurance are such as to allow him to meet any demands of private and public life," and Looker's conclusion, from observation, was "that he seems able to take more punishment than many men ten years younger." The published article containing these conclusions, along with a vivid narrative description of Roosevelt in action as governor, was promptly dubbed by Farley "a corker" that answered "fully" the question that had been so often raised. Thereafter, the question was raised far less often, and never again, during that campaign, with any important effect.[44]

Nine days after Farley's national tour ended, Roosevelt's annual state tour via the *Inspector* began—and in Farley's home county of Rockland. During the following eighteen days, with Eleanor and Earl Miller, now a sergeant, serving often as his legs and eyes and ears, he inspected hospitals, schools, prisons, barge-canal improvements, hydroelectric-power sites, and other state installations; had personal talk with many scores of private citizens about their special concerns; and held conferences with dozens of local political leaders about state political matters. Then, on August 13, he returned to Albany, where he plunged at once into final preparations for a special session of the legislature.

8

➤➤✕◄◄

The Presidential Candidate as Governor

I

ALL through this period of intensifying national politicking, it must be reiterated, the presidential candidate was a very active governor of New York, with by far the greater part of his time and energy devoted to his gubernatorial role. It was a role that would in any case have interacted strongly with his national candidacy; in the event, again to reiterate, it was substantially fused with the latter, especially so since every problem he faced as governor following his reelection was either a direct consequence of the national depression or was powerfully affected by it.

By the autumn of 1930, the most reliable indices agreed that unemployment had climbed above 4,000,000. This was approximately 9 percent of the total national civilian labor force; but since the labor force was concentrated in the large cities of the twelve most highly industrialized states, whence unemployment was obviously spreading, local unemployment was often two or more times the national average. There were scores of regular breadlines in Greater New York City, with new ones being started almost every day. There were also in New York City, and on a thousand street corners of other Eastern cities, ragged men, many of them war veterans, who peddled apples at 5 cents apiece —their pitiful occupation born of the bright idea of an official of the International Apple Shippers' Association, who sought thus to reduce profitably that year's great market surplus of apples. The apple peddler was destined to become one of the two most potent symbols of the Great Depression.[1] The other was the miserable cluster of shanties that increasingly appeared on wasteland in urban areas. Made of packing crates, scrap lumber, tin cans, tar paper, they provided the only shelter for thousands upon thousands of jobless men, many with wives and children. These shantytowns were dubbed Hoovervilles by Charles Michelson's propaganda machine, which was shifting toward its highest gear as 1930 drew to a close and which was in good part inspired and energized by Michelson's own personal dislike and contempt for Herbert Hoover the man.[2]

So Franklin Roosevelt's first major gubernatorial act following 1930's reelection was his reappointment and enlargement on November 15, 1930, of the Commission on Stabilization of Industry, which he had appointed eight months before. At that time, in March 1930, "our hope" had been "that the depression would be short-lived and that we should be spared the emergency of this present winter," he said publicly. On the basis of this "hope" he had asked the committee "to concentrate on the study of preventive measures" against unemployment in future depressions. The committee had done so, submitting to him two days before "a very important report on the possibilities." But it was now clear that the depression was deepening and unemployment increasing, and so he was not only enlarging the committee by appointing "persons expert in certain phases of relief work," he was also going to ask the legislature when it convened—this in accord with one of the planks he had dictated into the party platform—"to make this committee an official commission and to provide for its expenses, which up to this time have been borne by the individual members."* Further, he was expanding the committee's assignment, asking it not only "to coordinate and encourage . . . additional employment" and "to coordinate and prevent duplication" of housing and and clothing and feeding efforts on behalf of the unemployed but "also . . . to make plans for the establishment of loan funds on a sound and suitable basis, the loan funds to be under local management and direction and used for the purpose of sustaining those whose incomes are greatly reduced or entirely depleted by the unemployment situation." He was "convinced that such loan funds can be successfully and democratically administered if they are set up on a sound basis with the participation of banking and business interests."[3]

His words measure the depth and nature of his perceptions, at the moment, of the developing economic crisis and of the proper governmental action for alleviating its dire effects on individual citizens. Like Hoover, he insisted upon "the participation of banking and business interests" in top policy-making and administrative roles: he was yet inclined to accept as true those assertions of superior practical wisdom and managerial skill that businessmen were wont to make on their own behalf. Like Hoover, he insisted upon local responsibility for, and local control of, unemployment relief: he had little if any more inclination than Hoover, at that time, to accept as a direct governmental responsibility the administration of such relief.

But there was also and nevertheless perceptible in his word and deed, considered in their context, an important fundamental difference between Roosevelt and Hoover—essentially the same difference as had been manifest between a young Assistant Secretary of the Navy and President Woodrow Wilson aboard the *George Washington* on a February day in 1919.† Roosevelt had a factual vision, a humble vision. His outward look was seldom dimmed or blinkered by rigid ideological preconceptions or by egotistical willfulness. And he was far more sensitive to changes in environmental pressures and far more swiftly responsive to them than Hoover was, lacking any such resistance to novelty and innovation as was rooted in Hoover's character and training as an engineer. To a remarkable degree, as he approached his forty-ninth birthday, Franklin Roosevelt retained a child's openness to new experience, a child's reactive flexibility: he was psychologically prepared to do whatever presented itself to him as necessary or useful for the relief of human distress,

---

*His request that the committee be made an official agency was subsequently refused by the Republican majority of the legislature.
†See *FDR: The Beckoning of Destiny,* pages 560–561. Herbert Hoover, as he reveals in his *Ordeal of Woodrow Wilson,* felt a spiritual kinship with Wilson.

should the crisis continue. If certain basic concepts, including his flat identification of democracy with capitalism, remained by him unexamined and inviolable, these concepts being part and parcel of his religious commitment, the practical motivational beliefs and ideas he derived from them had at their heart a measure of tentativeness, of doubt. They were quite easily revised by him or, if necessary, totally disavowed.

Take, for instance, his insistence upon a "local" approach to unemployment relief, his aversion to the assumption by state or national government of responsibility for such relief. This was rooted in a Jeffersonian (states'-rights) belief in decentralized government that was in the process of revision—at least the way was being prepared for such revision—within a week or two of his announced continuance of the Commission on Stabilization of Industry. Frances Perkins then came to him with the suggestion that he invite to Albany the governors of neighboring Eastern industrial states for a conference on unemployment. He did so, after being assured by Frances Perkins, whom he had asked to check with the various state labor commissioners, that the governors were willing to come. The conference, which received national publicity, was held in the third week of January 1931, with the governors of Massachusetts, Rhode Island, Connecticut, New Jersey, Pennsylvania, and Ohio in attendance. To prepare for it, Frances Perkins summoned to Albany the University of Chicago's brilliant young economist Paul H. Douglas, whose annotated agenda, other documentation, and extensive oral briefings enabled Roosevelt to preside over the meeting in remarkably impressive fashion. No concrete practical proposals issued from the discussions of unemployment insurance (Douglas was among the nation's top authorities on unemployment insurance), the possible establishment of a central clearinghouse for employment information, and the advisability of uniformity of labor laws and corporate tax laws among the several states. But Roosevelt's economic orthodoxy was considerably jolted by his concentrated exposure to Douglas and other liberal economists who staffed the meeting, and he was never after as insistent as he had been before upon decentralized governmental ways of dealing with broad and basic economic problems. Clearly, such problems had no regard for political boundaries, and Roosevelt now opined that a uniformity of certain key legislation in "those of industrial states which include 47% of all the wage earners in the U.S."—that is, an abrogation of "states rights" to this extent —would be of benefit to "industry and workers as a whole."[4]

Or take, as another instance of his mental flexibility, Roosevelt's idea or belief that bankers were possessed of a morality somewhat higher than that of businessmen in general, were truly committed to managing the state's credit system in the public interest, and could therefore be trusted, when a portion of the system broke down, to repair it in ways that improved the system as a whole.

Roosevelt had acted according to this belief in the aftermath of the City Trust Company collapse. It will be remembered that he had pointedly refrained from endorsing the proposals made by the Moreland commissioner,

Robert Moses, at the conclusion of an unusually thorough investigation, regarding the urgent need for sweeping banking reforms (the abolition of private banks, the outlawing of affiliates formed solely for the purpose of speculating with depositors' money, the strict segregation of thrift from savings accounts, the subjection of thrift accounts to the same stringent regulations as were or should be applied to savings). Instead, Roosevelt had appointed a special commission, stacked with bankers and businessmen, to consider Moses' recommendations and make final ones of its own. It will be further remembered that when this commission predictably rejected every one of Moses' major recommendations,[5] substituting innocuous ones, Roosevelt had praised the commissioners for their "constructive" labors and had signed into law, with a show of pride in major accomplishment, the resultant four banking bills, none of which made any important change in banking practice. Finally it will be recalled that Moses, for whom Roosevelt felt strong dislike, had been deliberately snubbed in this procedure: not only had he not been appointed to the commission, as in common sense and simple justice he should have been, but the place he might have had on it *was given to a director and vice-president of the Bank of United States, whose organization and management had been singled out by Moses, in his report, for special censure!*

Almost everything about the Bank of United States was highly questionable, beginning with its misleading name. A state-chartered institution having no connection whatever with the federal government,* apart from its membership in the Federal Reserve System, it had been founded seventeen years before by a Jewish garment manufacturer whose son, Bernard K. Marcus, was now, in 1930, its president. The executive vice-president was Saul Singer. And the formidable promotional talents of these two, uninhibited by any scrupulous regard for truth telling but intimately joined with a penchant for daring gambles with other people's money, had caused the institution to grow rapidly all through the securities market boom of the Roaring Twenties. Numerous smaller banks had been absorbed through mergers, fifty-seven branch offices had been established in four boroughs of New York City, and more than 450,000 depositors had been acquired, most of them Jewish and nearly all of them, as in the case of City Trust, working people with small incomes: in 1930 well over 50 percent of the bank's $200,000,000 of deposits were in unsupervised thrift accounts; fully 350,000 of the deposit accounts were of less than $400. Nor had Marcus and Singer confined their entrepreneurial energy to orthodox banking channels: an intricate network of affiliates, some sixty of them, had been organized for purposes of speculation with depositors' money in real estate and other ventures, speculations that led to disastrous losses when the stock market crashed.

---

*The lobby decorations in the main office at 320 Fifth Avenue were designed to suggest otherwise. They included a large American flag, a huge oil painting of the U.S. Capitol, a gold model of the American eagle of impressive size, and a gold-lettered sign saying "Federal Reserve System." A goodly number of those doing business in this lobby were persuaded they dealt with an agency of the federal government.

Indeed, as early as mid-July 1929, a full three months *before* the Crash and less than two weeks after Joseph A. Broderick had assumed office as Roosevelt's state banking superintendent, examiners, more than a hundred of them, from the state banking department and the Federal Reserve Bank of New York had found the Bank of United States to be grossly mismanaged and its long-term solvency far from assured. Their report to Broderick, calling for drastic changes in the bank's operations and personnel, bluntly concluded that Marcus and Singer were unqualified to administer so huge an institution. Broderick, however, whose range of possible corrective action was in any case severely limited by existing banking law, had failed to take any decisive action. He had conferred with Marcus and Singer. He had seemingly accepted at face value their assurances that a general plan for the bank's overhaul, whereby the causes of criticism would be removed, was in the process of development. He had made no evident effort to see that such a plan was effected (actually no plan was even made) and, indeed, seemed to lose interest in the matter until a new examination of the bank, in August 1930, disclosed alarming discrepancies between its public financial statements and its actual financial condition. Far from having the $42,000,000 of capital, surplus, and undivided profit that it claimed, the bank had no surplus or undistributed profit whatever, and its capital was gravely impaired!

There followed desperate secret efforts to prevent the bank's collapse, while rumors of its shaky condition spread from the financial community to the public at large. Roosevelt himself became directly involved. On an October day he paused in his reelection campaign to confer secretly in his New York City home with representatives of four of the city's largest banks—Bankers Trust, Central Hanover, National City, and J. P. Morgan and Company—trying to persuade them to take over the faltering bank through merger. They did initiate negotiations toward this end with Marcus and Singer, which ultimately came to naught, while rising doubt and spreading fear spurred the withdrawal of some $60,000,000 of deposits from the Bank of United States over a two-month period. Then, on December 10, 1930, the failed effort of a Bronx merchant to sell his bank stock back to the Bronx branch manager from whom he had bought it sparked a rumor that he had tried to close out his account and had been unable to do so. Within an hour a frantic run began on the Bronx branch, spreading rapidly to other branches and, the next day, to the main bank itself. Hundreds of scared and increasingly unruly depositors, their anxieties heightened by Communist agitators, who joined the throng in the hope of provoking a riot,* were being kept in line by mounted police before the doors of 320 Fifth Avenue when, in the afternoon of December 11, there appeared on those doors a formal notice that the Bank of United States had been closed by order of State Banking Superintendent Broderick.[6]

It was the largest bank failure in the nation's history up to that time. It sent

---

*The national headquarters of the Communist Party were at 50 East Thirteenth Street, just around the corner from the main bank building. The agitators operated on orders from headquarters.

shock waves through the national financial community and ominously shook popular confidence in the credit structure (within two weeks, two other sizable New York banks were closed—the Chelsea Bank in New York City and the State Bank of Binghamton). It provoked angry public criticism of Broderick for his failure to act in defense of depositors when he first knew, for he now admitted he had known for fifteen months, that the bank was "shaky." It forced District Attorney Crain to institute grand jury proceedings to determine if there were grounds for criminal indictments of the bank's officers, though this did nothing to mollify a public that continued to view with disgust Crain's mishandling of the investigation of the magistrate's courts. And it incited Norman Thomas to wire Governor Roosevelt, releasing to the press his telegram, calling for a new Moreland Act investigation of the banking department.

The effect of all this upon Roosevelt as governor was an abrupt shift of policy ground.

He gave no sign of guilt over his appointment of Henry Pollock of the Bank of United States to his special banking commission; he gave not the slightest sign that he regretted having cavalierly rejected Moses' recommendations in favor of the do-nothing counsel of the bankers. He made no mention of his failure to recommend thrift-account protection to the 1930 legislature. Instead, he now remembered that he had been "greatly disappointed that [the] last legislature did nothing about thrift accounts," as he said "[c]onfidentially for your information" to Norman Thomas in a telegram (January 5, 1931) refusing the request for a new Moreland investigation but reporting that he had urged Crain to pursue vigorously the grand jury investigation. "I expect to recommend such action [on thrift accounts] to this legislature," he concluded.[7] He did so in a special message on March 24, 1931. "I believe that it is nothing more than ordinary good faith to the public that the legislature at this present session do something to initiate the safeguarding and protection of these thrift accounts," he said. "The people of the state not only expect it, but they have a right to demand it. . . . Any *further* [present author's italics] delay is inexcusable." And he went on to measure in unwontedly strong language his widening, deepening disillusionment with the banking community. "It is a matter of grave concern to the State that every one of these suggestions advanced [for the strengthening of the banking laws] has been strenuously opposed by some of the banking interests themselves," he said, "though I believe a majority of our bankers admit that something must be done. So far there has been visible only a campaign of opposition not only to this bill but to the other remedial bills offered this year by the Superintendent of Banks. . . . If the banking interests themselves had some substitute plan to correct the evils which lurk in our banking laws, more reliance might be placed on their wisdom. By merely blocking all reform, as they appear to be doing this year with your Honorable Bodies, they discredit any claim that their efforts are accompanied by a sincere desire to protect the depositors of the State."[8]

Fortunate, perhaps, for Roosevelt's reputation as a progressive reformer was the fact that his words on this matter, loudly spoken, fell upon deaf legislative ears—ears, however, that heard and heeded every whispered wish of New York's bankers. No thrift-account bill was passed by the Republican legislature in 1931 or 1932. This enabled Roosevelt to claim, if he chose to do so, that he had not publicly espoused this reform measure in 1930 because he knew there was then no chance of its passage, that he had instead waited until an untoward event, demonstrating to the public at large the urgent need for such reform, had created a climate of opinion favorable to its adoption, and that his then prompt and continued strong effort on behalf of small depositors had been frustrated by special-interest legislators who listened only to those who would speculate for their own profit with the hard-earned money of the "little" people. It should be added that Roosevelt himself, in his general views on banking, remained far more conservative than were most disinterested students of the credit structure in 1930–1932. For all his expressed concern to protect depositors, he favored no important structural change in the banking system, flatly opposing as "impractical" every deposit insurance scheme that was proposed for legislative action, as several were, during his second gubernatorial term.

II

MORE damaging to Roosevelt's reputation as a progressive reformer were his dealings as governor with the corruption of the New York City government, which was increasingly exposed, in incontrovertible factual detail, by the Seabury Investigation after it opened its public hearings. Yet here, too, Roosevelt manifested a swift response to pressures—a concern and talent for measuring pressure differences between opposing forces, then acting on calculations of the effect such differences might have upon his political fortunes—which contrasted sharply with Herbert Hoover's ideological rigidities.

Judge Seabury, a man not without ambition for national power and glory, announced to the first meeting of his full staff that his purpose was not only to inform the public about conditions in the magistrate's courts but also to arouse the public in ways leading to corrective action. This could not be done "through a series of graphs, charts, and reports," he said. "We must divorce this investigation, as far as possible, from legalistic machinery. There is more eloquence in the testimony of an illiterate witness telling of oppression suffered from legal processes than in the greatest sermon, editorial, or address ever written. Where preachers, editors, and lawyers have failed in arousing the public to a consciousness of unjust conditions these simple, unlearned witnesses will succeed."[9]

He prophesied truly.

Even those of the general public who wearily expected and thus partially condoned as "inevitable" such Tammany graft as Tuttle had exposed were generally shocked and sickened, in December 1930, by the Seabury revelations, from humble witnesses, of individual human tragedies consequent upon collusion between vice-squad police, bondsmen, lawyers, and magistrates in the "framing up" of women on morals charges. These charges were dropped or the victim was acquitted of them in court if she paid off her tormentors, but otherwise she was invariably convicted, then fined and jailed, no matter how flimsy or even nonexistent the evidence against her. Some policemen had grown wealthy from this racket: one had banked $90,000 in five years, and another, a lieutenant, $184,000. Some of the victims, unmarried girls and housewives of theretofore spotless reputation, had been driven to insanity or suicide. The public outcry against John Curry's Tammany and Roosevelt's patronage cooperation with it grew louder and angrier in the last month of 1930 than it had been at any time during the year before.

Tammany reacted according to form.

Dapper charming, gallant, chivalrous Jimmy Walker, mayor of the City of New York, "confessed" that he was "more or less shocked by reports of the framing of innocent women," he of course having had no prior inkling that so horrid or unfortunate a business (the "more" as against the "less" shocking) was possible in his city administration.[10] He then departed for a vacation in Palm Springs. New York City's police commissioner suspended every policeman whom stool-pigeon witnesses before Seabury had identified as a participant in the frame-up racket (there were twenty-eight of them) and ordered departmental trials of these men. District Attorney Crain announced an investigation of the vice squad, then proceeded in his usual halfhearted lackadaisical fashion to gather evidence against policemen accused of perjury and of otherwise falsifying evidence against helpless innocent women.

As for Governor Roosevelt, he was "deeply disturbed and greatly incensed" as he asked Judge Seabury to determine if "[s]omething should be done immediately" to correct the injustice done "women who have already been convicted and sentenced under . . . conditions of frame-up." Might not some of these cases be "reopened or brought before the governor with recommendations of executive clemency"? Seabury at once sent to Albany the names of six women, now on parole, who had served time in prison for alleged prostitution; he recommended that the governor issue a full pardon to each of them, which Roosevelt promptly did.[11] But, in private as in public communications, Roosevelt continued to refuse to budge from the narrow constitutional ground of "home rule," of local responsibility, which he had chosen as his defensive position when the first demands for executive action against the Curry-Walker regime had come to him, ground he had only slightly widened when, asserting an authority he claimed legally not to have, he took the Ewald-Healy case out of Crain's hands and assigned it to the state attorney general.

Henry Goddard Leach, editor of the influential *Forum* magazine,* wrote him a sharply worded letter accusing him, at least implicitly, of sacrificing moral duty to political expediency with regard to New York City. City government had completely broken down, said Leach, and if the state did not inter-

---

*Leach's wife, Agnes, was a leader of the Women's Division of the New York State Democratic Party and one of Eleanor Roosevelt's close personal friends.

vene to prevent urban anarchy, then the federal government, employing federal troops, must do so. Roosevelt replied with equal sharpness on the day that the Bank of United States was closed (December 11, 1930). He asked Leach to "run in and see me here [at 49 East Sixty-fifth Street] next Monday or Tuesday" because "I want to . . . get out of your head the idea that there is any question of political expediency in what I am driving at." He shared "100% . . . the thought that something must be done, but the answer is not State control or Federal control. That is moral cowardice [his use of the phrase is psychologically revealing] and heads the country straight for the type of government now in effect in Russia and Italy."[12] He then, without mentioning Leach's name, made public comment on Leach's disturbing letter in his second inaugural address (January 1, 1931), whose theme, obviously dictated by his worry over the New York City mess, was the necessity for improving local governments in order to preserve the decentralized authority of a truly democratic society. "Not long ago I received a letter from an eminent editor," he said, "telling me tearfully that all local government had broken down, and begging me as governor . . . to usurp and assume the functions of the officials duly elected by the communities themselves. . . . I cite this as an illustration of the present dangerous tendency to forget a fundamental of American democracy which rests on the right of a locality to manage its local affairs—the tendency to encourage concentration of power at the top of the governmental structure alien to our system and more closely akin to a dictatorship or the central committee of a communistic regime."[13] His implicit syllogistic reasoning to the effect that the City of New York and the Town of Hyde Park, since both were "localities," must have the same relationship with state government, a palpable legalistic absurdity, carried, of course, no conviction whatever in the minds of his critics. It did nothing to prevent, and indeed its sophistry encouraged, attacks upon him for failure to press a citywide investigation of the Walker regime. One such was made by the City Affairs Committee in a pamphlet issued on the day before Christmas, 1930, which Roosevelt chose to ignore but which stung and angered him all the same when he read it in Albany upon his return from Hyde Park, where, as always, he had celebrated the holidays with his mother, his wife, and his children.

Nor was his dubious defensive ground in any way solidified or widened; it was on the contrary loosened and narrowed, when, in the opening months of 1931, the magistrate's courts investigation and the Bank of United States investigation became mixed up together.

Exposed to the public gaze, in part by Norman Thomas in a much-quoted article in the *Nation*,[14] were interesting connections between the defunct bank's management and Tammany Hall politics. Prominent Tammanyites were on the bank's board. Samuel Levy, a Tammanyite recently elected borough president of Manhattan, had participated in a syndicate (pool) formed by the bank's chief officers to trade in the bank's stock, a syndicate large enough to rig stock prices. Max D. Steuer, the famous Tammany criminal lawyer who was now John Curry's chief counsel, had at various times in the past been Bernard

Marcus' attorney. He had been Warder's defense counsel when Warder was tried and convicted on charges of accepting bribes from City Trust management during his tenure as superintendent of banks; as banking superintendent, Warder must certainly have known and approved, or condoned, the Marcus-Singer practices that had led the Bank of United States to disaster. Was Broderick similarly guilty? Thomas rather more than hinted he might be. Broderick in September 1930 had permitted Marcus and Singer to issue a financial statement he must have known to be false, since he had by then received the report of the bank examination of the previous month.* And three months later, only days before the final collapse, he had authorized the opening of a new Bank of United States branch. The collapse having occurred, Max Steuer (his wife was permitted to withdraw $53,000 from the Bank of United States *after* closing hours on the last full day of the bank's life!) promptly became counsel of a hastily organized United States Depositors' and Stockholders' Association, a strange association, on the face of it, since the bank's stockholders and the bulk of its depositors had divergent if not opposing interests. Might not the stockholders be liable for the depositors' losses? Shortly thereafter, Steuer accepted Crain's invitation to serve as the district attorney's top assistant in the Bank of United States investigation, after Crain had been prodded toward vigorous action in this matter by the governor.

There could be no doubt among the knowledgeable that vigorous action *would* issue from Steuer's appointment, though it was unlikely to be pressed to any conclusion threatful of Curry-Walker interests. Steuer had been succeeded as Marcus' personal lawyer by a lawyer as brilliant as himself, Isidor J. Kresel, who had also subsequently become general counsel for the Bank of United States, in which capacity he had advised Marcus and Singer as to the legality of their intricate operations. Obviously Kresel, who had participated in the aforementioned syndicate formed to trade in the bank's stock, was now himself a likely object of criminal indictment, along with the men he had advised. And this fact added zest to the zeal with which Steuer entered upon his prosecutorial duties. Not only was Kresel a longtime and bitter personal enemy of Steuer's,† he was also, and had been from the outset, Seabury's

---

*Broderick later swore under oath that he first learned on September 18, 1930, from one of his examiners, that the bank's surplus had been wiped out.

†Some fifteen years before, Steuer had represented a musical-comedy actress named Edith St. Clair in an action brought by her against Abe Erlanger, a theatrical producer, for life support, she having been, she claimed, Erlanger's mistress. Kresel had represented the producer, who lost the case and thereafter paid dearly in cash for such favors as Miss St. Clair had granted him. But Erlanger would not have lost, an infuriated Kresel was convinced, if the actress had not given false testimony on the witness stand. Subsequently, evidently at Kresel's instigation, Steuer was brought up for disbarment on a charge of having suborned perjury (that is, of having coached Miss St. Clair to lie under oath), a charge of which he was finally, narrowly acquitted. Ever since, the two men had hated each other with a passion fed, one suspects, by the fact that each saw the worst features of himself reflected in the other. Each man was physically small, each far from handsome of face, each of gamecock disposition, and each a brilliant trial lawyer. Steuer, however, who was making $1,000,000 a year from his criminal practice in the late 1920s, evinced no such concern to serve the general welfare as Kresel had often evinced. The latter had interrupted his lucrative

right-hand man in the investigation of the magistrate's courts! Indeed, as the new year opened, he was so nearly an equal partner with the judge in this enterprise as to cause many to think of it as the Seabury-Kresel inquiry.[15] It appeared to Steuer, therefore, as it did to other rejoicing braves in Tammany wigwams, that whatever grievous injuries were now inflicted on Kresel must also injure the Seabury Investigation, and perhaps severely enough to discredit and abort it.

Steuer's design was frustrated, however, when Kresel, on February 10, 1931, resigned his post as Seabury's counsel in order, as he publicly stated, to avoid embarrassing the investigation with his personal troubles. "Kresel served with unflagging industry and devotion and he performed with outstanding skill and ability," reported Seabury to the Appellate Division in defiance of a hostile public opinion that rose high against the failed bank's counsel.[16] And though the replacement named for Kresel had abilities considerably smaller than his, the deficiency was offset by Seabury's own increased and redirected effort. The judge had theretofore operated largely *as* a judge, a referee in fact as in name: he now became an active investigator, with his staff, and a highly effective one. The work went on.

The net effect of all this so far as Roosevelt was concerned was to sharpen the already sufficiently sharp horns of his dilemma. There was a further swelling of the cry for direct gubernatorial action against a wickedness that directly, direly affected approximately half the population of the state and was assuredly not going to be removed by the city administration that perpetrated it. Though he continued to believe he could not win presidential nomination without the support, or lack of active enmity against him at least, of Tammany Hall, he must act against Tammany with a convincing semblance of all possible vigor if he was not to alienate a national public whose support he had to have to win the presidency. And the time to act was clearly *now*.

For in the same month as Kresel's resignation from Seabury's staff there occurred an event that demonstrated, more vividly than any earlier publicized event had done, the absolute contempt in which the law-enforcement agencies of the Curry-Walker regime were held by New York City's racketeers.

An attractive, evidently nymphomaniacal young woman named Vivian Gordon was found dead in the Bronx's Van Cortlandt Park. She had been strangled. The motive for the crime appeared clear when Seabury revealed that the victim had been questioned a day or so before in private by one of Seabury's assistants concerning her false arrest, some years earlier, on a vice charge.* Her informal preliminary testimony was deemed immensely important by Seabury. She was preparing to testify under oath, in detail, with concrete evidence,

---

private practice to serve as counsel for the New York State Assembly in the 1913 impeachment of Governor Sulzer (see *FDR: The Beckoning of Destiny*, pages 350–351); as special assistant attorney general of the United States investigating bankruptcy and antitrust matters; and as investigator for the Bar Association of shyster lawyering.

*Among the general public were many who wondered aloud if this police viciousness might not have led to Vivian Gordon's subsequent activities as a prostitute.

naming names and citing precise times and places, when she was murdered, and a week later her teenage daughter, who had apparently known nothing of her mother's underworld life and was shamed beyond bearing by its exposure, committed suicide. Thunderous indeed was the public clamor for state executive action that now arose. At its height, the City Club of New York formally petitioned the governor to remove from the district attorney's office "the incompetent, inefficient and futile" Thomas C. T. Crain. Again and again, Crain had "failed properly to conduct prosecutions for crimes . . . cognizable by the courts," had failed to expose "grafting in the Department of Purchase and crimes connected with the Board of Standards and Appeals," and had made misleading statements about the conduct of his official duties. So said the City Club's formal petition. Crain's operations as district attorney were chiefly notable for "inertia and timidity." So, a day or so later, said the City Affairs Committee, which had been originally organized in 1929 to support Norman Thomas' run for mayor of New York and of which the Reverend John Haynes Holmes, pastor of the Community Church, Rabbi Stephen S. Wise, and the philosopher John Dewey were leading members. " . . . popular cynicism and distrust of the processes of government have been greatly increased by the district attorney's statements on racketeering," and racketeering "could not flourish without political alliance." So said Norman Thomas himself.[17] As for the general public, it obviously had no confidence that Crain would effectively investigate the murder of Vivian Gordon or prosecute the murderers if they were arrested.

Thus Roosevelt found himself in approximately the same position he had been in when Crain's grand jury failed to find grounds for indictments in the Ewald-Healy case. He reacted in approximately the same way.

Crain and his sponsor John Curry were called to Roosevelt's New York City home and there confronted by the governor with the City Club charges. It was subsequently rumored that the governor gave Crain an opportunity to resign and that Tammany was enraged against Roosevelt, believing he had encouraged the filing of these charges in order to stifle Crain's Bank of United States investigation, which, if pressed, might lead to criminal indictment of the governor's banking superintendent. Publicly announced, following the meeting, was Crain's request for an immediate full investigation of the charges. And on March 8, 1931, in a move as calculatedly risky as his earlier use of Attorney General Ward had been, Roosevelt not only ordered this investigation but also asked Samuel Seabury, Tammany's *bête noire,* to conduct it as the governor's "commissioner under Section 34 of the public officers' law"—this in addition to the magistrate's courts investigation that Seabury continued to pursue. "You will, of course, note that the charges do not in any way involve the personal integrity of Justice Crain," Roosevelt was careful to point out in his charge to Seabury, "but relate solely to his competency to fulfill the office he holds."[18]

The ensuing investigation, which was vastly publicized, in good part by Crain's headline-hunting defense counsel, Samuel Untermyer, proved up to the hilt that Crain, if technically honest (he possessed inherited wealth), was totally unfit for his office. Seabury turned to Columbia's Professor Raymond A. Moley for help. He had read Moley's book, *Our Criminal Courts,* which was given to him by Basil O'Connor and which was "in part a summary of [Moley's] . . . findings and conclusions after ten years of study in law administration in various states,"[19] and he now asked Moley to make statistical analyses, graphically presented, of the district attorney's case record. The resultant evidence of incompetence was conclusive. Crain's standard practice, as explained by Herbert Mitgang, "was to indict defendants for major crimes and allow them to plead guilty of misdemeanors." Thus, of 1,279 indictments for grand larceny in 1930, 623 had resulted in convictions, of which 128 had been for lesser felonies and 423 for misdemeanors. Only 72 convictions had been for the crime charged. And in case after case specifically cited in the City Club petition, Crain's futility was evidentially demonstrated. Nevertheless, to the disgust of many reformers, Seabury's final report to the governor recommended that the City Club's petition for Crain's removal be denied.* "The question whether an elected public official should be removed is not determined by individual opinion as to what may promote public interest," concluded Seabury somewhat sophistically, having abundantly justified, with objective evidence, his own "individual opinion" that the public interest *would* be served by Crain's removal. "Proof, not opinion, is the standard which must be applied. . . . Public interests are to be served, but such interests cannot be truly served at the expense of injustice to an individual."[21] The governor of course accepted this recommendation: Crain continued as district attorney, with no perceptible increase in his effectiveness.

And by then (the final report of the Crain investigation was dated August 31, 1931) much else had happened to raise questions in critical minds about Roosevelt's commitment to good government.

One such major happening had been initiated on the evening of March 17, St. Patrick's Day, which was the twenty-sixth anniversary of Roosevelt's marriage to Eleanor and just nine days after he named Seabury his special commissioner. That evening Roosevelt attended a dinner of the Friendly Sons of St. Patrick at the Hotel Astor. He returned late to 49 East Sixty-fifth Street, where he found, waiting for him in the library, Rabbi Wise and the Reverend Holmes. They presented to him, on behalf of the City Affairs Committee, a petition of some 4,000 words wherein ten specific charges of gross negligence and incompetence were leveled in detail against James J. Walker as mayor of New York, on the basis of which the governor was asked to remove Walker from office. A few minutes later the two visitors left, being bowed out with no show of warmth by their host, who then himself departed for Grand Central,

---

*There were pragmatic reasons for the recommendation. Seabury had been informed that John Curry's Tammany was determined to nominate Crain for reelection, whether or not Crain was removed from office, and there was little doubt that Tammany's tight control of Manhattan's vote would ensure Crain's election victory. "We knew we would be left looking silly," remembered a Seabury assistant long afterward.[20]

where he boarded the 12:20 A.M. train for Albany. From Albany, seven days later, Roosevelt mailed the charges to Walker, who, his health reportedly broken under the incessant attacks made against him, was "recuperating" on Samuel Untermyer's estate in Palm Springs. The governor asked the mayor to reply to the charges in writing as soon as his health permitted.[22]

Walker did so some weeks later. He presented a 15,000-word document notable for its lack of logical organization, its glaring omissions, its failure to address in any meaningful way the specific charges, and for the malicious aspersions it cast upon the character and motives of his accusers. It was wholly of Walker's own composition. He had refused publicly the proffered help of a Tammany counsel, believing he had a better chance of leniency from a governor inclined toward leniency if his defense were strictly personal, *not* a defense by and of Tammany Hall.

And such belief would seem justified in the event.

For Roosevelt at once accepted the mayor's absurd brief as an adequate defense against the charges made. His privately expressed attitude toward Walker at this time was a tolerant mixture of exasperation and amusement, as if Walker were guilty of no more than a boyish mischievousness, aversion to work, and love of fun. (Toward Holmes and Wise, on the other hand, his privately expressed attitude was increasingly wrathful: he viewed their embarrassing public demands upon his office as personally hostile acts and was as inclined to impugn their motives as Walker was.) " . . . our little Mayor can save much trouble in the future by getting on the job, cleaning his own house and stopping wisecracks," he wrote Clark Howell, publisher of the Atlanta (Georgia) *Constitution,* on March 31, in a letter saying that "W.R.H. [William Randolph Hearst] . . . feels, I think, as I do"—this last in recognition of the fact that charming Jimmy was a favorite of Hearst's, defended by Hearst's two New York City papers against all attacks, and that Roosevelt yearned for the potent political support of Hearst's national chain of papers. "If he [Walker] does not do all this," Roosevelt's letter to Howell went on to say, "he can have only himself to blame if he gets into trouble."[23] From this it would appear that Walker, in Roosevelt's opinion, was not *yet* in "trouble." Certainly he would not be in any that was of the governor's making, or any the governor could protect him against, as was manifested on April 27, when, without making any investigation of his own or requiring the mayor to testify under oath, Roosevelt rejected the City Affairs petition, saying he found "insufficient evidence" to justify Walker's removal.

Reform leaders were again disgusted, of course. There was another spate of angry published denunciations of the governor's "cowardice," his evident willingness to sacrifice the general good to his personal ambition.

But the injurious impact of such denunciation upon Roosevelt's reputation as a progressive was, as so often happened with him, greatly cushioned by the ineptitude, the stupidity, the bad faith, of his partisan opponents. A long year had passed since the Republicans who dominated the legislature were first challenged to initiate an investigation of New York City's government, the governor having insisted that, if an investigation was needed, its conduct was properly a function of the legislative branch, not of the executive. During that long year, for various unstated reasons, a chief one being the vested interest that several Republican politicians had in the Tammany "system," the legislative Republican leadership had repeatedly refused the challenge, despite strong urgings to the contrary from W. Kingsland Macy. But now, at last, the challenge was accepted. On March 23, 1931, just as Roosevelt was about to forward the City Affairs charges to Walker—in other words, at the worst possible time for their partisan purpose of embarrassing the governor and, indeed, at a time when such action provided temporary relief from acute embarrassment—the Republicans pushed through the legislature a joint Senate-Assembly resolution to establish a special committee for "the investigation of the departments of the government of the City of New York." State Senator Samuel H. Hofstadter became the legislative committee chairman. An initial appropriation of $250,000 was made for the committee's operation, with another $250,000 allocated. Judge Seabury, with the governor's blessing, was appointed committee counsel, which meant he would actively conduct the investigation in conjunction with the two he already had in hand—that of the magistrates and that of Crain. And Roosevelt was enabled to justify on sound policy grounds, in late April, his inaction with regard to the City Affairs petition. Any investigation of his own, he was enabled to say, would be duplicative and confusing of the inquiry being made by the legislature.

Soon after, the Joint Legislative Committee placed Horse Doctor Doyle on its witness stand for questioning about his remarkably lucrative practice before the Board of Standards and Appeals. He was, of course, a recalcitrant witness. After it had been firmly established through bank records and banker testimony that his practice had netted him more than $1,000,000 in eight years, Doyle on advice of his attorney* refused to answer any questions concerning the fee-splitting whereby, obviously, his fortune had been acquired. Nor would he do so after the committee, having voted to grant him immunity from prosecution for self-incriminating testimony, threatened him with a contempt citation if he remained silent. The threat was then carried out: cited for contempt, Doyle was sentenced to thirty days in jail. But did the committee have constitutional authority to grant immunity? State Supreme Court Justice Benjamin Cardozo ruled that it did not when the Doyle case came before him on appeal. In Cardozo's opinion, which Seabury himself praised as "learned," the proper "way to compel disclosure as to conspiracies and attempts" was to embody the "grant of immunity in a statute." The legislature, when it convened, "may pass an act of amnesty with the approval of the Governor," whereupon Doyle "as well as other witnesses" would "be under a duty to

---

*Doyle's counsel, Samuel Falk, was a son-in-law of the Republican leader of New York County, Samuel Koenig, a fact that suggested to many that there was, if not actual collusion, no bitter hostility between Manhattan's Republican leadership and that of Tammany Hall.

declare the whole truth, irrespective of the number or nature of the crimes exposed to view."[24]

Seabury promptly drafted the indicated legislation and forwarded it to Roosevelt with a cover letter, wherein he pointedly called attention to the fact "that a portion of our party now in control of the City of New York has expressed its opposition" to the proposed statute. "Fortunately," the letter continued, "it lies within your power as Governor to convene a special session of the legislature to unite with you, regardless of party, in enacting a statute that will empower the Joint Legislative Committee in proper cases to grant immunity to witnesses to the end that the facts about graft and corruption in the City of New York may be disclosed. With great respect, I ask that you exercise this power." The letter's schoolmasterish tone could not but have irritated the letter's recipient, as did its pointing the path of duty in a way that implied Roosevelt's need for such direction, in a context that included Seabury's own growing national prominence (as a result of the New York City investigation he was beginning to be mentioned as a possible Democratic presidential nominee in 1932). Consulting on the matter with Rosenman and Lehman upon his return to Albany from the *Inspector* tour, Roosevelt may well have cast around a bit for some viable alternative to his doing what the judge requested. If so, he found none. He convened the special session in late August 1931 and told the assembled lawmakers that the "purpose of the proposed legislation meets with my entire approval" (the tameness of this endorsement displeased the New York *Times,* which felt he should have "flame[d] out in wrath against plunder").[25] When the bill sailed through with a sizable majority, he at once signed it into law, accompanying his signature with an essentially ironic commendation of the legislative leadership for its zeal in investigating local government, a zeal he hoped would extend to Republican-dominated local governments upstate.

III

BUT a New York legislature in extraordinary session was not limited by the state constitution to a consideration of the specific matter for which it had been convened; it might also consider other matters presented to it, in writing, by the governor. And at the very meeting with Rosenman and Lehman during which he decided he must accede to Seabury's request, Roosevelt also decided to seize the opportunity thus presented to him to shift popular attention away from the embarrassing subject of Tammany to the more important matter of relief for the unemployed, sharpening in the process an already sharp issue between himself and Herbert Hoover.

Not that his need for such diversion was the sole motive for the action he now took. Equally important were his humane instincts and his concern for the future of democracy as he assessed the human consequences of the collapse of the New Era.

For steadily, inexorably, terrifyingly, the national economy continued to spiral downward. A general survey published on December 28, 1931, by the Guaranty Trust Company of New York would report gloomily that "the year 1931, like 1930, has been one of swift . . . recession in the volume of business and prices" with the result that "the end of the year finds business activity at the lowest ebb since the beginning of the depression." This ebb was low indeed. The volume of stock-market transactions in 1931 was 29 percent smaller than that in 1930 and nearly 49 percent below that in 1929. Stock share prices declined to an even greater degree. The prices of railroad shares in 1931 were 48 percent below those in 1930 and 64 percent below those in 1929, while copper share prices in 1931 were only 45 percent of those in 1930 and only 16 percent of those in 1929. And the stock market now, in sharp contrast to that of the summer of 1929, reflected, if with far from mirror accuracy, actual conditions with regard to those "fundamentals" whose "soundness" incantative big-business spokesmen continued to assert, if with less and less assurance. Check transactions in 1931 were about 26 percent below those of 1930 and more than 44 percent below those of 1929. New building contract awards, which had totaled some $5.8 billion in 1929, had fallen to $4.5 billion in 1930, a drop of 42 percent, and they were 50 percent less in 1931 than they had been in 1930. The production of automobiles, steel ingots, copper, bituminous coal, and lumber in 1931 was but one third to one half of what it had been in 1929, despite which there continued to be "overproduction" of each of these commodities, measured, to a degree, by falling prices. Nor was there any sign in the securities market, transportation, or industry that 1932 would show an improvement over 1931. On the contrary, all signs pointed toward an acceleration of the downward trend. For instance, during the first nine months of 1931, new capital financing totaled only $1.6 billion, as compared with $4.5 billion for the corresponding period of 1930 and with $7.5 billion for the corresponding period of 1929, a drop of $5.9 billion, or nearly 79 percent, in two years.

Overproduction! This, it was generally agreed among leading policymakers, was the root-evil from which grew economic disaster. Irrelevant, since it could not be expressed in market purchases, was the need for food, clothing, shelter, by millions of impoverished citizens. The only remedy that these policymakers could clearly see was planned production control to limit output, thereby inducing price-lifting scarcities. This remedy could be applied with relative ease in large-scale manufacturing, where the number of competing units was relatively small and where a considerable measure of price-fixing cooperation, though illegal, had long prevailed, *provided* the antitrust laws were suspended or modified to permit specified "combinations in restraint of trade"—and there were not wanting powerful voices urging the Congress and administration to do precisely this. The American Bar Association in the spring of 1931 adopted a resolution asking for antitrust-law revision that would give the Federal Trade Commission "power to pass in advance on restraint of trade contracts, voluntarily submitted, and to grant immunity" from antitrust penalties to those whose contracts the FTC approved. The New York State Chamber of Commerce almost simultaneously adopted a resolution calling for modification of the Sherman and Clayton antitrust laws to permit necessary "collective action" by big-business men. In agriculture, however, insofar as planned scarcity could be achieved at all, and it could only be in that very small percentage of all agriculture that possessed large-scale organization, it could not be achieved so smoothly and subtly as in industry. Crudely destructive methods must be employed. Thus, when the Canners' League of California "found that the potential peach pack for 1931 would reach 17,000,000 cases, an increase of 4,000,000 cases over 1930, an agreement was reached to limit the pack to 9,000,000 cases." So the *American Year Book* for 1931 would report, going on: "To do this, the Canners' League decided to purchase 144,000 tons of surplus of the cling peach crop at $12 per ton and destroy the same. Besides, a reduction of 20 percent in acreage was decreed by peach growers, involving the uprooting of peach trees on 12,000 acres, for which the growers are to be reimbursed at the rate of $2.50 per tree. The canners contributed a fund of $1,500,000 to be used by the League in carrying out the measures for curtailment of production."[26]

The price situation for the nation's farmers was, in general, horrendous. On March 6, 1931, Alexander Legge resigned his post as chairman of the Federal Farm Board, in tacit recognition that the board's effort to stabilize major farm prices through open market purchases, joined with exhortation to farmers to produce less, was a dismal failure. Legge's successor promptly announced the Farm Board's discontinuance of wheat purchases and its intention to dispose of its entire wheat holdings (that is, to "dump" it) on foreign markets "as rapidly as possible without unduly depressing market prices." In November it was announced that, of the total wheat purchases of 330,000,000 bushels, the Farm Board still held 190,000,000 bushels unsold. As for the Farm Board's cotton purchases, totaling 1,319,809 bales, 1,310,789 bales remained unsold in November: there was no market whatever for cotton. A description of the agricultural economy to be issued at the end of 1931 by Hoover's Secretary of Agriculture, Arthur M. Hyde, who as the administration's spokesman should have been inclined toward "confidence"-breeding optimism, would be studded with such words and phrases as "desperate," "extremely serious," and "literally ruinous." By mid-1931 cotton prices had fallen to their lowest point since 1898, "with no proportionate decline in farm costs of production," largely because of a collapse of the export market for which the Hawley-Smoot tariff (as Hyde did not say) was partially responsible. "The supply [of cotton] for the 1931–32 season was well above the previous record supply of 1926–27, and more than twice as large as the world's consumption of cotton in 1930–31," reported Hyde. Similarly with wheat. During the seven years ending on July 1, 1930, the price of No. 2 hard wheat on the Kansas City market had averaged $1.28 a bushel. For the nation as a whole the price on October 15, 1930, was $0.65; on October 15, 1931, it was a mere $0.361, and there had been nothing like that great a reduction in wheat production costs, farm taxes, or farm indebtedness with accompanying interest payments. There had been, of course, *some* decline in the expenses of farm production—a decline, reported Hyde, of 15 percent—but the decline in gross farm income amounted to 25 percent, and this income had been far from adequate to begin with. "In January [1931]," said Hyde in a review of the situation, "the index numbers for the prices of representative farm commodities stood at 94, 6 percent below the pre-war (1909–1914) level. By October this index had declined to 68. In the same period [however] the index number of the prices paid by the farmers for commodities they usually buy declined only from 137 to 126. Relatively greater over-production in agriculture than in other industries is not the only cause of the familiar tendency of agricultural prices to fall sooner and lower than other prices in periods of depression. It is certainly, however, an important cause." In agriculture, Hyde explained, a "maladjustment between supply and demand" resulted "in a persistent accumulation of commodities," whereas "in manufacturing industries . . . [it] shows up in unemployment."[27]

And the New York Department of Labor statistics brought to Roosevelt's desk by Industrial Commissioner Perkins did measure a dramatic growth of unemployment in the state. Annual surveys of Buffalo, a typical industrial area, showed that the percentage of men able and willing to work who were without employment had increased from 6.2 in November 1929 to 17.2 in November 1930; it continued to rise rapidly (it would be 24.3 in November 1931 and 32.6 in November 1932). A million were unemployed in New York in the summer of 1931, by the most conservative estimate, while other statistics showed that the burden of relief grew huge beyond bearing for existing relief organizations, private or governmental. A canvass of forty-five New York cities, made by a legislative committee on unemployment relief, revealed that almost every city had spent as much or more for home relief in the first half of 1931 as it had for the entire year 1930, that such expenditures would undoubtedly remain on at least the same level for the year's second half, and that the direct hiring of labor by local governmental units "could not be appreciably increased."[28]

By his perception of the human misery that such information indicated— by the alarm and distress he felt in response to it—Roosevelt's conservative ideological aversion to providing state government relief to individual persons was overcome. He continued adamantly opposed to direct monetary payments ("the dole"), but, facing the bleak prospect of freezing cold and gnawing hunger for tens of thousands of his fellow citizens during the coming winter months, he now saw no humane alternative to the state's providing as much "useful work" as possible to those in desperate need, unable to find private or local governmental employment, or to the state's direct provision of "food against starvation and . . . clothing against suffering."[29] He concluded that a fully funded state relief program administered by a special agency was urgently needed for the bitter months ahead; he asked Sam Rosenman to draft a special message to the legislature saying so.

Rosenman did this writing, mostly at Hyde Park, during the third week of August.[30] His draft, which made use of surveys and recommendations by welfare professionals, was revised into final form only a day or so before

Roosevelt, having decided to gain for his message the greatest possible national attention, went in person before the legislature to deliver it—on the day (August 28) that he signed the immunity bill into law.

And national attention was indeed paid to the message's historic assertion, unprecedented for any American major party politician of presidential caliber, that democratic theory implies in an advanced technological society a "definite obligation" of government to care *not only* for "those who through accident or old age" are "permanently incapacitated" *but also* for "men and women incapable of supporting either themselves or their families because of circumstances . . . which make it impossible for them to find remunerative labor." The state, he said, is the "creature of the people," designed by them "for their mutual protection and well-being." The government, he said, "is but the machinery through which such mutual aid and protection are achieved." And it follows from this that "the duty of the State toward its citizens is the duty of the servant to its master." This "duty," he rather more than suggested, was not being performed by the federal government in a year when millions of Americans were driven into extreme poverty by forces beyond their control. "It is idle for us to speculate upon the actions which may be taken by the Federal Government, just as it is idle for the purposes for which we are here gathered to speculate about the causes of national depression," he said in words carefully chosen to point up Hoover's continued hostility to direct federal assistance of any kind to economically distressed citizens—words chosen also to suggest that the "national depression" was due in no small degree to Republican economic policies. "It is true that times may get better; it is true that the Federal Government may come forward with a definite constructive program on a truly large scale; it is true that the Federal Government may adopt a well-thought-out concrete policy which will start the wheels of industry moving and give to the farmer at least the cost of making his crop. The State of New York cannot wait for that. I face and you face and thirteen million people face the problem of providing immediate relief."

His own concrete proposal was for the establishment of a "commission of three persons to be appointed by the Governor without pay" whereby "unemployment and distress relief" in New York would be administered for an "emergency period" of seven months beginning on November 1, 1931. Stressing through redundancy the strictly limited term of this agency's life, he proposed to name it the Temporary Emergency Relief Administration, and he proposed to fund it with a $20,000,000 appropriation ("the estimated amount required to meet the needs of the coming year"), to be raised by a 50 percent increase in state income taxes. "It is clear to me that it is the duty of those who have benefited by our industrial and economic system to come to the front in such a grave emergency and assist in relieving those who under the same industrial and economic order are the losers and sufferers," he said. "I believe their contribution should be in proportion to the benefits they receive and the prosperity they enjoy." This suggested to the closely attentive that the speaker felt the prevailing order to be unfair if not actually exploitive and that, in his view, those who gained most from it would "come to the front" only under legal coercion. Yet the additional tax burden he proposed, distributed among 300,000 taxpayers, was certainly not onerous. A family head or any person with two dependents who earned less than $5,000 per annum (most citizens of the state received far less than that in 1931–1932) would pay no additional tax whatever; one making $10,000 would pay only $26 more; one making $30,000, an additional $102; one making $50,000, an additional $402; and one making $100,000, an additional $1,128. There should be few statutory limits upon the disbursement of the money so obtained, in Roosevelt's opinion. Under no circumstances should cash payments be made "to any unemployed or his family," and no person who had not resided in the state "for at least two years prior to the enactment of the statute" should be eligible for its benefits; otherwise "the widest latitude and discretion in the apportionment of the money and in its distribution" should be given the relief agency.[31]

With a fine show of personal disinterestedness, he suggested to the Republicans, immediately following the deliverance of his message, that they introduce the recommended legislation as a *Republican* measure. Thus they would share with him in a glow of nonpartisanship the political credit for an obviously necessary service of the general good. It was an offer that W. Kingsland Macy, now newly installed as Republican state chairman, urged his party's lawmakers to accept. "But Governor Roosevelt was blessed politically with a bitter and unintelligent opposition" and his "political luck did not fail him this time," Rosenman would later write.[32]

Infuriated by what they saw only as the governor's shiftiness and trickery, his squirming away from the horns of his Tammany dilemma, the Republican legislative leaders insisted upon introducing, in opposition to a Democratic bill that faithfully embodied the governor's recommendations, a bill that, as initially drafted, departed from the recommendations in several important ways. Known as the Wicks bill, it would place administration of the new program, not in a special agency that, freed of traditional bureaucratic red tape, could move swiftly and vigorously, but in the Department of Public Health, whose head was a Republican (this, protested Roosevelt, would tend to make relief a permanent function of the state instead of a " temporary emergency" one). It would establish flat rates of disbursements to town governments, which were mostly in Republican hands, instead of flexible rates to county and city commissioners of public welfare. It provided for an unlimited matching of local relief funds with state funds (this, protested Roosevelt, could force the state into bankruptcy). And it would raise the immediately needed money, not through income-tax increases, but through slashes in existing departmental budgets augmented by short-term loans, in other words, by a degree of deficit financing, and Roosevelt was opposed to deficit financing on moral grounds.[33]

The Republican design was to enact their bill promptly, as they had the votes to do, then adjourn, leaving the governor with a choice between going along or taking the blame for the state's failure to provide relief. But such design was, in the circumstances, easily frustrated, and in a way that greatly enhanced the governor's prestige at the expense of his opponents' prestige. Displaying angry outrage, Roosevelt threatened to veto the measure as soon as it reached his desk (his veto message, by simply telling the truth, would make the Republicans targets of popular wrath) and to call the legislators immediately back into another special session to do what must be done (the Republicans would bear sole responsibility for the needless extra expense). The opposition leaders then capitulated. They met in unhappy conference, they revised the Wicks bill into a form acceptable to the governor, they adjourned the session—all within twenty-four hours after Roosevelt's threat was made.

No other governor in the nation had moved so directly and forcefully into relief activity. And from none of his other gubernatorial actions, not even from his greatly publicized battle with the utility interests, did Roosevelt make greater gain over Hoover among the national electorate.

By September 29, when he left Albany for two weeks in Warm Springs, he had persuaded his good friend Jesse Straus to take the chairmanship of TERA, as the new agency established by the legislation was at once dubbed by the press. In early October, Straus, who accepted the appointment only on condition that he have a first-class deputy to run the agency, obtained as its executive director a professional social worker named Harry Hopkins, who had been for some years administrative director of the New York Tuberculosis and Health Association and had, in that position, favorably impressed, among others, Eleanor Roosevelt. A native Iowan, forty-two years of age, preternaturally bright of eye and thin and gangling of body ("an ulcerous type . . . intense, seeming to be in a perpetual nervous ferment—a chain smoker and black coffee drinker," as a New York co-worker of the time described him[34]), Hopkins proved at once to be the right man to deliver relief as swiftly as possible, with a minimum of overhead expense, to human beings urgently in need of it. His administrative style was as unorthodox as that which Roosevelt as governor was developing, though differing from Roosevelt's in basic motive and overall effect. If established bureaucratic procedures and the power flow lines depicted on the organization chart helped accomplish what he conceived to be his agency's main job, he followed them; if they did not, he ignored them. He was saved from censure for such violation of bureaucratic canons by his obviously selfless dedication to his task and by the efficiency with which he performed it. Roosevelt would be happy to appoint him Straus's successor, making him nominally as well as actually head of the state's relief program, when Straus resigned as TERA chairman in the summer of 1932: the governor would then realize that TERA had become a major asset to his presidential campaign (he could and did point to it with pride) and that for this fact Hopkins was in large part responsible.

For we may anticipate in our narrative what Roosevelt probably, and Hopkins certainly, expected in the fall of 1931, namely, the continuance of the relief agency well beyond its original seven-month term.

By the close of February 1932, more than 160,000 people were receiving relief through TERA, but an estimated 1,500,000 New Yorkers were out of work, an increase of some 50 percent in the state's unemployment during the last six months. Moreover, nearly all of the $20,000,000 allocated TERA was already spent, a full three months before the term date of June 1. Roosevelt, who by then had added his name somewhat belatedly to the lengthy list of governors openly advocating a massive federal public-works program (Senator Wagner had proposed such a program as a contingency plan even before the Crash of '29), felt himself forced by circumstances to act against his aversion to deficit financing. He prepared a special legislative message, delivered March 10, in which he called for the extension of TERA's "life and work" until January 1934, for a new appropriation of $5,000,000 from current revenues to carry it until November, and for a referendum on a $30,000,000 bond issue to finance it thereafter. He stressed the extreme reluctance with which he thus departed from "the pay-as-you-go policy," which "in normal times" was " the only proper way to provide funds for this purpose." A "deviation from that principle" was surely warranted, however, by the "conditions which now face us, in their gravity akin to war conditions."[35] The legislators, after some wrangling, did as he asked; the bond issue was overwhelmingly approved by New York's voters when it was presented to them as Proposition No. 1 on the November 1932 ballot.

IV

THE basic general pattern of the Democratic presidential nomination campaign had been tentatively discernible by the politically astute even before Roosevelt won his immense reelection victory. It had been subsequently confirmed in the minds of close observers by the differences that widened and deepened between Roosevelt and Raskob as the latter sought to dictate a conservative Democratic platform for 1932. It became clear for all in the fall of 1931, when a sorely troubled, embittered Al Smith publicly proclaimed his alienation from the man whom he had nominated for reelection, in the most glowing terms, barely a year before.[36]

Smith did so through a surprise attack upon one of Roosevelt's pet conservation measures, to wit, a constitutional amendment authorizing a $19,000,000 bond issue to be expended over an eleven-year period for the purchase of submarginal land and the planting upon it of forest trees.* It was a proposal that, in Roosevelt's view, did no violence to his principled aversion to deficit financing—it was not a "current expense" that therefore "should be borne from current funds"[37] but a long-term investment of state money. The proposal's purpose was so obviously meritorious, the cost of it so modest, that virtually no controversy had been provoked by it during its passage through two legislatures (a New York constitutional amendment proposal must be approved by two legislatures before being presented to popular vote). Conser-

---

*Some quarter-million acres of formerly farmed land were being annually abandoned by New York's farmers; only through reforestation could such land again become productive.

vation and sportsmen's organizations in the state strongly supported it. Republican as well as Democratic legislative leaders endorsed it; so did Chairman Macy of the Republican State Committee, along with Chairman Farley of the Democratic State Committee, rendering the measure nonpartisan. Favorable national attention was focused upon it by newspapers in every region, by mass-circulating magazines, and by such famous conservationists as Governor Gifford Pinchot of Pennsylvania. And Smith himself had given no sign that he disapproved of it; indeed, he had made no comment upon it whatever during the two years that had elapsed since the proposal was originally made. Hence the astonishment with which Roosevelt in Warm Springs learned on the morning of October 15 that Smith on the night before had attacked vehemently the proposed amendment in a speech to a Tammany rally and in a press statement immediately after. The measure, asserted Smith, was Socialistic: by allowing the state to cut and sell trees grown on the purchased acres it "put the state into the lumber business," in competition with private enterprise— this from the Al Smith who as governor had fought so valiantly for state ownership of hydroelectric-power sites! Its financing arrangement, said Smith, more cogently, was unwise if not unethical: abandoned land, if purchased, *should* be paid for from current funds annually appropriated. And, most cogently of all, Smith saw no justification for presenting such a measure as this in the form of a constitutional amendment rather than as a regular legislative bill: to "pile things into" the constitution in this way was to destroy a necessary distinction between the state's fundamental law and its general statutes.[38]

But Roosevelt and much of the public were at once aware that Smith's public argument against the measure did not express his basic reason for making it, the latter having nothing to do with conservation and everything to do with presidential politics.

Some weeks before, Ed Flynn, who had not then publicly announced his support for Roosevelt for President, had called upon Smith in the latter's princely office on the thirty-second floor of the nearly empty Empire State Building.* Before he announced his presidential preference, he said to Smith, he wanted as a longtime friend to know if Al still stood by the statement of total withdrawal from elective politics that he had made the day after 1928's Election Day. Al replied emphatically that he did, that "no one could induce him to enter the political arena again." For one thing, he was in "an extremely bad position" financially. Two of his sons and a nephew, unbeknown to him at the time, had speculated in a booming stock market with money they had been encouraged to borrow from the County Trust Company by that bank's president, James J. Riordan, a close friend of Smith's who had been one of the

---

*For several years after its "grand opening" in May 1931 the Empire State Building was only 20 percent occupied. One of the tenants was Belle Moskowitz, who operated a small public-relations firm in an office one floor below that of Smith's office. Her influence upon Smith had waned as Raskob's had waxed, but she still remained one of Smith's advisers on public affairs.

largest financial contributors to Smith's 1928 campaign. When the market crashed, they were ruined, as was Riordan, who committed suicide in early November 1929. Smith, who assumed the chairmanship of the board of County Trust, in an effort to reassure depositors as to the bank's solvency, had felt morally obliged to assume his family's indebtedness, and the consequence was a drawer full of notes which Smith fanned out on the desk top before Flynn, saying that they were "all debts that I must clear up" and that "it will probably take me the rest of my life" to do it. Smith said substantially the same thing to Lehman when Lehman, bothered as Flynn had been by divided loyalties, called upon him a little later.[39]

All this, of course, had been reported to Roosevelt by Flynn and Lehman. It confirmed his belief that Smith, at that time, had no intention of entering the lists as an active presidential candidate.

What, then, was the real meaning of the attack upon the reforestation measure? All one could be sure of was that Al, who could not but be tempted by the probability that Democratic nomination meant presidential election in 1932, who could not but wish that somehow the nominee would be himself, was declaring what he had more than hinted when he stood on Raskob's side against Roosevelt in last winter's controversy over the national committee's proper role, namely, that he opposed Roosevelt's nomination and would do what he could to block it. To this end, he proposed to measure his persuasive power over the state's electorate against that of his Albany successor. And the issue he had chosen for this trial of strength was by no means as disadvantageous to him, when viewed in prospect, as it would appear to have been when viewed in retrospect. The New York *Times* pointed out that every constitutional amendment proposed to New York's voters in the last decade had been voted down by a huge majority. And this one, involving a bond issue of substantial proportions, was being presented in an off-year of deep depression.[40] By such auguries, Smith's attack should be decisive of the proposal's defeat.

Certainly Roosevelt did not take the challenge lightly.

Immediately upon his return from Warm Springs to Albany, he mobilized all possible resources for the struggle. Every Democratic worker in the state received a letter from Farley, drafted by Roosevelt himself, urging strenuous efforts on the amendment's behalf. Every organization that could be enlisted as a pressure group *was* so enlisted, including the State Federation of Labor. Republican Chairman Macy, convinced of the proposal's merits, cooperated in efforts toward its adoption, matching Farley's letter with one of his own to Republican workers. He also made a radio address strongly favoring the measure's passage and damning Smith's attack upon it as wholly political, aimed against Roosevelt's presidential candidacy. Curry's Tammany, with which Roosevelt had been cooperating all along in patronage matters, resulting in the removal or barring of Smith men from official posts, refused to oppose Roosevelt on so unpromising an issue. Roosevelt himself went on the air to answer at length criticisms of the proposal.

And by all this, victory was won: the amendment was adopted on November 3 by a handsome majority.

V

Roosevelt then moved in characteristic fashion to soothe Smith's wounds while mitigating the popular impression of personal animosity between the two.

On November 10 he addressed to "Dear Al" a note saying that the "first trial balance of the budget" would be completed "next Monday the 16th" and that he was coming down from Albany to New York City that night. "Don't you want to run in any time on Tuesday or Wednesday the 17th or 18th to talk with me about it [?]," the note went on to say. "Come to lunch at 49 East 65 or else later in the afternoon. I go to Warm Springs [this for his traditional Thanksgiving there] Wed. evening at 6. Love to the family and my best to you."[41] Smith accepted the invitation. The two men lunched together on November 17, and numerous newsmen were of course on hand to report on what they, and Smith, expected to be a frank talk about intraparty politics.

And indeed, Roosevelt would have best served his wound-salving purpose by being frank and open with Smith about his presidential ambitions at this juncture. Smith had a right to expect it, who had twice had his name placed in presidential nomination by Roosevelt in national conventions, had won more votes than any other Democratic candidate in history, and was titular head of the party. What did Roosevelt have to lose by it? He had something to gain. There then yet remained some slight possibility of convincing Al that he, Roosevelt, really meant the flattering things he had said and continued to say in public about his gubernatorial predecessor—that he did in fact "look up" and not "down" at Smith, regretting those portions of his necessary cooperation with Curry's Tammany that resulted in official appointments of men unfriendly to Smith. By simply declaring what Smith knew to be true— that he ran for the nomination with all his might and would formally announce his candidacy early in the election year—and by then asking Smith's advice and opinions about the Roosevelt "boom" and about what was best for the party in 1932, Roosevelt would have removed some of the personal hurt that festered in Smith's sore spirit. He might have weakened a little Smith's ties with the party's right wing and won some measure of neutrality from Smith in the coming battle for delegates.

But Roosevelt's inclination toward deviousness, or at any rate against forthrightness, whenever dealing with anyone whom he regarded as a rival for power or a threat to his attainment of it was in this case encouraged by a residue of resentment over the attitudes occasionally evinced toward him in the past by Smith and by some of Smith's close associates. Moreover, he had been given some reason in recent days to believe that Smith might now be *irrevocably* committed to, if not actively involved in, the Raskob-Shouse "Stop Roosevelt" strategy.

Chicago was bidding high for 1932's Democratic National Convention, and on November 5 Chicago's Mayor Anton Cermak came East to confer with Smith, as well as with Raskob and Boss Frank Hague of Jersey City. Within an hour after his meeting with Smith, he told reporters that he wanted a Democratic presidential candidate who did not "pussyfoot about Prohibition," a remark generally interpreted as a slap at Roosevelt and an endorsement of Maryland's handsome, affable, and conservative Governor Albert C. Ritchie. Ritchie was at that moment calling loudly for repeal of the Eighteenth Amendment and insisting, in marked contrast to Roosevelt, that Prohibition was an issue at least as important as unemployment, if not more so. A few days later, Bernard Baruch praised Ritchie in a banquet speech as one "to whom the finger of fate seems to point as being perhaps destined to move" into the White House.[42] Roosevelt had no belief that this apparently developing conservative coalescence behind Ritchie meant that Ritchie would become a serious rival for the nomination. The Maryland governor was far too conservative to win the needed mass support amid deepening depression. But he could tie up delegate votes that Roosevelt would otherwise have, perhaps even enough of them, conjoined with those held by favorite sons, to deny Roosevelt the two thirds he must win on a very early convention ballot if he was to win at all. In the process of such tying up, Ritchie would serve as an excellent stalking-horse whose dropping to the convention floor would reveal, say, Newton D. Baker, Wilson's Secretary of War, a man of small physical stature but of great and deserved reputation, who was now a prosperous corporation lawyer in Ohio. By many leading opinion makers, including notably Walter Lippmann, Baker was deemed by far the best-equipped of all possible Democratic candidates for the White House. And Roosevelt, who knew that overtures had been made to Baker by Raskob emissaries, also knew that Baker, though wisely refusing to become an open candidate, had been by no means as emphatically and totally negative in his response as Owen Young had been when also approached by Raskob. Clearly, the Ohioan was available for a convention draft, and would welcome, even maybe connive for it. Probably, however, the way to him from Ritchie would be less direct than the one just considered. More likely, when Ritchie fell down, Al Smith himself would stand forth as a stalking-horse of much higher order (though perhaps believing himself to be *the* candidate of the conservatives, as most of them, too, would believe him to be)—one of sufficient size and strength to race Roosevelt into a convention deadlock. As a result, the delegates would turn to Baker as a compromise candidate, and probably before very many ballots had been taken, being moved to do so by horrendous memories of 1924. Those same memories, rankling in the minds of Smith and his supporters, would prevent the convention's ever turning to McAdoo, in Roosevelt's opinion.

Implicit in this strategy was the encouragement by Raskob and Shouse of favorite-son commitments or uninstructed delegations in as many states as possible. For this purpose, Shouse planned a trip to Alabama in late November or early December. So, at least, a chronically cynical and suspicious Louis

Howe told Roosevelt, probably on the morning of the very day that Roosevelt had Smith as a luncheon guest. Roosevelt believed him. He had been prepared to believe him by communications from Colonel House's longtime Washington friend Robert Woolley, who for many weeks had been warning both House and Roosevelt that a definite Smith-Baker coalition had been formed as soon as Owen Young rejected Raskob's overtures, that Baruch and Raskob were financing it, and that Shouse would operate as its chief tactician and traveling salesman. Howe proposed, and Roosevelt encouraged him, to write a letter to Shouse saying bluntly that this Alabama trip was deemed by him (Howe) a deliberately unfriendly act and, as such, unethical: no officer of the Democratic National Committee had any authority or moral right either to promote or discourage any presidential candidacy, directly or indirectly.[43]

This, then, is the context within which Roosevelt, hosting Smith at lunch on November 17, was bland, smooth, "charming," closely attentive to Smith's opinions on budget matters, and utterly silent upon the subject uppermost in both their minds. The effect was to add smart to Smith's hurt. When he departed the house, the ex-governor gave signs of seething with repressed anger. He was almost snappish with the reporters who crowded round him. "It was a good lunch," he said. What had they talked about? "We talked about state finances. That makes four words, don't it?" Had anything been said about politics? "Not a word."[44]

Some two weeks later, on December 2, six days after a well-publicized Thanksgiving celebration at the Warm Springs Foundation (where Roosevelt made an exuberant impromptu speech to his "gang" and again demonstrated his superb skill as a carver of roast turkey), Clark Howell called upon Smith at the Empire State Building for a lengthy private talk. At the outset, the publisher reminded his host that in 1928 he had been perhaps Smith's most influential supporter in the South, that he had stuck with Smith "through thick and thin," a fact that, he said, "warranted" perfect frankness between the two of them as they discussed national Democratic politics. Smith agreed. Howell then declared that Smith's attitude toward Franklin Roosevelt had become of pivotal national importance: it could either assure "an overwhelming Democratic victory next year" or "jeopardize the present prospect of sure success."

"With your support of him all opposition to him will vanish," Howell explained, "and his nomination will be a mere formality. The country expects you to support him, and it will not believe that you can possibly do otherwise."

Smith bristled. "The hell I can't!" he said, then quickly added that he didn't mean to say he would *not* support him. He was "for the party first" and would "support the man who seems best for the party."

But that man, Howell insisted, was obviously Franklin Roosevelt, who, if nominated, would carry every Southern state, "get perhaps three-fourths of the electoral votes of the states west of the Mississippi," and carry New York, New Jersey, Massachusetts, Connecticut, and Rhode Island. Smith shook his head. He "doubted" that Roosevelt could carry the Middle Atlantic and southern New England states. He ignored, significantly, Howell's interpolated assertion that Roosevelt would be *certain* to do so if Smith came out for him. He went on to say with considerable heat that "millions" in the Northeast "resented" the shabby way he, Smith, had been treated since 1928.

Treated by whom? Howell wanted to know. Did Smith have grounds for "personal hostility" toward Roosevelt?

"No," replied Smith, "socially we are friends. He has always been kind to me and my family, and has gone out of his way to be agreeable to us at the Mansion at Albany, but"—here Smith abruptly arose from his chair and stamped his foot—"Do you know, by God, that he has never consulted me about a damn thing since he has been Governor? He has taken bad advice and from sources not friendly to me. He has ignored me!"

And Smith's vehemence grew with what it fed upon. He slammed his fist down upon the desk top as he continued: "By God, he invited me to his house before he recently went to Georgia, and did not even mention to me the subject of his candidacy."

Obviously this was, in Smith's view, the ultimate snub. The ultimate insult.

The conversation ended inconclusively, with Smith emphasizing that he was neither *for* nor *against* Roosevelt and in no hurry to make up his mind one way or the other. Within an hour, Howell had sent a telegram to Roosevelt in Warm Springs informing him that a long conference with "Alfred" had been held and promising to "write details" later. The full report in letter form was mailed in the evening of that same day. "My recommendation," wrote Howell in conclusion, "is that you see him [Smith] upon your return to New York and talk with him on the subject. I think it will go a long way toward getting him in line. By handling him diplomatically I believe he will come around all right."[45]

But for this it was now too late. . . .

Two days after he received Howell's letter, Roosevelt received one from Shouse denying that Shouse was engaged in any "Stop Roosevelt" movement and angrily blaming "malicious" newspaper gossip for any belief anywhere that he *was* so engaged. Roosevelt replied to "Dear Jouett" on December 9, saying he felt "confident" that neither Shouse nor "John," being "the directing officers of the National Committee," would or could do anything so "unethical" as to attempt to " 'block Roosevelt' by encouraging uninstructed delegations or favorite sons." The trouble arose from the fact that "a great many . . . enthusiastic friends of mine in different states" had "jumped" to a contrary conclusion. "What many of them fail to realize is that I have in good faith lived up to my declaration that I am taking absolutely no part in any movement in my own behalf."[46]

Equally bland and insincere, or mendacious, was his reply from Albany ten days later to an obviously worried letter from Bernard Baruch in which Baruch "greatly resented" a report by Ernest Lindley in the *Herald Tribune* describing him as an ally of Smith and Raskob in a "Stop Roosevelt" campaign. Lindley, said Baruch, was misinterpreting the remarks Baruch had made about Ritchie in public. Ritchie had been a member of the War Industries Board, of which

Baruch was chairman during the war, and it was in this connection, at a get-together of former board members, that Baruch had praised him. Replied Roosevelt: "In regard to the national political situation, I am much in the position of one who sits on the side lines and has little personal interest but a great deal of concern as a Democrat and a citizen. . . . I do not need to tell you that I know you yourself would not engage in any surreptitious methods because you . . . realize that the situation from the national and the party viewpoint is too serious to engage in such tactics—and also because you personally are above them." But he went on to let Baruch know that he was perfectly aware of contemptuous remarks Baruch had made about him in conversations with influential people (for one thing, Baruch had repeatedly ridiculed Roosevelt as "the Boy Scout governor") and that he resented them: "But I cannot, of course, help knowing of the conversations of some people who profess friendship but nevertheless emit innuendos and false statements behind my back with the blissful assumption that they will never be repeated to me."[47]

Even the notably thick-skinned Baruch must have squirmed a little.

9

A "Brains Trust" Is Formed

I

WHEN Roosevelt, having returned from Warm Springs to Albany in mid-December, went down from Albany to Hyde Park for Christmas with his family, he felt that he was well on top of the situation. And when he surveyed the political scene from this cheerful perch as 1931 drew to a close, he saw little to disturb and nothing to dismay him.

More amusing than annoying were Raskob's current antics. The national committee chairman insisted upon a replay of the game he had lost the previous March: he had summoned the committee to meet on January 9, 1932, in Washington, to select the 1932 convention city (he was known to favor Chicago) and to reconsider the liquor proposal that had been tabled last March. As the New York *Times* had editorialized in late November, Raskob persisted "in the belief that the Committee and the Chairman should draft the party platform" and had gone so far as to assert in a published letter protesting the editorial that his belief was objectively justified by the Democratic Party's convention "Manual," wherein the committee was assigned the duty of recommending "policies or procedures for the consideration of the convention." On this Roosevelt made gleeful comment when he wrote to Ernest Lindley on December 4 in grateful appreciation of the "really grand job" Lindley had done on the just-published biography of him. "I am amused by the rushing into print of Brother Raskob," said Roosevelt. "I think someone will shortly skin him alive on this. I hope he will continue to write, talk and invent!" The Roosevelt forces were then in the process of eliciting from Congressman James Cannon of Missouri, compiler of the cited "Manual," a statement denying that the convention had ever, so far as *he* knew, conferred upon the Democratic National Committee any authority to participate in any way in the formulation of party policy or doctrine.[1]

Similarly stupidly ineffective would be Raskob's current polling of 80,000 contributors to the 1928 Democratic campaign, asking each to indicate what the 1932 platform should say about Prohibition. The poll results were perfectly predictable in that a large majority of the contributors, residing in wet urban areas, were themselves wringing wet: they had supported Smith for that reason. And Raskob's intended use of such results to force the committee to adopt his Prohibition-repeal resolution simply proclaimed once again his big-business man's belief in the divine right of Money to rule the Republic. Since this belief was highly unpopular, its every public expression served to diminish yet further a persuasive power that, in Raskob's case, had been severely limited to begin with. Farley encountered little difficulty as he again organized opposition to the Raskob proposal. Again he joined forces with Hull, Byrd, and others of the West and South. Again he obtained proxies from committee members unable to attend the meeting. And by Christmas he had in hand enough committee votes to defeat Raskob by a wide margin, with assurances of a wider margin still (new vote-pledges kept coming in) by the time the committee met.

On Raskob's performance Walter Lippmann made acid comment in a nationally syndicated column,* which Roosevelt almost certainly read in the New York *Herald Tribune* while breakfasting in bed at Hyde Park on the morning after Christmas. "Only a man without political instinct would have lent himself to an enterprise based on the premise that campaign contributors are a species of preferred stockholders," wrote Lippmann, and especially when everyone knew that Raskob "himself is by all odds the largest of the contributors." But Raskob's "spectacular amateurishness" would not be occupying "the center of the stage so continually," the columnist went on to say, if anyone else were "ready" and willing to do so. For instance: "A lot is said by the Roosevelt faction about 'economic issues' being 'paramount.' But what these paramount issues are they are careful not to say. Governor Roosevelt belongs to the new postwar school of politicians who do not believe in stating their views unless and until there is no avoiding it. . . . Where, for example, does he stand on the tariff, on reparations and debts, on farm relief, on taxation, on banking reform, on the railroad problem? I do not know. There is a vacuum where the paramount economic issues are supposed to be, and into that vacuum, where the angels, as it were, fear to tread, Mr. Raskob is continually rushing with his anti-prohibition schemes." Lippmann damned as "ignoble" and "deeply confusing of party action" the "new" political game that, as Roosevelt played it, "consists in gathering delegates first and adopting policies afterward to hold them together." Such procedure subverted the principles of popular government.[2]

Roosevelt could hardly have been pleased to read this, but neither could he have been greatly disturbed by the specific strictures made upon his operation. He had supreme confidence in his own sense of political priorities, tactics, and timing, born of his faith in God as beneficent Author of circumstances whose accurate perception by him either made or *was* his policy. He could do nothing actually to resolve national issues unless he won national office, which is to say, as he often did say to Rosenman, that his first task, on which all else depended,

---

*When the great brilliant New York *World* succumbed to "progress" and the Depression in February 1931, being then sold by the Pulitzer family to Roy W. Howard of the Scripps-Howard chain (Howard promptly killed it by merger with the *Telegram*), Lippmann, its editorial page editor, went over to the *Herald Tribune*. Thereafter, he contributed a thrice-weekly column on national and world affairs to this paper and its national syndicate. From the outset of his new career he was the most weighty, the most influential of all public affairs commentators, his commentary becoming one cause of the antipathy to columnists as a class that Roosevelt developed during his second gubernatorial term. The governor, who had shaped remarkably effective techniques for the management of straight news in his own interest, had and could have no such influence over the "think-pieces" of editorialists and columnists, the latter having, unlike editorialists, a large reading public and therefore constituting, from his point of view, a serious hazard.

was "to get elected." And to get elected he had best continue the basic strategy he had shaped in the aftermath of 1924's presidential election:* he should continue to avoid as much as possible issue-stands so precisely stated as to be divisive on any large scale, and he should continue to define and stake out as his own a position "just a little left of center," which was broad enough and sufficiently vague in its boundaries to serve as a gathering ground for an unbeatable "Roosevelt party" that included not only widely diverse elements of the current Democratic Party but also disaffected progressive elements of the Republican Party, along with a majority of those who deemed themselves politically "independent." Certainly he felt himself under no obligation to say anything about national issues, save as they directly impinged on state affairs, until he became an openly avowed presidential candidate.

But if Lippmann's specific criticisms left him unmoved, Roosevelt was disturbed by his awareness, the column reminding him, of the chief basic reason why the columnist so sternly disapproved of him.

For, more than all else, it was the governor's handling of the Tammany corruption issue that determined Lippmann's view of him as a sly slithering political animal, charming but guileful, amiable but unprincipled. This same issue was increasingly the severest test of Roosevelt's national candidacy, the gravest single threat to his election victory. And Roosevelt's unadmitted perplexity over it, his inability to discern cues or clues for action concerning it, was particularly acute at that moment: he knew that when he returned to Albany, he would find upon his desk a formal request from Judge Seabury that he remove from office the Honorable Thomas M. Farley, sheriff of New York County, on charges of corruption that seemed proved beyond reasonable doubt by an accompanying transcript of hearings that, when held the previous October, had been vastly publicized in the press.

This was, for Roosevelt in his situation, the bitterest fruit yet plucked by the Seabury Investigation, because Sheriff Farley was, to shift metaphors, the biggest fish yet caught in the Joint Legislative Committee's investigative net.

A Tammany Hall sachem, leader of the Fourteenth Assembly District, president of the Thomas M. Farley Association, friend of both Curry and Walker, the sheriff had contributed $20,000 to Roosevelt's gubernatorial re-election campaign at Curry's behest. He could afford it. In six years, during which his annual salary was $8,500, he had managed to accumulate nearly $400,000, as Seabury demonstrated through bank records and other incontrovertible evidence. Where had this money come from? Seabury wanted to know. From a "tin box" he kept in a "big safe," the sheriff replied. And how had the money got into the tin box? asked Seabury. Was it a "magic box" that generated cash? "It was a wonderful box," Farley admitted, and would admit no more. He was similarly amusingly mendacious, if also contemptuously so, when asked about the nature and function of the Thomas M. Farley Association. The association had a clubhouse. When police raided it at two o'clock

---

*See *FDR: The Beckoning of Destiny,* pages 779–785.

one spring morning, they found among the considerable number gathered there several well-known underworld figures and former associates of Arnold Rothstein. What were the association members doing in the clubhouse at that hour? asked Seabury of the sheriff. They were "busy packing baseball bats, skipping ropes, and rubber balls, because our May Day party took place next day," the sheriff replied. Seabury commended this rare dedication to a charitable cause. Nevertheless he wondered, "By any chance, did any gambling paraphernalia get mixed up with those rubber balls and other children's playthings?" Oh, absolutely not! said Farley. "There were canopies," he added, "and Maypoles."[3]

Such character-revealing insouciance under pressure was no doubt one reason why Sheriff Farley had become, like Jimmy Walker, "an idol of his people," as Roosevelt remarked to Raymond Moley some days later, a fact that of course complicated the governor's immediate problem.

He made this remark during a *tête-à-tête* luncheon in the state Capitol's executive office on a gloomy January afternoon. Moley had been summoned from New York City to talk about the work of the state's Commission on the Administration of Justice, which he headed, and about a speech on judicial reform that he was to write for Roosevelt's delivery before the New York City Bar Association on March 12. But the professor had also served Seabury in the New York City investigation, as we have seen. He knew precisely "what a spot the inexorable Seabury had selected for Roosevelt" in the Sheriff Farley matter. He knew that this "spot," bad enough in itself, was far worse in its indication of "what might come later should Seabury carry his investigation to a point where the issue of Mayor James J. Walker's removal was put to Roosevelt." And it was in this context, which included a seemingly casual reference by Moley to the presidential campaign, that the professor offered "to help in any way" he could. Roosevelt evinced gratitude. He would, he said, "be glad to call" for help later on, and his implication, or Moley's inference, was that the call might be for help well beyond the Farley case. Indeed, "[i]t seemed to me that Roosevelt had intimated, in a way peculiarly his own, that he might let me move in from the outer reaches of his circle pretty close to center," as Moley wrote years later. This was a delightful prospect for a professor whose vaunted practicality and hard-headedness did not preclude a romantic attraction toward power and the powerful; the prospect was more vivid in his mind's eye than "the river and the hills" were to his physical vision as his train bore him southward along the Hudson later that afternoon. Years later he confessed that it "occupied my thoughts every waking hour" during the weeks of suspenseful waiting that followed.[4]

For Roosevelt, these same weeks were increasingly tense, anxious, crowded.

On January 9 came the Democratic National Committee meeting in Washington. With respect to the Prohibition issue, it went well for the Roosevelt forces. By the evening of January 8, Jim Farley was able to tell all and sundry that more than 90 of the committee's 109 votes were firmly committed against Raskob's proposal, whereupon the committee chairman proposed and Farley readily accepted a face-saving "compromise." It was agreed that, instead of "recommending" the proposal to the national convention, the committee would merely "refer" it, accompanying it with the Raskob poll results, as relevant information. Moreover, Raskob was impelled to assert in a defensive public statement that "not a single member of this committee . . . knows of one thing that any of us has done to try to defeat or deter in any way those who . . . are promoting Mr. Roosevelt for the Presidential nomination,"[5] a palpably false assertion, amounting to a confession of guilt, whose effect was to strengthen popular belief in the inevitability of Roosevelt's nomination. Even more gratifying was the election of New Hampshire's national committeeman Robert Jackson, now one of Roosevelt's most fervent and effective supporters, to the strategically important post of committee secretary.

But as regards the main business of the meeting, which was to choose the convention city, the outcome was unfortunate from Roosevelt's point of view. He had hoped and his supporters had worked to have Kansas City chosen. Boss Thomas Pendergast of that city was friendly to him and could assure a gallery crowd similarly friendly. Instead, Chicago, favored by Raskob-Shouse-Smith, won out when it added $50,000 at the last moment to an already large bid. Roosevelt must now worry about the effects a hostile gallery might have upon delegates if the vote became close, for Cermak could pack the gallery with a noisy unruly mob whose sole concern was the immediate repeal of Prohibition and which, by that token and Boss Cermak's instructions, might boo every mention of Roosevelt's name.

To this bad news, worse was added by a communication Roosevelt received the next day from Louis Howe in New York City. "The enclosed Walter Lippmann article has been sent evidently to all the newspapers [the *Herald Tribune* published it on January 8] and is now being sent out in this form [as a leaflet] to the public generally," wrote Howe, adding ruefully, "I do not think there is anything we can do about it but I would advise you to read the article."[6]

Roosevelt at once did so—and writhed inwardly.

A few days before, on January 6, he had delivered his annual message to the legislature, one carefully designed to promote his national candidacy in the process of presenting his 1932 legislative program. He had spoken of a "domestic crisis which calls . . . for a unity of leadership and action as complete as if we were engaged in war." An aspect or element of this crisis was a sad divorcement of "personal liberty" from "economic liberty." The former "we have retained to a large degree, perhaps," he said, but the latter "we have lost in recent years" to "specialization of industry, of agriculture and of distribution." As an economic unit, the individual had become but a "cog" that could "move only if the whole machine is in perfect gear." Obviously the "machine" was now badly out of gear. There was an urgent need, which national leaders over "more than two years" had failed to supply, for "plans for the reconstruction of a better order of civilization in which the economic freedom of the individual will be restored." There was no justification, however, for any "extreme" of "pessimism" or despair, because the "American system of economics and government is everlasting."[7]

This message was the occasion of Lippmann's commentary.

"The art of carrying water on both shoulders is highly developed in American politics, and Mr. Roosevelt has learned it," wrote Lippmann. "His message to the Legislature, or at least that part of it devoted to his Presidential candidacy, is an almost perfect specimen of the balanced antithesis." When the governor called for "plans for the reconstruction of a better ordered civilization," he was appealing to such left-wing supporters as Senator Wheeler. When he proclaimed that "the American system" is "everlasting," he was appealing to such right-wing supporters as the New York *Times.* " . . . it is not easy to say with certainty whether his left-wing or his right-wing supporters are the more deceived. The reason is that Franklin D. Roosevelt is a highly impressionable person, without a firm grasp of public affairs and without very strong convictions. He might plump for something which would shock the conservatives. There is no telling. Yet when [left-wing] Representative Howard of Nebraska says he [Roosevelt] is 'the most dangerous enemy of evil influences,' New Yorkers who know the Governor know that Mr. Howard does not know the Governor. For Franklin D. Roosevelt is an amiable man with many philanthropic impulses, but he is not the dangerous enemy of anything. He is too eager to please."

In actual fact, Lippmann went on to say, Roosevelt was "an excessively cautious politician." He had been "Governor for three years, and I doubt whether anyone can point to a single act of his which involved any political risk. Certainly his water power policy has cost him nothing, for the old interests who fought Smith have been replaced by more enlightened capitalists quite content to let the state finance the development." In nothing else had he evinced any "willingness to attack vested interests," whereas in "one outstanding case" he had shown "the utmost reluctance to attack them." This case was that of Tammany Hall. "It is well known in New York, though apparently not in the West, that Governor Roosevelt had to be forced into assisting the exposure of corruption in New York City. It is well known . . . that, through his patronage, he has supported the present powers in Tammany Hall." Those powers did not like him, certainly, but they had with him a "working arrangement," as was manifest in last fall's battle over the reforestation amendment. " . . . it was the Tammany machine which gave the Governor his victory." Conceivably, Roosevelt "might . . . at some time in the next few months fight Tammany," but only if he decided that it was "safe and profitable to do so. For Franklin D. Roosevelt is no crusader. He is no tribune of the people. He is no enemy of entrenched privilege. He is a pleasant man who, without any important qualifications for the office, would very much like to be President."[8]

Perhaps only Louis Howe and Eleanor Roosevelt had any accurate notion of the personal hurt Roosevelt suffered from this public lashing, for he gave little private sign, and none publicly, that he was even aware of what the columnist had said. (Eleanor, who placed the article in her personal file for future reference, was inclined to believe he deserved some of it; within a few days she would become convinced he deserved all of it.) He did indicate his resentment of the denigration of his hydroelectric-power struggle, a resentment no doubt fed by his remembrance of the hearty congratulations Lippmann had sent him when he proclaimed victory over the power interests in January 1930. Morris L. Cooke of Philadelphia, the consulting engineer and power expert whom he had appointed a trustee of the New York Power Authority in May 1931, wrote him offering to address to Lippmann a statement setting aright the latter's distorted view of the governor's power record. "I hope you will write to Lippmann," Roosevelt replied on January 18. "In spite of his brilliance it is very clear that he has never let his mind travel west of the Hudson or north of the Harlem!"[9] Cooke may well have wondered what relevance this last remark had to the Lippmann critique. Did Roosevelt mean to indicate that Lippmann's continual harping on the Tammany theme revealed a parochial mind, one devoid of a sense of just proportions whereby the "local" scene could be accurately fitted into the "big national picture"?

II

CERTAIN it is that the chastisement had no corrective effect. Indeed, it might seem to some observers to have had an opposite effect, as if it had provoked an imp of perversity and a mood of stubborn defiance. For Roosevelt's every major public act during the weeks that immediately followed conformed precisely to the behavior pattern Lippmann had described and deplored.

On New Year's Day, 1932, William Randolph Hearst delivered over the radio a withering blast against the actual or possible presidential candidacy of Roosevelt, Baker, Smith, Young, or any other who, like those named, including Herbert Hoover, was a dangerous internationalist, committed to Woodrow Wilson's "visionary policies of intermeddling in Europe's conflicts and complications" through membership in the League of Nations. Hearst's own choice for the presidency, announced in his radio address and proclaimed the next day in a front-page editorial in every newspaper of his coast-to-coast chain, was John Nance Garner of Texas, Speaker of the House of Representatives. For Roosevelt, this was a disappointment of course. It did effectively stymie what had seemed up until then a potentially strong nomination drive through the Southwest and West by Oklahoma's colorful, controversial Governor William H. Murray, known everywhere as Alfalfa Bill, a ruthless, dictatorial man of sixty-two who affected the manners, while holding few of the principles, of an 1890s Populist. Moreover, Garner himself reportedly did not take his candidacy seriously and wanted no part in the "Stop Roosevelt" movement. But Hearst's announcement meant that the Texas delegation would not "instruct for Roosevelt," as Garner had thought, and said to Howe only a few weeks before, it would probably do. Roosevelt was thus deprived of 46 votes, and possibly of California's 44 votes as well, on the first convention ballot. Nor was this all. As the front-runner, Roosevelt became the target of further Hearst blasts. When some of his supporters, notably Senator Wheeler, denied he was any such internationalist as Hearst charged him with being, the publisher answered with a front-page editorial on January 17 quoting speeches Roosevelt had made in support of the League during the 1920 vice-presidential campaign; he also instructed his editors to mobilize local anti-League pro-American sentiment against the Roosevelt candidacy.[10]

This last was formally announced on January 22, when Roosevelt addressed to the secretary of North Dakota's Democratic State Committee a letter consenting to the presentation of his name "at your coming primaries as a candidate for the Democratic nomination for the Presidency." His letter was, in substance and style, precisely what Lippmann would have predicted. He fully appreciated "the honor that has been done me. . . . One who believes in new standards of Government to meet new problems, in the translation of forward-looking thought into practical actions, must welcome a chance to do his share toward that end." But as "Governor of a State containing nearly thirteen million people," he was, "especially at this time, obligated to a still higher duty. . . . Our Legislature is now in session. If I am to be faithful to this trust I must devote myself to the obtaining of progressive laws, and the immediate administering of executive duties in the interest of the people of this State. Were I now to divert my efforts in any degree by personal efforts in furtherance of my own political future, I would not only be untrue to my own convictions, but I would also stamp myself as one unworthy to be my party's choice as leader."[11]

About national issues, as he announced his national candidacy, he said not a word.

All the same, one such issue, the League issue as pointed up by Hearst, greatly worried him and Howe at that moment. And this worry increased when, on January 26, Newton D. Baker, in seeming response to Hearst's attack, retreated from his formerly firm and forward position in favor of League entry. "I am not in favor of a plank in the Democratic national platform urging our joining of the League," he told reporters as he boarded a ship for a Mexican vacation. "I think it would be a great mistake to make a partisan issue of the matter." He personally continued to favor America's entry and believed it to be ultimately inevitable, but only after a majority of the American people had become "satisfied as to the wisdom of such a course."[12] This straddle of the "matter" pleased neither friend nor foe of the League (certainly it failed to appease Hearst), a fact that gratified Roosevelt to the extent that it reduced Baker's political potency. But it also seemed a clear indication that Baker wanted the nomination, while demonstrating a necessity for Roosevelt publicly to face the League issue head on if he were not to risk a weakening of his candidacy that would proportionately strengthen Baker as a dark horse—and *this* was not gratifying at all.

One last effort was made to avoid the issuance of the indicated public statement. Farley, with Howe's permission, and perhaps at Howe's request, called in person at the offices of Hearst's New York *American* to tell the top

editor there that his paper's attacks upon Roosevelt were based on false information: Roosevelt had changed his mind about the League in recent years. The
tactic failed to work. It was, in fact, counterproductive. For Hearst promptly
published, on the front page of every Hearst paper, the fact of Farley's visit,
and made contemptuous personal comment upon it: "If Mr. Roosevelt has any
statement to make about his not being an internationalist he should make it
to the public publicly, and not to me privately."[13]

Two days later, on February 2, 1932, Roosevelt bit the bullet.

In an address to a convention of the New York State Grange in Albany—
a speech whose first draft was agonizingly crafted by Howe, with some help
from Colonel House—he tried to distinguish between *economic* internationalism, which he favored (save insofar as it called for cancellation or repudiation
of war debts owed the United States), and *political* internationalism, which he
opposed. He inveighed against the Hawley-Smoot Tariff and plumped for
"reciprocal methods" whereby "high tariff fences" could be lowered or
breached and a healthy world trade restored. This was designed to please such
internationalists as Cordell Hull, the fervent exponent of reciprocal trade
agreements, who, however, could not fail to be acutely distressed by what
followed. For Roosevelt's next words were designed, no doubt in a grim,
nervous spirit shot through with a sense of risk, to appease the rantingly
nationalistic Hearst. " . . . a trade conference with the other nations of the
world should not, by any stretch of the imagination, involve the United States
in any participation in political controversies in Europe or elsewhere," he went
on to say. Certainly it did not imply United States participation in the League
of Nations. Like "millions of my fellow countrymen" he had actively favored
America's joining the League in 1920, and for this he would make no apology.
"But the League . . . today," in part perhaps because the United States had
not joined at the outset, "is not the League conceived by Woodrow Wilson."
Instead, it had become increasingly "a mere meeting place for the political
discussion of strictly European political national difficulties," with "the principal members" showing "no disposition to divert the huge sums spent on
armaments into the channels of legitimate trade, balanced budgets and payments of obligations." Therefore, "American participation in the League
would not serve the highest purpose of the prevention of war and a settlement
of international difficulties in accordance with fundamental American ideals.
Because of these facts . . . I do not favor American participation."[14]

Nor was this the full extent of the concession he, who had gained his first
national fame as an exponent of Wilsonian idealism and the League, was
prepared to make.

To his repudiation of a position publicly maintained for a dozen years—to
this abject capitulation to a hateful and much hated man whose power of
inherited wealth was exercised in ways inimical to the essential processes of
democratic government—he was prepared, should Hearst demand it, to add
a statement saying he no longer favored U.S. participation in the World Court!
In other words, he was willing to retreat farther into isolationism than Harding

and Coolidge had done, for both these Republican Presidents, and Hoover also, had urged U.S. membership in the Court!

Fortunately for him, the publisher did not press him that far.

As it was, Roosevelt created a public sensation of a kind he could only suffer, and strained nearly to the breaking point the loyalty of many of his "most ardent and influential friends," as Colonel House warned him. Brilliant liberal journalists, who literally longed for the kind of candidate he professed to be when in a liberal mood, castigated him unmercifully in nationally read articles: Heywood Broun described him as "the corkscrew candidate," and Elmer Davis, as one "who thinks that the shortest distance between two points is not a straight line but a corkscrew."[15]

There was also private anguish—greater perhaps than Roosevelt had expected and been prepared to discount in advance.

Many of his personal acquaintances whose good opinion of him he cherished, including several longtime close friends, let him know that his speech was a contemptible performance. Eleanor was so furiously disgusted with him, despite Howe's attempts to explain to her the "facts of life," that she refused to speak to him for days. And her two closest friends, Nancy Cook and Marion Dickerman, with whom she shared the ownership of Todhunter and Val-Kill Industries, were only somewhat less disaffected. When he asked Agnes Leach (Mrs. Henry Goddard Leach) to lunch with him, hoping to persuade her to help "make peace" between him and his wife, she flatly refused. "That was a shabby statement!" she said. "I just don't feel like having lunch with you today." He was compelled to write defensive letters to other outraged Old Wilsonians, including some whose support was of major importance to him. Thus to Robert Woolley: "I had hoped you would understand. Can't you see that loyalty to the ideals of Woodrow Wilson is just as strong in my heart as it is in yours—but have you ever stopped to consider that there is a difference between ideals and the methods of obtaining them? . . . Here is the difference between me and some of my fainthearted friends: I am looking for the best modern vehicle to reach the goal of an ideal while they insist on a vehicle which was brand new and in good running order twelve years ago. Think this over! And for heaven's sake have a little faith."[16]

His exasperation, which during the following preconvention weeks and months flamed forth with unprecedented frequency and heat, was fed by unadmitted doubts and indecisions, whence sprang up abundant rationalizations, and joined with a growing resentment of his critics's refusal to accept them. Could they not see that their insistence upon absolutes in a world of relativities was absurd? How could they persist as they did in that "foolish consistency" that Emerson damned as the "hobgoblin of little minds"? *Why* their blindly stubborn refusal to think, as any successful politician *has* to think, in terms of practical possibilities, relative values, and an overall balance of forces pointed toward ultimate goals?

For it seemed to him perfectly clear that nothing of any value could have been gained or retained from his continued advocacy of League membership. Certainly it could not have effected such membership: he and Baker were in agreement that there was not the slightest chance, no matter what either of them did, that America would join the League now or in the foreseeable future. But he could point to several valuable practical results of his doing as he had done. His immediate purpose was achieved. Hearst, while continuing to support "Cactus Jack" Garner, ceased to make direct attacks upon him, which were especially dangerous to his candidacy in the South and West. Isolationist leaders were mollified, including the influential Progressive Republican Senator William E. Borah of Idaho—and isolationism was a majority sentiment in both parties, especially in the West and South. His overall candidacy was considerably strengthened: he gained far more support from fervent isolationism than he could possibly lose to fervent internationalism. Because of Baker's shift of position, League membership advocates among Roosevelt's supporters had in point of fact nowhere else to go with their votes if they wanted these votes to count in any practical way; they must stick with him whether they liked it or not. And, finally, the possibility was reopened that Hearst, after all, would support Roosevelt in the convention once it became certain that Garner would not be nominated—that Hearst would then encourage a shift of Garner's support to Roosevelt. But had this possibility ever been closed? Had it not always been a probability so great as to constitute a virtual certainty? Roosevelt himself seems not to have seen, what seemed to some of his critics perfectly obvious, that Hearst was bound in any case to do all he could to prevent the nomination of Smith, whom he personally hated, or of Newton Baker, whom he positively loathed, and would therefore inevitably turn to Roosevelt if ever the only likely alternative was the nomination of either of these two.

III

ON February 8, 1932, Alfred E. Smith, from his office in the Empire State Building, announced his "availability" for his party's presidential nomination. He would wage no "pre-convention campaign to secure the support of delegates," he said: it would be unseemly for him to do so, since he was titular head of the party. But if the convention "after careful consideration should decide it wants me to lead I will make the fight."

The announcement was not entirely unexpected.

It had been deemed unlikely, however.

To the Roosevelt camp it was profoundly disturbing, emphasizing the necessity for a virtually clean sweep of the upcoming primaries if Roosevelt's nomination was to be anything like the sure thing that Jim Farley was predicting. The New York *Times* editorialized that "what promised at one time to be a rather tame contest for the Democratic nomination will hereafter be bristling with excitement. When one of the contestants is named 'Al' Smith, none of the others can afford for an instant to be off their [*sic*] guard."[17]

Ten days after Smith's announcement, McAdoo announced his support of Garner.

An effect of this was to increase Roosevelt's already great reluctance to act

against New York City corruption in any way that might provoke outright
hostility from Tammany Hall, which could cost him not only New York's
ninety-six delegates but also, by sympathetic reaction, substantial portions of
the delegations in other states where big-city Democratic machines were a
dominant factor, such as Illinois, Indiana, New Jersey, and possibly even
Missouri. Roosevelt had every reason to fear the outcome of any truly equal
choice by Tammany between himself and Smith. Al had said harsh things,
certainly, about Curry and Walker. Indeed, much of the bitterness toward
Roosevelt that animated him derived from the governor's cooperation with
John Curry in ways that reduced Smith's political potency. Nevertheless,
Smith was himself emphatically a Tammany product. He was personally at
ease with Tammanyites as Roosevelt could never be; he had never fought the
machine as Roosevelt had done in the case of Blue-eyed Billy; he prudently
refrained from any public comment upon the Seabury Investigation exposures;
and he was under no official obligation to act upon these exposures. Roosevelt
was so obliged. He had immediately before him the case of Sheriff Farley. And
he cast about almost desperately for some formula whereby he could solve this
case without hopelessly antagonizing either Tammany or the forces of good
government.

He had publicly asked Judge Seabury if the charges against the sheriff were
preferred by him as counsel for the Joint Legislative Committee or by him as
an individual citizen. Seabury had replied stiffly that "my letter was an individual communication to the governor of the state."* Roosevelt had then submitted the charges to Farley. Weeks passed. Criticism of Roosevelt's failure to act
mounted. On February 1, Seabury addressed another letter to the governor,
commenting on the latter's recent "stirring address" about the country's need
"for leadership" and asking him to "furnish" some "in the present situation."
Seabury, whose yearning for the Democratic presidential nomination was now
palpable, wrote: "The People of New York County have no agency to which
they can appeal other than yourself. Every prosecuting agency within . . . the
greater city is in the control of Tammany Hall. Surely upon the facts you will
not fail to respond. . . . I feel that the people . . . are entitled to prompt action."
Still Roosevelt delayed. The Reverend W. Russell Bowie wrote him on February 11 in much the same vein as he had in November 1930 and received much
the same kind of answer.† To permit Farley to retain office would be outrageous, said Bowie; the governor should at once demonstrate the bold leadership he himself had just called for. Roosevelt asked his old friend to remember
"a certain magistrate by the name of Pontius Pilate, who acted upon public
clamor after first washing his hands"; he himself was resolved "not to let
politics interfere with my decisions as Governor, nor to deny the right to be
heard even to the meanest criminal in the State."[18]

*Seabury had asked the Joint Legislative Committee to present the evidence to the executive.
Tammany members of the committee had managed to block this move.
†See pages 180–181.

By that time he had in hand a "general rule," designed by Moley, to persuade Curry-Walker's Tammany that he was *forced* to act in this case as he was about to do, while at the same time persuading the general public that he acted with unprecedented boldness, according to principle. The principle itself was implicit in Seabury's investigative procedure. Said the governor: " . . . where a public official is under inquiry or investigation, especially an elected public official, and it appears that his scale of living, or the total of his bank deposits far exceeds the public salary which he is known to receive, he, the elected public official, owes a positive public duty to the community to give a reasonable or credible explanation of the sources of his deposits, or of the source which enables him to maintain . . . [such] scale of living. . . . While this rule may seem an enlargment of any previous ruling by a Governor of this State, it is time, I believe, that the standard of conduct of a public officer be put on a plane of personal as well as official honesty." Sheriff Farley notably failed to conform to this general rule when Roosevelt at last examined him in a public hearing on February 16. He gave no more satisfactory explanation than Seabury had obtained of the vast discrepancy between his public salary and his total income. But still Roosevelt delayed. Eight more days had passed before he finally issued the order removing Farley from office.[19]

Three weeks later, on March 17, 1932 (St. Patrick's Day, and Roosevelt's twenty-seventh wedding anniversary), he received from Rabbi Stephen Wise and the Reverend John Haynes Holmes of the City Affairs Committee a formal request that he remove from office John Theofel, chief clerk of the Queens County Surrogate Court, on the same grounds Roosevelt had applied to Sheriff Farley. And eight days after that came from the same gentlemen a request that he remove from office, in accordance with his newly announced "general rule," the Honorable James A. McQuade, sheriff of Queens County. Theofel, who had been unable to tell Seabury what duties he performed as chief clerk (actually he was the Democratic county leader and had put in office the surrogate he nominally served), had also been unable to explain how he had managed in just six years to increase his net worth by nearly $173,000—from $28,650 to $201,300. Similarly lucrative had been the post of Queens County register as occupied by McQuade, who had been elected sheriff in November 1931. As register, on an annual salary of $12,000, he had managed to accumulate $510,000 in a half-dozen years. How? By "borrowing" it a few thousand at a time, he said, from a great number of people, none of whom he was able to name in response to Seabury's questions. He claimed that he had been forced to borrow because he was the sole support of thirty-three other McQuades and that he had barely enough money "to do me the rest of my life if I die today."[20]

It is a measure of the strain Roosevelt was under at this opening of the crucial primary season and of the exasperation born of his doubtful indecision, his inability to discern clear cues or clues for action, concerning his relentlessly growing Tammany problem, that he, normally so remarkable for patience, sanguinity, and self-control, lost his temper completely at this juncture. And publicly! His official and moral obligation was only too clear. He should proceed as he had with Sheriff Farley, only more expeditiously—should submit the charges to the accused, give them opportunity to defend themselves in hearings before him, then remove them from office if they could not, as assuredly they could not, explain and justify the difference between their total incomes and their official salaries. Instead, on March 30, he addressed to Holmes and Wise a public letter in which he not only refused their requests on grounds palpably sophistic but also savagely impugned their motives in bringing the charges.* He found it "easy to question" their "good faith," and "to assume that you care more for personal publicity than for good government." He was "becoming convinced . . . that corruption in public office and unfit servants in public office are both far less abhorrent to you than they are to me." Their "rushing into print early and often, with extravagant and ill-considered language, causes many of our decent citizens to doubt your own reliance on law, on order and on justice." They "would be rendering a service" to the community that "at the present time you are not performing" if, instead of "asking your Governor to perform unconstitutional functions and to ignore the principles of representative government" (he stressed that McQuade had won election as sheriff *after* his alleged corruption had been exposed to the public gaze), they exerted themselves "patiently and consistently in pointing out to the electorate of New York City" the importance of "an active insistence" upon "better qualified and more honest and more efficient public servants."[21]

There can be no doubt that he regretted this outburst and was ashamed of it almost as soon as he read his letter in the newspapers. He received no praise for it and much blame in the press. And it may well have been with a sense of relief from self-disgust over this performance, if not of atonement for it and for his failure to press for meaningful bank reform in 1930, that in the following weeks, when political expediency could have tempted him toward passivity in the matter, he continued an active public defense of Banking Superintendent Joseph A. Broderick against criminal charges growing out of the Bank of United States collapse.

Roosevelt had been steadfast in Broderick's defense against loud and angry public clamor immediately after the bank failed. He had remained so when, in late June 1931, W. Kingsland Macy suddenly formally demanded Broderick's removal, claiming that the banking tragedy would not have occurred if Broderick had acted as duty required upon information brought him by "four of his examiners" in four "separately signed reports" in the summer of 1929. ("I do not accede to your request for a summary removal of the Superintendent of Banks," the governor had then tersely replied.) Roosevelt expressed outrage, and a furious resentment of Max D. Steuer, when the special prosecutor

---

*Louis Howe was furious with Roosevelt for this, knowing as he did how great and honorable were the public reputations of both Wise and Holmes. He bitterly blamed Sam Rosenman for not restraining "the boss" until sanity returned, as he was sure he himself would have done had he been at Roosevelt's side.

obtained, in late October 1931, from his special grand jury criminal indictments of Broderick for conspiracy and neglect of duty. He did all he could to bolster Broderick's morale during the anguished period of waiting for the trial to begin, wiring him "warm greetings" (from Warm Springs in December 1931) on his fiftieth birthday: "It must be awful to be so old. I will not equal it for another month."[22] And when the trial was under way in late April 1932, Steuer having completed his presentation of the case for the prosecution, Roosevelt insisted upon testifying in person for the defense. He did so at considerable personal inconvenience. The Governors' Conference was held in Richmond, Virginia, that year; Roosevelt addressed to it a "Tribute to George Washington" on Wednesday, April 27. His original plan had been to go then directly from Richmond to Warm Springs for his spring vacation. Instead, he came north again to testify for Broderick on April 29. On the witness stand, despite vehement objections from Steuer, all of them overruled, he assumed a considerable measure of personal and official responsibility for Broderick's alleged "conspiracy" and "negligence." He recalled that in the autumn of 1929 "there were approximately 200 banking institutions in the State of New York under the jurisdiction of *myself* [he stressed the personal reference] and the Superintendent of Banks that were in a somewhat weakened condition because of the stock market crash." It was utterly impossible, with the staff available at the time, to pay to each and every one of these the attention required for a truly adequate protection of depositors. He recounted his own efforts, a year later, to effect a merger of the Bank of United States with other banks, efforts that could be made only through delay of an official closing of the bank.

He thoroughly enjoyed Steuer's discomfiture as the special prosecutor, with a gesture of helpless disgust, refused to cross-examine the governor; he was immensely gratified when, on May 27, after nine days of testimony by Broderick and twelve hours of deliberation by the jury, his banking superintendent was declared innocent of the charges brought against him.[23]

IV

BY mid-March 1932, Raymond Moley had been permitted "to move in from the outer reaches . . . to [the] center" of the Roosevelt "circle," as he had dreamed of doing during the opening weeks of the election year.

He was eminently useful—as hard-working, self-disciplined, and well-organized in all his operations, hence as productive of usable materials, as Sam Rosenman. His hard, swift, practical intelligence; his pragmatic, flexible, anti-ideological attitudes, quickly sympathetic with Roosevelt's—though Moley's aversion to ideology, unlike Roosevelt's, was itself ideological; his basic conservatism, also akin to Roosevelt's, though perhaps more doctrinaire and less open to experimental variations; his remarkably wide range of factual information, extending far beyond the expertise in criminal-law administration which had first brought him to Howe's and Roosevelt's attention; his ability to grasp quickly and firmly the gist of complex problems, joined with a veritable genius for "boiling down" a huge seething caldron of fact and idea into succinct, forceful, clearly logical expository prose; his exhibited occasional literary eloquence and mastery of the telling word, the memorable phrase; his immense self-confidence and self-assurance, which augmented the force and persuasiveness of his counsels—all these had been either manifest or unmistakably indicated in the service he had given Roosevelt on increasingly frequent and important occasions since the autumn day in 1928 when Howe had introduced him to that year's Democratic gubernatorial candidate. His answer to the expected call for help in the Sheriff Farley case in early February, despite its invitation to further trouble, was recognized by Roosevelt as the best that could be devised in the circumstances: the removal formula and statement of principle won countrywide attention and approval for the governor. This had been followed by a well-crafted, thoughtful, scholarly critique of current judicial procedures ("The Road to Judicial Reform") prepared by Moley for Roosevelt's delivery on March 12 as a major address to the New York City Bar Association; it favorably impressed all who heard it, including some who disagreed with parts of it. Admittedly, Moley lacked the kind of warmth and generosity of spirit that attracts and holds great personal affection—he knew himself to be ill-equipped to run for elective office and had no desire to—but he understood party politics and the politician's temperament and outlook; he got on well with Roosevelt; and he also understood *personal* politics in general and practiced them to good effect in specific situations. On several occasions he had demonstrated to Roosevelt that he, in his own words, "could be trusted to handle awkward political situations with a reasonable amount of sense." He had smoothed out what could have been a rough embarrassment for the governor when the state Commission on the Administration of Justice was established. The final proof of his shrewd adroitness in the management of human relations, rooted more in manipulative intellect than in human empathy, was the fact that he remained on good terms with both Howe and Rosenman. He himself regarded this as a triumph of human engineering. "If either [of these men] had suspected that I was more than politely friendly with the other, if either had been given the slightest reason to resent any association of mine with Roosevelt at that crucial time, he would not have hesitated for a moment to block me off completely," Moley would remember years later. "It was lamentable but true that anyone, regardless of the contribution that he might have been able to make to Franklin Roosevelt, would have found the going hard unless he had appeased both these men."[24]

One may question whether Moley accurately assessed the motivating priorities of the two rivals, each of whom evinced a selfless devotion to Roosevelt considerably greater than Moley's. One may doubt that Roosevelt, who was acutely aware of his vulnerability as a candidate to the charges of mental vacuity that Lippmann and others hurled against him and who had several important speeches scheduled for the weeks just ahead, would have permitted either rival to "block off" any man as obviously qualified as Moley to help supply his need. But it is certain that there was no attempt at such blockage by either man at that "crucial time." Indeed, it was Rosenman himself, late on a mid-March evening when he and Roosevelt were alone together in the Executive Mansion study, who suggested the advisory arrangement that was being formalized to the minimum necessary degree on this Sunday in late April.

The 1932 session of the legislature had then just ended, delivering to the governor's desk the usual huge stack of thirty-day bills. One of its last acts had been the senatorial confirmation of Rosenman's appointment by the governor to fill a vacancy on the New York Supreme Court bench, an interim appointment (Rosenman would have to stand for election to the post the following November). Hence, it was in the knowledge that he himself, as soon as the thirty-day bills were disposed of, would enter upon new duties that would absorb time and energy he could otherwise have devoted to the presidential campaign that Rosenman spoke that night of the "awful fix" they would all "be in" if Roosevelt were "nominated tomorrow and had to start a campaign trip within the next ten days." Even if the candidate had had "a well-defined and thought-out affirmative program," which Roosevelt emphatically did not, "[i]t would be pretty hard [he meant 'impossible'] to get up intelligent speeches overnight on the many subjects you would have to discuss." Clearly there was immediate need "to get together some up-to-date information about the troubles with our economy," along with "some ideas on what to do about them," and since no such information or ideas had been forthcoming these last three years from the "successful industrialists" and "big financiers" whom presidential candidates normally consulted on economic matters, why not turn to the universities? College professors, with several of whom the governor had already had "good experiences," seemed to Rosenman less likely than business types to fear new departures "just because . . . [they] are new." Why not ask Ray Moley to recruit from among his Columbia colleagues* a group of men qualified "in different fields" to give expert advice? They could prepare memoranda and draft position papers on major issues, and Roosevelt could talk with them and learn from them in that way.[25]

Roosevelt had shown a reluctance to accept this suggestion similar to that he had shown when Flynn, refusing the campaign chairmanship, suggested Jim Farley instead. Perhaps it was similarly feigned, for the same kind of reason. At any rate, Rosenman was incited to argue strongly for his proposal, with Moley central to it, so that when Roosevelt finally agreed to it that night, he had greatly reduced the chance that acrimonious rivalry would arise from it between two men whose services were, in different ways, equally invaluable to him.

A few days later, Moley and Basil "Doc" O'Connor met with Rosenman in the latter's New York City apartment to discuss and approve a list of topics that Moley had prepared, each topic having beside it the name of a Columbia

---

*"Sam . . . loved Columbia University in a boyish and rather touching way . . . ," Moley later recalled.

University "expert." Beside "agriculture" was the name Rexford G. Tugwell; beside "tariffs," Lindsay Rogers; beside "credit," Adolf A. Berle, Jr.; and there were six or eight other topics and names.[26]

As things turned out, however, during the weeks that followed only Tugwell and Berle became permanently established with Moley in the core advisory group, whose nonacademic members continued to be Rosenman and O'Connor. These three Columbia professors, in other words, were key figures in a historic attempt to bridge that gap between Intelligence and Power that characteristically widens in twentieth-century polity—widens disastrously as physical power grows by leaps and bounds out of a rampantly advancing technology while the applied social intelligence necessary to control it for human purposes grows slowly or, during the last two decades, at least, not at all.

What, then, in addition to Moley's, were the mental attitudes, value systems, and general concepts that Intelligence was about to feed into this gap-bridging attempt?

V

TUGWELL was Moley's first recruit.

A native of rural New York, he was a 1915 graduate of the University of Pennsylvania's Wharton School of Finance and Commerce, where, like Frances Perkins a few years earlier, he had come under the immensely stimulating influence of the economics professor Simon Nelson Patten. Patten, an idealist in philosophy, was a pioneer theorist on the effects of modern technology, with its capacity to produce increasing abundance, upon a socioeconomic order developed, along with the "classical" economic theory that purported to describe it, in an age of scarcity. From him, Tugwell absorbed ideas basic to his subsequent work—that man is no mere function of his physical environment but, possessed of free will, can consciously change this environment; that the "economic man" of classical economics is therefore a distortive concept, materialistic self-interest being a far less powerful human drive than classicists taught; that, concomitantly, no "hidden hand" operates through a "free market," or ever did, to transform competitive greed automatically into general good; that, in fact, because of modern technology, there no longer *is* a truly free market in those areas of production and distribution most determinative of the general welfare; and, hence, that competition must be replaced by cooperation, *laissez-faire* economic individualism by planned collectivism, and emphasis on thrift by emphasis on consumption (one of Patten's magazine articles was entitled "Extravagance as a Virtue") if the new technology was to enhance rather than diminish the quality of individual lives and serve rather than master the human community.[27]

At the University of Washington, where he became an assistant professor of marketing in the School of Business after two years as an economics instructor at the University of Pennsylvania (1915–1917), Tugwell came under the influence of faculty colleagues who pioneered the application of psychology to social science. Chief among these was William F. Ogburn, who remained Tugwell's friend and colleague at Columbia for seven years (Ogburn came to Columbia in 1919, and Tugwell, in 1920) and whose concept of cultural lag became a major element, as well as a source of recurrent despair, in Tugwell's generally optimistic thinking. Others of Columbia's faculty who greatly influenced him were John Dewey as social and educational theorist, and Wesley Clair Mitchell, the outstanding student of Thorstein Veblen, whose essays in quantitative economics, especially his statistical studies of business cycles, aided Tugwell's understanding of New Era economics, and whom Tugwell regarded as "the bridge between classicism and instrumentalism in economics."

In 1927 Tugwell published his first important book, *Industry's Coming of Age.* In it he accepted the distinction Veblen made, notably in *The Engineers and the Price System,* between industry and business, and blamed the latter for the fact that wage increases did not keep pace with the increases in industrial production that resulted from scientific management (*à la* Taylor) and technological advance. The clear implication was a growing disparity between production and purchasing power, hence an increasing market overproduction. While writing this book, Tugwell began to wonder if national planning might not be more immediately feasible for American agriculture, under the impact of postwar and continuing farm depression, than for a presently prosperous business-controlled American industry. He began to concentrate on agricultural economics. And in the summer of that same year, 1927, he, with Stuart Chase, Paul Douglas, and seven other professors, accompanied a group of non-Communist trade unionists on a two-month visit to the Soviet Union. He returned convinced that Soviet agricultural policy, aimed at stimulating production, had little relevance to U.S. agriculture, whose problem was overproduction, and confirmed in his antideterminist philosophy, with particular reference to dialectical materialism. But he was also further confirmed in his conviction that national planning was necessary to make technology serve humane ends, that it was essential, even, to the prevention of technological catastrophe, and that America had much to learn from the Soviet experience with such planning. A year later, he became marginally involved in presidential politics: he was prevailed upon by a faculty colleague, Lindsay Rogers, who was advising Al Smith on tariff policy, to prepare a lengthy memorandum on the farm problem for the Democratic candidate's use.[28]

With the coming on of the Great Depression, and as it deepened through 1930 and 1931, Tugwell's insistence upon the immediate necessity for a planned economy grew almost shrill and, in at least one of his public statements, antidemocratic, protototalitarian. He addressed to the American Economic Association in December 1931 words suggestive of a doctrinaire Marxist's argument against "gradualism" and *for* revolution as the only means of effecting necessary social change.

Three months before, on September 16, in an address delivered to a meeting of the National Electrical Manufacturers Association in New York City,

Gerard Swope, president of General Electric, had proposed a scheme for industrial and commercial organization whereby market needs could be determined and production controlled on a national scale. At once immensely publicized as the Swope Plan, it called for the revision or suspension of antitrust laws to permit the formation of national trade associations, one for each kind of industrial or commercial activity. Every company engaged in interstate commerce that employed fifty or more people would be compelled by federal law to join the appropriate association if it didn't do so voluntarily within three years after the association was formed. These associations would collect and provide information (on inventories, prices, business volume, etc.) needed for planned production and growth, would establish codes of business ethics, would do other things needed for employment stabilization and efficient public service, and (this came in for special comment) would provide unemployment, life, and accident insurance, as well as old-age pensions on a contributory basis, with employers bearing at least half the cost. The associations would be loosely supervised by the Federal Trade Commission or a special federal agency with which each association would file quarterly and annual financial statements. A few weeks later, Henry I. Harriman, president of the U.S. Chamber of Commerce, announced a somewhat similar plan prepared by the Chamber's Committee on Continuity of Business and Employment. It was more specific than the Swope Plan in its call for antitrust revision to permit production limitation agreements among trade association members (at present such agreements were illegally "collusive"); but its chief departure from the Swope Plan was its proposal of a three-member fully staffed National Economic Council to investigate "fundamental" economic problems and to serve the associations in an advisory as well as "supportive," that is, public relations, capacity. Council members were to be chosen by a board that was itself chosen by the Chamber of Commerce, a board "representative of some such group of interests as . . . the United States Department of Commerce, the Chamber of Commerce . . . , labor, agriculture, manufacturing, banking, railroads, public utilities, distributive trades, the law, engineering, and professional economists." Harriman was opposed to "business planning by some all-powerful governmental board." He favored "business planning by business itself." And he found "economic council" to be a title preferable to "planning board" because it it did not imply "detailed and autocratic powers of control."[29]

But precisely this last was what was needed, declared Tugwell in his evidently *deliberately* shocking American Economic Association address. He dismissed with contempt, as "unrealistic," both the Swope and Harriman pronouncements. "Partial" planning through a national planning agency possessed of only "advisory" powers was useless, or worse; only "total" planning would "work," and total planning meant also total control. There must be "the laying of rough, unholy hands upon many a sacred precedent, doubtless calling for an enlarged and national police force for enforcement." In the end, "business will logically be required to disappear . . . [for] the essence of business is its free venture for profits in an unregulated economy." Industry would remain, and would become government! "When industry is government and government is industry," he said, echoing Veblen, "the dual conflict deepest in our modern institutions will be abated." Nor was there any time to lose, America being now on the verge of a social explosion. " . . . the future is becoming visible in Russia," he declared, echoing Lincoln Steffens; "the present is bitterly in contrast; politicians, theorists, and vested interests seem to conspire ideally for the provocation to violence of a long-patient people."[30] Yet this collectivist, though deeply sympathetic with much of the political program presented by Norman Thomas, did not consider himself a Socialist. It seemed to him of little importance whether the means of production were privately or publicly owned. In either case, actual control was in the hands of managers. What was important "beyond all else," he would declare in a later year, was "the achieving of publicly oriented direction whether of publicly or privately owned or operated agencies." (Norman Thomas would have replied that a "publicly oriented direction" is much less likely to be achieved through a private management ultimately responsible only to private owners, however widely dispersed, than by public servants whose operations are open to public scrutiny and subject to popular approval or censure.)

In general, Tugwell's was a holistic mind. He thought, he felt, in terms of total organism, was far less inclined toward analysis than toward connection and synthesis, had an instinctive aversion to atomism. He was also, in both mind and temperament, a romantic idealist: he would "bend the forces untamable; . . . harness the powers irresistible— . . . roll up my sleeves—make America over!," as he chanted in a Whitmanesque poem composed when he was a college senior.[31]

Tugwell was an unusually handsome man, still youthful in appearance at age forty-one. He was almost *too* romantically good-looking, some thought, with his wavy hair and rather "soulful" long-lashed eyes, though he was emphatically masculine in appearance and manner. And he had a vibrant personality whose effect upon social companions was "enormously stimulating . . . like a cocktail," to quote Moley. If inclined to use needlessly long and involved periods in prose intended for the eyes of academic colleagues, he had the ability to communicate ideas with clarity and force both in writings addressed to a general readership and in speech, the latter ability being especially important in his dealings with the ear-minded Roosevelt.

His initial contact with Roosevelt was on an evening in the third week of March 1932.

Tugwell and Moley came up from New York City by train to Albany in the afternoon, arriving at the Executive Mansion in time to dine with the Roosevelts and Missy LeHand. After dinner, the men went into the living room, where Roosevelt was uncomfortably seated, Tugwell thought, in the corner of a sofa so low he had to keep his withered legs stretched out before him and where Tugwell, responding to the governor's opening question about the relationship of agriculture to the general economic situation, held forth for almost two hours of almost uninterrupted talk, which ended only when Eleanor

Roosevelt, at midnight, "came in to call a halt." Moley was impressed. "I never saw Roosevelt listen to anyone as long as he did to you," said Moley to his protégé when the two said goodnight. And Tugwell, whose holism and romanticism had as one element an acute sense of history as dramatic process, was so excited that he lay awake for a long time in his bed that night.

The next morning his excitement was renewed and increased, becoming tinctured with a sense of "significance" and "consequence" (his own words), when Roosevelt, propped up in his narrow bed over which were scattered several of that morning's newspapers, his huge torso wrapped in an old gray sweater, a cigarette burning in the holder tilting up from his mouth, saw through his open bedroom door his two guests emerging from their rooms across the hall and shouted to them, in a cheery voice, an invitation to "come over." Tugwell was immensely relieved. He had gone to sleep half-convinced he had made rather a fool of himself in the Mansion living room with a "professorial . . . heavy . . . preachy" monologue. He had doubted he would ever be summoned again to the Mansion. But now it seemed to him that admission to the governor's bedroom meant admission to the governor's confidence, which meant he was entering a new and strange and rather frightening area of historic responsibility.

" . . . meeting him [Roosevelt]," Tugwell recalled long afterward, "was somewhat like coming into contact with destiny itself."[32]

And the impression Tugwell made on Roosevelt in that first meeting with him—an impression subsequently deepened in talk-filled evenings in Hyde Park as well as in Albany—was evident in the very first important speech that Roosevelt gave not long after, a ten-minute talk drafted by Moley for delivery over a national radio network during the Lucky Strike (cigarette) Hour on April 7. The speech's essential argument was provided by Tugwell's insistence that direct governmental action toward restoration of mass purchasing power was the major first step to take toward economic recovery; by his contemptuous commentary upon efforts to promote recovery by aiding big business, as in Hoover's newly established Reconstruction Finance Corporation, while doing nothing for farmers and others in distress (he likened this to an attempt to fertilize soil with manure placed in trees); and by his further insistence that chronic farm depression in the 1920s had undermined the New Era and brought on the Crash. "It is said that Napoleon lost the battle of Waterloo because he forgot his infantry—he staked too much upon the more spectacular but less substantial cavalry," said Roosevelt. "The present administration in Washington provides a close parallel. It has . . . forgotten . . . the infantry of our economic army. These unhappy times call for the building of plans that rest upon the forgotten, the unorganized but indispensible units of economic power, for plans . . . that build from the bottom up and not from the top down, that put their faith once more in the forgotten man at the bottom of the economic pyramid." Thus the key phrases of what became known at once and remains in history as the "Forgotten Man" speech. It called for federal action to restore "purchasing power to the farming half of the country" and to prevent mortgage foreclosures through aid to local credit agencies, and for tariff reductions and revisions aimed at a "reciprocal exchange of goods." It described the Reconstruction Finance Corporation as "[t]he two billion dollar fund which President Hoover and the Congress have put at the disposal of the big banks, the railroads and the corporations of the nation."[33] And it provoked a storm of controversy, being extravagantly praised by liberals and even more extravagantly condemned by conservatives, both Democratic and Republican. Radical demagoguery! This was the damning cry of Respectability across the land, and Moley worried lest Roosevelt flinch under these attacks, blaming Moley for exposing him to them. On the contrary, Roosevelt was pleased by the furor: it showed "that he is being taken seriously," as Moley wrote in a letter to his sister Nell, "and he realizes that the alienation of some standpatters is necessary if the campaign is to seem to the rank and file . . . something other than the usual campaign futilitarianism." "You ask what he is like," Moley's letter continued. " . . . One thing is sure—that the idea people get from his charming manner—that he is soft or flabby in disposition and character —is far from true. When he wants something a lot he can be formidable—when crossed he is hard, stubborn, resourceful, relentless. I used to think . . . his amiability was 'lord-of-the-manor'—'good-to-the-peasants'—stuff. It isn't that at all. He seems quite naturally warm and friendly. . . . The stories about his illness and its effect upon him are the bunk. Nobody in public life since T.R. has been so robust, so buoyantly and blatantly healthy as this fellow. . . . I've been amazed with his interest in things. It skips and bounces through . . . intricate subjects and maybe it is my academic training that makes me feel that no one could possibly learn much in such a hit or miss fashion. I don't find that he has read much about economic subjects. . . . This . . . seems to give Tugwell some worries because he wants people to show familiarity with pretty elementary ideas. But I believe that his [Roosevelt's] complete freedom from dogmatism is a virtue at this stage of the game. He will stick to ideas after he has expressed them, I believe and [sic] hope. . . . The frightening aspect of his methods is F.D.R.'s great receptivity. So far as I know he makes no effort to check up on anything that I or anybody else has told him."[34] This letter was written on April 12. On the following day, Wednesday, April 13, came the most vehement, bitter attack yet made on Roosevelt as presidential candidate. Addressing a Raskob-arranged Jefferson Day dinner in Washington, D. C., where Newton D. Baker also spoke, Al Smith referred to the "Forgotten Man" speech, without specifically mentioning it, as an attempt to incite class warfare, crying in a voice hoarse with outrage: "I will take off my coat and vest and fight to the end against any candidate who persists in any demagogic appeal to the masses of the working people of this country to destroy themselves by setting class against class and rich against poor!"[35]

To Roosevelt's next important public speech, Tugwell's contribution was more direct and extensive. This second speech, in which popular anticipatory interest was greatly heightened by Smith's outburst (Would Roosevelt respond? If so, how?), was to another Jefferson Day dinner, this one in St. Paul on the evening of April 18. Its first draft, whose central theme and some of whose key language had come from Tugwell, was already written when Moley rode up to Albany on the afternoon of Thursday, April 14, to work it into final form with Roosevelt. And when Moley read this draft on the train, with Smith's words of the night before still ringing in his ears, it struck him as precisely *right* for the occasion. A sober, reasonable, statesmanlike spelling out of certain implications of the Lucky Strike talk, it had in it no hint of defensiveness against Smith's attack, of course, since it had been completed before the attack was made. All the same, its insistence that none of the problems facing the nation could be solved in isolation, that each must be dealt with in terms of an overall "concert of interests" if it was to be truly overcome, answered beautifully Smith's implicit insistence upon the *single* interest of business, especially big business, as the center and focus of the nation's well-being. Roosevelt agreed with Moley on this in conferences that evening and the next day. The supposedly final draft speech was in the governor's hands by the afternoon of Saturday, April 16, when Moley boarded a train for Cleveland to spend a weekend with his mother and sister Nell. And with that draft both Moley and Tugwell were highly pleased.

They were less pleased with the speech that was actually given.* For within a few hours after Moley's departure Roosevelt read in the evening papers the sensational news of the imminent collapse of the $2.5 billion utilities empire of Chicago's Samuel Insull, which spread its network of power lines across thirty-nine states, controlled 6,000 central generating stations, and distributed over 10 percent of all the nation's electricity to more than 20 million customers. No man had loomed larger upon the American business scene during the New Era, than Samuel Insull, and none had been more glorified by New Era publicists. Born into a poor family in London, he had been brought to America in 1881, when he was twenty-one, as Thomas A. Edison's private secretary. He had subsequently employed a thorough knowledge of electrical technology, a tremendous capacity for hard work, and a rare genius for organization to serve an appetite for power and wealth that proved ultimately insatiable. A concomitant of his ambition—the usual concomitant of his kind of ambition—was a lack of concern for ethical practice. On his way to fame and fortune, and especially after his fortune was made, he had gone about as far as any one man had gone toward the destruction of essential elements of American democracy, earning as he did so the wrathful enmity of two Chicago civic reformers with whom Roosevelt would soon have important relationships, namely, the law partners Donald R. Richberg and Harold L. Ickes. Insull had effectively hired public servants—mayors, state legislators, regulatory board members, congressmen, governors, U.S. senators—to do his bidding in governmental halls, ensuring ineffectual regulation of utilities by state public service commissions and the Federal Power Commission. With overt and covert bribes he and

---

*Indeed, Tugwell told Moley afterward "that, to be honest, the production taken as a whole was terrible."[36]

his minions had introduced proutility antiregulatory doctrine into school text-books; had loosed upon an unsuspecting public a torrent of untruthful propaganda about utility rate making and profits; and had often denied print and radio media to critics of the sacred tenets of *laissez-faire.* They had piled atop operating companies one holding company upon another, each selling to an unwary uninformed unprotected public stock "secured" by the stock, similarly "secured," of the company immediately "under" it (Insull in 1932 was a board member of eighty-five companies, board chairman of sixty-five, president of eleven). They had then engaged in such cross-loaning of collateral among the dozens of Insull companies and such juggling of book entries and shiftings of assets as made it impossible for an army of CPAs to determine, later on, precisely *what* had been done. The one certainty was that the confused transactions had been in Insull's private interests and not in the interests of the ordinary stockholders in his companies. Roosevelt, with his active political interest in the public-power issue, was doubtless aware of one of the fragile dubious strands whereby Insull knit his empire together. The Roosevelt cottage in Warm Springs was lit with electricity generated and distributed by the Georgia Light and Power Company. This operating company was controlled by the Seaboard Public Service Company, which was controlled by the National Public Service Company, which was controlled by the National Electric Power Company, which was controlled by Middle West Utilities Company, which was controlled by Insull Utilities Investments, Inc. This last was the apex of the pyramid drawn on the empire's organization chart; every strand of control, every chain of command, led up to it. And it was Insull Utilities Investments that had, this day, been thrown into receivorship in what was by far the greatest single business failure in all American history!

Toward midnight of that Saturday, April 16, Moley was routed out of bed in Cleveland by a phone call from Albany. He was asked to board the governor's train when it passed through Detroit next morning. And all the way from Detroit to St. Paul, under Roosevelt's instruction, he worked on the draft speech, interrupting and fragmenting and severely slashing its initially smoothly flowing argument to permit the insertion of material about private utility financing and Roosevelt's electric-power policy. More work was done on the speech in St. Paul's Lowry Hotel on April 18. And to his Jefferson Day audience that night Roosevelt said, "It is an unfortunate fact . . . that largely through the building up of a series of great mergers and a series of great holding companies, the capital structure, especially in the case of the electric utilities, has been allowed to expand to an extent far beyond the actual and wise cash investment. It is a simple fact that in thousands of cases . . . electric utility companies have sought, and in many cases have succeeded in obtaining, permission to charge rates which will bring a fair return, not on this cash investment, but on a definite inflation of capital." He also reiterated his conviction that, though government should not engage in the business of power distribution from government-owned hydroelectric stations "if . . . private initiative and private capital" were willing to do it "for a reasonable and fair return" on capital actually and of practical necessity invested in distributive facilities, the government must certainly do so if "private individuals or corporations" insisted upon *more* than a "fair return."

But all was not lost, from Tugwell's point of view.

There yet remained enough of the structure and language of the original draft speech to cause the St. Paul effort to be known forever after as the "Concert of Interests" speech. Its key paragraph came after a comparison of the Hoover administration's "panic-stricken policy of delay and improvisation" in the face of economic crisis with the Wilson administration's constructive planning in the face of war crisis fifteen years before. Using Tugwell's language almost verbatim, Roosevelt said, "I am not speaking of an economic life completely planned and regimented [Tugwell thus cut his cloth to fit the man and the occasion]. I am speaking of the necessity that there be a real community of interests, not only among the sections of this great country, but among its economic units, and various groups in these units; that there be common participation . . . planned on the basis of a shared common life, the low as well as the high. In much of our present plans there is too much disposition to mistake the part for the whole, the head for the body, the captain for the company, the general for the army. I plead not for class control, but for a true concert of interests."[37]

The public's reaction to this speech was overwhelmingly favorable. Even Walter Lippmann, who interpreted it as "Governor Roosevelt's reply to Al Smith's warning," said in his column that the speech's "general sentiments" and discussion of "specific problems" evinced a "breadth of vision and an understanding of principles which are entitled to ungrudging praise."[38] And by such response Roosevelt was wholly confirmed in the high opinion he had already formed of Moley's service to him and of the service of those whom Moley had chosen as members of the advisory group.

VI

Of this group, Adolf A. Berle, Jr., had by this time become a member and was beginning to feed ideas and mental attitudes of his own into the mind of Franklin Roosevelt.

Four years younger than Tugwell and very different from him in appearance and background, Berle generally impressed others as being considerably younger than his thirty-seven years. His narrow-shouldered body had a somewhat unfinished look, as if its growth had been arrested in midadolescence, and his head appeared, by contrast with his torso, abnormally large, which augmented the general impression he gave of physical immaturity, though his general health was excellent and he was physically far stronger than he looked. His face was sharp-featured, sharp-eyed. His mouth, closed, wore a slightly smug, self-satisfied look, and it had in it an exceedingly sharp tongue, one that could pierce and slash sensitive psyches during his moments of irritation, though he seldom raised his voice. Not a few who had dealings with him were highly irritated by him. They deemed his manner arrogant and supercilious and looked upon him as a brash, cocky, obviously very bright schoolboy who had never quite grown up—a case of arrested emotional as well as physical development. Moley, who liked and admired him, nevertheless chuckled over somebody's description of him, years later, as an infant prodigy who remained an infant long after he ceased to be a prodigy, though in point of fact Berle never ceased to be a prodigy.[39]

His father, who had "a certain passionate energy" that "brought him into quite unnecessary conflict with all sorts and kinds of people," as the son once wrote,[40] was himself the son of a German immigrant of 1848. Adolf senior was a Harvard graduate, had taken a divinity degree at Oberlin, had been ordained a Congregational minister, and was serving a Boston church when Adolf junior was born. He continued in Boston through the first eight years of young Adolf's life, then served churches in nearby Salem and Shawmut for six years thereafter. The mother, née Mary Augusta Wright, the daughter of an Oberlin college professor of geology and theology, was a gentle soul, highly religious (she had done missionary work among the Sioux Indians before her marriage) but also highly intellectual. Life in the home of young Adolf's growing up was very much a life of the mind and spirit. Serious talk about "ideas" was the rule at the table; serious books by the score were in every room, it being the elder Berle's "theory" that no one should sit "in a comfortable chair" without finding "an interesting book within reach."[41] And both parents were concerned not only to encourage the intellectual growth of an eldest son who, in his earliest years, manifested genius, but also to encourage the development in him of moral sensitivity. They sought to instill in him the New England Calvinistic conscience by which each of them was ruled. They succeeded. Their son became when very young, and remained forever after, antihedonistic, anti-materialist, and as committed to helping those unable to help themselves as he was to reforming an economic system that created poverty by producing too much. For beneath his surface arrogance was much compassion; it would be felt by those who knew him in his relaxed, unchallenged moods, his students especially, and all children. His own student career could not have been more brilliant. Entering Harvard at age fourteen, he received his A.B. with highest honors when barely four months past his eighteenth birthday (1913), his M.A. from Harvard a year later, and his law degree from Harvard Law School, where his grade record was among the highest ever, in 1916. He then began to practice law, at age twenty-one, with the prestigious Boston firm of Brandeis, Dunbar, and Nutter.

Three years later he was in Paris as a member of the "expert staff" of the U.S. Peace Commission headed by Woodrow Wilson.

His intellectual brilliance had preserved him from shellfire after he'd enlisted in the Army Signal Corps very soon after American's entrance into the war. He was sent to officers' training school and in November 1917 was commissioned an infantry second lieutenant. He was then assigned to the Army War College in Washington, D.C., but was almost immediately placed on "inactive

duty" at the request of the War Industries Board so that he could go to the
Dominican Republic to search land titles and do other legal chores needed to
increase sugar production on the island. He acquired there a lifelong career-
influencing interest in Latin American affairs. Back in Washington, in the
summer of 1918, he was assigned to Army intelligence, where, through one of
those incredible flukes for which the military is notorious, he found himself
designated an expert in Russian economics. He quickly made himself into one,
of sorts, through intensive reading. And it was as a Russian expert that he went
to Paris. There he worked in a group that included, among others, Walter
Lippmann, William C. Bullitt, Isaiah Bowman, Samuel Eliot Morison, and
Christian Herter, and there he became one of the *Jeunesse Radicale* who
resigned from the commission in ostentatious protest against the terms of the
Versailles Treaty within days after they were announced.* It was "a futile
gesture," Berle recalled thirteen years later, but one for which he was "not
disposed to apologize. Inexperienced as we were . . . we did foresee . . . that
a treaty based on hatred and irritation . . . would produce nothing but long
drawn out misery."[42] His bitterness, his disillusionment, were profound.
" . . . I have come to the conclusion that no statement of ideals by anybody
will ever get any reaction from me again," he wrote his father from his room
in the Rue de Varennes on May 6, 1919. "If I can trust myself, I shall be happy;
if I trust anyone else, I shall be a fool."[43] And when he landed in New York
in July, honorably discharged after promotion to first lieutenant, his first major
act was to pen a savage indictment of the peacemakers, "The Betrayal at
Paris," which the *Nation* published the following month.

He was then twenty-four years old.

But if he was never again able to believe in any leader as he had believed
for a time in Woodrow Wilson, his essential Christian idealism, his concern
for social justice, remained unimpaired. When presented with an opportunity
to help the Pueblo Indians of New Mexico to defend their landholdings against
grab attempts by greedy interests in 1923, he at once seized it, though doing
so involved financial self-sacrifice. He took "a vacation" from the New York
City corporation law firm of Rounds, Hatch, Dillingham and Devoise, which
he had joined as an associate in the late summer of 1919.[44] He went to live with
the Pueblos for a while and worked out a plan, with implementing legislation,
which became national law. Under it, the Pueblos retain their land, with
mineral and water rights, to this day. He then left the Rounds firm to form,
in January 1924, in partnership with a lawyer he'd met in the Dominican
Republic, the law firm of Lippitt and Berle at 67 Wall Street. For three years
thereafter, until his marriage to Beatrice Bishop in December 1927, being
strapped for money (it took several years for the law firm to establish a good
business), he lived in Lillian Wald's famous Henry Street Settlement. There,

---

*See *FDR: The Beckoning of Destiny,* pages 567–570. Actually, technically, Berle as an army
officer could not "resign" his post, but he could and did ask to be relieved of his duties, a request
that, after some delay, was granted.

at Henry Street, he spent much of his free time working to good effect among neighborhood "slum kids," some of whom would remain profoundly grateful to him for the rest of their lives.

But it was his acceptance in 1925 of an invitation from the then brand-new Harvard School of Business to lecture one day a week in Cambridge on corporation finance that initiated the process whereby he was brought by Moley, seven years later, into the Roosevelt presidential campaign. For it was in connection with his lecture preparation that he began to contribute to the *Harvard Law Review* and, more frequently, to the *Columbia Law Review* articles critically descriptive of the growth and structure of large corporations, as well as articles on corporate financing practices that, though they violated no existing statute, did clearly violate ethical principles and threaten the good health of American democracy. The articles came to the attention of the Harvard economics professor William Z. Ripley, who, in a book he was writing, made extensive use of two of them, namely, "Problems of Non-Par Stock" (*Columbia Law Review*, January 1925) and "Non-voting Stock and 'Bankers Control' " (*Harvard Law Review*, April 1926). The book, *Main Street and Wall Street*, published in early 1927, created a great stir and was widely read. In that same year the Social Science Research Council, of whose organizing committee Ripley had been a member, began operations. With Ripley's encouragement and support, Berle applied to it for a research grant to study the modern corporation and its impact on society. Receiving the grant, with the stipulation that the research be conducted "in connection with some recognized university," he applied for and received a professorship at Columbia Law School. He also acquired as research assistant a young Harvard-trained economist named Gardiner C. Means, a candidate for a Harvard Ph.D. in economics, and, with contributions from Means so substantial as to make him an equal partner in the enterprise, completed the project in the form of a book entitled *The Modern Corporation and Private Property.*

The book, with Means listed as coauthor, had not yet been published when Moley tapped Berle for service as a Roosevelt adviser; it would not be published until the fall of 1932.[45] But much of its central thesis and supporting data was already widely known in the intellectual community, and especially among Columbia's law and social science faculties. Berle and Means had presented some of their findings as early as December 1929 in a paper entitled "Corporations and the Public Investor," presented at the annual meeting of the American Economic Association. Means had presented other findings in two articles, "The Growth in the Relative Importance of the Large Corporation in American Life" and "The Separation of Ownership and Control in American Industry," published in the *American Economic Review* (March 1931) and *Quarterly Journal of Economics* (November 1931), respectively.

At the beginning of 1930, reported Means in his *Economic Review* piece, the 200 largest nonfinancial corporations in the United States, each with gross assets of $80,000,000 or more (included were 97 industrial companies, 45 railroads, and 58 utilities), "controlled over 45 percent of the assets of all non-financial corporations, received over 40 percent of corporate income, controlled over 35 percent of all business wealth and between 15 and 25 percent of national wealth. Between 1909 and 1927, the assets of the two hundred largest increased more than twice as fast as the assets of other non-financial corporations. They reinvested a larger proportion of their earnings, secured a larger proportion of new capital in the open market, and increased in size through mergers. . . . If present rates of growth were to continue, 80 percent of non-financial corporate wealth would be in the hands of two hundred corporations by 1950." And in point of fact these "rates of growth" not only continued but accelerated. "Concentration appears to be proceeding more rapidly during depression than during prosperity," noted Berle in early 1932.[46] An overall consequence would be the virtually total replacement of what Means called the "trading market," that is, the "free market" of the classicists, by a "managed market," wherein it would be not *prices* but *production* that declined whenever demand decreased relative to supply.*

Berle studied in detail some of the effects of this development on the political process and the law. "Private property" as defined by Adam Smith had little or no application to the realities of the modern corporate world, he said, for there was a vast difference between an individual's ownership of a piece of tangible property and his possession of a "piece of paper" representing "little more than the loose expectation that a group of men, under a nominal duty to run the enterprise for his benefit and others like him, will actually observe this obligation." Certainly the individual stockholder had no means to *compel* performance of the named "duty": through a variety of legal devices he had been stripped "of virtually all his power within the corporation," such power being now the exclusive possession of corporation directors, officers, and, to a lesser degree, technicians in managerial posts. The stockholder's single decisive choice was between selling his stock and holding on to it. He must "look to the market" not only "for an appraisal of the expectations on . . . [his] security" but also "for . . . [his] chances of realizing them."[47] And even in the exercise of this meager power he was at the mercy of corporate directors and officers, who, possessed of prior "inside information" coupled with freedom to trade in the stock of their own companies, could and often did manipulate the market in ways that enriched them at the expense of the uninformed.

The social implications of this were disturbing, even frightening, to anyone committed to political democracy and human freedom. Some of them were

---

*The tendency was already manifested in statistical descriptions of economic changes between 1929 and 1932, though statistics enabling comparisons of trends in industrial production with trends in industrial prices are singularly difficult to obtain. It explains why, as Agriculture Secretary Hyde had pointed out (see pages 238–239), farm prices fell so much faster and farther than industrial prices between 1929 and 1932. Using figures for 1926 as an index number of 100, industrial production stood at 110 in 1929 and the cost of living at 97. By 1932, the comparable figures were 65 and 85. World wheat prices stood at 85 in 1929, at 42 in 1932. Note that industrial *production* fell much more than did the cost of living (wherein industrial prices are reflected) and that world *wheat prices* fell much more than the cost of living, wheat production remaining at approximately the same level during this period.

indicated in a document that was either the direct *incitement* of Moley's approach to Berle in early April 1932 or the direct *result* of that approach* —a memorandum written by Berle in collaboration with a young economist, Louis Faulkner, who was in the Security Research Department of the Bank of New York and Trust Company. Six hundred corporations now owned and operated 65 percent of all American industry, said the memorandum. Two hundred of them owned and operated nearly half. This meant "that some six thousand men, as directors of these corporations, virtually control American industry" as a whole; "eliminating the inactive directors, the number of men is reduced to not more than two thousand. These control perhaps 30% of the total national wealth; such wealth being the concentrated industrial wealth which dominates the life of eastern United States. . . . The true antithesis just now is not, as commonly stated, between the American system and Russian system. At the present rate of trend, the American and Russian systems will look very much alike within a comparatively short period—say twenty years. There is no great difference between having all industry run by a committee of Commissars and by a small group of Directors."[48]

Since this memorandum was destined to become one of the important papers in American history, as *The Modern Corporation and Private Property* would become one of the most influential books,† there is historical significance in the fact that in both the memorandum and the book there is a notable discrepancy or incongruity between description-of-problem and proposal-for-solution, or between diagnosis-of-ill and prescription-for-cure. The symptomatic and diagnostic description is bold, emphatic, sweeping, probing; the prescriptive solution is prudent to the point of timidity, tentative, narrow, superficial. And within the stated prescription itself there is a division and difference between the presentation of what *ought* to be done and the presentation of *how* to do it, the former being far clearer and firmer than the latter. Why this

---

*According to Berle's wife, Beatrice, he "was in a state of great ferment over the affairs of the world" in the early spring of 1932, was told by her that "he should find a customer for his ideas," and shortly thereafter "got together with some of the jr. economists of some N. Y. banks and they drew up a memorandum." Word of this "got around town and came to the notice of Raymond Moley." According to Moley, the memorandum was prepared at Moley's behest following a conference in Moley's office on April 25, 1932. Credence is given Beatrice Berle's account by the fact that Berle himself reviewed the diary entry (for October 6, 1932) in which it is given and made marginal notes that expanded upon and, in one instance, disagreed with what she said but that did *not* comment upon the statement quoted above. (See *Navigating the Rapids,* pages 50–51.) On the other hand, as all historians of the Roosevelt era know and are grateful for, Moley is in general scrupulously accurate in his presentation of specific fact and time sequence. (See *After Seven Years,* page 22.)

†In his review of it in the New York *Herald Tribune* (February 19, 1933), the historian Charles A. Beard averred that the book might "in time . . . be proclaimed the most important work bearing on American statecraft between the publication of the immortal 'Federalist' . . . and the opening of the year 1933. . . . Nothing less should be said in introduction to the public of this masterly achievement in research and contemplation." Wrote Max Ascoli of it in 1973, "It is difficult to describe what this book has done to the study of law and of economics in this country and all over the world. . . . [It] has acquired a sort of canonical quality, and, as with reproductions of traditional images of saints, real or marginal economists or sociologists feel obliged to give us their own versions."[49]

discrepancy? For one thing, of course, it is in general far easier to criticize than to create. For another, as would be much stressed by Marxist critics, Berle's wife was the daughter of a millionaire and Berle's was a Wall Street law practice: his private economic interests certainly militated against the holding of radical economic and political views and may well have inhibited his acceptance and unequivocal statement of what to others seemed the logical implications of the evidence he presented.

But the discrepancy is also due, and more so, to the nature of the Berle mind and temperament, which were very different from Tugwell's. Berle was certainly no atomist. He had no instinctive hostility to large-scale overall conceptions or to huge organizations of things and people. But neither was he a holist, naturally organismic in his thinking; grandeur *per se* had no strong attraction for him. His forte was analysis, not synthesis; he was far more perceptive of discrete elements of the prospect before him than he was of connections between or among them. Nor did he permit his imagination to soar in daring leaps while his soul vibrated, as Tugwell's often did, to a sense of destiny and the rhythms of history. He was in disposition a realist, not a romantic, with a profound distrust of the emotions as guides to conduct, his own most of all. Perhaps this was in tacit admission of what others deemed his emotional immaturity; perhaps it stemmed from his bitter observations of Woodrow Wilson's passionate idealism as it operated in 1919 to destroy great historic opportunities. In any case, having armed himself with hard specific facts, he was determined to keep his feet firmly on the ground as he advanced in rationally guided and measured steps toward goals small enough and near enough at hand to be, in their every feature, clearly and sharply definable.

The modern corporation was *not* a private enterprise, said Berle-Means. It was not absolutely owned, in the Adam Smith sense of "property," by either its stockholders or its executive management, nor even by the two together (the passive and active joined). For since its operations greatly affected the welfare of the community as a whole, the community as a whole "must" be involved in its decision-making processes and "must" be actively concerned with its control. But how? To what degree? Here Berle-Means, so precisely clear in their analytical descriptions, became lost in a fog of lawyer's prose: "When a convincing system of community obligations is worked out and is generally accepted, in that moment the passive property rights of today must yield before the larger interests of society. Should the corporate leaders, for example, set forth a program comprising fair wages, security to employees, reasonable service to their public, and stabilization of business, all of which would divert a portion of profits from the owners of passive property, and should the community generally accept such a scheme as a logical and human solution of industrial difficulties, the interests of passive property owners would have to give way." But what was meant by "must" and "would have to" in these sentences? Did they mean "must *necessarily*" or "would *inevitably*" through the automatic operations of a new kind of "hidden hand"? Or to put it another way, if "corporate leaders" failed to work out the indicated "program," would society do so and impose it upon them? If so, by what means? By socialization?

That Berle-Means inclined toward a "hidden hand" notion of "inevitability" seemed indicated by another passage in the book. The authors wrote that the survival of the corporate system seemed to require that " 'the control' of the great corporations should develop into a purely neutral technocracy, balancing a variety of claims by various groups in the community and assigning to each a portion of the income stream on the basis of public policy rather than private cupidity." Which seemed to echo Veblen's *Engineers and the Price System* without specifying how the "technocracy" was to be developed (would it be automatically generated?) in a way that would make it more sensitive to "public policy" than to "private cupidity."[50]

As for the Berle-Faulkner memorandum, having described "The Nature of the Difficulty" America was in, it proposed (1) "emergency" governmental measures to promote recovery from depression and (2) "long range" proposals to prevent depression's recurrence.

Among the "emergency" measures were proposals for the revitalization of "sterile" money—that is, hoarded cash, and deposits rendered stagnant by lending agencies' fearful need for "liquidity"—through increased security of savings and increased popular confidence in such security; for governmental loan and fiscal policies that would work toward providing relief for the unemployed while stimulating industry, largely through an increase of mass purchasing power, to increase employment; for reductions of local taxation to ease the urban and rural mortgage situations; and for the "federalization of marginal farms . . . by purchasing farms for taxes where the taxes are in default and the mortgagee, as frequently happens, is not prepared to take over the farm." There were two proposals for restoring health to the desperately sick railroads. One was for increased taxation of trucks, whose competition with railroads was unfair insofar as trucks, unlike railroads, did not maintain their own rights of way: Ripley had estimated that if railroads were replaced by trucks, "one ten-ton truck would pass every twenty seconds over every mile of improved road in the country," which meant that trucking could only supplement railroad freighting. The other proposal was for government financing of railroads joined with a consolidation of competing lines: " . . . if the government is to finance the railroad it can demand consolidation . . . and . . . abandonment of those lines which do not justify their economic existence." There was no suggestion of railroad nationalization.

In their introduction to the section on "long range" measures, Berle-Faulkner referred to Berle-Means. "The so-called 'cycle,' with periods of depression occurring in every decade, has reached a stage threatening to the safety of the American economic system," they wrote. "This is due to the fact that economic life has been, and still is, concentrating to a degree unparalleled in economic history. When most people are on farms, and business is small, a depression merely means a bad time. When most people are concentrated in cities, and most industry is concentrated in a few hundred very large units, depression means dislocation of the entire mechanism; millions of people literally without food and shelter; savings temporarily or permanently wiped out; wholesale misery and disturbance. There is a slow parallel between in-

creasing intensity of depressions in the cycles, and increasing economic concentration. Unless there is some reversal of trend, or some residual [*sic*]
control, some depression will ultimately cause a wholesale dislocation amounting to a revolution in fact, if not in name." Indeed, "[s]uch a dislocation could
take place next winter [that of 1932–1933]": there was about one chance in five
that it would! Which meant that the United States was now "[f]or the first time
. . . within hailing distance of revolution along continental European lines."[51]

As Berle and Tugwell both saw it, industrial concentration (collectivism)
was an inevitable consequence of the advance of scientific technology, though
Tugwell was far more emphatic on this point than Berle was. Neither of the
two accepted Brandeis' view that corporate "bigness" was more a creature of
permissive property law, which placed no restraints upon the operations of
power-lustful economic empire builders, than it was of technological "efficiency" and could therefore be undone and prevented by appropriate changes
in property law. Both not only stressed the fact that antitrust legislation had
notably failed "to discourage undue concentrations, and to protect small business," as the memorandum put it, they also asserted, especially Tugwell, that
such legislation was bound to fail, being unenforceable against the pressures
generated by technological advance within a private profit economy. Brandeis
to the contrary notwithstanding, the economic advantages (increased efficiency) of combinations and concentrations over small-unit production were
overwhelming and must *inevitably* lead to a mixture of monopoly and
oligopoly whose control in behalf of political democracy and the general
economic welfare was as increasingly difficult as it was increasingly necessary.

Nor was the process confined to industry. It operated also in agriculture, as
new and improved varieties of crops, breeds of livestock, fertilizers, pest-
controlling chemicals, farm machinery, and land-management techniques
were introduced by scientific technology. Here, too, larger and larger producing units were implied; here, too, the evident end would be combinations
sufficiently large to set prices through production controls. But because there
had been to begin with so many more competing productive units in agriculture than in industry (millions of farms compared with tens of thousands of
small industries) and because crop and livestock production was greatly
affected, as industrial production was not, by the weather and other factors
beyond human control, agricultural concentration proceeded more slowly
than industrial concentration. This speed differential resulted in chronic farm
depression, with a concomitant spread of rural slums and ruination of productive land through soil depletion and erosion, for it meant that the farmer must
sell his produce in a highly competitive market while buying industrial products, notably the increasingly expensive farm machinery he had to have, in
a managed one.*

---

*In talk sessions with FDR, Tugwell insisted, and Berle did not disagree, that it was the market
maladjustment between agriculture and industry that had brought on the Great Depression. The
farmer, with his shrunken purchasing power, had been unable to consume his proper share of

Thus the direly threatful "difficulty." How was it to be truly, permanently overcome?

Logically implied by the Berle-Means and Berle-Faulkner arguments, in the minds of many who studied them disinterestedly, was the need for profound structural changes in the economic system—changes that radically affected ownership and income-distribution patterns to ensure that mass production and mass consumption were properly matched; changes that made sure the general public and individual lives were served and not ruled or ruined by huge corporations that were "private" in name only but whose executive management had little or no public responsibility; changes that, overall, brought a planned, humanly purposive order out of the prevailing chaos of powerful forces. Clearly, America's choice in this matter was not between individualism and collectivism, not between *laissez-faire* and a planned economy, as Herbert Hoover would have Americans believe; it was between *kinds* of collectivism, *kinds* of concentrated productive power, *kinds* of economic planning. Operated in terms of the total human person, the collectives could become instruments of intelligently humane control over technology. Operated exclusively, as they now tended to be, in terms of the lowest common denominators, the physical appetites, of human beings, they could become instruments of a mindless domination of society *by* technology, with human lives and purposes subordinate to the machine's laws of operation, the machine's "convenience." And the choice between these alternatives must be made, could only be made, in the realm of public policy.

Such in general was the conclusion of members of the League for Independent Political Action, which Berle and Tugwell's Columbia colleague John Dewey had helped found, and of which Dewey was the first president, in early September 1929, nearly two months *before* the stock-market crash. It was the theme of a series of articles Dewey had contributed to the *New Republic* in March and April 1931, articles with such titles as "The Need for a New Party," "The Breakdown of the Old Order," "Who Might Make a New Party," and "Policies of a New Party." It was the theme of a book by Paul Douglas, *The Coming of a New Party,* the manuscript of which was delivered to its publisher while Berle-Faulkner were writing their memorandum and about which, after it came out in August 1932, Tugwell would have one of his most memorable private talks with Roosevelt. It was also essentially the theme of Stuart Chase's *A New Deal,* excerpts of which were published serially in the *New Republic* beginning June 29 (the book came out in August), though Chase had a far greater bias toward total national planning and control by "technocrats,"*

---

industrial goods. The disastrous offset of this inability had been inadequately secured American loans abroad, creating foreign markets for the domestic "surplus." And the realization that these loans were not going to be paid back, suddenly widespread in 1929, had caused the Crash.

*Chase's book, which went through four sizable printings within seven weeks after its publication, quoted as an epigraph in the front matter Veblen's *The Engineers and the Price System* (1921): "In effect, the progressive advance of this industrial system towards an all-inclusive mechanical balance of interlocking processes appears to be approaching a critical pass, beyond which it will somewhat along the lines of the Soviet Union's Gosplan, than either Douglas or Dewey. The latter, in their politics, were definitely "people-oriented" rather than "machine-oriented." They envisioned a People's (Populist) Party of laborers, white-collar workers, professional people, small-business men, and intellectuals; they insisted one was needed because (1) neither of the major parties was responsive to the needs of the great mass of the citizenry; (2) neither admitted that *laissez-faire* capitalism had collapsed, much less realized that the disaster provided opportunity for building a new and better order; and (3) the Socialist Party, with whose program as enunciated by Thomas both Dewey and Douglas were sympathetic, was so torn by factional strife and handicapped by long-nurtured deep-seated popular prejudices against its very name that it could not grow soon into a major force in American political life. The new party would consciously aim toward a cooperative society in which the individual realized himself as a creative element of human community, a society whose economy was planned and controlled by professionals truly representative of the needs and desires of the people as a whole.

No major structural changes toward such an end were proposed by Berle-Faulkner, however. Indeed, the memorandum's so-called "long range" proposals were only somewhat more so in actual fact than the "emergency" ones, and they penetrated but little farther toward root causes. The implicit general aim was to remove and prevent "abuses" of the prevailing system of production and distribution, rendering it more efficient and "fair" in its operations, without significantly modifying the class structure, that is, the self-perpetuating patterns of ownership and direction, that the system had generated. Certainly the adoption of *all* the suggested measures would not significantly increase social controls over technological applications, and it was predictable that those that would result in *any* such increase, however slight, would be hard put to pass through Congress against the organized hostility of big business.

Thus one "long range" proposal was for federal legislation requiring "[p]ublicity of corporate accounts and stock transactions" for all industries "concentrated to the point where properties are primarily represented by securities listed on stock exchanges or bond markets." Since the stock exchange is "in reality the paying and receiving teller window of a great savings bank" as well as "the measure of value of savings held by individuals and institutions the country over," it violated "the underlying function of these markets" to permit them to be manipulated, "especially by the individuals in charge of the industries in question." Enforced publicity would prevent this, in large part. The proposal had wide and strong support, even within the financial community: it could probably be adopted fairly easily. Another proposal was for sufficient federal regulation of security issuance to

---

no longer be practicable to leave its control in the hands of business men working at cross purposes for private gain, or to entrust its continued administration to others than suitably trained technological experts, production engineers without a commercial interest."

prevent the unloading of "unsound securities" upon an uninformed or misinformed public—to prevent, in other words, such outrages of common honesty and decency as the great Charles E. Mitchell of the National City Bank had recently admitted to, with no visible shame, in testimony before the U.S. Senate Committee on Finance, namely, the sale to individuals at substantial prices of foreign bonds known to be suspect and ultimately proved worthless.* There should be established, said the memorandum, a "Capital Issues Board which would perform the functions of a federal Blue Sky Commission, exacting full information about securities sold." This reform, too, had wide support even in financial circles and might therefore win early adoption. Also widely and firmly supported, hence also likely of adoption in the not so distant future, despite vehement opposition to them in certain quarters, were the memorandum's proposals for (1) formal recognition of the Soviet Union through negotiations that would open Russian markets for American goods, (2) tying war debt cancellation to new tariff agreements aiming toward free trade between Western European countries and the United States, and (3) tariff reduction or abolition in cases where a "scientific study" showed tariffs were needless or injurious when judged in terms of the general public good.

No such support was given, however, and no such probability or possibility of early adoption attended, the three Berle-Faulkner suggestions that would effect some degree, a small but significant degree, of actual structural change. One was for the establishment of central banking—a chain-banking system modeled after England's, Australia's, and Canada's whereby central administrative control would give "to each unit in the system the advantage of the liquidity of the entire system."† Another was for "amendment" of the antitrust laws "to permit consolidations and even monopolies at will," but with the proviso that when any industry was so concentrated that 50 percent or more of the interstate market for its product was dominated by two corporations "or less," with "corporation" defined to include any group of corporate units "under the same control," those corporations would "be subject to federal regulation." The third proposal was for government old-age, sickness, and unemployment insurance. "The theory that such insurance is unnecessary and unwise is based on the premise that individual action at liberty is the best safeguard of the individual," argued the memorandum. "Where businesses are largely [sic] small and competitive, this may be true. In concentrated industry, the individual has no real liberty of action; he is at the mercy of a uniform system with which he cannot possibly cope."⁵²

*Tens of millions were lost by individuals who bought foreign bonds through the National City Bank and National City Company, purchases promoted by every art of salesmanship and from which the underwriting institutions garnered substantial fees. The bank and company bought few of them (a mere $350,000 worth overall) to hold in their own vaults, a clear indication that they looked upon these securities as dubious investments.

†Canada, with its ten central banks and 3,000 branches, suffered not a single bank failure from 1930 through 1933. Upwards of 9,000 banks failed in the United States during this same period.

It was on a bright afternoon in early April that Berle made *his* first train journey to Albany in the company of Moley and Tugwell. He approached the throne of power in the Executive Mansion with considerably less awe and trepidation than Tugwell or even Moley had felt, for he had absolutely no desire for personal political power, covert or overt, and he shared with most academic intellectuals at that time a conviction that Newton D. Baker was far better suited for the White House than Franklin D. Roosevelt.

He indicated as much to Moley when the latter initially approached him.

"I have another candidate for president," he said, intending to refuse Moley's request.

Bluntness provoked sharpness.

"We're not asking for your political support," replied a nettled Moley, "which carries not the slightest weight in any case. What we'd *like* is your technical assistance."

Taken aback, Berle stared, then grinned as his sense of humor rose up to overwhelm his hauteur. Suddenly he laughed aloud, "nodded energetically, . . . and enlisted," as Moley later recalled.[53]

His preference for Baker remained, however, even after he had been repeatedly exposed to Roosevelt's mental processes and personal charm. It was *only* as a technical adviser that he was enlisted after he had justified his reputation for knowledgeable brilliance during the very first evening he spent in the governor's presence (the subject of discussion that night was monetary policy; Roosevelt was "flirting" with the "idea" of currency inflation, Berle would remember) and had also demonstrated qualities without which such brilliance would have had little immediate utilitarian value, namely, in Moley's words, "toughness of . . . mind, . . . energy, and . . . ability to organize material well."[54]

VII

ON Sunday afternoon, April 24, 1932, Moley and Roosevelt sat in easy chairs facing each other in the small first-floor sitting room of Roosevelt's East Sixty-fifth Street house. The governor, his thinning gray-streaked hair wreathed in smoke from the cigarette whose quill-stemmed six-inch holder was clenched between his teeth, dealt simultaneously with several matters, as was his wont. Last-minute preparations were being made for his trip to Richmond, Virginia, and for the Warm Springs vacation that was to follow, he having already prepared for his brief return to New York to testify in court on Broderick's behalf. He issued occasional directions to his dark-hued valet, Irwin McDuffie, who, packing for the journey southward, was in and out of the room. He glanced over and arranged some papers on the small table beside him. He gave the remainder of his divided attention to a seemingly casual conversation with pipe-smoking Moley.

"It seems a shame," said the governor, "that I must be away from New York for almost a month."

If he didn't go to Warm Springs now, however, he would be unable to do so until after the election, and he needed rest before "entering a campaign."

Moley, sucking his pipe, signified with a nod his sympathetic understanding.

But, continued the governor, why don't "you fellows" just "go ahead . . . as though I were here, seeing people and getting stuff together?" They might then put the "stuff" together in a memorandum and send it down for his study in Warm Springs. That way he would not "get too far behind in my homework." (Thus did he acknowledge the fact that he "went to school.")

Again Moley nodded. Fine, he said. But he was cautious. Whom precisely did Roosevelt mean by "you fellows"?

"Well, Sam, of course, and Doc, I suppose," Roosevelt replied. " . . . And Rex, and Berle."

Rex could "go on with his farm thing," though without being limited to that. Berle "could work up something on debt and finance," as well as on corporations and the stock market. As for Moley himself, "you put in whatever you want and pull the whole thing together so that it makes sense politically." He looked up at the professor, his eyes twinkling behind pince-nez spectacles. "Which makes you chairman, I guess, of my privy council."

His lips twitched, broadened. "My *privy* council!" he repeated. And roared with laughter.

He used the same phrase with the same wicked glee when he talked with Sam Rosenman that same afternoon, a few minutes after Moley had left the house. He also repeated his "hope my being away in Warm Springs will not stop any of you from going right ahead." He then underscored the deadline he had suggested to Moley, asking Rosenman to "come down for a week end" at Warm Springs three weeks hence, bringing with him the fruits of the "privy council's" labors.

He would not soon tire of a joke Moley found unfunny to begin with: he continued to call the advisory group his "privy council" until, in September, James M. Kieran of the New York *Times,* while covering the annual picnic for newsmen at Val Kill Cottage, reported for the first time the group's existence and the names of some of its members. Kieran dubbed it the "brains department." Four days later, enlarging on the subject in another despatch, Kieran referred to Moley as the "recognized chief" of Roosevelt's "brains trust." Roosevelt then abandoned the old label in favor of this new one, which, with the "s" generally removed from "brains," became famous in history.[55]

IO

-->>X<<--

The Genesis of a "New Deal" in the Campaign of 1932: Part One

I

THE next day, Tugwell, Berle, and Moley, meeting in Moley's small and crowded Barnard College office, mapped out the work they were to do for Roosevelt, with editorial assistance from Rosenman. Arduous indeed was the intellectual labor that ensued. A "detailed and specific" memorandum was prepared on each of eleven topics—"agriculture, tariff, banking, finance, money, international debts, power, relief, railroads, governmental economy, and presidential powers"—with each member of the triumvirate responsible for three or four of these. Each enlisted aid from others possessed of expert knowledge. Among them were Paul Mazur of Lehman Brothers;* Columbia's Howard Lee McBain, an authority on constitutional law; Columbia's James W. Angell, an authority on foreign exchange, who was a son of the president of Yale; Columbia's James C. Bonbright, Roosevelt's appointee to the New York Power Authority; Columbia's Joseph D. McGoldrick, an expert in government finance; and Henry Morgenthau, Jr., who worked with Tugwell on agricultural policy. Moley, in addition to the specific topical memoranda he had helped prepare, wrote out "a broad philosophic statement" to serve as a general introduction to the memoranda collection—a statement in which the phrase "a new deal" was used for the first time by a member of the Roosevelt entourage. The present depression, "[u]nlike most," had produced "as yet ... only a few of the disorderly manifestations," wrote Moley. But the "orderly and hopeful spirit" of the people that had thus far prevented "wild radicalism" was by no means inexhaustible. Real change was demanded. "Reaction is no barrier against the radical. It is a challenge and a provocation. It is not the pledge of *a new deal* [emphasis added]; it is the reminder of broken promises. Its unctious [*sic*] reassurances of prosperity round the corner are not oil on troubled waters; they are oil on fire." In its key passage the statement echoed, perhaps unwittingly, Bryan's "Cross of Gold" and an address Roosevelt himself had made at a banquet of the Democratic National Committee on May 29, 1919, when he was Assistant Secretary of the Navy. Bryan had said in 1896 that men must choose between two theories of government, one holding that "if you will only legislate to make the well-to-do prosperous, their prosperity will leak through on those below," the other (the "Democratic idea") holding that "if you legislate to make the masses prosperous, their prosperity will find

---

*This is the same Paul Mazur whose rosy view of New Era economics, change of mind following the Crash, and genius for garbled metaphor are presented on page 113.

its way up through every class which rests upon them." Moley said in 1932, "There are two ways of viewing the government's duty in matters dealing with economic life. The first sees to it that a favored few are helped and that some of their prosperity will leak through to labor, to the farmer, to the small businessman. This is the main theory of the Republican Party. It was the theory of the Federalists against whom Jefferson led his victorious party. And it is, I assert, the theory of some of those Democrats who are ready to call those who do not agree with it 'demagogues.' It belongs to the party of reaction, of Toryism, and now the party of ruined prosperity. But it is not, and never should be, the theory of the Democratic Party." Roosevelt in his 1919 address had spoken of a twenty-five-year battle between liberals (progressives) and conservatives (reactionaries) within each of the major political parties, a battle for control in which conservatism and reaction had triumphed in the Republican Party, while liberalism and progressivism triumphed in the Democratic Party. He had also spoken of the disastrous consequences for the Democracy of attempts in 1904 "to reconcile the conservative wing of the party" in the wake of the Bryanism of 1896 and 1900. He had concluded that "from that day on, it became evident that the Democracy of the United States was and is and must be a progressive Democracy." Moley echoed this belief as he now said that there was "no room in this country for two reactionary parties" and that the alternative to Republican reaction "should be a party of liberal thought, of planned action, of enlightened international principles, of . . . democratic principles."[1]

On May 19, the product of all this labor was packed into a suitcase that Rosenman took with him as he boarded a train for Newman, Georgia, where Roosevelt and Missy LeHand would meet him and then drive him forty miles to Warm Springs. It was a product of which the laborers were proud, and justly so: it added up to a fairly definite and coherent program for action against the depression in accordance with stated liberal principles. And for it Roosevelt was grateful, and by it he was relieved of some of his most profound anxieties, when he reviewed it with care and discussed it with Rosenman in detail on May 21. He was to give a major speech in Atlanta the next day, a commencement address at Oglethorpe University on which national attention would inevitably be focused. The memoranda he now reviewed, especially Moley's introductory one, confirmed him in the decision he had made to use practically verbatim, at Oglethorpe, a draft speech prepared for him by Ernest K. Lindley.

The genesis of the latter was both interesting and pyschologically revealing.

A week or so before, there had been a typically exuberant Rooseveltian picnic at Dowdell's Knob on Pine Mountain, above Warm Springs.* Guests of the governor and Missy that day were the four newsmen who had come

---

*Roosevelt owned a 1,750-acre farm atop Pine Mountain and had laid out across his land a road to the Knob, a remarkably lovely lookout point, which became for Warm Springs patients, and Roosevelt, *the* picnic place of the area.

down with them from New York City, including Kieran of the *Times* and Lindley of the *Herald Tribune*. The latter had staked a major portion of his professional reputation on Roosevelt's performing in accordance with the warmly admiring portrait drawn in *Franklin D. Roosevelt: A Career in Progressive Democracy*. He was personally stung by the charges of political hypocrisy and timidity that his *Herald Tribune* colleague Walter Lippmann currently hurled with persuasive force against the governor as presidential candidate. He was himself persuaded that Roosevelt's speeches thus far, save for perhaps two minutes of the "Forgotten Man," had been the opposite of bold and forthright in their expressions of conviction on issues. And he said so to Roosevelt, good-humoredly but seriously and emphatically, during the fun-filled afternoon on Dowdell's Knob. Roosevelt was defensive, Lindley persistent, and when the other three newsmen supported Lindley's view, Roosevelt issued a challenge. He had the Oglethorpe speech coming up. He had in hand for it only some biographical notes on James Oglethorpe that Moley had sent him. He needed a draft and, "if you fellows think my speeches are so bad, why don't *you* write one for me?" He looked hard at Lindley, who replied defiantly, "All right, I will!"

Lindley did so within the next two days.[2]

And so it was that Roosevelt addressed to "my fellow members of the Class of 1932" at Oglethorpe on May 22 words that marched as far to the left as had key phrases of the "Forgotten Man," and in greater density, while making their way toward a purely empirical, essentially noncommittal conclusion.

He spoke of the "gigantic waste" that had accompanied our industrial advance—"the superfluous duplication of productive facilities, the continual scrapping of still useful equipment, the tremendous mortality in industrial and commercial undertakings, the thousands of dead-end trails into which enterprise has been lured, the profligate waste of natural resources"—and asserted that "much of it . . . could have been prevented by . . . a larger measure of social planning." Such "forces" of control and direction as had been "developed in recent years" were concentrated "to a dangerous degree in groups having special interests . . . which do not coincide with the interests of our nation as a whole," small groups of men "whose chief outlook upon the social welfare . . . deserves the adjectives 'selfish' and 'opportunistic.'" Hence the "tragic irony," the "awful paradox" whereby, amid "a superabundance of raw materials" and more than ample yet idle facilities for the manufacture and transport of needed goods, "millions of able-bodied men and women, in dire need, are clamoring for the opportunity to work." He rejected "the theory that the periodic slowing down of our economic machine is one of its inherent peculiarities" that men must suffer because "to tamper" with the machinery would inevitably "cause even worse ailment." Acceptance of such theory "requires . . . greater faith in immutable economic law and less faith in the capacity of man to control what he had created than I, for one, have." Actually it was "well within the inventive capacity of man, who has built up this great social and economic machine," to ensure its working for the general welfare. He rather more than hinted at currency inflation as one means by which we might "again set into motion that machine." Certainly "we must meet straightforwardly" the fact that there had been in the last three years a "drastic change in the value of our monetary unit in terms of . . . commodities" and must choose between the alternatives that this "drastic change" presented to us. For it was "self-evident that we must either restore commodities to a level approximating their dollar value of several years ago or . . . continue the destructive process of reducing, through defaults or through deliberate writing down, obligations assumed at a higher price level."

He also more than hinted an acceptance of the then growing belief among liberal economists that America's was a "mature economy" and that this is what rendered social and economic planning so urgently necessary. " . . . it seems to me probable that our physical economic plant will not expand in the future at the same rate at which it . . . expanded in the past," he said. "We may build more factories, but the fact remains that we have enough now to supply all our domestic needs, and more, if they are used." The "oversufficiency" of capital, especially of "speculative" capital, had had as a concomitant "an insufficient distribution of buying power," which meant "that in the future we are going to think less about the producer and more about the consumer," shifting our national policy emphasis from capital to labor, from profits to wages. " . . . the reward for a day's work will have to be greater, on the average, than it has been, and the reward to capital, especially capital that is speculative, will have to be less." In these circumstances there was urgent need for "true leadership" that recognized the further urgent need "of planning for definite objectives."

But "[l]et us not confuse objectives with methods," said Roosevelt in what were evidently his own words, inserted in the Lindley draft, and he promptly repeated the admonition: "Do not confuse objectives with methods," which might itself have confused and alarmed some who heard him. It suggested a distinction between ends and means in the speaker's mind so sharp as to destroy a necessary connection between the two, so wide as to open a gap in what should, what must in the actual world, be a flowing continuity. In such a gap, all manner of contradiction might grow. Roosevelt at once made it clear, however, that he himself saw the dissociation of "objective" from "method" as simply the breaking of a chain of bondage, a release from fearful and foolish consistency into an area of multiple and multiplying options. Lifting high his head, raising his voice to singing pitch, he spoke the words for which his address would be chiefly remembered. "The country needs and, unless I mistake its temper, the country demands bold, persistent experimentation," cried Franklin Roosevelt. "It is common sense to take a method and try it: If it fails, admit it and try another. But above all try something." He hinted at ominous consequences if the prevailing governmental inaction continued; yesterday's reading and discussion of the Moley memorandum encouraged him to do so. "The millions who are in want," he said, "will not stand silently by forever while the things to satisfy their needs are within easy reach."[3]

The speech provoked reactions as strong, pro and con, as the "Forgotten Man" had done. Millions of distressed Americans heard its words as the speaker intended them to be heard—as a hopeful departure from the attitude of helplessness in the face of calamity, of abject submission to the incomprehensible uncontrollable "machine," which seemed to them to dominate the current administration. Others heard them as a confession that he who spoke them had no "definite objectives" in mind, much less any definite plans for reaching them. Among these last was an editorialist of the New York *Times,* whose opinion was published on May 24. The governor's "one firm conclusion," wrote the editorialist, "was 'above all try something.' " But something unspecified is not better than nothing," and Roosevelt's begging people to "try something" would only encourage a proliferation of pet nostrums and private panaceas. Experience had shown that "the man most to be avoided in a time of crisis is the one who goes about wringing his hands and demanding that something be done without explaining or knowing what can or ought to be done." Yet others were alarmed, not because the speech was vague and indefinite in its prescriptions, but for a precisely opposite reason: it seemed to them only too clear and definite in its indication that the speaker as President would abandon "sound money" in favor of "currency tinkering" (he might commit the ultimate sacrilege of taking America off the gold standard altogether!), joining this with measures that would effect drastic changes in income distribution patterns, drastic shifts in the foci of economic and political power. Virginia's Senator Carter Glass, one of the architects of the Federal Reserve system in the first term of Woodrow Wilson and the obvious choice for Secretary of the Treasury in any Democratic administration, was among those who felt this way.

Nor did the speech please Roosevelt's closest longtime friend and adviser. Louis Howe was, in fact, outraged: he phoned from New York City on May 23 to let the candidate in Georgia know that in his view the speech was an appalling piece of political stupidity. It was especially so in its ringing call for "bold, persistent experimentation." Such "radical" tone would no doubt gratify some who were already in Roosevelt's camp, people whose support for the nomination he could absolutely count on in any case. Others, however, would be frightened away by it. The speech would attract none to take their places, and Roosevelt, with the nominating convention only little more than a month away, could not afford to lose a single convention vote. He had already lost many that had seemed firmly in his grasp eight weeks ago.

Two days later, Roosevelt left Warm Springs for Albany, where he promptly met with Moley, Berle, Tugwell, Rosenman, and Angell in a long evening session at the Executive Mansion to discuss and largely adopt as his economic policy directive the Berle-Faulkner memorandum. A few days after that, on June 5, a Sunday, he held an unpublicized conference in Hyde Park with sixteen purely political advisers to make decisions on convention strategy, decisions that would be proved by the event to be of crucial importance.[5]

II

How did it happen that Roosevelt's candidacy, so brilliantly lighted by confident hope in early April, was shadowed by lowering clouds of misfortune in early June, his chance for nomination reduced from near certainty to little more than fifty-fifty?

He himself was in good part to blame—he whose greatest boast was his mastery of the art of politics.

The first state to list its delegates in the Roosevelt column was Washington, where Scott Bullitt of Seattle* did yeoman's labor on Roosevelt's behalf: Washington's sixteen votes had gone to the governor in state convention in early February. There had followed an unbroken string of Roosevelt triumphs —in New Hampshire, Minnesota, North Dakota, Georgia, Iowa, and Maine. The New Hampshire triumph, for which the superb politicking of the national committeeman and national committee secretary Robert Jackson was largely responsible, had been especially sweet: Al Smith's forces, strong in Manchester and other large New Hampshire towns, had waged a hard fight for the state and had been aided by an Election Day snowstorm, which reduced the rural vote, yet had won only 9,000 votes for their man, as compared with 14,500 for Roosevelt. Thus seven states were in Roosevelt's column by April 1, and the "Stop Roosevelt" movement, obviously demoralized, appeared on the verge of disintegration. Ralph Hayes, whose relationship with Newton Baker was somewhat analogous to Howe's with Roosevelt (Hayes had been assistant to the Secretary of War in Wilson's Cabinet), was operating as Baker's unacknowledged "dark horse" campaign manager, aided and abetted in this enterprise by Walter Lippmann. Hayes was near despair, agreeing with Lippmann in late March "that Roosevelt's strength has reached perilous proportions and is in danger of turning into a sweep." Soon after, two "favorite sons" removed themselves as obstacles to Roosevelt's nomination: Joseph T. Robinson of Arkansas, Smith's running mate in 1928, unequivocally withdrew from the contest, and Kentucky's Alben Barkley not only withdrew but also declared his support of Roosevelt. In addition, there were plausible rumors that Al Smith himself was considering a withdrawal of his statement of "availability."[6]

At this juncture, Roosevelt, with the advice and consent of Howe, decided to challenge directly the Raskob-Shouse control of party convention machinery.

In Chicago on April 4 a meeting of the Democratic National Committee's subcommittee on arrangements was held. It was authorized to choose the convention's temporary chairman, who would deliver the keynote address, would preside until the permanent chairman was chosen by the convention, and whose rulings from the chair, which could be overturned only by a two-thirds vote of the delegates, might be decisive of the seating of disputed

*He was of the Philadelphia Bullitts, a brother of William C. He died before that year, 1932, was ended.

delegations as of other highly important matters during the organization period. Though appointed by Raskob, most of the subcommittee members were for Roosevelt (the national chairman had been persuaded he could not weather the storm his choice of an anti-Roosevelt majority would have provoked); yet their voting of Shouse into the temporary chairmanship had seemed a foregone conclusion. He had canvassed for the post, no opposition to his selection had been indicated by Roosevelt's managers during the preceding weeks, and he had obtained enough seemingly firm vote commitments from subcommittee members during those weeks to assure his getting what he wanted.

He didn't get it, however.

Jim Farley, who was not a subcommittee member, and Bob Jackson, who was and who theretofore had been on friendly, even cordial, terms with Shouse, came as a team to Chicago, where, in the morning of April 4, a confident Shouse proposed himself as keynoter, citing past services to the party that surely entitled him to such honor. He mentioned only to dismiss reports in the "Republican press" during the last few hours that Roosevelt preferred Alben Barkley. Jackson then arose to make it clear that Roosevelt *did* prefer Barkley, also that the choice between Shouse and Barkley derived "political significance" from the fact that an organized attempt was being made to prevent Roosevelt's nomination.

Tempers at once rose high. There loomed another disastrous intraparty fracas.

In its impending shadow, Virginia's Harry Byrd suggested a compromise: the subcommittee would recommend Barkley as keynoter, such recommendation having the force of actual appointment, while recommending Shouse for the post of permanent chairman, the latter recommendation having no such actual force as the former. It *would* have such force, however, in the prevailing circumstances, if Roosevelt supported it, and Shouse promptly demanded that it be personally ratified by Roosevelt before the vote on it was taken. So Farley phoned Roosevelt in Albany, who listened carefully, calculatedly, to the proposed resolution, then approved it with a slight change of wording: "commend," he said, should be substituted for "recommend" in reference to Shouse. He explained at some length to Farley an alleged difference of meaning between the two words. It was a difference too subtle for Shouse to grasp, if, indeed, Shouse even noticed that a change had been made. (And *is* there any difference, really? By common usage, one is "commended" for past performance and "recommended" for future preferment, but if the two words are used in this sense, the substitution of "commend" for "recommend" makes nonsense of the compromise resolution. Only precise dictionary definitions would seem to apply here, archaic ones at that, and according to these, the two words are interchangeable: "commend" means "to recommend," and "recommend" means "to commend.") Hence, in the press announcement he issued at the meeting's close, Shouse simply said that the subcommittee had unanimously decided "to recommend . . . the selection of Senator A. W. Barkley for temporary chairman and of Jouett Shouse as permanent chairman of the convention," an outcome widely interpreted as either a defeat of Roosevelt's forces or else a magnanimous concession by Roosevelt to Raskob-Shouse.[7]

The latter interpretation was the more plausible at that moment. Certainly Roosevelt seemed in a position to be magnanimous. In Wisconsin on April 5, thanks in part to defections to him of La Follette Progressives, he won all twenty-six of the state's delegates, though he had been expected to lose at least five to Smith. He was now expected to make a clean sweep of the remaining New England delegations. And despite the fact that the California primary, upcoming on May 3, had become a three-man race—Garner, Smith, Roosevelt —predictions were being confidently made that Roosevelt would win California's forty-four delegate votes, thus assuring his nomination on the first ballot. Party unity behind the leader was being called for by prominent Democrats, including some who had been fervent supporters of Smith. One of them was Nevada's Senator Key Pittman, who said on the front page of the New York *Times*, three days after the Chicago subcommittee meeting, that "selfish friends" had maneuvered Smith into a "humiliating position" and, for his sake as for the party's, should cease promoting his candidacy. This statement may have been the final encouragement of Roosevelt's managers to announce the next day that they were breaking their prior agreement with Connecticut's Governor Wilbur Cross, a Smith supporter, to divide Connecticut's delegation between Smith and Roosevelt when it was chosen in state convention; instead, they now wanted *all* of Connecticut's delegates, voting as one for Roosevelt under the unit rule.[8]

But this last note of supreme confidence was sounded at the high point of Roosevelt's nomination campaign. From that point the fall was swift and, in the view of the convention's two-thirds rule, dangerously far.

Instead of withdrawing from the race, Al Smith, as we have seen, his symbolic brown derby now definitely discarded in favor of silk hat and tails, was provoked into an intensely active campaign by the alleged "demagoguery" of Roosevelt's Forgotten Man. On April 9 he published vehement letters to his supporters in Connecticut, Pennsylvania, and California denouncing as false propaganda allegations that he was not a serious candidate. He was a forceful presence at the New York State Democratic convention that met in Albany in mid-April to select delegates-at-large to the national convention; and he was himself named a delegate-at-large (Roosevelt had declined nomination to such a post out of a "delicacy" he had hoped Smith would share). Moreover, he was unmistakably demonstrated to be, in a meeting dominated by John Curry, Tammany's preference over Roosevelt for the presidential nomination, despite his past attacks upon the Curry-Walker regime and despite Roosevelt's attempts to appease that same regime. One evidence of this was the distinct setback dealt Roosevelt when, without consulting him in advance, the state convention leaders pushed through a Prohibition-repeal resolution that Roosevelt in his circumstances could not do other than emphatically endorse, yet whose "wringing wet" language seemed designed to offend his supporters in the dry Democracy of the South, the West, and rural America generally.[9]

Clearly, then, little or nothing had been gained by Roosevelt's otherwise costly dealings, or refusals to deal, with New York City's "local problem." As a matter of fact, faced with the growing probability that Seabury would soon demand Walker's removal on incontrovertible grounds of corruption, the governor as candidate was in a far weaker position, a far more dangerous situation, than he would have been if he had *not* continued patronage cooperation with Curry, had *not* manifest a reluctance to remove Sheriff Farley, had *not* flatly refused to remove Sheriff McQuade, had *not* publicly denounced civic reformers who pressed him to act, had *not* cavalierly dismissed last year the charges preferred by these same reformers against the mayor, but had instead acted promptly, directly, forcefully, as he was officially empowered and obligated to act, against evident criminality.

And this state convention setback was for him but the beginning of a series of misfortunes.

In the following week Roosevelt was forced to reap the crop of bitter weeds sprung up from seed he himself had impulsively grasped and sown with a reckless hand upon the stony soil of Massachusetts when he yielded to the blandishments of Boston's colorful, charming, corrupt Mayor James M. Curley during his train ride from New York City to Boston in June 1931. The political alliance he formed then had been strengthened with personal familial ties when Curley "adopted" Roosevelt's eldest son, James, as a business and political protégé. The mayor helped establish James in the insurance business in Boston; he guided—or misguided—James, who became his father's official state campaign manager, through the intricacies of Bay State politics. And it was at Curley's insistence that Roosevelt entered the Massachusetts primary and then, instead of safely contenting himself with second-choice commitments from delegates, permitted the mounting of an intense campaign against Smith in a state whose predominantly Catholic Democracy was overwhelmingly and passionately devoted to Al. Too late for retreat or compromise did Roosevelt realize that Massachusetts' Governor Joseph B. Ely and Senator David I. Walsh, between whom and Curley was bitterest enmity, were the truly dominant figures in Commonwealth Democracy and that Curley, as Bob Jackson wrote to Roosevelt, had no political force whatever outside the metropolis. On primary day, April 26, Roosevelt's by-then expected defeat turned out to be of unexpectedly, humiliatingly huge proportions: Smith trounced him three to one![10]

Nor was his Massachusetts humiliation relieved by the outcome of Pennsylvania's presidential primary and delegate race, also held on April 26. He had been expected to defeat Smith in Pennsylvania by a wide margin. But there, too, his fortunes had become intermingled with those of a politician, the once all-powerful Joseph Guffey, who headed one of two warring factions. In consequence, he emerged with only a narrow victory over Smith in the preferential primary and with only forty-odd of the state's seventy-eight delegates instead of the sixty-odd that had been predicted for him.

These events so shadowed Roosevelt's path to Chicago that its end in the convention was obscured. Through the gloom he denied existed, Jim Farley claimed still to see clearly, straight ahead, a first-ballot Roosevelt nomination; but Louis Howe, his nerves tightened to near breaking point, saw no such thing. He shuddered at the now distinct possibility that his beloved Franklin would not be nominated at all! And this possibility loomed larger to present vision as the shadows deepened in the days immediately following. On May 2, Rhode Island announced itself a Smith state: a party convention there rejected a pro-Roosevelt delegation by the humiliating vote of 173 to 23, which meant ten delegate votes for Smith. The next day, in the California primary, John Nance Garner won the state's forty-four delegates (in the final tally Garner had 214,000 votes, Roosevelt 169,000, and Smith 137,000) in circumstances that alienated McAdoo from Roosevelt, dangerously, for Roosevelt's California managers, in their quest for votes, had formed a political alliance with two former Smith supporters who remained McAdoo's enemies. On May 17, by state convention, Connecticut gave its sixteen delegates to Smith, and New Jersey, by primary vote, did the same on that same day with its thirty-nine. The losses were insufficiently offset by Roosevelt victories in the Midwest and West, victories owing something to cynically duplicative promises of vice-presidential preferences made to governors and senators by Roosevelt representatives. Roosevelt-instructed delegations were won successively in South Dakota and Kansas, where Governor Harry H. Woodring was instrumental in stifling the pro-Baker efforts of Jouett Shouse of Kansas City; in Wyoming and Arizona, where Isabella Greenway operated effectively; in New Mexico and Montana, where Senators Wheeler and Walsh dominated; and in Oregon, Nevada, Colorado, and Utah, whose Governor Dern was said to be a virtually certain Roosevelt running mate. But all these victories added up to only ninety-two delegates, only six more than the eighty-six he had counted on winning but had instead lost to Smith in New England and Pennsylvania.

A long-distance phone call made at this time from Smith's Empire State Building executive suite to McAdoo's law office in Los Angeles was ominous for Roosevelt. Herbert Bayard Swope, former editor of the New York *World,* * speaking for Smith with Al and his daughter, Emily Warner, at his elbow, wanted to know if McAdoo was interested in blocking Roosevelt's nomination. McAdoo indicated he was, *provided* he was included in the conference of Democratic leaders who would then, in a deadlocked convention, choose the nominee. Smith assured him he would be. The bitter rivals of the 1924 convention then agreed to meet for a strategy talk in Chicago at the opening of the convention of 1932.[11]

And these troubles were neither the sum nor the worst of those Roosevelt's candidacy now faced.

Simultaneous with the close of the primary season was the end, and climax, of the Seabury Investigation. Closer, ever-closer to the mayor himself had come the searching probe, still sharply pointed despite unremitting efforts by

*He was a brother of the General Electric president, Gerard Swope, author of the Swope Plan.

committee Tammanyites to blunt it. Last summer it had opened to public view the fact that Walker, like Sheriff Farley and others, possessed a wondrous "tin box," a safe-deposit box jointly held by him and one Russell T. Sherwood, who, knowing he was about to be subpoenaed by the Joint Legislative Committee, fled the country in August 1931. Sherwood went to Mexico City; he flatly refused to return, but it was subsequently revealed that he, as Walker's financial agent, between January 1, 1926, and the date of his flight, had deposited for the mayor nearly $1,000,000 in the safe-deposit box and in various bank and highly secret brokerage accounts. Some of the money had come from the Equitable Coach Company, a highly dubious enterprise that, with Walker's help, at a time when it owned not a single bus, had obtained a franchise to operate a bus line on New York City streets. Equitable had also provided Walker with a letter of credit at the Chase National Bank, drawn upon by him to finance an expensive European vacation. Tiles for the walls of subway stations were sold to the city by a firm in which Paul Block, who owned a string of newspapers, had substantial interest, and it was from Block that the mayor received $246,683 over a two-year period. ("Mr. Block for several years . . . manifested a very genuine friendship for me," said Walker. "Mr. Block's life has been characterized by generosity.") J. A. Sisto was a senior partner of a Wall Street brokerage firm that owned a considerable portion of the Checker Cab Corporation, which sought and obtained from the city administration certain street advantages for its taxis. From Sisto the mayor received through an intermediary an envelope containing $26,000 in bonds, the alleged profit from a brokerage account opened by Sisto in his and Walker's name, though Walker had put not one cent into it. All these facts and others equally damaging had been spread upon the record, through greatly publicized sworn testimony and documentary evidence, when, on May 23, 1932, a subpoena was served upon the mayor by the Joint Legislative Committee, calling upon him to appear before that committee in the New York County courthouse on May 25, bringing with him all records of his personal financial transactions since January 1, 1926.

On the appointed day, in a blaze of national publicity, and before a roomful of his supporters, Walker mounted the witness stand. He brought with him an innocuous fraction of the records called for, claiming he had been unable to find the rest. He put on a brave show, delighting his immediate audience with wisecracking diversionary tactics. But all his fully exercised genius for obfuscation and dissimulation could not obscure his failure to answer satisfactorily a single one of the embarrassing questions put to him by a remarkably patient, persistent, truth-armed, and self-controlled Judge Seabury. When his two days on the stand ended, though his supporters cheered him as loudly as before, he was fully exposed to all reasonable disinterested men as a lying crook, wholly unfit for the office he held.

There ensued some days of rancorous public dispute between Seabury and Roosevelt. The former let it be known through the press that he considered his job done, that the "next move" was the governor's. The latter, abruptly flooded with private and public demands that he remove Walker forthwith, let it be known that in his view Seabury sought deliberately to embarrass him. And it was certainly true that if the governor were to "act on his own initiative now," with the nominating convention only weeks away, he would "run the risk of being accused of political opportunism," as the New York *Times* said on June 3, adding that the "political effect of Mayor Walker's case upon Governor Roosevelt's chances of winning his party's nomination cannot be minimized." Roosevelt then announced, on that same day, that he *could* not act until he was officially apprised of the charges and the evidence gathered by the investigative committee. "The only information before the governor is in the form of very incomplete newspaper stories," he complained. " . . . If the evidence in any case now before the legislative committee, in their judgment or that of their counsel, warrants, it is time for the legislative committee and their counsel to stop talking and do something. It is not the time for political sniping or buck passing."[12]

One evening during this brief anxious waiting period, Marion Dickerman experienced a flaring manifestation of the frustration, the helpless anger over the Walker case that seethed behind Roosevelt's outward show of calm confidence. She, who was to go to Chicago as the delegate Caroline O'Day's alternate, had driven up to Albany from Val Kill Cottage in her Buick that afternoon to receive from the governor's hand confidential letters having to do with convention preparations she was to deliver in person to Roosevelt lieutenants in western New York. The early June day was glorious, the river and woods and hills along Route 9 had never appeared more beautiful, and she arrived at the Executive Mansion in a glowing happy mood that matched, she believed, that of Roosevelt and Missy, with whom she dined, the three of them alone, in the Mansion's breakfast room. After the meal, Missy went to her typewriter to "catch up" on her work, and Roosevelt invited Marion to "stay on" as a silent witness to an "important conference" he was to have with three national Democratic politicans, who, in Marion's later recounting of the episode, remained unnamed. Perhaps he felt in need of spiritual support—felt that the presence of a longtime member of the innermost circle of his intimates, a witness intelligently appreciative of his performance, would help him bear with grace pressures he knew would be heavy and emotionally abrasive. For his visitors came in hard uncompromising mood. They told the governor he *must* remove Walker from office at once. Public morality and practical necessity joined in demanding it: the governor's presidential nomination was impossible without it, for *never* would the convention choose as standard bearer a man in thrall to Tammany! Roosevelt was unmoved. Smilingly, courteously, having listened with what Marion deemed a marvelous calm to statements as tacitly insulting as they were emphatically made, he refused to promise the action called for. His visitors departed angrily, shortly before midnight, leaving behind an air that shuddered with threatful predictions. Whereupon Marion, greatly agitated, sprang up to express the conviction that had grown in her out of the visitor's argument. "They're right, Franklin!" she cried. "You know they are! You can't possibly—" And was struck into silence by the cold fury that suddenly blazed out at her from his eyes and by a voice that cut like a whip as he raised it to an intensity of pitch she'd never heard before, telling her that he would *never* let it be said that he had climbed to power on the back of another! He said other things, furiously accusatory. She shrank away. And when he saw how really frightened she was, he brought himself back under control and, calm again, told her that such decisions as this were his and his alone to make. She was soothed, at peace with him, when she went up to her bed. But never, never so long as she lived, would she forget the pure terror for her of that moment of wrath![13]

When the governor met with sixteen political leaders at Hyde Park on Sunday, June 5, 1932, the shadows cast upon Roosevelt's cause by the Walker case, added as they were to other shadows cast since early April, were dark indeed, darker than was realized by Howe, Farley, Flynn, or even Jackson. Honor, as some would say, withered in the gloom.

As the agenda for the meeting was being prepared, Howe and the other three of the governor's closest advisers regarded as settled the question of who would become the convention's permanent chairman: Jouett Shouse must be named, by the terms of the April 4 compromise whereby Alben Barkley had been named temporary chairman. Honor required it and practical need did not overwhelmingly oppose it, in the view of these four, none of whom then believed that Shouse as presiding officer could do fatal harm. And with this assessment Roosevelt, at the outset, was inclined to agree. Fortunate for his candidacy was the presence in the Hyde Park living room that day of powerful Democratic senators from Western and border states—Cordell Hull of Tennessee, Clarence D. Dill of Washington, and Burton Wheeler and Thomas Walsh of Montana—whose constituency equated Tammany with the Devil and who themselves measured more accurately than his other advisers the further erosion of as yet uncommitted delegate strength that would almost certainly result from the Walker case, no matter how the governor now handled it. They were convinced that Roosevelt's chance for nomination under the two-thirds rule was now too slim to survive rulings from the chair hostile to his interests. Should an attempt be made, then, to abolish the two-thirds rule? This could be done by a simple majority of the convention—and Roosevelt's candidacy would have more than a bare majority support when the convention opened. Not everyone who favored his nomination, however, would also favor the rule's change. A substantial portion of his support was from the South, in whose "peculiar" sectional interest—that of maintaining white supremacy in the face of the Fourteenth Amendment—the two-thirds rule had been adopted in the first place, and the proposal of change was bound, in the circumstances, to provoke dangerously plausible charges that desperate and unfair tactics were being employed by the Roosevelt forces. So a final answer to the question was put off until the delegates gathered in Chicago. This meant that the two-thirds rule would probably still be in effect at nomination time, which further meant, as the senators insisted, that Shouse *must* be denied the seemingly promised chairmanship. Wheeler made the point emphatically. "If Shouse becomes chairman," he said to Roosevelt, "*you* will not become President!" The upshot was a decision to promote Wheeler's Montana colleague Walsh into the permanent chairmanship* and have Farley announce this decision to the press at once, so that the furor it provoked would have time to die down before the convention opened. Farley did so within an hour after the conferees, having agreed to ask newspaperman and historian Claude G. Bowers to make the Roosevelt nomination speech, and having decided upon Arthur Mullen of Nebraska as floor leader, had taken their departure. The reporters were reminded, and in turn reminded the public, of the language of the subcommittee resolution that Roosevelt had approved, to wit, that Shouse was "commended," not "recommended," for the post he sought.[14]

Such sly slipperiness added to the disgust that Walter Lippmann felt, and expressed in a nationally syndicated column dated June 7, 1932.

It was a column about the Walker case.

"There has been something distinctly queer in Franklin D. Roosevelt's mental processes throughout this affair," said Lippmann. "He seems most deeply irritated at the fact that the Seabury investigation has been producing testimony which compels him to choose between condoning corruption and striking it." Admittedly, the governor's was a painful, hazardous dilemma. If he acted at once upon the Seabury findings, removing the mayor from office before the national convention opened, he would be accused of sacrificing justice to personal ambition: " . . . to try James J. Walker before a man who stands to profit enormously by convicting him is a revolting spectacle." On the other hand, "Tammany and its allies will have a large vote in Chicago," and Roosevelt's failure to act at once on the Walker matter would evince a fearful subservience to Tammany, in the view of the public at large. It was all a "squalid mess" for which the governor's "own weakness and timidity" were solely responsible. "If months ago he had done what he should have done, if he had broken with Tammany and put himself unequivocally at the head of the forces struggling for good government, there would be no dilemma today. . . . He elected, instead, to play an intricate game with Tammany, to act against corruption only when he was forced to do so, to feed Tammany patronage, to consort with the Tammany bosses, and to go along with Tammany in trying to discredit Mr. Seabury and the active forces fighting Tammany corruption." He had thereby "lost his moral freedom." Concluded Walter Lippmann: "The trouble with Franklin D. Roosevelt is that his mind is not very clear, his purposes are not simple, and his methods are not direct. A clear-headed, simple, and direct man would not have landed himself in the confusion which now prevails as between Albany and City Hall. . . . He himself has had to drag

---

*Walsh had been permanent chairman of the disastrous 1924 Democratic National Convention and had then presided with notable and well-remembered fairness and parliamentary skill.

the question of Mayor Walker's removal into the Presidential campaign."[15]

On June 8, having as committee counsel asked the Hofstadter Committee to present fifteen specific charges of Walker criminality and the evidence for them to the governor, and having been refused by the committee's Democratic (Tammany) majority, Seabury presented them himself in his "individual capacity as a citizen of the State of New York." He had, he said publicly, "no request or petition to make with reference to this matter," his only desire being that the governor deal with it "solely on its merits and regardless of other consequences."[16] For more than a fortnight thereafter, while popular clamor for Walker's removal rose ever higher, the Seabury report reposed in the governor's office, where, the public was informed, it was being carefully checked by legal counsel. Not until June 24, which was eight days after a remarkably lackluster Republican National Convention in Chicago had nominated with no enthusiasm a Hoover-Curtis ticket, was the Seabury report forwarded to Jimmy Walker by Roosevelt. By that time Democrats were already gathering in Chicago, where the party's national convention would open three days hence—already they engaged in maneuvers of major importance to the convention's outcome—and the mayor said he would reply to the charges after he had returned from Chicago, he being a convention delegate.

So it was that Roosevelt arrived at the hour of decision with a clear majority of the convention delegates, numbering over 650, instructed or otherwise committed to vote for him, but still shy by some 100 votes of the needed two thirds. And he could not have been more grievously burdened by the Walker case at this juncture if his most implacable enemies had dictated, from first to last, his gubernatorial management of it. Nothing seemed to have been gained by his "intricate game." The hostility toward him by Curry-Walker's Tammany could hardly have been greater than it was, and its effectiveness was almost certainly greater than it would have been if he had long ago declared war on corruption. Such war, properly conducted, would have reduced the Tiger's potency. And much had been lost by this same "intricate game." Ugly corrosive questions now ate into his formerly bright and shining national reputation as a progressive—and if the number of his convention supporters was not considerably less than it would otherwise have been, the *fervor* of their support certainly was.

III

SELF-DOUBT, especially doubt of his ability to read providential cues accurately and respond to them properly in terms of the grand providential design, must have occasionally assailed him as, alone in the darkness of night, half asleep, half awake, he was caught defenseless against a sense of loss, of danger, of impending failure. He must then have measured painfully the difference between his brilliant prospects in early January and his actual situation in late June and have admitted to himself (he would admit to no one else) that the sad decline in his fortunes was due mostly to his own miscues, his own

mistaken decisions or failures to decide. Had he *fatally* muffed his assigned
lines? But such doubt and guilt were thrust aside, or pushed down below the
threshold of consciousness, by his will and mind when he was wide awake, in
which state he also resisted all temptation to blame others, for his grievous
losses, even when others clearly deserved blame. The telegram he dispatched
to Mayor Curley, in response to one *from* Curley, on the day after his Massachusetts humiliation, was characteristic: "I am not the least bit down-
hearted," he said, "and you need not be either. You are right that a skirmish
does not win a battle. I do not need to tell you how grateful I am for all that
you have done."[17] To the general public he gave no anxious sign whatever; he
appeared wholly relaxed, serene, good-humored, confident, secure. And even
to his circle of intimates the signs he gave of stress were far-spaced and muted.
He laughed much. He frowned seldom. He radiated optimism. He seemed the
tirelessly energetic epitome of great good health—this crippled man who,
under constant pressure, which he welcomed and gloried in, was easy and
frequent prey to obscure viral respiratory infections. Quite possibly his brief
moment of rage against Marion Dickerman was unique.

Nor was this appearance of his contradicted by any action, secretly made,
in the world of concrete realities. His every practical design upon the immediate future presumed an impending triumph.

Since early June his intimates had known of his decision to break with the
tradition, born of the primitive communications system of the early Republic,
whereby a presidential nominee was required silently to wait in pretended
ignorance of his selection until, weeks after the event, he was formally notified
of it by an official delegation. This, in 1932, was *literally* foolish, as Roosevelt
acutely sensed, in that it seemed designed to fool and bemuse the populace in
a way perfectly consistent with Herbert Hoover's public attitude toward the
depression, his public statements about its cause and cure. Roosevelt himself
would have none of it. Nominated, he proposed to go at once before the
convention to accept the honor in person from those who bestowed it. Moreover, he would do so in the most dramatic possible fashion, descending upon
Chicago, godlike, out of the heavens. Practical necessity required this of him.
He could hardly wisely ask dead-tired conventioneers to remain in session for
the extra day needed for his journey by rail from Albany. Hence he had
ordered a Ford trimotored plane to be parked ready for takeoff at the Albany
airport, a plane large enough to transport him and a considerable party to the
convention city. He well knew that the flight of itself alone would be a vivid
symbolic gesture, signifying personal daring and courageous precedent-shattering leadership, since flying in that year was yet a novel and, in the popular
view, a hazardous mode of travel, from which the timid shied away. No
President, no campaigning candidate for the presidency, had ever flown before.

Part and parcel of this decision was Roosevelt's assignment of Moley, early
in June, to the writing of a nomination acceptance speech that, being radio-
broadcast nationally, would launch the election campaign before the nominating convention had adjourned. It could well become, Roosevelt realized, the

most important of all his campaign utterances: it would almost certainly have the largest radio audience. He therefore ordered it to be, not a typically "rousing" piece of convention oratory, but a sober issues-and-policy statement addressed to the country as a whole, setting the tone of his campaign and introducing, in necessarily sketchy fashion, much of the subject matter to be developed in later pronouncements. Moley devoted the bulk of his time and energy for two long weeks to the writing of this statement. He drew heavily upon the "privy council" memoranda of May 19, especially upon his own summary-introduction of these. He also incorporated language furnished by Tugwell, blaming the depression on income maldistribution. And he placed the product of this labor in Roosevelt's hand early in the week before the convention opened. The initial draft speech, though saying in general what Roosevelt wanted to say, and in the way he wanted to say it, ran far too long, totaling more than 9,000 words; but by Saturday, June 25, when he and Tugwell entrained for Chicago, Moley, following Roosevelt's specific marginal instructions, had shortened and revised it into nearly final reading copy. The finishing touches would be put upon it by Rosenman, who remained at Roosevelt's side in Albany, and by Roosevelt himself, who, as was his custom, would pen a peroration (to be revised by Rosenman) in his own hand.[18]

IV

MEANWHILE, in the Madison Avenue headquarters of the "Friends of Roosevelt," Louis Howe suffered intensely. No contrast could have been sharper than that between Roosevelt's mood and the darkening, increasingly irritable and irascible mood of his chief of staff as the latter approached the climax, the make-or-break point, of his entire life. It was as if every fearful doubt and terrible anxiety that Roosevelt might have felt, yet seemed not to feel, was imposed as a spiritual burden upon this sickly man, who, incredibly, had become Roosevelt's alter ego.

But *was* Howe still truly the alter ego?

He himself was increasingly unsure of it.

Indeed, a major part of his abundant trouble was the insecurity he now felt in the role he had played, and in the close symbiotic relationship he had had with his beloved Franklin, through the last two crowded decades. He had a bitter gnawing sense of being gradually inexorably set aside, displaced by men who rushed forward, all undeserving, to pluck fruits of triumph from a tree he himself had planted, so he believed, and nourished with his nerve and blood in times when it would otherwise certainly have perished. His jealous hatred of Rosenman, thinly disguised as a conviction that Sam lacked the judgment and skill and guts required to keep Franklin "on the rails" at crucial moments; his covert resentment of the growing persuasive power exerted by Moley and the other professors of the Brain Trust, a resentment that Moley could not remove, for all his trying; his highly imaginative suspiciousness whereby lurking enemies were seen everywhere, whispering conspiracies were heard everywhere, and poisonous betrayal spread through every dark—all these grew now close to the outermost bound of mental health without ever quite reaching the realm of the pathological. For though he sucked Sweet Caporal smoke into his tortured lungs from morning till night while scheming endlessly, worrying incessantly, fretting over small details as over large concerns, and was constantly on the verge of total collapse, his general judgment remained shrewd and he continued to labor prodigiously at a high level of efficiency.

Howe left nothing to chance that might conceivably be controlled. He was security-conscious to a fault.

He personally prepared dozens of pink index cards on Texans of alleged political potency, noting pertinent facts about them, one card for each individual, and used these to check and guide Colonel House's dealings with a state political situation that House no longer understood as well as he thought he did. (The cards would interest and amuse future historians. Said the one on Albert S. Burleson* of Austin: "Disgusted, tired, ready to die. . . . Violent wet. . . . Admires Al Smith. . . . No following." Said the one on Fort Worth's Amon G. Carter: "Non-committal. . . . Powerful. . . . King-maker type. . . . Loud. . . . Breaks with everyone." On U.S. Senator Tom Connally of Texas: "Politician—no convictions. . . . Friendly but non-committal. . . . *Tremendous* influence. . . . Fears N.Y. City situation." On Houston banker Jesse H. Jones:† "Money. . . . For himself first, last and all time. . . . Ambitious. . . . Promises everybody everything. . . . Double-crosser." On San Antonio's colorful Maury Maverick: "Hot-headed. . . . Factional local politics. . . . Influential. . . . Friendly." Of a few others he noted that they were "honest," as if this quality were rare, and of yet others he wrote that "early support of FDR would be *bad,*" meaning they would antagonize delegates otherwise inclined toward Roosevelt.[19]) On his office wall was a huge map of the United States, on which, within each state, the date of its primary or state convention was listed. When a state's delegation was won by Roosevelt, that state was colored with pink crayon on the map. By late June, the number of states so colored was impressive, and the area colored, even more so, and Howe then ordered a duplicate of the map to be prepared for hanging on the wall in Farley's Chicago hotel suite for the persuasive edification of delegates visiting this "reception center" of the Roosevelt convention headquarters. He composed a one-and-a-half-minute "inspirational" message to committed delegates, had Roosevelt read it in his most warmly intimate tones into a recording microphone, then had a pressing of it mailed to each of these delegates, along with a personal letter from the candidate and a personally inscribed photograph of him. He also "worked out an excellent system for keeping us informed" in Chicago of what the opposition was doing and hoped to do secretly; in consequence, "we were seldom caught napping," as Farley later recorded.[20] He thus capitalized upon

*Burleson had been Postmaster General in Woodrow Wilson's Cabinet.
†Hoover had recently appointed Jones as the Democratic member of the Reconstruction Finance Corporation (RFC) board.

the wide network of confidential communicants, thousands of them scattered across the nation, with concomitant files of specific personal information about them as individuals, which resulted from the tremendous "personal" correspondence he had carried on in Roosevelt's name and with Roosevelt's active cooperation since 1920. He was at great pains to protect the confidentiality of communications, those received and those made. He arranged to have not one but three adjacent rooms in the Chicago Stadium assigned to the Roosevelt forces, so that Jim Farley, holding conference in the middle one of the three, with the other two locked against interlopers, would be protected against eavesdropping. He ordered one of his agents to stay in these rooms night and day until the convention opened, to guard against possible usurpers or installers of listening devices.

Louise Hackmeister, whom everyone called Hacky, had been Howe's highly skilled and absolutely trustworthy telephone switchboard operator since the 1928 gubernatorial campaign; she was sent by Howe to Chicago to manage the Roosevelt headquarters switchboard in the Congress Hotel, paying special heed to the private line that Howe had installed between the Executive Mansion and his own corner suite on the Chicago hotel's seventeenth floor. To this private line was attached a loudspeaker in the suite's living room, to be switched on when individual delegates or groups of delegates were present who might be inspired by Roosevelt's intimately friendly voice addressing them from Albany, directly, by name. Access to this suite, the nerve center of the entire Roosevelt operation at the convention, would be more carefully controlled than was that to Farley's suite in another part of the hotel or Flynn's in yet another part, the three selected suites being deliberately widely spaced for increased information-gathering and delegate-influencing efficiency. Guarding its doors, admitting only those who ought to be admitted, would be Louis' son Hartley and his able faithful personal secretary, Margaret "Rabbit" Durand.*

It was not until the late afternoon of Thursday, June 23, several days after Farley and Flynn had arrived in Chicago, that Howe entrained on the Twentieth Century Limited for the convention city. He was accompanied by Nancy Cook and Marion Dickerman, whose company he had demanded even though they had made Pullman reservations on another train—reservations which they had to cancel only a couple of hours or so before departure. And at the table the three shared in the Limited's dining car that evening he was very much the Louis Howe the two women had long known and loved, a sensitively intelligent, wittily humorous, robustly imaginative man, possessed of great kindness and compassion, a man thus greatly different from the Howe whom others, outside the Roosevelt circle, thought they knew. When he said goodnight, having arranged to breakfast with his two companions in this car the next morning, he

---

*So nicknamed by Howe after she had given him warning signals one day from behind a visitor's back—wigwagging signals, like a rabbit's twitching ears.

seemed more cheerful and relaxed than he had been for weeks before.

The next morning, however, he failed to appear at the breakfast table.

Marion and Nancy grew alarmed.

They sent for the conductor and followed him to Howe's stateroom.

And when the door was opened they were shocked by the sight of him lying desperately ill in his bed, gasping for breath, his face the color and texture of crinkled gray paper. They had seen him under severe asthma attack before—even in his best health he coughed and wheezed a great deal—but never had they seen him like this! They believed him to be dying. They exchanged horrified knowing looks with the conductor: arrangements must be made, as soon as they arrived in Chicago, to rush from station to hospital this man whose life's meaning depended upon events of the next few days in which his own active participation was required for a successful outcome. He himself was convinced of this; so were the two women. The ghastly bitter irony of it, joined to their loving empathy with the sick man, and with Franklin Roosevelt, struck deep into their souls.

But then, before their eyes, a seeming miracle occurred.

Louis Howe, his willpower so intensely focused as to be almost a visible energy, drew himself upright in bed, brought his theretofore helpless panting under control, and began to breathe regularly if rapidly and shallowly through his nostrils instead of through wide-open mouth. A faint ruddiness returned to his dead-gray cheeks. He showed irritation at this invasion of his privacy, ordering the two women and conductor out of his room, so that he might shave and dress. He ordered, too, that the morning newspapers be brought him as soon as they were aboard.[21]

And perhaps nothing could have been better calculated to revive him than the top-headlined story in these morning papers.

Early in the preceding day in Chicago, Mayor Frank Hague of Jersey City, the floor manager of Smith's convention forces, had asserted in a lengthy public statement that, of all possible Democratic candidates, Roosevelt was the weakest. The governor, according to Hague, "has no chance of winning" since he "cannot carry a single state east of the Mississippi and very few in the Far West." Farley had at once made a soft reply, its language dictated to him over the phone from Albany: "Governor Roosevelt's friends have not come to Chicago to criticize, cry down, or defame any Democrat from any part of the country. This, I believe, is sufficient answer to Mr. Hague's statement." That statement, however, deemed a violation of nomination campaign ethics, infuriated leaders of the Roosevelt forces, who a few hours later gathered to organize and make final plans for the impending struggle.

Farley had had misgivings about holding, for this purpose, so large a meeting (some sixty-five people were present); they were at once proved justified. For hardly had the meeting got under way when Louisiana's colorful, often clowning, but always highly effective demagogue, Senator Huey Long,* was

---

*Long, who was loudly calling for income limitation and wealth redistribution as Depression-corrective measures, doubted Roosevelt's liberalism. But the New York governor was clearly more

on his feet to propose a resolution committing Roosevelt forces to a floor fight for abolition of the two-thirds rule. Farley, chairing the meeting, was dismayed. The timing was all wrong. It had been agreed at the Hyde Park conference that no such move would be made without the prior express approval of Roosevelt personally and that, if made at all, it should be very shortly before or actually at the convention session during which the rules was formally adopted. This would surprise the "Stop Roosevelt" leaders; they, who had nothing in common save their hostility to Roosevelt, would not have time to coalesce and organize their opposition before the rules vote was taken. As it now was, if Long's resolution was adopted, the opposition would have ample time in which to gain recruits, and a defeat on this issue, leaving the two-thirds rule intact, would be tantamount to Roosevelt's loss of the nomination. Farley tried to explain this to the gathering. He sought to declare the motion lost for want of a second. But Long sprang again to his feet to second his own motion and, stripping off his coat, delivered in sweat-soaked shirt-sleeves "a stem-winding, rousing stump speech that took his listeners by storm," as a rueful Farley later recorded. Hull spoke then in support of the resolution. So did Wheeler, Josephus Daniels, and Connecticut Democratic leader Homer Cummings. And when the vote was taken, Long's motion was carried almost unanimously.[23]

This was the news Louis Howe read on that Friday morning, June 24, as the Limited roared through Gary and East Chicago, then slanted northwestward along Lake Michigan into Chicago itself. He read, too, statements harshly condemnatory, on moral grounds, of this allegedly typical piece of Roosevelt trickery, which seemed only too consistent with the "violation" of Roosevelt's "promise" to Jouett Shouse. These statements came from Al Smith, John W. Davis, and James M. Cox, all former presidential candidates; from McAdoo and Texas' Sam Rayburn, who deplored this effort to change the rules in the middle of the game; from Carter Glass, who damned it as a cheap "gambler's trick"; from Newton D. Baker, who, ominously, declared in Cleveland that "[s]ensitive men would find it difficult to defend a candidate who started out with a moral flaw in his title." And what Howe read (it was all a damnable stinking mess; how the *hell* had Jim let it happen?) could not but trigger a flow of heart-stimulating bronchi-relaxing epinephrine into his bloodstream.

When he stepped off the train, he still looked "like death" to Jim Farley, who had come to the station to meet him. He seemed miraculously recovered, however, to his two traveling companions. He was upright. His dark brown eyes flashed the fire of an aroused spirit, a challenged intelligence. He moved under his own power through the station into the already hot and sultry

---

progressive than his opponents; he was being supported by Huey's good friend Burton K. Wheeler. When Long ascertained that Nebraska's George W. Norris, whom Long idolized, was also supporting Roosevelt, he announced (in early May 1932) that, following Norris' advice, he and the Louisiana delegation, which he as national committeeman headed, would vote for Roosevelt's nomination. The announcement was made in Atlanta from the railway car in which Long was riding from Washington to New Orleans.[22]

morning street, asking brusque questions as he did so, and after he had entered Farley's chauffeured limousine with Jim and Nancy and Marion, and was riding with them to the Congress Hotel, none dared so much as to hint that he should have a doctor look him over, much less that he check in at a hospital.[24]

V

THE Democratic National Convention of 1932, now about to open, the most consequential of all political conventions since 1912, will be for most who participate in it a vast blurred confusion. They will experience it as a succession of excitements, sweat-soaked, soul-draining, qualified and separated by periods of utter boredom and intense irritation, and they will be unable to discern through the thickening fog of oratory, of tobacco smoke, of weariness, any pattern or order beyond the bare minimum prescribed by the printed agenda.

Not so for Louis McHenry Howe, the hero-worshiping disciple of Thomas Carlyle who comes now to his moment of truth.

From Room 1702 of the Congress Hotel, the suite he miserably occupies, from which he emerges seldom, and never to go outside the hotel until the convention's final day, this sick little man views the convention from first to last as an unfolding drama whose ending is highly uncertain until it comes but whose general plot, despite its complexity, is clear enough. Every event of the drama carries with it to him, at the very instant of its occurrence, a weight of significant meaning that derives from the perceived dramatic plot as a whole, as well as from the temporal and physical setting in which the drama is played out.

For Chicago swelters in droughty summer heat that must be suffered full force by almost everyone in town, unmitigated by air conditioning save in drugstores and theaters, and it wallows in an economic and psychological depression deeper than most great cities suffer. The effects of the collapse of the Insull utilities "empire" upon an already profoundly troubled community have been dire indeed. Seven hundred thousand of the city's workers are unemployed. In dozens of Hoovervilles scattered across Cook County, a discarded humanity huddles in shacks built of discarded materials. Many myriads of others live scarcely better in ill-ventilated slum tenements and in tacky row-houses crowding mean streets for miles west of narrow Gold Coast. South of the Loop, along Lake Michigan's shore, almost within sight of the window of Howe's suite seventeen floors above Michigan Avenue, hungry men scavenge for garbage to eat, sometimes fighting over it. The city's treasury is empty, and the city's credit exhausted: $20,000,000 is owed in back pay to 14,000 Chicago schoolteachers, hundreds of whom are in the clutches of loan sharks, who extort from them, with threat of maiming violence, interest at 42 percent. And the banking system is rapidly breaking down. Thirty-two suburban banks and eight of the Loop's smaller ones closed their doors within fifty days after the failure of Insull Utilities Investments; now the five largest in the Loop are gravely threatened because the weakest of them, the Central Republic Bank and Trust Company, is on the verge of collapse.

Of this last, though it is shrouded in secrecy so far as can be, whispering rumors may reach the ears of Louis Howe this fateful weekend. Central Republic is the "Dawes bank," organized thirty years before by Charles G. Dawes. Just three weeks ago this same "Hell n' Maria" Dawes, in Washington, abruptly resigned his post as Hoover-appointed president of the RFC, to the utter astonishment of his fellow board members, and ten minutes after was on a train bound for Chicago. He is now on La Salle Street, a few hundred yards from the Congress Hotel, angling obliquely but definitely, desperately, for a huge RFC loan to his bank, whose board chairmanship he has assumed. There are dangerously heavy runs on every Loop bank within hours after Howe checks into Room 1702—runs that will resume on the morrow. Jesse Jones, he of the false promise and the double cross, according to Howe's index card on him, witnesses the tail end of them at noontime of Saturday, June 25, when he arrives in Chicago as a Texas (Garner) delegate to the convention. The next morning, he as an RFC board member is called on at his hotel by a tensely anxious Melvin A. Traylor, executive head of Chicago's First National Bank, who whisks him to a meeting of the city's top banking executives, some three dozen of them, in Central Republic's boardroom. Dawes, pale and despairing, is present. Dawes tells them all that his bank, insolvent, will not open tomorrow. Whereupon Jones does what he has been called there to do: he telephones Herbert Hoover urging that an RFC loan be made and expressing a willingness to assume personal responsibility for it if Hoover will approve. Hoover, who has retreated from Washington's sultry heat to his Blue Ridge Mountain camp on the Rapidan River, *does* shortly approve, with no such wrench of "free enterprise" principle as might be expected by the literal-minded. So shortly before dawn of Monday, June 27, just hours before the Democratic National Convention opens, Dawes is assured of a government loan of $90,000,000. His bank will open after all! (Be it noted that $90,000,000 is only $5,000,000 less than Central Republic's total deposits at that moment, that it is three times the amount RFC will lend state governments in all 1932 for the relief of human beings who are unemployed, and that, even so, it will not suffice: soon Central Republic will close its doors forever.)[25]

Rumors of this there may be, as said, for Louis Howe. A repercussion of it, important to his immediate vital enterprise, there certainly is.

He and Farley, the latter especially, for many weeks have been maneuvering, cajoling, prodding, bargaining, for Illinois' fifty-eight delegates, currently but obviously temporarily pledged to Illinois Senator J. Hamilton Lewis as favorite son. Lewis evinces no desire for them, no wish to retain them. And on Saturday, via telegram to a Springfield newspaperman, from Washington, where Congress remains in session, Lewis unexpectedly unconditionally releases them. A copy of the telegram is rushed to Farley's suite, where Howe happens then to be. "Carried away with happiness and enthusiasm," Farley is at once convinced that "the band-wagon rush" to Roosevelt has begun. A first-ballot nomination is now assured! A dour, sour Louis Howe doubts it, and says so. He does not sufficiently protest, however, Farley's impulsive decision to summon newspaper reporters at once and read Lewis' telegram to them, thus implying that the senator withdraws in Roosevelt's favor and that Roosevelt can now count upon a substantial number if not all of Illinois' votes. The falsity of such implication is quickly demonstrated. The great banker Melvin Traylor, a conservative Democrat, was a hero in the press that weekend in the way that Richard Whitney was on Black Thursday of 1929, a hero not for his role in saving Central Republic, a wholly unpublicized operation, but because he has bravely pushed his way through an angry fearful crowd of depositors bent upon withdrawing their deposits, in the lobby of his bank on Saturday morning, and mounted the pedestal of a marble pillar in that awesome temple of finance, from where, with confidence-breeding show of confidence, he assured the tempestuous crowd that First National, a pillar of Chicago since the Civil War, will continue so to be, seemingly thereby saving not only his own bank but also others. His prestige is at its highest when Mayor Anton Cermak comes to him begging him to assume Ham Lewis' vacated place as favorite son. Or has it been for some time arranged by Cermak, undoubted boss of the Illinois delegation, that the banker will step forward when the senator steps back? At any rate, Traylor promptly accepts the proffered honor with its commitment to him of fifty-eight votes he knows to be coveted by Franklin Roosevelt and that he suspects may ultimately go to Newton Baker.[26]

These maneuverings sharply displease Howe, of course. But they are for him a relatively minor concern that weekend.

His major concern, his overriding concern, is to effect a withdrawal with as much grace and as little loss as possible from the untenable position taken on the two-thirds rule.

That it *is* untenable—that total repudiation of it is an absolute necessity—has been his conviction since first he read of it. A contrary view is put forward by the eternally optimistic Farley, who, while regretting that the move was untimely made, points to the fact that "we could lose almost a hundred votes off our total [committed delegate] strength" and still retain the majority needed for rules change. He quotes soothing words from Roosevelt, who, over the phone, has told him "not to worry, to let things drift along."[27] Howe snorts dissent and disgust. Says he, in effect: "We'll lose *more* than a hundred votes on this issue, if we press it; we'll lose damn near the whole South." This same prediction, emphatically made also by Senator Josiah W. Bailey of North Carolina, who, within an hour or so after Howe's arrival at the hotel, comes storming into the Roosevelt headquarters "thoroughly enraged at what we had started," as Ed Flynn will remember,[28] is yet further supported, with frightening statistics, by a New York *Times* survey of delegate opinions, conducted on Saturday. Roosevelt himself is by then convinced, not less by his own political instinct than by Howe's emphatic assertion, that withdrawal is necessary. The withdrawal must be carefully made, however, in a way that will be construed as principle affirmed, not weakness confessed, in a way that does not offend those strong Roosevelt supporters who mistakenly initiated this losing battle, and in a way that leaves the door ajar for a rules change if the convention threatens to become deadlocked.

Only a published statement by Roosevelt himself can achieve in single impact such divergent aims. On Monday morning it issues from Albany—a telegram from governor to campaign manager, made public at the Chicago headquarters just as National Committee Chairman Raskob, on the podium in Chicago Stadium, officially opens the 1932 convention.

"The need of the nation—the need of the world—in these distressing days requires avoidance of personal animosities and discussion of procedures and calls for concentration and attention on principles and leadership . . . ," says Franklin Roosevelt. "I believe and always have believed that the two-thirds rule should no longer be adopted. It is undemocratic. Nevertheless, it is true that the issue was not raised until after the delegates to the convention had been selected, and I decline to permit either myself or my friends to be open to the accusation of poor sportsmanship. . . . I am accordingly asking my friends in Chicago to cease their activities to secure the adoption of the majority nominating rule. . . . I ask this of those delegates who are honoring me with their support and who number many more than a majority. I trust, however, that the committee on rules may recommend some rule to ensure against the catastrophe of a deadlock or a prolonged balloting."[29]

The statement is adroitly worded—a strong honorable man, disdaining easy triumph at the risk of honor, reminds the world that he is strong enough to triumph in any case. However, it is not *quite* straightforward, is not *quite* what it seems to be, and out of the gap between its apparent and actual effects springs serious trouble, at once!

Roosevelt supporters control the rules committee. Under the lead of committee chairman Bruce J. Kremer of Montana and Huey Long, they interpret the closing sentence of Roosevelt's telegram as an admonition, which they hasten to obey. They adopt a resolution formally recommending that the two-thirds rule not apply beyond six convention ballots: on the seventh, if a seventh becomes necessary to nominate, majority rule shall prevail. Again, tumult! Roosevelt's opponents loudly cry that this committee operation is of a piece with other Rooseveltian trickery and deceit in that it furtively snatches back with sinister left hand what is seemingly proffered by a right hand of good fellowship and fair play. Looms immediately the specter of a floor fight that Roosevelt cannot afford to lose, yet has little chance to win! Howe has anguish of spirit to match anguish of body as Farley rushes before the rules committee to plead in person for an immediate rescinding of the pernicious resolution.

"Drop the issue!" begs Farley of Kremer-Long and colleagues.

"Drop it absolutely, unequivocally!" he desperately begs.

And but narrowly wins his way.

For only after "considerable wrangling" does the committee "finally" do what is needful to be done, and "the long headache . . . [is] over at last."[30]

It is well for Louis Howe on this Monday of the convention's opening that he knows naught of yesterday's meeting, in Bernard Baruch's suite in the Blackstone Hotel, between Alfred E. Smith and William Gibbs McAdoo, with Baruch and Herbert Bayard Swope also present, a meeting arranged weeks ago through long-distance phone conversation between Smith and McAdoo.

For at this meeting the bitter rivals of 1924 have buried deeply, beyond possibility of retrieval, in a common ground of hostility to Roosevelt, hatchets they formerly used on one another. So, at least, believes Al Smith, who has said to McAdoo, citing specific evidence for his contention, that state after state colored pink on Farley's famous map has a delegation whose commitment to Roosevelt is too weak to last beyond three or four ballots, that after these four ballots, switches will certainly be made, and that therefore, if McAdoo can and will hold California in the Garner column through four ballots, "we've got him [Roosevelt] licked." Then Smith, McAdoo, and a few others "can sit down around a table and get together on a candidate." The candidate so chosen will definitely *not* be Al Smith: " . . . my candidacy is out the window," said he, who could hardly have expected McAdoo to so far forgive 1924 as to connive toward Smith triumph in 1932. Neither will it be McAdoo, for a similar reason in reverse, though no mention was made of this, and McAdoo may continue to nurse secret hope. It could conceivably be Garner, in circumstances highly improbable. But Baker it almost certainly *will* be—a near-certainty that went emphatically unspoken by Smith yesterday in deference to the known lack of friendship between Baker and McAdoo, who differ widely on matters of foreign policy. (In point of fact, Smith, Raskob, Shouse, Hague, Lippmann—even John Curry and Adolf Berle, Jr., marginally —have for many weeks been concerting strategy, loosely, with Baker's man Ralph Hayes, to prevent Roosevelt's nomination and secure Baker's.) Did McAdoo explicitly pledge himself to cooperation with Smith along the indicated lines? Did he definitely promise to notify Smith in advance of any shift of the California's delegation's vote? Smith will say yes and McAdoo no to both questions, in future acrimonious controversy. But certainly the meeting ended on a cordial note, with a handshake that *seemed* to betoken a gentleman's agreement.[31] Yes, it is well that none of this is known to Howe—best that he continue to believe, on this first convention day, that political cooperation between Smith and McAdoo is unlikely to the point of virtual impossibility. He has, surely, anxieties enough already!

In Room 1702, with a direct phone line to FDR at his fingertips always, when not in hand, the desperately sick little man is prostrate. Seldom is he on his feet or even seated upright in a chair on this opening convention day or through feverish nights and days thereafter. For the most part, coatless, his stained tie loosened and his collar opened round his scrawny neck, he lies on bed, sofa, floor, bureau top, where he feels he gets more air, struggling for breath, his drawn gray face blasted by the wind of two electric fans. Every now and again he is doubled over, his chin brought near his knees, by a frightful paroxysm of coughing, yet smokes another cigarette immediately after. He smokes incessantly. But he also continues to function incessantly and effectively. Somehow he manages to keep close track of convention-floor proceedings via a radio, its volume turned low, while simultaneously conducting brusque conversations with those who are admitted in almost constant stream by his doorkeepers, and conversations, too, several each hour, over the phone. He is deferred to by Farley and Flynn and the floor manager Mullen; they make no major move without consulting him. He is deferred to by Ray Moley, who makes 1702 his Chicago headquarters. Through him flow nearly all personal messages to and from FDR. Not without objective reason, therefore, does he deem himself heart and head of the Roosevelt convention operation, and suffers in consequence all the agonies of a crucifixion, which, in his own fever-blazed eyes, must appear ignominiously slavish if it does not become gloriously salvational.

All the while that he listens with half an ear to Alben Barkley's passionately eloquent keynote address—a full two-hour indictment of the Hoover administration delivered in the highest style of Kentucky oratory—he worries about tomorrow's convention session in which two contested Roosevelt delegations, those of Minnesota and Huey Long's Louisiana, will or will not be seated. If Huey plays the clown before the entire convention as he had just done before the credentials committee, which nevertheless recommends the seating of his delegation, whose legal right to it is clear, then a delegation hostile to Roosevelt may be accepted in outraged reaction to Long's antics, reducing by twenty votes Roosevelt's delegate strength and quite possibly determining the loss also of Minnesota's twenty-four-vote delegation. In that event, Roosevelt's nomination becomes impossible. Hence goes forth from Howe to Flynn to Long's good friend Burt Wheeler to Long himself an urgent plea for civilized decorum and reasonableness. Probably it is unnecessary. For all his rambunctious foolishness, Long is very far from being a fool, and his own astuteness must tell him to make, as in fact he does make before the whole convention on Tuesday, a sober and convincing argument whose result is the seating of his (the Roosevelt) delegation by a vote of 638¾ to 514¼. Immediately thereafter the pro-Roosevelt Minnesota delegation is seated by a somewhat wider vote margin.[32]

But removal of this anxiety means, for Howe, no slackening of tension.

For now comes, at once, the decisive moment of the crucial struggle for the permanent chairmanship.

It is a struggle whose outcome is very much in doubt, in Howe's feverish mind, as he listens to Washington's Senator Dill and South Carolina's Senator James F. Byrnes nominate in glowing terms Tom Walsh. Jouett Shouse is eloquently, gracefully nominated by courtly John W. Davis.[33] Shouse will doubtless gain sympathetic support as a result of Roosevelt's loudly denounced "commend-recommend" deviousness. Howe has been told that some strong Roosevelt supporters feel compelled by prior commitment and a sense of fair play to vote for the party secretary, whose hard work to build up the Democracy these last years surely deserves reward. If many feel this way, Roosevelt's cause is doomed. And Howe, nervously keeping score in Room 1702 as Farley does on the convention floor while the teller makes his roll call of states, cannot be certain of Walsh victory until eighteen states' votes, Missouri's being the eighteenth, have been counted. The final victory margin of 626 to 528 is too narrow to sustain that prediction of first-ballot triumph for Roosevelt that Farley, even on this second convention day, continues publicly to make, but it demonstrates a gratifying firmness of Roosevelt support, and it averts disaster. As he watches through his mind's eye a dignified impressive Senator Walsh being formally escorted from the floor to the podium amid loud applause, then listens to Walsh's dignified, impressive, and reasonably short acceptance speech, Howe can relax a bit.

For little or no anxiety need be felt by him, or by Flynn or Farley, over the party platform, whose consideration is the convention's main business on Wednesday. It is a document that displeases and even disgusts Tugwell and others among Roosevelt's supporters, who deem consistency a virtue, believe promises should be kept, and worry lest needed domestic economic action be prevented by international monetary agreements of a kind Hoover seems only too eager to make; but it presents no threat to Roosevelt's nomination, hence no worry for such as Howe.

This platform is a model of brevity, as Roosevelt has insisted it should be, to contrast with the Republican one, which is a monster of verbosity. It also places its major emphasis on economic issues, as Roosevelt has insisted it should. Having been chiefly drafted by the Old Wilsonians Cordell Hull and A. Mitchell Palmer, of the infamous Palmer Raids, it proclaims itself a "covenant with the people [the phrase calls to mind Covenanter Woodrow Wilson] to be faithfully kept by the party," then opens with an indictment of "the disastrous policies pursued by our Government since the World War." They are policies "of economic isolation, fostering the merger of competitive business into monopolies and encouraging the indefensible expansion and contraction of credit for private profit at the expense of the public," policies that have "ruined our foreign trade, destroyed the value of our commodities and products, crippled our banking system, robbed millions of our people of their savings, and thrown millions more out of work, produced widespread poverty and brought Government to a state of financial distress unprecedented in time of peace." The only hope of national salvation "lies in a drastic change in economic governmental policies." Yet the Democratic prescription for a Depression cure, here formally announced, is cautiously conservative by the standards of 1932 and would not have seemed radical or even advanced to either the Bull Moosers or the New Freedom advocates of twenty years ago. Called for is an annual balancing of the federal budget; "an immediate . . . reduction of governmental expenditures . . . to accomplish a saving of not less than twenty-five percent in the cost of Federal Government"; the preservation of "a sound currency . . . at all hazards"; the "removal of government from all fields of private enterprise"; strengthened antitrust laws and their "impartial" enforcement; a "competitive tariff for revenue" (what a "competitive tariff " may be goes unexplained); "unemployment and old-age insurance," but under "state laws" rather than federal ones; "expansion of the federal program of useful construction affected with public interest, such as adequate flood control and waterways"; and "an international monetary conference [one has been proposed by the British Government and agreed to by the Hoover administration] . . . to consider the rehabilitation of silver [this London has *not* proposed; Western silver politicians have] and related questions." All in all, though it goes before the convention bearing Roosevelt's stamp of warm approval, this is such a platform as the corporate lawyer Newton Baker might stand and run on more easily, one would think, than can the champion of the Forgotten Man, the proponent of "concert-of-interests" national planning, the exponent of "bold, persistent experimentation."*

The only plank in it worthy of debate on the convention floor is the one on Prohibition. In its original form, this plank is neither more wet nor more dry than the one the Republicans adopted after acrimonious party-splitting argument: it calls simply for resubmission of the question to the electorate, and is thus expressive of the "moist" stance Roosevelt has generally adopted when free to choose. It is therefore, as expected, vehemently attacked by "dripping wet" Democrats, who want the platform to demand explicity "the repeal of the Eighteenth Amendment." Their chief spokesmen are Smith and Ritchie, both of whom make impassioned speeches. And when they win their way by a huge majority of 934¾ to 213¾, they believe they have dealt a blow to Roosevelt's candidacy while demonstrating their own vote-getting potency. They are badly mistaken. If anything, Smith has suffered another fall from Roosevelt's mastery of political jujitsu. For Roosevelt has cannily stood aside from the controversy, letting it be known that he cares not how his delegate supporters vote on so relatively unimportant a matter; he'll cheerfully abide by the result, whatever it may be. Hence the lopsidedness of the decisive vote merely demonstrates that Prohibition, a lost cause, is by that token no longer a viable issue within or between the two major parties. Those politicians who have given it priority over economic concerns are clearly out of step with the times.

But if all this is mere spectacle for Louis Howe, he is again under extreme pressure by the time it ends, and under even heavier pressure during the two nights and two days that follow. He is also more continually prostrate in the relentless sweltering heat as he keeps close track of increasingly frantic scurryings and scramblings after delegates votes, and exerts over these such directive control as circumstances permit.

When the presidential nominating speeches begin on Thursday, June 30, Roosevelt's assured delegate strength is no greater than when the convention opened. By every measure of probability, and with every passing hour, his prospects shrink while Baker's enlarge, a fact attested to by the increasing prominence with which the Ohioan's name is displayed in newspaper stories speculative upon the convention's outcome. The powerful national Scripps-Howard newspaper chain has endorsed Al Smith, but Howe has been told by

---

*Baker-supporting Walter Lippmann proclaimed in his column that "[t]he resolutions committee has done the best job in any national convention for at least twenty years."[34]

his informants on the Indiana delegation that the publisher Roy Howard has promised Scripps-Howard support to the Indiana state Democratic ticket *provided* Indiana casts at least eight votes for Baker on the first three convention ballots. Smith, then, is being used by Howard as a stalking-horse for Baker, and Indiana was one of the three states, Illinois and Ohio being the other two, deemed most likely, just a few days ago, to switch to Roosevelt before the final tally of the first ballot, thus initiating the essential bandwagon rush. Now Indiana must be written off, as Illinois was when Traylor replaced Lewis as favorite son, and as Ohio must also be when that state's favorite son, Governor White, who has earlier seemed inclined to release his fifty-two votes to Roosevelt after a token complimentary vote, tells Farley he can no longer do so, having "come to an understanding" with fellow Ohioans Baker and James M. Cox. By Thursday evening a Baker campaign headquarters had been opened in Chicago by Cleveland's Colonel Leonard P. Ayers, and every delegate has in hand reprints, distributed by Roosevelt foes, of two June 29 newspaper columns hostile to Roosevelt. One of these, the liberal Heywood Broun's nationally syndicated "It Seems to Me," cites instances of Roosevelt's deviousness to support the conclusions that the New York governor, if nominated, "will go before the country as the corkscrew candidate of a convoluting convention." The other, Walter Lippmann's nationally syndicated "Today and Tomorrow," says that, since "Smith is not here to win the nomination for himself," and since Roosevelt's followers, though numerous, "are in no sense fanatically devoted to him," obviously developing Smith-Roosevelt deadlock can be easily avoided, and the national interest can be best served, by turning to "Newton D. Baker of Ohio," who is not only "the real first choice of more responsible Democrats than any other man" but also "an acceptable second choice to almost everyone."

There is now sharp, tension-producing disagreement between Howe and Farley concerning strategy. Farley favors concentration on the Texas delegation, whose switch to Roosevelt would bring over the California delegation as well—ninety votes in all, enough to clinch the nomination. Such a switch cannot be effected simply by Garner's withdrawal from the race; it might not be made even if Garner then urges it, since most Texans, firmly committed to Cactus Jack, have small liking for Roosevelt and great suspicion of his dealings with hated Tammany. No, the Texans will come over to the governor only if their own man is promised the vice-presidency, and Roosevelt, knowing this, is perfectly agreeable to a Roosevelt-Garner ticket. He has said so to Farley. Farley has said so to Silliman Evans and Sam Rayburn, two key men on the Texas delegation, in secret conference.* And the response of these two has been, to Farley, highly gratifying, even elating. Rayburn of course reiterated the Texans' intention "to nominate Speaker Jack Garner . . . if we can," but he also frankly acknowledged Roosevelt to be "the leading candidate" and added that "[w]e don't intend to make [this convention] . . . another Madison

---

*Rayburn, as head of the Texas delegation, is Garner's floor manager.

Square Garden." Farley interprets this to mean that the Garner forces have taken and will take no part in the "Stop Roosevelt" strategy of Smith-Raskob-Shouse, and this interpretation is bolstered in his mind by reports from Daniel Roper of his and Cordell Hull's conversations with McAdoo, who has promised to try to engineer a California switch to Roosevelt, "and that will mean Texas too," *if* Garner is given second place on the ticket.[35] (Evidently McAdoo's doubts about a deadlock's probable result grow in proportion to a deadlock's likelihood.)

But by all this a suspicious Howe is unimpressed. The Texans employ precisely the tactics they *would* employ, he says, if their aim were to bemuse and deceive.

Garner, he insists, is no mere favorite son, no mere bargaining counter; he is a serious candidate whose powerful backing and fanatical support will not permit his withdrawal until more ballots have been counted than Roosevelt's candidacy can possibly survive. The fact that Rayburn and Evans conferred secretly with Farley *might* mean something if such a meeting had been sought by them. It hadn't been, however. It had been held in response to Farley's initiative and had ended with no promise or commitment of any kind by the Texans; they'd not even indicated an interest in the vice-presidency. And as regards this last, Farley will do well to heed the warnings of his fellow Irish Catholic Ed Flynn, who is convinced Garner would be almost the worst possible running mate for Roosevelt in the party circumstances of 1932. The wounds of 1928 are far from healed, and Texas inflicted some of the deepest. The hatred that rural Protestant Texas has for Catholics and Tammany, which unprecedentedly caused Democratic Texas to vote Republican in 1928, is more than matched by the hatred Smith's Catholic supporters have for that rural Protestant Texas of which Garner is the personification. Which is to say that Garner's vice-presidential nomination, far from reconciling the Smith faction and reuniting the party, will or would widen the party split and lead, quite possibly, to Hoover's reelection in November.

Hence Howe's conclusion: Farley squanders desperately needed resources of time and and energy in a bootless wooing of the Texans. Far better would it be to concentrate on Virginia, whose favorite son, Harry Byrd, during the Democratic National Committee's subcommittee meeting of April 4, promised Flynn and Farley the delivery of Virginia's twenty-four votes to Roosevelt whenever they were needed.

So sharp is the disagreement that Howe has consulted Roosevelt about it over the phone, his presentation of the case being immediately followed by Farley's, and Roosevelt, characteristically, has refused to accept either proposal as exclusive of the other. Instead, he splits the difference, telling Howe to continue the pursuit of Virginia and Farley to continue the pursuit of Texas, a division of negotiating strength that Howe knows to be dangerous in the extreme at this juncture. Another twist is thus given the rack on which Howe's spirit lies stretched in agony, drawn near the point of break and death, as his sweat-soaked body lies in agony upon a hotel bed, wheezing, coughing, gasping, while the radio beside him pours into his ears the ceaseless speech and noise of the convention.[36]

He hears that Alabama has yielded to New York for the purpose of making a nomination. To the podium with its battery of microphones comes now not eloquent and colorful Claude Bowers, who as a staff member of a Hearst paper has felt compelled to decline the invitation to speak for a rival of Hearst's own candidate, Jack Garner, but plain John E. Mack of Poughkeepsie, who, twenty-two years ago, together with Tom Lynch, sponsored a youthful Franklin Roosevelt's first run for public office. A good man, a warm friend, is Judge Mack but, alas, no public speaker. His way of presenting Roosevelt's name does nothing to inspire the delegates or lighten Howe's dark mood. Nor is that mood lightened by the prolonged but, Howe feels, insufficiently enthusiastic floor demonstration that follows, whose theme song, "Anchors Aweigh," personally chosen by the sailor Roosevelt for this occasion, is played much too slowly by band and organ, as if it were a funeral march, over and over again, its every note a hammer blow on Howe's taut nerves, until at last he gasps out to Rabbit Durand, "For God's sake tell 'em to play something else!" What else? asks the faithful Rabbit, who is his chief medium for messages to the convention floor. "Oh, something lively, for God's sake!" replies Howe. Whereupon Flynn makes a suggestion. "Okay, then," says the unhappy Howe, "tell 'em to play 'Happy Days Are Here Again,' " and so thrusts into history the song that will be ever after associated with FDR.[37]

Following the Roosevelt demonstration are other nominations, other demonstrations. Massachusetts Governor Ely's speech nominating Smith is the most eloquent, and the Smith demonstration, in which galleries packed by Cermak with a Smith claque vociferously join, is the most heartfelt and enthusiastic. And there are more to come, a parade of favorite sons, plus hours of seconding speeches, when the convention recesses until eight o'clock.

To 1702 during this dinner recess come Farley, Nancy Cook, and Marion Dickerman, the latter two doing what little they can to ease things for Louis. They tidy up a bit the messy rooms, they relieve Hartley Howe and Rabbit as doorkeepers, and Marion orders up a quart of chocolate ice cream, which Farley and Howe eat seated on the floor while Farley reports his latest approach to Sam Rayburn. It seems to Howe a fruitless approach (Bob Jackson's latest approach to Byrd has been similarly barren), with Rayburn again indicating no interest in the vice-presidency and again refusing to attempt a switch of Texas to Roosevelt before the first ballot vote is announced from the chair. " . . . we just must let the convention go on for a while," Rayburn has said. Recalling Sam's earlier remark that the Texans have no intention of perpetuating another Madison Square Garden, Farley sees hopeful significance in the fact that the Texan *did* ask how long the Roosevelt lines can hold without a break. And what has Farley replied? "Three ballots, four ballots, maybe five." Howe shakes his head gloomily. Surely Farley's estimate of durable strength is highly optimistic in view of the narrowness of the margins by which Pat Harrison's Mississippi and Joe Robinson's Arkansas are bound to Roosevelt under the unit rule and in view of the known fact that, with every caucus of the two delegations, rebellion against the unit rule grows stronger. Well, admits Farley, holding the line beyond three ballots *would* be difficult, but then it won't be necessary! Assailing Howe's gloomy disbelief, addressing the desperate wish to believe by which this gloom is qualified, Farley points out that "in all the history of the Democratic Party" no man has "received the huge vote" that will be Roosevelt's on the first ballot without being then nominated at once, which is to say there will be a crumbling of the opposition's fragile line, there will be shifts of key delegations to Roosevelt, before the first ballot is finally recorded.

The two men then talk, without arriving at a firm conclusion, about the timing of this first ballot, a burning question for consideration on so fervid an evening, yet one the Roosevelt leaders must at once decide, since they control a majority of the delegates.

Obviously the hour will be very late, it will be after midnight, possibly well into early Friday morning, before the last word of the last seconding orator is spoken, the last noisy parade ended. Shall the convention then recess until tomorrow afternoon, or shall it proceed uninterruptedly into the balloting? Howe inclines to favor the latter. So does Farley. They reason that the very lateness of the hour may work in Roosevelt's favor: bone-tired delegates may insist upon finishing the nomination business as quickly as possible, so that they can go to bed, and the only way they can do that is by nominating the front-runner. To delay the ballot, on the other hand, may invite grave trouble: Roosevelt's opponents will interpret delay as a sign of weakness and, during the hours of recess, will redouble their attempts upon the most vulnerable of the Roosevelt delegations.

With this reasoning most of the Roosevelt leaders agree when, a few hours later, they confer round the cot on which Farley lies near exhaustion in his stadium headquarters while another meaningless demonstration is being dragged out to unconscionable length on the convention floor. So does Roosevelt with "strong, reassuring voice . . . like a tonic for jangled nerves" (so Farley will always remember) when consulted in Albany over Howe's direct line.[38]

This, then, is the decision—to drive straight ahead.

And it is adhered to despite the fact that dawn light has streaked Lake Michigan's horizon (the stadium clock shows the time as 4:25 A.M.) before an impassive Chairman Walsh, looking up into nearly empty galleries and over a smoke-fogged paper-littered convention floor with hundreds of vacant chairs upon it, bangs down his gavel to announce the next order or business.

"The clerk," says he, "will now call the roll."

Immediately, the delegates stream back into their seats. The galleries refill. Following which nearly two hours are consumed as one anti-Roosevelt delegate after another demands a person-by-person poll of his or her delegation. (Tammany's John Curry does so, of the largest delegation of all, voting of course for Al Smith, as does Jimmy Walker, whose brave defiance of the governor's power to remove him from office raises a loud cheer from the galleries.) And when the ballot is at last completed, it proves inconclusive. Roosevelt has 666¼ votes, 89 more than a majority but 104 less than two thirds. Smith, his nearest rival, has 201¾, Garner 90¼, with the remaining votes scattered among favorite sons, save for Indiana's 8½ votes for Baker, ominously premonitory for Roosevelt supporters, since Baker's name has not even been formally placed in nomination.

And there are, to Farley's surprise and bitter disappointment, no switches!

The second ballot is begun before any delegate can move for recess. It is almost as time-consuming as the first, and similarly inconclusive. Roosevelt has at its end 677¾ votes, a gain of 11½, 6 of these from Missouri (whose favorite son is James M. Reed), thanks to Kansas City's Boss Tom Pendergast. Smith now has 195¼, while Garner holds at 90½ and Baker retains his 8½.

And *again* there are no switches!

Farley is now, for the first time, desperately afraid, especially when the Roosevelt floor leader, Arthur Mullen, in the face of strong protests from jubilant anti-Roosevelt leaders, feels forced to withdraw his motion that the convention recess till 4:00 P.M. The third ballot must now proceed, and there is strong likelihood that Mississippi, again acrimoniously caucusing, will break away, either rescinding its unit rule to permit the delegates to vote as they please or retaining it and transferring its twenty votes to Baker. That will mean the loss of Arkansas and probably Alabama as well. But by the slenderest of chances, thanks in good part to threatful pressures upon Pat Harrison by Huey Long, whose persuasive power spills across Louisiana's borders into the electorates of both Mississippi and Arkansas, Mississippi *does* hold on the third ballot, at whose end Roosevelt has scored another slight and, in the circumstances, insignificant gain, thanks again to Pendergast's Kansas City machine, winning 682.79 votes. Smith's vote shrinks slightly, to 194½, while Garner's increases by 11, to 101¼.

Bright hot sunlight pours through the stadium windows as Chairman Walsh announces these results. The time is 9:15 A.M. on Friday, July 1, when, upon McAdoo's motion, quickly seconded by Mullen, the convention recesses until 8:30 that evening.[39]

Louis Howe, who has suffered through the long night and will suffer through the crucial hours ahead such anguish of spirit, mind, and body as he has not before known in a life shot through with pain and suffering, is now sick almost to death. Between his two electric fans, set now to blast air directly against his face, and with the radio beside him now turned off, he lies upon a mattress he has had dragged into the center of 1702's living room, and again he looks like death to Jim Farley, all skin and bone, and his skin dead-pale, with only his hollow eyes seeming alive, though blazingly so, darkly and feverishly burning, when Farley comes to him for a strategy conference shortly before eleven o'clock, accompanied by a half dozen of the most "trusted leaders," including Ed Flynn and Pennsylvania's Joe Guffey. Nancy Cook and Marion Dickerman are already there, having come to 1702 directly from the stadium, pausing only to snatch a hurried breakfast in the Congress Hotel coffee shop. Howe sounds like death, too. A wheeze akin to a death rattle is in his quick shallow breathing and in the faint voice with which he greets his visitors, at least one of whom later opines he'll not last out the day. He remains dead-prone, making no effort even to sit up. Farley, to hold private talk with him, must motion the others to stand back out of earshot while he himself lies down upon the carpet to whisper through cupped hand into Howe's ear his view of the situation and of what must now be done. All efforts by the top command to woo Virginia or any other state delegations save the two committed to Garner must be abandoned, says Farley. "We must stake everything on Texas; it's our only chance." And Howe, without lifting his head, nods and whispers his agreement that no other course seems now possible, not adding that this course, too, seems to him unlikely to succeed.

There ensues, through the noon hour and all the hours of a long hot afternoon, such a welter of simultaneous and near-simultaneous events, each event deemed crucial by those actively involved in it—such a multitudinous swarm of weary agitated spirit-and-flesh into and out of meetings in a half-dozen Chicago hotels, especially the Congress and the Sherman House—such a prolonged flurry of seemingly historically decisive long-distance phone calls, from Chicago to Hearst's San Simeon palace in California, from San Simeon to Chicago and Washington, from Washington to Chicago, from Chicago to Albany—such a complicatedly hectic swirl of all these as will defy the attempts of future historians to tell the story in any strictly chronological, causally sequential order. And not until early evening will there come clear into the mind of the sick man in 1702 a sense of an actually definitive event leading to a single certain conclusion.

True, Jim Farley returns to Howe within an hour after their prone and whispered consultation to report an end to all their anxieties: the event is already now decided in the happiest possible fashion—the nomination is "in the bag." For Farley has just met again secretly with Sam Rayburn in Pat Harrison's Congress Hotel apartment, a brief meeting, over in a few minutes, at the end of which, responding to Farley's frankly desperate plea for a Texas switch now, Rayburn has said, "We'll see what can be done." Farley, ecstatic, is astonished by the impassivity with which Howe receives this news, Howe saying merely, "That's fine," with not the slightest change of facial expression. What incredible self-control! thinks Farley at the time. "What a man!" writes Farley in his memoirs.[40]

But in point of fact, Howe's joy is severely limited by his realization that Rayburn's word, in itself noncommittal, after all, is by no means the *last* word on this matter. Garner's delegates, most of whom won their seats through spirited contests against Roosevelt men, are bound to him by strong emotional ties. Only Garner personally can release them—and Garner has not been heard from. Nor will he be through all the afternoon by anyone in Chicago save Rayburn, who keeps strictly to himself whatever it is that Garner tells him.

Meanwhile a flood of telegrams from "folks back home" descends abruptly

upon Roosevelt delegates, urging them to turn from the New York governor
to the *real* choice of the people, Newton D. Baker. This is worrisome to Howe,
who by early afternoon is sufficiently, amazingly, recovered from his morning
prostration to move again about the suite and meet on his feet, or seated, the
incessant demands upon his attention.* Clearly the telegraphic flood is no
spontaneous outpouring of popular sentiment: it has quite obviously been
contrived by utilities corporations (Baker's law firm has one of the largest of
these as a client), which fear Roosevelt's power policy, and it may do more
to brand Baker the candidate of "the interests" than to win him delegate votes.
On the other hand, in the absence of countermeasures, it *might* provoke
disaffections, and Roosevelt at this point can afford no loss whatever. So Howe,
by phone with Roosevelt, sees to it that a long telegram comes that afternoon
from Roosevelt to his Chicago supporters, urging them to stand firm.

Simultaneously he is kept informed of frantic and futile efforts by Roosevelt
leaders, by Smith leaders, by Smith himself, to communicate with Jack Garner.
The Speaker cannot be reached either in the Washington Hotel apartment
which is his capital home, or in the Speaker's private room of the Capitol;
always "out" or "unavailable," he responds not at all to pleas that he call back.
And Howe's anxiety over this lack of decisive word is not reduced but rather
increased by his knowledge of a phone call made early this morning, at seven
Chicago time, five California time, to William Randolph Hearst by the Massachusetts millionaire Joseph P. Kennedy, who has been associated with Hearst
in the movie business. Kennedy, supporting Roosevelt, in a panic after the
second ballot, warned the lord of San Simeon that Roosevelt cannot win unless
Hearst does something to help and that Roosevelt's defeat will mean the
triumph of Smith or Baker, either of them disastrous from Hearst's point of
view. Kennedy's reported impression is that Hearst will at once get in touch
with Garner to urge Garner's withdrawal in Roosevelt's favor. But if this has
been done, why the lengthening deathly silence? By late afternoon, Howe is
again deep in the slough of despond.

A pity that we who retrospectively share his suite 1702 cannot also share
with him our restrospective knowledge that Hearst did indeed act promptly
upon Kennedy's warning. At eleven o'clock, Washington time, in this morning
of July 1, George Rothwell Brown, head of the Washington bureau of the
Hearst newspaper chain, talked with Garner in the Speaker's Capitol room,
conveying Hearst's suggestion that Garner withdraw. Garner has replied that
he intends to do so. And so he does, in a phone call to Rayburn at three o'clock,
Washington time, in the afternoon: "Sam, I think it is time to break this thing
up. . . . Roosevelt is the choice of the convention. . . . The nomination ought

---

*Again and again during his sickly manhood Louis Howe manifested amazing powers of recupera-
tion, bouncing back from the point of death seemingly through sheer willpower. Once, while being
anesthetized for surgery in a Boston hospital, he actually *did* die, according to attendant physicians, who worked in vain for two hours to revive him. "Then he came to of his own accord,"
as FDR wrote "Dearest E" on June 21, 1925, "blinked an eye & in apparently a few seconds was
perfectly all right again."[41]

to be made on the next ballot." In this, Garner is motivated by no desire for the vice-presidency, which he deems worth no more than "a bucket of warm spit," as he says disgustedly to an associate.* He would much prefer to continue in his powerful post as House Speaker. But he fears that a compromise presidential candidate will lose the election, his acceptance of the vice-presidency seems essential to Roosevelt's nomination, and so he, who has said he'd do "almost anything" to put a Democrat again in the White House, makes what he regards as a personal sacrifice.[42]

But of this Howe knows nothing. There is for him no assurance of happy outcome until he learns the result of crucial early-evening caucuses by the Texas and California delegations in adjoining rooms of the Sherman.

They are turbulent sessions, both of them. Neither has a certainly predictable issue.

Rayburn, on his way to the Texas caucus, which is scheduled for 6:30 P.M., meeting McAdoo in the Sherman lobby, tells him of Garner's decision, then announces it to the assembled Texans, provoking a storm of protest that comes near overwhelming his leadership. Only by a narrow margin, 54 to 52, with some two dozen delegates absent, many of whom are Garner diehards whose absence is due to their current negotiations on Garner's behalf with other delegations, does Texas vote to switch to Roosevelt under the unit rule. There is similar angry protest in the California caucus, which assembled at 7:00 P.M. In it *no* final vote is taken. Instead, an explosive situation is defused by appointment of a four-member steering committee empowered to decide if and when a shift of California's vote should be made. This committee, dominated by McAdoo, who now fears that Smith may yet somehow become the nominee if the decision is made "around the table" after only four ballots, and who believes that Roosevelt, for all his faults, is the candidate most in accord with Progressive principles, then promptly decides to do as Garner requested.

And so now, at last, it truly *is* all over! What Howe listens to over his radio when Chairman Walsh at nine o'clock at last gavels the noisy excited convention into working order is a drama of known end.

Yet it is by no means devoid of dramatic interest!

The Texas-California switch is a remarkably well-kept secret when the roll call of the fourth ballot begins. The "Stop Roosevelt" coalition leaders have no inkling of it. They do know that Mississippi's single swing vote has been lured away from Roosevelt: Mississippi in caucus has decided by that one vote to give its twenty to Baker. This certainly means further Roosevelt losses, possibly even a general exodus of weakly committed states from the Roosevelt ranks before the final tally is announced. The governor is through! Hence the surprise, the sudden tension and alarm, when the fourth state in the alphabetical listing is called and McAdoo asks for unanimous consent to explain California's vote.

Never has the vast throng been so quiet as when McAdoo begins to speak,

*Or did he say "a bucket of warm piss"? Accounts vary.

and never have the galleries been so noisy—an ominous roaring noise—and never have the delegates on the floor been so vociferously demonstrative as both audiences become when they realize the significance of McAdoo's opening words: "California came here to nominate a President of the United States. She did not come here to deadlock the convention." For nearly half an hour thereafter the galleries howl their fury at McAdoo, that trim wiry figure out of the Wilson years who stands now very straight, his head lifted defiantly, a sardonic smile upon his face, until a thoroughly angry Chairman Walsh at last summons Mayor Cermak to the podium with orders to silence his unruly fellow townsmen. Cermak does so, with difficulty. Then McAdoo mockingly thanks the galleries "for the compliment they have paid me," hastily adding, however, that he has no wish to "cause . . . wounds," that "[t]hose of 1924 were created against my wish," that Democrats ought to "fight Republicans" instead of one another, concluding with the decisive pronouncement: "California casts forty-four votes for Franklin D. Roosevelt."

Then, the bandwagon rush!

At ballot's end only the delegations of Connecticut, Massachusetts, New Jersey, and Rhode Island, under the unit rule, plus 63 of New York's 94 votes, 14½ of Pennsylvania's 76, and 2 of Wisconsin's 26—190½ votes in all—remain in Smith's column. By then, Smith himself, stunned, embittered, angry, has left the hall without releasing his delegates, thus preventing the traditional unanimity of convention final choice.

It is 10:32 P.M. of July 1, 1932, when Chairman Walsh proclaims that Franklin D. Roosevelt, having received 945 votes, is "the nominee of this convention for President of the United States," a proclamation soon followed by the chairman's reading to the convention of a telegram from Albany saying that the nominee will come by airplane to Chicago on the next day to receive the formal notification of his nomination and to address the delegates.[44]

So it is that Louis Howe's moment of truth becomes, at long last, a moment of triumph.

And how does he respond to this glorious fruition, this self-justifying fruition, of twenty years of intense, anxious, unremitting labor?

With joy, surely!

Yet with surprisingly meager show of it.

And with no such release from tension as one would expect.

Indeed, his anxiety over his future status and role in the inevitably expanding Roosevelt entourage gnaws now more deeply into his soul than ever in immediate consequence of that for which he has so long labored, so that the happy relief with which other exhausted men tumble into bed that night for long hours of a sleep too profound for dreams is denied him.

Some time past, Sam Rosenman delivered to Moley over the private line from Albany to 1702 an edited text of the address Roosevelt will present to the convention and nation the next day. A trusted stenographer, doubly sworn to secrecy, took the phoned speech down in shorthand, then typed it out, and

Moley, reading the transcript, was delighted to find that no substantive changes had been made in the draft speech he had given into Roosevelt's hand just before his departure for Chicago. Extensive cuts had been made, of course. A peroration had been added. But the central ideas, the essential language, remain intact in this draft, and they are ideas and language that Howe has known were going into the speech, since Moley was at pains to keep him informed of every step in the drafting. Hence Moley's "amazement" when Howe, shown the phoned text, "rasped that the speech simply wouldn't do . . . wasn't appropriate to such an occasion." Why not? In good part, evidently, because Sam Rosenman's "hand" can be seen by Howe "in every paragraph of this mess," a view in which he persists despite Moley's assertion that Sam has had little more than an editor's role in the draft's preparation. But there is another reason also, as Moley surmises: Howe is desperately, touchingly desirous of "a major role in the crowning oratorical climax of his idol's career." Surely this is his right! Has he not earned it a dozen times over? Hence his emphatic insistence that "a whole new speech" is required and that he himself (*"Mein Gott!* Do I have to do everything myself?"*) must write it.

It is this, then, that keeps him from badly needed sleep during the long hours of night that follow the nomination. Somehow he manages to summon "enough energy out of the crannies of his frail anatomy" (Moley's words) to dictate to Rabbit Durand a draft speech whose substance is a point by point exposition of the Democratic platform and whose contents, on the morrow, he will refuse to show to Moley or anyone else, save the man for whom he prepares it.[45]

Nor is this the sum total of his anxiety on this night of triumph.

Just as he is about to begin the speech dictation, two visitors, intimates of the innermost circle, come to him from the convention hall. Nancy Cook and Marion Dickerman are eager to share with him a triumph to which, over the years, they have made some (as he has made enormous) contribution; but they come, too, for another purpose. Yesterday morning, the morning of the day of the nominating speeches, which seems now *very* long ago, Nancy received from Eleanor Roosevelt a long, passionately troubled, deeply troubling letter, and it has been decided, not without a painful balancing of private against public obligations, that the letter *must* be shown Howe.

The hurt, love-seeking Eleanor during the last decade has confided many an intimate secret in the two women, her closest friends and working associates. Many a letter has she written each of them when the three were separated, expressive of her love for them, her need for their love, and of her resentful fear of being personally obliterated by the demands of her husband's career. Yet it has always been clear to Nancy and Marion, has been made clear to them by Eleanor herself, that her expression of feelings in overt act is and will ever be severely disciplined and even often denied by her stern commitment to duty. For instance, one night in 1926, when the three of them sat before a glowing fireplace in Val Kill Cottage, Eleanor confessed to her two friends her deepest hurt, that of Lucy Mercer, yet did so in a curiously detached, emotionless, matter-of-fact fashion, as if she described something observed rather than participated in—an interesting natural phenomenon determined by electrical attractions and repulsions. Her friends understood that she was thus calmly neutral in her account, not because she no longer felt the hurt—she did, her friends knew she did—but in accordance with moral standards self-imposed by act of will. She wanted and needed their sympathetic understanding, but not at the price of alienating them from FDR, forcing them to side with her against him in ways that would inhibit their threesome teamwork toward fulfillment of his high destiny. For by that year they all realized fully that, like it or not, they were involved in history. Each had a historical role of greater or lesser importance to play and could play it best only if she had accurate knowledge of FDR the man, accepted him as the man he was, and accepted also with compassionate understanding the relationship that existed between him and Eleanor.

But there is no such objectivity, no willed detachment, in the long letter that came yesterday into Nancy's hand and was promptly shared, of course, with Marion. There is no thoughtfulness whatever in it, and nothing of self-discipline. Eleanor simply lets go of herself, of standards, even of a sense of reality, as she pours out in tumbled incoherent phrases her fear of the sentence of death that will be imposed on her if her husband wins the presidency. She cannot bear to become First Lady! Every atom of her being rebels against the prospect of being a prisoner of the White House, forced, scourged, onto a narrow treadmill of formal receptions, "openings," dedications, teas, official dinners, and there denied any chance of being simply herself, or doing any of the things she most wants to do. She won't do it! She'll run away with Earl Miller—never mind the fact that Earl has just become engaged to Ruth Bellinger and that Eleanor has been arranging, against her mother-in-law's contemptuous disapproval, a wedding ceremony for him at Hyde Park. She'll flee with Earl, who loves and respects her as Franklin never did, nor her sons. She'll file suit for a divorce from Franklin!

Thus the epistle that Nancy hands to Louis Howe, who, quite apart from his status anxiety, has been suffering a tense fear that something might yet go terribly wrong, queering the nomination or the chance for election. His fear feeds upon what he now reads. His pale face darkens. Deep down, he is reasonably sure that this ghastly effusion is a temporary aberration from which Eleanor will quickly recover, if she hasn't already. He knows her so well, he who is a loved and trusted friend of *both* Franklin and Eleanor, hence a bridge of mutual sympathy, a medium of communication, between the two of them. They've gone through so much together—the Lucy business, the polio agony, subsequent family crises by the score. He's seen her break down before, but he's also seen her always come erect again and stand erect under pressures that would crush most people. She'll do it this time, too! Her Puritan conscience will not let her do otherwise. He's sure of it.

All the same . . .

Abruptly he tears the scribbled sheets in two, rips these into shreds, then dribbles passion in tatters through his long sensitive fingers into a wastebasket.

"You are not to breathe a word of this to anyone, understand?" he orders sternly. "Not to *anyone.*"[46]

VI

ROOSEVELT and his party boarded the Ford trimotor plane, poised for flight into cloudy windy skies at Albany's airport, shortly before 7:30 in the morning of Saturday, July 2. Aboard with him when the plane took off were four of his children—Anna (now Mrs. Curtis Dall), James, Elliott, and John—Rosenman, Missy, Grace Tully, Guernsey Cross, Gus Gennerich, Earl Miller, and Eleanor.

During the last hectic days in the Executive Mansion, Eleanor had given no sign to her observers of the inner turmoil, the passionate rebellion, that had dictated her wild letter. Indeed, some had remarked in her a strange calmness, a remoteness from present circumstances, as if she were interested in the convention proceedings but not personally emotionally involved in them. Such men as Ray Moley use pipesmoking, the endless fiddling with bowl filling and bowl emptying and stem draft, as a defense against self-revelations during moments of stress. Such women as Eleanor Roosevelt use knitting needles to the same end. And all through the long night of nominating speeches and balloting, as she listened to the radio with her husband and others of the family circle, which included the "official family," as well as his mother, up from Hyde Park to be at her son's side when he was anointed, all through those hours her hands were busily knitting, and most of her attention seemed absorbed by, a turtleneck sweater intended for Louis Howe.[47]

There was one person, however, who the next day had some inkling of what Eleanor really felt at that time. Lorena Hickok of the Associated Press was one of the score or so reporters assigned to cover—occupying a makeshift newsroom in the Executive Mansion garage—the front-runner and his family during the convention. A large woman of blocky build, thirty-nine years old, rather coarse-featured and loud-voiced, grossly overweight (she weighed close to 200 pounds), she had not the appearance of a person acutely sensitive to the feelings of others. One of the top woman reporters in the nation, she was accustomed to being treated, she wanted to be treated, as "one of the boys" by her journalistic colleagues, nearly all of whom were male. Yet she at once sensed "something wrong" in Eleanor's mood when she and the AP Albany bureau chief, Elton Fay, having accepted an impromptu invitation from Eleanor, breakfasted alone with her on a Mansion side porch at noon of the crucial Friday, July 1. Eleanor was gracious enough. If she seemed not to want to talk much, neither did her two guests: all three were very tired after their all-night vigil. But Lorena Hickok felt waves of suffering emanating from the other woman; she was both surprised and astonished by them, and deeply puzzled. "That woman is terribly unhappy about something!" she exclaimed to Fay as the two walked away from the Mansion. Fay shrugged. Of course the candidate's wife was disappointed by those first three ballots, said he, and worried about the upcoming fourth. Lorena Hickok shook her head. That might be part of it, though somehow she doubted it. She was sure there was something else.[48]

The flight plan called for refueling stops at Buffalo and Cleveland, and a landing in Chicago at around 1:30 P.M., enabling Roosevelt to rest in the Congress Hotel while the convention, called again into session at two o'clock, went through the formality of nominating John Nance Garner as Democratic candidate for Vice-President of the United States. This done, the presidential nominee would proceed to the convention hall for his acceptance speech.

And surely Roosevelt must by now greatly need rest.

Not perhaps since his polio ordeal had he known darker hours than those of the night of June 30–July 1, sitting in his shirt-sleeves beside the radio in the Mansion study, enveloped in a thickening cloud of tobacco smoke (he smoked one cigarette after another all night long) and a deepening cone of unwonted silence, seldom broken by him save for phone calls to and from Chicago, wherein his words and tone of voice were invariably confident, cheerful. Darker still for him had been most of the sunlit hours of the preceding day. Only an hour or so after he'd gone to bed following the convention's recess, Rosenman had had to rouse him from sleep to take several important Chicago phone calls that had piled up, and the substance of these, and of following ones, weighed so heavy upon his spirit that by five o'clock in the afternoon he was, almost unprecedentedly for him, crushed down into utter despair.

No sign of his despondency had he given Rosenman, or anyone else in the Mansion.

But at 5:20, or thereabouts, seated alone in his study, he had placed a phone call to Newton D. Baker. "It now looks as though the Chicago convention is in a jam and that they will turn to you," he had said, as soon as Baker was on the line. "I will do anything I can to bring that about if you want it."

One must assume that Baker was taken aback. As Roosevelt may have surmised, Baker had long had decidedly mixed feelings about becoming President in such parlous times, and in the state of his health. "After all I am sixty and have had warning experience [he'd had a heart attack four years earlier]," he later explained to a friend. His doubts about it had increased in proportion to his chance of nomination, and so had his determination to accept nomination *only* if it were a genuine draft. Hence his response to Roosevelt, after brief hesitancy, had been a demurral. He claimed that he had not been following closely the proceedings in Chicago but that, "on the basis of any such information as I have," Roosevelt ought not to give up; certainly he, Baker, did not want Roosevelt's endorsement of a Baker candidacy at that point, though he appreciated the generosity of the governor's offer.[49]

It was barely an hour later, just as Roosevelt, Rosenman, Missy, and the others were about to enter the dining room for the evening meal, that Roosevelt had taken the phone call from Chicago informing him that Garner had withdrawn and that Texas and California were caucusing on the question of shifting their votes to him. The assembled dinner group had witnessed his reaction to this, had heard his words ("Good! Fine! Excellent!") and seen the sudden broad grin that spread across his countenance, like sunlight breaking through a dark cloud. Obviously he had heard good news! What it was, however, he had teasingly refused to say. In the dining room he had asked that the dining table be moved closer to the phone in the serving pantry, whose cord was too short to reach him in his accustomed place at the table's head; he had done this rather than change his place at table because to do the latter might "change his luck," as he had explained, thereby reminding his companions, who needed no reminder, that he was "superstitious about . . . small things" (Rosenman's words), these being to him signs of great ones. Thus all at table had known that he awaited a phone call of the highest importance. "F.D., you look just like the cat that swallowed the canary," Missy had said, provoked by his teasing silence.

Then, in a few minutes, had come the call—suspense ended, anxiety ended, by news of the Texas-California switch—with joy shared by all save Eleanor, who hid her feelings well. Joy unconfined.[50]

Far less joyous, both as symbol and experience, was the flight into the West by a man who had no love of flying, who preferred a slow train to all other modes of travel over land; for it was a rough flight, not without danger, and might be deemed as darkly portentous, symbolically, as it was expressive of precedent-shattering audacity. From the moment of its takeoff in Albany, the trimotor flew into stiff head winds, which greatly slowed its westward progress. Beyond Buffalo, the air was turbulent, the plane buffeted by squalls. Roosevelt managed several naps as the hours passed, to Rosenman's amazed admiration. Rosenman himself was busy making further cuts in the speech to be delivered by the "man of steel nerves" who napped beside him—cuts responsive to radio reports that the waiting delegates were increasingly restive, that some had already left town. And it was well that the candidate slept, well for him that the triumph so narrowly won, and perhaps *because* it was so narrowly won, ending prolonged anxiety, acted as both stimulant and relaxant upon his nerves; for there was certainly no rest for him after the plane at last landed in Chicago, at 4:30 P.M., some three hours behind schedule.

A vast and vastly excited throng awaited him at the airport. He was so rudely jostled—his hat was knocked off, his glasses nearly so—that he remained upright on his steel-braced legs, then made his way to a waiting automobile on the strong arm of Gus Gennerich, with great difficulty. Yet he remained in high good humor. He laughed. He waved. He recognized by shouted name ("Rex! Ray! Jim!") men with whom, through such public recognition, he shared the triumph they had helped him win.* He even managed to respond with grace and kindness to the incredible, the impossible demand immediately made upon him by Louis Howe, who on this afternoon, for the first time since entering the Congress Hotel, emerged from it, and in better

---

*An exhausted Ed Flynn had left Chicago for New York City as soon as Roosevelt was nominated.

shape than he had been in when he came to town, for all his prolonged
life-threatening ordeal! Howe, in unprecedented thrust of self upon popular
attention, seated himself beside the candidate in the automobile. Howe at once
placed in the candidate's hand the draft speech dictated the night before,
saying, "It's much better than the speech you've got now. You can familiarize
yourself with it while you ride to the convention hall." Roosevelt looked at him
in amazement, muttering in a swift aside, "But dammit Louis, *I'm* the candidate!" Then, immediately sensing something of what the little man beside him
was feeling, this man whose whole life had become absorbed into his own, he
said in Rosenman's hearing—Rosenman having by then been warned by a
nearly frantic Moley of Howe's mad purpose—"All right, Louis, I'll try to read
it over while we're riding down." Fortunate in the immediate thereafter was
his remarkable ability to divide his attention, to do several things simultaneously, for he did skim through the Howe manuscript while at the same time
waving his hat and smiling upon the hundreds of thousands of people who
lined the streets through which he rode. By the time he arrived at the stadium,
he had come to a decision. The bulk of Howe's draft was unusable, but the
first page of it was not radically different from the opening page of the revised
Moley draft (Howe had had this draft at hand as he dictated his own) and it
led equally well into the main body of the latter.

So on the stadium stage, as he awaited Chairman Walsh's introduction of
him, he substituted the first page of Howe's draft for the first page of the Moley
one.[51] And when he began his prepared speech, after an ad-libbed apology for
being late ("but I have no control over the winds of Heaven, and could only
be thankful for my Navy training"), it was with an emphatic redundancy that
critical listeners deplored as evidence of an imprecise if not illogical mind.
"The appearance before a National Convention of its nominee for President
. . . is unprecedented and unusual, but these are unprecedented and unusual
times," said he.* He paid obligatory tribute to "the great, indomitable, un-
quenchable, progressive soul of . . . Woodrow Wilson," many of whose "captains, thank God, are still with us, to give us wise counsel." He praised the
party platform as "an admirable document" that he accepted "100 percent"
and went on to present a speech that seemed appallingly ill-organized to most
who listened to it, or later read it, with close critical attention. The drastic
cutting of the original draft had removed virtually all transitions, and material
ruthlessly inserted—on Prohibition, the farm problem, taxes, the tariff, reforestation, and economy in government—now interrupted and prevented thematic development. Moreover, the reforestation insert manifested "a careless-
ness inexcusable in a state paper," as Tugwell would later say, proposing as
it did the "employment" of "a million men" to plant trees on "marginal and
unused land" across the nation. "Yes, I have a very definite program for
providing employment by that means. I have done it, and I am doing it today

---

*The Moley-Rosenman draft opened: "The appearance before a National Convention of its
nominee is unusual. But these, I submit, are unusual times."[52]

in the State of New York." (Four days later, the national press would carry a statement by Secretary of Agriculture Hyde, approved by President Hoover, pointing out that New York's forestry program, which called for reforesting a million acres in fifteen years, currently employed seventy-two men full time and 272 part time and that, since one man could plant a thousand trees a day, a million could plant a billion: "All the baby trees in the country today could be put in the ground in three hours.") The few extendedly coherent statements remaining in the speech, dealing in broad terms with economic policy, were mostly verbatim transcripts of Moley's May 19 memorandum and, with language revision, of the memorandum Tugwell had given Moley during the speech drafting, joined with some words about the farm problem derived from a telegram Tugwell had sent Roosevelt shortly before the convention opened.

Nevertheless, the address as a whole, beautifully delivered, was effective of Roosevelt's overall purpose. It gave an impression of concern for the welfare of the common folk as against special favors for the well-to-do, and of a determination to make badly needed changes in an economic system that had proved as impractical as it was immoral, yet also of a firm commitment to the private profit system ("[l]et us use common sense and business sense"). As for the peroration, it became immediately famous. "Never before in modern history," said Franklin Roosevelt, "have the essential differences between the two major parties stood out in such striking contrast as they do today. Republican leaders not only have failed in material things, they have failed in national vision. . . . Throughout the nation, men and women, forgotten in the political philosophy of the government of the last years, look to us for guidance and for a more equitable opportunity to share in the distribution of national wealth. . . . Those millions cannot and shall not hope in vain. *I pledge you, I pledge myself, to a new deal for the American people. . . .* * This is more than a political campaign; it is a call to arms. Give me your help, not to win votes alone, but to win in this crusade to restore America to its own people."[53]

Then the politicking—the kind of personal politicking that Roosevelt was better equipped for, and more skilled in, perhaps, than any other man of presidential stature since Henry Clay.

He shook hundreds of hands as he made his difficult way out of the auditorium, hundreds more after he'd arrived at Howe's suite, which now became his quarters, too, in the Congress Hotel. Among those he greeted was Charles Michelson, the highly talented Democratic National Committee publicity director, who, under orders, had covertly cooperated in the Raskob-Shouse "Stop Roosevelt" enterprise while developing a "Smear Hoover" campaign of

---

*Italicized by history. On Sunday, July 3, newspapers carried a cartoon by Rollin Kirby showing a farmer leaning on a hoe (evidently a pictorial reference to Edwin Markham's famous poem "The Man With the Hoe," itself inspired by a Millet painting) as he gazes up, with mingled puzzlement and hope (Millet-Markham's peasant looked at the ground in brutish despair), at an airplane passing overhead, Roosevelt's plane, with the words "New Deal" emblazoned on its wings. Within days the words had become firmly attached as a label to the new dispensation that Roosevelt promised—a development unforeseen by any who had worked upon the acceptance speech.

unparalleled effectiveness. "Glad to see you aboard the ship," said Roosevelt with a broad smile and just a touch of good-natured irony.[54] He also heartily approved Howe's acceptance earlier that day of support from Bernard Baruch. Baruch had brought with him to Room 1702 his protégé, Brigadier General (Retired) Hugh S. Johnson, a colorful, explosively energetic, remarkably able, if also erratic and alcoholic, man of fifty years. A West Point graduate who had served in Mexico during the futile pursuit of Pancho Villa, he planned and administered the draft in 1917 and then became head of Army Purchasing and, as such, the War Department's representative on the War Industries Board, which Baruch chaired. After the war, he was associated first with George N. Peek in the Moline Plow Company; he was coauthor with Peek of the McNary-Haugen Plan,* whereby a federal export corporation would buy farm surpluses for sale ("dumping") abroad, with a tax on producers (an "equalization fee") to make up the difference between the world price and a higher domestic price arbitrarily set by a governmental agency. Then he was involved with Baruch in various business enterprises. Johnson, suggested the ceaselessly insinuating, blandly imperturbable, and incredibly thick-skinned Baruch,† would be useful as an idea man and speech writer in the upcoming campaign, serving with Professor Moley. And this suggestion, too, was accepted with much show of gratitude by Roosevelt, despite his perfect awareness of Baruch's power-seeking motive and his strong suspicion that he accepted, or *seemed* to accept, a potential enemy into his camp, it being predictable that the great financier would vehemently oppose certain kinds of governmental action, those of an inflationary nature for instance, which Roosevelt felt he would probably, as President, have to take.

For "party unity" was, now more than ever, the candidate's watchword. A reduction of factional animosities, insofar as these could not be wholly removed, was his overriding immediate aim. And to that end he displayed an eagerness to forgive and forget past attacks upon him and to welcome as allies in the war upon Hoover Republicanism men who had been his bitter enemies only yesterday.

Thus, when he performed with zest and charm that evening before a massive press conference, he seized the opportunity to heal, as far as possible, the breach between himself and Al Smith, who had checked out of the Congress a full hour before his train time that afternoon in order to avoid meeting the man who superseded him as titular head of the party. Roosevelt frankly proclaimed his disappointment at not being able to confer with his "old friend Al," as he had frankly proclaimed his "hope" of doing so when he spoke the previous night to reporters in Albany. Within an hour after Smith's departure from Chicago, Roosevelt had assigned to Mrs. Sam (Dorothy) Rosenman, who remained in Albany, the task of soothing Al's hurt feelings to the extent, at

---

*See *FDR: The Beckoning of Destiny,* page 750.
†Tugwell would never forget, nor cease to be disgusted by, Baruch's greeting as he entered Howe's suite: "Well, boys, we won!"[55]

least, of preventing a party-splitting statement by him to the reporters who would press him for one when his train arrived at Grand Central. She had long been one of Al's favorite people. She was a close friend of State Supreme Court Justice Sheintag, who was one of Al's warm friends,* and she persuaded Sheintag to board Smith's train at Harmon, New York, from where all the way to New York City the judge would make his argument against an act that would be at least as damaging to Smith's reputation and prestige as it would be to Roosevelt's candidacy. The argument would evidently be effective: Al would refuse to make any public statement whatever at Grand Central.

Shortly after his press conference, Roosevelt went to the Gold Room of the Congress, where, at a dinner meeting ordered in accordance with his insistence upon "action *now*," the Democratic National Committee replaced Raskob with Jim Farley as committee chairman. Control of the party machinery was firmly in Roosevelt's hands when, addressing the assembled Democratic chieftans, he lavishly praised "my very good and old friend, John Raskob," and "my old friend, Jouett Shouse," asserted his confidence that a "united party" would now "meet the Republican leadership," and, looking up at the Gold Room clock, closed dramatically: "The campaign starts at ten o'clock tonight!" Then, back in Room 1702 of the Congress, he socialized with party stalwarts, cementing relationships, as the saying goes, for two solid hours.

And for nearly two hours after the last stalwart had left, in an inner room of the suite, while Tugwell and Doc O'Connor waited in the adjoining room, Roosevelt conferred alone with Moley ("I'm not even a little bit tired," he said buoyantly to the professor), outlining the issue side of his campaign in such detail that Moley, when he took his leave, had with him several pages of scribbled notes. Moley had wondered how or if the advisory group would function once the nomination was secured. Now he knew. He had Roosevelt's solemn assurance that he would continue as "privy council" chairman in full charge of speech preparation ("there will be no drafts or suggestions that aren't cleared through you"), and that "policy" and "politics" would be kept in distinct and separate compartments of the campaign organization, with Jim Farley in charge of the latter. As for Howe, about whom Moley specifically asked, he would operate on the political side, with Farley, said Roosevelt, and have little or nothing to do with Moley's operation.

A few days later in New York City, Farley, in a "heart-to-heart" talk with Moley, pledged his allegiance to the candidate's design. " . . . I'm interested in getting him the votes—nothing else," said Jim to the professor. "Issues aren't my business. They're yours and his. You keep out of mine, and I'll keep out of yours." The two shook hands on it.[57]

*See page 174.

-->>X<<-

The Genesis of a "New Deal" in the Campaign of 1932: Part Two

I

WITHIN three weeks thereafter the campaign organization was in place and efficiently operative.

In New York City's Biltmore Hotel were the official campaign headquarters, presided over by Farley, whence issued the abundant campaign literature that Howe had prepared, now added to by Charlie Michelson—posters, pamphlets, flyers, broadsides, whose distribution among field workers was carefully rationed to assure their actual use as vote getters. At Farley's side was Molly Dewson, to whom, thanks to Eleanor, was assigned the task of recruiting women into the Roosevelt ranks. Closely associated with Molly were women with whom Eleanor had long worked in New York politics: Caroline O'Day, Nancy Cook, Frances Perkins (when her official duties permitted), Marion Dickerman, and a dozen others. Eleanor herself had an office across the street from the Biltmore in the old "Friends of Roosevelt" headquarters, which Howe continued to occupy; here, as in Albany, Val Kill Cottage, and during her nationwide campaign travels, she was soon "covered" full time by the Associated Press reporter Lorena Hickok, who had requested this assignment. In the governor's office in Albany, with a branch of equal size in Howe's New York City office, was a vastly expanded letter-writing mill, directed by Howe, whereby "personal" answers by the hundred were made to the letters now daily flooding the presidential candidate, each answer bearing Roosevelt's "personal" signature, forged by someone trained in the art.* Headquartered in a three-room suite of the Roosevelt Hotel by late July were Moley and the other policy advisers, who had earlier been cramped and scattered among Moley's, Tugwell's, and Berle's Columbia offices. The suite had been hired for their use by the generous Jesse Straus, who was now director of the Business and Professional Men's League for Roosevelt. Here consultations were held, a huge correspondence dealt with, interviews by the dozen conducted daily, and some drafting done, though most of the actual speech writing was done elsewhere, in the relative peace and quiet of the drafter's own home or office.

---

*Howe's letter writers were supposed to confine themselves to friendly, noncommittal acknowledgments of receipt. Letters calling for more complicated answers, with statements on policy, were supposed to be turned over to Moley, whose advisory group prepared answers that were actually reviewed and signed by the candidate himself. Howe's letter writers often went beyond their terms of reference, however. " . . . every time I looked over the stacks of replies they turned out I would find what seemed to me dangerous commitments to this policy or that . . . ," Moley would later write. Fortunately, none of these dangerous replies fell into Republican hands.[1]

In general the Roosevelt-ordered separation of "politics" from "issues" as operating functions of the campaign was strictly maintained. On the two or three occasions when the candidate's pledge to Moley was seriously violated, the violator, as might be expected, was Louis Howe. Though he tried, Howe was not always able to prevent flaring expressions of his hurt resentful rebellion against the assignment to others of roles that had been formerly exclusively his own. After one such episode he apologized to Roosevelt in writing: "Sorry I injured Moley's feelings and upset your orderly plans on speeches."[2]

II

SECRETARY of Agriculture Hyde's attack upon Roosevelt's proposal of reforestation as an antidepression measure was published on Wednesday morning, July 6. In Albany, Roosevelt saw it in a half-dozen papers as he breakfasted in bed, smoking the first two or three of that day's thirty-odd cigarettes. He laughed about it when, wheeling himself into the Executive Mansion, where Moley, Tugwell, and O'Connor awaited him, he took note of their glum expressions. Admittedly, he had made a mistake. The reforestation notion had just "popped" into his head while he was flying to Chicago, and he had thrust it recklessly into a draft speech that Rosenman was at that very moment struggling to shorten. He ought not to have done it; he regretted bruising the fruit of Moley's meticulous labor. But there would be no serious consequences. There might have been if President Hoover had "taken this on" personally, as Roosevelt in Hoover's place would certainly have done: the Democratic presidential candidate in that case would have been forced to confess error of a kind damaging to vote-getting prestige.[3] But Hoover, characteristically, had deemed such action beneath the dignity of his office. A subordinate had replied, one whose general prestige was low indeed, especially among country folk directly concerned with land use—and a discredited Secretary of Agriculture could be safely ignored by a major party nominee for President of the United States.

That is what Roosevelt did.

Simultaneously he made news of his own, in smothering abundance.

From his meeting with his speech advisers that Wednesday morning, during which they were instructed to prepare basic language "on the half-dozen big issues" for presentation to him two weeks hence, he went to a press conference, where he announced that he and his sons James, Franklin junior, and John were embarking the following week on a long-planned sailing cruise through New England coastal waters in a forty-foot yawl, the *Myth II,* hired by him "because it was cheap."[4] The holiday would last "about a week." The next day, in the evening, he gratefully and gracefully accepted the honor of a homecoming triumph accorded him by thousands of people who trekked with lit torches through Albany's streets to the Executive Mansion, a celebration rendered nationally newsworthy by the significant fact that Albany's Tammany bosses had organized it. Why had they? Was a major segment of Tammany "surrendering" to Roosevelt even before he had acted on the Walker case? Or was this a stratagem for "capturing" his support of the gubernatorial ambitions of Albany's Tammanyite Mayor John Boyd Thatcher? The next day, Friday, Roosevelt motored south from Albany along the old Albany Post Road, with the lordly Hudson shimmering away at his right hand, the Taconic Hills rolling far away to his left, down into the landscape of his boyhood, where another homecoming triumph awaited him, this one accorded him by Hyde Park neighbors at the homeplace of his farmer, Moses Smith. And yet another victory-and-homecoming celebration was held on Saturday, July 9, at the Big House of Hyde Park, with thousands gathered on the spacious lawn from all over the state senatorial district (Putnam, Dutchess, Columbia counties) that in 1910 had elected him to his first public office. On that same day he dispatched to Herbert Hoover in the White House, and released for publication in Sunday's papers, a lengthy telegram,* the one in which he offered in a spirit of self-sacrificial public service to abort his New England cruise and come to Washington "on forty-eight hours notice" for a conference with the President on New York's interest in the St. Lawrence seaway pact, which was reportedly in the final stages of negotiation between the State Department and Canada. It was an offer he knew Hoover would refuse, as Hoover promptly did: its purpose was to point up the sharp difference between President and governor regarding hydroelectric power, Hoover's opposition to governmental enterprise in this field continuing as adamant as it was increasingly unpopular, especially since the Insull collapse. The difference was further emphasized by Roosevelt's release to the press, simultaneously with his telegram, of a New York Power Authority report charging the State Department with a deliberate attempt to frustrate New York's efforts toward cheap electricity for the people by assigning to the state an excessively high proportion of the total St. Lawrence project construction costs. From Hyde Park to New York City came Roosevelt on Sunday, to spend that night in the Sixty-fifth Street house.

And early on Monday morning, July 11, with Roosevelt at her wheel and his sons hoisting sail, *Myth II* was towed out from her Port Jefferson anchorage to catch a stiff breeze across Long Island Sound, beginning a cruise that, if leisurely, was not notable for peaceful contemplative solitudes.[5]

The yawl reached New Haven's Morris Cove on the first day's running, Stonington on the second, and Cuttyhunk Pond in the third; Roosevelt had planned to make Naushon Island the third day, to spend the night with his maternal cousins, the Forbeses, who owned the island, but a brisk northeast wind had slowed him. *Myth II* was followed at no great distance by the *Marcon*, chartered by reporters, as well as by a luxurious steam yacht, the *Ambassadress*, chartered by Jesse Straus, whose guest passengers included at various times Joseph P. Kennedy, William H. Woodin, and others whom *Time* magazine called "tycoons," as well as Farley, Ed Flynn, other politicians, and the musical comedy star Eddie Dowling, who was organizing theater people in support of Roosevelt. Nor were the two following boats the only guarantee that there would be no loneliness of father and sons upon an immensity of

*See pages 100–101.

ocean, under an immensity of empty sky. For the sky was often *not* empty: seaplanes bearing photographers often swooped low overhead.

There were no planes on the fourth day (Thursday), however. That was a day of heavy fog and slight breeze on Buzzard's Bay, with hours of almost flat calm, during which *Myth II* crept northward at a snail's pace past Fairhaven, where Roosevelt as a boy had spent many of his happiest hours, in the attic of the big Federal-style house built by his seafaring great-grandfather Warren Delano, and on his great-grandfather's stone pier; past several beaches off which, as a boy and youth, he had swum in water warmed by the Gulf Stream; past the seacoast village of Marion, where, five years before, after weeks of almost unbearably strenuous exercises performed under the tutelage of the physician who had devised them, he had come the closest he would ever come to walking again, *really* walking, without braces on his legs—past all these on a shore hidden from his sight by fog until at last he dropped anchor in Sippicon Harbor at the top of the bay. There he told reporters that, unable to make this summer the tour of state institutions that had been his annual custom, he was asking Lieutenant Governor Lehman to do so, an announcement understood to mean that he intended Lehman, *not* Albany's Mayor Thatcher, to be his successor in the governor's chair. The fog lifted while he slept that night. And on the following day he again moved through scenes from his past. They were scenes visible now to his actual sight and not just to his mind's eye. For the day was clear and bright as *Myth II*, her sails furled, was pushed by her small auxiliary motor up the Cape Cod Canal, with Roosevelt waving to crowds upon the bridges under which he passed as he had waved to many thousands along the banks on a day in July 1914 when Austrian troops invaded Serbia, Russia and Germany mobilized, all Europe was about to burst into flame, and he, as Assistant Secretary of the Navy, stood upon the bridge of the destroyer *McDougal*, leading a parade of destroyers up and down this canal as part of the ceremonies formally opening it. Thereafter *Myth II* ran beautifully before a favoring wind all day long, across Massachusetts Bay past Boston to Marblehead, off which her anchor was dropped as the sun went down. She ran equally well on Saturday, July 16, around Cape Ann and up New Hampshire's brief coastline to Portsmouth, where Bob Jackson, Colonel House, and a galaxy of New Hampshire political luminaries awaited him.

That night was the last night spent by him aboard *Myth II*. The next day, with his cruise ended, he went by motorcade to Hampton Beach, pausing on the way at Little Boars Head, where James and his wife, Betsey, were summering in the home of her father, Dr. Harvey Cushing, and where Betsey brought out in her arms to her father-in-law's car her infant daughter, Roosevelt's grandchild, to receive his joyous blessing. At Hampton Beach, where Bob Jackson had arranged things with his usual efficiency, he was introduced to a crowd of 50,000 by New Hampshire's governor, who found it fitting that Roosevelt's first campaign speech should be made in the state whose primary had started him on the road to nomination. Roosevelt, however, thought it *not* fitting to "talk politics" on Sunday in New England, and said so. He was reminded of a visit made to Portsmouth during the Spanish-American War by Assistant Secretary of the Navy Theodore Roosevelt, who had then remarked the presence in Portsmouth's harbor of the whole of a naval reserve squadron sent there to protect the Navy base. How come no ships were out on patrol? asked TR of a young naval officer. The officer, a New Englander, had found the question strange. "It's Sunday, you know," he had replied.[6]

Thus did Franklin Roosevelt's "nonpolitical" talk tacitly remind his audience of his familial relationship with TR.* And all that day, Sunday or no, he continued the politicking for which his cruise had been designed as much as it had been for recreation.

At almost every anchorage he had received aboard his boat New England political leaders who had fought tooth and nail against him and for Al Smith during the primaries and convention. "I not only understood but admired the loyalty of Rhode Island Democrats to our old friend Al Smith," he had said to reporters after a cordial visit with J. Howard McGrath, Democratic state chairman of Rhode Island, who boarded *Myth II* at Stonington, Connecticut. "I am confident they will give me the same loyal support." And on this Sunday, July 17, after motoring from Hampton Beach to the Beverly Farms, Massachusetts, home of Colonel House, he met with Governor Ely and other Massachusetts Democrats at Swampscott. Felix Frankfurter, who was on friendly terms with Ely, in a phone conversation with Roosevelt while the latter was homeward-bound from Chicago, had urged the nominee to invite Ely, who was a national committeeman as well as governor, to come to Albany or Hyde Park for a visit. Roosevelt, smarting from things Ely had said during the speech nominating Smith, had been reluctant to do so but had finally promised to "do something" along the lines Frankfurther suggested.[7] Now he did it. In a face-to-face meeting, exercising all his charm, he indicated his awareness that the alliance he had formed with Curley had been a grievous error, his eagerness to let bygones be bygones, his hope Ely would do the same. Ely, warming to the nominee, responded in kind. The next day, after a night at Little Boars Head, Roosevelt spent several hours with Colonel House at Beverly Farms, taking care to be photographed by a battery of news cameras as he sat with the colonel on the porch of the latter's home. The gesture signified his continued commitment to "Wilsonian ideals," his continued close association with men who had greatly figured in Woodrow Wilson's administration, a signification underlined when, having motored from Beverly Farms to Albany, he welcomed Bernard Baruch as his houseguest in the Executive Mansion that Sunday night.

By then it was clear to knowledgeable observers that *Myth II* had not only facilitated a restoration of party unity, with Roosevelt firmly in command, it had also alienated a yet-sulking Al Smith from major sources of his political

---

*His words might also remind listeners that Portsmouth, New Hampshire, became world famous when TR as President, mediating the quarrel between Russia and Japan, held there the peace conference ending the Russo-Japanese War of 1905.

potency while increasing the pressures upon him, by his own friends, to grasp the hand of comradeship that Roosevelt repeatedly, ostentatiously, held out to him.

Nor was this all.

The cruise had gone far toward nullifying the effectiveness of any attempt by Republicans to exploit in clandestine ways the question of Roosevelt's health—so far, indeed, as to render the health issue possibly more damaging to Hoover than to Roosevelt insofar as its raising might invite invidious comparisons. For the daily accounts filed by reporters of doings aboard the yawl, the photographs of captain and crew appearing in newsreels and the rotogravure sections of Sunday papers, made no reference to the pulling and hauling by which Roosevelt was moved up and down companionways, then shifted from place to place on deck. Their abundant descriptions and pictorializations were of a robust, highly skilled blue-water sailor, the beloved and tirelessly energetic father of strong handsome sons who were themselves remarkably active. This portrait of a big muscular self-confident man, with sun-tanned vigor and a laughing zest for life, contrasted sharply with the tense anxiety and seemingly flabby physique,* the fear-soaked gloom, the consequent inability to act in any way not prescribed by blueprint or even to smile convincingly, that characterized the Great Engineer now presiding so miserably, from the White House, over a nation's misery.

It was a contrast soon sharpened by a peculiarly ugly episode in Washington to a point deeply penetrative of the national consciousness and in ways fatal to what little personal liking for Herbert Hoover yet remained in the land.

III

EARLY in May 1932 a group of some 300 unemployed World War veterans in Portland, Oregon, led by a thirty-four-year-old former AEF (American Expeditionary Force) sergeant named Walter W. Waters, boarded the empty cars of a freight train to begin a "march on Washington" emulative of Coxey's Army of 1894. Organized in quasi-military fashion as companies, platoons, and squads and clad in portions of their old uniforms (khaki tunics, canvas leggings, overseas caps), they called themselves Bonus Marchers or the Bonus Expeditionary Force (BEF), since their purpose was to apply pressure upon Congress for immediate payment of a veterans' bonus that by previous congressional enactment was not due until 1945.

A bill to effect such payment through the issuance of $2.4 billion of fiat money† had been introduced in the House by Texas Democratic Congressman Wright Patman, himself a veteran (he'd been a machine gunner in the war).

---

*Whenever Hoover put on weight, the first pound of it puffed out his cheeks, so that in facial portraits he always appeared far more overweight than he actually was.
†That is, paper currency that, though legal tender, had no backing by gold or silver and bore no explicit promise of redemption in specie.

It was agitated for by veterans, had the support of others who inclined to favor *any* proposal that would increase mass purchasing power, and was of course vehemently opposed by Herbert Hoover. It was also opposed by many who had no ideological aversion to a controlled inflation in the circumstances but deplored an inflationary measure designed for the special benefit of a segment of the body politic. Roosevelt was opposed to it on principle. "I do not see how, as a matter of practical sense, a government running behind two billion dollars annually can consider the anticipation of bonus payments until it has balanced the budget," he said in a public statement in April 1932, subscribing thereby to the priorities of the President whom he attacked for "piling up huge deficits."* He reiterated his principled opposition when Huey Long phoned him from the Chicago convention hall during the dark night (June 30–July 1) of the nominating speeches and first balloting. Identifying himself as "the Kingfish" and addressing Roosevelt as "Frank," though the two men had thus far never met, Long asserted that if Roosevelt would at once issue a statement favoring the bonus, he would at once be nominated, whereas if he did not he would never be. "I'm afraid I cannot do that because I am not in favor of a soldiers' bonus," Roosevelt replied. Long was disgusted. "Well," he said, "you are a gone goose."[9] As for Patman himself, he flatly denied that his proposal would initiate an inflationary spiral akin to Germany's in 1923, as critics charged. "We are willing to tie to a 40 percent gold basis," he said. On that basis, he went on, $10 billion of paper currency could be supported by the gold ($4 billion of it) that yet remained in the U.S. Treasury, and since only $5.5 billion of paper was now in circulation, an additional $2.4 billion would leave the total well below the danger point.[10]

The departure and initial progress of Waters and his men, unimpeded by officials of the railroads—the Northern Pacific, the Union Pacific—whose freights they rode, were little noticed in the nation's press. In East St. Louis, however, on May 21, their attempt to board a Baltimore and Ohio freight was frustrated by railroad security guards in ways that humiliated and angered them. In an ugly mood they began to uncouple cars, slash air hoses, and grease rails in the marshaling yard. National Guard units were called out. A bloody confrontation was avoided when sympathetic, but also frightened, East St. Louis citizens presented the angry hungry men with 200 pounds of sausage, simultaneously providing trucks to transport them across Illinois into Indiana —and by then the Bonus Expeditionary Force, with its "Battle of the B & O" substantially won, had become national front-page news. Other unemployed veterans in every region of the country were incited to "hit the road" to Washington. When the West Coast contingent arrived in the capital on Sunday, May 29, having been given truck transportation by nervous state and local officials through eight days and across five states beyond Illinois, they found

---

*Hoover, whose administration's deficits were due to declining revenue, *not* increased expenditure, insisted that "the urgent question today is the prompt balancing of the budget. When that is accomplished I propose to support adequate measures for relief of distress and unemployment."[8]

upward of a thousand veterans already there, waiting to join them in their unique lobbying effort. Many thousands more were on their way. Walter Waters remained the leader, the spokesman. "We are going to stay here until the bonus bill is passed," he said firmly on the day of his arrival and again and again thereafter, his words echoing ominously, increasingly so, through corridors of power at both ends of Pennsylvania Avenue.

Soon well over 20,000 men, hundreds of them with their wives and children, were suffering Washington's sweltering summer heat as members of the Bonus Army. There arose on a sunbaked floodplain across the Anacostia River from the city proper, within plain sight of the Capitol dome, which was dazzling white in sunlight and spotlighted at night, one of the nation's largest Hoovervilles,* a huge collection of shacks constructed of the usual Hooverville materials, interspersed with tents, sprawled along "streets" jocularly, ruefully, ironically named. Other veterans by the hundred moved into a dozen or more small Hoovervilles in the district and into condemned, partially demolished buildings owned by the government in downtown Washington, buildings soon to be razed to permit construction of new government offices. Considering the strain they were under, the physical misery investing them, though this was often less than they'd suffered "back home," these men were remarkably orderly and well behaved—too much so to please the editor of their own newspaper, the *B.E.F. News,* which soon began publication ("Are you . . . curs and cowards?" cried a representative *News* editorial. "Or are you men?"). Many or most had come here less out of a clear and definite hope than because they were so terribly lonely and helpless at home, had nothing else to do, nowhere else to turn. They were normally law-abiding, recognized the need for social organization, were more prone than most to patriotic emotions, and they willingly subordinated themselves to Waters, who demonstrated high if increasingly authoritarian leadership qualities: on the Anacostia Flat, latrines were dug, sanitary measures imposed, chow lines organized, drunkenness prohibited, orders against panhandling enforced, and, in general, a semimilitary discipline maintained. The veterans also accepted, with gratitude and initial surprise, the friendly help and advice of the District of Columbia's superintendent of police, a tall, trim-figured World War veteran named Pelham D. Glassford. He was a man of rare compassion, good sense, patience, and self-control, who, though he privately deplored their coming, was determined to give these impoverished folk a "fair shake."† He restrained the fear-motivated bellicosity of the three presidentially appointed district commissioners who were his immediate superiors and whose only answer to the "invaders" from first to last was forcible eviction. He solicited donations from

---

*New York City had a considerably larger one on the Hudson River immediately below Morningside Heights, some sixty miles downstream from Hyde Park.
†A West Point graduate, Glassford, after serving as colonel of the 103rd Field Artillery, became the youngest brigadier general in the AEF until Douglas MacArthur achieved brigade command in late June 1918. He had had no police experience whatever when in November 1931 he was appointed to the district police superintendency.

well-heeled Washingtonians to provide desperately needed food, clothing, and medical supplies; arranged a policemen's boxing match, which raised $2,500 for the veterans; contributed $750 of his own money. And his persuasive argument, conjoined with his firm drawing of the line against unacceptable conduct, helped Waters to prevent violently provocative responses by the veterans to disappointments, frustrations. The almost daily demonstrations before the Capitol were peaceful. So were the occasional ones before the White House, where Herbert Hoover repeatedly refused Waters' requests for an audience and, indeed, gave no public sign of awareness that the BEF existed (there was, however, a noticeable augmentation of White House security forces).

On June 15, the House of Representatives, with its substantial Democratic majority, passed the Patman Bill 206 to 176. Many congressmen who did not actually favor the measure voted for it, cynically, in the expectation that the Senate, organized by Democrats with the narrowest possible margin, would reject it. Two days later, the Senate did so. All through the long hot afternoon of that June 17, while senators debated the proposal, the Bonus Army members were assembled in full force upon the Capitol plaza facing the Senate chamber. Their ominous presence was often noted in the senators' floor speeches. Nevertheless, when the vote was taken shortly after nightfall, the defeat of the measure was by an overwhelming majority—62 to 18. Even then, order was maintained. Waters mounted a pedestal beside the Capitol steps. "Comrades!" he cried to the tensely waiting throng. "I have bad news." The subsequent prolonged chorus of angry boos was silenced by Waters' imperious gesture. A stanza of "America" was sung by his order. Then the men "dispersed to billets" in marching platoon order. Within minutes the plaza was empty and silent beneath the star-spangled sky.[11]

Thereafter, a few thousand veterans drifted away from Washington, some taking advantage of the offer of a free ride home made to New Yorkers by Governor Roosevelt in June and to all by the federal government a short time later. Most, however, 12,000 to 15,000, stayed on even after Congress adjourned in mid-July. Internal dissension grew in proportion to the BEF's loss of purpose. There had arrived on June 10, to lead the handful of Communists in the BEF,* one John T. Pace of Detroit, who came under Comintern orders to seize control of the "movement" from Waters, then use it to provoke riots that would in turn provoke bloody retaliations and thereby "radicalize" the populace. He had at the outset no success. The Communist intrusion was bitterly opposed by men who prided themselves on their "Americanism": on one occasion a kangaroo court sentenced Communist agitators to ten lashes apiece with a belt, followed by expulsion from the Anacostia Flat; on another, a half-dozen Communists were beaten up and thrown into the Anacostia River.

---

*They were fewer than one hundred according to John Pace's own testimony before the House Un-American Activities Committee in 1949, Pace having by then left the party and allied himself with the cold warriors of that year.

Waters' authority was repeatedly, emphatically reaffirmed. But by the time Congress adjourned, it was evident to Glassford, as to others, that Waters was losing control, not only of the men but also of himself. A fanatic gleam appeared in his hard blue eyes. With Mussolini's Black Shirts and Hitler's Brown Shirts obviously in mind, he began to call himself an ex-Socialist, like Mussolini, and to talk of transforming the BEF into the Khaki Shirts of America, dedicated to direct political action. And as his megalomania grew, his leadership was of course more and more resented, resisted, repudiated. There developed a rudimentary polarization between left and right extremism among men who were, as individuals, nonideological and even, normally, apolitical. Communist agitations became, in consequence, more effective. John Pace may have been largely responsible, as Waters bitterly charged, for the decisive incident Glassford had tried so hard to prevent—a violent confrontation of Bonus Marchers and police.

This was on Thursday, July 28, a day whose sultry heat encouraged rash irritability.

Shortly before nine that morning, at Waters' order, veterans occupying four government buildings on Pennsylvania Avenue assembled for a meeting. Waters told these men that, in a session the previous afternoon, the district commissioners had given them four days (a deadline of Monday, July 31) for evacuation of the buildings; he urged them to move to a camp that had been established on Alabama Avenue S.E. But before he could complete his argument he was handed by Glassford's secretary a Treasury Department order, just issued, demanding *immediate* evacuation. Waters, reading the order aloud, exploded wrathfully. "You've been double-crossed!" he cried. This of course vitiated his immediately following plea that the men, even so, obey the order peaceably. They booed him. They flatly refused to budge. They called for help from Camp Anacostia and other camps. When Glassford arrived sometime later to enforce the order, with a hundred police, he found upward of 3,000 angry sullen men in the street, being "egged on" by John Pace's Red agitators. Glassford, who was himself angered by an order he believed deliberately designed by Secretary of War Patrick Hurley to provoke an incident that would justify martial law, encountered resistance as he did his duty. At first it was passive; then it became violent. In a five-minute melee, ended by Glassford's shouted and laugh-provoking suggestion that they all "break for lunch," several policemen were injured, one seriously, by flying brickbats and stones, and several veterans were clubbed by police after one of the buildings had been repossessed. Glassford then, on the blue motorcycle he habitually rode, sped to the Board of Commissioners' office with a plea for postponement of further execution of the order until tempers had had time to cool and reason could prevail.

Instead, the commissioners at once formally notified the President of the United States that a "dangerous" situation had been created "during the past few hours" by the "unlawful acts of a large number of so-called 'bonus marchers,' who have been in Washington for some time" (the commissioners implied that the presence of these "so-called" had naturally been beneath the President's notice theretofore).* They informed him that in the police superintendent's "opinion" the police could maintain order from now on only "by the free use of firearms" (Glassford, personally opposed to army intervention, would later deny having expressed any such "opinion") and that they were "therefore" requesting "that they be given the assistance of Federal troops."[12] This request was at once granted by a President who had refused every request by BEF representatives for audience with him. Through Secretary Hurley to the Army Chief of Staff went the necessary order.

The Chief of Staff was General Douglas MacArthur, a theatrical, passionately willful personality, possessed of simplistic mind, immense courage, awesome ego, profoundly antidemocratic attitudes, and a convenient conviction, shared with the President, that the Bonus Marchers were a subversive criminal rabble among whom were few "real" veterans. He consequently insisted upon commanding the operation in person, rejecting out of hand the unasked-for advice of his aide, Major Dwight D. Eisenhower, who pointed out that such action would offend congressmen before whom a staff chief must defend proposed army budgets. "There is incipient revolution in the air!" cried Douglas MacArthur. A national emergency demanded that the nation's highest ranking officer "go into active service in the field."[13] And so, clad in dress uniform, booted and spurred, with eight rows of ribbons and two medals on his tunic, and with his reluctant aide at his side, he marched six tanks and nearly 1,000 troops (an infantry battalion, a cavalry squadron, each mounted cavalryman with flashing saber in hand, each infantryman with fixed bayonet, gas mask, and tear-gas bombs)† up Pennsylvania Avenue from a rendezvous point near the White House, late in the afternoon. He marched them against an "incipient revolution" manifest not in abstract "air" but on concrete pavement and hard-packed urban wasteland by a crowd of desperately poor men who, unarmed and wholly disorganized, women and children among them, could only taunt, jeer, throw a few stones, and then retreat ignominiously, their eyes streaming, as fogs of tear gas swept over them and the ranked bayonets advanced.

Never before, in all the history of the Republic, had the U.S. Army attacked American citizens, by presidential order, in the national capital. Inevitably, though Hoover would later assert that "not . . . a person was injured," scores were injured seriously enough to require emergency treatment in hospitals.[14] A sick baby died after breathing tear gas. By 7:15, the Bonus Marchers were

---

*The "danger" was certainly augmented by the commissioners' refusal to accede to Glassford's request. When Glassford returned from the commissioners' office to the Pennsylvania Avenue trouble spot, he ordered four of his men into one of the occupied buildings to stop a fist fight that had broken out between two veterans on the second floor. The four policemen were attacked inside the building. One, threatened with a brickbat, pulled his revolver and fired wildly. "Stop the shooting!" shouted Glassford. He was at once obeyed. But two bleeding veterans lay then on the floor, one dead, the other dying. This was the only fatal violence that day.
†The cavalry was under the command of Major George S. Patton, Jr. Major Eisenhower, during the operation, was MacArthur's liaison with Glassford, whose police were superseded.

driven from the city proper, their shanty-bivouacs put to the torch behind them. By midnight they had been driven out of the District of Columbia, MacArthur having ignored specific orders *not* to cross the Eleventh Street Bridge. Every shanty on the Anacostia Flat was burned to the ground: the fire's red glow could be seen on the horizon by Herbert Hoover as he looked out through White House windows. The pitiful remnants of the BEF streamed then through the night along Maryland roads, homeless refugees whose only belongings were on their backs and in their hands, reminding some observers of Belgian villagers fleeing the advancing Hun in the summer of 1914. They had nowhere to go.

And as if to make sure that they received no sympathy and a bare minimum of help from officials and citizens of the towns through which they passed, their characters were maligned, their bona fides as veterans denied, in press statements by an administration whose public silence about them had been absolute till now. "An examination of a large number of names discloses the fact that a considerable part [of the so-called Bonus Marchers] are not veterans: many are communists and persons with criminal records," the President had told reporters that morning, immediately after issuing his order to Secretary Hurley. He now gave the press another statement: "A challenge to the authority of the United States Government has been met, swiftly and firmly. . . . We cannot tolerate the abuse of Constitutional rights by those who would destroy all government. . . . Government cannot be coerced by mob rule." MacArthur held an impromptu press conference at midnight, during which, as if to forestall presidential censure of his gross insubordination,* he heaped praise upon the "force and vigor" with which the President had acted after having with "extraordinary patience . . . gone to the very limit . . . to avoid friction and trouble." Said MacArthur: "That mob . . . was a bad-looking mob. It was animated by the essence of revolution." Its members "were about to take over in some arbitrary way . . . the direct control of the government." They were "insurrectionists." As for their claim to be war veterans: " . . . if there was one man in ten in that group today who is a war veteran it would surprise me."[15]

IV

Franklin Roosevelt read about all this in a half-dozen newspapers as he smoked in bed in the morning of Friday, July 29, in Albany's Executive Mansion.

The previous evening he and Tugwell, who was spending the night in the Mansion, had talked about the radio address to the nation that he was to broadcast from "my own home, away from the excitement of the campaign," on Saturday evening, July 30. This, his first major speech since the acceptance,

---

*But was it *truly* insubordination? Hurley and MacArthur doubtless knew that Hoover wished above all to be rid of the Bonus Marchers and would therefore be more relieved than angry to have his restraining order ignored.

consisted of extended readings from the Democratic platform with interpolated comments reaffirming in detail the candidate's "100 percent" acceptance of what Tugwell deplored as a highly conservative, unrealistic, self-contradictory policy document: the draft speech was substantially the one Howe had produced, then tried vainly to persuade the candidate to use, in Chicago. Tugwell was very unhappy about it.[16] But when Tugwell awoke early Friday morning, he found in his mind language that, inserted in the speech, might improve it somewhat—language neatly linking criticism of Republican tariff policy with an insistence, as Roosevelt did insist, upon full collection of war debts owed the United States. He had this language on paper in his hand when, answering Roosevelt's invitation called across the hallway, he entered the governor's bedroom at 7:30. He was unable to present what he had written, however, until a considerable time had passed.

For Roosevelt's mind was full of that morning's Bonus Army news, and he talked of it at length, in tones of outrage and disgust. His hand rested upon a full page of pictures in the New York *Times* as he told Tugwell what Hoover *ought* to have done, what he himself in Hoover's place *would* have done, in response to the undoubted threat that the veterans, if only by their presence in such numbers and circumstances, presented to law and order in the national capital. Hoover should at once have acceded to Water's request for audience, welcoming the opportunity to explain in frank face-to-face talk the administration's position on the bonus and welcoming, too, any suggestions Waters might have for dealing with a situation Waters himself must recognize as intolerable for any extended period. Similarly when Pace showed up before the White House with 200 noisy demonstrators. They had been met precisely as Communist agitators wanted them to be met, with barred gates and a show of force. How much better would it have been for Hoover to send coffee and sandwiches out from the White House kitchen to the demonstrators, simultaneously inviting Pace and a comrade or two to come in for a talk! Surely at the very least governmental provision should have been made to feed and shelter these poor people outside the District for a few days after their eviction. Evidently no such act of human warmth and kindness was possible for Herbert Hoover. He whom Roosevelt himself had deemed a Great Humanitarian, back in the days when Hoover administered immense war relief programs, was in reality deficient, disastrously deficient, in generous human instincts. He was cold, hard. He disliked people, especially the common folk. And at the root of his dislike was fear. Years ago someone had suggested that a fitting epitaph for Herbert Hoover would be: "Here lies a man whose dominant passion was fear." Felix Frankfurter had recently described him as "the most timid man who has been in the White House since Buchanan." And with this assessment Roosevelt thoroughly agreed. "There was nothing left inside the man but jelly," he said to Tugwell; "maybe there never *had* been anything."[17]

More talk ensued that day along this line during what Tugwell later described as "a fairly typical Albany family luncheon." "Present were Eleanor, Missy Le Hand, and, I think, the Tully sisters, Grace and Paula," Tugwell would remember. Roosevelt called attention to a curious remark of Pat Hurley's made at that midnight press conference wherein MacArthur proclaimed himself the instrument of national salvation. The eviction operation was "a great victory" and "Mac . . . the man of the hour," Hurley had said, then added a strange self-admonition: "But I must not make any heroes just now." What had Hurley meant? Roosevelt thought he knew and was about to explicate when, the luncheon finished and he on the verge of transfer from his seat at table to his wheelchair, he was informed by a servant that Huey Long was on the phone, calling from Louisiana. He grinned broadly. "I'll take it here," he said and, to the others, as the phone was placed on the table beside him, "Listen to this! It'll be good!" It was. Long talked into a phone with the same pitch and volume he employed in platform speech: his every word was clearly audible across the room from the receiver Roosevelt held at a careful distance from his ear. And what he had to say was an angry, profanity-laced denunciation of Roosevelt for neglecting the people "who got you nominated," especially Long himself, while cultivating such "stuffed shirts" as Owen Young, Baruch, and other "crooks that got us into this mess in the first place." Long resented the "run-around" he was getting from Howe and Farley; they refused him the campaign money he needed, refused to approve the plans he'd made to campaign on Roosevelt's behalf throughout the country.* Roosevelt responded with soothing words ("[e]veryone appreciates what you've done"), indicated his intention to make full use of Long's talents once the fall campaign got under way, and then, hanging up, shared with the others a loud laugh over Kingfish buffoonery. He quickly sobered, however. Actually, Huey Long was far from being a joke, he said seriously to Tugwell. Exercising an almost hypnotic influence over crowds, absolute self-confidence, remarkable shrewdness, and utter ruthlessness in political battle, the Kingfish had made himself dictator of Louisiana. He now aspired to national power in a time when many had lost faith in democracy and talked of the need for an American Mussolini. Huey Long, said Roosevelt, was "the second most dangerous man in the country." The *second*? asked Tugwell. Who, then, was the first? "Douglas MacArthur," replied Roosevelt promptly. The haughty general might seem stupid to sophisticated minds who read in the press his simplistic pronouncements on public questions—they were always pronouncements, never mere comments—but he was *not* stupid. He was highly intelligent, a brilliant soldier, whose contempt for "the masses," whose view of himself as hero and savior, and whose eagerness to substitute force for persuasion in his pursuit of personal power and glory were all manifest in the previous day's strut up

---

*A speaking schedule was ultimately arranged for Long that took him "into states believed already lost or so firmly committed to Roosevelt that he couldn't possibly do any harm," Farley explains in *Behind the Ballots,* the "old-timers at headquarters" being afraid he "might upset the apple cart" as he nearly did with his forcing of the attack on the two-thirds rule in Chicago. " . . . we underrated Long's ability to grip the masses," Farley admits. " . . . he put on a great show and everywhere he went, especially in the larger cities, we got the most glowing accounts of what he had accomplished for the Democratic cause. . . . We never again underrated him."[18]

Pennsylvania Avenue, yesterday's excess of humiliating violence upon the Anacostia Flat. It was this, a vague sense of MacArthur-as-threat, that had prompted Pat Hurley's strange remark about not making "any heroes just now."[19]

Yet from this appalling episode Roosevelt the politician drew personal satisfaction. He was frank about it in his talk with Tugwell that day: Hoover's reelection, theretofore unlikely, now became nearly impossible and would have been wholly so save for one thing, the one serious embarrassment of Roosevelt's own campaign, namely, the still-unresolved Walker case.

About this last, however, the anxiety was now acute.

When Roosevelt arrived in his Capitol office that Friday morning, he found upon his desk Jimmy Walker's long-delayed reply to the Seabury charges. It was totally unsatisfactory, of course, and this time there was no possibility of pretending otherwise. He must open the long-dreaded and long-postponed public hearing within a few days, must then act decisively upon his findings, in circumstances that rendered whatever decision he made hazardous to the success of his campaign.

Warning advice, as assertive as it was contradictory, had for weeks poured in upon him, and would continue to do so. If he removed the mayor, he would lose New York certainly, Massachusetts and New Jersey probably, and Illinois and Connecticut quite possibly, endangering an electoral college majority. So he was told by Curry and friends, by many another professional politician, and by his own erstwhile law partner Basil O'Connor.* If he did *not* remove the mayor, he would lose "many independents and Republicans [who] are favorably inclined to you at this time." So wrote Harold L. Ickes from Chicago, speaking a prevailing sentiment among Western and Midwestern liberals whose votes could be the margin of victory or defeat. Felix Frankfurter, who was his houseguest in Albany on Saturday and Sunday, July 30 and 31, told him that "the facts ineluctably compel removal of the mayor," going on, however, to indicate an awareness that "the facts" of themselves alone would not do the job. "I have no doubt," concluded the courtier Frankfurter, "that the kind of opinion you would write would put the matter . . . in language of such unanswerable austerity that it would not be possible to put any other interpretation upon your action than as the performance of a sad but inescapable duty." Walter Lippmann was similarly convinced as to the compelling facts and the kind of action they compelled, repeating in his column: "Governor Roosevelt . . . must not only do justice as a judge but he must convince the people as a leader that justice has been done."[20]

Clearly the governor would be as much on trial as the mayor was when the

---

*But Roosevelt could hardly have deemed O'Connor's advice disinterested, or wholly determined by Roosevelt's perceived interest, since O'Connor was Walker's lawyer. He was of course disqualified by his Roosevelt connection for service as Walker's counsel at the hearing, the latter assignment going to John Curtin.

hearing began, and for this trial by ordeal Roosevelt prepared himself with great care. He retained as his special counsel a brilliant lawyer, Martin Conboy (the fact that Conboy was a prominent Catholic layman was not irrelevant to Roosevelt's choice of him[21]), refreshed his own knowledge of the rules of evidence and judicial procedure, thoroughly familiarized himself with the evidence of misfeasance and malfeasance that Seabury had developed, and obtained detailed briefings from Conboy on the law as it pertained to gubernatorial powers of removal and to the kind of hearing he proposed to hold. It must be *his* hearing, held for the sole purpose of enabling *him* to decide in the public interest. It must not be permitted to become, as Walker's counsel would assuredly try to make it, a kind of higher court review of lower court action, necessitating a recall of all the hundred-odd witnesses who had presented before Seabury testimony damaging to the mayor. By the opening day of the hearing, Thursday, August 11, which happened to be the day of Hoover's formal acceptance of the Republican nomination (attention was thereby diverted from Hoover's opening address of the campaign), Roosevelt felt himself as ready for the ordeal as he could possibly be.

He was nervous all the same and showed that he was, which was highly unusual, when he emerged from his private office in the Capitol at 1:30 in the afternoon and made his way slowly, painfully, on creaking braces, before a hushed and intently watchful crowd, to his desk in the Executive Chamber. He was grim-faced. Perspiration gleamed upon his cheeks and brow. When he tried to lower himself inconspicuously into the governor's chair, his muscular arms gave way: he dropped down heavily. His voice was uncharacteristically weak and quavering as he announced that, preliminary to the formal questioning, he would try to "simplify matters and save time" by reading "a little statement with regard to procedure."[22]

This initial quaver, however, may have been due less to nervous tension than to exasperation born of a realization, angry, resentful, that his anguished progress, shocking to many who witnessed it, had made him the object of a pity tinged with contempt. And perhaps, as he then heard his voice trembling in his ears, he responded to it as an actor responds to the cuing voice of another, correcting thereby his own performance. At any rate, before he had completed his opening statement, he had firmly established himself in the role for which he had so carefully prepared—a stellar role in what one of Seabury's biographers would describe as "high drama, enacted before an audience of millions."* He was in full command of himself. He was in full command of his situation.

And he continued to be through the days and the two long weeks that the hearing lasted. Smilingly or sternly, as occasion demanded, he parried the thrusts of Walker's counsel, who tried with all his might to make the hearing an adversary proceeding (Roosevelt vs. Walker) but succeeded only in pointing up Roosevelt's patience, decency, skill, and judicial fairness. "To manhandle

---

*Herbert Mitgang, *The Man Who Rode the Tiger*, page 283.

a situation of this sort into a proceeding which is . . . dignified, pointed, and fruitful, is an achievement of the first order," he was told in a note dated August 17 from the lawyer Adolf Berle, who had theretofore been, as we have seen, doubtful of the governor's capacities. "It is doubly so since you have not the buttress of a codified procedure which supports judges on the bench."[23] In good part by sheer force of personality he managed to transform potential catastrophe into something approaching triumph, his public stature increasing in proportion to Walker's shrinkage under his calm, relentless questioning.

In the end he did not even have to announce the flat either/or decision he had so long dreaded making.

On the night of September 1, with the hearing scheduled to reopen the next day (it had been recessed till then on August 29, to enable Walker to attend his brother George's funeral), Roosevelt sat in his Executive Mansion study discussing the Walker case with Rosenman, Moley, O'Connor, Farley, and several others. Farley and O'Connor urged him to let the mayor off with a stern reprimand, an option Roosevelt had already wishfully considered and rejected regretfully ("No, that would be weak," he'd said aloud to himself in Moley's hearing). Roosevelt shook his head. Matters would have to "take their course," he said, his words clearly indicating his conclusion that the mayor must be removed. O'Connor was disgusted. "So you'd rather be right than President!" he said with an anger to which Roosevelt soberly, good-humoredly responded, "Well, there may be something in what you say."

At that instant, as if on cue, in a providential reward of virtuous conduct, the phone rang at Roosevelt's right hand. It was a call informing him that James J. Walker had just resigned his office as mayor of the City of New York, "the same to take effect immediately."[24]

V

THEN the fall campaign. . . .

Two major campaign addresses had already been delivered during weekend recesses of the Walker hearing. In Columbus, Ohio, on Saturday, August 20, Roosevelt had made a slashing attack on Hoover's economic policies, employing an "Alice-in-Wonderland" parody, the original draft for which was Berle's, to point up the disastrous absurdity of high tariffs conjoined with huge loans abroad to prop up foreign markets for "surplus" American goods.[25] The speech *seemed* to argue for a drastic lowering of tariff walls; it *was,* in its rather lame conclusion, as Tugwell deemed it, a commitment by Roosevelt to increased public-protecting federal regulation of national banks, stock exchanges, and holding companies. A week later, in Sea Girt, New Jersey, he reiterated his personal commitment to the Prohibition-repeal plank of the Democratic platform, ridiculed Hoover's temporizing on this issue, and, most important of all, received impressive public assurance of the support of "Boss" Hague, Al Smith's manager in Chicago—for Hague had arranged this rally of more than 100,000 people.

The major campaigning, however, was scheduled to begin on September 14, with an address on agricultural relief in Topeka, Kansas, Roosevelt's first major appearance in a speaking tour through Western states to the Pacific coast, then back again.

His decision for such a tour, rivaling in strenuosity the one he had made as a vice-presidential candidate a dozen years before, was taken against the advice of virtually every leading Democratic senator and congressman, including many whose own reelection was closely linked to his success. These urged upon him a "front-porch" passivity, especially after the Bonus Marcher eviction, arguing that he had nothing to gain and much to lose, perhaps everything to lose, from an arduous campaign. Circumstances, the chief one being the now-overwhelming personal unpopularity of Herbert Hoover, must inevitably elect him ("All you have to do is stay alive 'til November," said Jack Garner[26]), *unless* he made a bad mistake, and the chance for such a fatal error would be greatly increased amid the hurly-burly of the campaign trail. Witness a weary Hughes's tactical error in California in 1916! It had given the state, and the election, to Wilson.* Certainly none could fault Roosevelt for remaining at home, attending to his duties as chief executive of the most populous state in the Union. This advice, however, received in the shadow of the then-impending Walker hearing, was rejected in part because it ignored what then seemed likely effects of this hearing on public opinion. They were effects whose offsetting might well require persuasive appearances by Roosevelt before huge crowds all across the land.

And in any case, he must look beyond election victory to the exercise of governing power.

If he depended wholly upon existing state and local Democratic organizations to "get out the vote" for him, he would be beholden to them in ways he did not care to be. He needed them, but he wanted them to be his instruments, wanted, as he had been consciously trying to do for a decade, to create a *Roosevelt* party committed to his brand of Progressivism, and he could do this only if he was more effective than they at vote getting in terms of a vaguely stated program for action. Also, after three years of deepening depression and principled opposition to doing anything on the national level to help a suffering citizenry, the country badly needed that show of human concern and optimistic courage that Roosevelt was sure he, in public appearance and speech, could

---

*The Republican Party in California was split into two ferociously warring factions when Hughes campaigned there in August 1916. Conservative regular Republicans fought tooth and nail to deny nomination for the U.S. Senate to California Governor Hiram Johnson, who had rejoined the Republicans after running as the Progressive Party's vice-presidential candidate in the Bull Moose campaign of 1912. These regulars had full control of the party machinery, and a tired Hughes permitted them to take him over completely; they sponsored his meetings, and he in his speeches made not a single sympathetic reference to Johnson or the progressives. This outraged progressives in both major parties in every state; Hughes lost progressive votes which, had he retained them, would have enabled him to carry California, New Mexico, North Dakota, and New Hampshire, all of which went to Wilson by exceedingly narrow margins. As it was, Wilson won 277 electoral votes, Hughes 254.

supply. Finally, there were his own personal needs as potential President, joined to the pure joy, for him, of a vigorous campaign. With his distrustful aversion to generalizations and abstractions, he needed direct individual contacts with the people he aspired to govern, needed an immediate feeling experience of the vast sprawling Republic with its widely various local and regional moods. As for the joy, it was literally recreative. Something electric and wonderful happened when he stood before a crowd. He addressed it, not as a single mass entity, but as a gathering of uniquely individual persons, with each of whom, somehow, he established a vital connection, curiously intimate —and along this connective line there was massive feedback whereby he himself was inspired, revivified, spiritually nourished.

Substantial preparations for his tour were completed and much of the actual language of his speeches was down on paper before the Walker hearing had ended. They were the product of strong diverse pressures playing upon the candidate's largely intuitive sense of national feeling, historic direction, and immediate political necessity.

Urged upon him by Bernard Baruch, who contributed some $60,000 to the party campaign funds, were big-business *laissez-faire* policies, with major emphasis on government economy and a balanced budget. Baruch argued directly through a memorandum he submitted to Roosevelt in mid-July; he did so indirectly through his personal representative on the speech-writing team, Hugh S. Johnson, and, somewhat surprisingly, through Louis Howe, whose overriding fear now was that the Brain Trust professors would entice the candidate into issue-stands that would cost him the conservative vote he had to have to win. The Baruch memorandum was turned over to Moley, Tugwell, and Berle for comment, the last writing Roosevelt on July 20: "Most of the practical proposals seem like sound common sense. . . . [But when] he gets under principle, B.M.B. poses the essential issue between the two wings of the party. Like most eastern business men, B.M.B. wants to permit free play to business, which in practice means freedom to six or eight hundred large corporations and banks to fight out among themselves the ultimate mastery of the situation. He believes individuals must suffer for and rectify their own mistakes. Unfortunately, the result reached is that the 'forgotten men' suffer for the mistakes of the industrial leaders, who come off relatively unhurt."[27]

Tugwell's opposition to Baruch's program was stronger than Berle's, being buttressed by a greater dislike and distrust of Baruch personally than Berle evinced.* Yet his own major campaign proposal, in a memorandum written in his father's house on the shores of Lake Ontario immediately following the Chicago convention, might seem to have been influenced by the success in 1918 of the War Industries Board, which Baruch had headed—might later seem to

---

*Contemptible, in Tugwell's view, were the speculations by which Baruch had acquired much or most of his huge fortune. Through intimate contacts with high government officials (he was reputed to "own" sixty congressmen), he was supplied with prior privileged information on shifts of government policy, enabling him to "bet" on "sure things" on the exchanges.

point toward a national experiment of which Baruch, at its launching, would enthusiastically approve in general. Certainly it was partially emulative of the proposal Henry I. Harriman had announced on behalf of the U.S. Chamber of Commerce in the fall of 1931.* Tugwell stressed the fact that, thanks to the technology involved, an "industrial enterprise today" must plan its factories, acquire its raw materials, and assemble its labor force "far ahead of demand," hoping "that somehow customers will appear." Such blind leaps in the dark had landed the country in the present depression; such a depression could be cured, its recurrence prevented, only by effective economic planning on a national scale; and such planning, matching production to consumption, was properly a function of government, since the only alternative was "nation-wide monopolies, with definite contractual relations among themselves . . . ; and the dangers in such a scheme are obvious." Tugwell proposed, therefore, "a Federal Economic Council" of twenty-one economists and industrial representatives "attached to the Executive, and operating under his direction to secure the needed co-ordination." It would be "at first" an information-gathering body: "[i]t is not proposed to have the government run industry; it is proposed to have the government furnish the requisite leadership; . . . and rise to the challenge of planning that concert of interests of which I have spoken before." But once it was "set up, the federal government ought to press for a reorganization of industry somewhat on the model of the Federal Reserve System in banking. The antitrust acts can be repealed and each industry can be encouraged to divide itself into suitable regional groups on which will sit representatives of the Economic Council." Of course, there were "administrative and constitutional difficulties" to be overcome, but if "they seem to you burdensome . . . I would remind you that something like thirty billions of national income has been sacrificed annually now for three years to the gods of chance."[28]

On this, too, Berle made comment, in a memorandum to Roosevelt dated August 17. "The liberal wing of the party, particularly the intellectuals, are very firm in favor of an economic council," he wrote. "In theory, of course, they are right. Practically, all responsible students agree that the present industrial situation can result only in one of two ways. Either the government steps in through some form of economic administration; or the business machinery, by consolidation, merger, or the like, evolves an irresponsible economic government of its own." But the difficulties in the way of developing an effective council seemed to Berle far greater than Tugwell admitted; he regarded as practically unattainable the coercive power to implement plans at which Tugwell tacitly aimed. "No mechanism covering the ground has existed, except in war time," he said. "I think the line has to be the slow development of a group which will collect, coordinate and continuously interpret economic information, rendering opinions to the president of [sic] the congress at intervals. As these judgments show themselves wise, the group could gather authority and public confidence."[29]

*See page 270.

Radically different from the policies urged either by big business or by the national economic planners—also less insistently and assertively argued within the inner circle but instead there implied or indirectly indicated (by Frankfurther for one, on occasion, and by the New York City lawyer Max Lowenthal, who was a Frankfurther protégé)—were small-unit *laissez-faire* policies inherited from Populism, Bryanism, and the Brandeis-Wilsonian New Freedom of 1912–1915. These emphasized strict enforcement of antitrust law to break up monopoly and oligopoly, a strengthening of regulatory agencies to restore and then maintain free competition among reasonably small units in the marketplace, monetary manipulations—inflationary in immediate effect—to enable debt payment and encourage enterprise by smaller businesses, and drastic tariff reductions aiming toward an immediate great increase in international trade. All of this added up loosely to form a general program, or approach, having a considerable political potency and, hence, persuasive power with the candidate himself. Various facets of it were subscribed to with varying emphasis by such "silver" senators as Burton Wheeler and Nevada's Key Pittman; such Midwestern Progressives as Nebraska's George Norris and Wisconsin's Robert M. La Follette, Jr.; such demagogues as Huey Long and the Detroit "radio priest," Father Charles E. Coughlin, whose national radio audience grew by leaps and bounds; and such free-trade ideologues as Cordell Hull.

Nor was it without respectable support in the intellectual community.

Irving Fisher's rosy view of the stock market on the eve of the 1929 Crash had tarnished his reputation for prescience, but he remained justly recognized as a brilliant monetary theorist. And in that summer of 1932 his proposal to forsake the gold standard in order to "reflate" and then stabilize the currency in terms of a "commodity dollar"—a proposal fitting neatly into what might be called neo-Brandeisianism—strongly recommended itself not only to a multitude of farmers and a considerable number of businessmen but also to many economists. Wesley C. Mitchell was sympathetic toward it. So was Cornell's George F. Warren, the farm management specialist who had helped write Roosevelt's state reforestation legislation and who, as a leading member of the state Agricultural Advisory Commission, greatly influenced the thinking of Henry Morgenthau, Jr. With Frank A. Pearson as coauthor, Warren was completing that summer a book, *Prices,* in which he argued that, through "manipulation of the gold content" of the dollar by means of governmental gold purchases at prices set somewhat higher than the prevailing market price, a proportionate rise in general prices could be achieved, the ultimate objective being that stabilized "commodity dollar" at which Fisher aimed, a dollar "that has a constant buying power, not for one commodity but for all commodities, managed in accordance with a price index."[30]

Moley, Berle, and Tugwell, however, were as one in their hostility toward this general approach, if for differing reasons. To Tugwell, as has been said, the Brandeisian insistence upon the "curse of bigness" was an exercise in sentimental nostalgia, wholly unrealistic in its refusal to accept the inescapable socioeconomic implications of technological advance. Berle, thoroughly orthodox in his monetary views, while conceding that a "certain amount of inflation

... exists" and that "a certain additional amount is inevitable," was strongly opposed to any deliberate inflation of the currency, seeing its effect to "be a steadily mounting cost of living without accompanying rise in wages, ultimately reacting heavily against the whole urban population . . . except the fortunate few who own either stocks, real estate, or commodities, in large quantities."[31] Moley was especially fearful of the consequences of immediate drastic tariff reductions. Not only would such an abrupt lowering of tariff walls cause massive dislocations among theretofore protected enterprises, significantly increasing employment, but it would also decrease the American government's freedom to institute emergency economic recovery programs in proportion as it increased the necessity for an international approach to depression problems. It thereby played into the hands of Herbert Hoover, who in the preceding several months had discovered that the depression was initiated and recovery prevented, not by failed American business and governmental policies (the two were fused in the 1920s), but by "blows from abroad"—delayed effects of the World War for which no American government could be held responsible.

Seated at the center of this tangled web of policy proposals, the focus of intense and opposite persuasive pressures, Roosevelt remained smilingly at ease, serenely inscrutable. Whitmanesque in his zestful openness to a variety that, being limitless, included contradictions, and in his "yea-saying" to all and sundry (rarely did he speak a flat "No!"), he was absolutely confident of his ability to ameliorate, accommodate, and "weave together" antagonistic counsels and personalities in ways that would not only enable him to "get elected" but also, on the ground he had chosen "a little left of center," keep open to him the widest possible range of options once he was in office. Often his own speech writers were not sure where he stood, what his real convictions were or, indeed, if he had any, on the issues with which they had to deal—and this despite the many long evening sessions they had had with him in Hyde Park and Albany, during which basic issue-questions were supposed to be thrashed out. Often an initial draft speech, prepared with only meager and sometimes contradictory hints from him of what he wished to say, became an arduous, hazardous attempt to make up his mind for him. And inevitably his writers, in their pride of craft, suffered from his habit of revising their scripts in ways that rendered trackless and fragmentary the arguments they had labored to develop coherently—rendered vague, susceptible of contrary interpretations, the issue-statements they had struggled to make clear, precise, definite. At least one of the writers, Tugwell, deplored what he sensed as a shift of role after Chicago from the honestly educative and investigative to the contemptibly sophistical. "We had started out to explain things and to deduce from the explanation what ought to be done," he would remember long afterward.[32] "We were reduced now to . . . contriving ingenious accommodations to prejudice and expediency." The writers even wondered, on occasion, with dismay, whether the candidate had a sufficiently firm grasp of key issues to understand, *really* understand, what it was that a draft speech said about them.

An instance of this that became famous, when later related by Moley, concerned the tariff.

At a meeting of seven policy advisers with Roosevelt on the night of August 4 in the Albany Executive Mansion,* it was decided that seven or eight set speeches would be given during the fall campaign, each to deal with one major issue. The tariff speech was assigned to Moley for drafting. It was a difficult assignment. Thanks to Hawley-Smoot, the Republicans were especially vulnerable that year on an issue that had also become, during the last decade, profoundly divisive of the Democratic Party, and Moley was unable to determine with which side of the division Roosevelt himself stood. Not with any certainty. He therefore conceived his task to be one of lambasting the Republicans for protectionism run riot, but without repudiating economic nationalism (this, which involved a considerable measure of protectionism, should instead be tacitly affirmed) or, on the other hand, without dangerously alienating the economic internationalists, the almost religiously fervent free traders, within the party. Of the latter, Cordell Hull was the chief oracle. So Moley dispatched to Tennessee, to obtain Hull's view of what a tariff speech should say, a man whom Roosevelt had first met on the train taking him back to New York from Warm Springs in May 1932 but who Moley had been led to believe (by Roosevelt) was an old and dear friend of the governor's, one whose counsel the governor greatly valued.[33]

This man was Charles W. Taussig, head of the American Molasses Company, whose familial connections† and special business interests inclined him toward free-trade principles but whose presence at policy-discussion meetings should have educated him, in Moley's view, regarding the flexible, selective approach to foreign-trade problems which the New Deal in general would require. Instead, Taussig became a mouthpiece for Hull; he returned from Tennessee with a draft speech on which he and Hull had collaborated, calling for an immediate flat 10-percent reduction of *all* tariffs. Moley found this wholly unacceptable. So did Hugh Johnson, who then stayed up all night dictating to a series of stenographers in the Roosevelt Hotel suite a speech proposing a gradual selective lowering of tariff walls through bilateral international negotiations. By means of "old-fashioned Yankee horse-trades," wrote Johnson, certain foreign products, those least competitive with U.S. products, would be permitted entry to U.S. markets in return for the permitted sale abroad of "our most oppressive domestic surpluses," these being, of course, agricultural.

The two draft speeches proceeded from radically different philosophies. They differed totally in style. They contradicted each other in their practical proposals. Yet when Moley presented both to Roosevelt in early September,

---

*Present were Rosenman, Moley, Tugwell, Berle, Hugh Johnson, Max Lowenthal, and O'Connor.
†He was a nephew of the famous Harvard economist F. W. Taussig, a free-trade advocate who believed the best prescription for depression cure was an immediate drastic reduction of tariffs and a vastly expanded international trade.

the governor, having apparently read both with care in Moley's presence, airily suggested that the professor "weave the two together!"

Moley was appalled.

"But it can't be done!" he cried. He explained why.

"Well, then," said Roosevelt, unperturbed, "let it go until we get on the train. We'll see what we can do about it there."[34]

In the end he gave two major tariff speeches, in Seattle on September 20 and in Sioux City, Iowa, on September 29, the latter a revision of the Johnson draft, on which Moley worked, on Roosevelt's orders, with Montana's Walsh and Nevada's Pittman, both of whom were high-tariff men. In Seattle the talk was of a "negotiated tariff" based on "the simple principle of profitable exchange" or "fair barter" between two nations. In Sioux City the candidate reiterated his "reciprocal tariff" proposal and vigorously called for a reduction of the "outrageously excessive rates" of Hawley-Smoot. But this last was, in context, an all-too-obvious sop to the Hull group, for Roosevelt also objected to the "stigmatization" of the Democratic Party "as a free trade party" and insisted that Democrats had always favored tariff walls high enough to protect "the prosperity of American industry and American agriculture."[35] In later speeches, wherein he mentioned the tariff in passing, he backed yet farther away from free-trade principles. Had he been concerned to educate the public on public questions he might have pointed out that high tariffs on products of which there was a huge domestic-market surplus served no function whatever. What possible economic incentive could there be, tariff or no, for importing such products? But Midwestern and Western producers of huge wheat and corn-hog surpluses had been long conditioned to believe that their very survival as farmers depended upon high-tariff protection. They would find persuasive Herbert Hoover's doomful campaign assertion that if tariff protection was removed, "the grass will grow in the streets of a hundred cities, a thousand towns; the weeds will overrun the fields of millions of farms . . . their churches and schoolhouses will decay." And so Roosevelt, who seemed actually to believe that his Sioux City speech was, as he told Moley, "a compromise between the free traders and the protectionists,"[36] took pains thereafter to assure farmers that he opposed any reduction of *agricultural* tariffs.

On the tariff question in general, said the all-too-principled Herbert Hoover in a campaign address, Roosevelt's was "the dreadful position of the chameleon on the Scotch plaid."[37]

Somewhat similar to this experience of Moley's, raising the same question about the candidate's mental grasp, was Tugwell's experience with farm policy, the subject assigned him for speech writing at the August 4 meeting.

In issue-discussion sessions with Roosevelt, Tugwell had abundantly expressed his disapproval of the McNary-Haugen (Peek-Johnson) approach to farm relief. Its reliance on the "dumping" abroad of American farm surpluses was bound to be self-defeating, since foreign governments would promptly raise tariff walls too high to be "dumped" over, and even if it caused a farm price rise, that rise was bound to be temporary, wiped out by the increased production and consequent renewed surpluses that the initial price hike would stimulate. There was nothing in McNary-Haugen to prevent this. No, said Tugwell, farmers could obtain a "fair price" for their produce—that is, could achieve "parity" with industry, the concept of "parity" being then a novel one —*only* if they did what big industry had long done to raise prices and then maintain them at an advantageous level: they must control production in order to match it to a market demand that was estimated *in advance* of production. It was of course impossible for them to do this, operating as 6,500,000 wholly independent productive units; they must form effective combinations. And such combinations could be brought about only under the aegis, and through the agency, of government.

But how was the needed farmer-government cooperation to be achieved? What new institutional devices were required?

A definite if highly complicated answer to these questions had been worked out a few years back, largely by the economist John D. Black, who dubbed it the Voluntary Domestic Allotment Plan. Elements of it were included in two bills—Hope-Norbeck and Rainey-Norbeck—that were before the Congress that summer, but Tugwell had no clear understanding of it until it was explained to him in detail by Professor Milburn L. Wilson of Montana State College and Henry A. Wallace,* hybrid-corn breeder and editor-publisher of *Wallace's Farmer* in Des Moines, Iowa—this at a national conference of agricultural economists to which Tugwell had gone as Roosevelt's emissary in late June, frankly in search of a program that would entice Midwestern and Western farmers away from their traditional Republicanism into the Roosevelt camp. Soon convinced not only of the practical efficacy but also of the political potency of Domestic Allotment, Tugwell had attempted to explain it over the phone to Roosevelt in Albany. The attempt failed. After a long half hour of listening and questioning, Roosevelt had said with a laugh that he would have to "take your word for it that it's the latest and most efficient model."[38] He asked Tugwell to wire him "two or three hundred words" on the matter. These, revised and inserted at almost the last moment into the Chicago acceptance speech, committed the nominee to a program to "reduce surpluses" through "voluntary" production control by farmers, and committed him also if blurredly, *against* surplus dumping abroad. Immediately after the convention, Wilson was brought by Moley and Tugwell to Albany, where he made a highly favorable impression on both the governor and Eleanor, for Wilson's was a wide-ranging country philosopher's mind joined with a remarkably lovable personality. He explained Domestic Allotment and assessed its politi-

---

*Wallace's namesake father, founder of the periodical he edited, was a former Bull Mooser who became Secretary of Agriculture in the Harding Cabinet that included Hoover as Secretary of Commerce. Under the elder Wallace, who clashed frequently with Hoover on policy matters, the U.S. Department of Agiculture had been reorganized and greatly improved as an agency of service to farmers. The junior Wallace, a lifelong Republican, protesting his party leadership's indifference to the plight of the farmer amid the "Republican Prosperity," had loudly voted for Al Smith in 1928.

cal appeal in a way that persuaded Roosevelt to make it the central feature of his agricultural program.

This was all to the good in Tugwell's judgment.

But as he began working on the initial draft of what would become the Topeka farm-policy speech, he made a dismaying discovery. Twice in recent months Roosevelt had published his approval of the essential feature of McNary-Haugenism, namely, surplus dumping abroad. He had done so early in 1932, when he endorsed the resolutions of the newly formed National Farm Conference, one of which called for dumping. He had done so again, specifically and explicitly, in an article published in *Liberty* magazine, in its June 25, 1932, issue. Headed "I Indict the Administration: We Need a Complete About-Face on the Question of Foreign Debts, the Tariff, and Farm Relief . . . ," this piece was one of a series ghost-written by Earle Looker* and evidently not even read with any care by Roosevelt, their ostensible author, before they went into print, though each of them made emphatic policy pronouncements. Nor was this all. On July 28, 1932, the publisher Covici Friede of New York issued a 107-page book, *Government—Not Politics,* by Franklin D. Roosevelt, a collection of magazine articles, the bulk of them Looker's contributions to *Liberty;* one of these was the piece endorsing surplus dumping. Tugwell, working away on his draft speech, using as basic material a long memorandum written by Wilson and carefully reviewed by Henry Wallace, could only hope the Republicans took no notice of the contradictions between what Roosevelt would soon say and what he *had* said in the immediate past about farm economics. He was immensely relieved when *Government—Not Politics,* the "only book by the Democratic nominee for the Presidency," as its jacket erroneously said, attracted little reviewer attention and few readers.

As for the speech finally given on the Kansas Capitol grounds to some 20,000 people perspiring under a broiling September afternoon sun, it was, in Moley's words, "the direct product of more than twenty-five people!" Among them, in addition to those already named, were Morgenthau, who had been assigned the task of enlisting farm organization leaders in Roosevelt's cause; Clifford V. Gregory, editor of the influential *Prairie Farmer;* Berle, who contributed language about farm indebtedness; Hugh Johnson, who characteristically responded to Moley's request for suggestions by dictating an entire speech, of which portions were used verbatim; Moley, of course, who did the final "putting together" and wrote most of the argument for "interdependence" as a necessary condition of individual "independence" in the modern world (his argument that "our economic life today is a seamless web" derived much from Tugwell's organismic "concert of interests" approach); and finally, Roosevelt himself, who, with blue pencil as his shears, cut the cloth others had woven to fit his own pattern. He also dictated introductory material describing himself as a "farmer" of Hyde Park and Georgia's Pine Mountain, and inserted into the body of the draft striking phrases, including one that echoed

*See page 220.

Abraham Lincoln: "This nation cannot endure if it is half 'boom' and half 'broke.' "[39]

Not one of the direct contributors to it, save Roosevelt and Moley, who conceived it altogether in terms of political effect, was wholly pleased with the final product. Nor was either of the two principal farm organization leaders, Edward A. O'Neal, president of the American Farm Bureau Federation, and John A. Simpson, president of the Farmers' Educational and Cooperative Union (the Farmers' Union, as it was generally called), with both of whom Roosevelt had had personal consultation regarding the farm problem and to each of whom he had listened with close and seemingly agreeable attention as they advised him what to say in public speech. He had conferred with O'Neal at Hyde Park on July 20 and with Simpson in Columbus on August 20, receiving no radical advice from the former, whose organization represented the larger, richer farmers of the corn-hog Midwest and the cotton South, but receiving strongly worded inflationary, anti–big business advice from Simpson,* whose organization represented the smaller, poorer farmers, many of them tenants, whose general outlook reflected that of 1890s Populism. O'Neal, listening to and then reading the Topeka speech, worried some lest Roosevelt incline too far toward Farmers' Union inflationary doctrine; whereas Simpson, reacting to the same speech, among others, feared that Roosevelt might be at heart a hard money man who, in office, would not inflate at all. And of the myriad thousands who heard him in Topeka and over the radio, not one knew, there was much subsequent argument about, precisely what Roosevelt meant when he pledged himself to a "national plan" for agriculture aimed at restoring "agriculture to economic equality with other industries" and giving "to that portion of the crop consumed in the United States a benefit equivalent to a tariff sufficient to give . . . farmers an adequate price." He failed actually to outline any such plan; he confined himself to "specifications" for its design. The plan, he said, "must provide for the producer of staple surplus commodities . . . a tariff benefit over world prices which is equivalent to the benefit given by the tariff to industrial products," but do so in such a way "that the increase in farm income . . . will not stimulate further production." The plan must be self-financing. It must avoid dumping abroad. It must use "existing agencies" and be as decentralized as possible in its administration. It "must operate as nearly as possible on a cooperative basis, and its effect must be to enhance and strengthen the cooperative movement." Finally, it "must be, insofar as possible, voluntary."[40] From all this, major questions dangled, unanswered: did he propose crop-acreage reductions? If so, through what mechanisms?

Yet if no one deeply concerned with the farm problem was wholly satisfied by what Roosevelt said, neither was anyone wholly displeased or antago-

---

*According to Frank Freidel, he pointed out to Roosevelt that some 200 one-pound loaves of bread, worth $20 at prevailing grocery-store prices, could be made from the three bushels of wheat for which a farmer received $1.

nized by it, and Eastern businessmen who had feared that the candidate might give way to "radical" farmer pressures were immensely relieved by it. Tugwell himself came to realize that in this speech as in others, however shoddy their intellectual content, Roosevelt the politician knew exactly what he was doing. A studied vagueness on those matters about which dispute was sharpest enabled the disputants to read into the candidate's words whatever they wanted him to say. A vigorous emphasis persuaded everyone of the distinct possibility if not probability that Roosevelt in office truly *would* act on the problem of farm surpluses, vigorously, realistically, in sharp contrast with Hoover's merely exhortative Farm Board and his "disposition . . . to set proponents of one plan off against proponents of another" in order to justify government refusal to accept any farm plan whatever.[41] Perhaps most important of all was the impression made on farmers by the speaker's personality: by his infectiously buoyant smile, his characteristic gestures—arms outstretched, head tossed back, strong jaw outthrust—his vibrant voice saying warmly, sincerely, "My friends . . . "; You all know . . . "; "You have felt in your own lives and experiences . . ."; "You know better than I . . . " They concluded that, whether or not this new man was smarter or better informed than Herbert Hoover, he was certainly kinder, more friendly, and far more concerned about their plight.

The hope thus restored in breasts that had been drained of it, though a thin and doubtful hope, was sufficient to dampen for the time being what had become a near-revolutionary fire then spreading through the corn belt, a fire whose sparks flew high and far across the Missouri into the dry wheatland and grassland of the plains.

Even as Roosevelt spoke, farmers armed with clubs and pitchforks were patrolling every road leading into Sioux City, Iowa, turning back with whatever force was needed trucks loaded with farm produce. They were members of the newly organized Farmers' Holiday Association, whose founder was a sixty-five-year-old former Populist named Milo Reno, long a dominant figure in the Iowa Farmers' Union. For years Reno had been preaching the necessity, if all else failed, of an "organized refusal" by farmers to market products for which they were paid less than the cost of production; his words inspired action, an ominously contagious action, in the spring and summer of 1932. Iowa dairy farmers went on strike, violently preventing the delivery of milk to distributors in Sioux City and Council Bluffs. The impoverished unemployed of great cities, their children undernourished (a recent U.S. Public Health Service publication declared that "over six millions of our public school children do not have enough to eat"[42]), could read and see pictures of rivers of milk flowing across highways and down roadside ditches from thousands upon thousands of ripped-open milk cans.

Of such activity, despite Reno's call in early October for a general farm strike throughout the Midwest, there was a marked decline following Roosevelt's Topeka pronouncement. Farmers were now disposed, as Election Day neared, to "wait and see."

VI

AT Salt Lake City on September 17, Roosevelt talked of "rehabilitating" America's sick railroads, proposing "regulation by the Interstate Commerce Commission of competing motor carriers" and a relaxation of that part of antitrust law requiring competing railroad lines where traffic was insufficient to support two lines. At Portland, Oregon, on September 21, he discussed public utilities, proposing public development of Boulder Dam, Muscle Shoals, the Columbia River, and the St. Lawrence power site as "a national yardstick to prevent extortion against the public and to encourage wider use of . . . electric power"; he also reiterated that water power "should belong to all the people" and proposed legal abolition of "the so-called reproduction cost theory of rate-making," replacing it with the "actual money-prudent investment principle as the basis for rate-making." At San Francisco on September 23, he discussed in historicophilosophical terms the nature of individual freedom and of progressive government in the America of 1932. At Detroit on October 2, on his way back from his Western swing, he talked of "social justice through social action," reasserting his commitment to "old-age insurance—old-age pensions." At Pittsburgh on October 19, he gave at last the conservative speech that Louis Howe had been urging him to make during the Western tour (Howe's insistence, his refusal to take no for an answer, had become annoying to the candidate), indicting the Hoover administration for piling up "unprecedented deficits in spite of increased taxation" and reasserting his "absolute loyalty" to the Democratic platform's economy plank, that is, to an immediate 25-percent reduction of federal expenditures and an annually balanced budget thereafter. At Baltimore on October 25, he made the bitterest of all his attacks on Hoover, saying he waged "a war . . . against the 'Four Horsemen' of the present Republican leadership—the Horsemen of Destruction, Delay, Deceit, Despair," and further saying, in reply to Hoover's blaming of a Democratic House for fiscal irresponsibility, that "after March 4, 1929 [with the Crash coming in the following October, with four years of deficit thereafter], the Republican Party was in complete control of all branches of the Federal Government—the Executive, the Senate, the House of Representatives and, I might add for good measure, the Supreme Court as well." This last was a departure from his prepared text,* an impulsive interpolation that he soon had

---

*The prepared text said merely: "After March 4, 1929, the Republican Party was in complete control of all branches of the government." Roosevelt could not truthfully have charged Hoover with narrow partisanship, or even with insistence upon a general agreement with his own political philosophy, in the making of Supreme Court appointments. Hoover's first such appointment was Charles Evans Hughes as Chief Justice. His second nominee was John J. Parker, a Southern Democrat, whom the Senate rejected because Parker had made anti-Negro comments and had as judge upheld an injunction enforcing a yellow-dog labor contract. Parker rejected, Republican Owen J. Roberts was appointed instead, an extreme conservative but one who had attracted favorable notice from liberals through his prosecution of Teapot Dome oil scandal cases. Then had come the appointment of the brilliant liberal Benjamin Cardozo of New York, a Democrat and a Jew.

good reason to regret. It provoked outraged protest from Bar Association officials and from Hoover himself, who, in a campaign address, called it an "atrocious slur" on the Supreme Court, revelatory of Roosevelt's reckless demagoguery, his subversive attitude toward the highest tribunal (he would "politicize" it), his lack of ethical sensitivity. In Boston on October 31, where he was with difficulty persuaded by Moley and Marvin McIntyre, his campaign public relations man, *not* to insert in his speech angry responses to Hoover's attack that Frankfurter and Jimmy Roosevelt had written out for him, Roosevelt spoke of "immediate relief for the unemployed" as "the immediate need of the hour," and of "long-range planning" to increase purchasing power and provide "permanent employment." In New York City's Madison Square Garden on November 5, he closed out his formal campaign with a survey and summing up of what had gone before.[43]

Of all these speeches, only two were extended coherent statements, and of these two, only one spoke Roosevelt's own mind, his own personal conviction.

The San Francisco speech, given at noon before that city's exclusive and prestigious Commonwealth Club, had its genesis in a Berle memorandum to Roosevelt dated August 15. In it, Berle, having estimated Roosevelt's election chances at only somewhat "better than even"—an estimate that seems incredibly pessimistic until one remembers it was made during the opening days of the hazardous Walker hearing—asked the candidate to "reckon" with the possibility of defeat. "In that event, you still have your political career to think of," wrote Berle. "Should the campaign go off merely as a series of scattering issues, defeat would probably end your career, as it did the careers of Cox, Davis, and even Al Smith. Should you, however, quite definitely become the protagonist of an outstanding policy, your significance in American public life would continue—as did that of Bryan and Theodore Roosevelt. . . . Obviously the line is, therefore, to make some statement analogous to Woodrow Wilson's 'new freedom' speech." Inevitably, Berle was asked to draft such a speech. He did so in his New York City home, collaborating with his wife, Beatrice, who "did a powerful lot of pruning and rewriting" of his "very sloppy" first draft, as she recalled long afterward. The final product, which the Berles thought of forever after as the "New Individualism" address, was reviewed by Baruch and Johnson, who made no changes in it, and then airmailed on September 19 to Roosevelt and Moley aboard the campaign train.[44]

Delivered with far fewer excisions and revisions than most Roosevelt draft speeches underwent, though Moley later remembered otherwise,[45] this speech was the least characteristically Rooseveltian of all his 1932 campaign utterances, being somber in mood, and philosophical, not only in the sense of a serene acceptance of clearly defined necessity, but also in the sense of seeking out fundamental causes or patterns of historical event, an enterprise toward which Roosevelt had little natural inclination or attraction.

A reassessment of the nation's basic political aims in the light of two overwhelmingly important developments was called for, he said. One development was the settlement of the West, the disappearance of the frontier. The other was the increasing concentration of economic power in giant privately managed corporations. By these developments new significance was given Jefferson's distinction* between "two sets of rights, those of 'personal competency' and those involved in acquiring and possessing property." By "personal competency" Jefferson meant "the right of free thinking, freedom of forming and expressing opinions, and freedom of personal living." Personal rights, in Jefferson's view and in the basic theory of American democracy, had a clear priority over property rights, since they constituted that individual "liberty" whose "blessings" the Constitution was designed to "secure." Theoretically, they could not be abridged but "must be protected at all hazards." Property rights, on the other hand, being creatures of man-made law rather than of God or the Natural Order, not only could but must be initially defined and then continually redefined in terms of that "general welfare" of which individual "liberty" partakes and that the Constitution was designed to "promote." But though theoretically the relationship between the two sets of rights is one of harmonious end and means, in actual practice it has been since the earliest days of the Republic an adversary relationship marked by frequent bitter confrontations. Witness the "great political duel" between Hamilton and Jefferson— with Hamilton stressing property and Jefferson the people, Hamilton stressing centralized national sovereignty and Jefferson decentralized state sovereignty —the duel whence "came the two parties, Republican and Democratic, as we know them today." All the same, a tolerable balance between the two sets of rights could be maintained within a meaningful concept of "individualism" (this became "the great watchword of American life") for as long as wealth was primarily land, land was fairly widely and equally distributed among a multitude of freeholders, free land was at hand for the taking in the West, and the nation's industry and commerce were divided among myriads of small independent entrepreneurs. But this state of affairs proved historically short-lived. It was shattered by the Industrial Revolution. The spread of a network of railroads across the land, the unprecedentedly swift and wasteful exploitation by "financial Titans" of immensely rich natural resources, the swift driving of the Western frontier to its drowning death in the Pacific, and the simultaneously swift rise of "industrial combinations" to the status of "great uncontrolled and irresponsible units of power within the State" were all brought about within a few decades in the name of an "individualism" that was increasingly glaringly a misnomer, since it referred more and more to the activities, not of individual human beings, but of corporations whose "personality" was a legal fiction.†

"It still is true that men can start small enterprises, trusting to native

---

*He made it in the summer of 1776, a few weeks after his writing of the Declaration of Independence, when America, as he said, had "no paupers" and "few who could live without labor," those few being possessed of only "moderate wealth."

†It was a fiction deliberately designed, as Roosevelt-Berle might have added, to blur the distinction between people and property, thereby extending to the latter the "rights" and "blessings" of "liberty" that are constitutionally guaranteed the former.

shrewdness and ability to keep abreast of competitors," said Roosevelt-Berle, "but area after area has been preempted altogether by the great corporations, and even in the fields which still have no great concerns, the small man starts under a handicap. The unfeeling statistics of the last three decades show that the independent businessman is running a losing race. . . . [P]lainly we are steering a steady course toward economic oligarchy, if we are not there already." Hence the urgent need "for a reappraisal of values." Since "[o]ur industrial plant is built" if not in fact "overbuilt," a "mere builder of more industrial plants, a creator of more railroad systems, an organizer of more corporations is as likely to be a danger as a help. The day of the great promoter or the financial Titan . . . is over. Our task now is not discovery or exploitation of natural resources, or necessarily producing more goods. It is the soberer, less dramatic business of administering resources and plants already in hand, of seeking to reestablish foreign markets for our surplus production, of meeting the problem of underconsumption, of adjusting production to consumption, of distributing wealth and products more equitably, of adapting existing economic organizations to the service of the people. The day of enlightened administration [Berle's draft had said, 'The day of the manager'] has come." But from certain logical implications of this argument, which Norman Thomas as the Socialist candidate for President was preaching across the country at that very moment and which Berle himself had pointed toward in his memorandum on the "economic council" idea, the Commonwealth Club speech backed away. *Not* called for by Roosevelt-Berle was any radical transformation of the social or economic order, any governmentally planned and administered reorganization of big finance and big industry along cooperative lines. We "should [not] abandon the principle of strong economic units called corporations, merely because their power is susceptible of easy abuse. In other times we dealt with the problem of an unduly ambitious central Government by modifying it gradually into a constitutional democratic Government.* So today we are modifying and controlling our economic units. As I see it, the task of government is to assist the development of an economic declaration of rights, an economic constitutional order. This is the common task of statesmen and businessmen."

No other speech of the campaign made so deep an impression on America's intellectual community. None other was so permeated with the autumnal mood of the post-Crash years, the sense of things ending, contracting, freezing into a fixed pattern. None other stated so clearly the "mature economy" thesis that was central to the thinking of America's most influential economic theorists of the 1930s, and central also, or basic, to much of the New Deal to come. But the mood was *Berle's* mood, the thesis was *Berle's* thesis. Had Roosevelt

*Referred to was the "national Government" of George III, whose tyranny had "become a threat in the 18th century." Ignored was the fact that the "modification" of this into American constitutional democracy, far from being "gradually" accomplished, was effected through a revolutionary war.

truly shared them he would not have replaced Berle's opening language as he did with: "Sometimes, my friends, particularly in years such as these, the hand of discouragement falls upon us. It seems that things are in a rut, fixed, settled. . . . But then we look around us in America, and everything tells us that we are wrong. America is new. It is in the process of change and development. It has the great potentialities of youth."[46]

No such gap between Roosevelt's own mind and that of his speech writer is evident in his Pittsburgh address. In later years, when its words were quoted against him to prove up to the hilt that he broke a campaign promise most solemnly made, he "frequently complained . . . that this speech was one of the few he ever made—even in the heat of a campaign—without adequate time for discussion and consideration," according to Rosenman, who in those later years professed a conviction that the address would never have been made "in the form that it took" if Roosevelt had had "time to give the issue more thought." Actually no speech of the campaign was drafted farther in advance of its delivery than this one. Hugh Johnson dictated it in the second week of September, checked it with Baruch, and had Jim Farley deliver it personally to Roosevelt in Ogden, Utah, on September 17. If it remained wholly unrevised (and it did) up to the very day it was given, when some minor stylistic changes were made, this was not because the speaker had not read it with care. Nor was it because he knew nothing of arguments currently being made by followers of John Maynard Keynes against the budget cutting and balancing he now vehemently espoused. So, at least, claims Moley. " . . . he was wholly aware of its [the speech's] implications when he made it," writes Moley. "He knew the alternatives because, while none of us, then [of the Brain Trust], was a member of the 'borrow and spend' school, we had honestly presented its arguments to him. So far as it is possible for anyone to be positive of anything, I am sure that the speech, as delivered, represented Roosevelt's wholehearted views on government finance."[47]

And, as delivered, that speech excoriated Hoover for a billion-dollar increase in federal expenditures within four years, for the "unprecedented bureaucracy in Washington," for an "unbalanced budget and . . . continued failure to take effective steps to balance it," and, in general, for his neglect of the obvious fact that a nation, like a family, must live within its means. "I regard reduction in Federal spending as one of the most important issues of this campaign. . . . It is the most direct and effective contribution that government can make to business." He himself proposed to balance the budget "by reorganization of existing departments, by eliminating functions, by abolishing many of those innumerable boards and those commissions which . . . have grown up as a fungous growth on American government," and by the "Federal tax on beer" that would be imposed when "the Democratic platform pledge is enacted into legislation modifying the Volstead Act." He hastened to add that the "Democratic platform . . . opposes the return of the old-time saloon." He also, in evident fear that his pledge to reduce expenditures might arouse vote-denying anxieties among the impoverished, interpolated an "at-the-same-time" statement that was at wide variance with, if not in actual contradiction of, his address's general tone and central argument. Said he: "If starvation or dire need on the part of any of our citizens make necessary the appropriation of additional funds which would keep the budget out of balance, I shall not hesitate to tell the American people the full truth and ask them to authorize the expenditure of that additional amount."[48]

VII

THE last rally was in Poughkeepsie on election eve.

For nearly two months he had been certain of his election victory. His last lingering doubt about it had been dissipated when, just as he was about to board the train in Albany to begin his tour of the West, he received the almost incredible news that the Democrats had won Maine's state elections, something that hadn't happened since the Civil War (gleefully he had quoted the traditional Republican slogan, "As Maine goes, so goes the nation"). The only question remaining thereafter, as regards election outcome, concerned the width of his victory margin.

And his optimistic estimate of this had not been reduced when Hoover, in response to the Maine news, scrapped his earlier plan for a passive campaign and prepared with his own brain and hand, in painful labor, nine major speeches, making the first of them in Des Moines on October 4 and the last in Madison Square Garden on October 31, with dozens of rear-platform and other small talks in between. These constituted virtually the whole of the Republican presidential speaking campaign that year. Calvin Coolidge, pitiful in his bewilderment over the turn of events since 1929, "burnt out," as he sadly confessed, and soon to die, was with difficulty prevailed upon to make one speech in Hoover's behalf. He was almost the only topflight Republican politician to do so, and his single effort was a poor one. Hoover's speeches, on the other hand, were good, most of them, as compositions. They were soundly structured; they had clarity, coherence, and occasional flashes of eloquence; they were always perfectly logical in their deductions of policy from principle. They lacked color and sparkle, however. They were substantially negative in argument and irritatingly moralistic in their negativism, being full of reasons why proposed action ought not, hence must not, be taken. And what hope they held out for change for the better measured small against the fear they expressed of a change for the worse. Indeed, fear of change was their dominant note. "My countrymen, the proposals of our opponents represent a profound change in American life—less in concrete proposal, bad as that may be, than by implication and evasion," said Herbert Hoover in Madison Square Garden. "Dominantly in their spirit they represent a radical departure from the foundations of one hundred and fifty years that have made this the greatest country in the world."[49] Roosevelt well knew that such words would be more likely in the circumstances to lose than to gain votes: they would be interpreted to mean that nothing could be done about the depression without disturbing the "foundations" of the Republic, and they would either not be believed or they would encourage a conclusion that the "foundations" *should* be disturbed. Men hungry and cold could not subsist on a diet of abstractions, however lofty in tone. They needed tangible food, clothing, shelter, and if radical departures were required to supply these, Hail Radicalism!

Roosevelt, moreover, had now actively behind him a Democracy strong and united as it had not been in any presidential election since 1916. An unwitting agent of this party unification, helping greatly to heal the breach between Roosevelt and Al Smith for the time being, was Tammany's vindictive and none-too-intelligent John Curry. At the New York Democratic State Convention in late September, Curry overplayed his hand. He denied to Rosenman the nomination for state Supreme Court justice, which would normally be Rosenman's automatically by virtue of his interim appointment to that post by a Democratic governor. He did this despite a telegram to him from Roosevelt, who was then campaigning in Sioux City, expressing the "personal hope that Rosenman will receive designation." (The next day, Roosevelt wired Rosenman: "The fellow who is behind in the first quarter mile is very likely to finish first. I am . . . terribly disappointed but you will remember that I have a long memory and a long arm for my friends.") But when Curry moved to block the nomination of Roosevelt's gubernatorial choice, Herbert Lehman, and to nominate instead Albany's Mayor Thatcher, he ran head-on into Smith, whom Lehman had strongly supported financially and otherwise during Smith's gubernatorial campaigns, also in 1928, when Lehman had been Smith's choice for lieutenant governor. If Lehman were denied the governorship in 1932, stormed Smith at Curry, "I'll run myself for Mayor of New York in 1933, and smash you." "On what ticket would you run?" asked Curry, provoking a Smith reply of withering scorn: "Hell, on a Chinese laundry ticket." Curry had then given in, and the stage was set for a public reconciliation between Smith and Roosevelt. It had taken place in Albany's vast armory, where Roosevelt, having just returned from his Western tour, appearing on the platform for the state convention's closing session, was approached by the delegate Al Smith, hand outstretched. "Hello, you old potato!" Al was reported to have said in an Associated Press dispatch read by tens of millions. What he actually said was, "Hello, Frank, I'm glad to see you," with Roosevelt replying, "Hello, Al, I'm glad to see you too—and that's from the heart." Subsequently, Smith had made, before huge crowds, several speeches in support of both Lehman and Roosevelt.[50]

Hence it was a man knowing himself to be the next President of the United States who on the evening of November 7, 1932, addressed his "friends and neighbors of all political parties here in Dutchess County," as he had done at the end of "every political campaign" for twenty-two years, and addressed also an unseen audience of millions, for he spoke into the microphones of a national radio network. There was nothing of exultation, much of humility and selfless dedication in what he said. He summed up the "impressions" made upon him during his national travels, the "vivid flashes" that "tell us of the essential unity of things." He said, "A man comes to wisdom in many years of public life. He knows well that when the light of favor shines upon him, it comes not, of necessity, that he himself is important. Favor comes because for a brief moment in the great space of human change and progress some general human purpose finds in him a satisfactory embodiment. To be the means through which the ideal and hopes of the American people may find a greater realization calls for the best in any man; I seek only to be the humble emblem of this restoration. If that be your verdict, my friends of America and my next-door neighbors of Dutchess County, and that be the confident purpose behind your verdict, I shall in the humility that suits such a great confidence seek to meet this great expectation of yours. With your help and your patience and your generous good will we can mend the torn fabric of our common life."[51]

In the afternoon of Election Day, Roosevelt and Eleanor, who had come up to Hyde Park from her Todhunter School class that morning to cast her ballot, went together to the polls in the Town Hall, where after voting they posed for newspaper and newsreel photographers. In New York City a few hours later, at the Sixty-fifth Street house, they hosted a buffet supper for family, friends, and a few newspaper people. Among them was Lorena Hickok, who had covered Eleanor throughout the campaign for the Associated Press and between whom and Eleanor had grown a friendship of rare and increasing intimacy. (They had in common intensely unhappy childhoods, though Lorena's was far more horrendous than Eleanor's had been: her father, a man whose ungovernable temper had lost him one job after another, forcing him to move his family from one little town to another across the Midwest, was a sadist who beat her without mercy and, on one occasion, raped her. When some hint of this horror came to Eleanor through her longtime personal secretary and friend, Malvina [Tommy] Thompson, with whom Lorena had compared childhoods during a night train ride, she characteristically extended sympathy, compassion.) Eleanor greeted Lorena at the door with a kiss and a soft-spoken, "It's good to have you around tonight, Hick."[52] After the buffet, the entire party went to the Democratic National Headquarters in the Biltmore Hotel to receive by radio, telegraph, and telephone the election returns.

The earliest of these indicated a Roosevelt sweep, though Louis Howe, in a strange dark mood, professed not to believe it. We may guess at the emotions that swirled in raging conflict through the spirit of this sickly little man in those hours; we can know only that he refused to share the mounting tumultuous triumphant joy of the Biltmore crowd. He went across the street to his little office in the old "Friends of Roosevelt" headquarters and remained there in seclusion with his wife, Grace, and son Hartley until, at eleven o'clock, Eleanor and Jim Farley came to fetch him. At midnight, Roosevelt presented himself to a wildly cheering throng in the Biltmore ballroom. Beside him on the platform stood Farley and Howe, the "two people in the United States more than anybody else who are responsible for this great victory."[53]

And it *was* great, certainly, greater than Hoover's landslide triumph over

Smith four years before. Winning 22,815,539 votes to Hoover's 15,759,930, Roosevelt carried forty-two states with 472 electoral votes. The six states going to Hoover, with 59 electoral votes, were Pennsylvania, Delaware, Connecticut, New Hampshire, Vermont, and (reverting to pattern) Maine. In the new Congress, Democrats would outnumber Republicans 60 to 35 in the Senate and 310 to 117 in the House. And as Norman Thomas had feared, and the Socialist spokesman Nathan Fine now admitted, "the reputed progressiveness of Franklin D. Roosevelt" had denied to the Socialist Party the great gains "expected . . . in the third year of a devastating depression."[54] Socialism, which had won 6 percent of the popular vote in 1912 and 3.2 percent in 1920, won less than 3 percent in 1932. Yet the gains actually made were representative of national trend and mood, and one may be sure that Franklin Roosevelt took note of them—took note of the fact that in straw votes among college students prior to the election, Thomas ran neck and neck with Roosevelt for first place in the North, neck and neck with Hoover for second place in the South; took careful note also of the intellectual *quality* of Thomas' support, which included, as Tugwell had stressed in conversations with him, John Dewey, Paul Douglas, Stuart Chase, Reinhold Niebuhr, Oswald Garrison Villard. Also noted was the fact that in the election itself, Norman Thomas, the candidate of a party of barely 10,000 members that by devious technicalities was even denied a place on the official ballot in five states,* a party whose total national campaign expenditure was a mere $50,000, won 899,935 votes, nearly four times the number won in 1928. Roosevelt may further have noted, as significant of the left limit of political possibility, the fact that the Communist Party candidate won only 70,000 votes, though Communism claimed the allegiance of a growing number of professional intellectuals, including, tentatively and, as it turned out, briefly, the writers Theodore Dreiser, Sherwood Anderson, Edmund Wilson, Waldo Frank, and John Dos Passos.

*Florida, Idaho, Louisiana, Nevada, and Oklahoma.

12

-»>X«<-

Interregnum: Into the Winter
of Our Discontent

I

ELEANOR Roosevelt had been among those seated on the platform from which her husband broadcast his Poughkeepsie speech on election eve. She, who had done no overt campaigning for her husband (her doing so would be in "bad taste," it had been decided) but had made several speeches for Lehman and many public appearances at her husband's side, came up from New York in her own car to attend this last rally. She refused, however, to spend the night in Hyde Park: she had a nine o'clock class at Todhunter School the next morning and insisted upon meeting it, though this meant a midnight drive back to the city. And as she drove southward into the cold dark of the first hour of Election Day—perhaps it was while she drove on Riverside Drive past that sprawl of helpless misery upon the riverbank, below Morningside Heights, known as Hoover Village—she ruminated aloud to her companion in the car, Lorena Hickok. "Of course Franklin will do his best if elected," she said, her "if" being more expressive of secret wish than of actual uncertainty. "He is strong and resourceful. And he really cares about people. The federal government will have to take steps. But will it be enough? *Can* it be enough? The responsibility he may have to take is something I hate to think about."[1]

Franklin Roosevelt, too, remained that night in somber mood. Having returned from Poughkeepsie to Hyde Park, he sat with Raymond Moley before an open fire while Eleanor journeyed through the night. The two were virtually alone in the Big House—all the family and most of the servants were gone to the city—and they *felt* loneliness, of a kind, insofar as each was acutely aware of the freezing dark, full of dangers, that spread in vast extension all around their tiny island of warmth and light. Moley would never forget "the play of the firelight" across Roosevelt's "strong, mobile face," and how "utterly calm" was this man who, they both knew, must soon assume historic burdens as heavy as, and, because of their slipperiness, more difficult to bear than, Lincoln's had been, or Washington's. "There was no excitement, . . . no petty sense of impending personal triumph," Moley wrote years later. "We . . . talked quietly of the campaign, of the gathering economic storm clouds—the tumbling prices, the mounting unemployment."[2]

Nor was Roosevelt's mood less somber when, some twenty-four hours later, having returned from the Biltmore's tumultuous victory celebration to the quiet of his New York City town house bedroom, he was helped to bed by his oldest son, James. He made then one of his rare revelations of innermost feeling, an almost unique revelation that what he felt was a fear of personal inadequacy in the face of personal challenge.

"I'm just afraid I may not have the strength to do this job," he said. "After you leave me tonight, Jimmy, I am going to pray. I am going to pray that God will help me, that He will give me the strength and the guidance to do this job and to do it right. I hope you will pray for me, too, Jimmy."[3]

II

FOR there was no sign whatever of that "bottoming out" and initiation of recovery that, according to classical economic theory, was bound to occur if the workings of "natural law" were not "interfered with" by government and that, since the Hoover administration had certainly *not* "interfered" in any fundamental way, should surely by now be occurring. Instead, economic conditions that had seemed almost impossibly bad to the editors of *The Guaranty Survey,* issued by the Guaranty Trust Company of New York, at the end of 1931 were worse by far and continued steadily to worsen in these closing weeks of 1932.

"Measured by almost any of the accepted standards of economic activity," *The Survey* would say in its December issue, "the year 1932, taken as a whole, was a period of deeper depression than 1931." The volume of check transactions in 1932 was a third smaller than in 1931, was less than half what it had been in 1930, and was but 38 percent of what it had been in 1929. The volume of stock-market transactions showed a similar precipitous decline: in 1932 it had been 29 percent smaller than in 1931, some 45 percent smaller than in 1930, and almost 58 percent smaller than in 1929. Steeper still was the decline in the amount of new capital financing: it totaled only $255,855,975 for the first nine months of 1932, as compared with $1,628,950,773 for the corresponding period of 1931 (for the first nine months of 1930 and 1929 it had been $4,474,761,601 and $7,466,588,928, respectively). Similarly, and alarmingly, with new building construction. The first nine months of 1932 had new building contracts awards of only $1,057,363,700, as compared with $2,562,707,800 for the same period in 1931, a decline of 59 percent—and 1931's total had been a third less than for the comparable period of 1930 (1932's total was less than a fourth the total for 1929). And indeed the credit system through which new ventures were financed was itself crumbling. It had never been strong. There had been over 6,000 bank failures involving deposits of some $1.7 billion during the golden years of the New Era. But with the Crash had come a terrifying rush of bank closings—1,345 in 1930, of which the greatest was the Bank of United States; 2,298 in 1931; and over 1,200 thus far in 1932. The governor of Nevada had been forced to declare in October what was euphemistically, ironically, called a "bank holiday," closing his state's banks for several days by executive decree to save them from disastrous "runs."[4]

Production figures for automobiles, gasoline, copper, coal, lumber, cement —for virtually every mineral or manufacture—were drastically below those of 1931, which were themselves drastically lower than those of 1930, as "production control" was increasingly effected by big-business cooperative action in defiance of antitrust law. Suspension of the latter was called for even more vociferously in 1932 than it had been in 1931. Thus, on March 10, 1932, representatives of the copper industry, meeting in New York City, agreed to curtail production of copper by 20 percent of the rated mining capacity—a reduction of about 12,500 tons per month. The American pig-iron industry operated in 1932 at less than 16.5 percent of its rated capacity, and the steel industry, at a little over 19 percent of capacity. Of nonagricultural products, the total production in 1932 was half what it had been in 1929.

Estimates of the number of unemployed in the autumn of 1932 varied widely, but the lowest—11,901,000, retrospectively made by the Bureau of Labor Statistics—amounted to 24 percent of the total civilian labor force that year. Other estimates were considerably higher. The American Federation of Labor estimated 12,870,000, or something over a fourth of the labor force. The Cleveland Trust Company estimated 13,416,000. The Alexander Hamilton Institute estimated 14,728,000. Highest of all was the Labor Research Association's estimate of 16,783,000—well over a *third* of the total labor force! When the Soviet Union's Amtorg issued from its New York City office a call for "6,000 skilled workers" to go to Russia for a term of years, more than 100,000 Americans at once applied, this in late 1931. When Birmingham, Alabama, advertised for 750 ditch diggers, resident in the city, to work ten-hour days at a daily wage of $2, more than 12,000 at once applied, this in early 1932. Statistics showed a halt, even a reversal, of that population flow from country to city that had prevailed since the early years of the century, as myriads of the unemployed fled the city to seek their livelihoods on the land. The total farm population increased in 1930, for the first time in a quarter century. It increased again in 1931, and yet again in 1932, when urban centers lost and rural areas gained some 400,000. But this town-to-country movement represented, overall, no alleviation of the misery that drove the urban unemployed into the countryside: the land they moved to was necessarily the poorest, the cheapest —"precisely the areas which should not be farmed," as Secretary of Agriculture Hyde put it—and even on the best of land, farmers in that year could not make ends meet.[5]

For agriculture as a whole was, like industry, in far worse shape in 1932 than it had been the year before. Unlike industry's, agriculture's production remained high, it was about the same as it had been during the 1920s but with augmented catastrophic effect upon farm prices and gross farm income. The latter had been a little less than $12 billion in 1929, which was considerably less than 6.5 million farm families would have received if the total national income had been equitably distributed. It fell to $9.347 billion in 1930, was less than $7 billion in 1931, and was down to slightly more than $5 billion in 1932. "Farms cannot be quickly shut down like factories," explained Secretary Hyde, going on to point out that this fact, calamitous for farmers, "was . . . a blessing to urban groups" in that, by lowering the price of food and clothing, it made "life easier for wage earners with reduced incomes." By the same token, it lessened "the burden of unemployment relief." Admittedly, it was not "philanthropy" but "necessity" that caused the farmer to become "the great shock-absorber

... in hard times," but the fact that he did so become "should be remembered when farmers seek governmental relief."[6]

Certainly the farmers themselves, as Hyde did *not* say, were increasingly rebellious against what they deemed a scapegoat role—and rebellious in ways that boded ill for the immediate future. As a wave of mortgage foreclosures rolled high and ever higher across the land in the closing weeks of 1932, as larger and larger portions of the farm community were transformed into rural slums, there was more and more open talk of a possible violent revolution in the farm belt come spring. The talk was loudest, the organization for it strongest, among men who had been recently more conservative politically, more strongly committed to law and order, than most Americans, namely, the smaller corn-hog and dairy farmers of the most fertile areas of the Midwest. There would be at the very least a renewal and augmentation of the violence that had swept over western Iowa in August and September, unless effective farm relief was forthcoming by next summer. And no shadow of impending event lay darker on Roosevelt's spirit than this one as he sat with Moley, on the eve of his election, before an open fire.

But equally dark, and heavy upon the spirit, was the shadow cast by the relief crisis in general. Herbert Hoover's principled opposition to the provision of federal living aid to the unemployed had been stubbornly maintained well into the spring of 1932, as was his insistence that federal aid should go only to business, the relief of individual human distress being properly a local or state function only (he had been forced to abandon his initial belief that it was properly a function of private charity only). The President had done all that his office gave him power to do against a bill, the La Follette–Costigan bill, that would have provided federal grants to states for relief purposes and that went down to defeat in February 1932. Only under extreme political pressure had he signed in July a bill authorizing the RFC to lend $300,000,000 to needy state and local governments for relief distribution, emphasizing as he did so that the "loans are to be based upon absolute need and evidence of financial exhaustion."[7] By the end of 1932, only $30,000,000 of the authorized $300,-000,000, or just one-third the amount of the single RFC loan to the Dawes bank of Chicago in June, would be actually allocated to the states for relief.

Yet there was not a city and scarcely a town in the nation in which the relief system favored by Hoover had not completely broken down by early 1932 under burdens many times heavier than this system had ever had to bear before. During 1932, in city after city and county after county, the number of families on relief doubled or tripled while available relief funds increased but 20 to 30 percent, according to a survey of forty-four cities "and adjacent areas" made by the American Association of Social Workers. Only one out of four of the totally unemployed was receiving any relief whatever in the fall of the year, and the help given this relatively lucky one was but a fraction of that needed to maintain a decent standard of living. The survey also revealed that $17,500,000 a month was being expended by these surveyed localities for the relief of 3,000,000 people, an average of about $5.80 per person per month. Nor could local governments do any more than they were now doing in the way of relief: nine tenths of their income derived from real-estate taxation, and this narrow tax base grew narrower still, and more fragile, as real-estate income declined. " . . . rentals, in most places, are down about 20 percent" and real-estate tax delinquency was up by 20 to 30 percent, said the noted business economist Sumner H. Slichter of the Harvard Business School as he testified before a congressional committee on the "self-evident" need for "national assistance."[8]

The human effects were ghastly. An eleven-day gap separated the total exhaustion of private relief from the initiation of public relief, itself wholly inadequate, in Philadelphia in April 1932. The executive secretary of the Community Council of Philadelphia told a congressional committee of an intensive study made by his organization of ninety-one families "to find out what happened when the food orders stopped." One woman borrowed a half-dollar from a friend and used it to buy stale bread at 3½ cents a loaf, "and that is all they had for eleven days except for one or two meals." Another woman fed her family vegetables that fell from wagons as they moved along the docks and fish that was given her by fish vendors on one or two occasions. Yet another family subsisted on two meals a day, of which one (breakfast) consisted of bread and coffee, and the other, of bread and raw or cooked carrots. In most cases families went without any food whatever for a day or two at a time. When public assistance began in May, in Philadelphia, some 55,000 families were on the relief rolls; they received $4.23 per family per week. In Birmingham, Alabama, "[t]he scale of relief ranges for an average family of four and three-tenths persons from $2.50 to $4 a week," according to testimony by Representative George Huddleston before a congressional committee.[9]

Children went hungry in every corner of the land. The offspring of sharecroppers in the single-crop South had long suffered from poor and insufficient food; now the serious cases of malnutrition and undernourishment multiplied. In Chicago, in the spring of 1931, when the Board of Education announced the exhaustion of funds for the payment of teachers, it was discovered that teachers had been contributing from their salaries to provide free lunches for 11,000 hungry children, and this was but a small part of the numbers in the school system who were clearly insufficiently nourished. The condition worsened drastically in 1932. In the bituminous coalfields of West Virginia and Kentucky, the American Friends Service Committee, weighing schoolchildren to determine which should be fed from the committee's limited funds (no child was fed who was not at least 10 percent underweight), discovered that in one school ninety-nine out of a hundred were at least 10 percent underweight. In many other schools, 85 to 90 percent were underweight. In the best-fed of the coalfield school populations, 20 percent were underweight. There had been, of course, "a steady decline in the health conditions in these areas" over the "past three years," testified Clarence E. Pickett, the committee's secretary, in congressional hearings. There was marked mental retardation among the undernourished children. "We find drowsiness, lethargy, and sleepiness."[10]

Yet there was a glut of food everywhere in the land! Elevators and storage bins were bursting with grain, the stockyards jammed with cattle, hogs, sheep! And this bitter paradox of poverty amid plenty, and *because* of plenty, bred grave doubts about the virtues of "free enterprise," the beneficence of the "profit motive," and the logic of the "capitalist system," in hundreds of thousands of informed, sensitive men and women who were not themselves in dire need. Oscar Ameringer, a journalist of liberal persuasion, editor and publisher of an Oklahoma City periodical, spoke for these when, in testimony before a subcommittee of the House Committee on Labor in Washington in 1932, he reported on a three-month tour of twenty states that he had just completed. He had seen "numbers of women searching for scraps of food in the refuse piles of the municipal market" of Seattle, had seen the next day "thousands of bushels of apples rotting in the orchards," had been told of forest fires set "by unemployed workers and bankrupt farmers" so that they could "earn a few . . . dollars as fire fighters," had seen "men picking for scraps of meat in the garbage cans of Chicago"* and had then dined in a Chicago restaurant with a Western sheep rancher who "said he had killed 3,000 sheep this fall and thrown them down the canyon because it cost $1.10 to ship a sheep and then he got less than a dollar for it," had seen in Oklahoma, Texas, Arkansas, and Louisiana "fine staple cotton rotting" in the fields "by the hundreds and thousands of tons." Concluded Ameringer: "The farmers are being pauperized by the poverty of the industrial populations, and the industrial populations are being pauperized by the poverty of the farmers. Neither has the money to buy the product of the other, hence we have overproduction and underconsumption at the same time in the same country."[11]

Nor was doubt about the "system" the only or most negative attitudinal response to the "system's" painfully obvious breakdown. There was angry disgust also, as well as a strong disposition to *personalize* the causes of the collapse, that is, to describe these as the acts or refusals to act of evil men, who, in positions of power and authority, had continuously robbed, cheated, exploited, and lied to the American people. Such feeling permeated the testimony of a spokesman for the American Federation of Labor before the same Senate committee as listened to Clarence Pickett on child hunger in the coalfields. "I say to you gentlemen, advisedly, that if something is not done . . . starvation is going to continue [and] the doors of revolt in this country are going to be thrown open," testified Edward F. McGrady of the American Federation of Labor, who was assuredly no radical, as he inveighed bitterly against the Hoover administration's insistence upon a balanced budget as the most press-

---

*"In Chicago a committee investigated city garbage dumps and then reported: 'Around a truck which was unloading garbage and other refuse were about thirty-five men, women and children. As soon as the truck pulled away from the pile all of them started digging with sticks, some with their hands, grabbing bits of food and vegetables' " (Edward Robb Ellis, *A Nation in Torment*, p. 242). Ellis also, on pages 242 and 243, quotes Edmund Wilson on the Chicago scene: "A private incinerator at Thirty-fifth and La Salle Streets which disposes of garbage from restaurants and hotels has been regularly visited by people, in groups of as many as twenty at a time, who pounce upon anything that looks edible before it is thrown into the furnace."

ing need for recovery. If there was continued refusal, in the interest of a balanced budget, "to provide food for these people [the unemployed] until they do secure work, as far as I personally am concerned, I would do nothing to close the doors of revolt if it starts. . . . It would not be a revolt against the government but against the Administration."[12] Such feeling also permeated several of the popular songs published that year.* Thus a song called "The Happy American," by an anonymous lyricist:

> *How happy to be an American,*
> *One of the chosen breed,*
> *Who live in a land of abundance,*
> *Where no one is ever in need.*
> *As long as a man is willing to work*
> *He is bound to get on well,*
> *And there are two chickens in every pot—*
> *There are, like Hell!*
>
> .   .   .   .
>
> *How happy to be a citizen*
> *Where the voice of the people rules,*
> *Where there are no grafters in office,*
> *Nor corporation tools;*
> *Where justice, the right of everyman,*
> *No one can buy or sell,*
> *And the courts are the poor man's refuge—*
> *They are, like Hell!*

Perhaps it was the same anonymous lyricist who reacted as follows to the press statement issued by Secretary of War Hurley on the night the Bonus Marchers were driven out of Washington:

> *"Only two courses were open,*
> *As anyone can see;*
> *To vindicate law and order*
> *Or yield to anarchy."*
> *Granted!—the Chiefs of Government*
> *Cannot tolerate mobs—*
> *But isn't it strange you never thought*
> *To give the workless jobs?*
>
> .   .   .   .
>
> *"Only two courses were open"—*
> *To the Higher Racketeers*
> *Who look on human suffering*

---

*"If you can sing a song that will make people forget their troubles and the depression, I'll give you a medal," said Herbert Hoover in the White House to the radio singer Rudy Vallee in the spring of 1932.[13]

With lofty well-fed sneers.
And thus will your names be noted
By history's merciless pen:
"They knew how to rise to Power,
But not how to act like Men!"

Of such topical songs, however, the most popular by far in that dying season of a disastrous year was a bitterly nostalgic verse by E. Y. Harburg set to a sad haunting tune by Jay Gorney entitled "Brother, Can You Spare a Dime?" Doubtless hundreds of thousands of Americans, sitting beside their radios, listened to it during the long hour that Roosevelt and Moley sat in quiet serious talk before the fireplace at Hyde Park:

They used to tell me I was building a dream
And so I followed the mob—
When there was earth to plow or guns to bear
I was always there—right on the job.
They used to tell me I was building a dream
With peace and glory ahead—
Why should I be standing in line
Just waiting for bread?

   .   .   .   .

Once I built a railroad, made it run,
Made it race against time.
Once I built a railroad,
Now it's done—
Brother, can you spare a dime?"[14]

III

WAS there no hope?

Certainly none could be found by the great mass of Americans in the pronouncements of those once-revered spokesmen for the New Era who, remaining utterly committed to "pure capitalism," could only stress over and over again the iron necessity of more contraction, more retrenchment, more suffering by the dispossessed.*

---

*Is the capacity for human suffering unlimited? asked Senator Robert M. La Follette, Jr., of Albert H. Wiggin, chief executive of the Chase National Bank, during Senate subcommittee hearings on a bill to establish a national economic council, in May 1931. "I think so," Wiggin replied. The great banker was of course absolutely opposed to the proposed bill, being convinced that economic planning is an "impossibility" because "[h]uman nature is human nature" and "we are [therefore] bound to have conditions of crisis once in so often." It goes without saying that Wiggin's own capacity for suffering was unmeasured by the depression: he in fact made money out of the misery of others when he sold short his own bank's stock.[15]

Nor was much definite hope offered elsewhere that was not predicated upon an admission or assertion that the theretofore prevailing order—now moribund if not actually already dead—must be replaced by an order radically different.

Of proposals so predicated, however, there was no lack—and one of them, though it had no persuasive power whatever over the minds of Roosevelt and Moley,[16] was of such immediate plausibility that it had aroused great and increasing popular excitement by election eve of 1932. During the weeks that followed it would become the most talked-about, written-about topic in the land.

It was called Technocracy, a word coined in 1919 as a meld of "technology" and "democracy" by a Berkeley, California, inventor named William H. Smyth. It had the merit of addressing directly what was perceived by many to be the central problem of Western civilization, namely, that of adjusting social and economic institutions to the logical implications of a continuously advancing scientific technology in ways that served truly human purposes. It had a primary text in Thorstein Veblen's *The Engineers and the Price System* (1922), wherein Veblen argued that the "price system," that is, the profit system, institutionalized as nonproductive "business" and personified by nonproductive "businessmen," prevented realization of the abundance that modern technology was capable of providing for all and *would* provide for all, if only businessmen, whose concern was with private profit, were replaced by engineers and technicians, whose concern was with general efficiency, as the prime decision-makers of the economy. And of course Technocracy had its leading figure, its prophet, without whom it would not have impinged as it did upon the public mind.

He was a self-styled "engineer"* named Howard Scott. A colorful, dramatic, forceful, authoritarian, emotionally unstable personality (under pressure he inclined toward paranoia), he had once been a partner in a small floor-wax manufacturing firm in New Jersey, had lived for the last dozen years in New York City's Greenwich Village, and had personally known Veblen during Veblen's last years. He had become a well-known Village "character" during the 1920s. His favorite haunt was Lee Chumley's speakeasy, where, having doffed the broad-brimmed hat and leather overcoat he customarily wore on the street, he sat night after night in blue serge suit, blue shirt, and red necktie, spouting heretical economic views interspersed with romantic tall tales about his past. Immensely self-assured and self-assertive, occasionally harsh of manner, he was addicted to dogmatic statements, which were delivered in a language generally more impressive when listened to than when read in cold print and which, whether heard or read, often lay heavy on the remembering mind as impenetrable lumps of verbiage. Thus he once "explained" that technocracy's "methods are the result of a synthetic integration

---

*He had, in fact, no professional engineering credentials whatever. He once confessed to Margaret Mead that his formal schooling had ended in the ninth grade.[17]

of the physical sciences that pertain to the determination of all functional sequences of social phenomena."[18] But he had native intelligence. He was armed with a central idea that not only passed consistency tests for truth but could also be buttressed, or so it appeared, by masses of objective statistical data. And some of his published expressions of this idea made a great deal of sense to a great many people, including a number of distinguished minds. Several of these were attracted into a Scott-organized Committee on Technocracy, among them Stuart Chase, whose persuasively argued pamphlet *Technocracy: An Interpretation* soon became the most widely read of technocratic tracts. He was joined by Harold Loeb, former editor-publisher of the literary magazine *Broom* (a nephew of Solomon Guggenheim, a grand-nephew of one of the founders of the investment banking firm of Kuhn, Loeb, he was cruelly caricatured as "Robert Cohn" in Hemingway's *The Sun Also Rises* [1926]); the economist Leon Henderson of the Russell Sage Foundation; and, most important for Scott's immediate purposes, Professor Walter Rautenstrauch of Columbia University's department of industrial engineering. Rautenstrauch, with the blessing of Columbia's president, Nicholas Murray Butler, arranged office space for Scott on the university's campus and helped him recruit a corps of unemployed engineers and architectural draftsmen to make, with an abundance of charts and graphs, an Energy Survey of North America, prerequisite for the establishment of American technocracy.

It was the Energy Survey that had initially attracted wide popular attention to Technocracy and its prophet. Scott had announced it at a press conference sponsored by Columbia's industrial engineering department in late August 1932, and it had at once recommended itself to newsmen as a major "story." Since then, with accelerating intensity, the public had been bombarded through newspapers and magazines and radio with statistics on the growing productive capacity of modern technology, along with apocalyptic statements of what this meant, as dire threat or shining promise, for the immediate future.

The threat was of a chronic, growing technological unemployment or, as a special committee of the Society of Industrial Engineers would put it in early 1933, "unemployment of technology."* Scott predicted 20,000,000 unemployed within eighteen months "if present trends continue," for the number of man-hours needed to achieve a given quantity of production dramatically declined year by year. Thus, technology now enabled one man to produce in one hour as much pig iron as 3,000 man-hours had produced in 1840. In decades past, a single man in one minute could roll perhaps a dozen cigarettes; a few years back, he could produce 500; now he could produce 3,000. Only

---

*The select committee submitted a report on the "Economic Significance of Technological Progress" along with a memorandum on Technocracy, saying, "The advent of the new mode of production alters the position of labor and management in industry. Productivity of labor is determined more and more by the nature of technological process. . . . Failure to recognize this fact has resulted in . . . deterioration of earning capacity. . . . The inadequate purchasing capacity of the majority of the population restricts the market necessary for the full utilization of the existing means of production."[19]

208 workers operating giant drop forges were now producing 10,000 auto frames daily in a single Milwaukee plant, enough to supply the needs of the whole auto-making industry, displacing thousands of workers. Five brick-making plants employing but a hundred men could produce in 1932 as many bricks a day as 2,370 plants employing thousands had made as recently as 1929. And under construction, according to a Technocracy press statement, was a *totally* automated rayon factory in New Jersey, one that could operate twenty-four hours a day without a single worker in the plant, its every dye change and other operation controlled by one man seated at a pushbutton panel in company offices across the Hudson, in New York City.*[20]

But as great as the threat, or even greater, was the promise of material well-being held out by the new technology, if only the outmoded "price system" were replaced by scientific management. The first step, now being taken, was to determine accurately the available natural energy, actual and potential, on the North American continent. The second was to determine, presumably by scientific poll taking, the economic wants and needs of the American people. The third was to determine accurately the volume of needed and wanted goods that could be produced within given time units if industrial and agricultural technology ran at "the continuous full load" that was "necessary to produce at lowest physical cost." The fourth step was to divide the total volume of production thus arrived at by the number of people and then distribute goods fairly among the latter. (The question of what constituted "fairness" in this context was imperfectly addressed: virtually nothing was said about how services were to be measured in energy terms. Indeed, Scott barely recognized the fact that service employment increased as goods-producing employment decreased. He made no move toward measurement of the extent to which the former might offset the latter during the years ahead if, to use a favorite phrase of his, "present trends continue.") The distribution system called for the substitution of energy certificates for gold-backed dollars. These would be issued at centrally located distribution centers, each representing a given number of ergs or joules or larger units of energy measurement. The assigned value of each item produced would also be expressed in energy units. And the total of the issued certificates would represent the total amount of energy expended in the production of all the goods that were available, thereby ensuring a

---

*Roosevelt, if he read this, may have been reminded of an excursion into automation that he and Henry Morgenthau, Jr., had made as speculative investors in 1928. The two had acquired stock in a holding company called Consolidated Automatic Merchandising Corporation (Camco), which proposed to establish a national chain of stores in which vending machines wholly replaced clerks as dispensers of small-item merchandise. The few such stores opened several months before the Crash lost money from the start, in part because the very idea of "clerkless" stores was repulsive to many potential customers and in part because the vending machines too often malfunctioned, bringing down upon themselves the smashing wrath of the customers they cheated. (See *FDR: The Beckoning of Destiny,* pages 706–708.) But if this raised doubts in Roosevelt's mind about the validity of some of technocracy's claims, they were doubts that technocrats would have answered with the assertion that Camco's failure simply proved the impossibility of realizing the benefits of modern technology within the prevailing "price system."

precise match of production to purchasing power. In effect, the national economy would be transformed into a single vast machine whose efficient operation would enable every American to enjoy a standard of living ten times higher than that prevailing in 1929 while working, on the average, only sixteen hours a week.

And what of the decisive control of this vast machine?

It was to be in the hands of a central committee of engineers. They would establish priorities, allocate resources, and make work assignments, not willfully or wishfully, not even thoughtfully, but "scientifically"; their "decisions" would be statistical calculations of wants, needs, capabilities. "Administration, in a technocracy," explained Harold Loeb in a book he was writing during the last weeks of 1932, "has to do with material factors . . . subject to measurement. Therefore popular voting can be largely dispensed with. It is stupid deciding an issue by voice or opinion when a yardstick can be used."[21] And the "yardstick," one must emphasize, as Loeb did, would be exclusively the property of the central committee and its chain of command, for only engineers knew how to make or use it.

Here it was, in response to such statements as Loeb's, revelatory of the authoritarianism (the engineer as dictator) implicit in the technocratic view of social process, that Technocracy at the very height of its enormous faddish popularity encountered its strongest opposition. Most minds that had been classically, humanistically educated found Loeb's use of the words "issue" and "administration" to be itself "stupid." Such minds were very sure that anything properly called an "issue" was compounded of differing ideas, value judgments, moral intuitions, perceived interests—and the notion that these might be weighed and measured like pig iron or electricity was manifestly absurd.* Similarly with "administration." In the view of anyone profoundly committed to democracy, "administration" had essentially nothing to do with "material factors"; these could simply be placed, moved, removed, manipulated. It had everything to do with human beings, each unique in total personality and hence, *in toto,* unmeasurable; each endowed with free will and hence, in his behavior, only very partially predictable; each to be considered always and only as an end served by social process, never as mere means. Part and parcel of such view was a conviction that engineers as a class, far from being peculiarly fit to govern, were peculiarly unfit to do so since, as a class, they were narrow- or single-minded specialists, highly trained vocationally but otherwise uneducated. " . . . we have had enough of engineers, great or otherwise," was Heywood Broun's sour comment upon both Technocracy and Herbert Hoover, and Broun's sentiments were soon echoed and enlarged upon by Al Smith. Said Smith publicly: "As for substituting engineers for political leaders in the running of the country, I cannot refrain from mentioning the

---

*In an article in the December 1932 issue of *The Living Age* magazine (Quincy Howe its editor), Scott himself wrote that, while "the phenomena involved in the functional operation of a social mechanism [sic] are metrical," there is "no metrical equivalent" for "value."

fact that we have finished an era of government by engineers in Washington."[22]

On the other hand, the very authoritarianism that democratic idealists found repugnant was what most strongly attracted many an addict of "law and order," many a national planner of the left as of the right.

It attracted, as has been said, the leftist Stuart Chase, Veblen's most articulate disciple, who was enthralled by the alleged successes of Soviet Russia's first Five Year Plan. Wrote Chase, somewhat incoherently, in his *A New Deal,* published just as Technocracy was achieving its first national publicity: "At last, in 1932, the perpetual motion machine [which Americans had believed themselves 'aboard' prior to 1930] has stripped its gears, and economic change has acquired psychological imperative. For this reason, all generalizations based on the past about what Americans will or will not do, about impotence and corruption of government, the impossibility of political realignments, all the windy phrases about the imperishable traditions of democracy and the immaculate conception of the Constitution, stand suspect and tottering. Anything may happen—even the running of a redesigned economic machine by those most competent to run it." The last sentence of *A New Deal* was a rhetorical question: "Why should Russians have all the fun of remaking a world?"[23]

Initially, Technocracy also attracted, tentatively, certain big-business men who, like Columbia's President Butler, were enthralled by the alleged successes of Mussolini's corporate state and were inclined to identify themselves with the Fascist elite. A retired president of the National City Bank invited Scott to be his weekend guest on his country estate. The retired banker's wife asked Scott to serve as a key member of a National Planning Board that she proposed to organize. The president of the giant pharmaceutical firm E. R. Squibb & Company invited Scott to address a big-business men's dinner that the Squibb president hosted in New York City's exclusive Metropolitan Club. In early January 1933 a group of big-business men arranged for Scott to address them at a formal dinner in New York City's Hotel Pierre, as well as a glitteringly prestigious array of invited guests—some 400 "leading capitalists, bankers, industrialists, economists, and artists," as a New York *Times* reporter would put it. Arrangements were also made to broadcast Scott's speech from the Pierre over a radio network to a national public eager for an authoratative, definitive statement of Technocracy's analyses and proposals.[24]

Alas for Howard Scott, that dinner was not only the climax but also the end of his and Technocracy's active influence on the public mind. Held on January 13, 1933, it was a fiasco.

The guest of honor appeared in his standard uniform of blue serge suit, dark shirt, and red necktie, thus proclaiming his freedom from conventions in a way tacitly insulting to his immediate listeners, virtually all of whom were in formal evening attire. His speech was even less formal, and far less neat, than his dress. Impressively entitled "The Place of Science and Technology in Modern Civilization," it was a harsh, turgid, rambling, jargon-filled harangue of a kind that his alcoholic listeners in Greenwich Village speakeasies had found impressive but that exposed him to his present audience as an arrogantly pretentious fraud. He made sweeping doomful statements, one after another, but presented no data in support of them. He "failed to be explicit about the social order he proposed," as the *Times* reporter complained. He received embarrassingly brief, widely scattered applause when his harangue ended. And when written questions were called for, only five were sent to the podium, none indicating that the questioner took Scott or his message seriously.[25]

The next day, the American Engineering Council issued a statement denying that Technocracy had its official approval or represented any considerable body of professional engineering opinion. On January 17, Nicholas Murray Butler issued a statement denying that Scott or Technocracy had any academic connection whatever with Columbia. Professor Rautenstrauch perforce followed suit, announcing his resignation from the Committee on Technocracy and ordering Scott to vacate his campus office space. Columbia's industrial engineering department, it was said, would conduct its own "energy survey." Simultaneously, Harold Loeb, Leon Henderson, and almost all other self-proclaimed technocrats of established reputation dissociated themselves from Scott, most of them becoming members of the Continental Committee on Technocracy, formed and headed by Loeb. Those continuing to accept Scott's leadership joined his newly formed Technocracy, Inc.

And so it was that Technocracy as a "movement," having divided into bitterly quarreling factions, sank abruptly into oblivion, so far as the general public was concerned, barely six months after it had received its first mention in the press.

Yet the furor was not without historic effect or significance.

There remained of it, in the public mind, a sense of the seemingly limitless power and abundance that might flow from a planned, humanly purposive control of scientific technology, a sense, too, of the appalling waste of both human and environmental resources that *did* actually flow from the present control of high technology by profit-motivated enterprise. For the technocrats had talked much of a systematic suppression by "business" of inventions that would produce consumer goods of immensely greater durability and efficiency than those now available, such as shoes that would last a lifetime or a carburetor that would reduce automobile gasoline consumption by 90 percent, in order to maintain a profitable market demand. They had laid heavy stress upon the distortion of consumption patterns, and of human behavior in general—the drugging of the critical faculties, the lowering of moral and aesthetic standards—that mass advertising accomplished to the extent, almost precisely, that it was effective in selling consumer goods. And joined with these cultural residues of Technocracy was an increasingly angry popular impatience with those who continued to insist that the deepening depression was a "natural" calamity, in the face of which men were helpless.

The furor, just in itself, manifested a willingness, even an eagerness, on the part of the public to accept drastic changes in the socioeconomic structure, a belief that almost *any* change would probably be for the better since things in general could hardly be worse, either as trend or actuality. " . . . people right now are in a mood to grab at anything," wrote the entertainer Will Rogers in a nationally syndicated column about Technocracy, published on December 22, 1932. "They are sure of one thing and that is that the old orthodox political way of running everything has flopped. There is not a man in the whole world today that people feel like actually knows what's the matter. If there was he would be appointed [to] dictatorship unanimously by the whole world."[26]

IV

CERTAINLY the new President-elect, in the closing weeks of 1932 and the opening ones of 1933, did not appear in the national public eye as the longed-for Man of Destiny. Insofar as he was a shining light, it was mostly by contrast with the gloom that spread round Herbert Hoover, and the light he cast was flickering, uncertain, like that of a candle whose flame, feeding on desperate hope, was imperfectly shielded against chill night winds of doubt.

There was now a repetition on a national scale of the questioning opinion that had played about him in New York State when he first assumed his gubernatorial role—though now, alas, no decisive answer to the questions could obtain until increasingly troubled weeks and months had passed.

All agreed that he was amiable, affable, kind, a "cultured gentleman," as Professor James Hart of Johns Hopkins wrote of him within four weeks after his election victory. All agreed that he had been (he remained until January 1, 1933) a generally successful governor of New York. But it was also pointed out that as governor he had built on foundations firmly laid by a brilliant predecessor, that he would have no such advantage when he entered the White House, where he would inherit a crumbling structure for whose reconstruction or replacement he must develop his own blueprints, and, most disturbingly of all, that portions of his gubernatorial record raised grave doubts about his forthrightness, his moral courage, his commitment to principle, doubts that his presidential campaign did more to reinforce than to remove.

Indeed, critically observant eyes saw nothing in that campaign proving him to be other than the shrewd "balanced-antithesis" politician, opportunistic and slippery in his dealings with large issues, whom Walter Lippmann had descried, described, and deplored a few months before. " . . . his intellectual grasp does not seem to be of the first order," wrote James Hart, who also sensed a possible lack of "firmness and decision" and "a danger of over-playing the game of politics." Clearly, in Hart's opinion, the campaign had not proved him to be "equipped with the stuff of which strong and courageous leadership is made." On the other hand, it had not proved that he was unequipped either. One could only wait and see, meanwhile drawing hope from history, for, as Hart concluded, "the presidency has proved men of less character than he to have potentialities hitherto unrevealed." The latter wishful, hopeful, doubt-ridden notion was permeative of the public mind during those anxiously waiting weeks. It was pungently expressed by the famous Kansas editor William Allen White in a letter to Theodore Roosevelt, Jr., on February 1, 1933. "Your distant cousin is an X in the equation," wrote White. "He may develop his stubbornness into courage, his amiability into wisdom, his sense of superiority into statesmanship. Responsibility is a winepress that brings forth strange juices out of men."[27]

As for Walter Lippmann, he was now of somewhat different mind about Roosevelt than he had formerly been. He continued to fear and say that Roosevelt was too "impressionable," too "eager to please," too fond of politics as a "game" ("he . . . is likely to be ultra-political almost to show his own virtuosity"), and "so little grounded in his own convictions that almost everything depends on the character of his . . . advisers." He said these things in a letter to Felix Frankfurter in mid-September 1932. Yet barely two weeks later, in early October, less because he was attracted to Roosevelt than because he was repelled by Hoover (the latter's reelection, he realized, might provoke violent revolution), he had announced in his column his intention to vote for Roosevelt, whose abilities had "either been underrated" in the past or had matured in recent months. Soon after the election, Lippmann went so far as to approve the advantages Roosevelt had gained through the very strategy of ambiguity and noncommitment that, prior to the nominating conventions, Lippmann had damned as cowardly, dishonest, "ignoble." "Luckily for him [that is, Roosevelt] the public has not been taught to look upon him as a superman," wrote Lippmann in mid-November. " . . . Luckily for him he has not made or had to make very many specific pledges to the voters which will rise to plague him. He has ample power."[28]

And he knew how to keep it!

His performance during the mounting crises of the interregnum would continue to deny to critical observers any firm assurance that he had an adequate "intellectual grasp" of issues, but it would abundantly demonstrate to such observers his sure instinct for power, his jealousy of it, his skill in defending his possession of it against determined attempts to limit the number and range of his options.

He began to do so even before he arose from his bed in his Sixty-fifth Street house on the morning after the election. Raymond Moley found him there, the breakfast tray having been cleared away, "contemplating the President's telegram of congratulations," as Moley later wrote. In that telegram Herbert Hoover had said: " . . . I wish for you a most successful administration. In the common purpose of all of us I shall dedicate myself to every possible helpful effort." On the back of it, Franklin Roosevelt had penciled a reply: "I appreciate your generous telegram. I want to assure you that subject to my necessary duties as Governor during the balance of this year, I hold myself in readiness to cooperate with you in our common purpose to help our country." About this last, however, which was considerably more committal than Hoover's closing sentence, he had in Moley's presence second thoughts. He crossed out "during the balance of this year" and "in readiness to cooperate with you in," substituting for the latter the phrase, "ready to further in every way." He then handed the telegram to Moley, who, perfectly attuned to, and indeed partly responsible for, Roosevelt's wariness, wrote on the back of the telegram's envelope a yet more innocuous if not utterly meaningless reply. Dispatched at once and then released to the press it said, "I appreciate your generous telegram. For the immediate as well as for the most distant future I join in your gracious expression of a common purpose in helpful effort for our country."[29]

He was similarly wary and resistant of attempts by public speculators to hurry him into Cabinet making. "No decision has been reached and no decision will be reached in regard to any appointments for at least two months," he announced from his Albany office on Thursday, November 10, adding that "until January 1, 1933, the greater part of my time will be occupied with my duties as Governor of the State of New York." And on the day after that he cancelled his usual four o'clock press conference, saying there would be a "lid on" news for the time being. He was not feeling well when he did this. A few hours later he was decidedly ill, with a feverish catarrhal infection that kept him abed in the Executive Mansion for the next five days, delaying his departure (he had planned to leave on Friday, November 18) for his annual Thanksgiving vacation in Warm Springs.

On the second day of his illness, or early on Sunday morning, November 13, he received and read in bed a lengthy telegram from Herbert Hoover, who was then returning to Washington by train from his home in Palo Alto, California, where he had gone to vote and for a much-needed rest following the election. The telegram, for which no historic precedent existed, proposed a seemingly strictly limited cooperation between President and President-elect, during the interregnum, on a specific foreign-policy matter of which no issue had been made during the campaign. The matter concerned Allied war debts to the United States. On its face, Hoover's proposal was wholly reasonable, wholly statesmanlike, wholly selfless. It would so recommend itself to most of the public best informed on public affairs. To Roosevelt's quick intuition, however, it glinted of risk, it stank of danger. It rang alarm bells in his mind. Within minutes after he had perused the message he was telling Raymond Moley about it over the telephone (Moley was at home in New York City) and asking the professor to come at once to Albany to discuss what should be done.

Moley obeyed the summons. He was at Roosevelt's side by early afternoon.[30]

V

THE specific problem faced by the two men that day was part and parcel of a much wider, deeper problem of world economic relations. At its heart was the question of how and when, if ever, the nations of the earth should restore the international gold standard, whereby, for a half century prior to the Great War, currency exchange rates had been stabilized, with salutary effects upon world trade. Roosevelt himself repeatedly declared, and only half facetiously, that he didn't know what the gold standard was. Indeed, he would assert in a press conference, airily, dismissively, that "*nobody* [present author's italics] knows what the . . . gold standard really is."[31] But it is in fact easy to describe, and some knowledge of it is necessary to our understanding of the issue that now arose between Hoover and Roosevelt, with determinative effects upon world history during the months ahead.

In its pure original form, as distinguished from postwar varieties, it was exclusively a *gold-coin* standard governed by a half-dozen strict rules.

(1)   Actual gold money must be payable on demand.

(2)   The basic monetary unit must be a fixed quantity of gold of a specific quality (the pound sterling before 1914 was 113 grains of gold nine-tenths fine, the dollar was 25.8 grains, the French franc was 290.32 milligrams, etc.).

(3)   Holders of gold bullion must be permitted to have it coined into money, free, save for a small seigniory charge.

(4)   Anyone possessing gold coins must be free to melt them down.

(5)   Subsidiary or collateral forms of money—bank notes and the like—must be maintained at a purchasing value parity with gold bullion.

(6)   There must be no restriction whatever upon the export or import of gold bullion.

So long as the system operated in accordance with these six rules, it fixed within the narrow limits of actual gold-shipment costs the value of each currency in terms of all other currencies. Fluctuation beyond these limits was impossible. If, for instance, the 113 grains of fine gold that backed the pound sterling could be purchased in New York for $4.8666, the dollar value of the pound could not be *less* than $4.8666 minus the cost of shipping 113 grains of gold from London to New York or *more* than $4.8666 plus the cost of shipping 113 grains from New York to London. This meant that no nation on the gold standard could inflate or deflate its currency by more than a small percentage unless there were an equivalent inflation or deflation in other gold countries. International gold movements would prevent it.

The whole arrangement was consistent with, if it did not actually exemplify, that faith in the *automatic* beneficence of a system of checks and balances, disinterestedly designed but thereafter operating independent of overall human decision-making, that animated eighteenth-century English social philosophers, notably Adam Smith, a faith whose obverse and probable cause was a distrust of "human nature," a doubt that individual men would or could, in their day-to-day exercise of "free will," subordinate their selfish passions to a rationally defined general good. And to many who looked back from the early 1930s upon the gold standard's operation between 1870 and 1914—particularly upon its operation during the last twenty years of the period—this faith seemed justified by the event. The complementary doubt seemed equally if not more justified by the events that followed.

For the gold standard of the second half of the nineteenth century and early twentieth century did contribute directly and importantly to a stable international order that other factors threatened to disrupt. It encouraged world trade by curbing assertive economic nationalism. It even pointed, vaguely, toward an eventual world government of some kind insofar as it promoted the international economic interdependence that technological advances implied and, also, monetary community—virtually a single world currency—among the nations of the earth. And the world thus stitched together with threads of gold, its prosperous stability maintained in delicate balance by a typically English civility (the English had invented the gold standard, and English gentlemen "played the game according to the rules"), had indeed become by the summer of 1914, as Winston Churchill remembered it, "fair to see" and even "very brilliant." Travelers could move about in it with a freedom that would seem marvelous to later generations, crossing national frontiers with neither passport nor visa. A golden glow of confidence and optimism bathed the social scene, there being a general persuasion that reason must inevitably be sustained, social morality improved, and calamitous folly prevented by a continuous Progress having science and technology at its heart. "Were we after all to achieve world security and universal peace by a marvelous system of combinations in equipoise . . . , of checks and counter-checks upon violent action?" asked Churchill rhetorically decades later, as he described the mood of his generation in 1914. "Would Europe . . . thus grouped, thus related, unite into one universal and glorious organism capable of receiving and enjoying in undreamed-of abundance the bounty which nature and science stood hand in hand to give?"[32]

Myriads of Europeans would have answered these questions with a hearty affirmative in June 1914.

And many of these myriads were killed soon after, cut off in their youth and prime, when history returned a tragically different answer.

Every nation in the world was off the gold standard by the end of the Great War. All the original belligerent countries had to suspend specie payments and issue paper to cover their huge borrowings from their own central banks and from nonbelligerents who could supply their deficiencies of war matériel. Creditor nations, of whom the United States was by far the greatest, maintained their currencies at a parity with gold, but each of them violated the gold standard to the extent of imposing an embargo on gold shipments. The United States did so through a 1917 Trading With the Enemy Act, whereby the President was authorized to embargo at his discretion during a national emergency. (This act had never been repealed: forgotten by almost everyone, it yet remained on the statute books, a fact soon to become important to Franklin Roosevelt and the nation.) After the war, the United States slipped easily back into a pure gold-coin standard. But though surviving millions of Europeans longed for a renewal of the prewar Golden Age (so they now remembered it) and deemed the gold standard a central and essential theme of that happy time, any return to it proved impossible for the erstwhile belligerent nations through a half-dozen years of anguish. The Versailles Treaty militated against European recovery. The harshly punitive war reparations that it demanded of Germany, coupled with American insistence that Allied war debts be paid in stipulated installments whether or not Germany actually made the scheduled payments (it was in fact unable to do so), ensured financial chaos.

Not until the Dawes Plan of 1924 scaled down German reparations payments to realistic proportions and provided the Weimar Republic with American loans of $200,000,000 in gold—this following the incredible German inflation of 1923, whose miseries had encouraged the failed Munich Beer Hall Putsch of a theretofore little-known Adolf Hitler and his young Nazi Party—not until then were European currencies enabled to return to a gold base. The return thereafter was wholesale. Within three years the gold standard was as prevalent over the world's commerce as it had been before the war. It was not, however, the *same* standard as had earlier prevailed, perfectly uniform among the nations. There were significant differences among the nations in the way they returned to gold and in the kind of gold backing they now gave their currencies, differences that rendered gold considerably less effective than it had formerly been as a stabilizing influence upon both domestic and international exchange.[33]

Britain, going back on gold in 1925, restored the pound sterling to its prewar gold content of 113 grains, an evident and mistaken reassertion of nineteenth-century British imperial pride (Winston Churchill was then Chancellor of the Exchequer) in that it greatly increased the value of the pound in terms of other currencies but had severe internal deflationary results. All other former belligerents save Germany stabilized their currency at approximately the lowest point of its postwar depreciation—that is, with a far smaller content of gold per monetary unit than it had formerly had (Germany replaced its worthless paper with a new gold-backed monetary unit, the rentenmark). For instance, the French franc, the Belgian franc, and the Italian lira, when stabilized in 1926 and 1927, contained, respectively, 58.95 mg, 41.85 mg, and 79.18 mg of gold as compared with the 290.32 mg each had contained in 1914. *No* formerly belligerent European nation returned to the gold-coin standard. England and France adopted what was known as the gold-bar, or gold-bullion, standard, whereby circulating money was redeemable upon demand in gold bullion but not in gold coins, of which none were minted. Other countries, including Germany, Italy, and Belgium, adopted a so-called gold-exchange standard, whereby the country's domestic currency was not always and necessarily convertible into gold but might be converted into the currency of a foreign country that was on a solid gold standard. In other words, the foreign country's gold became the gold of ultimate redemption, and as it happened, Britain's foreign exchange constituted a major part of the reserves of gold-exchange countries by decade's end.

The return to gold signaled and had some causal connection with the European economic recovery that followed, generating the prosperity everywhere evident to Eleanor Roosevelt, Nancy Cook, and Marion Dickerman when they had visited Europe in 1929. It was, however, as Francis Hirst then warned the traveling ladies, a prosperity precariously balanced upon a slender, fragile, crumbling base. It was very much dependent upon American loans, whose ultimate repayment was rendered impossible by high and rising American tariff walls and whose continuance, in the face of manifestly dubious security for them, reflected not only a maldistribution of U.S. national income but also the virtually total lack of governmental, public-protecting securities market regulation. These loans, much reduced by American stock-market speculation through the first nine months of 1929, practically ceased altogether following the stock-market crash in October. For some eighteen months, short-term credits, swollen by gold-exchange operations as they could not have been by either the gold-coin or gold-bullion standards, partially filled the vacuum in European finance left by the withdrawal of American money. But in late May 1931 the Kreditanstalt of Vienna, one of the largest private banks on the Continent, suddenly collapsed. The immediately following panic withdrawals of short-term credits from Britain, from Germany, from all Central Europe, sent the whole of the European economy into a tailspin. Upon Britain's gold reserves the draining pressure was at once intense; they began to melt away at an alarming rate, presaging Britain's forced abandonment of the gold standard and an inevitably consequent worldwide flight from gold, again, into unstable managed paper currencies.

In a frantic effort to prevent this, all through a long summer of growing anxiety, the U.S. government very actively participated.

Herbert Hoover was deeply emotionally involved. Not only was his commitment to gold of a religious nature (he spoke of the metal as a sacred substance "enshrined in human instincts for over 10,000 years"[34]), he had also persuaded himself in recent months that the roots of the American depression *must* lie, most of them, in foreign soil. Otherwise they would be traced to the acts and policies of the American big-business community, which the Republican Party represented. And he now seized upon the European financial debacle, which others deemed a consequence of America's financial debacle, as evidence of the truth of his thesis. He responded swiftly. On June 30, 1931, within three months after the Kreditanstalt's failure, he formally proposed a one-year moratorium on all war debts and reparations payments to ease the anguish of, as he stressed, "worldwide" depression. His proposal was accepted with alacrity by all interested parties save France, and France, under strong pressure from London and Washington, was soon forced to accept it. Hoover also encouraged the U.S. Federal Reserve System, whose governors may have needed little encouragement, to extend large credits to the Bank of England, as did the Bank of France.

But all this did not suffice.

On September 14, 1931, sailors of Britain's Atlantic fleet, on shore leave at Invergordon, met in angry protest against the government's newly announced cuts in navy pay, deemed essential to Britain's retention of a gold-backed pound. The next day the sailors refused to put to sea for the scheduled autumn exercises, though they peacefully boarded and worked their ships when the government, promising a full investigation of their grievances, cancelled the exercises and dispersed the ships to their home ports. The near-mutiny, magnified by the press into a full-scale one, sent shock waves around the world.

It was portentous of social revolution. It signified a serious threat to freedom of the seas, for of this the Royal Navy had been the chief guarantee for 200 years. And it provoked a wave of selling on every nation's stock exchanges, which in turn caused increased withdrawals of foreign balances in London. Within five days the last of Britain's credits had been exhausted. On Monday, September 20, 1931, Great Britain suspended its gold standard by act of Parliament.

What had been fearfully anticipated by international financiers and traders now became, for them, a nightmarish reality. Australia, Argentina, and Mexico had been forced off gold shortly before Britain was. Fourteen other countries were driven off within weeks, including Norway, Sweden, Denmark, Finland, Portugal, Canada, India, and Japan. Seven more countries, including Greece, Chile, and Peru, had abandoned gold in 1932. The moment each country left gold, the currency of each was of course abruptly devalued in terms of the currencies of the remaining gold countries, the chief of which were the United States, France, and Germany. For instance (the most important of instances), the pound sterling, worth $4.8666 in August 1931, fell to $4.28 on September 22, to $4.10½ on the day after that, and to $3.25, or about 70 percent of its former parity, in November. It rose the following month to $3.37, thereafter fluctuating widely, swiftly, unpredictably, above and below this point—it stood at $3.72 in April 1932 and at $3.27 in December. The fluctuations of other managed or "floating" currencies were similarly swift and wide.[35] Every international commercial transaction became now far more difficult and hazardous than it would have been two years before, *immensely* more so than in early 1914, not only because of monetary instability but also because of the tariffs, exchange controls, quotas, import restrictions, trade agreements, and other checks upon trade that began to be imposed in bristling array by governments seeking to protect their economies against what Hoover called "shocks and set-backs from abroad." An already sadly shrunken foreign market for U.S. goods was further contracted.

Thus, by that mid-November day of 1932 when Roosevelt and Moley conferred over Hoover's lengthy telegram, an increasingly exclusive and combative economic nationalism was dividing the commercial world. And as economic crisis produced political crisis, as economic distress bred psychological illness, there was an ominous resurgence of aggressive militarism, especially in Japan (which made imperialistic war on China), Italy (Mussolini was building a navy and air force of alarming size), and Germany (a moribund Weimar Republic was staggering off history's stage while Hitler waited in the wings). The Hawley-Smoot Tariff had of course greatly encouraged the disastrous trend. Indeed, Hoover's signing of this bill into law in June 1930, using six *gold* pens, was what finally convinced Japan that the United States was determined to prevent any legitimate peaceful expansion of Japanese trade and that it was therefore necessary for Japan to conquer markets by force. Nor had Hoover done anything to abate or mitigate the surge of economic nationalism, he did precisely the opposite, when he made the maintenance of a high protective tariff a central issue of his reelection campaign. It was an issue on which, as we have seen, he was very confusedly and confusingly opposed, insofar as he was opposed at all, by Roosevelt. Hoover was nationalistic, too, as was Roosevelt, in his stand on war debts. Despite his moratorium proposal, the President had refused to agree with the six-nation Lausanne Conference* in early July; since German reparations and Allied war debts were as a practical matter inextricably linked, cancellation of the former, which the conference proposed, implied cancellation of the latter and was, as a matter of fact, contingent upon this. Hoover and Roosevelt agreed with Coolidge and Wilson that the United States had no concern whatever with reparations, having demanded none at war's end. The war debts to the United States, on the other hand, were debts of honor; they *must* be paid. "A year ago in recommending to the Congress the ratification of the moratorium," said Hoover in his message to Roosevelt, "I . . . pointed out that debts to us bore no relationship to debts between other nations which grew out of the war."[36]

Yet the President who thus embraced protectionism with some passion (witness his "grass-will-grow-in-the-streets" campaign statement) and who otherwise espoused policies of economic nationalism, was simultaneously an economic *internationalist* insofar as he was convinced, publicly at least, that the depression, being worldwide in extent and international in cause as a consequence of the massive economic dislocations of the Great War, could be cured only through cooperative international action. Early in the summer of 1932, even before the Republican National Convention nominated him for a second presidential term, Hoover committed the United States to full participation in the World Monetary and Economic Conference,† originally scheduled to open in London in January 1933 but now postponed to an unspecified date. High on the conference agenda would be the proposal of international currency stabilization by means of a reinstituted worldwide gold standard. Hoover's administration was also playing "a leading part" (his words) in the World Disarmament Conference, which had opened in Geneva on February 2, 1932, and whose General Commission, still in session, was attempting in mid-November to end the stalemate that had resulted when Germany demanded, in drastic revision of the Versailles Treaty, "equality of rights in matters relating to armaments."‡ He had emphasized bipartisanship in his approach to these international endeavors by naming a prominent Democrat as chief U.S. delegate to the Disarmament Conference and, also, as a member of the organizing commission of the World Economic Conference. This Democrat was Norman H. Davis, a strikingly handsome silver-haired man of fifty-three who had been Assistant Secretary of the Treasury under Wilson. As

---

*Represented at Lausanne were Great Britain, France, Belgium, Italy, Germany, and Japan.
†The idea for such a conference was born at Lausanne, where the United States was not represented.
‡A five-power formal recognition "in principle" of the justice of the German demand would be signed on December 11, enabling the German delegates to return to a conference they had boycotted for five months.

conservative as Hoover in his economic views, he had been a leading advocate
of the League of Nations since its founding, and was now, in Moley's unfriendly words, "the darling of the internationalists of both parties."[37] Hoover
was continuing his bipartisan approach to foreign affairs when he wrote out
his long message to Roosevelt and dispatched it on the evening of November
12 as his train passed through Yuma, Arizona.

VI

As for Roosevelt, he accepted as generally valid the traditional maxim that
partisan politics should cease at the national frontier. During the presidential
campaign he had made no attack on Hoover's conduct of foreign affairs. But
bipartisanship could prevail in foreign policy only if, or to the extent that, a
hard and fast line was drawn between foreign and domestic affairs, and it was
because he knew that no such line was now drawn by Hoover, nor perhaps
could be in present economic circumstances, that alarm bells rang in his mind,
and ever louder, as he read through Hoover's surprising message.

Its opening words informed Roosevelt, who already knew from press reports, that Great Britain had just asked in effect for an extension of the foreign
debt moratorium, which had just expired, over the period necessary for a
thorough review of the entire "regime of intergovernmental financial obligations . . . now existing." Other debtor nations were about to make similar
requests. This not only meant an indefinite postponement of the debt installment payments due the United States on December 15 (those of Britain and
France totaled a little less than $119,000,000), it also clearly presaged debtor-
nation requests for either (1) a reduction, if not outright abolition, of the
remaining debts or (2) negotiation of methods of debt payment other than
direct gold or gold-equivalent transfers. And the executive now had no room
for maneuvering in response to such requests. When Hoover presented his debt
moratorium proposal to Congress for ratification in 1931, he recommended the
establishment of a new debt commission "to deal with situations that might
arise owing to the temporary incapacity of any individual debtor to meet its
obligations . . . during the period of world depression." The House and Senate,
however, in their joint resolution ratifying the one-year moratorium, had
"expressly declared [it] to be against the policy of the Congress that any of the
indebtedness of foreign countries to the United States should be in any manner
cancelled or reduced; and nothing in this joint resolution shall be construed
as indicating a contrary policy or as implying that favorable consideration will
be given at any time to a change in the policy hereby declared." Since establishment of a new debt commission *would* be so construed, and *would* have such
implication, Hoover's recommendation had been emphatically rejected. This
meant that "[a]ny negotiation [of debt payments in forms other than gold
transfers] . . . is limited," wrote Hoover to Roosevelt, " . . . and if there is to
be any change in the attitude of the Congress it will be greatly affected by the
views of those members who recognize you as their leader." Hoover was

therefore "loath to proceed with recommendations to the Congress until I can have an opportunity to confer with you personally," and he suggested that such conference be held "during the latter part of next week," when, he understood, Roosevelt would be passing through Washington en route to Warm Springs.

The President-elect, it was clear, was being asked to share responsibility with the President for decisions only the latter had legal authority to make. This was risky enough for Roosevelt when limited to the highly emotional question of war debts. But war debts were not all that Hoover wished to discuss at the proposed meeting. "There are also other important questions as to which I think an interchange of views will be in the public interest. The building up of world stability is, of course, of the greatest importance in the building up of our recovery." And the President went on to mention in this connection the upcoming World Economic Conference ("[w]hile this conference may be begun during my Administration, it is certain that it will not be completed until after you have assumed office") and the continuing World Disarmament Conference, whose success would serve "a great economic purpose, as well as the advancement of world peace."[38]

The "of course" in Hoover's statement about recovery could not but have sharpened Roosevelt's and Moley's awareness of danger, their consequent wariness of cooperation with the lame-duck President. It implied that President-elect Roosevelt must accept as an accurate description of fact what candidate Roosevelt had ridiculed as the "boldest alibi in history," namely that "our troubles come from abroad." (" . . . our opponents have . . . become almost frantic in their insistence that this entire sequence of events [leading to depression] originated abroad," Roosevelt had said in Pittsburgh. "I do not know where; they have never located 'abroad,' but I think it is somewhere near Abyssinia.")[39] It further implied an effort by Hoover, perhaps without wholly conscious motivation, to commit Roosevelt to a foreign economic policy that might severely limit the New Deal's freedom of domestic action on depression problems.

Hence the very careful wording of the telegram that was dispatched from Albany on Monday, November 14, and delivered to the President on his train in Pratt, Kansas. In it Roosevelt said that he had been "confined in the house with a slight cold" and so didn't know just when he would be leaving for Warm Springs but that he would be "delighted to confer" on a "wholly informal and personal basis" and would phone Hoover as soon as he was able to say definitely when he would be in the capital. It would be "helpful to have your views" when he, Roosevelt, met with "Democratic leaders of the present Congress late this month in Warm Springs," but he made no implied promise of an attempt to persuade them toward Hoover's "views." Instead, he hoped Hoover himself would meet with these same congressional leaders "at the earliest opportunity, because, in the last analysis, the immediate question raised by the British, French and other notes creates a responsibility which rests upon those now vested with executive and legislative authority."[40]

The Hoover-Roosevelt meeting took place on Tuesday, November 22, in the Red Room of the White House,* with Moley at Roosevelt's side and Secretary of the Treasury Ogden Mills at Hoover's side. It was no easy, relaxed, happy occasion, despite Roosevelt's attempts to lighten the proceedings. "Everyone smoked somewhat nervously, President Hoover on a fat cigar," as Moley later remembered. Hoover could not bring himself to look directly at his principal guest (he only glanced at him from time to time), or even to address him directly, as he launched upon an impressively well-organized, detailed historical exposition of the debt question. Instead, during a monologue lasting nearly an hour, he fixed his gaze first upon the Great Seal of the United States, which was woven into the thick red carpet, then upon Moley, who was made distinctly uncomfortable by it. He concluded on a note of urgency, if not crisis. *Either* debt cancellation *or* default of payment in the weeks just ahead would have strongly adverse effects upon international credits, deepening world depression. On the other hand, if the debt question were settled, Britain would be enabled to return to the gold standard, leading the way for other countries currently "off gold" and providing solid basis for worldwide business recovery. What Hoover now proposed, therefore, was the idea Congress had rejected last year, namely, a reconstituted debt commission empowered to negotiate with representatives of the debtor nations. The commission would consist of three senators, three representatives, and three presidential appointees, with the President-elect joining the President in selecting the last. Roosevelt's approval of the idea would assure its acceptance by the Democratic leadership of the lame-duck Congress. And to Hoover and Mills it appeared that Roosevelt personally *did* approve—he smiled, he nodded, he said yes, though vaguely, as if perhaps he meant only that he understood what had been said—until he turned to Moley, tacitly inviting the professor's extended verbal response to the proposal. Moley, speaking for Roosevelt, did *not* approve. Instead, improvising with swift adroitness upon what he knew to be a central theme of Roosevelt's interregnum strategy, that of noncommitment, he suggested firm insistence upon full payment of the December 15 debt installments, accompanied by a statement of the four principles governing the Hoover administration's dealings with war debts that Hoover had just stated, principles wholly acceptable to Roosevelt: (1) the debts were business obligations, not political obligations, (2) each nation's debt was a unique transaction between that nation and the United States, to be considered independently of other national debts to the United States, (3) there was no connection between German reparations to the Allies and Allied debts to the United States, and (4) the United States was prepared to consider any nation's actual or professed inabil-

*Accompanying Roosevelt on the Baltimore and Ohio's Capitol Limited from New York City, in addition to Moley, were Louis Howe, Jim Farley, and, of course, his constant companion and personal bodyguard, Gus Gennerich. At Washington's Union Station he was officially greeted, on behalf of the President, by his first cousin, Warren Delano Robbins, to whom fifteen-year-old Franklin Roosevelt had been guide and mentor when twelve-year-old Robbins entered Groton's I Form in the fall of 1897. Robbins was now the State Department's Chief of Protocol.

ity to pay its debt. The latter consideration called, of course, for international negotiations but not necessarily for a special debt commission, whose establishment would require congressional permission. Why not conduct the necessary conversations through the State Department's normal channels of diplomacy?

There was, then, no meeting of the minds on the debt question between the outgoing and incoming administrations. When Roosevelt that evening, in his Mayflower Hotel suite, greeted Democratic leaders of Congress (the final session of the 72nd Congress was to open December 5), he told them he had entered into no agreement with the President beyond concurrence in the President's insistence that the December 15 installment payments must be made. He then listened to, and gave every sign of approving, the congressional Democrats' intention to propose in the lame-duck session a severely limited legislative program, its main items being the legalization of beer having an alcoholic content of 3.2 percent, taxation and governmental economy measures aimed at balancing the budget, and some measure of farm relief. The next day, he and the President issued separate statements about their White House meeting, neither indicating that anything had been accomplished beyond an exchange of views.[41]

But this was by no means the end of the matter.

Hoover underrated Roosevelt in much the same way as Al Smith and Robert Moses and many another actual or potential rival for power had done, and as Lippmann had done. When Secretary of State Henry L. Stimson phoned the White House immediately after the Red Room meeting, the President reported that he and Mills "had spent most of their time in educating a very ignorant" if also "well-meaning young man."[42] Accordingly, he refused to accept or even recognize the fact that his effort to commit Roosevelt to his own brand of economic internationalism had been decisively rebuffed. Instead, he continued this effort with increased forcefulness and decreased flexibility. On December 15, Great Britain, under strong protest and with continued urgent request for a general review of the debt question, met its scheduled debt-installment payment of $95,550,000 in gold. France, however, defaulted on her payment of $19,261,432. And this occasioned another long telegram from Hoover to Roosevelt, dispatched on Saturday, December 17.* In it, the President again insisted that special "machinery" must be "erected" immediately to deal with debt problems, since the "routine machinery of diplomacy neither affords the type of men required nor can they give the time from other duties which such discussions require." He reiterated that debt problems could not "be dissociated from the problems which will come before the World Economic Conference and to some extent those before the Conference on World Disarmament. As the economic situation in foreign countries is one of the dominant depressants of prices and employment in the United States, it is urgent that the World Economic Conference should assemble at as early a date as possible.

---

*Roosevelt was then in Hyde Park. He had returned to New York from Warm Springs some ten days before.

The United States should be represented by a strong and effective delegation. This delegation should be chosen at an early moment." His implied suggestion (he was not explicit on this point) was that the debt negotiations be conducted by members of the delegation chosen for the World Economic Conference, a delegation including not only members of Congress but also "some of the old or new members of the delegation to the arms conference." In that way, "these three important questions" could "be given coordinate consideration." He concluded with words that seemed to some in the Roosevelt camp threatful and were, consequently, resented: "I shall be informing the Congress of the economic situation and the desirability of the above proposed machinery for dealing with these conferences. I should be glad to know if you could join with me in the selection of such delegation at the present time or if you feel that the whole matter should be delayed until after March 4th."[43]

Roosevelt did not reply to this communication until the evening of Monday, December 19, though, or perhaps because, he had been informed that the President's message would by then, on that day, have been delivered to Congress. This presidential message stressed abandonment of the gold standard as a major cause of the continuing downward spiral of world prices. International currency stabilization on a new gold standard was, therefore, a major prerequisite for world economic recovery. The message also announced Hoover's proposal to appoint at once a special commission to deal with the interrelated problems of international debts, disarmament, and the world economy. Roosevelt, responding to all this, was very sure that the three "questions" that the President tied so closely together would "be found to require selective treatment." He suggested, therefore, that disarmament be pressed along the policy line ("[y]our policy is clear and satisfactory") already laid down and that the debt question be pursued, either through "the existing machinery of diplomatic service" or through special appointees of the President, in ways designed to determine "facts" and explore "possibilities" but not to fix "policies binding on the incoming Administration." "As to the economic conference: I am clear that a permanent economic program for the world should not be submerged in conversations relating to disarmament or debts. I recognize, of course, a relationship, but not an identity. Therefore, I cannot go along with the thought that the personnel conducting the conversations should be identical." Nor would he agree to an early appointment of permanent delegates to the conference. Instead, "I must respectfully suggest that" this matter and that of finally determining the conference agenda "be held in abeyance until after March 4th." He was sure the President would "recognize that it would be unwise for me to accept an apparent joint responsibility with you when, as a matter of constitutional fact, I would be wholly lacking in attendant authority.[44]

Yet still Hoover persisted. Within hours after he read Roosevelt's reply, the President dispatched to the President-elect, on December 20, yet another telegram, this one quite consciously designed to make Roosevelt appear a "mere politician" in a situation calling for high statesmanship. Wrote Hoover: "I have your telegram expressing the difficulties which you find in cooperation at the present time. In the face of foreign conditions which are continually degenerating agricultural prices, increasing unemployment and creating economic difficulties for our people, I am unwilling to admit that cooperation cannot be established between the outgoing and incoming Administrations which will give earlier solution and recovery from these difficulties. . . . My frequent statements indicate agreement with you that debts, world economic problems and disarmament require selective treatment, but you will agree with me that they also require coordination and preparation. . . . There is thus no thought of submerging the World Economic Conference with other questions, but rather to remove the barriers from the successful issue of that conference. With a view to again making an effort to secure cooperation and that solidarity of national action which the situation needs, I would be glad if you would designate Mr. Owen D. Young, Colonel House, or any other men of your party possessed of your views and your confidence . . . to sit with the principal officers of this Administration in an endeavor to see what steps can be taken to avoid delays of precious time."[45]

Roosevelt was not moved. Unpersuaded of any such direct causal connection between "foreign conditions" and the American depression as Hoover alleged, he felt no such need as Hoover felt to deal with these "conditions" at once. " . . . the difficulties," he said in a telegram sent to the White House on December 21, " . . . are not in finding the means or willingness for cooperation, but rather in defining clearly those things concerning which cooperation between us is possible." No effective decisions on these international questions could be made by him before March 4, he reiterated. "There remains . . . only the possibility of exploratory work and preliminary surveys." These last he would be "glad" to have go forward. "However, for me to accept any joint responsibility in the work of exploration might be construed by the debtor or other Nations . . . as a commitment, moral though not legal, as to policies and courses of action. The designation of a man or men of such eminence as your telegram suggests would not imply mere fact-findings; it would suggest the presumption that such representatives were empowered to exchange views on matters of large and binding policy."[46]

Even this did not bring the exchange to an end.

The next day, an angry Hoover informed Roosevelt by wire that, since there had been in the press "so many garbled versions" of the communications between them, for which, he implied, Roosevelt was responsible, he was releasing the telegrams for publication. He did so with an accompanying blunt statement, accusatory in tone: "Governor Roosevelt considers that it is undesirable for him to assent to my suggestions for cooperative action. . . . I will respect his wishes." It was now Roosevelt's turn for anger. As soon as he saw the Hoover statement on Thursday afternoon, December 22, he wrote out in pencil, for immediate release to the press, a denial of its imputation. He was "rather surprised," he said, by the White House statement. "It is a pity not only for this country but for the solution of world problems that any statement or intimation should be given that I consider it undesirable to assent to cooperative action on foreign problems." He had made "the definite suggestion" that the President select "representatives to make preliminary studies," had asked "to be kept advised" of the progress of these, and had "offered to consult with the President freely between now and March 4th." He hoped "that this practical program and definite offer of co-operation will be accepted."[47]

VII

THE exchange, in overall effect, was not fortunate for Roosevelt's personal prestige with the public at large. Especially unfortunate was his remark to reporters, after leaving the White House, that war debts were "not my baby" since he'd not be President until March 4. The Detroit *Free Press* spoke the judgment of millions when it editorialized on November 24 that Roosevelt's "refusal to cooperate," joined with his subsequent disavowal of parental responsibility for "baby," indicated a "lack of largeness and vision . . . disquieting in a person about to become Chief Executive." Said the Baltimore *Sun* on the same day: " . . . Mr. Roosevelt might wisely have given thought to the possibility that this baby . . . may soon grow up into an unruly stepchild, permanently lodged under his roof, and disposed to play with matches." Secretary Stimson recorded in his diary the opinion that Roosevelt had made himself "look like a peanut" compared with the President, whose telegrams had been "dignified and on a high plane of unselfishness."[48] Certainly the exchange was not reassuring to those who looked anxiously, longingly, toward the President-elect, hoping to see greatness in him. They saw instead and at most mere cleverness of political maneuvering, and even of this they might well have doubts.

Nor was Roosevelt's stature increased in the public eye, or popular trust in him enhanced, by his other publicized words and deeds as the old year died and 1933 was born.

At Warm Springs, at Albany until his successor, Herbert H. Lehman, was inaugurated governor of New York, at Hyde Park, in Washington's Mayflower Hotel, in his private car on railroad journeys, he talked with a steady stream of visitors—congressional leaders, business leaders, labor leaders, farm organization leaders, publishers, and publicists—each of whom tried and failed to discover what his specific programs would be, yet each of whom left him saying for publication, and often believing, that he was deeply sympathetic with the visitor's views if he did not, in fact, share them. Several reports of these conversations gave the impression that he was a conservative of the conservatives, one who gave a higher priority to reduced spending and a balanced budget than to providing jobs and relief for the unemployed. So rigid, on occasion, seemed his adherence to the economy plank of his party's platform and to the hard line of his Pittsburgh speech that even Cordell Hull, one of the platform's chief draftsmen, became alarmed and urged through an intermediary that Roosevelt adopt a more progressive line. If, on the other hand, the visitor were a liberal, the impression carried away was of a man who clearly subordinated property rights to human rights and was prepared to take bold new departures. Always, however, it was an *impression* that was carried away, never an absolute conviction. Thus California's elderly Progressive Senator Hiram Johnson, commenting on his private talk with the President-elect, spoke of "what I think was his ready agreement, generally speaking, with progressive principles." Inevitably encouraged was an already widespread suspicion that Roosevelt, of himself alone, stood for very little, that he was indeed as "ignorant" as he was "well-meaning," that he had no settled plans of his own for attack upon the depression. "When I talk to him," said Huey Long to a reporter in mid-January 1933, "he says 'Fine! Fine! Fine!' But Joe Robinson [notoriously conservative and Long's arch-enemy in the Senate] goes to see him the next day and again he says 'Fine! Fine! Fine!' Maybe he says 'Fine!' to everybody."[49]

The one certainty about him, now recognized nationwide, as it had been statewide in early 1929, was his possession of immense personal charm. A day or so after Huey Long spoke the above-quoted words of disparagement, he had a private conference with Roosevelt in the Mayflower and was, for the moment, completely won over. He entered the suite in a belligerent mood, intending, he said, to "talk turkey." He emerged a half hour later, all smiles, to say glowingly to reporters, "He is the same old Frank. . . . all wool and a yard wide." Hiram Johnson, too, was glowing when he emerged from *his* private interview. "I like Roosevelt immensely," he wrote to a friend. "I like his good humor, his geniality, his genuine smile." Similarly with crusty old Carter Glass of Virginia, father of the Federal Reserve, whose commitment to the gold standard and against any kind of "tampering with the currency" was of religious fervor and who was considered to be, almost certainly, the next Secretary of the Treasury. Arthur Krock, the New York *Times*'s Washington bureau chief, watching with awe Roosevelt's January wooing of congressional leaders of all stripes and shades of political opinion, reported that it was "a skillful, even a miraculous performance."[50] Many others said much the same in print. In sum, however, these reports did more to augment than to allay doubts in critical minds about Roosevelt's essential character. Such consciously exercised charm ("skillful performance") was so seldom joined, in one's experience, to a tough decisiveness or any capacity for sustained mental effort, was so often joined with deviousness, employed as a literally *beguiling* charm for purposes of deception, trickery, fraud.

Nor was confidence in Roosevelt bolstered by his seemingly vacillating and certainly ineffectual dealings with lame-duck legislation. On the contrary, these dealings, as reported in the press, encouraged the dim view of him as a man so empty of solid conviction and so full of a gaseous wish to please that he went with every wind, however light and shifting.

Take, as a prime example, his handling of the outgoing President's proposal of new taxes to balance the budget. For the fiscal year 1933 Herbert Hoover presented to Congress a budget that, though it called for reductions of nearly 18 percent in controllable expenses, was still some 10 percent out of balance.

This deficit the President proposed to make up with a 2½-percent general manufacturers' sales tax on virtually every item save food. Roosevelt tacitly approved the slash in expenditures. He could hardly do otherwise, being himself publicly committed to a much larger cut. And he seemed initially to have no objection to Hoover's tax program, for he made no public pronouncement against it, whereas he had let it be known that he favored Democratic support of new taxes that would enable his own administration to avoid deficit financing during its first year. Accordingly, House Speaker (and Vice-President-elect) Garner announced his support of the sales tax and began to use the considerable powers of the Speaker's office to coerce reluctant Democrats into a favorable vote. Aligned with him were leading Democratic conservatives, including Bernard Baruch, who was soon calling for "sacrifice . . . frugality," the taxation of "everybody for everything," and Al Smith, who went so far as to favor a manufacturers' sales tax high enough to permit a cut in income taxes.[51] From spokesmen for farmers, laborers, retailers, and liberal opinion in general, however, came loud cries of protest. The proposal was vehemently attacked for its manifest unfairness, since a disproportionate portion of the new tax burden would be borne by those economically least able to bear it, and for its equally manifest deflationary effect, since it must inevitably further reduce an already drastically shrunken consumer market. Roosevelt remained publicly silent on the matter for many days. Not until he learned that Garner and the chairman of the House Ways and Means Committee were using his name in support of the measure, claiming they acted in accordance with his known wish, by which time it was abundantly clear that budget balancing through a sales tax would cost him far more politically than would a budget deficit—not until then did he take a definite stand. Through "sources close to the governor" he then, in late December, professed amazement that anyone could believe he had ever favored a sales tax: in point of fact he was prepared openly to break with Democratic congressional leaders if they continued to press for its passage.

A few days later, on the evening of January 5, he met in his New York City home with Representatives Garner and Rayburn, Senators Robinson and Hull, and a half-dozen other senators and representatives of generally conservative opinion to review and make final decision (so said political reporters) concerning the Democratic legislative program for the remainder of the lame-duck session. The press interpreted the meeting as evidence of the President-elect's determination to push through (1) the budget-balancing tax legislation (in lieu of the sales tax it would necessarily involve a sharp increase in income taxes); (2) the farm legislation whose "specifications" he had outlined in his Topeka speech (the leading farm organizations were now generally agreed upon the voluntary domestic allotment plan promoted by Milburn L. Wilson and Henry A. Wallace, though this continued to be opposed by George N. Peek and Hugh Johnson, coauthors of McNary-Haugen); and (3) legislative authorization of the governmental reorganization powers, including authority to impose salary and staff reductions, which the executive would need to achieve a 25-percent cut in federal expenditures—all this to obviate the necessity for a special session of Congress after he took office. For Roosevelt had publicly stated his wish for nine months of executive action, free of the need to deal with legislation, at the outset of his administration. He was therefore blamed—it was taken as evidence that he could not lead, much less master, a Democratic Congress—when none of this proposed legislation was enacted. All had failed, and ludicrously, by mid-February. It was by that time clear that a special session could not be avoided.

Similarly and simultaneously weak, vacillating, and ineffectual appeared Roosevelt's renewal in early January of foreign-policy dealings with the Hoover administration.

On December 22, the same day Hoover and Roosevelt issued their counter-accusatory press statements, Norman H. Davis arrived in America from a recessed Disarmament Conference in Geneva. In a shipboard interview he announced to the press that the World Economic Conference's Preparatory Commission would conclude its meetings in January. The conference itself, he said categorically, would open in April. The statement was given authority by Davis' membership in the Economic Conference's organizing body, and this last, joined to his role in Geneva, seemed to make his pronouncement a tying together of disarmament, debt settlement, and currency stabilization in precisely the way Hoover insisted they must be. Moley and Tugwell were highly displeased—also alarmed, insofar as they were uncertain about Roosevelt's clarity and firmness of purpose. For in that season's crisis circumstances, the two Brain Trusters were especially fervent economic nationalists, suspicious that every effort of the outgoing administration to obtain foreign-policy commitments from Roosevelt was an effort to abort the New Deal. They were consequently strongly of the opinion that the Economic Conference, if held at all (they wished that it need not be), should have its opening delayed as long as possible. The new administration must have time in which to launch its economic recovery program, time in which to establish it with sufficient firmness to render the monetary aspects of it non-negotiable internationally. And Roosevelt was of the same opinion. He had indicated as much to Edmund E. Day and John H. Williams, the two "expert" representatives of the United States on the Preparatory Commission, when Tugwell brought them to consult with him at Hyde Park on Sunday, December 18. He made no public objection to Davis' pronouncement, however. Instead, he yielded to Davis' insistence upon an exclusively private talk with him in Albany on the day after Christmas, then cancelled a meeting with Day and Williams scheduled for the following day (Roosevelt had suggested to Tugwell a conference on December 27 of Davis, Day, Williams, and Tugwell). This meant that Day and Williams sailed for Europe on December 28 to participate in renewed meetings of the Preparatory Commission, uninstructed in any definitive way as to the upcoming administration's policies.

Moreover, by the time of the Davis meeting, Roosevelt, with the active assistance of both Davis and Frankfurter, was arranging for a private conference with Secretary of State Stimson, who was eager for it but had some difficulty obtaining the permission he needed from the President, since Hoover's dislike and distrust of Roosevelt grew now toward the pathological. That difficulty cleared away, Stimson accepted Roosevelt's invitation to lunch at Hyde Park on Monday, January 9, and was alone with the President-elect for some five hours. "The Governor did everything to make the interview pleasant, and his hospitality was very agreeable," wrote Stimson in his diary that Monday evening. " . . . we had no difficulty in getting on. . . . I was much impressed with his disability and the brave way in which he paid no attention to it whatever."[52] The fact that this meeting was held was at once greatly publicized.* What the two men talked about was not publicized at all. But two days later Roosevelt announced his approval of embargoing arms shipments to warring nations. (Hoover, on January 10, had urged Congress to ratify a Geneva convention calling for such an embargo.) A few days later, Roosevelt let it be known, in offhand fashion, that he had agreed to meet again on the foreign debt question with President Hoover. (Why, for God's sake? worried Moley and Tugwell. Was he about to reverse his stand on this matter?) And a few days after that, he announced what was in effect an endorsement of a major and highly controversial element of the Hoover administration's foreign policy, one about which Hoover himself had doubts, namely, the so-called Stimson Doctrine.

A year before, on January 7, 1932, in reaction to Japan's forcible seizure of Manchuria from China, a conquest begun in September 1931, the Secretary of State had formally declared that the United States would recognize "no situation, treaty, or agreement" achieved by force in violation of the 1928 Declaration of Paris, that is, the Kellogg-Briand Pact, "outlawing" war. It was a declaration that, in context, reaffirmed the 1899 Open Door policy for China as written into the Nine-Power Treaty signed in 1922 at the Washington Conference on Naval Limitations. Insofar as it had any substantive meaning, it threatened the use of economic and even, ultimately, military sanctions against Japan, an implication Stimson himself fully intended, since, in his private opinion, "it is . . . almost impossible that there should not be an armed clash between two such different civilizations."[53] The announced doctrine had no deterrent effect upon the militarists now in control of the Japanese government. Neither did a report of the League of Nations' commission of inquiry, the Lytton Report, which charged Japan with aggression in Manchuria and recommended a restoration of Chinese sovereignty over the region, with international safeguards of Japanese economic interests there. By the time this report was issued, in October 1932, Japan had set up a puppet state, Manchukuo, incorporating Jehol with Manchuria. And on the January day when Stimson lunched with Roosevelt, Japanese forces were pressing southward from the Great Wall of China toward the port of Tientsin, from

---

*Roosevelt's original wish was that his meeting with Stimson go unpublicized, but Hoover announced it to the press.

which, and the area surrounding it, Chinese troops would soon be forced to withdraw.

A week later, on January 16, 1933, with the League of Nations about to begin, in Geneva, formal consideration of the Lytton Report with a view to its acceptance as Far Eastern policy, Stimson emphatically reiterated his doctrine in a formal communication to European foreign offices. He also, in press reports, broadly hinted that his stated policy had the President-elect's approval. Such approval, assuring continuity of U.S. foreign policy on this matter, must of course encourage not only League acceptance of the Lytton Report but also incorporation of the nonrecognition formula, with all that it implied, in the League's final policy statement. And what Stimson had hinted, Roosevelt promptly confirmed. On January 17, besieged in his New York City home by reporters clamoring for a statement, he handed them a penciled note, dashed off in their presence, saying that though "[a]ny statement relating to any particular foreign situation must of course come from the Secretary of State . . . ," he was "wholly willing to make it clear that American foreign policy must uphold the sanctity" of treaties, this being "a cornerstone on which all relations between nations must rest."[54]

These developments brought Moley and Tugwell to the edge of despair. "To say I was sick at heart over what was happening would be the epitome of understatement," remembered Moley six years later. "I was also completely baffled. Was Roosevelt really ignorant of the implications of what he was doing?" On January 18 the two men came together to 49 East Sixty-fifth Street and were closeted for hours with the President-elect. With Tugwell doing most of the talking, they argued vehemently against "a commitment which may lead us to war with Japan," as Tugwell put it. Roosevelt remained unmoved. He calmly admitted that war was possible. He even indicated, as if in echo of Stimson's luncheon talk, that war might ultimately prove inevitable, given Japan's aggressively imperialistic ambitions, and that "it might be better to have it now than later." Tugwell was horrified. He spoke of Japan's desperate need of assured markets, because of population pressure and rapid industrial growth. Backed by Moley, he "expressed some doubts whether Japanese imperialism was much worse than British." But he and Moley were forced at last to realize that they argued in vain. Roosevelt's decision was made. Moreover, it was evidently a deeply *felt* decision, highly personal, for he spoke of the commercial and sympathetic ties that his family, the Delano side of it, had formed with the Chinese people in the days of the clipper ships. The sympathy remained profound. How, then, asked Roosevelt, "could you expect me not to go along with Stimson on Japan?"[55]

There remained to be saved, if possible, in Moley's view, the New Deal's freedom to act, untrammeled by foreign commitments, upon domestic depression problems—and on this matter, at least, Moley's worst fears were allayed when at Roosevelt's request he accompanied the President-elect to Washington for the second meeting with Hoover on January 20.

Anxiously, through the last four weeks, Moley and Tugwell had watched

Norman Davis' apparently growing influence over Roosevelt's thinking about European relations. The suave, prestigious, physically impressive, imperviously self-assured Davis was not only at one with the Hoover administration as regards the intermingling of debt conversations with other matters in preparation for the London Conference, he also repeatedly imposed himself upon the President-elect, his impositions seemingly unresented and certainly unrepulsed. To Moley's acute displeasure, Davis was aboard the train that bore Roosevelt, Moley, and Tugwell from New York City to Washington on January 19. Was he there by Roosevelt's invitation? Moley wondered. If so, why? His presence was unconnected with the upcoming White House, meeting, according to a statement Roosevelt made to reporters in New York City, and in Washington a few hours later, responding to a specific question, Roosevelt said to reporters that Davis would *not* attend the next day's conference. Moley remained anxious, however, and with good reason. For at the Mayflower Hotel next morning, after Moley and Tugwell had had a heated and inconclusive argument with Davis on the question of linkage between debt conversations and preparations for London—and just as Roosevelt and Moley were about to leave the hotel for the Hoover meeting—Davis came to Roosevelt and asked "point-blank" if the latter wouldn't like to have him come along to the White House. Moley was furious. The request seemed to him outrageous of Roosevelt's prerogatives and insulting to Roosevelt personally. But Roosevelt gave not the slightest sign of displeasure; instead, he replied "good-naturedly" that Davis might come along if he wished.

And at the White House, Davis was no such silent witness as Moley felt he ought to be, given the circumstances: he "lacked the sensibility to keep from chiming in with the Hoover, Stimson, and Mills arguments." It was Roosevelt who kept silence, sitting at ease in an easy chair, smoking cigarettes, smiling now and again, nodding his recognition of points made, while an aroused Moley parried the thrusts of the Hoover group and made thrusts of his own, arguing with all possible force the case for the position Roosevelt had taken in his December 19 telegram to the President. It seemed to a somewhat exasperated Moley that Roosevelt was thoroughly "enjoying this high-powered barrage." It also seemed to him "hours" before Roosevelt put an end to it with a flat, unequivocal statement "that discussions of the debts and of other matters must be separate" and that no decision on Economic Conference delegates or agenda could be made until after March 4.[56]

Absolutely nothing had been accomplished by the meeting, so far as Moley and Tugwell could see, save the disillusionment of Stimson, who had believed he had Roosevelt "in his pocket" and who took out his frustrations on the two Brain Trusters a few hours later, after Roosevelt had boarded the train for a trip south. Why, then, had Roosevelt agreed to the meeting? Tugwell and Moley could only wonder.

Others thought they saw the motive, and saw it as unedifying: to them, Roosevelt seemed to have been moved, not by any desire to achieve public good, but by a shrewd politician's felt need to remove from his name any stain of "uncooperativeness" that might have been left upon it by his earlier communications with the President.

And indeed, by this time, there were close students of international affairs who, surveying the whole of Roosevelt's performance *vis-à-vis* Hoover, were utterly dismayed by it. There seemed to them little doubt that, had there been the will on Roosevelt's part and clear ideas in Roosevelt's head, a way could have been found for cooperation between the two administrations that would have increased the chances for success of the upcoming World Economic Conference *without* jeopardizing the effectiveness of the new administration's domestic program. As a matter of fact, in their view, a proper coordination of well-planned domestic and foreign economic programs should increase the effectiveness of both, speeding world recovery. The stakes were high—were recognized at the time to be of the highest, including perhaps the very survival of Western civilization. (The English writer H. G. Wells, then enormously influential in Anglo-American public opinion, saw it so and said so in a prophetic work, *The Shape of Things to Come,* to be published in September 1933.) For the failure of the Economic Conference to stem the rising tide of economic nationalism, joined with the failure of the Disarmament Conference to stem the accompanying rising tide of militarism, could not but increase the likelihood, it might well mean the inevitability, of a Second World War.*

VIII

YET when Roosevelt turned his attention to questions of natural-resource conservation and hydroelectric power—questions in which he had been actively interested since before he entered politics and about which he had gathered much information and developed strong feelings—he ran straight and true to long-professed principle. He also manifested a capacity to dream great dreams and see visions grand. He did so on the very next day after his White House meeting, when he inspected the giant Wilson Dam and nitrate plant at Muscle Shoals on the tumultuous Tennessee River in northern Alabama, a trip he viewed as being of major importance and for which he did all he could to achieve maximum press coverage.

The day was a long one. From his train, early in the morning of January 21, he rode in an open car, though the air was chilly, because he could see better from an open car and be better seen by the crowds gathered here and there

---

*The term "Second World War" came as an initially shocking novelty into the popular mind of the early 1930s, a time when most people strove to believe that no such horror as the Great War could possibly be repeated. The term was introduced by a best-selling large-format book of 1914–1918 photographs—horrifying scenes of war deaths and mutilations and ruins—selected and ironically captioned by Laurence Stallings, a veteran of the famed U.S. Fifth Marines (he may have seen Roosevelt in August 1918 when the Assistant Secretary of the Navy, touring the Western Front, reviewed a battalion of the Fifth in a village near Nancy). Stallings had collaborated with Maxwell Anderson to write the play *What Price Glory?,* had written a bitter antiwar novel entitled *Plumes* and the scenario for *The Big Parade,* one of the great motion pictures of the 1920s, before he published his book of photographs. His title for this last was *The First World War.*

along his way. With him was his daughter, Anna. She was now separated from the reactionary stockbroker whom she had married in 1926;* she made her home in the Sixty-fifth Street house with her two children, six-year-old Anna ("Sisty") and three-year-old Curtis ("Buzz"), and would move with her children into the White House, come March 4. But his principal guest was good gray Senator George Norris of Nebraska, the greatest of all warriors for public hydroelectric power. Norris had been invited for this trip in a mid-December letter wherein Roosevelt had hinted that his interest in Muscle Shoals was wider than that "possibility of fertilizer manufacture" with which Alabama's Senator John H. Bankhead was "chiefly concerned."[57] And the hopes thus raised in the brave old man were raised higher still when Roosevelt, pausing at the town of Sheffield on the Tennessee's southern shore, spoke extemporaneously to a crowd of people who were "almost . . . 'my neighbors,' " as he said, "because, from my little cottage at Warm Springs, from Pine Mountain which lies back of it, I can look into Alabama." He had come, the President-elect went on, because the Muscle Shoals development and that of the Tennessee Basin were "as a whole . . . national in their aspect and are going to be treated from a national point of view."[58] It was a theme he enlarged upon in two other impromptu speeches, that morning and afternoon, in the river towns of Florence and Decatur, and in extended conversations with Alabama officials and members of his own traveling group. He stood with George Norris atop Wilson Dam. He looked down upon sluiceways through which most of the mighty river roared without turning a wheel, without generating a watt of power. And he shouted above the roar his displeasure, his distress even, at this vast waste of public money and of an enormously valuable natural energy resource. He vowed that the waste would now end. "This should be a happy day for you, George," he said loudly into Norris' ear, and Norris eyes filled with tears as he replied that this was for him a joyous day indeed: "I see my dreams come true."[59] The idle steam auxiliary plant was visited, along with the idle nitrate plant, each a huge facility (everything at Muscle Shoals "was at least twice as big as I ever had any conception of it being"), Roosevelt gathering through his ears from a succession of expert informants much factual data about what he saw with his eyes. His interest was unflagging. His curiosity was seemingly insatiable.

It was late afternoon when he turned southward from the river's shore.

He rode then for hours through waning daylight into evening, down across the central body of Alabama. Night had fallen when, in Montgomery, he stood upon the "sacred spot" (he called it so) where Jefferson Davis in February 1861 "took oath of office as the President of the Confederacy." From the portico of Alabama's capitol he looked out over a dimly lit sea of faces spread across the lawn below him, and he spoke again extemporaneously, for the fourth time

---

*She had married Curtis Dall, she later remembered, less out of love for him than out of a desperate need to escape from a home rendered miserably unhappy by the constant friction between her mother and grandmother.

that day, his words pointing toward a regional developmental project of far greater scope than George Norris had dared, out loud, at least, to dream about. "My friends, I am determined on two things as a result of what I have seen today," said Franklin Roosevelt. "The first is to put Muscle Shoals to work. The second is to make of Muscle Shoals a part of an even greater development that will take in all of that magnificent Tennessee River from the mountains of Virginia to the Ohio and the Gulf. . . . Muscle Shoals gives us the opportunity to accomplish a great purpose for the people of many States and, indeed, for the whole Union, because there we have an opportunity of setting an example of planning, planning not just for ourselves but planning for the generations to come, tying in industry and agriculture and forestry and flood prevention, tying them all into a unified whole over a distance of a thousand miles so that we can afford better opportunities and better places for [living] for millions of yet unborn."[60]

From Montgomery he went on that same night east and north, across the Chattahoochee River into Georgia and for miles along the foot of Pine Mountain to his Warm Springs cottage. There he remained for a dozen days and nights, receiving visitors in thick unending stream. One of them was Sir Ronald Lindsay, the British ambassador, whose visit became the occasion of loud denunciations of the President-elect's alleged encroachment upon congressional prerogatives in the matter of war debts. They were denunciations that fed popular doubt of Roosevelt's ability to dominate legislators of his own party.

And by the fortnight's end it was clear that his Muscle Shoals expedition had done little to help his prestige with the general electorate. Surprisingly slight was the impact made upon the public mind by the brave words spoken at Montgomery. Even journals of liberal opinion that had long crusaded for the public operation of Muscle Shoals gave but perfunctory attention and praise to Roosevelt's announcement of his intention to achieve precisely this, and to do so as an element of unified regional planning on a scale and of a kind unprecedented. A shining promise, surely, to those who cared. But also a distant one, far from certain of fulfillment—and so much else was going on of immediate and ominous importance!

The world scene steadily darkened.

In Germany on January 28 General Kurt von Schleicher was forced, in good part by Nazi intrigues, to resign as German Chancellor after only fifty-seven days in office. His fall effectively ended the Weimar Republic. Two days later Adolf Hitler was appointed Chancellor by an aged and senile President Paul von Hindenburg, who also decreed, at Hitler's insistence, that new German elections be held on March 5. Thereafter, day after day, Americans read in their newspapers of cruel Jewish persecutions and of brutal, often fatal assaults upon political opponents by gangs of uniformed Nazi thugs in the streets of German cities. The Nazi-controlled police stood idly by. Obviously Hitler strove thus to assure his party a clear majority at the polls (the German electorate was divided among a half-dozen parties), thereby "legitimizing" the iron dictatorship he was determined to impose in any case. Nor did eyes outraged by Nazi violence see happier sights when they turned to the Far East. There a full-scale Sino-Japanese war now loomed as Japan made new harsh demands upon a Chinese government increasingly inclined to resist them. Every passing day made the Stimson Doctrine more anxiously meaningful to Americans. In Geneva that doctrine continued to encourage the Assembly of the League of Nations toward favorable action on the Lytton Report, despite the British Foreign Office's manifest reluctance to stand firm beside the U.S. State Department in the matter of sanctions, while embittered Japanese delegates hinted more and more strongly that the Rising Sun might soon withdraw its light altogether from a League that, God knew, was gloomy enough already and, in its gloom, only too feeble and despairing. There issued from the Disarmament Conference now and again cautiously optimistic reports. "Progress" was "being made," according to Norman Davis. But such vague allegation carried scant conviction against the definite fact of Japan's growing military might and aggression, Italy's naval expansion, France's stubborn insistence upon the punitive portions of the Versailles Treaty, and Hitler's rise to power with all that that portended in view of his long-avowed purpose of scrapping the treaty and rearming Germany to the teeth.

The domestic scene also steadily darkened.

To the miseries of the actually totally impoverished, the unemployed whose life savings had been wiped out long ago and whose number increased daily, were added miseries of anxiety among those who still had savings deposited in banks. Their number shrank as, by the thousand, they decided that tangible cash hidden in a mattress at home was preferable to mere signs of it (pledges) made by banks (bankers) whose soundness (honesty) was highly dubious. And of course by their action of withdrawal they often assured the bank failure they feared. An apprehensive public noted that even the largest, most prestigious financial institutions were now threatened. Thus the Hibernia Bank and Trust Company of New Orleans, the third largest bank in Louisiana, was saved only through swift forceful action, on February 3 and 4, by Huey Long, a close friend of Hibernia's president. The bank had made heavy loans to a group of insurance companies that had failed despite RFC aid. The fact became known via a congressional-floor speech by New York's Representative Hamilton Fish. A catastrophic run on Hibernia would have been made on Saturday, February 4, had not Long's henchman Governor Oscar K. Allen proclaimed that day to be a statewide legal holiday, in celebration of the sixteenth anniversary of the severing of diplomatic relations between the United States and Germany! (In point of fact, the diplomatic break occurred on February 3, 1917, but Long, desperate for a holiday excuse and unable to discover a single American historical event dated February 4, declared that so momentous an action as this severing *must* have taken two days.) The Saturday closing gave Huey Long time in which to arrange a transfer of $20,000,000 in cash to Hibernia from the RFC and the Federal Reserve System. The bank was enabled to open on Monday, February 6, with no renewal, for the time being, of panic withdrawals. The Hibernia crisis had been darkly portentous, all the same. By the second week of February 1933, as Ernest K. Lindley would write, "it was a nice question which would crack first: the twisted framework of the credit structure or human endurance."

And by then, too, as Lindley would also write, "[c]onfidence in . . . [Roosevelt] was clearly waning."[61]

13

~>>X<<~

Interregnum: The Crisis

I

FOR what was the President-elect of the United States doing while the great world in which he was to act fell to pieces?

So far as the general public could see, he did nothing that contradicted persistent and now increasingly persuasive rumors of his superficiality of intellect, his adolescent humor, his frivolous "playboy" proclivities—rumors allegedly emanating from people who had long known him well in his private capacity. After a near-fortnight of relaxation in sun and heated swimming pool (it was thus that the general public saw him at Warm Springs), Roosevelt, on the evening of Friday, February 3, boarded a special train for an overnight ride down to Jacksonville, Florida. There, on the morrow, he would embark on another near-fortnight of relaxation—a twelve-day fishing cruise down Florida's coast to the Bahamas aboard one of the largest, most luxurious private yachts afloat, Vincent Astor's famous *Nourmahal.*

Some of the doubt about him would have been allayed had the doubters been permitted to see and hear him during the opening hour or so of his southward train ride. Moley and Ed Flynn were with him in the drawing-room coach, and as the miles of darkness clicked by outside the windows, he talked over with them his ideas for the inaugural address, whose initial draft Moley was assigned to prepare. Moley took notes of what Roosevelt said: "1. World is sick. 2. America is sick. Because failure to recognize Eco. changes in time vast development of machine age in 20 years from point of view of replacing manpower [have] moved faster than in 100 years [before] producer capacity in agri—capacity in industry outrun consumption. . . . Time to face the facts and get away from idea we can return to conditions of 29–30. . . . What is needed is action along . . . new lines. . . . Action. . . . Action. . . . [If necessary] I shall ask Cong for . . . broad executive powers to conduct a war against the world emergency just as great as the powers that would be given if we were invaded by a foreign foe."[1] Neither of Roosevelt's companions had doubts that night of his seriousness of purpose, or of his personal force. He dominated them, both formidable men; he appeared in full command of himself and his situation.

But, of course, this experience of him was denied the generality of men, and even Ed Flynn was assailed by certain doubts when, the next morning, he stood on Jacksonville's municipal dock at Commodore Point watching the *Nourmahal*'s departure. She was a gleaming white beauty of a ship, virtually a small liner with her 263 feet of length, her diesel-powered speed of 16 knots, her cruising range of 19,000 miles. Lined up along her rail were Vincent Astor and his five guests, all wealthy men, all in holiday attire, all in boyishly exuberant mood. Flynn regarded them sourly. He was particularly struck by a gaudily striped blazer worn by Mr. George St. George of Tuxedo Park. "The Hasty Pudding Club puts out to sea," said Ed Flynn, with more than a hint of contempt in his voice.[2] He wished, as others of Roosevelt's political associates wished, that the President-elect had chosen, in this dark winter of discontent, a less ostentatiously privileged mode of relaxation, that his holiday companions had not all been of that social elite which leftists damned as the "exploiting class," and especially that his host had not been scion of a family whose huge income derived in good part from Harlem slum property. About Vincent Astor, and about the fact that the Astor and Roosevelt families had marital ties between them,* left-wing journalists could, and did, make acid comment.

Nor would derogation be confined to left journalism. The fervently right-wing *New York Sun,* whose Republicanism was fanatical, soon printed in its then-famous "Sun Dial" column a "poetic" composition entitled "At Sea With Franklin D." One stanza of it said:

> *They were just good friends with no selfish ends*
> *To serve as they paced the decks;*
> *There were George and Fred and the son of Ted†*
> *And Vincent (he signed the checks);*
> *On the splendid yacht in a climate hot*
> *To tropical seas they ran*
> *Among those behind they dismissed from mind*
> *Was the well-known Forgotten Man!*[3]

During the following days, there was no public word at all of activities aboard the *Nourmahal.* Newsmen assigned to cover the President-elect were "among those left behind . . . dismissed from mind"; they were denied even radio contact with him. This meant there was no published reaction from him to the dark news that came, first as rumor, then as fact, out of the wintry glooms of Michigan during the long Lincoln Birthday weekend that began at noon on Saturday, February 11.

For while Roosevelt and his companions loafed through sun-soaked days over the Great Bahama Bank, desperate men in bitterly cold Detroit strove

---

*The marital ties between the Delano, Roosevelt, and Astor families were formed in the latter half of the nineteenth century. Franklin Delano, Sara Delano (Mrs. James) Roosevelt's beloved uncle, after whom she named her only son, was married to William Astor's sister Laura. James Roosevelt (Rosy) Roosevelt, FDR's half-brother, married as his first wife Helen Schermerhorn Astor, whose mother, Mrs. Wiliam Astor, was *the* Mrs. Astor, who ruled New York City high society as none other before or after her. Helen Astor died young (Rosy remarried), after producing two children, one of whom, Taddy, FDR's half-nephew, created a great scandal when, in 1900, he married a notorious prostitute, "Dutch Sadie" Meisinger. See *FDR: The Beckoning of Destiny,* pages 33 and 137.

†"George" was George St. George, "Fred" was Justice Frederic Kernochan, of New York and Tuxedo Park."The son of Ted" was TR's son Kermit, whose presence on this cruise, as boon companion of the Democratic Roosevelt, did not please his Oyster Bay relatives and was notably displeasing to his mother, TR's widow.

behind the scenes to prevent the failure of the huge Union Guardian Trust Company, whose collapse might bring down the whole of Michigan's credit structure, and much else besides. That Union Guardian was insolvent, rendered so by a long run of bad management and bad luck, had become undeniable by the time the bank doors closed on Saturday. Those doors could open again on Tuesday, February 14 (Monday was a legal holiday, since Lincoln's birthday fell on Sunday that year), only if Henry Ford promised *not* to withdraw the $7,500,000 he had on deposit in Union Guardian while General Motors and Chrysler each deposited there, as they would do if Ford "went along," an additional $1,000,000. This would enable the RFC to loan Union Guardian some $35,000,000, enough to keep it open for some time to come.* But Henry Ford, whose loathing and distrust of bankers was profound, flatly refused the necessary promise. Worse, he threatened that if Union Guardian failed to open on Tuesday, he would promptly close out the Ford Motor Company's $25,000,000 account with First National of Detroit, Michigan's largest bank, thus assuring its downfall. And his flinty heart was unsoftened by a telephoned plea from President Hoover or by almost tearful pleas from two Hoover emissaries, Secretary of Commerce Chapin and Under Secretary of the Treasury Arthur A. Ballantine. Michigan's Governor William A. Comstock had no choice but to issue, at 1:32 in the morning of Tuesday, February 14, an order closing all 550 banks in his state for eight days, with no assurance of their opening even then, thereby immobilizing $1.5 billion of deposits made by some 900,000 people.[4]

By Wednesday evening, when the *Nourmahal* ended its cruise in Miami (it was seven o'clock when she tied up at the dock), fear was spreading out from Michigan over the whole of the American financial community, sparking withdrawals by frightened depositors everywhere in the land. The credit foundations of the American economy, so long fissured with distrust, were now on the verge of crumbling into dust. The evening paper that Ray Moley read as he waited at dockside to board the *Nourmahal,* he having come down from the North to report orally to Roosevelt on negotiations with prospective Cabinet appointees, was filled with ominous news.

But aboard the yacht there was no hint of anxiety or of any serious concern whatever. Moley found Roosevelt still seated at the dinner table, where a festive farewell dinner had just been completed. A group of reporters surrounded him. To them he said nothing of public affairs. He would talk only of his vacation, and of this, he indicated, grinning mischievously, with some

---

*By February 1933, in consequence of congressional legislation pushed into passage by Speaker of the House Garner, the amounts and recipients of RFC loans, theretofore highly "confidential," were being fully publicized. In the December 1932 issue of *Harper's Magazine,* John T. Flynn published an exposé article, "Michigan Magic," in which it was unmistakably implied that Secretary of Commerce Roy D. Chapin had used his office to influence loans to Detroit financial institutions in which he was personally interested. (Chapin was a former top executive of the Hudson Motor Company.) All this was making the RFC far more cautious, far more reluctant to make loans without proper security, than it had formerly been.

reservations: he had locked away the ship's log, he said, to keep its contents from the reporters' prying eyes. He did want them to know he'd had a perfectly grand dozen days in the Caribbean sea and sun, had done a lot of fishing, a good deal of swimming, with his shipmates. "I didn't even open the briefcase," he went on, with the sly glee of a truant schoolboy. "We went to a different place each day. . . . One day we had an all-day trip to the middle bight of Andros Island after bone-fish. The only difficulty is that you can't talk and fish for bone-fish. . . . We only fished for bone-fish one day."[5]

When the press interview ended, Moley was left alone with Roosevelt to present his confidential reports.

II

THE President-elect's Cabinet making, if not actually haphazard, had had no overall design so far as Moley could see, and no one save Louis Howe and Roosevelt himself was more intimately or decisively involved in the process than he. Each choice was apparently made for its own unique reason, independent of other choices, with no concern for the ease or difficulty with which those chosen could work together, with less concern for political philosophy than might have been expected, and with virtually no concern for the wishes of Democratic city bosses, though Ed Flynn was of course closely consulted. Yet there were a few general guidelines. Roosevelt wanted a wide range of economically interested and politically ideological points of view—those of the businessman, the farmer, the worker, the professional man, the social reformer —to be represented by advocates bound to him personally by ties of loyalty. He paid some heed to geographic distribution. East, West, Midwest, and South should, if possible, have Cabinet representation. He would appoint no one who had actively, strongly, publicly opposed his nomination, no matter what qualifications that prospect might have. He was leery of most of the "big names" most prominently mentioned in the press as possible appointees. He was especially leery of "names" representative of big industry, big finance, or big corporation law. Thus he gave no serious consideration to Cabinet positions for Baker, Baruch, McAdoo, and Norman Davis, all of whom, especially Baruch and Davis, were urged upon him. He did originally intend to appoint R. H. Macy's Jesse Straus to Commerce, a post Straus's uncle had held in TR's Cabinet. But McAdoo insisted that his friend Daniel C. Roper, who had been McAdoo's floor manager during the catastrophic 1924 convention and had done much to assure Roosevelt's nomination in Chicago, *must* receive a Cabinet appointment. And Roosevelt, who liked Roper personally, recognized Roper's superlative skill as political manipulator, and could not afford McAdoo's enmity, quickly agreed. So Roper became Secretary of Commerce. (Roosevelt then exercised all of his charm to soothe Straus into acceptance of the ambassadorship of France as a consolation prize.) For a time, Roosevelt considered General Electric's Owen D. Young for State. But rumors that Young was being considered provoked cries of protest from Western Progressives, whose antipathy to giant utility company executives was as great as it was undiscriminating. It became clear that Young could not be confirmed without a nasty Senate floor fight in which the executive would be pitted against some of the strongest potential legislative supporters of the New Deal; at which point Roosevelt was glad to receive a letter in which Young asked not to be considered, for personal reasons. By then Roosevelt had about decided, and he did immediately thereafter decide, to ask Cordell Hull, whom Louis Howe was promoting, to come in as Secretary of State.

To many, including Moley, who had a direct personal interest in the matter, this last seemed a strange choice. Several longtime Senate colleagues of Hull's deemed him wholly unqualified for the conduct of foreign affairs or for the administration of a large department. Five of them told Moley so, begging him to pass the word to Roosevelt, who was then in Warm Springs. Worshiping at the shrine of Adam Smith, Hull was convinced that free trade was the source of all good and tariffs the root of all evil in international relations. The "one string to his bow," as one Senate colleague complained, was tariff reduction; he had no understanding of issues between economic nationalism and internationalism that the new administration would have to face, and he "was unable to handle men well." But when Moley conveyed these sentiments to Warm Springs by phone from Washington, Roosevelt dismissed them decisively.[6] He obviously intended to conduct foreign affairs himself. And for the kind of Secretary of State needed in such a case, several of Hull's qualifications were outstanding. He had what Roosevelt called a "fine idealism." There was no question of his personal integrity, his commitment to the general good as he saw it. If he stood low on the competence scale employed by the five complaining senators, he stood high in the esteem of the Senate as a whole and would be a valuable vital link between the executive and the legislature. Most important of all, perhaps, was the fact that the perpetual sadness of Hull's facial expression accurately bespoke a capacity for silent, passive, patient long-suffering as great as any that Chase National's Wiggin could have wanted* for those whom he and his fellow bankers had defrauded, a capacity whose full exercise might be called for in a Secretary of State whom the President often ignored and continually bypassed in ways that could not but be personally, publicly humiliating. Such humiliation, Moley knew, was definitely in the cards for Hull if he accepted the post.

For the President-elect was anxious to continue into his administration the active services of his three main Brain Trusters. To this end he sought federal appointive offices for them having few specific or onerous statutory duties and from which they would have direct frequent access to the White House, regardless of the power foci and flow lines depicted on organization charts. Berle was asked to become Federal Trade Commissioner, an offer at once refused, though Berle promised to continue to carry out specific New Deal assignments. Roosevelt asked Tugwell to become Assistant Secretary of Com-

*See footnote on page 384.

merce, a post Tugwell had not yet definitely refused, though he fully intended to, when Henry A. Wallace accepted appointment as Secretary of Agriculture. This was among the easiest of all Cabinet choices for Roosevelt to make, despite the fact that his close friend Henry Morgenthau, Jr., longed for the post; Wallace was the overwhelming favorite of the leading farm organizations. Immediately, Wallace asked Tugwell to come in as *his* Assistant Secretary, and Tugwell, who had formed with Wallace a warm, mutually admiring friendship, agreed to do so, though with no intention of remaining long in the government. What made the Hull choice so personally important to Moley was Roosevelt's urgent insistence that Moley accept the post of Assistant Secretary of State, the one office in the whole of the federal establishment, so far as Roosevelt had been able to determine, to which *no* statutory duties whatever had been assigned.

What, then, would his duties be? Moley wanted to know. He pressed for specifications in writing before accepting a post fraught with obvious dangers, and Roosevelt finally yielded to the extent of dictating and signing a job description. It was of broad sweep, certainly! Moley listened to it, then read it, with a mingling of astonishment, pride, and apprehension. His duties would include the handling of "foreign debts, the world economic conference, supervision of the economic adviser's office [the remarkably able Herbert Feis was currently the economic adviser] and such additional duties as the President may direct in the general field of foreign and domestic government." Moley protested. Surely Hull, with whose tariff stand, the central theme of Hull's politics, Moley disagreed, must strongly object to this arrangement as soon as he learned its details! Roosevelt shook his head. "Hull knows all about it," he said. "There'll be no misunderstanding with him if he takes the job." But when Moley, worried by newspaper speculations about his official role, sought for his own protection to release the signed job description to the press, he was refused permission. It was one thing for Hull to know "all about" the arrangement. It was quite another thing, in that it would embarrass Hull, for the world know about it. And Hull had not yet finally accepted the offer, which had been definitely made in the third week of January, when Moley boarded the *Nourmahal* on the evening of February 15.[7] The senator, indeed, was showing more reluctance to accept than seemed required by the ritualistic coyness that tradition prescribes for such transactions. To Moley, who conducted the negotiations with him, he said nothing about what must have been the chief question in his mind, namely, that of his standing and authority with relation to Roosevelt and Moley himself, should he take the post. Instead he spoke of the high cost of the social entertainment normally required of a Secretary of State. A large house would have to be bought or rented and staffed with servants. A Secretary's salary would not begin to cover the cost, and Hull was not a wealthy man. Louis Howe proposed a way to remove this obstacle. It was that career diplomat William Phillips, who *was* a wealthy man and also a longtime personal friend of Roosevelt's (he had been an Assistant Secretary of State when Roosevelt was Assistant Secretary of the Navy), be appointed

Under Secretary of State, a post for which he was eminently suited, with the understanding that *he* would do most of the necessary official entertaining.

This proposal, whose acceptance by Roosevelt would probably mean Hull's acceptance of State (he did accept, at any rate, when Phillips was named Under Secretary), was one of the three major items in the oral report that Moley made to the President-elect during their few minutes together at the dinner table on the *Nourmahal.* Five definite Cabinet choices, inclusive of Wallace for Agriculture, had by then been made, each formally offered and accepted, or soon to be, including the Roper offer that was made and accepted a week later. Jim Farley's appointment as Postmaster General had been a foregone conclusion by Election Day. Also clear by then was the need to find a place for Utah's Governor George Dern, disappointed of the promised Vice-Presidency: a Cabinet post was assured him, probably as Secretary of War, which he did become. The post of Attorney General had been offered to Montana's Senator Walsh in the hopeful expectation that he, preferring to stay in the Senate, would refuse it, enabling the appointment of a man more noted for liberalism, possibly Wisconsin Governor Phil La Follette. Instead, Walsh was clearly in the process of accepting, though he took his own sweet time about making the acceptance definite (the seventy-three-year old Walsh was being married that winter to a woman much his junior). Determined to have a woman in the cabinet, being influenced in this by Eleanor, her Val-Kill colleagues, and Molly Dewson, Roosevelt easily decided upon Frances Perkins for Secretary of Labor, despite the prevailing view that Labor was almost as exclusively "masculine" in its job requirements as War or Navy. There remained Interior, Treasury, and Navy to be chosen, and it was the status of negotiations over the first two of these choices that constituted the remainder of Moley's oral report.

Interior was deemed properly to belong to a Western Progressive, nominally Republican, whose support had been a major element of the "Roosevelt coalition," and it had been first offered to Hiram Johnson, who at once refused it. It was then offered to Senator Bronson Cutting of New Mexico, who had been born and raised in much the same privileged circumstances as Roosevelt and had been subjected, in boyhood and youth, to much the same molding influences. An Easterner by birth, a product of Groton and Harvard, he had contracted tuberculosis in his young manhood, had gone to the desert Southwest to recover early in the century's second decade, as had Moley (the shared experience provided an empathic base for communication between the two during their negotiating talk), and had remained there. At age forty-four his health was still precarious, his strength slender. This was a cited reason for his reluctance to accept the proffered post. But his real reason, as Moley suspected, was his doubt that Roosevelt was a true liberal, his fear that Roosevelt in action might prevent social changes and subvert social principles to which Cutting himself was deeply, passionately committed. And the doubt remained even though Cutting and Wisconsin Senator Bob La Follette had come down together, by invitation, to Warm Springs and had been wooed there with talk of the progressive policies Roosevelt intended to pursue.[8] Moley thought it possible, and now reported to Roosevelt the probability, that Cutting's refusal of the post would be made definite, final, when Cutting, as had been arranged, boarded Roosevelt's train in Washington during Roosevelt's journey from Miami to New York.

As for Treasury, Roosevelt was virtually compelled to offer it to Virginia's elderly Carter Glass, who had held the post under Wilson, had made his reputation as *the* Democratic authority on fiscal matters, and was a powerful national political force. Roosevelt was also virtually compelled to continue pressure upon the senator to accept after Glass had demurred during the hurried conversation between the two men in Washington on January 19. Like Cutting, Glass cited health reasons for refusing the honor; but clearly *his* real main reason was his suspicion that Roosevelt, far from being too conservative, was not conservative enough on currency questions, was not sufficiently strongly committed to the gold standard, and hence might devalue the dollar. He asked of Roosevelt, he asked of Moley, firm assurances that there would be no inflation of the currency. He didn't get them. "So far as inflation goes," said Roosevelt to Moley, "you can say we're not going to throw ideas out of the window simply because they are labelled inflation." And this was, or seemed for the moment to be, finally decisive. When Moley next talked to Glass, he was told definitely by the "old boy," as Roosevelt called him, that the offer was refused. "Even if there were no other objection," said the senator, "my own health [he had also cited his wife's frail health] and the heavy social burden that would fall on my wife would preclude my acceptance." He then placed in Moley's hand a sealed letter to Roosevelt, dated February 7, to be delivered when the President-elect disembarked at Miami. Moley was greatly relieved. So was Howe. The two promptly happily radioed the news to the cruising President-elect.*

The matter was not thus ended, however.

Baruch and other party conservatives, privately informed of Glass's decision, at once begged him to reconsider. They were desperately worried by the developing bank crisis, they perfectly agreed with Hoover as to the need for a publicly announced "sound money" commitment by the incoming administration, to "restore confidence," and they believed that Glass's acceptance of Treasury would be tantamount to such announcement or, at least, would be so deemed by the "investing public." Moreover, Glass gave signs of wavering: it was anybody's guess what he would say on the matter when he, too, by arrangement, boarded Roosevelt's homebound train in Washington. And it was in awareness of this that Howe and Moley on February 14 concocted and radioed to Roosevelt on the *Nourmahal* a cryptic message. "Prefer a wooden roof to a glass roof over swimming pool," it said. Roosevelt was puzzled for a moment by the apparent reference to an indoor swimming pool that was being constructed for him at the White House. Then, catching the meaning,

---

*Such messages, always code-worded to prevent leaks to the press, were signed "Luhowray."

he "roared with laughter," as Moley learned from Roosevelt's own lips on the evening of the following day.[9]

For Roosevelt, too, had been toying with the idea of asking Will Woodin to take Treasury if Glass refused it, an idea that had occurred to Moley and Howe in late January and about which they had grown enthusiastic. Woodin was no such single-minded monetary ideologue as Carter Glass, no such rigid conservative: he had wide humanistic interests and a flexible mind. Yet his appointment to Treasury would be approximately as reassuring to the business community as Glass's. Incongruities were focused upon, if not harmonized within, his person. Soft-spoken, shy-mannered, unimpressive in physical appearance—he stood perhaps three inches taller than tiny Louis Howe and was almost as frail-looking as Howe—Woodin, on the evidence, cared little for money *per se* or power *per se.* He did care, passionately, for music. He was a skilled performing musician, on piano, violin, and guitar; he was a composer, whose published works included *The Covered Wagon Suite, The Oriental Suite,* several nursery songs, for which he wrote the verses, and "The Franklin Delano Roosevelt March," newly written for the inaugural. But he was also president of the American Car and Foundry Company and, since assuming that post in 1916, had abundantly demonstrated his administrative ability and hard-headed business shrewdness. Congruous with his big-business career and private fortune of many millions was his Republican Party affiliation during the first four decades of his voting life. Incongruous, and sensational in its impact upon his fellow members of Philadelphia's and New York's Union League clubs, was his defection from this party to support Roosevelt for governor in 1928, the year of Hoover's greatest triumph, of the New Era's happiest moments, and of Woodin's own sixty-first birthday. His extremely active support of Roosevelt ever since had been of inestimable value to the Democratic candidate, moneywise and otherwise, doing much to persuade businessmen that Roosevelt was no such "radical" as Raskob and his ilk alleged but was, instead, business's "enlightened" friend. Of Woodin's personal loyalty to Roosevelt there was no question: rooted in love of the man, it was absolute.

III

WHEN Moley had completed his reports, he moved with Roosevelt and others of the party from the yacht to three automobiles that had been drawn up on the dock.

And when they entered these, they entered upon an hour of clock time that would ever after loom as years in the memories of most who directly experienced it—an hour that would also become a historical moment, fixed by deep shock in the national consciousness and endowed there with symbolic meaning.

Roosevelt was already late for a kind of "welcome home" celebration that had been scheduled for nine o'clock in Miami's Bay Front Park. Many thousands had long been assembled in the park, and a group of dignitaries also waited there, seated in the bandstand. Among these last was Chicago's Mayor Anton Cermak. He came to discuss with Roosevelt the possibility of easing his city's continuing financial crisis with an RFC loan; but he also came, and primarily, as Roosevelt well knew, to mend political fences badly damaged by the rowdy Cermak-organized gallery support of Al Smith at the convention.

In the lead car, a touring car with its top down, Roosevelt was seated beside his official host, Miami's mayor, a few minutes after nine. In that same car rode his personal bodyguard, Gus Gennerich, and Marvin H. McIntyre, the thin cadaverous fifty-four-year-old newspaperman and newsreel journalist who had been the press contact man for Roosevelt during the 1920 vice-presidential campaign, had been brought into the 1932 campaign by Howe after he'd lost a Pathé-newsreel job, and was now slated to be the President's appointments secretary. The second car, also open, carried only Secret Service men. The third and last car was a sedan too small to hold comfortably Astor, Moley, Kermit Roosevelt, and two other men who were jammed into it. Twenty minutes later the small cavalcade arrived at the park, where the crowd was now immense. Roosevelt's car and the other cars were slowed to the pace of a walking man as they moved down a narrow lane cleared through the throng. Then, having come abreast the bandstand, the lead car halted, with the car bearing the Secret Service men not far behind and that in which Moley and Astor rode about seventy-five feet back. The night grew loud with the cheers and applause of a crowd now standing, though some hundreds had theretofore been sitting in rows of flimsy chairs and benches facing the bandstand. Quiet descended as Roosevelt was hoisted up onto the top of the back seat, this being done so swiftly, so expertly by Gennerich that most of the crowd didn't realize it was made necessary by almost totally withered legs. He was introduced by Miami's mayor with the brevity, the simple unadorned naming of title, proper for a President-elect of the United States, and was handed a loudspeaker.

He spoke into it words no more memorable than those he had given his newspaper interviewers aboard the yacht.

"I am not a stranger here because for a great many years I used to come down here," he said, referring to the many weeks he had spent each winter, from 1923 through 1926, on a houseboat, first the rented *Weona II,* then the purchased *Larooco,* in Florida waters, swimming and sunning and doing special exercises to strengthen his polio-blasted legs. " . . . I have had a very wonderful twelve days fishing in these Florida and Bahama waters. It has been a wonderful rest and we have caught a great many fish. I am not going to attempt to tell you any fish stories [the crowd laughed on cue], and the only fly in the ointment on my trip has been that I put on about ten pounds [more cued laughter]. I hope very much to come down here next winter and see you all and have another ten days or two weeks in Florida waters. Many thanks."[10]

Almost before his last word was spoken—certainly before he could acknowledge the crowd's applause in his accustomed manner, with his head back, a wide smile on his face, his right hand lifted to wave—Roosevelt was accosted by a man who had clambered up on the car's back, surprisingly unhindered in this by the Secret Service. The man was one of "the talking picture people," as Roosevelt later put it, and he told the President-elect to turn around and repeat for the recording camera (Roosevelt had had his back to it) his little speech. Moreover, incredibly, he refused to take Roosevelt's prompt flat no for an answer. "But you've *got* to!" he protested. "We've come one thousand miles for this!" The smile faded from Roosevelt's face. "I'm sorry, it's impossible," he said coldly, dismissively, and slid down into the seat.

As he did so he saw Mayor Cermak approaching, hand outstretched, and he took that hand in hearty shake. The two talked together for a few seconds, arranging to meet a little later for a private talk in Roosevelt's private railway car, which now waited at the Miami station to return him to New York City. Cermak then moved off a few feet behind the car and stood there with a Secret Service man named Robert Clark beside him while someone approached the President-elect, a man carrying what Roosevelt later described in typical hyperbole as "a telegram five or six feet long."

He was destined never to know what that curious telegram contained.

For just as the man carrying it had begun to explain its contents, he was interrupted by a sharp report, which Roosevelt, leaning forward and a little to his left, interpreted as an exploding firecracker, which Moley, seventy-five feet away, interpreted as a car backfiring, and which initiated one of those moments that flash instantaneously through immediate experience but may become, in retrospect, very long, being thick with simultaneous event, heavy with the significance of fatal might-have-beens.

Four more sharp reports followed the first in rapid succession. There were shouts, screams of pain and terror, a blur of violent action, and at the initiating center of it all sat Franklin Roosevelt, whose enforced immobility might be expected to make him peculiarly vulnerable to flinching nervousness as he realized, all at once, that what he had heard was a gun and that he was almost certainly that gun's intended target. He showed no excitement whatever. Only an alert attentiveness. Calmly, precisely observant, a fact that comes clear in the account of the episode he dictated a few hours later, he acted with a commanding decisiveness in response to his swiftly accurate perceptions of what he saw. First, he saw the man with the telegram being pulled away, yanked away from the car, whose motor roared as the driver started it and shifted into gear—saw in that same instant that the back of one of Bob Clark's hands had been deeply scratched and was bleeding—then saw that Cermak, marble white of face, tottering, with blood on his shirtfront, was being held up by Clark. Instantly he surmised that a bullet had creased Clark's hand on its way into Cermak's chest and that Cermak, not he, had been the gunman's intended victim. The car was now moving, gathering speed; immediately he ordered the driver to stop and, with imperious gestures, ordered the men beside Cermak to ease the wounded man into the car beside him.

"Providentially," as Roosevelt later said, the car had moved some thirty feet beyond the spot where Roosevelt had spoken, for over that spot the excited crowd now closed in and "it would have been difficult to . . . get out."

As it was, they were clear of the crowd in a few seconds.

And all the way to the hospital, which was quite a long way, Roosevelt sat with his left arm around Cermak, holding the stricken man in what he knew to be the correct position for one who had suffered a chest injury (he had learned a good deal about anatomy and medical practice during his long struggle to walk again), talking to him continuously, though at first he believed he was talking to a dead man. For while he talked he felt with his right hand for Cermak's pulse and could find none. "For three blocks I believed his heart had stopped." But then, suddenly, Cermak, who had been slumped limply in the seat, straightened up and began to breathe, and his pulse surged surprisingly strong under Roosevelt's fingertips. Thereafter his pulse steadily improved. "Tony, keep quiet," said Roosevelt. "Don't move. It won't hurt you if you keep quiet." And went on to say confidently, over and over again, that everything was going to be all right, that Cermak was doing just fine, that they'd be at the hospital in just a few minutes (" . . . encouragement of that sort is often the thing which will save a man when he is near death from shock," commented a nationally prominent surgeon to newsmen the next day[11]), until in fact they *were* there, at the emergency entrance of the Jackson Memorial Hospital, whence Cermak was rushed to the operating table.

Meanwhile, in Bay Front Park, the car in which Astor and Moley were seated was immobilized for a time by the crowd surrounding it. Roosevelt had not seen and would never see the man who had done the shooting, saying later that "the second time the car moved forward I saw a melee down on the ground and I assumed he [the gunman] was in that." But Astor, Moley, and the others in their car soon saw him. Into their car, too, a wounded man had been taken, a young man with a superficial head wound whom Astor held in his lap. So when the gunman, who had had much of his clothing torn off him, was plucked from the ground and brought to that car by three burly policemen, there was no room for him inside. He was therefore thrown roughly across the trunk rack at the car's rear, where two of the policeman sat on him while the car slowly forced its way through and finally clear of the crowd, then raced toward the hospital. The third policeman made the trip on the car's running board, Moley holding him there by his belt. To all in the car the ride seemed, as it had to Roosevelt, unconscionably long, but when it was ended, Moley was immensely relieved to see Roosevelt coming out of the hospital on the arm of Gus Gennerich—a Roosevelt who appeared perfectly calm and was (Moley had not theretofore been absolutely certain of this) without the slightest injury.

All of them in the Roosevelt party were then escorted to a room at the rear of the hospital, where they remained through a long hour, piecing together their separate impressions into a reasonably coherent if incomplete story of what had happened and receiving from time to time reports on the condition of the shooting victims, all of whom were brought to the same hospital. Each of the five shots had found a different victim, and two of these, in addition to

Cermak, were in critical condition. One was a New York City policeman, William Sinnott, assigned to Roosevelt's guard detail, who had been shot through the head. The other was Mrs. Joseph H. Gill, wife of the president of the Florida Light and Power Company, who had been shot in the abdomen. Reports also came from the city jail on the nineteenth floor of Miami's sky-scraper City Hall, where the gunman, having given his name as Giuseppe Zangara, was locked in a cell. During this waiting period Moley watched Roosevelt closely for signs of delayed nervous reaction to mortal danger, now that the danger was past and the need to maintain appearances diminished. He saw no such sign. There was no departure from a normal tone of voice and rhythm of speech as Roosevelt spoke his continuing belief that this gunman, this Zangara, who might well be, with a name like that, a Chicago gangster, had aimed to kill the mayor of Chicago, not the President-elect. Otherwise, surely, Zangara would have shot while Roosevelt was speaking, a perfect target atop the car seat.

And this was the conclusion Roosevelt gave his wife when, at about 10:40 P.M., he called her, at 49 East Sixty-fifth Street in New York City, from the hospital.

Eleanor had been engaged in public speech at the Warner Club on West Forty-fourth Street when the first news of the assassination attempt was received by New York newspapers. She left the club without having heard the news. Not until she arrived at the Sixty-fifth Street house did she learn, sketchily, what had happened, first from the agitated stammering butler who met her at the door, then from her daughter, Anna, and then, somewhat more fully, from a newspaper reporter. She received the news calmly, almost with a shrug. "These things are to be expected," she remarked as she reached for the phone to place a person-to-person call to Miami. She was unable to get through. Neither was Louis Howe. But scarcely had Howe hung up after his attempt when the phone rang with a call from Roosevelt to his wife. Husband and wife conversed perfectly calmly for a minute or so. "He's all right," she said to a reporter after she'd hung up. "He's not the least bit excited."[12] Nor was she. A few minutes later she left the house to go to Grand Central Station. There she boarded a train (it left at 11:35) for Ithaca, New York, where next day she was to speak at Cornell University's annual Farm and Home Week.

At about the time his wife arrived at Grand Central, Roosevelt arrived back at the *Nourmahal* to spend the night, having postponed till the next day his departure for New York. And there it was, in the yacht's grand saloon, that the ever-watchful Moley was presented with a final and to him now astonishing display of Roosevelt's nervous control.

Everyone knew by then that it was definitely Roosevelt, not Cermak, whom the gunman had meant to kill. Moley had been sent to interview Zangara in his cell, to check out the possibility that he was the executing arm of a conspiracy. Eagerly, volubly, Zangara had made a full statement of his act and motive. "I hate all presidents . . . , and I hate officials and everybody who is rich," he had said, expressing as his only regret the failure of his attempt on the President-elect's life. (How, Roosevelt wondered, could he possibly have missed? While shooting, he could not have been more than twenty feet away.) Roosevelt's companions, therefore, "were prepared, sympathetically, understandingly, for any reaction that might come from . . . [him] now that the tension was over and he was alone with us." They themselves were let down, their nerves frayed, and they showed this in their manner. Roosevelt, however, remained unmoved. "There was nothing—not so much as the twitching of a muscle, the mopping of a brow, or even the hint of a false gaiety—to indicate that it wasn't any other evening in any other place," recalled Moley years later. " . . . I have never in my life seen anything more magnificent."[13]

When the President-elect went to bed at two o'clock, he fell at once soundly asleep. The Secret Service man guarding his stateroom testified to this. He remained asleep until somewhat later than his usual rising time the next morning.

IV

From newspaper accounts that next morning Roosevelt was able to fill in the missing elements of the story of the assassination attempt—learned how and why the attempt had failed and substantially all that history would ever know about the man who had tried to kill him.

Giuseppe Zangara, nicknamed "Joe" upon his emigration from Mussolini's Italy in 1923, had come early to Bay Front Park the night before. He wanted, in his own words, "to be as close as possible to the President-elect." He found, however, that he had not come quite early enough: hundreds were already gathered before the bandstand, and he could not place himself in the foremost row of the crowd as he had planned to do. He had to remain in the second row, where he dropped down on a bench to wait through the nearly two hours intervening between his arrival and Roosevelt's scheduled appearance.

An utterly insignificant little man he seemed, sitting there. Of all the thousands of people soon packed around him—of any crowd whatever, as he himself had long since realized, bitterly—none other was less impressive in appearance. Square-jawed, hollow-cheeked, dark-eyed, black-haired, plain-featured, swarthy of complexion, he lacked any facial distinction that would offset the impression made by his physique, which was meager: when drawn up to his full height (he always held himself rigidly erect when on his feet), Zangara stood barely an inch over five feet tall, and he was proportionately narrow of body. Similarly unimpressive was he by the standards that normally measure human importance. Negatives described his general condition. No longer youthful at age thirty-three, a bricklayer by trade, he was unemployed, unmarried, uneducated, unfriendly (therefore friendless), unmoneyed—and most decidedly unwell. On the bench, he was unable to sit still. Sometimes he huddled forward, elbows on knees. Sometimes he sat straight up or leaned against the bench back, while his right hand gripped in his coat pocket, as if for dear life, or dear death, the butt of the revolver he had bought for $8 in a pawnshop on North Miami Avenue two days before. (The arrant stupidity of permitting any American to arm himself at any time with a handgun would be much commented upon, editorially, in the days immediately following.[14]) He fidgeted constantly. But no change of position could ease his agony for more than a few seconds. "Maybe it was the excitement," he later said. At any rate, he could not remember a time when his suffering was more intense than now, though severe stomach pain had been his virtually constant companion since his early childhood. He felt, he later indicated, as if a red hot poker were thrust, twisting, into his abdomen.

A pitiful creature, you would have said, seeing him there. But *merely* pitiful.

Yet there is a sense in which he would have been highly significant even if he had not violently erupted for a brief bloody moment, as he was about to do, on history's stage. For even if he had remained passive in his misery upon a park bench, utterly alone in the crowd—in any crowd save when absorbed into it, his individual will and consciousness dissolved—this unemployed little man with a bellyache would have been both symbolic and representative of the depression's human waste. As it was, pain-racked, desperate, a revolver in his pocket and murder in his heart, his brain a blazing coal of hateful rage, he signified the vast social danger inherent in depression misery. He personalized, individualized, a deadly sickness that was spreading, horribly, terrifyingly, through all the civilized world. Hatred was the organizing principle of his life. It was the very core of his being. Born in Calabria in the first year of history's bloodiest century, he had begun "to hate very violently" while he was yet "a little boy in school," as he would say, speaking in abrupt spasms of words, within an hour after his act of violence. He hated his "richer schoolmates who had money to spend" and "privileges" denied him and who later, when he was in his teens, "went to school while I worked in a brick factory . . . and burned myself." By then his hatred was fused with the chronic pain of an ulcerated stomach (an autopsy would show that his ulcers caused serious adhesions) and had become focused upon kings, prime ministers, presidents, "no matter from what country," upon any and all who possessed official power, official authority, and were by that token, in his view, the torture agents of "capitalists." He would "kill them all" if he could.

Thus was prepared the fateful encounter between historic darkness and light, between nihilism and optimistic faith, which began when Roosevelt's car came to a halt barely sixteen feet in front of Zangara at 9:30 P.M. The little man was then on his feet, wild-eyed and sweating, his drawn revolver at his side, fully prepared to kill, he had planned to kill, while the President-elect was speaking. Typically, he was frustrated by the people in front of him, all of whom now rose also to their feet. They formed a wall of humanity too high for him to see over ("I'm such a little fellow I didn't have a chance"), until some of them sat down after Roosevelt, his little talk completed, had himself slid down into the car seat. Then Zangara sprang up onto the bench before him. He was wildly excited, his perceptions blurred by his excitement. Afterward he remembered of that moment only that the bench he stood on "wob-bled," that "the gun started to shake" when he "pointed it at Mr. Roosevelt," that he "pulled the trigger anyway," he couldn't "remember how many times," and that he was then on the ground, his breath knocked out of him by the frenzied, clothes-rending, pummeling men piled atop him.

He didn't know until the next day, when the newspapers told him, as they told Roosevelt, that his aim had been spoiled by a woman who had seized his shooting arm and forced it upward.

She was Mrs. Lillian Cross, wife of Dr. W. F. Cross, physician and surgeon, who lived at 1069 Northwest Second Street in Miami, a no-nonsense woman of forty-eight years, physically small (though a bit taller than Zangara, she weighed only one hundred pounds), with remarkably swift reflexes in keeping with the alert intelligence that showed in her eyes through the glasses she wore. Because of her shortness, she had clambered up onto the bench where she'd been sitting "to get a better look" at the President-elect after he sat down; she was standing there when Zangara jumped up behind and a little to the right of her. He almost toppled her to the ground. She turned to protest just as he raised his pistol, aiming it over her right shoulder. "My mind grasped immedi-ately what he was up to," she told reporters an hour or so later. "I said to myself, 'Oh! He's going to kill the President!' " Horror of the kind that freezes many people had upon her a galvanizing effect. Her handbag was in her right hand but in an eye-wink's time she had "switched it to my left hand and caught him by the arm" just as he pulled the trigger. The firing, within an inch or two of her right ear, deafened that ear temporarily and smudged her cheek with gunpowder, "but I held on."[15]

And so Roosevelt lived on.

Cermak did not. Nor Zangara. And the brief remainder of their life stories may as well be told here.

When Roosevelt presented his inaugural address a little over two weeks later, Anton J. Cermak listened to it over the radio in his Miami hospital room, though he was now sick unto death. During the preceding ten days he had suffered through colitis, then pneumonia; now he had gangrene in his punc-tured lung. Two days later, on March 6, 1933, shortly before seven in the morning, he died.

Joe Zangara was then still lodged in the Miami jail.

He had been convicted and sentenced to eighty years' imprisonment for the shooting of three of his victims but had not yet been tried for the shooting of Mrs. Gill, who remained in critical condition, or for the shooting of Cermak. He was now rushed to trial on a charge of first-degree murder in the Circuit Court of Miami, where, on March 9, before Judge Uly O. Thompson, he defiantly proclaimed his guilt in a statement shot out from the witness stand in machine-gun spasms of words. "I want to kill all capitalists," he cried in his high-pitched voice. "Because of capitalists people get no bread. . . . I feel this way since I fourteen years old. . . . I have stomach pains since I six years old. I mad at capitalists. They got education. My stomach hurts since I six years old. . . . I feel I have a right to kill Mr. Roosevelt. . . . It was right. I know they give me electric chair but I don't care—I'm right."

On March 10, before pronouncing sentence, Judge Thompson took occasion to express his "firm conviction that the Congress of these United States should pass" strict gun-control legislation. "Assassins roaming at will through our land—and they have killed three of our Presidents—are permitted to have pistols. And a pistol in the hands of the ordinary person is a most useless weapon of defense. No one can foresee what might have happened had Zangara been successful in his attempt." (One sure thing is that John Nance Garner would have become President of the United States on March 4, 1933: the Twentieth Amendment, which went into effect on February 6, 1933, set January 20 as inauguration day and made the Vice-President-elect the Chief Executive if the President-elect died.) Judge Thompson then sentenced Zangara to death in the electric chair during the week of March 19. "You is crook man, too!" screamed Zangara at the judge. "I no afraid. You one of the capitalists." He was taken, heavily guarded by a squad of machine gunners, to the death house on the Florida State Prison farm at Raiford, where, in the morning of March 20, while the nation's attention was focused upon the momentous opening acts of the New Deal, he was executed.

He remained defiant to the last. He contemptuously refused the proffered ministrations of the prison chaplain ("I no want minister, there is no God"), walked with a firm pace, head high, shoulders back, to the electric chair, and lost his composure only when, seated, he looked around the death chamber and saw no photographers. "No cameramen?" he asked. "No movie to take picture of Zangara?" The prison superintendent said none was allowed. "Lousy capitalists!" screamed Zangara. "No picture—capitalists, no one here to take my picture—all capitalists lousy bunch of crooks." And he sagged in the chair. But he straightened up as the headpiece was placed over him, shouting, "Goodbye. Adios to all the world." Then, tauntingly, his voice muffled by the headpiece, he said, "Push the button."

The sheriff of Dade County did so at precisely 9:15 A.M.[16]

V

IN the morning of Thursday, February 16, when the valet Irwin McDuffie brought to Roosevelt the tie rack from which was selected each day the tie he would wear, Roosevelt reached out for the same one he'd worn the day before. McDuffie shook his head. "This morning," he said firmly, "we won't put the red tie on." Whereupon, as McDuffie remembered long afterward, Roosevelt "laughed and laughed," then accepted the tie McDuffie chose for him.[17]

Soon thereafter he left the *Nourmahal* for the railway station, stopping on the way at Jackson Memorial Hospital to visit the shooting victims—all of them save Mrs. Gill, whose condition, though she eventually recovered, remained that morning far too critical to permit her seeing anybody. With

Cermak ("I'm glad it was me instead of you," said Cermak) he talked optimistically for several minutes about the possibility of federal aid to pay the $20,000,000 of back pay that Chicago still owed its schoolteachers. With Bill Sinnott, whose head wound, it was now evident, would not be fatal, he was jocular: "I . . . told him they couldn't hurt him with a bullet in the head. I left orders for them to starve him and take off at least twenty pounds."[18]

And throughout that day and the next, with almost his every word and gesture reported by the press and radio to a shocked, closely attentive nation, the President-elect continued perfectly exemplary in the cool disdain, the cheerful contempt, for danger, the manifest total faith in Divine Providence, with which he reacted to his close brush with death. (In his soon-dispatched telegram of thanks to Mrs. Cross he spoke of the "Divine Providence" whereby "it now appears that . . . the lives of all the victims of the assassin's disturbed aim will be spared."[19]) He continued concerned about those who suffered from bullets meant for him; otherwise, on the evidence, the previous day's incident was dismissed wholly from his mind.

His train left Miami at 10:15 A.M. After lunch he napped for a couple of hours in his stateroom to make up for sleep lost the night before. In the early evening, in Jacksonville, where the Houston banker Jesse Jones, an RFC board member, came onto the train for conference with him, he had a phone brought aboard so that he could talk to Miami doctors about Mrs. Gill's condition and Cermak's. With Jones he later talked about a possible RFC loan to Chicago and about the Michigan bank holiday and its repercussions throughout the country. There was a brief interruption when the train passed through tiny Nahant, Georgia, to enable James and Betsey Cushing Roosevelt to see him for five minutes, having driven over from Thomasville, thirty miles away, where Betsey's father, Dr. Harvey Cushing, had a winter home. Roosevelt retired to his stateroom shortly before midnight.

At 8:10 the following morning, Friday, February 17, in Richmond, Virginia, Roosevelt came out of his stateroom in pajamas to shake hands with Virginia's Governor John G. Pollard, come to pay a courtesy call, and with Cordell Hull, who then rode with him to Washington. In the capital, Bronson Cutting and Glass came aboard, as arranged, to ride with him to Baltimore, where both got off. During this brief ride, Cutting made definite his refusal of Interior and Glass all but made final his refusal of Treasury, having tried once again, and again in vain, to obtain from the President-elect firm assurances that there would be no "tampering with the currency." At Philadelphia, Roosevelt's son Elliott and daughter, Anna, and Missy LeHand came aboard to accompany him on the last leg of his journey. He arrived at 4:10 P.M. in Jersey City, where he was met "by one of the most elaborate police guards ever accorded an individual," as the New York Times reported. Upward of a thousand police, detectives, and Secret Service men surrounded him at the station; during the drive to his home, where he arrived shortly after five o'clock, his car, itself carrying several bodyguards, was preceded by seven and followed by seven that were entirely filled with his guardsmen—an absurd excess of protective zeal, in his view, and one he'd not tolerate in the future.

At his home, to reporters who found him "bronzed, vigorous, confident," he said he planned no future curtailment of his public appearances but made no specific mention of the Miami incident.

"I'm feeling fine and have had a fine trip," he said.

Then, said the *Times,* he "at once plunged into work."[20]

He did so with his personal prestige, his effectiveness as national leader, greatly enhanced.

His "superb personal conduct," joined with "the shudder of the country at the thought of what might have been, "rallied the entire nation behind him" and "buried all doubts and quibbling," as Ernest K. Lindley would write a few months later. In Frank Freidel's words, it "brought a surge of national confidence in him as had none of his other actions since the election."[21]

And never, not even during the dark late winter of 1861, were the American people more greatly in need of confidence in a leader than they were during the long fortnight, climactic of dissolution and disillusionment and despair, which separated the assassination attempt from the inaugural.

On Saturday evening, February 18, Roosevelt was guest of honor at a dinner in the Hotel Astor given by a group of political reporters. The after-dinner entertainment, like that of Washington's famed Gridiron Club, consisted of satirical skits performed by the newsmen. Roosevelt was thoroughly enjoying one of them when, just an hour before midnight, a Secret Service agent came to him and handed him, as unobtrusively as possible, an envelope bearing the seal of the President of the United States. Within it was another envelope addressed in the hand of Herbert Hoover to "President-elect Roosvelt [*sic*]"; it contained a ten-page handwritten letter from Hoover. Roosevelt skimmed it swiftly, with no apparent diversion of his happy attention from the skit performance, then handed it under the table to Moley. Moley, at once grasping the missive's dire significance, looked up from it to Roosevelt with much the same kind of astonishment, as well as admiration for an almost incredible display of nervous control, as had flooded over him in the Miami hospital and aboard the *Nourmahal* three nights before. Roosevelt gave not the slightest sign of shock or even concern over what Hoover had so agitatedly, portentously written him. Nor did he do so when, an hour later in his Sixty-fifth Street house, he discussed the message with a small group of his advisers.[22]

Undoubtedly one reason for this was the letter's tone, which was far better designed to infuriate than to persuade or frighten Franklin Roosevelt.

"A most critical situation has arisen in the country of which I feel it is my duty to advise you confidentially," it began. " . . . The major difficulty is the state of the public mind, for there is a steadily degenerating confidence in the future which has reached the height of general alarm. I am convinced that a very early statement by you upon two or three policies of your Administration would serve greatly to restore confidence and cause a resumption of the march of recovery." And Hoover went on to render explicit the insult that was implied by his use of the words "restore" and "resumption." There had been a "restoration of confidence" in early 1932, he said, as a result of "the passage of [Administration] measures for credit expansion," the chief of these being the act establishing the RFC. The "recovery" then begun had "continued until it was interrupted by the aggregate of actions in the House of Representatives [of which the Democrats were in solid control] last spring [which] again spread fear and practical panic across the country." Only when it became evident that the administration would prevail against disruptive Democrats on such matters as gold-standard maintenance, the soldiers' bonus, and federal aid to unemployed individuals—only then did "confidence" return, and the "country resumed the march of recovery." There was immediately "a rise in . . . prices, production, industry and employment" along with a return of "gold . . . from abroad." (Most Americans had remained unhappily unaware of the cited "rise," which others deemed too slight and spotty to have any significance of trend.) This "recovery" had "continued during the summer and fall," until, with the election, "there began another era of interruptions to public confidence which have finally culminated in the present state of alarm and . . . transformed a distinct upward movement into a distinct downward movement." The crying need was for "assurances" only Roosevelt could give that, under the incoming administration, "there will be no tampering or inflation of the currency; that the budget will be unquestionably balanced, even if further taxation is necessary; that the Government credit will be maintained by refusal to exhaust it in the issue of securities."[23]

An epistle so "cheeky," as Roosevelt called it,* neither required nor encouraged the courtesy of an immediate reply, and Roosevelt made none for eleven days.

During those days he completed his Cabinet. He had already completed, by January 20, his immediate personal staff. Missy LeHand was of course continuing as his personal secretary, with Grace Tully her chief assistant. Louis Howe, equally of course, was to be Secretary to the President. The press secretary would be Stephen T. Early, who had covered the Navy Department for the Associated Press during Roosevelt's tenure as Assistant Secretary and had been advance press secretary for Roosevelt during the 1920 vice-presidential campaign. Marvin McIntyre, as already said, would be appointments

---

*That Hoover's letter was in good part motivated by a wish to impale Roosevelt on the horns of a dilemma is made clear by a "confidential" memorandum addressed to Republican Senator David A. Reed of Pennsylvania on February 20. Hoover in this memorandum defined the current "alarming state of public mind" as a "breakdown of public confidence in the new administration now coming in." The American people were terrified by the prospect of "inflation, an unbalanced budget, and governmental projects which will surtax the borrowing power of the Government," and the only way "to stem the tide" was "assurance . . . at once by the new administration that they have rigidly opposed such policies. . . . I realize that if these declarations be made by the President-elect, he will have ratified the whole major program of the Republican Administration; that is, it means the abandonment of 90% of the so-called new deal. But unless this is done, they run the grave danger of precipitating a complete financial debacle. If it is precipitated, the responsibility lies squarely with them for they have had ample warning—unless, of course, such a debacle is a part of the 'new deal.' "[24]

secretary. On Sunday, February 19, Glass made absolutely final his refusal of Treasury, whereupon the post was offered to Will Woodin, who, after an hour-and-a-half taxi-cab ride through Central Park in the company of Basil O'Connor, during which O'Connor overcame his manifold doubts and objections, accepted the next day.[25] The Woodin and Hull appointments, promptly announced (they were the first Cabinet appointments to be announced, with the others following at intervals of a day or two), soothed some of the alarm aroused in conservative breasts by Glass's refusal. More of it was soothed by the announcement that Arizona's Representative Lewis Douglas, whose commitment to gold, government economy, and a balanced budget was as religiously fervent as Hoover's or Glass's, would become Director of the Budget. Glass's refusal of Treasury determined Roosevelt's choice for Secretary of the Navy. There were here two decisive factors. First, Harry F. Byrd, the dominant figure in Virginia politics, had let it be known that he wanted a Senate seat for himself. He would have taken Glass's vacated seat had Glass entered the Cabinet; he would now almost certainly run against and defeat Glass's senatorial colleague, Claude Swanson, in the 1934 primary if Swanson ran; and Roosevelt at that point believed that the strong-willed, strong-minded Byrd, whom he yet deemed a "friend," would be more useful to him in the Senate than Swanson, an "amiable party hack," as correspondents called him, who always "went along." Second, and on the other hand, the seventy-year-old Swanson had made the Navy his legislative specialty, had chaired the Senate Naval Affairs Committee during the war, and was thus well-equipped for the Navy post whereas he was, in Roosevelt's view, ill-equipped for the chairmanship of the Senate Foreign Relations Committee, a post that would be his in the new Congress if he remained in the upper chamber. Much better suited for Foreign Affairs was Nevada's Key Pittman, who was second in line for it after Swanson. So Navy went to Swanson. There then remained only Interior to be filled, and Roosevelt, now under intense time pressure, filled it in remarkably casual fashion. Some weeks before, he had asked Senators Johnson, Cutting, and La Follette to suggest someone sharing their Progressive views to work with Moley on preparations for the war-debt talks with foreign representatives that were to be held in Washington in the spring. It was a request that measured the distrust Roosevelt now had of advice on such matters from Wall Street's international bankers and from the similarly minded Norman Davis. The three senators promptly named Harold L. Ickes, the Chicago lawyer and civic reform leader, a Progressive Republican whom Johnson had been promoting for the post of Commissioner of Indian Affairs. Roosevelt had never met him, when, at Moley's request, he came to New York City on February 21. The next morning he was one of a group that, at 49 East Sixty-fifth, conferred with Roosevelt (that is, listened to Roosevelt's opinions) about the debt problem. As far as Moley could later recall, the only word Ickes spoke during that morning's meeting was his name, after Roosevelt had pronounced it incorrectly. Immediately after the conference, Ickes and the President-elect had perhaps five minutes of private talk together. No more than that, certainly.

Hence Moley's astonishment when Roosevelt told him a few hours later that he'd have to find another war-debt adviser because Harold Ickes was going into the Cabinet as Secretary of the Interior. Explained Roosevelt: "I liked the cut of his jib."[26]

During those hectic days, too, the inaugural address was put into nearly final shape.

A first draft of it had been written on February 12 and 13 by Moley, making use of the notes he had taken during the train ride southward from Warm Springs to Jacksonville on the night of February 4. This draft, revised, then revised again, and a typewritten copy made of it (Moley never dictated a speech; he always composed in longhand on ruled yellow legal-sized tablets), went with Moley on Monday, February 27, to Hyde Park, where, after dinner that evening, it was placed in Roosevelt's hand for his first reading of it. Moley and Roosevelt were then alone together in the library, seated before a flaming fireplace, as they had been on election eve, and again there was the sense of solitude and strange quiet in a tiny island of warmth and light surrounded by a vast sea of wintry cold. Such sense could not but be even stronger for these two on this night than it had been on the earlier one, for this night was darker still, and swept by storms more severe, all across America.

Upon the card table at which Roosevelt sat in his "governor's chair" while he perused the draft speech lay a letter just received from the Morgan Bank partner Tom Lamont. It declared that the banking crisis was now become an unmitigated national disaster; the situation "could not be worse." And what Lamont said had been said in different words by every other prominent figure in the financial world who had written or phoned the President-elect or his advisers, as many had, during the last three days. History would confirm the dire estimate. A total of 389 banks had failed in the land since the first of the year—241 in January, and 148 in February. It was obvious this number would have been multiplied but for the severe deposit-withdrawal restrictions or total bank holidays imposed in recent weeks by government edict in Iowa, Michigan, New Jersey, Indiana, Maryland, and Arkansas. On this black Monday night, twenty other states were on the verge of ordering all their banks closed, and it was "impossible to contemplate the extent of the human suffering" and the "social consequences" that must at once follow such "denial of currency or credit to our urban populations," as Lamont claimed. It was like "cutting off a city's water supply"; there would be "[p]estilence and famine."[27] The situation was exacerbated by the congressional order issued in January of full publicity for all RFC loans, past, present, and future, an order sparked by congressional outrage over the size and circumstances of the reluctantly disclosed loan to the "Dawes bank" in Chicago last June. This certainly militated against the RFC's purpose of bolstering the national credit structure: the request for an RFC loan became now tantamount to a public confession of weakness on the part of the requesting bank, inciting a rush of withdrawals larger than the loan itself could offset.

Also exacerbating the situation, insofar as they further eroded what was left of popular confidence in the integrity and intelligence of great bankers and big businessmen in general, were two public hearings currently being conducted by committees of the U.S. Senate.

One of these was a relentless probing by the Senate Banking and Currency Committee into the top management of two of America's most famous banks. In January the committee's new counsel, a brilliant and indefatigable lawyer named Ferdinand Pecora, called upon Charles G. Dawes for testimony as to the relationship between his now-closed Central Republic Bank of Chicago and the vast enterprise of Samuel Insull. Dawes was forced to admit that nearly 90 percent of Central Republic's deposits had been on loan to Insull companies when the Insull "empire" collapsed, though Illinois law prohibited any bank from lending more than 10 percent of its deposits to a single borrowing entity. The Insull companies would seem to have constituted a single legal entity, being all tied together by one giant holding company and managed, in terms of ultimate policy, by a single man. Asked Pecora: "Mr. Dawes, would you say that making these loans . . . , if they didn't constitute a violation of the letter of the laws . . . violated the spirit of those laws?" Dawes would *not* say it, yet could not convincingly deny the statement's truth. In February, Pecora launched an inquiry into the affairs of the National City Bank, which was the second largest in the nation; the affiliated National City Company, which was the largest investment house in the nation; and the mighty Charles E. Mitchell, that titan of finance who had done so much to thwart the Federal Reserve's effort to curb stock-market speculation in 1929* and who was the top executive of both bank and company (the two had practically identical directorships, though the company was the largest single trader in the bank's stock: it was against federal law for a national bank to market securities). Day after day, Pecora elicited from Mitchell and colleagues testimony that damned them in the public mind as liars, cheats, and swindlers on a grand scale, albeit they operated generally within the letter of loosely drawn laws. What Mitchell called "creative" marketing (he likened it to the "manufacture" of finance capital) was shown to consist all too often of deliberately false advertising of extremely risky stock and bond issues, those of Latin American governments especially, joined with high-pressure salesmanship in reckless disregard of truthfulness by Mitchell's "young men," as he called them. The profits for Mitchell and his fellow directors had been huge. The great banker's income had been over $4,000,000 in 1929, and on this, by "selling" stock to his wife at a loss (he subsequently "repurchased" it, of course, at the selling price), he managed to avoid payment of any federal income tax whatever. "If you steal $25, you're a thief," commented the *Nation* on Pecora's revelations. "If you steal $250,000, you're an embezzler. If you steal $2,500,000, you're a financier." *Commonwealth* remarked that, compared with Mitchell, Al Capone was "a bungler."[28]

The other confidence-depleting Senate hearing, launched in mid-February,

*See pages 114, 144–145.

was an inquiry by the Senate Finance Committee into the causes and cure of the depression as seen by captains of industry, finance, higher education, and the press. It had been originally conceived by Mississippi's conservative Pat Harrison as a means of counteracting "radical" tendencies among the populace through maximum publicity for the sound advice, the practical wisdom, of America's most successful men of affairs. What was perforce publicized instead was an appalling lack of ideas, and of generous instincts, among those who had been in almost exclusive control of national economic policy for the last dozen years. One after another they came to the witness table—the presidents of U.S. Steel, Weirton Steel, Mutual Life, Prudential, the Pennsylvania Railroad, the First National Bank of New York, along with the financier Baruch, the corporation lawyer John W. Davis, the educator Nicholas Murray Butler, the publisher Paul Block (Jimmy Walker's gift-giving friend)—and there they revealed in their various ways that they had no idea what had gone wrong but were very sure it was not the "system" or their management of it. Capitalism was the economic expression, the only true economic expression, of human freedom; by "human freedom" was meant the free expression of "human nature"; it was "human nature" to oscillate between optimism ("boom") and pessimism ("bust"); and as everyone knows, "you can't change human nature." But what about the current mass unemployment, bankruptcy of small business, ruin of farmers, collapse of relief, and general poverty growing steadily deeper as piles of "surplus" grew steadily higher? Could nothing be done about these? Nothing, chorused the great captains, in effect —nothing beyond balancing the budget through drastic cuts in government expenditures. Called late to testify was Ickes' erstwhile law partner, Donald R. Richberg, who was an attorney for the railroad brotherhoods. He was coldly contemptuous of preceding witnesses. "I submit," he said, voicing the opinion of millions, "that every conspicuous leader of affairs who has appeared before this committee and has attempted to justify the continuance of the present political economic system unchanged, with its present control unreformed, is either too ignorant of facts, too stupid in comprehension, or too viciously selfish . . . to be worthy of any attention in this time of bitter need for honest, intelligent, and public-spirited planning for the rehabilitation of our crumbling civilization."[29]

These, then, were the things spoken of on this pitch-black night of February 27, 1933, by the bitter wind that swirled around the house at Hyde Park, sighing through the naked boughs of great trees on the lawn, moaning across icicled eaves, wheezily rattling the tightly closed and shuttered windows. And thus the vortex of forces, signified by Tom Lamont's letter, which centered upon the card table where the opened letter now lay and where Franklin Delano Roosevelt sat, beside a glowing fireplace, perusing the initial draft of the inaugural address he must deliver to a nearly paralyzed nation just five days hence. He approved Moley's handiwork. Forcefully, succinctly, the draft speech phrased not only the ideas expressed on the night train ride to Jacksonville but also ideas emergent from talks with Howe, Flynn, Moley, and others since Miami. Moreover, the *tone* seemed right, and at this juncture, tone was every bit as important as idea content. So Roosevelt proceeded to make the draft his own by copying it in his own hand on one of Moley's yellow legal-sized tablets.* As he did so, he read sentences aloud, testing words and phrases for ease of delivery and probable audience effect, while at the same time impressing them on his thought, absorbing them into his feeling.

Half sitting, half lying on the long couch facing the fireplace, Moley made suggestions now and then and answered questions; but mostly he watched, listened, and deeply felt the presence of History here, closely gathered and focused upon the man he watched. Significantly, he had no feeling that this historical moment was *his* essentially, or predominantly, as he might well have felt had his relationship with Roosevelt been more typically that of "ghost-writer" or "idea-man" with public figure. It was Roosevelt's moment. *He* dominated, and not just because of circumstance, the great office he was about to assume, but also, and more, by force of personality. Of character. As the tall pendulum clock struck eleven, Moley took out of his pocket the notebook he always carried and began to scribble into it jagged impressions: "I have been here since last night almost alone w. him. Everyone happy. Missy, Mac (dressed up) . . . , 4 of us dined together. Margaret [a stenographer otherwise unnamed] Missy F.D.R. & I. . . . Talk of [Ben] Franklin (he was shallow) Jefferson best. T. R. range of his knowledge Wilson. . . . " The notes ended on a stark sure note. Wrote Moley: "A strong man F.D.R.—"

By one o'clock in the morning of Tuesday, February 28, the inaugural address was substantially in the form in which it would be delivered. It lacked concluding words, which, it had been agreed, should be religiously prayerful. Moley had not presumed to draft them: Roosevelt regarded his religion, his personal relationship with God, as very much his *private* affair; he cloaked his religious feeling in thick-layered reticence and generally avoided public worship because he loathed being stared at as he said his prayers. The closing words, then, must be originally as well as finally Roosevelt's own, and he now wrote them: "In this dedication of a Nation we humbly ask the blessing and the guidance of God. May He protect each and every one of us." Then, after a pause, he crossed out of the first sentence "and the guidance" so that he might write as the very last sentence: "May He guide me in the days to come."[30]

Two days later he at last replied to the agitated handwritten letter he had received from Herbert Hoover eleven days before.

He was prodded into doing so by the arrival at Hyde Park, around noon on March 1, of another special Secret Service messenger, bearing a second letter to him from Hoover concerning the banking crisis, written the day before.

---

*One reason for doing so, Roosevelt explained to Moley, was that Louis Howe was coming up from New York City the following morning and would "have a fit" if the speech draft he reviewed was not in Roosevelt's own hand.

"It is my duty to inform you that the financial situation has become even more grave and the lack of confidence extended further than when I wrote to you on February 17th," the letter began. "I am confident that a declaration even now on the line I suggested at that time would contribute greatly to restore confidence, and would save losses and hardship to millions of people." But Hoover's major purpose was, he wrote, to suggest that a special session of Congress be called "quickly after March 4," and to place himself "at your disposal to discuss the situation upon your arrival here or otherwise."

Roosevelt dictated his reply while the special messenger waited for it.

"I am dismayed to find that the enclosed which I wrote in New York a week ago did not go to you, through an assumption by my secretary that it was only a draft of a letter," he said. "Now I have yours of yesterday and can only tell you that I appreciate your fine spirit of cooperation and that I am in constant touch with the situation through Mr. Woodin [he had sent Woodin to Washington for a conference with Mills and other administration figures as soon as Woodin accepted Treasury]. . . . I am inclined to agree that a very early special session will be necessary. . . . I get to Washington late tomorrow night and will look forward to seeing you on Friday."

The enclosure was also dictated while the messenger waited. Possibly it was dictated from an earlier draft; certainly the typist, under instruction, dated it February 19, 1933.

"I am equally concerned with you in regard to the gravity of the present banking situation," it began, "—but my thought is that it is so very deep-seated that the fire is bound to spread in spite of anything that is done by way of mere statements. The real trouble is that . . . very few financial institutions anywhere in the country are actually able to pay off their deposits . . . and the knowledge of this fact is widely held." He "had hoped to have Senator Glass' acceptance of the Treasury post—but he has definitely said no this afternoon—I am asking Mr. Woodin tomorrow." If Woodin accepted, the announcement of his appointment and of Hull's as Secretary of State would be made the following day. "These announcements may have some effect on the banking situation, but frankly I doubt if anything short of a fairly general withdrawal of deposits can be prevented now."[31]

VI

AND by the latter fact he remained, in Moley's view, and Woodin's, not to mention Hoover's and Mills's, remarkably undisturbed. He gave no sign to his intimates that he was "equally concerned" with Hoover over the "gravity" of the "banking situation." He seemed in fact quite serenely *un*concerned and uninvolved in any profound personal sense, certainly unworried and unafraid, as if he, awaiting his cue to go to the center of the stage, watched from the wings a drama of whose happy outcome he was certain. Or, to use his own metaphor, he seemed truly to believe that the "baby" was wholly Herbert Hoover's until noon on March 4, there being nothing achievable through the "cooperation" Hoover kept calling for that Hoover as President could not achieve without it.

For instance, nothing Roosevelt could do would either increase or diminish the President's legal authority to restrict gold exports, control foreign exchange transactions, and prohibit the paying out of gold by banks in exchange for paper money. Either the President could or he could not do these things under the grant of executive authority made by the 1917 Trading With the Enemy Act.* Hoover was as familiar as Roosevelt was with that act's terms and with the question of whether or not it had automatically expired at war's end (certainly it had never been formally repealed); for Hoover had given some consideration to a use of its powers during the gold-drain crisis that had followed Britain's suspension of its gold standard. Indeed, he was being urged at that very moment to invoke it by Treasury Secretary Mills, Under Secretary Ballantine, and Adolph Miller of the Federal Reserve Board. If instead he chose to follow the negative advice of Attorney General William D. Mitchell and Senator Glass, both of whom believed the act no longer valid, neither of whom wanted the President to do what the act, if valid, gave power to do—if he chose to follow this advice, the choice was his. As for Roosevelt, he had weeks ago asked Tugwell to explore the possibility that executive powers residual from wartime legislation could be exercised in the present emergency. Tugwell had been told by State Department economist Herbert Feis of the Trading With the Enemy Act. And Senator Walsh, the designated Attorney General, had been asked for his legal opinion as to the act's current validity. Walsh's reply to this request awaited Roosevelt at 49 East Sixty-fifth Street when, in the afternoon of Wednesday, March 1, he came down to the city from Hyde Park on the first leg of his journey to Washington. In a communication from Florida, where the senator, having been married in Havana barely a week before, was about to board the train that would take him and his much younger bride† to the inaugural, Walsh expressed some personal doubt that the act remained in force but promised an official opinion legally justifying Roosevelt's action, should Roosevelt invoke its powers. Roosevelt then decided that he *would* invoke these powers as soon as the presidential authority was his.

But such decision-making ruffled not at all the placid sun-sparkling waters of his spirit, being neither more nor less important, in his evident view, than the decisions he made about the inaugural parade and balls (he was much involved in the planning of these) during his consultations with Rear Admiral Cary T. Grayson, who had been the White House physician during the Wilson administration and was now, by Roosevelt's choice, the general chairman of the Inaugural Committee. *Nothing* ruffled him. Neither by tone of voice nor

---

*See page 395. The act was revised by congressional action in September 1918, evidently with the purpose, not openly stated by the revision's authors, of adding permanently to the powers reserved for presidential use in times of emergency.

†She was, until she became Mrs. Walsh, Senora Maria Nieves Perez Chaumont de Truffin, the wealthy widow of a Cuban banker and sugar planter.

facial expression, by no slightest sign of tension, did he reveal inward anxiety or anything but an absolute smiling confidence in his capacity to deal successfully with whatever might come. Others drew abundantly upon his cheerful calm, his optimistic courage, his sure strength.

Whence did he derive his own?

Late in the afternoon of Thursday, March 2, a day of raw cold, he went by limousine with siren-screaming police escort from Sixty-fifth Street to a ferry slip on the West Side, near the tip of Manhattan; was ferried across the slate-gray wind-whipped Hudson; then boarded the special train of the Baltimore and Ohio that would take him to Washington. He remained serene, confident, but in somber mood, as he had been on Election Day. The halfdozen newspapers he had perused as he breakfasted in bed that morning told of a banking crisis mounting to fatal climax. Half the states in the Union had decreed bank holidays, and many more were certain to do so in the hours just ahead. Credit, the lifeblood of the economic system, flowed now so meagerly through America that the Republic had virtually ceased to function as a vital organism and lay prostrate, paralyzed, seemingly moribund in the fearful cold. Death was everywhere. Soon after he'd read the morning's news, Roosevelt received, among a multitude of calls from panic-stricken governors, bankers, big industrialists, a phone call telling him that the man he had chosen to be Attorney General was dead. Senator Walsh's bride of barely a week had found him lying dead of a heart attack upon the Pullman car floor when she awoke that morning. Roosevelt had had no time to indulge whatever personal grief he may have felt over the loss of a man he had certainly greatly admired. He must find a new Attorney General at once. He had done so, with Howe's help, by shifting Connecticut's Homer S. Cummings from the governorship of the Philippines to the Cabinet. He had then at once asked Cummings to prepare an official opinion on the Trading With the Enemy Act's validity and saw to it that all the information thus far gathered on the matter was placed, in a folder, in Cummings' hands.

Night fell.

At Roosevelt's invitation, Jim Farley, whom Roosevelt knew to be a man of great and simple religious faith, came to the last car of the special train to sit beside the President-elect in his stateroom, the two of them alone together for the most part. And to Farley the President-elect talked, not of financial crisis or of the multitudinous problems of economic breakdown for whose solution he would be responsible in two days' time, but of God, and the determinative effect of men's faith in God.[32] More important than any planned operation for the solution of the present crisis was a great people's religious faith, said Franklin Roosevelt. Ultimately the salvation of the United States depended upon the American people's active belief in Divine Providence, their seeking and acceptance of Divine guidance. He himself proposed to launch the New Deal with a prayer: his first public act on inauguration day would be his attendance at a worship service conducted at St. John's Episcopal Church, across Lafayette Square from the White House, by the Reverend Endicott

Peabody, the rector of Groton parish, the headmaster of Groton School. Farley listened, deeply moved, even awestruck. The man beside him shone with an inward light.

And outside the train windows was night.

Deep, dark, wintry night. . . .

→>>X<←
Acknowledgments

IN the Acknowledgments of help in the writing of the first volume of this history, I remarked that my book had been, "of its kind, a more than normally solitary labor." The same is true of this present volume.

A writer who chooses to live and work as I do on a New England "farm" of meadow and garden, rocks and trees, must purchase his peace and quiet amid landscape beauty at the price of remoteness from others engaged in literary or scholarly pursuits. Had I worked in a university setting, where most historical writing is done in our time, I would no doubt be acknowledging here the help of numerous colleagues who vetted my work in progress in return for my vetting of theirs. Such cooperative exercise would, I am sure, have resulted in a better book in some ways. On the other hand, and in other ways, it might have resulted in a worse book—or so I tell myself, defensively. Prudential considerations might then have blurred definitions now relatively sharp and clear, a willingness to draw precisely the conclusions that seem to me logically implied by evidence might have become qualified by felt peer pressures toward a safe conformity with established views, and such individual distinction as my prose may have would almost certainly have been replaced in some degree by the cautious neutrality, the deliberate avoidance of distinction, that characterizes the writing of doctoral theses.

At any rate, in my actual situation, I have been more exclusively dependent upon the published work of my predecessors in the field of scholarship where I labor than I would have been had I been able to discuss problems face-to-face with subject-matter authorities, and I am deeply conscious of my great debt to these predecessors. I have tried to indicate its magnitude and nature in specific citations in my Notes. Especially heavy are my debts to Bernard Bellush's *Franklin D. Roosevelt as Governor of New York*; Ernest K. Lindley's *Franklin D. Roosevelt: A Career in Progressive Democracy,* a work whose objectivity and high quality in general are remarkable in view of the fact that it was conceived and written as a campaign biography; Samuel I. Rosenman's *Working With Roosevelt*; Raymond Moley's *After Seven Years* and *The First New Deal,* the latter of which corrects a false view of FDR's writing of his first inaugural address that FDR himself fostered; Frances Perkins' *The Roosevelt I Knew*; Eleanor Roosevelt's *This Is My Story* and *This I Remember*; the first three chapters of Basil Rauch's excellent pioneering *History of the New Deal*; Alfred B. Rollins, Jr.'s, *Roosevelt and Howe,* an indispensable work of original scholarship that is also incisively written; Rexford G. Tugwell's *The Democratic Roosevelt* and *The Brains Trust,* which are particularly valuable for their psychological insights into FDR; Edgar Eugene Robinson's *The Roosevelt*

Leadership, 1933–1945, of which the opening part is a highly critical assessment of FDR as New York governor; Elliott A. Rosen's *Hoover, Roosevelt, and the Brains Trust,* which sheds much new light on the interregnum and is a valuable corrective of the memoirs of Raymond Moley, whose *First New Deal* was produced under the prodding and with the active assistance of Rosen; Arthur M. Schlesinger, Jr.'s, brilliant *The Crisis of the Old Order,* which is the first volume of his *The Age of Roosevelt;* James MacGregor Burns's fine *Roosevelt: The Lion and the Fox;* and finally, and in many ways most importantly, Frank Freidel's *Franklin D. Roosevelt: The Triumph* and his *Franklin D. Roosevelt: Launching the New Deal,* the third and fourth volumes of his masterful biography of FDR, which, upon completion, bids fair to become the definitive scholarly work on this subject. All these works are cited in the Notes. Two that are not cited there, yet had important influence upon my thinking about FDR, are Otis L. Graham, Jr.'s, *An Encore for Reform: The Old Progressives and the New Deal* and Richard Hofstader's *The American Political Tradition,* especially the chapters entitled "Herbert Hoover and the Crisis of American Individualism" and, of course, "Franklin D. Roosevelt: The Patrician as Opportunist." The latter confirmed in me, while brilliantly defining, an attitude toward my subject that I as a very young man working in a New Deal agency felt forced, against my will, to assume.

Every writer about FDR draws heavily, of course, upon the rich resources and wonderfully helpful and efficient staff of the Franklin D. Roosevelt Library at Hyde Park. The abundant and precisely annotated use my predecessors have made of that library has drastically reduced the number and duration of my own visits to Hyde Park, but every visit I have made there has been as enjoyable as it was profitable, and every specific question I have put to the library staff through correspondence has been promptly answered in full detail. Mentioned in my Notes is a question about Hoover's famous letter to Roosevelt about the developing banking crisis in February 1933, which Frances M. Seeber, supervisory archivist, swiftly answered. I wish here to thank her for that, since I find to my chagrin that I failed to do so by letter; and also to express my gratitude to librarian Joseph Marshall and to William Emerson, director of the library, for the many helpful kindnesses they have shown me over the years.

Another rich resource upon which FDR scholars heavily draw, and for which I am very grateful, having made considerable use of it, is Columbia University's Oral History Collection, to which I was introduced many years ago by the late Louis Starr, then director of Columbia's Oral History Research Office. Greater still is my debt of gratitude to the late Tilton M. Barron, director of the Goddard Library at Clark University, without whose special service to me I could not possibly have completed this work while continuing to live as and where I do. And only somewhat smaller than these debts is the one I owe Ellen Howe and her efficient staff at the Goodnow Memorial Library in Princeton, Massachusetts.

The award of a fellowship by John Guggenheim Memorial Foundation helped me financially through two difficult years on this project, in 1974–1975, and this help I here most gratefully acknowledge.

Finally, I wish here to express profound thanks to my beloved wife, Florence Olenhouse Davis, whose support during long dark periods has been unfailing, and to my editor, Robert D. Loomis, Vice-President and Executive Editor of Random House, for the more than support—the active help, the highly intelligent criticisms, the full exercise of superlative editorial skills—that he has given me.

KSD
Princeton, Massachusetts

Notes

This book is concerned less with the discovery and presentation of hitherto hidden facts about Franklin Roosevelt and his years than it is with comprehending in interpretive ways, from a clearly defined point of view, factual information that has long been at hand in vast bulk. My hope and belief are that such comprehension may help us better understand what is happening in American life today. My book is also intended for a general rather than a scholarly specialized readership. I have therefore decided to dispense with the extensive bibliography prepared for inclusion here. It would add at least ten pages to a work already sufficiently lengthy while serving, so far as I can see, no useful purpose. Most of the titles on my list are necessarily the same found in the literally hundreds of Roosevelt–New Deal bibliographies already printed and readily available to students, including the bibliography for *FDR: The Beckoning of Destiny, 1882–1928,* which is the first volume of the present history. Moreover, though several works consulted for general historical context and thematic program are not specifically cited in the following Notes, most of the titles I used *are* so cited.

Prologue: Midstream: October Ferry to Hoboken

1. Samuel I. Rosenman, *Working With Roosevelt* (New York, 1952), pp. 15–16, describes Roosevelt's appearance and manner during the ferry crossing.

2. Mrs. James Roosevelt, as told to Isabelle Leighton and Gabrielle Forbush, *My Boy Franklin* (New York, 1933), p. 18.

3. Franklin D. Roosevelt, "The Roosevelt Family in New Amsterdam Before the Revolution," a 1901 manuscript written for a Harvard class assignment; now in the Franklin D. Roosevelt Library, Hyde Park.

4. Every close Roosevelt associate who has attempted a psychological analysis of him and published the conclusions—notably Eleanor Roosevelt, Rexford G. Tugwell, Frances Perkins—has stressed FDR's simple but strong religious faith as a determining factor of his temperament, a basic conditioner of his major acts. His mother (Mrs. James Roosevelt, *op. cit.,* pp. 15–16) tells of the boy Franklin's serene conviction that a wren he wished to add to the bird collection he was making would remain perched in a tree several hundred yards from the Hyde Park house while he sauntered up to the house to get his bird gun.

5. Daniel W. Delano, Jr., *Franklin Roosevelt and the Delano Influence* (Pittsburgh, 1946), is a principal source of information on FDR's maternal ancestry.

6. Mrs. Susan Lesley, *Memoir of the Life of Mrs. Anne Jean Lyman* (Cambridge, Mass., privately printed, 1875), is another principal source of Roosevelt maternal ancestry information.

7. Grenville Clark, *Harvard Alumni Bulletin,* vol. 48, April 28, 1945, p. 452.

8. Undated letter, Louis Howe to FDR, FDR, Group 9, Franklin D. Roosevelt Library.

9. Miss Marion Dickerman, in repeated personal interviews when she and I worked together on a book based on her recollections, during 1973, is a principal source of my information concerning Howe's part in this matter. Miss Dickerman's information came from Eleanor Roosevelt.

10. Eleanor Roosevelt, *This Is My Story* (New York, 1937), tells the polio story in a chapter entitled "Trial by Fire," pp. 328–352. The friend to whom FDR communicated his sense of having been "abandoned" by God was Frances Perkins. See Frank Freidel, *Franklin D. Roosevelt: The Ordeal* (Boston, 1954), p. 100.

11. Franklin D. Roosevelt, "Introduction" to *Whaleships of New Bedford* (Boston, 1929), by Clifford W. Ashley, pp. iv–v. All of the preceding direct quotes are from this introduction.

12. Famous during Roosevelt's lifetime was his personal preference of past simplicities over present complexities and of country over city life, along with his immunity to attraction by machinery and new gadgetry.

13. One may observe, since the observation is relevant to essential purposes of the present work, that Spengler would not have gone to the great trouble of writing his book had he really basically believed what he so perversely and emphatically asserted, namely, that ideas, systems, conceptualized beliefs, are without consequence or effect in the "actual" world. (He suggests at one point that Archimedes was "less effective" in the "history of actuality" than the ignorant soldier who slew him.) For Spengler was certainly a lover of Power; he was eager to gain and exercise it in typically Germanic (that is, terrifying) fashion. Basically he knew as well as you or I that ideas do have practical consequences, that between Truth and Fact, to employ the dichotomy he stresses, there is a reciprocal relationship that is continuously operative. Witch-burning depends upon a conceptualized belief in witches and is impossible without this. Jew-burning depends upon a conceptualized belief that the Jews are an alien people, unassimilable, and is impossible without this. No one of sensitive intelligence could read Spengler after the 1940s without smelling the gas chambers of Auschwitz. The quotation about "the logic of space" and "the logic of time" is from Oswald Spengler, *The Decline of the West,* vol. 1 (New York, 1926), p. 7. The quotations about "destiny-men" and "causality-men" are from vol. 2 (New York, 1928), pp. 16–17.

14. Elliott Roosevelt, ed., *F.D.R.: His Personal Letters, 1905–1928* (New York, 1947), p. 135. Hereafter *Letters, 1905–1928.*

15. It is evidently impossible to explicate Spengler in truly logical (that is, mutually exclusive) terms. Everything runs together. Having established to the best of your ability the proper pitch and tonal scale (that is, your *feeling*) of Spengler's philoso-

phy, you must "let yourself go" to "do your thing" with the language or style he employs. You can only hope thereby to produce an accurate impression (or feeling) of his meaning.

16. Spengler, *op. cit.,* vol. I, p. 142.

17. Eleanor Roosevelt, *op. cit.,* pp. 149–150.

18. Telegram, FDR to Alfred E. Smith, September 30, 1928, FDR, Group 17, Franklin D. Roosevelt Library.

19. Telegram, Louis Howe to FDR, September 26, 1928, FDR, Group 17, Franklin D. Roosevelt Library.

20. Elliott Roosevelt, *Letters, 1905–1928,* p. 346.

21. Eleanor Roosevelt, *op. cit.,* p. 346.

22. Interviews with Marion Dickerman, 1973.

23. Ernest K. Lindley, *Franklin D. Roosevelt: A Career in Progressive Democracy* (New York, 1931), pp. 18–21, is a highly circumstantial account of Roosevelt's "drafting" for the nomination by one who was present in Rochester at the time. Lindley's account was confirmed in part by my conversations with Marion Dickerman, who heard of the Rochester proceedings in detail from her friends Nancy Cook and Eleanor Roosevelt on October 2 and 3, 1928.

One: From Warm Springs to Albany

1. Telegram, Louis Howe to FDR, October 2, 1928, FDR, Group 17, Franklin D. Roosevelt Library. Quoted in Alfred B. Rollins, Jr., *Roosevelt and Howe* (New York, 1962), p. 235, and in Freidel, *op. cit.,* p. 255.

2. Telegram, Eleanor Roosevelt to FDR, October 2, 1928, FDR, Group 17, Franklin D. Roosevelt Library. Freidel, *op cit.,* p. 255. Rollins, *op. cit.,* p. 235. Joseph P. Lash, *Eleanor and Franklin* (New York, 1971), pp. 317–318.

3. Lash, *op. cit.,* p. 317.

4. Letter, Louis Howe to FDR, October 2, 1928, FDR, Group 17, Franklin D. Roosevelt Library. Quoted in Rollins, *op. cit.,* pp. 236–237.

5. New York *Post,* October 2, 1928. New York *Herald Tribune,* October 3, 1928. Lindley, quoting Al Smith, *op. cit.,* p. 21. The quote from the New York *World* is also in Lindley, p. 21.

6. Elliott Roosevelt, *Letters, 1905–1928,* pp. 647–648, quoting FDR's October 5, 1928, statement.

7. New York *Herald Tribune,* October 9, 1928. Quoted in Freidel, *op. cit.,* pp. 260–261.

8. Edward J. Flynn, *You're the Boss* (New York, 1947), p. 70. Arthur M. Schlesinger, Jr., *The Crisis of the Old Order* (New York, 1956), p. 388.

9. Flynn, *op. cit.,* p. 70.

10. Ernest K. Lindley, *The Roosevelt Revolution* (New York, 1933), pp. 298–300. Schlesinger, *op. cit.,* p. 400.

11. Rosenman, *op. cit.,* p. 14.

12. *Ibid.,* p. 16.

13. *Ibid.*

14. *Ibid.*

15. *The Public Papers and Addresses of Franklin D. Roosevelt* (13 vols., New York, 1938–1950). Vol. I: 1928–1932, pp. 20–21. Hereafter PPA, 1928–1932.

16. *Ibid.,* pp. 27, 29–30.

17. Box 32, Howe Papers, Franklin D. Roosevelt Library. Quoted in Bernard Bellush, *Franklin D. Roosevelt as Governor of New York* (New York, 1968), p. 17.

18. Rosenman, *op. cit.,* p. 17.

19. *Ibid.,* pp. 17–18.

20. *Ibid.,* pp. 19–20. PPA, 1928–1932, pp. 30–31, 37–38.

21. Rosenman, *op. cit.,* p. 22.

22. PPA, 1928–1932, pp. 38, 41, 43.

23. *Ibid.,* pp. 44–51.

24. *Ibid.,* pp. 67, 68, 71.

25. Rosenman, *op. cit.,* p. 22. PPA, 1928–1932, pp. 53–54.

26. New York *Times,* November 5, 1928.

27. Smith probably derived his embittered remark from reports of a speech made by the famed Kansas editor William Allen White at a dinner in Salt Lake City in March 1927. Said White: "As a Kansas farmer told me, 'No man will ever tell his beads in the White House.' " Attacked editorially in an official Catholic publication for his statement, White replied defensively that it was but a "rustic phrasing" of

a "political fact." See Walter Johnson, ed., *Selected Letters of William Allen White* (New York, 1947), pp. 267–268. According to Frances Perkins, *The Roosevelt I Knew* (New York, 1946), p. 46, Smith made this same remark to her while in "a reflective mood many years later." Emily Smith Warner and Hawthorne Daniel, *The Happy Warrior* (New York, 1956), tell, pp. 226–227, of Emily's phoning Herbert Bayard Swope for confirmation of reports from the South.

28. Flynn, *op. cit.,* p. 71.

29. PPA, 1928–1932, p. 29.

30. Rosenman, *op. cit.,* p. 26. Flynn, *op. cit.,* pp. 71–72.

31. Perkins, *op. cit.,* p. 48.

32. Elliott Roosevelt, *F.D.R.: His Personal Letters, 1928–1945,* part I, p. 9. Hereafter *Letters, 1928–1945.* Letter, FDR to Archibald Roosevelt, November 19, 1928. Quoted in Freidel, *op. cit.,* p. 268.

33. Elliott Roosevelt, *Letters, 1928–1945,* p. 8.

34. Samuel Lubbell, *The Future of American Politics* (New York, 1952), pp. 35–36. On the evidence, Howe and Roosevelt reached the same conclusion as Lubbell here presents, as they pondered the meaning of the election results.

35. Flynn, *op. cit.,* p. 211.

36. Herbert C. Pell to FDR, January 4, 1929, Franklin D. Roosevelt Library. Elliott Roosevelt, *Letters, 1928–1945,* pp. 24–25.

37. *Ibid.,* pp. 5–6.

38. *Ibid.,* p. 7.

39. *Ibid.,* p. 17.

40. Quoted in Lash, *op. cit.,* p. 320.

41. Elliott Roosevelt, *Letters, 1928–1945,* p. 772. Lash, *op. cit.,* p. 323, quoting letter from Eleanor Roosevelt to FDR, November 22, 1928.

42. James Roosevelt, with Sidney Shalett, *Affectionately, F.D.R.: A Son's Story of a Lonely Man* (New York, 1959), p. 210, quoting letter from Eleanor Roosevelt to FDR, November 22, 1928.

43. New York *Times,* November 8, 1928. Matthew Josephson and Hannah Josephson, *Al Smith: Hero of the Cities* (Boston, 1969), p. 400.

44. Letters, Eleanor Roosevelt to FDR, November 13, 19, 1938. Quoted in Lash,

op. cit., p. 323. Freidel, *Franklin D. Roosevelt: The Triumph* (Boston, 1956), p. 17.

45. Rosenman, *op. cit.,* p. 29.

46. Grace Tully, *F.D.R., My Boss* (New York, 1949), pp. 37–39.

47. Rosenman, *op. cit.,* p. 29.

48. *Ibid.,* pp. 29–30.

49. New York *Times,* November 28, 1928.

50. Elliott Roosevelt, *Letters, 1928–1945,* p. 14.

51. Rosenman, *op. cit.,* p. 31.

52. Warner and Daniel, *op. cit.,* p. 240. Elliott Roosevelt, *Letters, 1928–1945,* p. 772.

53. Perkins, *op. cit.,* p. 55.

54. Elliott Roosevelt, *Letters, 1928–1945,* p. 772.

55. *Ibid.,* p. 773.

56. Flynn, *op. cit.,* pp. 75–76.

57. Perkins, *op. cit.,* pp. 52–53.

Two: The New Governor: Is He Tough Enough?

1. New York *Times,* January 1, 1929.

2. *Ibid.,* January 2, 1929. Josephson and Josephson, *op. cit.,* p. 402.

3. PPA, 1928–1932, pp. 75–80, gives the inaugural address in full.

4. PPA, 1928–1932, pp. 80–86, excerpts from the annual message.

5. New York *Times,* January 14, 15, 1928. Freidel, *Roosevelt: The Triumph,* p. 33, says in a footnote that the actual number of replies received "was about a thousand," not the 3,000 FDR proclaimed.

6. Elliott Roosevelt, *Letters, 1928–1945,* pp. 26–31, prints FDR's letter to Nicholas Roosevelt in full.

7. Perkins, *op. cit.,* p. 62.

8. Lindley, *Franklin D. Roosevelt,* p. 337.

9. *Ibid.,* pp. 339–340.

10. Perkins, *op. cit.,* pp. 90–91.

11. Elliott Roosevelt, *Letters, 1928–1945,* p. 19.

12. New York *Times,* January 18, 1929.

13. Freidel, *Roosevelt: The Triumph,* p. 32, quoting letter from FDR to Casper T. Gee, March 12, 1929, and letter from Gee to FDR, February 19, 1929.

14. Flynn, *op. cit.,* p. 78.

15. New York *Times,* January 17, 18, 1929. *Public Papers of Franklin D. Roosevelt, Forty-eighth Governor of New York* (4 vols., Albany, 1930–1939), vol. I, pp. 683–685. Hereafter PPG.

16. Elliott Roosevelt, *Letters, 1928–1945,* p. 39.

17. New York *Times,* March 6, 1929.

18. PPA, 1928–1932, pp. 171–178, has message in full.

19. New York *Times,* March 15, 1929.

20. Max Freedman, ed., *Roosevelt and Frankfurter: Their Correspondence, 1928–1945* (Boston, 1967), p. 41. Letter, FDR to Frankfurter, July 5, 1929.

21. Elliott Roosevelt, *Letters, 1928–1945,* p. 44.

22. *Ibid.,* pp. 44–45. Lindley, *Franklin D. Roosevelt,* p. 249.

23. Freidel, *Roosevelt: The Triumph,* pp. 58–59, citing New York *Post,* March 29, 1929; New York *Herald Tribune,* March 29, 1929.

24. PPG, 1929, p. 143. PPA, 1928–1932, describes the budget issue from FDR's point of view, pp. 239–340.

25. Lindley, *Franklin D. Roosevelt,* p. 246. New York *Times,* February 29, 1929. Bellush, *op. cit.,* pp. 41–43.

26. Lindley, *Franklin D. Roosevelt,* pp. 246–247. New York *Times,* March 14, 1929.

27. New York *Times,* March 10, 1929. Bellush, *op. cit.,* p. 43.

28. Freidel, *Roosevelt: The Triumph,* p. 58, citing New York *World,* March 28, 1929.

Three: The Answer: A Highly Qualified "Yes"

1. Elliott Roosevelt, *Letters, 1928–1945,* p. 44.

2. PPA, 1928–1932, pp. 541–547, has address in full.

3. Freidel, *Roosevelt: The Triumph,* p. 64, quoting letter from George W. Wickersham to FDR, April 6, 1929.

4. PPA, 1928–1932, pp. 342–343.

5. New York *Times,* April 27, 1929. Freidel, *Roosevelt: The Triumph,* p. 64.

6. Bellush, *op. cit.,* p. 52.

7. PPA, 1928–1932, p. 348.

8. Elliott Roosevelt, *Letters, 1928–1945,* p. 48.

9. *Ibid.,* pp. 22–24.

10. New York *Times,* July 8, 1929.

11. New York *Times,* July 5, 1929. New York *Post,* July 6, 1929.

12. *New Leader,* July 13, 1929. Bellush, *op. cit.,* p. 213.

13. Letter, FDR to Felix Frankfurter, July 5, 1929, in Freedman, *op. cit.,* p. 41.

14. *Ibid.,* p. 40.

15. Bellush, *op. cit.,* pp. 216–217.

16. Franklin D. Roosevelt, "The Real Meaning of the Power Problem," *Forum,* December 1929, pp. 327–332.

17. New York *Times,* January 6, 8, 1930. Bellush, *op. cit.,* p. 217. Freidel, *Roosevelt: The Triumph,* p. 108. Lindley, *Franklin D. Roosevelt,* p. 251.

18. Herbert Hoover, *Memoirs: The Cabinet and the Presidency, 1920–1933* (New York, 1952), pp. 122–123.

19. New York *Times,* January 2, 3, 1930. Freidel, *Roosevelt: The Triumph,* pp. 107–108. PPA, 1928–1932, pp. 91–92.

20. New York *Times,* January 8, 1930. Freidel, *Roosevelt: The Triumph,* p. 108.

21. New York *Times,* January 15, 1930. Freidel, *Roosevelt: The Triumph,* p. 109. Bellush, *op. cit.,* p. 219.

22. Freedman, *op. cit.,* p. 44. Bellush, *op. cit.,* p. 219.

23. *New Leader,* January 18, 1930. Bellush, *op. cit.,* pp. 220–221, quoting letter from FDR to Norman Thomas, January 24, 1930.

24. PPA, 1928–1932, pp. 203–205.

25. Bernard K. Johnpoll, *Pacifist's Progress: Norman Thomas and the Decline of Socialism* (Chicago, 1970), p. 17, quoting Thomas' testimony in *Hearings,* 1920, State of New York, Assembly Committee on the Judiciary, p. 1672.

26. Elliott Roosevelt, *Letters, 1905–1928.*

27. Gene Fowler, *Beau James: The Life and Times of Jimmy Walker* (New York, 1949), p. 240.

28. Johnpoll, *op. cit.,* p. 63.

29. Flynn, *op. cit.,* p. 55.

30. PPA, 1928–1932, p. 76. PPG, 1929, pp. 710–713.

31. PPA, 1928–1932, pp. 367–370.

32. See *FDR: The Beckoning of Destiny,* pp. 372–374, for a discussion of Bismarck's Germany as a model for TR's New Nationalism, the influence of German natural-resource conservation policy upon FDR's thinking in 1912, and Bismarck's deliberate use of state welfare programs to offset and frustrate Socialism.

Four: The Last Summer of the Golden Glow

1. This advertising, like other promotions by the American Tobacco Company in those years under the ineffable and incredible George Washington Hill, was quite terrifyingly effective. Candy manufacturers were so badly hurt that they sued for damages, and got them.

2. All direct quotes are from the "Foreword" to Benito Mussolini's *My Autobiography,* pp. xi, xvii, xix. The book, written at Child's suggestion, was published in New York in 1928 after serialization in the *Saturday Evening Post.* Richard Washburn Child, as poet, further rhapsodized on p. xix: "He [Mussolini] is a mystic to himself. I imagine, as he reaches forth to touch the reality of himself, he finds that he himself has gone a little forward, isolated, determined, illusive, untouchable, just out of reach—onward!" In the immediately preceding sentence, Child wrote: "One closes the door when one leaves him, feeling . . . that one could squeeze something of him out of one's clothes." But Child was only somewhat more rhapsodic on the subject of Mussolini than was Thomas Lamont, who became treasurer of the Italy-American Society and, on behalf of the House of Morgan, did all he could to promote American investments in Fascist Italy. As for Otto Kahn, he praised Mussolini for having "substituted efficient and energetic and progressive processes of government for Parliamentary wrangling and wasteful, impotent bureaucracy. He has engen-

dered among the people a spirit of order, discipline, hard work, patriotic devotion and faith." Will Rogers, in his syndicated newspaper column, in the summer of 1929, said he had "never seen a thing that . . . [Mussolini] has done that wasn't based on common sense. He has done more constructive things in his country since the war than any hundred men in any other country."

3. Quoted in *Time*, January 28, 1929.

4. Paul M. Mazur, *American Prosperity: Its Causes and Consequences* (New York, 1928), pp. 263, 266, 267. The banker Mazur's genius for garbled metaphor, almost the equal of Warren G. Harding's, is so delightful that the temptation to quote him at too great length is almost irresistible. On p. 3, for instance, he manages to incorporate five distinct implicit metaphors, each wholly exclusive of the others, in two sentences. "There is no reason to believe that the major part of American history will be created elsewhere or come from some other source [than industry]," he writes. "Industry is too definitely the marrow of our thought and outlook, too subtly interwoven with the fibers of our survival, to play a secondary role." It is worth noting that Mazur changed his tune in a book, *New Roads to Prosperity*, published in New York in 1931. He then no longer believed in the general beneficence of the businessman's unmitigated pursuit of private profit. He spoke instead (pp. 95–96) of the "tragic lack of planning that characterizes the capitalistic system," saying that it was "a reflection upon the intelligence of everyone participating in the system." Mazur became one of those Raymond Moley consulted when formulating Brain Trust proposals for FDR in early 1932.

5. *Time*, May 27, 1929. The survey was published in book form, in two volumes, under the title *Recent Economic Changes in the United States* (New York, 1929). Its introduction made bitterly ironical reading during the following year, for it stressed price stability as a prevailing fact due to business management "prudence," bankers's "skill," and foreign market "expansion." There had been "no serious cyclical fluctuations" during "the period under review" (1922–1929); a "dynamic equilibrium" of "economic forces" had been achieved; and there was no sign of serious trouble ahead. "Our situation is fortunate, our momentum is remarkable." See pp. xiii, xvii, xx, and xxii of the cited book.

6. New York *Times*, February 3, 1929.

7. *Time*, May 20, 1929.

8. Chapter I of *America in Midpassage*, by Charles A. Beard and Mary R. Beard (New York, 1939), describing the United States in the 1920s, is entitled "The Golden Glow."

9. J. Joseph Huthmacher, *Senator Robert F. Wagner and the Rise of Urban Liberalism* (New York, 1968), pp. 58–61. New York *Times*, May 6, 20, 1928.

10. Elliott Roosevelt, *Letters, 1928–1945*, p. 60.

11. John J. Raskob, with Samuel Crowther, "Everybody Ought to Be Rich," *Ladies'*

Home Journal, August 1929. Crowther was Henry Ford's public-relations man and the author of an adulatory biography of Ford.

12. Elliott Roosevelt, *Letters, 1928–1945,* pp. 42–43.

13. Eleanor Roosevelt, *This I Remember* (New York, 1949), p. 349.

14. Several items of the Val Kill Cottage furnishings—some of the silver, some of the pewter that Nancy handcrafted, several of the products of Eleanor's incessant knitting—bore the initials of the first names of the three friends, "E. M. N." (*not,* be it noted, "M. E. N.")

15. Caroline O'Day was remarkable even among Eleanor's generally remarkable friends. Born on a Georgia plantation, of the Southern aristocracy (her maternal grandfather was the Confederate General Eli Warren), she had early displayed an unusual talent for music and painting, had been an art student of Whistler's, had had some pictures accepted by the Paris Salon in 1898 and 1900, was a superb etcher, and had with reluctance abandoned a career in art to become the wife of Daniel O'Day, who became a vice-president of Standard Oil and an extremely wealthy man but who nonetheless encouraged, if he did not share, his wife's political and economic liberalism. He died in 1916. She remained under Whistler's influence to the extent that all her life she dressed only in black and white. She also saw the political and social world in which she operated as black and white, good vs. evil. But hers was a compassionate nature and vision, inclined to define evil as a mere absence of good, which would have been there but for ignorance or misunderstanding or illness. She had been one of the most ardent suffragettes in the 1910s. She had proclaimed her opposition to war, at risk of federal prosecution under the Alien and Sedition Law, in 1917 and 1918. Her luxurious home in Rye, New York, was frequently visited by Eleanor and used as a meeting place by organizations of which Eleanor was an active member. In 1924, though she held high office in the state Democratic Party and perforce worked for the party's presidential candidate, her personal choice for President was Robert M. La Follette of that year's revived Progressive Party. She probably voted for La Follette.

16. The "rough diamond" quote is from "The Reminiscences of Marion Dickerman," Oral History Research Office, Columbia University.

17. The "covertness" did not prevent Sara Roosevelt's frank expression of her view of this matter to her intimates. Marion Dickerman, who had no great liking for Earl Miller herself, knew of it and mentioned it to me. J. B. West in his *Upstairs in the White House* (New York, 1973) speaks of it.

18. Lash, *op. cit.,* p. 341.

19. There are in Marion Dickerman's private collection, as I write this, many as-yet-unpublished photographs, still and movie, taken by Nancy Cook of the intimate Roosevelt entourage at Val Kill and elsewhere. In the movie sequences especially the visual evidence of the joy Eleanor took in her friendship with Earl Miller is clear. She positively glows with unwonted happiness in several of them. It is to be hoped

that these pictures will eventually become part of the collections of the Franklin D. Roosevelt Library.

20. The story of this unhappy dinner, and the various quotes within my recounting of it, derive from personal interviews with Marion Dickerman in 1973, supplemented by "The Reminiscences of Marion Dickerman," Oral History Research Office, Columbia University. Lash, *op. cit.,* pp. 329–330, also tells of it, having derived his information from interviews with Miss Dickerman, Franklin D. Roosevelt, Jr., and John Roosevelt.

21. Eleanor Roosevelt, *This I Remember,* p. 56.

22. PPG, 1929, p. 745.

23. Charles Michelson was a brother of the light-speed-measuring Nobel Prize–winning physicist Albert A. Michelson, whose collaborative Michelson-Morley experiment aimed at measuring "ether drift" sparked, by its negative result, Einstein's development of the theory of relativity.

24. Elliott Roosevelt, *Letters, 1928–1945,* p. 55.

25. *Ibid.,* p. 53. Roosevelt's implication that Shouse's acceptance of the party post involved great personal sacrifice is hardly borne out by the facts. Shouse's salary, paid by Raskob, was $50,000 a year from 1929 through 1932, in addition to which he was to share in the profits of a "business syndicate" formed by Raskob, presumably a stock pool of the kind later outlawed. In the event, the syndicate made no profit because of the stock-market crash, but Shouse could not have foreseen this when he made his "self-sacrificial" decision. See Elliot A. Rosen, *Hoover, Roosevelt and the Brains Trust* (New York, 1977), footnote 8, p. 387. And not irrelevant to an assessment of the deprivation Shouse suffered in consequence of his "unselfishness" is the fact that he had married an extremely wealthy heiress, the daughter of Boston's Lincoln Filene.

26. Letter, Herbert Lehman to FDR, April 30, 1939, Governor's Personal File, Franklin D. Roosevelt Library.

27. Elliott Roosevelt, *Letters, 1928–1945,* prints FDR's letter to Howe answering one (unavailable) from Howe to FDR. FDR says (May 8, 1929), "The boom for Herbert is all to the good—I agree with you" (p. 55). The book's editor explains the meaning of this in an editorial note.

28. The bulk of the City Trust Investigation Report is incorporated in that curious pastiche of official reports, memoranda, and (evidently) dictated personal commentary by Robert Moses, published by McGraw-Hill (also, in departure from current normal practice, copyrighted by the publisher instead of the author), in 1970, as a book by Robert Moses entitled *Public Works: A Dangerous Trade.* The "City Trust Investigation" constitutes Chapter 8 (pp. 639–683) of this strange work.

29. New York *Times,* July 14, 1929, reporting speech given July 13.

30. Address at State College of Agriculture, Cornell University, February 14, 1930, PPA, 1928–1932, p. 142.

31. New York *Times,* August 16, 1929. PPA, 1928–1932, pp. 477–489.

32. The specific adjusted price figures are from a list of thirteen stocks whose gain from March 3, 1928, to September 3, 1929, was worked out by or for Frederick Lewis Allen, who published it on p. 353 of *Only Yesterday* (paperback edition). The Standard Statistics Company figures are given on p. 28 of Broadus Mitchell, *Depression Decade: From New Era Through New Deal, 1929–1941* (paperback edition).

33. Eleanor Roosevelt, *This I Remember,* p. 59.

34. Personal interviews with Marion Dickerman, 1973 and 1974. Francis W. Hirst's writings exerted a considerable influence upon Walter Lippman who in his *The Good Society* (1937), which contains a cogent Brandeisian critique of such New Deal experiments in collectivism as the NRA (strangely enough, Lippmann does not mention Brandeis in this book), acknowledges a special debt to Hirst's *Liberty and Tyranny.* Eleanor Roosevelt and Helena Hirst became fast friends. In her Oral History Research Office transcript, Miss Dickerman tells how two years after this London meeting, when FDR was clearly established as front-runner for the Democratic presidential nomination, the Hirsts came to America, where Francis Hirst was scheduled to deliver a series of lectures at Harvard. Aboard ship, however, he fell seriously ill and had to be taken by ambulance to a New York City hospital when the ship docked. Eleanor then had Helena Hirst come stay at the Sixty-fifth Street house, which was "partially open," as Miss Dickerman says, "because of Eleanor's being there during her Todhunter teaching days each week." When Hirst was released from the hospital, he and his wife were invited by Herbert Hoover to stay in the White House during his convalescence. Both the Hirsts were "steeped in history," which added to their enjoyment of the White House, but Helena, despite her husband's position, "had no conception whatever of American politics," according to Miss Dickerman. When she said goodbye to the Hoovers, having thanked "Herbert" for "one of the great experiences of our lives," she added the hope that, "when we come back, if you're not here, the Franklin Roosevelts will be."

35. Marion Dickerman's Oral History Research Office transcript, augmented by personal interviews, 1973 and 1974. Lash, *op. cit.,* p. 333, speaking of toasts drunk in Luxembourg, quotes a letter from Eleanor to FDR in which she says she "joined in, in Evian water!"

36. The quote seems doubly a propos at this point because it is from an essay by John J. Ingalls, the Kansas Republican Senator of the Gilded Age, who also wrote that the "purification of politics is an iridescent dream" dreamt only by masculine females and feminine males. His vehemence stemmed from the threat to his political life and personal reputation (he as a politician was far from "pure") posed by a rising Populism. It was in a happier vein that he wrote: "Grass is the forgiveness of nature—her constant benediction. Fields trampeled with

battle, saturated with blood, torn with the ruts of cannon, grow green again with grass."

37. Eleanor Roosevelt, *This I Remember,* pp. 59–60.

38. Interviews with Marion Dickerman, 1973 and 1974. In her Oral History Research Office transcript she tells how she and Eleanor visited the cathedral "remembering well parts of Henry Adams' *Mont-Saint-Michel and Chartres* which we had read at Campo."

39. Marion Dickerman's Oral History Research Office transcript tells of this boat ride, which she described to me in interviews as a "religious experience." *"Immensi tremor oceani"* is inscribed on the collar of the Order of Saint Michael, which Louis XI created, as Henry Adams says on the first page of *Mont-Saint-Michel and Chartres.* Of Eleanor's feminism, her revolt against male domination, her letters to Marion Dickerman and Nancy Cook during these years (letters in Marion Dickerman's possession) provide abundant evidence.

40. Eleanor Roosevelt, *This I Remember,* p. 60.

41. Henry Adams, *The Education of Henry Adams,* pp. 390, 499 (Modern Library edition).

42. New York *Times Book Review,* September 29, 1929.

43. New York *Times,* September 1, 1929.

Five: The Coming on of the Great Depression

1. New York *Times,* October 12, 1929.

2. Accounts vary as to the precise size of Whitney's Steel bid. Newspaper and magazine accounts at the time generally say he bid for 25,000 shares, and so do most of the books that tell of the Crash—for example, Matthew Josephson's *The Money Lords* (New York, 1972) and Edward Robb Ellis' excellent *A Nation in Torment* (New York, 1970). But Frederick Lewis Allen in his carefully researched *Only Yesterday* (New York, 1931) gives the figure as 10,000, and this is the figure John Kenneth Galbraith uses in his *The Great Crash* (Boston, 1955). Charles A. Beard and Mary R. Beard, *America in Midpassage* (New York, 1939), p. 57, prudently refrain from giving a figure. It is certain that Whitney actually purchased only 200 shares of Steel, leaving the balance of his order with the Steel "specialist," that is, the Exchange member who executes such orders by other brokers. He did the same with the other bids. If the stock rose above the price bid before the purchase order (and Steel quickly rose above 205, closing at 206 for a net gain of 2 points for the day), the order itself, of course, remained unexecuted. How much of the pool's cash was actually spent was known only to Whitney and the pool members.

3. This was evidently a conducted chorus, as John Kenneth Galbraith points out in *The Great Crash,* p. 11. The bankers' consortium appears to have urged upon these

mightiest the importance of immediate firm reassuring statements to "restore confidence." Galbraith refers to a *Saturday Evening Post* article (December 28, 1929) by Garet Garrett reporting an effort to persuade President Hoover to make a statement *specifically* supporting the stock market, as President Coolidge had done when criticism of the amount of brokers' loans threatened to cause a market break. Hoover refused. On this Friday, a Boston investment trust prepared a large advertisement that appeared over the weekend in the *Wall Street Journal.* It said: "S-T-E-A-D-Y Everybody! Calm thinking is in order. Heed the words of America's greatest bankers."

4. New York *Times,* October 26, 1929.

5. Quoted, from a contemporary newspaper account, by Josephson, *op. cit.,* p. 103.

6. New York *Times,* October 30, 1929.

7. Herbert Hoover, *Memoirs: The Great Depression 1929–1941* (New York, 1952), p. 17, tells of sending for Richard Whitney soon after the 1929 inauguration to "urge that the Exchange itself curb the manipulation of stocks. I informed him that I had no desire to stretch the powers of the Federal government by legislation to regulate the Stock Exchange—that the authority rested only in the Governor of New York, Franklin D. Roosevelt." Hoover identifies Whitney as President of the Exchange, though in fact Whitney did not become Exchange head until 1930; in 1929 he was vice-president.

8. F. Scott Fitzgerald, *The Crack-Up,* edited by Edmund Wilson (New York, 1945), p. 21.

9. Prophets of the New Era of course tried hard to convince themselves and others that "fundamental" changes in the economic system had rendered the "business cycle" obsolete. In the immediate aftermath of the Crash, Samuel Crowther composed an article entitled "Why We Are Prosperous," which appeared in *Reader's Digest,* January 1930. "There are just two great dangers to the continuance of prosperity," wrote Crowther. "The first is the false idea that business is still governed by a cycle of boom and bust, and the second is that the leaders of business will think that the country is broke because some of their friends are."

10. Edmund Wilson, *The Shores of Light: A Literary Chronicle of the Twenties and Thirties* (New York, 1952), p. 498.

11. Though the high point for the stock market as a whole was reached on September 3, 1929, a good many issues climbed above their September 3 prices during the recovery that followed the September 5 break. " . . . indeed, on September 19th the averages as comprised by the New York *Times* reached an even higher level than that of September 3rd," writes Allen, *op. cit.,* p. 355.

12. Hoover, *Memoirs: The Great Depression,* p. 30. On p. 11 of this work Hoover tells how, as Secretary of Commerce, he had protested to both President Coolidge and Secretary Mellon against the credit-inflating decisions of the Federal Reserve Board

in 1927, urging them to "send for Crissinger [Daniel R. Crissinger, the thoroughly incompetent Harding-appointed governor of the Federal Reserve Board] and express alarm at the situation," as Hoover himself had done to no effect. Coolidge declined. So did Mellon, who "seemed to think my anxiety was alarmist and my interference unwarranted." The quotations about the conferences that I use are from *Ibid.*, pp. 42, 43.

13. In *The Great Crash,* Galbraith has a great deal of fun describing what he calls the "no-business meeting"—the meeting called to give the impression something is being done when in fact nothing is. He places the Hoover economic conferences of late 1929 in the "no-business" category. Though amusing, this is not, I think, an accurate historical judgment. Actually, the Hoover conferences of November were remarkably productive of effective decisions, even amazingly so, given the circumstances and involved personnel.

14. "The vigorous measures undertaken by the Government to combat the downward tendency in business have also interjected an element of uncertainty. . . . Never before have public agencies interceded in such a direct and intensive way to alter the course of business, and the results [are] unpredictable." So said the management of the Guaranty Trust Company of New York in *Commercial and Financial Chronicle,* vol. XXX, no. 3367, January 4, 1930, p. 21. Quoted in Broadus Mitchell, *Depression Decade* (New York, 1947), p. 32.

15. The quoted statements in this paragraph are, in order, from the New York *Times,* November 1, 1929; New York *Times,* November 22, 1929; New York *Times,* December 11, 1929; Schlesinger, *op. cit.,* p. 163 (also Robert Goldston, *The Great Depression* [Indianapolis, 1968], p. 45, paperback edition, among other books); Mitchell, *op. cit.,* p. 31. Mitchell is quoting aforementioned issue of *Commercial and Financial Chronicle.*

16. New York *Times,* November 1, 1929. William Starr Myers, ed., *The State Papers and Other Public Writings of Herbert Hoover,* vol. 1 (New York, 1934), pp. 145, 146.

17. *Ibid.,* p. 289.

18. Ellis, *op. cit.,* p. 127.

19. Perkins, *op. cit.,* p. 94.

20. *Ibid.,* p. 95.

21. *Ibid.,* p. 94.

22. *Ibid.,* pp. 95–96.

23. Elliott Roosevelt, *Letters, 1928–1945,* p. 92.

24. Telegram, FDR to Victor Watson, New York *American,* October 24, 1929, Box 127, Private Correspondence of FDR, 1928–1932, Franklin D. Roosevelt Library.

Quoted in Freidel, *Roosevelt: The Triumph,* pp. 96–97; cited in Bellush, *op. cit.,* p. 127.

25. William Starr Myers and Walter H. Newton, *The Hoover Administration,* p. 29.

26. New York *Times,* December 10, 1929. Quoted in Freidel, *Roosevelt: The Triumph,* pp. 96–97.

27. PPA, 1928–1932, p. 87.

28. Norman Thomas, "The Banks of New York," *Nation,* February 11, 1932.

29. Perkins, *op. cit.,* p. 97.

30. Interviews with Marion Dickerman, 1973. Perkins, *op. cit.,* p. 94.

31. New York *Times,* March 30, 1930.

32. PPA, 1928–1932, pp. 447–449. It is hard to believe that one portion of this statement was not concocted tongue-in-cheek. "I count on the industrialists of this State to strive to overcome recurring unemployment in their industries with the same good will as they overcame so many adverse conditions, such as industrial accidents, industrial diseases, child labor, long hours, etc.," said Roosevelt, who knew well that New York's kind-hearted broad-minded industrialists had fought tooth and nail against every effort to shorten hours, abolish child labor, and compensate employees for industrial accidents when measures to do so were proposed in the legislature.

Six: Triumphant Balancing Act, on a Tightrope in a Rising Wind

1. New York *Times,* March 6, 1930. According to Rosen, *op. cit.,* pp. 27–29, who derives his conclusions from a study of the Raskob Papers, Eleutherian Mills Historical Library, Greenville, Del. (he cites correspondence between Irenée Du Pont and Raskob), Raskob's 1928 alliance with Al Smith and subsequent takeover of national Democratic Party machinery "stemmed basically from the thinking of Pierre S. du Pont, president of E. I. du Pont de Nemours & Co., who determined during World War I to wage a fight against Woodrow Wilson's decision to levy heavy taxes on corporations and incomes. Du Pont opposed taxation of the productive sector of the American economy and preferred that the burden of taxation should be borne by the lower classes, not by those who created the jobs. Sometime in the ensuing decade . . . , Pierre du Pont decided, as did John J. Raskob, a key executive in the Du Pont company, Christiana Securities, and General Motors, that the solution lay in the legalization of beer. When, in November 1927, Voluntary Committee No. 28 of the Association against the Prohibition Amendment (AAPA) maintained in a report that a tax on beer, dependent on Prohibition repeal, would yield $1.3 billion, permitting a 50 percent reduction in income and corporation taxes, Raskob and the Du Ponts arrived at two major decisions. They financed the AAPA with a half million dollars annually beginning in 1927 in order to bring about Prohibition repeal. Then, they captured control of the bankrupt Democratic party,

which had been thrashed in 1924, and envisaged it as a conservative instrument in national affairs." Pierre and Irenée Du Pont and Raskob were among seventy "extraordinarily wealthy and powerful members of the business community" who by 1928 had been "recruited for membership on the Board of Directors of the AAPA." Al Smith, after his 1928 nomination, "agreed . . . with Raskob and Irenée Du Pont that our society required a reduction of government interference in big business." As interpreted by Raskob to Irenée Du Pont, "this meant . . . high tariffs and reduction of Interstate Commerce controls over the management and operation of railroads. The only difference between the two major parties, Raskob concluded, was the wet and dry question." Thus the "Prohibition issue functioned as a smoke-screen . . . for an economic program that advocated," among other things, "the empowering of the Federal Trade Commission to grant immunity from antitrust prosecution in cases where it was decided that a given combination or merger was not inimical to the public interest," and "a liberalization of regulatory legislation to allow trade practices aimed at elimination of destructive competition." The Raskob–Du Pont program also called for the "private operation of public utilities under 'fair' (minimal) public regulation and the leasing to private industry ('not public operation') of Muscle Shoals." Al Smith could not publicly have supported the latter proposal without reversing completely his earlier, highly popular stand for public ownership of hydroelectric sites, and Rosen cites no evidence that he, Smith, ever accepted the specific Raskob program items in private agreements with Raskob. See also George Wolfskill, *The Revolt of the Conservatives: A History of the American Liberty League, 1934–1940* (Boston, 1962). Wolfskill cites the *Annual Reports of the President of the Association Against the Prohibition Amendment* in support of his contention that big business did indeed deliberately make use of the Prohibition issue as a smokescreen for its program to reduce corporate and personal income taxes and to reduce or eliminate governmental regulations imposed on big-business activities.

2. New York *Times,* April 27, 1930.

3. *Ibid.* Elliott Roosevelt, *Letters, 1928–1945,* p. 130, evidently quoting a Wheeler statement given reporters after the meeting, has Wheeler saying that "if the Democratic Party of New York will reelect Franklin Roosevelt Governor, the West will demand his nomination for President and the whole country will elect him."

4. "Many of these editorials cry down the thought that the power question will become a leading national issue, and yet in crying it down they give the impression that their one fear is that it will become a great national issue," wrote Roosevelt to Wheeler, June 3, 1930. Elliot Roosevelt, *Letters, 1928–1945, op. cit.,* p. 129.

5. Lash, when selecting the personal FDR letters for the volume nominally edited by Elliott Roosevelt, included the letter to Nancy Cook but omitted the one to Nicholas Roosevelt. The latter, dated May 19, 1930, is in the Governor's Personal File, Franklin D. Roosevelt Library. The former is on pp. 121–122 of Elliott Roosevelt, *Letters, 1928–1945.*

6. Elliott Roosevelt, *Letters, 1928–1945,* p. 129.

7. Chicago *Journal of Commerce,* May 10, 1931. Quoted in Bellush, *op. cit.,* p. 229.

8. New York *Times,* July 1, 1930.

9. New York *Times,* July 1, 6, 1930. Perkins, *op. cit.,* p. 107. Two weeks after the Governors' Conference, Perkins herself, in a memorandum to FDR dated July 15, 1930, recommended that he "go cautiously when talking about unemployment insurance by that name. Unemployment reserves is safer and more educative for the present." The memo-letter is in Box 37, Private Correspondence of FDR, 1928–32, Franklin D. Roosevelt Library.

10. PPG, 1930, pp. 171–172. Lindley, *Franklin D. Roosevelt,* pp. 265–266. Freidel, *Roosevelt: The Triumph,* pp. 129–130.

11. Elliott Roosevelt, *Letters, 1928–1945,* p. 136.

12. Lindley, *Franklin D. Roosevelt,* pp. 266–267. Herbert Mitgang, *The Man Who Rode the Tiger: The Life of Judge Samuel Seabury* (Philadelphia, 1963), p. 212. Bellush, *op. cit.,* p. 155.

13. Quoted in Lindley, *Franklin D. Roosevelt,* p. 268.

14. Elliott Roosevelt, *Letters, 1928–1945,* p. 136.

15. Lindley, *Franklin D. Roosevelt,* pp. 269–270.

16. Mitgang, *op. cit.,* p. 173.

17. Lindley, *Franklin D. Roosevelt,* p. 272.

18. PPA, 1928–1932, pp. 320–321.

19. New York *Times,* September 27, 1930. Lindley, *Franklin D. Roosevelt,* p. 276. Bellush, *op. cit.,* p. 158.

20. New York *World,* September 18, 1930. Bellush, *op. cit.,* pp. 159–160.

21. New York *Times,* September 21, 1930. Freidel, *Roosevelt: The Triumph,* p. 150.

22. Rosenman, *op. cit.,* p. 42. PPG, 1930, p. 792.

23. Freidel, *Roosevelt: The Triumph,* pp. 161–162.

24. Letter, FDR to James A. Walker, September 27, 1930, Governor's Official File, Franklin D. Roosevelt Library. Lindley, *Franklin D. Roosevelt,* p. 277.

25. Lindley, *Franklin D. Roosevelt,* p. 277.

26. Roosevelt's defenders, of course, denied, with great emphasis, that the "official act" limitation was designed to present a loophole for Tammanyites when they again went before the grand jury with offers to sign immunity waivers, but the governor's reiterated stress on the crucial phrase makes the denial unconvincing. Roosevelt was certainly anxious to prevent, if he could, any such general "fishing expedition" as Todd was eager to conduct, which the unlimited immunity waiver would have facilitated.

27. New York *Times,* May 2, 1930; San Francisco *Chronicle,* May 31, 1930, as quoted in W. A. Swanberg, *Dreiser* (paperback edition, New York, 1967), p. 437. Letter, C. H. McCarthy to FDR, July 31, 1931, as quoted in Bellush, *op. cit.,* p. 130. New York *Times,* August 21, 22, 1930, and Ellis, *op. cit.,* p. 141.

28. Elliott Roosevelt, *Letters, 1928–1945,* pp. 119–120.

29. Letter, W. Russell Bowie to FDR, October 4, 1930, Governor's Personal File, Franklin D. Roosevelt Library. Freidel, *Roosevelt: The Triumph,* p. 153.

30. Elliott Roosevelt, *Letters, 1928–1945,* pp. 146–148.

31. James A. Farley, *Behind the Ballots: The Personal History of a Politician* (New York, 1938), p. 53.

32. New York *Times,* October 1, 1930. Lindley, *Franklin D. Roosevelt,* p. 278.

33. PPA, 1928–1933, pp. 399–404.

34. Kansas City *Star,* October 8, 1930. Freidel, *Roosevelt: The Triumph,* p. 157. Alfred B. Rollins, Jr., *Roosevelt and Howe,* (New York, 1962), p. 292.

35. Rollins, *op. cit.,* p. 287. Molly W. Dewson Scrapbook, "Politics, 1932–1933," Mary W. Dewson Papers, Franklin D. Roosevelt Library.

36. New York *Herald Tribune,* October 1, 1930.

37. New York *Times,* October 19, 1930. Lindley, *Franklin D. Roosevelt,* pp. 35–36.

38. New York *Times,* October 19, 1930. Bellush, *op. cit.,* p. 164–165. PPA, 1928–1932, pp. 408, 411, 417, 419, 426.

39. PPG, 1930, p. 755.

40. PPA, 1928–1932, pp. 432–444.

41. Farley, *op. cit.,* p. 63. New York *Times,* November 3, 1930. Elliott Roosevelt, *Letters, 1928–1945,* p. 152.

42. New York *Times,* November 5, 6, 1930.

Seven: The Governor as Presidential Candidate

1. Lash, *op. cit.,* p. 336. Eleanor's attitude (or attitudes, for they were curiously mingled) toward Missy comes clear, or as clear as may be, in her personal correspondence with Nancy Cook and Marion Dickerman. For instance, when Eleanor visited her husband at Warm Springs in April 1926, she expressed to Marion, as she had before, her dislike of rural Georgia—its slovenliness, laziness, incompetence, and poverty (not to mention, as she often did, the viciousness of the white Southerner's attitude toward the Negro)—and her disapproval of her husband's decision to buy the Warm Springs resort. "Missy . . . is keen about everything here of course!" she added, acidly. Lash, in *op. cit.,* p. 510, says that, though "hurt by Missy's role" in her husband's life, "she was sorry for Missy, for Missy, too, was a victim of this fascinating man's concentration upon himself and his objectives."

2. Rosenman, *op. cit.,* p. 48.

3. *Ibid.*

4. Interview with Louis A. Depew, Sara Roosevelt's chauffeur, quoted in John Gunther, *Roosevelt in Retrospect* (New York, 1950), p. 229.

5. Lash, *op. cit.,* p. 341, derived his information from an interview with Earl Miller and a letter from Eleanor Roosevelt to Maude Gray, July 12, 1930.

6. New York *Times,* November 6, 1930.

7. Farley, *op. cit.,* p. 62.

8. Rosenman, *op. cit.,* p. 48.

9. New York *Times,* November 6, 1930.

10. Elliott Roosevelt, *Letters, 1928–1945,* pp. 161–162.

11. Flynn, *op. cit.,* p. 82. Flynn has Roosevelt going on to say, in addition to the words I quote, "on the Democratic ticket," as if there were any chance of his nomination on the Republican one.

12. Letter, FDR to Hugh Gibson, January 2, 1920, Roosevelt Papers, Franklin D. Roosevelt Library.

13. Louis B. Wehle, *Hidden Threads of History: Wilson Through Roosevelt* (New York, 1953), pp. 81–82.

14. Flynn, *op. cit.,* p. 84.

15. *Ibid.*

16. Farley, *op. cit.*, p. 69. James A. Farley, with Walter Trohan, *Jim Farley's Story* (New York, 1948), p. 7. Letter, Farley to FDR, November 29, 1930; quoted in Freidel, *Roosevelt: The Triumph*, p. 174. Elliott Roosevelt, *Letters, 1928–1945*, p. 153.

17. Farley, *Behind the Ballots*, pp. 69–70. Rollins, *op. cit.*, p. 312.

18. Charles Michelson, *The Ghost Talks* (New York, 1944), p. 137.

19. Isabella Selmes and Eleanor met in 1902, when Isabella was only sixteen but already a famous beauty. She was the sensation of New York Society in the year of her "coming out," married Eleanor's close friend Bob Ferguson (he was eighteen years her senior), moved to the Southwest, where Ferguson died of tuberculosis years later, then married John C. Greenway. Eleanor's *This Is My Story* portrays Isabella as perhaps the closest of the friends she made in the early 1900s and retained through later years.

20. Elliott Roosevelt, *Letters, 1928–1945*, pp. 180–181.

21. *Ibid.*, p. 179.

22. New York *Times,* March 3, 4, 1930.

23. Farley, *Behind the Ballots op. cit.*, p. 76.

24. Cordell Hull, *Memoirs* (New York, 1948), vol. I, p. 145.

25. Elliott Roosevelt, *Letters, 1928–1945*, pp. 181–182.

26. Franklin K. Lane, *Letters* (Boston, 1922), p. 267. See Louis W. Koenig, *The Invisible Presidency* (New York, 1960), pp. 190–191; Harvey Wish, *Contemporary America* (New York, 1955), pp. 158–159; and Schlesinger, *op. cit.*, p. 33.

27. Letter, FDR to Colonel Edward M. House, October 8, 1928. Quoted in Rosen, *op. cit.*, p. 16.

28. Elliott Roosevelt, *Letters, 1928–1945*, p. 201.

29. *Ibid.*

30. New York *Times,* March 30, 31, April 18, 1931.

31. Letter, Eleanor Roosevelt to FDR, May 9, 1931. Quoted in Freidel, *Roosevelt: The Triumph*, p. 216, and Lash, *op. cit.*, p. 345. Eleanor Roosevelt, *This I Remember*, p. 64.

32. Charles G. Dawes, *Journal as Ambassador to Great Britain* (New York, 1939), pp. 346–347. New York *Times,* May 28, 1931. "Elliott accompanied father on that trip and of course met a lady and enjoyed a shipboard romance," writes James Roose-

velt, *My Parents: A Differing View* (Chicago, 1976), p. 227. "Father teased him unmercifully. Finally, one night, father assigned him to dance with Rosa Ponselle, the ponderous opera star, who nearly broke Elliott's back when the ship lurched and she fell on him."

33. Rosen, *op. cit.,* pp. 20–21, gives a detailed account of this meeting, quoting Robert Jackson diary, June 11, 1931. A copy of the diary is in Rosen's possession.

34. New York *Times,* June 13, 1931

35. Letter, E. M. House to Robert Woolley, June 14, 1931. Quoted in Freidel, *Roosevelt: The Triumph,* p. 203.

36. New York *Times,* June 14, 1931.

37. New York *Times,* June 17, 1931.

38. Farley, *Behind the Ballots,* p. 81.

39. *Ibid.*

40. Freidel, *Roosevelt: The Triumph,* p. 207.

41. Farley, *Behind the Ballots,* p. 87.

42. Letter, McAdoo to House, January 10, 1931. Quoted in Rosen, *op. cit.,* p. 17.

43. Elliott Roosevelt, *Letters, 1928–1945,* pp. 210–212.

44. Earle Looker, "Is Franklin Roosevelt Physically Fit to Be President?" *Liberty,* July 25, 1931. Letter, Farley to Roosevelt, July 17, 1931, quoted in Freidel, *Roosevelt: The Triumph,* p. 211.

Eight: The Presidential Candidate as Governor

1. Hoover, in his *Memoirs,* vol. 3, p. 195, makes self-revealing comment on this: "Some Oregon or Washington apple growers' associations shrewdly appraised the sympathy of the public for the unemployed. They set up a system of selling apples on the street corners in many cities, thus selling their crop and raising their prices. *Many persons left their jobs for the more profitable one of selling apples* [present author's italics]. When any left winger wishes to indulge in scathing oratory [directed toward 'the eternal damnation of Hoover'], he demands, 'Do you want to return to selling apples?' "

2. Charles Michelson frankly expresses his loathing of Hoover personally in *The Ghost Talks.*

3. PPA, 1928–1945, pp. 451–452.

4. Freidel, *Roosevelt: The Triumph*, p. 196, quoting a penciled note, January 23, 1931, in Governor's Official File, Franklin D. Roosevelt Library.

5. Tacitly assumed by the special banking commission was that "higher morality" on the part of bankers that Roosevelt himself then assumed. The commission's major premise, whence derived its conclusion against any regulation of banking practice, was the familiar contention of political conservatives that "morality" cannot be "legislated." Governmental supervision could not transform a dishonest man into an honest one nor an insolvent institution into a solvent one; the public could protect itself by dealing with bankers who possessed "character, integrity and ability." (Unacknowledged was the fact that a "dishonest" man is inclined toward honest behavior in proportion as he is convinced that otherwise he will suffer grievous penalties [losses], whereas an "honest" man may be tempted toward dishonesty by the knowledge that its risks are virtually nil while its profits are enormous. Actually, of course, "morality," as the special commission implicitly defined it, was "legislated" when murder, rape, and robbery were legally defined as crimes.)

6. *Annual Report of Superintendent of Banks*, State of New York, part I, December 31, 1930, p. 46. John T. Flynn, "The Bank of United States," *New Republic*, vol. 65, pp. 288–291, January 28, 1931. Ellis, *op. cit.*, pp. 108–110. Milton Friedman and Anna Jacobson Schwartz, *A Monetary History of the United States, 1867–1960* (Princeton, N.J., 1963), pp. 309–311. The merger negotiations were initially stalled upon an exorbitant price set by Marcus and Singer on Bank of United States assets. But this price was soon lowered, and George L. Harrison, governor of the New York Federal Reserve Bank, worked out a plan for merging the Bank of United States with Manufacturers Trust, Public National, and International Trust, with Clearing House banks subscribing $30,000,000 in new capital funds to the new institution. All major parties had agreed to this reorganization plan and the Federal Reserve Bank had actually issued a statement in which the directors of the merged institution were named when, on December 8, the Clearing House banks refused to put up the $30,000,000, despite almost tearful pleas by Broderick. The banking superintendent was convinced the big bankers cold-bloodedly decided to let Bank of United States collapse because those hurt would be, for the most part, merely "little people." He reminded them "that only two weeks before they had rescued two of the largest private bankers of the city and had willingly put up the money needed," according to the testimony presented by him at his trial in the spring of 1932.

7. Freidel, *Roosevelt: The Triumph*, p. 190, quoting telegram from FDR to Norman Thomas, January 5, 1931, Governor's Official File, Franklin D. Roosevelt Library.

8. PPA, 1928–1932, p. 537.

9. Mitgang, *op. cit.*, p. 176.

10. *Ibid.*, p. 185.

11. *Ibid.*

12. Elliott Roosevelt, *Letters, 1928–1945*, pp. 162–163.

13. PPA, 1928–1932, p. 96.

14. Norman Thomas, "The Banks of New York," *Nation,* February 11, 1931.

15. Mitgang, *op. cit.,* pp. 198–199.

16. *Ibid.* Kresel was subsequently indicted and tried for perjury allegedly committed during the trial of Marcus and Singer, who were found guilty of numerous criminal offenses in their conduct of the affairs of the Bank of United States and sentenced to the penitentiary. Kresel's defense lawyer was John W. Davis, the 1924 Democratic candidate for president, whose successful labors (Kresel was found not guilty after years of court battle) are told of in some detail in William H. Harbaugh, *Lawyer's Lawyer: The Life of John W. Davis* (New York, 1973), pp. 303–313.

17. New York *Times,* February 28, March 1, 3, 4, 31, 1931. Mitgang, *op. cit.,* pp. 204–205.

18. FDR's letter is quoted in full in Mitgang, *op. cit.,* p. 206.

19. Mitgang, *op. cit.,* p. 176, quoting Moley, who was interviewed by Mitgang.

20. Quoted in Mitgang, *op. cit.,* p. 215.

21. Commissioner Seabury's report to the governor, August 31, 1931. Quoted in Mitgang, *op. cit.,* p. 214.

22. Lindley, *Franklin D. Roosevelt,* p. 297. Fowler, *op. cit.,* p. 218. New York *Times,* March 19, 1931. Bellush, *op. cit.,* p. 271.

23. PPG, 1931, pp. 455–484. Bellush, *op cit.,* p. 271. New York *Times,* April 28, May 1, 1931. Elliott Roosevelt, *Letters, 1928–1945,* pp. 186–187.

24. Mitgang, *op. cit.,* pp. 226–227.

25. New York *Times* editorial, August 26, 1931. Quoted in Mitgang, *op. cit.,* pp. 227–228.

26. *The Guaranty Survey,* December 28, 1931. S. S. Huebner, "Economic and Business Conditions," in *American Year Book: Record of the Year 1931,* pp. 306–309. William F. Notz, "Control of Production," *American Year Book: 1931,* p. 332.

27. Lloyd M. Short, "Federal Administrative Commissions," p. 17, and Arthur M. Hyde, "Conditions of Agriculture," *American Year Book, 1931,* pp. 395–397.

28. Bellush, *op. cit.,* p. 131, citing David M. Schneider and Albert Deutsch, *History of Public Welfare in New York State, 1867 to 1940* (Chicago, 1941), p. 295.

29. PPA, 1928–1932, p. 461.

30. Rosenman, *op. cit.,* p. 50.

31. PPA, 1928–1932, pp. 461–466.

32. Rosenman, *op. cit.,* p. 51.

33. Freidel, *Roosevelt: The Triumph,* p. 220, quotes a letter FDR wrote at this time (September 2, 1931) to Lewis A. Lincoln: "I can tell you frankly that I am disturbed by this morning's news that the President's policy seems to be to borrow money, over one billion dollars, to pay the current treasury deficit because this merely puts the burden of this unemployment cycle on future generations."

34. Statement by Jacob A. Goldberg, secretary of the Tuberculosis and Health Association, quoted in Robert E. Sherwood, *Roosevelt and Hopkins,* p. 29 of paperback edition.

35. PPA, 1928–1932, p. 471.

36. "No man has accomplished more in the office he occupies than Franklin D. Roosevelt," said Al Smith in his speech nominating Roosevelt for reelection in September 1930. "He has a clear brain and a big heart. For his humanity, the love and devotion he has shown the poor, the sick and the afflicted, Almighty God has showered down on his head the choicest graces and His choicest blessings."

37. PPA, 1928–1932, p. 471.

38. New York *Times,* October 15, 1931. Elliott Roosevelt, *Letters, 1928–1945,* p. 228.

39. Flynn, *op. cit.,* p. 86. Josephson and Josephson, *op. cit.,* p. 420.

40. New York *Times,* October 17, 1931.

41. Elliott Roosevelt, *Letters, 1928–1945,* p. 229.

42. New York *Times,* November 13, 1931. Quoted in Freidel, *Roosevelt: The Triumph,* p. 236.

43. Letter, Robert Woolley to FDR, September 18, 1931; cited in Rosen, *op. cit.,* pp. 23–24. Letter, Howe to Shouse, November 19, 1931; cited in Freidel, *Roosevelt: The Triumph,* p. 238.

44. New York *Times,* November 18, 1931.

45. Elliott Roosevelt, *Letters, 1928–1945,* pp. 229–232.

46. *Ibid.,* p. 240.

47. *Ibid.,* p. 244.

Nine: A "Brains Trust" Is Formed

1. Elliott Roosevelt, *Letters, 1928–1945*, p. 239.

2. Walter Lippmann, *Interpretations, 1931–1932* (New York, 1932), pp. 257–259.

3. Mitgang, *op. cit.*, p. 240. The clubhouse was a notorious gambling den.

4. Raymond Moley, *After Seven Years* (New York, 1939), p. 2.

5. New York *Times*, January 10, 1932.

6. Elliott Roosevelt, *Letters, 1928–1945*, p. 252.

7. PPA, 1928–1932, pp. 112, 124. It is interesting to compare Roosevelt's remarks on the loss of "liberty" through "specialization" with what Ortega y Gasset has to say about the modern "specialist" as a new species of "barbarian," who, as the type of "mass-man," threatens not only personal liberty but civilization itself. See chapter 12 of *The Revolt of the Masses* (New York, 1932), entitled "The Barbarism of 'Specialisation.' "

8. Lippmann, *op. cit.*, pp. 260–262.

9. Elliott Roosevelt, *Letters, 1928–1945*, p. 254.

10. Freidel, *Roosevelt: The Triumph*, p. 250. Chicago *Herald-American*, January 17, 1932.

11. PPA, 1928–1932, p. 623.

12. New York *Times*, January 27, 1932; *Literary Digest*, February 6, 1932, p. 8; Rosen, *op. cit.*, p. 99. By this time, Baker's candidacy was being covertly but strongly promoted by Walter Lippmann and by several major newspapers, including the Cincinnati *Enquirer*, the Richmond *News-Leader*, the Des Moines *Register-Tribune*, and the Cleveland *Plain-Dealer*. The last, on December 3, 1931, which was Baker's sixtieth birthday, devoted much of its editorial space to Baker. Among the sobriquets suggested for him by *Plain-Dealer* correspondents was "New Deal" Baker, Diehl being Baker's middle name. See C. H. Cramer, *Newton D. Baker* (Cleveland, 1961), p. 236.

13. Freidel, *Roosevelt: The Triumph*, p. 250, citing, indirectly, Chicago *Herald-Examiner*, January 17, 1932

14. New York *Times*, February 4, 1932. PPA, 1928–1932, pp. 155–157. The latter is an excerpt from the speech whose subject is described as "Revival of world trade—Reciprocal trade agreements." It does *not* include the portion repudiating FDR's former stand on the League of Nations.

15. Heywood Broun's most famous use of the "corkscrew" phrase was in a column published July 1, 1932, wherein he described FDR as "the corkscrew candidate of a convoluting convention." Elmer Davis' comment was in his "The Collapse of Politics," *Harper's Magazine,* September 1932.

16. Lash, *op. cit.,* pp. 346–347. Interviews with Marion Dickerman, 1973–1974. Letter, FDR to Robert Woolley, February 25, 1932; cited in Rosen, *op. cit.,* p. 110.

17. New York *Times,* February 9, 1932. Quoted in Warner and Daniel, *op. cit.,* p. 252.

18. Letter, FDR to J. Russell Bowie, February 15, 1932; quoted in Freidel, *op. cit.,* pp. 257–258. Mitgang, *op. cit.,* pp. 240–241.

19. PPA, 1928–1932, pp. 582–583.

20. Mitgang, *op. cit.,* p. 236.

21. PPG, 1932, pp. 290–293.

22. Bellush, *op. cit.,* p. 118. Elliott Roosevelt, *Letters, 1928–1945,* p. 279.

23. New York *Times,* April 30, 1932. Bellush, *op. cit.,* p. 119.

24. Moley, *op. cit.,* p. 7.

25. Rosenman, *op. cit.,* pp. 56–59. Moley, *op. cit.,* pp. 5–9, asserts that Rosenman claims too much credit for the arrangement—or was assigned too much in press interviews quoting Rosenman (*Working With Roosevelt* was published in 1952, thirteen years after Moley's book)—but I find Rosenman's circumstantial account convincing.

26. Moley, *op. cit.,* p. 9. Rosenman, *op. cit.,* pp. 58–59.

27. Joseph Dorfman, *The Economic Mind in American Civilization,* vol. 5 (New York, 1959), pp. 502–515. Daniel M. Fox, *The Discovery of Abundance: Simon N. Patten and the Transformation of Social Theory* (Ithaca, N. Y., 1967), pp. 82–88. Bernard Sternsher, *Rexford Tugwell and the New Deal* (New Brunswick, N.J., 1964), pp. 4–5. Simon N. Patten, *Essays in Economic Theory* (New York, 1924), edited by Rexford G. Tugwell.

28. Sternsher, *op. cit.,* pp. 6–10. Tugwell's friends and associates Wesley C. Mitchell and William F. Ogburn (the latter left Columbia to go the University of Chicago in 1927) were leading members of the Research Committee on Social Trends appointed by President Hoover soon after his inauguration in 1929. The committee's 1600-page two-volume report, *Recent Social Trends in the United States,* published in 1933, had a major impact on socioeconomic thinking in America during the Depression decade and some influence on governmental policy.

29. "Committee Report" (1931), in *Establishment of a National Economic Council: Hearings Before a Subcommittee of the Senate Committee on Manufacturers,* 72nd Congress, first session, p. 194. Quoted in Dorfman, *op. cit.,* p. 633. Hoover, who as Commerce Secretary had promoted the trade association idea, reacted with horror to the Swope Plan. It was "thoroughly unconstitutional," would lead to "gigantic trusts such as we have never dreamed of in the history of the world," and amounted to an attempt to "smuggle fascism into America through the back door," as he wrote to Solicitor General Thomas Thacher. He was no less horrified by the Harriman proposal and successfully opposed Harriman's effort to revise (abrogate) the Sherman and Clayton Acts. See David Burner, *Herbert Hoover* (New York, 1978), p. 234.

30. R. G. Tugwell, "The Principle of Planning and the Institution of Laissez-Faire," *American Economic Review,* supplement, March 1932.

31. Widely quoted, generally sneeringly, in the anti–New Deal press of the 1930s, the verse is in Sternsher, *op. cit.,* p. 5.

32. Rexford G. Tugwell, *The Democratic Roosevelt* (Garden City, N.Y., 1957), p. 213.

33. PPA, 1928–1932, pp. 624–627.

34. Moley, *op. cit.,* pp. 10–11.

35. New York *Times,* April 14, 1932. "This is no time for demagogues," said Smith. "At a time like this, when millions men and women and children are starving throughout the land, there is always the temptation to some men to stir up class prejudice. . . . Against that effort I set myself uncompromisingly. I protest against the endeavor to delude the poor people of this country to their ruin by trying to make them believe that they can get employment before the people who would normally employ them are also again restored to conditions of normal prosperity. A factory worker cannot get his job back until business conditions enable the factory owner to open up again, and to promise the great masses of working people that they can secure renewed employment by class legislation is treachery to those working people, to the principles of the Democratic party, and to the United States itself."

36. R. G. Tugwell, *The Brains Trust* (New York, 1968), p. 50.

37. PPA, 1928–1932, p. 632. Tugwell, *The Brains Trust,* p. 48.

38. Lippmann, *op. cit.,* pp. 275–276. There was an aftermath to this speech that was acutely embarrassing to Moley. He had used verbatim three sentences from a memorandum written by Lindsay Rogers about the effects of the Hawley-Smoot Tariff. He had phoned Rogers from St. Paul to read to Rogers that portion of the speech dealing with tariff problems and ask for Rogers' comment or criticism. Rogers made none. But Rogers had given a copy of this same memorandum to Al Smith, who had used in his Jefferson Day speech in Washington precisely the same three sentences that Roosevelt used in St. Paul. On April 22, the New York *Post*

printed the St. Paul and Washington speech excerpts side by side under the heading "A Deadly Parallel." Moley was in agony over the furor that followed. He assumed that Roosevelt was squirming with embarrassment as he, Moley, would have done had he been caught plagiarizing; he expected Roosevelt to dismiss him from the campaign entourage. Actually, Roosevelt did not even ask for an explanation and, when Moley volunteered one, listened impassively, "smiled ruefully, and said he supposed we'd better put the incident out of our minds." Moley thought this a manifestation of "one of the loveliest facets of Roosevelt's character: he stood by his people when they got into a jam." It may also have manifest a value-priority system radically different from Moley's, or any intellectual's: Roosevelt placed no such value on ideas and originality of idea as Moley did—was, indeed, inclined to regard writers and their productions on his behalf as tools of only somewhat higher order than a typewriter and a typist. See Moley, *op. cit.,* pp. 16–17.

39. Moley, *op. cit.,* p. 18. My view of Berle has been influenced by that of Berle's longtime friend and neighbor in Stockbridge, Mass., the Reverend Douglas Krumb-haar, who is now a friend and neighbor of mind in Princeton, Mass.

40. Beatrice Bishop Berle and Travis Beal Jacobs, eds., *Navigating the Rapids, 1918–1971: From the Papers of Adolf A. Berle* (New York, 1973), p. 4.

41. *Ibid.*

42. *Ibid.,* p. 14. Letter, Berle to John Bassett Moore, July 27, 1932.

43. *Ibid.,* p. 11.

44. The law firm had as one of its clients the South Puerto Rico Sugar Company, which had a subsidiary in the Dominican Republic, and it was Ralph Rounds, a senior partner of the firm, who had asked the War Department to place Berle on "inactive duty" so that he could clear land titles in the Dominican Republic in early 1918.

45. Shortly after *The Modern Corporation and Private Property* was published, efforts were made by big business to suppress it. Berle tells the story in a diary entry for June 27, 1947, which appears on pp. 21–22 of *Navigating the Rapids*. The original publisher was the Corporation Clearing House, a law-book publishing firm whose stock was owned by the Corporation Trust Company. Shortly after publication day, writes Berle, "a representative of the Corporation Clearing House called on me to say that they thought they could not handle the book properly and wished to transfer the contract to some other publishing company and arrangements were finally made to transfer the contract to Macmillan." What had happened, Berle learned in 1947 from a Mr. Darr, who had handled the book for the Corporation Clearing House, was that "one of the large corporation clients of the Corporation Trust Company (Darr believes the General Motors Corporation) read a review of the book and then called on the Corporation Trust Company, explaining that in the view of that corporation no such book ought to be published. The Corporation Trust Company agreed that they would require CCH to drop it at once. This CCH did. . . . It would be interesting to know whether a corporation of that size and standing

would do the same thing in 1947." In this connection it is "interesting" to recall General Motors' response to Ralph Nader's *Unsafe at any Speed* decades later: the corporation hired detectives to find or manufacture "dirt" about Nader, making a special effort to "smear" him as a homosexual.

46. Berle and Jacobs, *op. cit.,* p. 45.

47. Adolf A. Berle, Jr., and Gardiner C. Means, *The Modern Corporation and Private Property* (New York, 1932), p. 277.

48. Berle and Jacobs, pp. 45–46.

49. Max Ascoli, "Introduction" to *Navigating the Rapids,* p. xix.

50. Berle and Means, *op. cit.,* p. 356.

51. Berle and Jacobs, *op. cit.,* p. 356. Berle's view of the modern corporation as no longer "private" was in some degree anticipated and influenced by John Maynard Keynes' "The End of Laissez-Faire," in *Essays in Persuasion,* published by Keynes in 1926. On pp. 314–315 of this book, Keynes said that business corporations "when they have reached a certain age and size . . . approximate . . . the status of public corporations rather than of individualistic private enterprise," and predicted an increasing separation of management from ownership. Keynes believed that corporation managers would become more concerned with "the general stability and reputation of the institution" than with "the maximum of profit for the shareholders" and that this would tend to transform the corporation into an agency serving the general welfare. There is, of course, an offset or counter to this beneficent tendency, which Keynes neglected to mention, namely, the evidently unbridled personal greed of corporation managers as a class. Being in a position to determine their own salaries and bonuses and perquisites, without consultation with shareholders, a number of them in America have "earned" over $12 million per annum over the last several years. One of them "earned" well over $22 million in 1984. The managers are also encouraged by the present legal setup to engage in merging, or takeover, operations, which add nothing to the nation's income but a great deal to their own, and which have produced concentrations of economic power that are grave threats to our free institutions.

52. *Ibid.,* pp. 47–48.

53. Moley, *op. cit.,* p. 18.

54. *Ibid.*

55. Moley, *op. cit.,* pp. 21–22. Rosenman, *op. cit.,* p. 64. New York *Times,* September 6, 10, 1932. Rosenman, *op. cit.,* p. 81, says that the actual originator of the phrase was Louis Howe, who used it derisively (out of his jealous hatred of Rosenman) in conversation with Roosevelt, who in turn used it in talks with newspaper reporters, one of whom "used the phrase in his news article next day." Tugwell, *The Brains Trust,* p. 6, opines that Howe "may indeed have been the originator" but that

Kieran deserves "credit for acuteness" in seizing upon it and using it for the first time in public prints.

Ten: The Genesis of a "New Deal" in the Campaign of 1932: Part One

1. Moley, *op. cit.*, p. 23, footnote. Louis W. Koenig, *Bryan* (New York, 1971), p. 197, quoting the "Cross of Gold" speech. Kenneth S. Davis, *FDR: The Beckoning of Destiny*, pp. 607–608.

2. Rosenman, *op. cit.*, p. 65. Moley, *op. cit.*, p. 24. Tugwell, *The Brains Trust*, pp. 103–105

3. PPA, 1928–1932, p. 646.

4. Tugwell, *The Brains Trust*, pp. 104–105.

5. Berle and Jacobs, *op. cit.*, p. 32. Rosen, *op. cit.*, p. 237.

6. Letter, Ralph Hayes to Newton D. Baker, March 25, 1932; quoted in Rosen, *op. cit.*, p. 218. New York *Times*, April 1, 7, 1932. Freidel, *Roosevelt: The Triumph*, p. 278.

7. Rosen, *op. cit.*, pp. 218–222. Flynn, *op. cit.*, p. 98. Farley, *Behind the Ballots*, p. 104. Freidel, *Roosevelt: The Triumph*, pp. 291–292.

8. New York *Times*, April 7, 8, 1932. Warner and Daniel, *op. cit.*, p. 242.

9. New York *Times*, April 16, 1932. Freidel, *Roosevelt: The Triumph*, p. 282.

10. New York *Times*, April 27, 1932. Rosen, *op. cit.*, pp. 225–228.

11. New York *Times*, April 27, May 3, May 18, 1932. Warner and Daniel, *op. cit.*, p. 253.

12. New York *Times*, May 26, 27, 28, 1932. Mitgang, *op. cit.*, pp. 254–265.

13. Interviews with Marion Dickerman. Kenneth S. Davis, *Invincible Summer: An Intimate Portrait of the Roosevelts*, based on the recollections of Marion Dickerman, pp. 97–101.

14. New York *Times*, June 6, 1932. Freidel, *Roosevelt: The Triumph*, p. 293. Rosen, *op. cit.*, pp. 237–239.

15. Lippmann, *op. cit.*, pp. 248–251.

16. New York *Times*, June 9, 1932. Mitgang, *op. cit.*, p. 264.

17. Elliott Roosevelt, *Letters, 1928–1945*, p. 274.

18. Moley, *op. cit.*, pp. 26–27. Rosenman, *op. cit.*, p. 74. New York *Times*, June 30, 1932.

19. Louis McHenry Howe, Box 55 (Democratic National Convention), Franklin D. Roosevelt Library.

20. Farley, *Behind the Ballots*, p. 129.

21. Interviews with Marion Dickerman. Davis, *Invincible Summer*, pp. 102–103.

22. T. Harry Williams, *Huey Long* (New York, 1969), p. 573.

23. Farley, *Behind the Ballots*, pp. 116–117. Schlesinger, *op. cit.*, p. 299. Williams, *op. cit.*, p. 577.

24. Davis, *Invincible Summer*, p. 103. Farley, *Behind the Ballots*, p. 117.

25. Ellis, *op. cit.*, pp. 201–204. Schlesinger, *op. cit.*, p. 238.

26. Ellis, *op. cit.*, pp. 202–203. Farley, *Behind the Ballots*, p. 121.

27. Farley, *Behind the Ballots*, p. 117.

28. Flynn, *op. cit.*, p. 90. There is discrepancy between Flynn's and Farley's accounts of Howe's initial attitude toward the two-thirds issue. Farley has Howe tending to agree with him about the possibility of winning the fight, at the outset, but Flynn writes: "Just to rub it in, Louis Howe, who had just arrived, told us exactly how foolish he thought we had been to go out on such a limb. It was imperative, he told us, to withdraw as gracefully as possible before it broke with our weight." Farley, in his account, is naturally concerned to have others share responsibility with him for the "mess." Flynn's account squares with the known facts about Howe's mind and temperament.

29. Quoted in Farley, *Behind the Ballots*, p. 119.

30. *Ibid.*, pp. 123–124.

31. Frank R. Kent column, "The Great Game of Politics," Baltimore *Sun*, November 18, 1932, gives in circumstantial detail the story of the meeting between Smith and McAdoo. Quoted in Rosen, *op. cit.*, pp. 246–248.

32. Chicago *Tribune*, June 29, 1932. Columns of Arthur Brisbane and Claude G. Bowers in Chicago *American*, June 29, 1932; quoted in Williams, *op. cit.*, pp. 579–580.

33. Schlesinger, *op. cit.*, p. 301. Harbaugh, *op. cit.*, p. 339.

34. Lippmann, *op. cit.*, p. 308.

35. Schlesinger, *op. cit.*, p. 307, quoting Daniel C. Roper, *Fifty Years of Public Life.*

36. Farley, *Behind the Ballots,* pp. 135–136. Rosen, *op. cit.,* p. 255, deriving his information from letters and interviews with Robert Jackson, says that Byrd "was 'playing both ends against the middle' in the form of a Baker-Byrd ticket."

37. There are varying accounts of this episode by people in a position to know the truth. I substantially follow Lela Stile's account in her *The Man Behind Roosevelt: The Story of Louis McHenry Howe* (Cleveland, 1954), pp. 181–182. Flynn, *op. cit.,* p. 100, says *he* was the one who suggested the change, because "Anchors Aweigh" as played by "that particular group of musicians" sounded like a "funeral march."

38. Farley, *Behind the Ballots,* pp. 139–140.

39. Interviews with Marion Dickerman. Farley, *Behind the Ballots,* pp. 140–143. New York *Times,* July 2, 1932. Tugwell, *The Brains Trust,* pp. 250–253. Freidel, *Roosevelt: The Triumph,* pp. 292–293.

40. Farley, *Behind the Ballots,* pp. 145–146.

41. Davis, *Invincible Summer,* pp. 47–48. The operation was on Saturday, July 18, 1932, and was, judging from Roosevelt's letter, extremely serious, since Louis made a will before going to the "Mass. Homeopathic Hospital" in Boston. " . . . went on operating table with 3 anaesthetists in attendance—They gave him gas, he went under quietly, then they gave him the ether & his heart stopped. He was to all intents and purposes 'dead.' They worked over him for two hours, using every known restorative, & as there was no sign of life they gave him up & started to send a telegram announcing his death." It was then he came to. "He was of course sick & considerably shaken, spent that day & Sunday in the Hospital and came on to N.Y. with a trained nurse on the Sunday night train. So there was no operation! He has persuaded the doctors to let him work it out as he did the previous attack [?], but to give him something to make him sleep when the pain is very bad. . . . By the way, Louis wants no one told about his narrow escape!"

42. Bascom N. Timmons, *Garner of Texas* (New York, 1948), pp. 165–167. Rosen, *op. cit.,* pp. 261–265. Farley, *Behind the Ballots,* p. 147. Freidel, *Roosevelt: The Triumph,* pp. 309–310.

43. Timmons, *op. cit.,* p. 167, says, "Actually there is some question whether the Lone Star delegation ever voted to go to Roosevelt." New York *Times,* July 2, 1932. Rosen, *op. cit.,* pp. 264–265.

44. New York *Times,* July 2, 1932. *Official Reports of the Proceedings of the 1932 Democratic National Convention* (Washington, D.C., 1932). Freidel, *Roosevelt: The Triumph,* pp. 310–311.

45. Moley, *op. cit.,* pp. 28–31. Rollins, *op. cit.,* pp. 346–347. Rosenman, *op. cit.,* p. 73, says Howe phoned him in the evening of July 1 asking to see the acceptance speech in its then form before Roosevelt arrived in Chicago. "So, before I went to bed, I asked Grace Tully to read the text of the entire revised speech over the private wire

to a stenographer in the Roosevelt headquarters in Chicago. In Chicago it was transcribed and given to Howe." But, according to Moley, Howe already had read this draft—or one slightly different—several days earlier. "During the agonizing six days of the convention my chief job was to get Louis to approve this speech," writes Moley, *op. cit.,* p. 29.

46. That the letter spoke of Eleanor's leaving Franklin and running off with Earl Miller was told to me by Marion Dickerman, who, however, *still* regarded it as privileged confidential information, not for publication, when I wrote this (she has since died). Lash, who obtained his information from Marion, recounts the episode, or rather mentions it, on p. 351 of *Eleanor and Franklin.* I tell of it in *Invincible Summer,* pp. 107–108, omitting the Earl Miller reference at Marion's insistence.

47. Lash, *op. cit.,* p. 349.

48. Lorena Hickok, *Reluctant First Lady* (New York, 1962), pp. 32–33.

49. C. H. Cramer, *op. cit.,* p. 252. Cramer's information came from interviews with Baker. No mention of this phone call is made by Farley, Flynn, Moley, Schlesinger, or, as far as I know, any other writer save Rosen.

50. Rosenman, *op. cit.,* pp. 72–73, an eyewitness account. Tully, *op. cit.,* pp. 51, 53, also an eyewitness account.

51. New York *Times,* July 3, 1932. Rosenman, *op. cit.,* pp. 76–77. Moley, *op. cit.,* p. 33, has Howe handing FDR his draft speech while the two sat on the platform of the convention hall, but FDR himself told "many times . . . with great glee . . . how he waved his hat and read the speech at the same time" while driving to the stadium.

52. In container no. 483 of the FDR speech file in the Franklin D. Roosevelt Library is the much-reprinted March 25, 1933, memo in which FDR tells, somewhat inaccurately, of the final putting together of the acceptance speech. It is attached to the original draft (the Moley-Rosenman one), to which is appended the opening page from Howe.

53. PPA, 1928–1932, pp. 647–659. The Hyde statement on reforestation is in New York *Times,* July 7, 1932.

54. Michelson, *op. cit.,* p. 10.

55. Sternsher, *op. cit.,* p. 42; derived from Sternsher's interview with Tugwell.

56. New York *Times,* July 4, 1932. Freidel, *Roosevelt: The Triumph,* p. 316. *Proceedings of the 1932 Democratic National Convention,* pp. 596–597.

57. Moley, *op. cit.,* p. 36.

Eleven: The Genesis of a "New Deal" in the Campaign of 1932: Part Two

1. Moley, *op. cit.,* p. 40.

2. *Ibid.,* p. 37.

3. Tugwell, *The Brains Trust,* pp. 329–330

4. New York *Times,* July 7, 1932. Tugwell, *The Brains Trust,* p. 333.

5. New York *Times,* July 12, 13, 14, 15, 16, 17, 18, 1932, carries accounts of the cruise. Tugwell, *The Brains Trust,* pp. 337–347. Freidel, *Roosevelt: The Triumph,* pp. 329–33.

6. Tugwell, *The Brains Trust* p. 344.

7. New York *Times,* July 18, 1932. Freidel, *Roosevelt: The Triumph,* p. 333. Tugwell, *The Brains Trust,* p. 346. Freedman, *op. cit.,* pp. 74–76.

8. PPA, 1928–1932, p. 809. Ellis, quoting Hoover, *op. cit.,* p. 159.

9. Rosenman, *op. cit.,* pp. 69–70.

10. Ellis, *op. cit.,* p. 159.

11. New York *Times,* June 16, 18, 1932. Consulted for the general story of the Bonus March were Hoover, *Memoirs,* vol. 3 (New York, 1952); J. H. Bartlett, *The Bonus March and the New Deal* (Chicago, 1937); Donald Lisio, *The President and Protest: Hoover, Conspiracy, and the Bonus Riot* (New York, 1974); William Manchester, *American Caesar* (Boston, 1978); Kenneth S. Davis, *Soldier of Democracy* (New York, 1945); Burner, *op. cit.;* Paul Y. Anderson, "Tear-Gas, Bayonets, and Votes," *Nation,* August 31, 1932; Ellis, *op. cit.;* Schlesinger, *op. cit.*

12. Hoover, *Memoirs,* vol. 3, p. 227.

13. Manchester, *op. cit.,* p. 150

14. Hoover, *Memoirs,* vol. 3, p. 226.

15. *Ibid.,* p. 228.

16. Tugwell, *The Brains Trust,* pp. 383–384. Among those outraged by the July 30 radio address was J. David Stern, publisher of the Philadelphia *Record,* who in a letter to Roosevelt dated August 1, 1932, told Roosevelt he was considering a withdrawal of his newspaper's support because of the speech's "conservatism." "Your emphasis on the importance of balancing the budget with a view to maintaining a sound currency would put you in line with the most conservative of financiers, who believe in allowing the deflation to run its course," wrote Stern. " . . . It is my impression

that the weight of enlightened economic thought takes the opposite view from that expressed by you." (Stern believed John Maynard Keynes to be "the greatest economist living today"; he said so in testimony before the U.S. Senate Finance Committee hearing, *Investigation of Economic Problems,* in early 1933.) Stern's letter was turned over to Berle and is now in Berle Papers, Franklin D. Roosevelt Library.

17. Freedman, *op. cit.,* p. 87. Tugwell, *The Brains Trust,* p. 358.

18. Farley, *Behind the Ballots,* p. 171.

19. Tugwell, *The Brains Trust,* pp. 425–426, 430–434. New York *Times,* July 9, 1932.

20. Letter, Ickes to Roosevelt, July 8, 1932; quoted in Freidel, *Roosevelt: The Triumph,* p. 334. Freedman, *op. cit.,* pp. 80–81. Lippmann quoted in Mitgang, *op. cit.,* p. 291.

21. Moley, *op. cit.,* pp. 25–26, says that he suggested Conboy to Roosevelt and that Conboy's acceptance of the assignment was a "political coup" because Conboy "was, like Walker, a Catholic of Irish extraction and a member of Tammany."

22. New York *Times,* August 12, 1932. Mitgang, *op. cit.,* pp. 285–286.

23. Berle and Jacobs, *op. cit.,* p. 60.

24. Rosenman, *op. cit.,* p. 83. Moley, *27 Masters of Politics,* pp. 209–211. Schlesinger, *op. cit.,* pp. 422–423. Mitgang, *op. cit.,* pp. 296–297.

25. Berle and Jacobs, *op. cit.,* p. 60.

26. Timmons, *op. cit.,* p. 168.

27. Berle and Jacobs, *op. cit.,* p. 51.

28. Tugwell, *The Brains Trust* pp. 525–528, includes as an appendix the entire text of "Proposal for an Economic Council."

29. Berle and Jacobs, *op. cit.,* p. 59.

30. George F. Warren and Frank A. Pearson, *Prices* (New York, 1933), p. 176.

31. Berle and Jacobs, *op. cit.,* pp. 55–56.

32. Tugwell, *The Brains Trust,* p. 385.

33. Moley, *After Seven Years,* p. 47. In the Charles W. Taussig file of the Franklin D. Roosevelt Library is a letter from him to Roosevelt mentioning the train ride and sending Roosevelt a copy of a privately printed book Taussig had written on the history of the molasses industry, a topic of interest to Roosevelt because his great-

great-grandfather Isaac "the Patriot" Roosevelt made a fortune in this business in the eighteenth century.

34. Moley, *After Seven Years,* pp. 48–49.

35. PPA, 1928–1932, pp. 725, 767–769.

36. Moley, *After Seven Years,* p. 51.

37. Quoted in, among many others, Burner, *op. cit.,* p. 315.

38. Schlesinger, *op. cit.,* p. 403, quoting Tugwell, "New Deal Memoir," chapter 1.

39. Moley, *After Seven Years,* pp. 44–45. Roosevelt's description of himself as a "farmer" in Hyde Park led the Republican National Committee to distribute to the press aerial photos of his Hyde Park estate, with detailed description, in picture legend, of coach house, gardens, swimming pool, etc.

40. PPA, 1928–1932, pp. 699, 704–705.

41. *Ibid.,* p. 703.

42. *Ibid.,* p. 772, quotes from the U.S. Public Health Service publication.

43. *Ibid.,* pp. 711–780, 831–842. New York *Times,* October 27, 1932. New York *Herald Tribune,* October 27, 1932, comparing prepared text with what Roosevelt actually said regarding Republican control of the Supreme Court.

44. Berle, and Jacobs, *op. cit.,* pp. 62–70, includes speech as drafted by the Berles and telegram from Adolf Berle to Roosevelt, "attention Moley," September 19, 1932.

45. Moley, *After Seven Years,* p. 58, asserts in a lengthy footnote that he urged Roosevelt "to sum up . . . his political philosophy" before the Commonwealth Club, to which Roosevelt had originally intended "to deliver merely a brief and unimportant greeting," and that he (Moley) had in early August "asked Berle to make a draft of the ideas we had all been discussing from April through to September." He further asserts that the Berle draft then "passed through the same mill that every other speech went through, and was not finally completed until the early morning before it was given." Moley's memory is, in this case, faulty, as a comparison of the draft in Berle and Means, *op. cit.,* and the text of the speech actually given clearly shows.

46. PPA, 1928–1932, p. 743.

47. Moley, *After Seven Years,* p. 62.

48. New York *Times,* November 1, 1932. PPA, 1928–1932, pp. 799, 810.

49. New York *Times,* November 1, 1932.

50. Farley, *op. cit.*, pp. 176–178. Rosenman, *op. cit.*, p. 84. Elliott Roosevelt, *Letters, 1928–1945*, p. 302. Josephson and Josephson, *op. cit.*, p. 442.

51. Moley, *After Seven Years*, prints as Appendix A, pp. 401–402, the entire text of the Poughkeepsie talk, which is, as he footnotes on p. 65, "conspicuous by its absence" from PPA, 1928–1932.

52. Doris Faber, *The Life of Lorena Hickok, E. R.'s Friend* (New York, 1980), pp. 92–93.

53. Rollins, *op. cit.*, p. 363, citing *Time,* November 21, 1932, issue.

54. Nathan Fine, writing on "Socialism" in *The American Year Book: Record of the Year* 1932, p. 541.

Twelve: Interregnum: Into the Winter of Our Discontent

1. Hickok, *op. cit.*, p. 55.

2. Moley, *After Seven Years*, p. 65.

3. Roosevelt and Shalett, *op. cit.*, p. 232.

4. *American Year Book: 1932*, pp. 314, 315, 316. Federal Reserve Board, *Annual Report*, 1930, 1931, 1932, cited in Mitchell *op. cit.*, pp. 128, 129.

5. *American Year Book: 1932*, pp. 342, 443, 444. *Business Week,* October 7, 1931, pp. 32–33. Representative George Huddleston of Alabama in testimony *(Federal Cooperation in Unemployment Relief: Hearings)* before a subcommittee of the Committee on Manufactures, U.S. Senate, 72nd Congress, first session, pp. 239–240. Testimony of H. L. Lurie before La Follette–Costigan Committee, January 1933, reprinted in David A. Shannon, ed., *The Great Depression* (Englewood Cliffs, N.J., 1960), p. 39. *American Year Book: 1932,* p. 404.

6. *American Year Book: 1932*, pp. 424, 399.

7. Hoover, *State Papers and Other Writings*, vol. 2, p. 236. Cited in Schlesinger, *op. cit.*, p. 241.

8. Shannon, *op. cit.*, p. 37.

9. *Ibid.*, pp. 45–47, 49, reprints testimony by Karl de Schweinitz and Representative George Huddleston before a subcommittee of the Committee on Manufactures, U.S. Senate, 72nd Congress, first session, 1932.

10. *Ibid.*, pp. 43–54, reprints testimony of Clarence E. Pickett before a subcommittee of the Committee on Manufactures, U.S. Senate, 72nd Congress, first session, 1932.

11. *Ibid.*, pp. 26–28, reprints testimony of Oscar Ameringer in *Unemployment in the United States: Hearings,* before a subcommittee of the Committee on Labor, House of Representatives, 72nd Congress, first session, 1932, on H.R. 8088, pp. 98–99.

12. Quoted in Schlesinger, *op. cit.,* p. 176, from Senate Committee on Manufactures, *Federal Cooperation in Unemployment Relief: Hearings,* 72nd Congress, first session, 1932.

13. *Time,* April 2, 1932. Cited in Schlesinger, *op. cit.,* p. 242.

14. Susan Winslow, with Wendy Holman, *Brother, Can You Spare a Dime?* (New York, 1969), pp. 23, 24, 34. "Brother, Can You Spare a Dime?" by Jay Gorney and E. Y. Harburg, © 1932, by Harms, Inc. The song was the hit tune of a revue, *Americana,* produced in New York City in mid-October of 1932.

15. Beard and Beard, *op. cit.,* p. 109, and Schlesinger, *op. cit.,* p. 178, quoting Senate Manufactures Committee, *Establishment of a National Economic Council: Hearings,* 72nd Congress, first session, 1932.

16. Moley doesn't mention Technocracy in his published memoirs, nor does Roosevelt in the personal letters of public papers (published). Neither does Tugwell in his *The Democratic Roosevelt, The Brains Trust,* or other personal histories of the New Deal era—and this despite Technocracy's close affinity and even identity with many of Tugwell's main ideas. Berle, on the other hand, "saw some good" in Technocracy, as Ellis puts it in *A Nation in Torment,* p. 228.

17. Margaret Mead, *Blackberry Winter* (New York, 1972), pp. 187–188. Cited in J. C. Furnas, *Stormy Weather* (New York, 1977), p. 213.

18. Quoted in Ellis, *op. cit.,* p. 220.

19. Quoted in Beard and Beard, *op. cit.,* p. 41. Scott's views on technological unemployment were supported by Frederick C. Mills in *Economic Tendencies in the United States,* published in 1932 by the National Bureau of Economic Research, pp. 292ff. Mills's study revealed that, while the physical volume of industrial production had increased at the rate of 3.9 percent a year between 1901 and 1913, the volume of employment in industry had increased by only 2.7 percent per year. The discrepancy between production increase and employment increase was much greater following the Great War. The volume of manufactured goods increased at the rate of 4.5 percent a year between 1922 and 1929, while the volume of employment increased only 1 percent annually. The study further showed that per hour increases in worker productivity had not been matched by increases in per hour wages for workers but were instead reflected in increased profits for businessmen. Between 1922 and 1929 the net income of corporations increased 7.3 percent annually, and the profits of financial institutions increased 16.2 percent annually. The average earnings of industrial employees during these years increased only 1.6 percent annually. See Mitchell, *op. cit.,* p. 112.

20. Mitchell, *op. cit.,* pp. 111–112. Ellis, *op. cit.,* p. 221.

21. Harold Loeb, *Life in a Technocracy: What It Might Be Like* (New York, 1933), p. 97. Quoted in Furnas, *op. cit.,* p. 221.

22. Broun column quoted in Ellis, *op. cit.,* p. 225. Alfred E. Smith, "The New Outlook," *New Outlook,* January 1933. Quoted in Schlesinger, *op. cit.,* p. 463.

23. Stuart Chase, *A New Deal* (New York, 1932), pp. 251, 252.

24. New York *Times,* January 14, 1933.

25. *Ibid.*

26. Quoted in Ellis, *op. cit.,* p. 223.

27. *American Year Book: 1932,* p. 12. Walter Johnson, ed., *Selected Letters of William Allen White* (New York, 1947), p. 329.

28. *Literary Digest,* November 19, 1932, p. 7. Quoted in Freidel, *Franklin D. Roosevelt: Launching the New Deal* (Boston, 1973), pp. 16–17.

29. Moley, *After Seven Years,* p. 67. Edgar Eugene Robinson, *The Roosevelt Leadership, 1933–1945* (Philadelphia, 1955), p. 82., describes the original document now in Box 8, President's Secretary's File, 1933–1935, Franklin D. Roosevelt Library. *New York Times,* November 10, 1933.

30. Moley, *After Seven Years,* p. 68.

31. FDR Presidential Press Conference, no. 1, March 8, 1933.

32. Winston S. Churchill, *The World Crisis, 1911–1918* (abridged and revised edition, London, 1943), p. 107.

33. Descriptions of the various gold standards adopted after World War I and of gold weights per monetary unit derive from the National Industrial Conference Board, "The Gold Standard: Recent Developments and Present Status," a memorandum dated May 5, 1933; M. L. Burstein, *Money* (Cambridge, 1963), pp. 26–27; Edwin Walter Kemmerer, *Gold and the Gold Standard* (New York, 1930), pp. 35–39.

34. Herbert Hoover, *Addresses Upon the American Road, 1933–1938* (New York, 1938), p. 30.

35. Goronwy Rees, *The Great Slump: Capitalism in Crisis, 1929–1933* (New York, 1970), pp. 198, 256, 257.

36. *Ibid.,* p. 201. PPA, 1928–1932, p. 874. Roosevelt's personal attitude toward the war debts varied with the times and circumstances. In 1926 he composed for a public speech "A Parable on War Debts," which, telling the story of a flint-hearted country banker (analogous to the United States as "Uncle Shylock"), condemned the war-debt policy of the Coolidge administration and Coolidge's famous comment "Well,

they hired the money didn't they?" See *FDR: The Beckoning of Destiny,* pp. 806–807.

37. Moley, *After Seven Years,* p. 90.

38. PPA, 1928–1932, p. 878.

39. *Ibid.,* p. 803.

40. *Ibid.,* pp. 876–877.

41. Moley, *After Seven Years,* pp. 72–77. The same story is told in greater circumstantial detail in Moley's *The First New Deal* (New York, 1966), pp. 27–35. Freidel, *Roosevelt: Launching the New Deal,* p. 35. New York *Times,* November 23, 24, 1932.

42. Stimson diary, November 22, 1932; quoted in Freidel, *Roosevelt: Launching the New Deal,* p. 35.

43. PPA, 1928–1932, p. 879.

44. *Ibid.,* pp. 880–881.

45. *Ibid.,* pp. 881–882.

46. *Ibid.,* p. 883.

47. Freidel, *Roosevelt: Launching the New Deal,* pp. 42–43. New York *Times,* December 23, 24, 1932.

48. Stimson diary, December 13, 1932; quoted in Freidel, *Roosevelt: Launching the New Deal,* p. 45.

49. *Time,* January 23, 1933; cited in Schlesinger, *op. cit.,* p. 452.

50. New York *Times,* January 22, 1933.

51. Senate Finance Committee, *Investigation of Economic Problems: Hearings,* 72nd Congress, second session, 1933. Cited in Freidel, *Roosevelt: Launching the New Deal,* p. 57.

52. Quoted from Stimson diary in Freidel, *Roosevelt: Launching the New Deal,* p. 118.

53. Quoted from Stimson diary in Freidel, *Roosevelt: Launching the New Deal,* p. 120.

54. New York *Times,* January 18, 1933. Freidel, *Roosevelt: Launching the New Deal,* p. 120. Moley, *After Seven Years,* p. 94.

55. Moley, *After Seven Years,* p. 95. Freidel, *Roosevelt: Launching the New Deal,* pp. 121–122, quoting from Tugwell diary.

56. Moley, *After Seven Years,* pp. 97–98.

57. Letter, FDR to George Norris, December 14, 1932. Quoted in Freidel, *Roosevelt: Launching the New Deal,* p. 164.

58. PPA, 1928–1932, p. 886.

59. New York *Times,* January 22, 1933.

60. Edgar B. Nixon, ed., *Franklin D. Roosevelt and Conservation, 1911–1945,* vol. 1, p. 133. PPA, 1928–1932, pp. 888–889.

61. Lindley, *The Roosevelt Revolution,* pp. 69, 47.

Thirteen: Interregnum: The Crisis

1. Moley, *The First New Deal,* pp. 100–103, contains facsimiles of notes taken on the train. Flynn, *op. cit.,* p. 124.

2. Freidel, *Roosevelt: Launching the New Deal,* p. 168.

3. Roosevelt and Shalett, *op. cit.,* p. 278.

4. The story of the Michigan crisis is told in detail by Susan Estabrook Kennedy in *The Banking Crisis of 1933* (Lexington, 1973), pp. 76–102. It is extremely doubtful that a state governor had legal authority to close national banks, but the closing order went unchallenged.

5. New York *Times,* February 16, 1933. Among the items in the well-stuffed "briefcase" that allegedly remained unopened was a lengthy letter from Pennsylvania Governor Pinchot concerning the national "forest problem." It argued for nationalization of upward of 100,000,000 acres of forest land and 50,000,000 acres of abandoned farm lands. Wrote Pinchot: "Voluntary private forestry has failed the world over. There is absolutely no reason to assume that it will succeed in the United States. . . . Private forestry in America, as a solution to the problem, is no longer even a hope. Neither the crutch of subsidy nor the whip of legislation can restore it. The solution of the private forest problem lies chiefly in large scale public acquisition of private forest lands." See Nixon, *op. cit.,* pp. 129–132, 134.

6. Moley, *After Seven Years,* p. 114. In *First New Deal,* pp. 86–93, Moley tells in much greater detail the story of Hull's appointment and gives the names of four of the five senators, each a powerful voice in foreign affairs, who objected strenuously to Hull for State. The four were Carter Glass, Claude Swanson, Thomas J. Walsh, and Key Pittman. "The fifth is still living [1966] and must be unnamed here."

7. Moley, *After Seven Years,* pp. 116, 118.

8. Freidel, *Roosevelt: Launching the New Deal,* p. 151. Freidel has Roosevelt talking with Cutting on February 20 at "the Washington station" about Walsh's appoint-

ment, but this is evidently a typographical error. The date must have been January 20.

9. Moley, *After Seven Years,* p. 122.

10. New York *Times,* February 16, 1933. All the direct quotes on the following pages are from this same issue of the *Times.* The paper reported Roosevelt's own account of incident, verbatim, on February 17, 1933.

11. The surgeon was Dr. Hugh H. Young, on the staff of the Johns Hopkins University medical school, who is quoted in the February 17, 1933, issue of the New York *Times.*

12. New York *Times,* February 16, 1933

13. Moley, *After Seven Years,* p. 139.

14. See, for instance, "Heavy Cost of $8 Pistol," *Literary Digest,* March 18, 1933, pp. 26–28.

15. Mrs. Cross's verbatim account is in New York *Times,* February 16, 1933.

16. All details of Zangara's trial and execution are from New York *Times,* March 10, 11, 21, 1933.

17. The Irwin McDuffie story is from Max Hall, "A Hero to His Valet," *Emory University Quarterly,* October 1947. Quoted in Schlesinger, *op. cit.,* p. 466.

18. New York *Times,* February 17, 1933.

19. The FDR telegram to Mrs. Cross is in New York *Times,* February 20, 1933.

20. New York *Times,* February 18, 1933.

21. Lindley, *The Roosevelt Revolution,* p. 47. Freidel, *Roosevelt: Launching the New Deal,* p. 174.

22. Moley, *After Seven Years,* pp. 139–141. Moley, *The First New Deal,* pp. 140–141.

23. Hoover's letter was first published in *The Saturday Evening Post,* June 8, 15, 22, 29, 1935, in a series of articles by William Starr Myers and Walter H. Newton, later included in their book *The Hoover Administration: A Documented Narrative.* Frances M. Seeber, supervisory archivist of the Franklin D. Roosevelt Library, told me (August 1981): "We cannot locate any correspondence between Herbert Hoover and Franklin Roosevelt wherein Herbert Hoover asked for the return of the original longhand letter [it is in the President's Personal File 820 in the library] or copy of the same." It is obvious, however, that *either* Hoover asked for and received a copy of his letter from Roosevelt *or* he had a copy made of the original longhand before he mailed the letter. Otherwise Myers and Newton could not have reprinted it.

24. Myers and Newton, *op. cit.,* p. 341.

25. Farley, *Behind the Ballots,* p. 206.

26. Moley, *After Seven Years,* pp. 126–127.

27. Letter, Thomas W. Lamont to FDR, President's Personal File 70, Franklin D. Roosevelt Library. Cited in Freidel, *Roosevelt: Launching the New Deal,* pp. 187–188.

28. Kennedy, *op. cit.,* p. 126, quotes *Nation* and paraphrases *Commonwealth.*

29. Schlesinger, *op. cit.,* pp. 458–459, quoting from Senate Finance Committee, *Investigation of Economic Problems: Hearings,* 72nd Congress, second session, 1933.

30. Moley, *The First New Deal,* pp. 96–124, gives authoritative detailed account of the preparation of the inaugural address, with insert reproducing the manuscript that FDR prepared with his own hand. A generation of historical scholars was befuddled, until Moley's *First New Deal* came out, by the fact that FDR attached to his handwritten version a memorandum on White House stationery, dated March 25, 1933, saying, "This is the original manuscript of the Inaugural Address as written at Hyde Park on Monday, February 27th, 1933. I started in about 9:00 P.M. and ended at 1:30 A.M. A number of minor changes were made in subsequent drafts but the final draft is substantially the same as this original. /s/ Franklin D. Roosevelt."

31. Myers and Newton, *op. cit.,* pp. 344–345, reproduces the FDR letter, as does Moley, *The First New Deal,* pp. 143–144, and many others. Writes Moley, *The First New Deal,* p. 144: "Roosevelt's second letter [the cover letter apologizing for the delay of transmittal of the allegedly earlier letter] . . . was by internal evidence written on March 1 and delivered on the same day, by means of which I have no evidence. At the Hyde Park library the stenographic notes from which these letters were typed show that both were dictated on the same day, March 1st.

32. Farley, *Behind the Ballots,* pp. 207–208.

Index

About the Author

A biographer of Eisenhower, Lindbergh, and Adlai Stevenson as well as a novelist, KENNETH S. DAVIS was awarded the prestigious Francis Parkman prize for *FDR: The Beckoning of Destiny,* which was also a nominee for the National Book Award. He has received a Guggenheim Fellowship among other awards and fellowships.

A graduate of Kansas State University, with a master of science degree from the University of Wisconsin and an honorary doctor of letters degree from Assumption College, Mr. Davis has been a journalism instructor at New York University, a war correspondent attached to General Eisenhower's personal headquarters, special assistant to the president of Kansas State University, a member of the State Department's UNESCO Relations Staff, editor of the *Newberry Library Bulletin* in Chicago, an adjunct professor of English at Clark University, and a visiting professor of history at Kansas State University.

He and his wife now live in Princeton, Massachusetts.